ETHICS, LAW,
AND
BUSINESS

ETHICS, LAW, AND BUSINESS

William Arthur Wines
Oxford, Ohio

LEA
2006

LAWRENCE ERLBAUM ASSOCIATES, PUBLISHERS
Mahwah, New Jersey   London

Senior Acquisitions Editor: Anne Duffy
Editorial Assistant: Rebecca Larsen
Cover Design: Kathryn Houghtaling Lacey
Full-Service Compositor: TechBooks

This book was typeset in 10/12 pt. Janson Text, Italic, Bold, and Bold Italic.
The heads were typeset in Base9, Base12, and Stone Sans.

Lawrence Erlbaum Associates, Inc., Publishers
10 Industrial Avenue
Mahwah, New Jersey 07430
www.erlbaum.com

Library of Congress Cataloging-in-Publication Data

Wines, William A.
Ethics, law, and business / William Arthur Wines.
    p. cm.
  Includes bibliographical references and index.
  ISBN 0-8058-5496-7 (pbk. : alk. paper) — ISBN 0-8058-5495-9 (cloth :
alk. paper) — ISBN 0-8058-5740-0 (instructor manual : alk. paper)
  1. Business ethics.   2. Professional ethics.   3. Social responsibility of
business.   I. Title.
  HF5387.W565   2006
  174′.4–dc22

                                      2005029196

Printed in the United States of America
10 9 8 7 6 5 4 3 2 1

Dedication

This book is dedicated to the memory of Willa Wines (1916–1992)—mother bear, fiercely loyal, resilient but fragile—who made certain, in every way, that "her boys" got the formal education that life had denied her; and to the memory of Harold Glen Wines (1911–2001), a rare and precious man among men: son, husband, father, grandfather, warrior-scholar, a fighter who never learned to hate, a true *mensch*.

Rest in Peace.

CONTENTS

CHAPTER 15   Rise of Regulation and Corporate Social Responsibility   239

CHAPTER 16   Workplace Issues I: Employment Versus Personal Dignity   256

CHAPTER 17   Workplace Issues II: Designing a Better Organization   287

CHAPTER 21   Success and the American Dream   348

PART 6   APPENDICES   373

PREFACE

This book is a work in progress. As the noted French poet Paul Valery (1871–1945) wrote, "A poem is never finished, only abandoned."[1] So it is with books. This book has been in gestation for more than a decade. Parts of it have been reworked, and portions of it have been presented at academic conferences. Now, all these pieces have been fitted together, and new materials have been added to provide a textbook in ethics, law, and business.

A question that deserves a response is, Why another book on business ethics? The answer is that it was needed for the course on Ethics, Law, & Business that I teach at Miami University. When I mentioned the book to colleagues, they expressed an interest in the materials. There are no shortages of books and some excellent works on ethics, law, and business. However, there was not one or even any combination of two that provided the necessary coverage in an eminently readable style.

It has been said that there are two types of scholarly minds: those that find distinctions and those that find common themes. My mind tends to find similarities and see relationships between ideas. Consequently, several themes run through this text.

First, there is interplay between moral philosophy and law.[2] I have tried to highlight some of the areas in the text where such interplay is strongest. Second, research has established a link between the study of disquieting topics and an increase in moral reasoning skills.[3] Some of the controversial materials in this book are introduced for that reason—to challenge the reader to push the edges out of his or her comfort zones. Third, business is a vast, complex social organization that has tremendous power. Such an enterprise should be managed by those who are sensitive to the moral dimension. Much of the material presented here is designed to heighten the reader's sensitivity to the moral domain.

A final theme that underlies much of my effort but that may not be readily apparent is my firm conviction that we need to prepare business students for leadership roles in our communities. This is a task that business schools have not adequately addressed. We prepare our students for their first jobs and to some degree for careers, but we do not accept responsibility for our society turning to business leaders, rightly or wrongly, for leadership. Business managers, almost invariably, are asked to run for city council, school boards, planning and zoning boards, and many public offices. Before they walk across the stage at commencement, we might do well to, at the very least, make them somewhat conversant with the continuing problems in American society. This book makes that attempt by addressing such topics as free speech, violence, affirmative action, and public education.

My perspective may not be your perspective. So, I ask you to consider much of what is presented here as one opinion—an informed and educated opinion—but merely one person's opinion, when all is said and done. Take from it what you find useful and leave the rest. There should be ideas in here that you find provocative, ideas that stimulate your curiosity to learn more. If

---

1. http://www.quotemeonit.com/valery.html accessed on November 8, 2002.
2. EDMUND CAHN, THE MORAL CHOICE: RIGHT AND WRONG IN LIGHT OF AMERICAN LAW (Midland ed. 1981).
3. *See, e.g.*, Edward J. Conry & Donald R. Nelson, *Business Law and Moral Growth*, 27 AMERICAN BUS. L. J. (Spring 1989) at 1–39.

your curiosity has been aroused by new ideas, then the effort that went into this book will not have been in vain.

Part of the function of higher education is to make students curious for the rest of their days. The terminology currently popular in higher education circles is "life-long learners." I prefer curiosity. In this respect, education can be likened to an inoculation, and we all know people on whom the inoculation did not "take." Unhappily, some of those who are not curious include holders of doctoral degrees.

Another function of higher education and one that has been neglected by many colleges is the fostering of adults who are prepared to participate meaningfully as citizens in this republic of ours. I hope this work helps you realize the significance of the research by Robert Bellah et al. that points to the conclusion that one cannot have a meaningful nor satisfying public life without a meaningful and satisfying private life and vice versa.[4] It follows then that one does not get an education exclusively for one's own benefit.

A well-educated younger generation is a gift that a society gives itself and is a blessing to the world. As the noted British intellectual G. K. Chesterton (1874–1936) observed, "Properly speaking, there is no such thing as education. Education is simply the soul of a society as it passes from one generation to another . . . , and that transition may be called education."[5]

A truly educated individual is, in a very real sense, a citizen of the world. On a planet where an estimated 30,000 people die daily of starvation,[6] we are in need of more global citizens and fewer parochial thinkers.

Finally, a college degree should indicate that the recipient has taken control of his or her intellect and is prepared to chart the future direction of his or her intellectual growth. This means much more than merely securing employment on graduation. Probably we all know people who hold college degrees but who are not curious, do not read actively, and do not participate meaningfully in citizenship. My wish for you, the readers encountering this book, is that your lives will be fuller, happier, and more meaningful than theirs.

---

4. ROBERT N. BELLAH *et al.*, HABITS OF THE HEART: INDIVIDUALISM AND COMMITMENT IN AMERICAN LIFE (1985) at 162–163.

5. Illustrated London News (July 5, 1924) as found at http://quotes.liberty-tree.ca/quotes.nsf/quotes5/6756b6481763dcab85256ec900589d60 (last visited on December 22, 2004).

6. http://www.freelanceworkexchange.com/archive/issue90.html accessed on May 27, 2003. In 2001, there were over 10 million deaths from starvation worldwide, and it is estimated that approximately 4 billion people suffer from malnutrition. http://www.jvpnet.com/latest.html cached. Enter "Starvation worldwide" in a Yahoo search engine and it will produce over 72,000 sites.

ACKNOWLEDGMENTS

The author wishes to acknowledge the contributions over the past three decades of the many college students who have helped him shape his understanding of this material and his role as an educator. He is also grateful to Professor J. Brooke Hamilton III, Professor Terence J. Lau, Professor Robert D. Ley, Professor R. Larry Reynolds, Sandra Ward Angell, Sue Axtell, and Robert G. Wines, Esq., for their friendship and encouragement. Among many good research assistants, the author acknowledges the especially diligent help of Carrie Russell, M.B.A. '03; Samir Bhatias, M.B.A. '04; Andres Ocariz, M.B.A. '04; and Jason Tate, M.A. '05—all of Miami University.

The author is deeply grateful to Professor Joseph A. Petrick, Director of the Institute for Business Integrity of Wright State University, for his excellent comments and helpful suggestions on an earlier draft of the manuscript. He thanks Paula Hensley, senior administrative assistant in the Finance Department at Miami University, for her unflagging efforts in support of this and numerous other projects. He also wishes to acknowledge the untiring support of Ms. Susan Hurst. Finally, he wishes to acknowledge the excellent job done by Anne Duffy, Senior Editor at Lawrence Erlbaum Associates, in shepherding this work to publication. Any omission of other persons who have helped along the way is purely unintentional and reflects a failure of memory, not a lack of appreciation. The mistakes remaining and the responsibility for the ideas expressed herein remain solely those of the author. Nothing herein should be construed as reflecting the views or policies of Miami University, the Trustees of Miami University, or the State of Ohio.

William Arthur Wines
Oxford, Ohio
October 6, 2005

ETHICS, LAW,
AND
BUSINESS

PART 1

Basics of Ethics, Law, and Business

CHAPTER

1

Introduction to Basic Concepts in Ethics, Law, and Business

> Each world revolution has begun with some just complaint about moral wrongs
> in the prevailing political, social, or religious system.
>
> —Norman F. Cantor[1]

In the United States in 1999, over 1.5 million Americans were arrested for driving under the influence (DUI).[2] In 2001, that number declined to 1.4 million.[3] However, Mothers Against Drunk Driving (MADD) estimated that only 1 arrest is made for every 88 DUI incidents.[4] In 2001, 1,461 people were killed in automobile crashes that involved alcohol-impaired or intoxicated drivers who had at least one prior DUI conviction.[5] In 2002, 17,419 people died in alcohol-related traffic accidents.[6]

This abuse of alcohol is just one of many examples where the interests of business, society, and government intersect and sometimes conflict. In 2002, the retail dollar sales for the alcohol beverage market climbed 6.3% to $137.2 billion.[7] The states and the federal government all receive tax monies from those sales.[8] For thousands of years, human beings have been drinking alcoholic beverages.[9] However, with the advent of the automobile, people who mix drinking with driving have put the safety of the public—that is, the general welfare—at risk. In its role as the promoter of the general welfare,[10] what should the government do about this problem?[11] Should society expect the government to solve the problem, or are there actions we the people can take

---

1. NORMAN F. CANTOR, THE CIVILIZATION OF THE MIDDLE AGES (HarperPerennial ed. 1994) at 244.
2. ABC News Tonight with Peter Jennings, Orlando, FL affiliate CH. 9 on December 27, 2000 at 6:30 p.m. EST. The actual number given was 1.511 million arrests.
3. MADD, *Did you know?* Accessed at http://www.madd.org/stats/0,1056,1784,00.html on August 30, 2004.
4. *Id.*
5. *Id.*
6. *Alcohol-Related Traffic Deaths Rise for Third Year in Row, According to Latest Government Data (July 17, 2003).* Accessed at http://www.madd.org/news/1,1056,6896_print,00.html on January 12, 2005.
7. *U.S. Alcoholic Beverage Industry Sales Grow in 2002—Brief Article*, FOOD & DRINK WEEKLY (Mar. 10, 2003). Accessed at http://www.findarticles.com/p/articles/mi_mOEOUY/is_9_9/ai_98655477 on September 2, 2004.
8. For example, in FY 2001–2002, the State of Florida Division of Alcoholic Beverage and Tobacco generated nearly $1 billion in license fees, taxes, and other forms of revenue. *Division of Alcoholic Beverages and Tobacco*. Accessed at http://www.state.fl.us/dbpr/abt/index.shtml on September 2, 2004.
9. The first alcoholic beverages were fermented. Scenes showing fermentation appear on pottery made in Mesopotamia (modern-day Iraq) as early as 4200 BC. WORLD BOOK ENCYCLOPEDIA (1990), vol. 1 at 337. Brandy was probably the first distilled alcoholic beverage and dates from approximately the year 100. *Id.*
10. *See* Preamble to the U.S. Constitution.
11. Compare what Sweden has done about drunken driving to the U.S. response. In the United States (by state law), the limit for driving under the influence (DUI) has within the past two decades generally dropped from a blood-alcohol content (BAC) of 0.10% to 0.08%. In Sweden, the BAC was lowered in 1990 from 0.05% to 0.02%. Drivers with a BAC over 0.1% now risk imprisonment. In Sweden, drunken driving is considered a serious crime, and one of the results of this social attitude is that it is fairly rare compared to the other countries. An estimated 1 of every 1,000 drivers is drunk in traffic in Sweden. *See, e.g.,* Lars Aberg, *Long Time Effects of a Lowered Blood Alcohol Limit in Sweden.* Accessed at http://www.druglibrary.org/schaffer/Misc/driving/s15p2.htm on January 17, 2005. For comparison, one author says that each year in the United States, 1 driver out of every 100 is *arrested* for DUI: "more people than for any other crime." *"Repeat DWI Offenders in the United States.* Accessed at http://www.nhtsa.dot.gov/people/injury/traffic_tech/1995/TT085.htm on February 2, 2005.

short of passing new laws? Should the alcoholic beverage industry accept any responsibility for this problem?

A second example of issues that arise at the intersection of law and business occurred in the winter of 2000–2001 in Boise, Idaho. The City Council had passed an ordinance that made landlords responsible for detecting and reporting illegal drug activity to the local police.[12] The proposed penalty for failure to report included forfeiture of the property. In January 2001, property owners' associations and others sponsored a media campaign bitterly denouncing this so-called transfer of police work to ordinary citizens.[13] Was this an appropriate demand for local government to make on people in the real estate rental business?

THE CONCEPT OF LAW

Law is much more than an accumulation of rules. Some believe that law is a process by which disputes are resolved.[14] Yet, law is more than merely such a process. Law, more broadly understood, is the skeleton that gives a society shape and form. The two goals of law as it seeks justice are predictability and flexibility. These goals are necessary for laws to be both observed and respected. Laws must be stable and predictable to allow people of good will to monitor their actions to stay within the law; laws must be flexible to meet the needs of a changing and evolving society. Yet, these two valuable goals conflict. This inherent conflict provides much tension within the institution of the law. More on this tension is found in Chapter 2.

ETHICS AND MORALS DISTINGUISHED

Law is frequently intertwined with a society's morality. Some aspects of morality are so widely held, so universal, that a society will enact laws enforcing those aspects—putting the weight of government and the machinery of the law behind them. Some examples are the moral injunctions against homicide, the importance of keeping promises, not bearing false witness, and respecting the person and the property of others. Yet, law is a secular institution, and morality, even in very homogeneous societies, varies widely. Consequently, law is not a good vehicle for the enforcement of a broad spectrum of moral values because once we move beyond the narrow band of universal moral principals consensus breaks down. In addition, in the United States, law is generally observed

---

12. *See, e.g, Boise Mayor Faces Controversies in Office*, ID. STATESMAN (January 13, 2001) at 5A. The ordinance was passed on a 6–0 vote on December 19, 2000, and is now in effect in Boise.
13. *See, e.g.*, radio ads running during the week of January 8, 2001, on Radio 104.3 FM in which a speaker imitating President Clinton supports Mayor Cole's attempt to "snoop on tenants" and then laughs, saying, "I've snooped on some tenants myself in my day." The message ends with the simulated voice of President Clinton advising Mayor Brent Coles that "the extra police you requested are in the mail." In addition to the radio campaign, Mayor Coles received many telephone calls; during one 12-day span in December, the mayor's office logged in 186 calls to his hotline about the drug cleanup ordinance. All but 18 were critical. Gene Fadness, *Boise's Mayor Has Tough Month*, ID. STATESMAN (January 13, 2001) at 1A.
14. *See, e.g.*, K. N. LLEWELLYN, THE BRAMBLE BUSH (1960, orig. ed. 1930) at 12. Professor Llewellyn writes, "This doing something about disputes, this doing of it reasonably, is the business of the law. And the people who have the doing in charge, whether they be judges or sheriffs or clerks or jailors or lawyers, are officials of the law. *What these officials do about disputes is, to my mind, the law itself.*" Id.

by the people out of respect for the institution; voluntary compliance is the rule—not the exception.

Morals can be understood as *prima facie* rules for good behavior. *Prima facie* is a legal term that in this context means that moral principles are like trump in a card game: The moral principle prevails unless it is overruled by a higher moral principle. Ethics, in contrast, is the cognitive, reasoned, and systematic application of moral principles in situations in which that application is unclear or moral principles conflict.

There are **two basic types of ethical dilemmas**.[15] An *ethical encounter of the first* kind involves a situation where one knows right and wrong but has difficulty deciding whether to follow one's moral principle. *An ethical encounter of the second kind* addresses a conflict between two valid moral principles. An example may involve a conflict between your obligations (moral duties) to your family and your obligation to your employer (a moral duty). Both are legitimate, and both parties insist on your presence on Wednesday evening at 6 p.m. Which do you pick? How do you choose? There is no magic solution to ethical encounters of the second kind. One has to examine and weigh the choice each time. The discomfort that results from having to examine each conflict on its merits may be why some ethics books and some instructors prefer to stick to the first kind of dilemma, in which they can always argue for baseball, apple pie, and Chevrolet.

All decisions do not implicate the moral domain.[16] Some decisions are morally neutral. For example, a person who owns two pairs of shoes has to decide which pair to wear; that choice does not invoke a moral dimension. In contrast, a doctor may have to perform triage, deciding which of several patients gets immediate medical attention and which waits. That decision has implications for the moral domain. A jury may have to decide whether to impose a death sentence or to sentence a convicted felon to life without parole. That decision has moral implications. We examine these matters in greater detail in Chapter 3 and other later chapters.

The epigram at the beginning of this chapter by Norman F. Cantor talks about world revolutions springing from "some just complaint" in the prevailing systems; interestingly, Cantor does not mention economic systems as the basis for a world revolution. In the Middle Ages, economics was not yet a social science. However, in modern times, we may be witnesses to a revolution in economics. The rise of economic society and the evolution of capitalism may, perhaps, be a world revolution about to go global. Whether another world revolution will arise out of the culminating stage of capitalism is an engaging question.

JUST WHAT IS BUSINESS?

Business can be defined as any "commercial, industrial, or professional dealings."[17] The purpose of this book, however, is to take an expansive position on the concept of business so as to err on the side of overinclusiveness.

---

15. For an excellent discussion of these two types, *see* Jonathan B. King, *Ethical Encounters of the Second Kind*, J. BUS. ETHICS (no. 5, June 1986) 1–11

16. Defining the moral domain—that is, the nature of morality—is impossible. However, as James Rachels has pointed out, there is a widely accepted concept of a minimal morality. "Morality is, at the very least, the effort to guide one's conduct by reason—that is, to do what there are the best reasons for doing—while giving equal weight to the interests of each individual who will be affected by one's conduct." JAMES RACHELS, THE ELEMENTS OF MORAL PHILOSOPHY (3rd ed. 1999) at 19.

17. THE AMERICAN HERITAGE DICTIONARY (2nd college ed. 1985) at 220.

"Who's winning?"

From *The New Yorker*, circa 1973.

Consequently, in this book, business includes nonprofit, for-profit, and governmental activity when it falls into the general area of proprietary functions. By proprietary functions, I mean the production, distribution, or sales of goods or services so long as the activity or practice does not fall within the realm of traditional governmental activity.[18] Thus, when the City of Milwaukee runs a water department and sells drinking water, it is business; when the State of Idaho runs liquor dispensaries and sells whiskey, it is business as well. However, when the City of Milwaukee collects taxes to pay for sewers and streets, it is not engaging in a business activity, but rather a governmental function. This book recognizes no artificial distinction among for-profit business, nonprofit business, and governmental business; it lumps them all together as business. Business, thus liberally understood, is the dominant social institution on the planet Earth today.[19]

THE IDEA OF SOCIETY

Society can be understood as "a community, nation, or broad grouping of people having common traditions, institutions, and collective activities and

---

18. We adopt this distinction from the majority opinion in *Garcia v. San Antonio Metropolitan Transit Authority et al.* 469 U.S. 528 (1985).

19. *See, e.g.*, CHARLES DERBER, CORPORATE NATION: HOW CORPORATIONS ARE TAKING OVER OUR LIVES AND WHAT WE CAN DO ABOUT IT (1998) at 35–48. Derber describes the decline since the 1950s of the "countervailing powers" (labor unions and prominently the federal government) together with the globalization of corporations leading to an uncontested global dominance of huge corporations. *Id.*

interests."[20] There are, of course, other definitions of society, but for our purposes this definition is the most useful. The study of societies is called sociology, which can be defined as a social science in which the "long-run aim is to discover the basic structure of human society, to identify the main forces that hold groups together or weaken them, and to learn what conditions transform social life."[21]

At least four contrasting models have been established as starting points for the study of society: consensus, conflict, structure, and process. Although most sociologists share a general perspective, these four models demonstrate some of the important differences in emphasis and outlook. The consensus model gives considerable weight to the persistence of shared ideas, whereas the conflict model or approach holds that society is best understood as an arena of actual and potential conflicts. Another source of tension in sociology stems from choices in how society is broken down into components for study and where scholars place their emphases. Some sociologists emphasize social structures, and others insist that the individual be kept as the center of attention. The latter school is known as symbolic interactionism.[22]

Strictly speaking, structure versus process is a false dichotomy because there can be no structure without process. Neither does it make much sense to study process without examining the nature of the framework within which choice and action take place. However, the difference in emphasis is significant: Symbolic interactionists argue that the heart of social reality is the human being trying to make sense of social situations. The implication of a structural emphasis is that individuals are seen as shaped by the forces that are applied to them, by their social backgrounds, and by their group memberships.

WHAT IS GOVERNMENT?

Government can be defined as the act or process of controlling policymaking in a political unit or agency.[23] Government is also commonly thought of as a "governing body or organization" or "those persons who comprise the governing body."[24] We Americans have always had a distrust of government, going back, I suppose, to the bad relations we had with George III during our colonial period.

As Thomas Hobbes pointed out in *Leviathan*, in the absence of government, a state of nature would exist in which there would be "no arts; no letters; no society; and which is worst of all, continual fear and danger of violent death; and the life of man [would be] solitary, poor, nasty, brutish, and short."[25] Men and women band together to promote their mutual safety and general welfare. Without government, property could not exist; there would only be naked possession.

WHY IS POLITICS IMPORTANT?

We look at politics because politics is "the art or science of government" or, perhaps, more explicitly "the art or science concerned with guiding or influencing

---

20. MERRIAM WEBSTER'S COLLEGIATE DICTIONARY (10th ed. 1995) at 1115.
21. L. BROOM & P. SELZNICK, SOCIOLOGY (5th ed. 1973) at 3.
22. *Id* at 9.
23. *Id*. at 569.
24. *Id*.
25. THOMAS HOBBES, LEVIATHAN (1651), pt. 1, ch. 13.

governmental policy."[26] In the United States, we have a representative form of government in which one of the obligations of citizenship is to participate in government. Thus, a discussion of politics is unavoidable in a study of law, ethics, and business. Legalizing marijuana is an example of a policy decision made by the government and determined by politics. Our political values are driven by our personal values. The determination of our personal values is a subject we discuss later. Our politics is also driven by our belief as to what the appropriate role of government should be in a free society.

THEORIES OF GOVERNMENT (THE STATE)

Following Frederick D. Sturdivant (formerly Riklis Professor at Ohio State University), we will posit and discuss five main theories of the state: pluralist, Marxist, welfare, libertarian, and modern cynic.[27] The pluralist perspective holds that the function of government is to maintain a rough balance between conflicting groups, such as consumers and retailers, labor and management, debtors and creditors, etc. The notion is one of government as an umpire making sure that no one side has dominance, even including the federal government, which would enable it to impose its will and, hence, probable injustice on its policy opponent; the pluralist view of government is the dominant view among American political scientists at this time. The idea of shared power and the concept of checks and balances are as deeply rooted in U.S. society as the Constitution. Sources of this line of thought can be traced to James Madison's work on *The Federalist Papers*.

Until the proletariat[28] rises and takes power, the capitalist state is merely the tool of the rich and powerful that they use to dominate the state and exploit the workers. This is the Marxist view of the capitalist states. As one University of Colorado political scientist has argued,

> Through the control of the media and educational institutions, but more important, through its control of the forms by which people labor and earn their living, the dominant class finds its ideas permeating the social order. In feudal society, for example, ideas conducive to the stability of the feudal order, such as sanctity of land, of the serf-landlord relationship, and of mutual loyalties, dominated social thought. In capitalist societies, ideas requisite to the maintenance of capitalist economic arrangements dominate social thought: the rights of private property, competition, free enterprise, consumption, and individualism.[29]

The state, from this perspective, becomes the means by which the major economic actors protect their dominance against threats to their position, whether such threats arise from the downtrodden masses, impersonal economic forces, or radical academic thinkers. The underlying assumption is that powerful economic forces represented usually by business dominate not only the economy of a nation but also its ideology and political processes. In this vein, it may

---

26. *Supra* note 7, at 901.
27. FREDERICK STURDIVANT, BUSINESS AND SOCIETY (rev. ed. 1981).
28. The proletariat is "the class of industrial wage earners who, possessing neither capital nor production means, must earn their living by selling their labor." THE AMERICAN HERITAGE DICTIONARY at 990.
29. EDWARD S. GREENBERG, SERVING THE FEW: CORPORATE CAPITALISM AND THE BIAS OF GOVERNMENT POLICY (1974) at 24 as quoted in FREDERICK STURDIVANT, BUSINESS AND SOCIETY (rev. ed. 1981) at 49.

be interesting to note how little news coverage Ralph Nader's campaign for president of the United States generated in the years 2000 and 2004 and also how Nader was excluded from the national debates and kept off ballots in various states. Perhaps, his views on regulating corporate America did not sit well with some decision makers in our society?

Another often-used illustration of the unfairness of capitalist states is the contrast between the penalties meted out to white-collar criminals and those assessed against so-called street criminals. As Ralph Nader noted in his introduction to Charles Derber's disturbing book on corporate power, now that the U.S. culture is a corporate culture, "we grow up corporate," meaning we accept unthinkingly corporate assumptions about most matters. These assumptions extend to the meaning of words so that "violence" excludes corporate violence, "crime" excludes corporate crime, and "welfare" excludes corporate welfare.[30] Yet, as Frederick Sturdivant noted two decades ago, the take from "home improvement frauds alone (not to mention other forms of fraud, as well as price fixing, embezzlement, forgery, and other varieties of commercial theft) nearly equals the annual dollars generated by street crimes."[31]

White-collar crime dwarfs street crime, yet the perpetrators of street crimes fill the prisons, whereas most white-collar criminals walk.[32] In Texas recently as noted by CBS "60 Minutes," a black man was sentenced to 80 years in prison for allegedly dealing one-eighth ounce of cocaine; in comparison, two top executives of the Fruehauf Corporation were sentenced to 4 months of public service for "conspiring to defraud the federal government of some $12 million in excise taxes."[33] The mastermind of a $100 million oil swindle was fined $19,000, ordered to pay $100,000 in restitution, and sentenced to 1 day in the federal section of the Tulsa, Oklahoma jail.[34] The examples go on. Look at the inside trading scandals and the penalties meted out to Michael Milken[35] and others. Examine the Watergate scandal and the penalties served by top White House aides who betrayed the public trust.[36]

---

30. CHARLES DERBER, CORPORATE NATION: HOW CORPORATIONS ARE TAKING OVER OUR LIVES AND WHAT WE CAN DO ABOUT IT (1998) at ix.

31. STURDIVANT, *supra* note 27, at 50.

32. *Id.* at 50–53.

33. *Id.* at 51.

34. *Id.*

35. Michael Milken, the junk bond king from Drexel-Burnham-Lambert, paid a $1 billion fine and served about 22 months in a federal minimum security prison on charges of securities fraud. Initially, Milken was sentenced to 10 years; but that was reduced when it was argued that Milken should not serve a longer sentence than Ivan Boesky, his Wall Street friend who gave him up to the feds. *See, e.g.*, Don Oldenburg, *Dishonest Executives Face Serious Jail Time*, THE WALL STREET JOURNAL ONLINE. Accessed at http://www.careerjournal.com/services/print/?url=http%3A//www.careerjournal.com/myc/l on January 21, 2005. The charges against Enron Chief Financial Officer (CFO) Andrew Fastow alone added up to a potential sentence under the Federal Sentencing Guidelines of almost 1,000 years. *Id.* Mr. Fastow cut a plea bargain under which he agreed to cooperate with prosecutors and received a 10-year prison sentence for pleading guilty on January 21, 2004 to two counts of wire and securities fraud. Mr. Fastow had been facing a 98-count indictment and an April 2004 trial date. *Fastow and His Wife Plead Guilty*. Accessed at http://cnnmoney.printthis.clickability.com/pt/cpt?action=cpt&title=Fastow+pleads+guilty on January 21, 2005.

36. Counsel to the President, John Dean, served 4 months in witness protection because he cooperated with the Congress and the prosecution. In March 1974, seven former members of President Richard M. Nixon's administration or of the Nixon 1972 reelection committee were indicted on charges of conspiracy to obstruct justice in the Watergate break-in of June 17, 1972. In January 1975, former Domestic Chief Counsel John D. Erlichman, White House

The welfare theory of the state does not use the concept of welfare in the pejorative sense. Rather, proponents of that theory argue that it is the job of the government to do for people what they cannot do for themselves. The modern positivist state is active and intervenes in society to improve the lives of its citizens and others around the world. From this perspective, the state is a positive force: "The state is an unselfish instrument of the common welfare; it is designed to alleviate potential hardship caused by economic displacements, technological change, and the like."[37] The period between 1952 and 1977 in Great Britain has been used to argue for the effectiveness of this policy.[38]

On the American side of the Atlantic, a welfare state perspective has been much criticized not only in books[39] but also at the polls. To be elected, Democrats have had to move toward the right and support such policies as welfare-to-work reform, school vouchers, right to life, and the death penalty. The election of Ronald Reagan to the White House in November 1980 marked a significant swing of political fortunes toward the conservatives not only in the ranks of the Republicans but also on the Democratic side of the ballot. The election of William Jefferson Clinton did not mark so much a change in public attitude as an endorsement of the politics of pragmatism. The election of George W. Bush in November 2000 validated a "compassionate conservatism" marked by a conservative government that left compassionate acts to individuals who felt so moved. The reelection of George W. Bush in November 2004 seems to have marked the start of a 4-year effort to reshape the American experiment more along lines reflecting the ideology of the neoconservatives. However, the divisions in the American electorate may represent a serious potential obstacle to President Bush's remodeling effort.[40]

The libertarian perspective views the state as "conceived in violence" and "born to power."[41] In 1788, a year after the Constitutional Convention,

---

Chief of Staff H. R. "Bob" Haldeman, and Attorney General John N. Mitchell were each convicted of conspiracy, obstruction of justice, and perjury. They were sentenced to prison terms of 2.5 to 8 years. The sentences were later reduced to 1 to 4 years. One estimate is that the total criminal convictions resulting from Watergate totaled about 30. THE WORLD BOOK ENCYCLOPEDIA (1990), vol. 21 at 144–145.

    Erlichman voluntarily entered prison in 1976, and Haldeman and Mitchell—having exhausted their appeals—entered prison the next year. *See, e.g., Watergate Scandal.* Accessed at http://www.en.wikipedia.org/wiki/Watergate on January 21, 2005. All three were released after serving approximately 18 months. *See John D. Erlichman Sighted in Arizona.* Accessed at http://www.doney.net/aroundaz/celebrity/ehrlichman_john.htm on January 21, 2005. Erlichman died in 1999. *Id.* John Mitchell died in 1988, Bob Haldeman died of cancer in 1993, and former President Richard M. Nixon died in 1994. The Watergate scandal can be understood to be the gravest Constitutional crisis in U.S. history.

37. *See* STURDIVANT, *supra* note 26 at 56.
38. *See, e.g.,* BERNARD D. NOSSITER, BRITAIN: A FUTURE THAT WORKS (1978) as cited in STURDIVANT, *supra* note 14, at 56–57.
39. *See, e.g.,* CHRISTOPHER LASCH, THE CULTURE OF NARCISSISM (1979) and ALAN BRINKLEY, LIBERALISM AND ITS DISCONTENTS (1998).
40. George W. Bush became the first candidate since 1988 to receive a majority of the popular vote. Mr. Bush, who was sworn in for a second term on January 20, 2005, by an ailing Chief Justice William Rehnquist, won by the smallest margin of victory for a sitting president in U.S. history. His margin was 2.5% of the votes. In terms of absolute number of votes, Mr. Bush won by the smallest margin (approximately 3 million votes) since Harry S. Truman won in 1948. Mr. Bush received approximately 62 million votes, and Mr. Kerry got approximately 59 million votes out of the 122,267,553 votes cast on November 2, 2004. *U.S. Presidential Election, 2004.* Accessed at http://en.wikipedia.org/wiki/U.S._presidential_election,_2004 on January 12, 2005.
41. R. M. MACIVER, THE MODERN STATE (1929) as cited in STURDIVANT, *supra* note 14, at 48.

Thomas Jefferson wrote to a friend, "The natural progress of things is for liberty to yield and government to gain ground."[42] Adam Smith believed that the government had three natural functions: (1) protection of property and enforcement of laws, (2) national defense, and (3) the building of such public works as were in the common welfare but that could not be supported by private means. Libertarians would probably not disagree much with the observations of the man from Kirkcaldy.

About 1849, Henry David Thoreau, the student of Ralph Waldo Emerson, wrote, "I heartily accept the motto, 'That government is best which governs least'; and I should like to see it acted up to more rapidly and systematically. Carried out, it finally amounts to this, which I also believe, 'That government is best which governs not at all.'"[43] That sentiment could easily devolve into something like the contemporary bumper sticker that humorously declares, "Anarchy is better than no government at all." However, I doubt that Thoreau meant to go down that road.

In the eyes of libertarians, the modern state is nothing more than a continuing effort by the government to extend its control over society and reduce personal freedom. Thus, most libertarians believe that what is called for is a night-watchman-type of government. In pursuit of that minimalist concept of government, libertarian candidates for office often call for such policies as privatizing education and prisons.

A modern cynic sees government existing not so much for any reasonable or defensible purpose but merely to extend its own sway. This view is really not a formal school of thought or even much of a political science position as it is a negative reaction to growing governmental regulation. It is frequently expressed by someone frustrated or angry over red tape, rising taxes, or governmental waste. The underlying assumptions are that all politicians are generally crooked and deceitful, that public officials and employees are lazy, and that the public is generally being taken for a ride.[44] Whether based on fact or only on anger and frustration, cynicism toward government is a rapidly growing position and one liable to have an impact on American society for better or worse.

THE AMERICAN CULTURE OF VIOLENCE

"Violence is as American as cherry pie."[45] So spoke H. Rap Brown in Baltimore on the occasion that resulted in his conviction for inciting to riot.[46] In a periodical published shortly after the end of World War I, A. Phillip Randolph, the father of the modern black civil rights movement, declared, "Make wars

---

42. STURDIVANT, *supra* note 26, at 48.

43. HENRY DAVID THOREAU, *On the Moral Duty of Civil Disobedience*, in WALDEN (orig. publ. 1849, Signet ed. 1960) at 222.

44. *See* STURDIVANT, *supra* note 26, at 58.

45. Thomas Merton meditated on this quotation in his essay, *Faith and Violence*, THOMAS MERTON, THOMAS MERTON ON PEACE (1971) at 199-202. In part, he observed, "Rap Brown's statement...is steeped in the pungent ironies which characterize the new language of racial conflict.... Yes, violence is thoroughly American and Rap Brown is saying that it is in fact the real American language. Perhaps so, perhaps not. But in any event, it is the language the Black American has now elected to speak. Oddly enough, he instantly got himself a much better hearing when he did so." *Id*. at 199.

46. *See also* QUOTATIONS IN BLACK (Anita King, ed. 1981) at quotation # 1146 citing H. RAP BROWN, DIE, NIGGER, DIE (1969).

unprofitable and you make them impossible."[47] Yet, organized warfare is only one aspect of violence in American society and an increasingly small part of it over the past 40 years. What we now face is an epidemic of violence sweeping across the landscape of this great country[48] in which young and old, rich and poor are perpetrators and victims.[49]

---

47. QUOTATIONS IN BLACK, *supra* note 1, citing Asa Phillip Randolph, *The Cause and Remedy of Race Riots*, THE MESSENGER (September 1919).

48. Psychologist Dave Grossman reaches this conclusion after a book-length analysis of killing and violence in American society. He states, "Between 1985 and 1991 the homicide rate for males fifteen to nineteen increased 154 percent. ... In Vietnam a systematic process of desensitization, conditioning, and training increased the individual firing rate from a World War II baseline of 15 to 20 percent to an all-time high of up to 95 percent. Today a similar process of systematic desensitization, conditioning, and vicarious learning is *unleashing an epidemic, a virus of violence in America* [emphasis added]." DAVE GROSSMAN, ON KILLING: THE PSYCHOLOGICAL COST OF LEARNING TO KILL IN WAR AND SOCIETY (1995) at 304.

49. As of December 31, 2001, there were 1.3 million adults in state and federal prisons. Bureau of Justice Statistics, U. S. Department of Justice, Criminal Offenders Statistics, *Summary Findings*. Accessed at http://www.ojp.usdoj.gov/bjs/crimoff.htm on January 11, 2004. Federal prison inmates were likely to be older and more were serving time for drug offenses than state prisoners; 24% of federal prisoners were age 45 or older versus 13% for state prisoners, and in 2000 57% of federal inmates were serving time for drug offenses as opposed to 21% of state inmates. *Id.* at p. 3. According to the Federal Bureau of Investigation's *Uniform Crime Reports*, the crime rate index decreased 1% between 2001 and 2002, and it fell a whopping 25% from 1993 to 2002. Bureau of Justice Statistics, U.S. Department of Justice, Crime and Victims Statistics, *Summary Findings*. Accessed at http://www.ojp.usdoj.gov/bjs/cvict.htm on January 11, 2004. These numbers should be viewed with substantial caution, however. Dr. Grossman pointed out some of the problems with U.S. crime statistics in the following passage:

> There is some confusion about crime reporting in America, generally due to the fact that there are two crime reports produced each year by the U.S. government. One report is compiled by the FBI based upon all crime reported by law-enforcement agencies across the nation. In recent years this report has reflected a steady *decrease* in overall crime and a steady *increase* in violent crime, as reflected in the graph on page 300.
>
> The other annual crime report is based on a national survey of crime victims and reports its findings according to the number of crimes per household. ... The data in this report also have potential for error (probably in the direction of underreporting), since they are based on a subjective assessment on the part of an increasingly jaded population being surveyed. Nevertheless, in 1994 this survey reflected a 5.6 percent increase in violent crime.
>
> The fact that the crime victim survey reflected a significant increase in violent crime in the same year that the FBI reported a small decrease supports a school of thought which holds that the FBI report has also increasingly underreported crime. ... There is evidence to indicate that in many high-crime areas attacks and assaults that would have received immediate attention thirty years ago (for example, drive-by shootings in which no one is hit and beatings in which no one is killed) are routinely ignored today." DAVE GROSSMAN, ON KILLING (1995), *supra* note 20, at 346–347.

Even putting aside problems with data, most of which tend toward underreporting, the data tend to support the idea that crimes are committed against all ages, all races, and all gender groups in this country. For instance, Table 4 labeled "Personal crimes, 2002" indicates that there were 3.0 crimes of violence committed against females over age 65 years per 1,000 individuals in that group; there were 3.9 crimes of violence against males over 65 per 1,000 individuals; for every male between 12 and 15 years of age, there were 46.1 crimes of violence per thousand; and for every female between 12 and 15 years of age, there were 42.6 acts of violence per thousand. Bureau of Justice Statistics, U.S. Department of Justice, *Criminal Victimization in the United States, 2002 Statistical Tables*. Accessed at http://www.ojp.usdoj.gov/bjs/cvict.htm on January 11, 2004.

For all persons, both genders, the total rates of crimes of violence per 1,000 were 23.1 crimes (Table 2); for males, the rate was 26.1; and for females, the rate was 21.5 crimes. *Id.*

To support such a sweeping conclusion, the term "violence" needs to be understood in a much broader and inclusive way than it has historically been understood. Violence is, of course, the use of physical force so as to injure or abuse.[50] Yet, violence is much more. Physical violence can be organized on a grand scale; then it goes by the name of "war." Yet, we need to expand our viewpoint to encompass concepts ranging from "unnecessary harm"[51] to "sentient creation," usually a form of environmental violence. For instance, is it defensible from a justice standpoint to consume resources at a rate that exceeds sustainable levels of consumption? Can that be viewed as the moral equivalent of stealing from our grandchildren's trust fund?

Economics should be included as a potential source of organized violence against nature, people, communities, and societies. Is it an act of violence when a corporation, as one recently did in the Cincinnati area, waits until the morning shift workers arrive to tell them that the plant has closed down permanently?[52] Is it an act of violence when a plant relocates out of the country and leaves a town with roads, schools, sewers, streets, and sidewalks to be paid for by long-term debt? Is it an act of violence for the plant to be relocated and to leave former employees with equity in houses that suddenly have no market?

Analyzing these data by race and type of crime (Table 5) produced the following: crimes of violence per 1,000 White people aged 12 years and up were committed at a rate of 22.8; for Blacks, the comparable rate was 27.9; and for others the rate was 14.7. *Id.* For household burglaries (Table 21), the rate of burglaries per 1,000 households for Whites with household income $75,000 and more was 21.7; for Blacks with an income of $75,000 and more, the rate was 18.0; for Whites with income of less than $7,500, the rate was 44.9 per thousand; and for Blacks with an income of less than $7,500, the rate was 75.6 per thousand. *Id.*

When it comes to homicide, the differences in race and age between victims are stunning. In the United States in the year 2001, there were 13,752 murder victims (Table 2.4) according to the FBI; of those, 6,446 were Black; and of those, 5,350 were Black males. Federal Bureau of Investigation, Department of Justice, *Uniform Crime Reports.* Accessed at http://www.fbi.gov/ucr/o1cius.htm on January, 11 2004. Of the 13,752 murder victims (a number not including the victims of the September 11th events in Pennsylvania, Washington, D.C., or New York City), there were 220 infants under the age of 1 year; 269 victims aged 75 years or over; and 2,651 victims aged 20 to 24—of whom 2,299 were males. *Id* at Table 2.5.

I do not intend to limit this note to Department of Justice statistics, particularly because I am urging broader parameters in the study of violence and specifically inclusion of acts of economic violence. The numbers of victims and perpetrators of acts of economics violence are much harder to determine—especially because some of the acts that I would include are not presently even considered crimes. However, one episode from 2001 serves to support my thesis, even if only in an anecdotal manner. When Enron imploded in a sea of hidden debts, inflated profits, and accounting skullduggery in 2001, millions of investors lost billions of dollars. Some Enron employees lost all their retirement savings; and 4,500 employees in Enron's retail energy unit lost their jobs. Kristen Hays, *SEC Has Collected $324 Million in Enron-Related Fines So Far,* THE MIAMI HERALD (July 29, 2003). Accessed at http://www.miami.com/mld/miamiherald/business/6410537.htm on January 11, 2003. In comparison with the total fines to the date of this article ($324 million), the losses are staggering; the aggregate amount sought in damages just in the shareholder lawsuits filed in Houston, Texas, is over $25 billion, more than 75 times the total fines held by the SEC. *Id.*

50. MERRIAM WEBSTER'S COLLEGIATE DICTIONARY (10th ed. 1995) at 1319.
51. Unnecessary harm has the negative implication of "necessary" harm. It may be that killing a fish to feed a hungry person or a bear is a form of necessary harm, or that burning dead wood to warm a family may be necessary harm, even though the dead limbs provide shelter to various grubs and insects. The idea of necessary harm came to my attention from Norm Bowie's writing. *See, e.g.,* NORMAN E. BOWIE & RONALD F. DUSKA, BUSINESS ETHICS (2nd ed. 1990) at 73.
52. Announced on ABC local news, Tuesday, October 22, 2002, Channel 9 at 6 p.m.

The concept of sentient creation was raised to the level of an entity with moral standing by the utilitarian philosophy of Bentham and Mill.[53] In the early 1970s, skeptics laughed at the notion that trees and whales should be entitled to legal standing[54] and representation. Thirty years later, the idea may not be laughed away as easily. Global capitalism has raised the specter of decimation of forests and mountains and even aquaculture in its relentless pursuit of profit. Many of the countries where the greatest harm has been done are also among the poorest. Consequently, some of us may argue that global capitalism, in certain times and places, has treated the ecosystem of this planet in the same manner that the U.S. cavalry treated the indigenous people of the United States less than 150 years ago.[55]

Most of us think reflexively about violence as physical violence. Similarly, the tenth edition of Webster's Collegiate Dictionary defines "violence" first as "exertion of physical force so as to injure or abuse (as in effecting illegal entry into a house)."[56] In the second definition, violence is defined as "injury by or as if by distortion, infringement, or profanation: outrage."[57] The third definition of violence is "intense, turbulent, or furious and often destructive action or force <the ~ of the storm>."[58] It would be correct usage to talk about the violence of global capitalism in the third sense: Global capitalism can be understood as a very destructive force that is causing damage to established economies and to social structures worldwide.[59]

Finally, economic power exercised through marketing can be used to convey images, which through repetition become embedded in American society and culture. Many of these images are neutral or inane. Some, however, have been rightly challenged as potentially damaging to groups in our society or as aiding the sale of goods or services that may be unnecessarily harmful to the environment. For example, look at the images of women used by Madison Avenue marketing firms to sell just about everything from automobiles to chewing tobacco. Some feminists and others have challenged the use of these images on the grounds that they promote the sexual harassment of women[60] and even violence toward women[61] by objectifying them.

The use of female images to market goods and services,[62] although pervasive in U.S. marketing, is also strikingly associated with violent sports and violent forms of entertainment. The exact nexus is not clear, but the frequency of the combination seems to exceed mere coincidence. The NFL Dallas Cowboy "cheerleaders" in their revealing costumes are one example. More

---

53. *See, e.g.,* JAMES RACHELS, THE ELEMENTS OF MORAL PHILOSOPHY (4th ed. 2003) at 97–101.
54. *See Sierra Club v. Morton* 405 U.S. 727 (1972) wherein Justice Douglas in dissent argues that "these environmental issues should be tendered by the inanimate object itself." *Id.* at 752. *See also* Christopher Stone, *Should Trees Have Standing? Toward Legal Rights for Natural Objects,* 45 S. CAL. L. REV. 450 (1972).
55. *See, e.g.,* DEE BROWN, BURY MY HEART AT WOUNDED KNEE (1970).
56. MERRIAM WEBSTER'S COLLEGIATE DICTIONARY (10th ed. 1995) at 1319.
57. *Id.*
58. *Id.*
59. *See, e.g.,* WILLIAM GREIDER, ONE WORLD READY OR NOT: THE MANIC LOGIC OF GLOBAL CAPITALISM (1997) and DAVID KORTEN, WHEN CORPORATIONS RULE THE WORLD (1995).
60. *See, e.g.,* Joyce Hollyday, *Selling Sex and Beer,* SOJOURNERS (Feb.–Mar. 1992) at 4.
61. *See, e.g.,* IN HARM'S WAY: THE PORNOGRAPHIC CIVIL RIGHTS HEARINGS (Catherine A. MacKinnon & Andrea Dworkin, eds., 1997).
62. This practice has long been the subject of a large amount of critical commentary. *See, e.g.,* CRITICAL STUDIES IN MEDIA COMMERCIALISM (Robin Andersen & Lance Strate, eds., 2000); and JEAN KILBOURNE, DEADLY PERSUASION: WHY WOMEN AND GIRLS MUST FIGHT THE ADDICTIVE POWER OF ADVERTISING (1999).

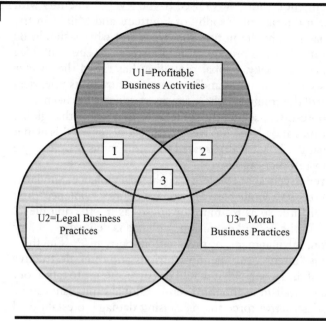

pedestrian examples can be found locally. Look, for example, at the "Meanest Man Contest" held quarterly near Ross, Ohio, at Stricker's Grove Hall.[63] Although 14 states have outlawed such contests, Ohio sanctions them. In such contests, so-called ring girls conduct a lingerie auction during the second intermission and sashay about advertising the auction between rounds.[64] One writer described the outfits as "slinky" and described the modeling as a "fan favorite for years."[65]

AN INTEGRATION MODEL OF PROFITS, MORALS, AND LAW

Without denying that profits are a requirement for the survival of for-profit enterprises, the corporate social responsibility position argues that business should be willing to make some trade-offs at the margin to be good citizens, (i.e., be "socially responsible"). Assuming this position without proving it (for now), a set of Venn diagrams for business profits, law, and ethics[66] might look like Figure 1.1.

Obviously, this drawing is not to scale, but it does point out some interesting concepts. The ideal target area for business operations is represented by the shaded area in the middle (3). Area 1, which represents business activities that are profitable and legal but not moral, might include both activities that are amoral (i.e., morally inert or neutral), together with activities that are

---

63. Kevin Kelly, *Who's the Meanest of Them All? Contest Offers Chance To Be a Fighter for a Night,* CINC. ENQUIRER (December 18, 2004) at C1.
64. *Id.* at C7.
65. *Id.*
66. The idea is based on a very similar Venn diagram used in EDWARD J. CONRY, GERALD R. FERRERRA, & KARLA H. FOX, THE LEGAL ENVIRONMENT OF BUSINESS (1986) at 30.

immoral. For instance, some child advocates and some advocates of nonviolence might argue that running "Meanest Man" contests falls into Area 1. Area 2, which would be smaller if this drawing were made to scale, includes business activities that are moral and profitable but illegal, such as producing marijuana for treating side effects of chemotherapy in cancer patients.

CONCLUSION

This chapter introduces concepts of ethics, law, and business and the themes that are basic to this book. It defines politics and five models of the state. One of the continuing themes, the pervasiveness of violence in our culture, is introduced in the last section. I argue that a persistent ethos of violence against human beings and against the environment has been gaining ground in this country and around the world for many decades. The failure to embrace a standard of sustainability means simply that we are using up more than our generation's fair share of the earth's provisions. Ultimately, we may come to see that economics without compassion "becomes merely a highly developed form of violence."[67]

---

67. MATTHEW FOX, A SPIRITUALITY NAMED COMPASSION AND THE HEALING OF THE GLOBAL VILLAGE, HUMPTY DUMPTY AND US (1979) at 177. *See also* WILLIAM A. WINES, *Does Capitalism Wear a White Hat or Ride a Pale Horse? Physical and Economic Violence in America and a Survey of Attitudes Toward Violence held by U.S. Undergraduate Business Majors Compared to Ohio Valley Quakers*, **forthcoming in** SOUTHERN UNIVERSITY LAW REV. (Fall 2005).

CHAPTER 2

Law and Jurisprudence

DEFINITIONS AND FUNCTIONS

Law has been defined many ways in many contexts. Professors Berman and Greiner listed four main functions for law in their textbook, as follows:

> In speaking of law, then, we have in mind a special type of process of restoring, maintaining or creating social order, characterized by formality (in the sense indicated: that is, by relative deliberateness, definiteness, etc.), whose main general functions are (a) to resolve disputes, (b) to facilitate and protect voluntary arrangements, (c) to mold and remold the moral and legal conceptions of a society and (d) in the Western tradition, at least, to maintain historical continuity and consistency of doctrine.[1]

For our purposes, law can best be understood as the main social institution that provides for nonviolent dispute resolution. Professor Karl Llewellyn uttered the most famous and succinct statement of this concept in his opening lectures at Columbia Law School in 1929 and 1930.[2] In a much debated passage, Professor Llewellyn declared,

> What, then, is this law business about? It is about the fact that our society is honeycombed with disputes. Disputes actual and potential; disputes to be settled and disputes to be prevented; both appealing to law, both making up the business of the law. . . . This doing something about disputes, this doing of it reasonably, is the business of law. And the people who have the doing in charge, whether they be judges or sheriffs or clerks or jailers or lawyers, are officials of the law. *What these officials do about disputes is, to my mind, the law itself.*[3] (italics in original)

We can better appreciate this approach to defining law when we understand that forerunners to trial by jury involved trial by battle, trial by ordeal, and wager of law.

Trial by battle rested on the assumption that "right makes might." It implicitly held that the Almighty Ruler of the Universe would side with the party who was telling the truth in the dispute about who owned the brown cow. Thus, the so-called truth-teller, counting on divine intervention, could proceed in confidence to battle the nontruth teller. An extension of this approach came into being when the parties in interest no longer had to go into battle themselves, but could appoint a Paladin to fight for them; the assumption was that "right makes might" could also work in a tag-team situation or through agency.

Trial by ordeal was the mainstay of the Star Chamber and the Spanish Inquisition. Its underlying assumption is that a person would rather perish than die and face the Day of Judgment with a lie on his or her lips. Consequently, one could try someone for heresy, for example, merely by placing that person in a painful position and interrogating him or her. Especially, it was thought, someone would not admit to heresy or witchcraft, conditions that would imperil one's soul and possibly prohibit the benefit of last rites and burial in sacred ground. Another consideration was that the penalty for heresy and

---

1. H. J. BERMAN & W. R. GREINER, THE NATURE AND FUNCTIONS OF LAW (4th ed. 1980) at 36.
2. K. N. LLEWELLYN, THE BRAMBLE BUSH (1960) at 7.
3. *Id.* at 12.

witchcraft was burning at the stake. The dunking stool in Massachusetts was a last vestige of this approach; it was a double dead end when the prosecutor(s) were convinced of a person's guilt. Either that person drowned from being held under too long after giving the so-called wrong answer or she ended up being toasted.

Trial by wager of law was an interesting phenomenon. Under wager of law, a man who was a party to a dispute "could wage his law" by taking an oath that the brown cow was his. If his oath was supported by the required number of "compurgators"—that is, oath-helpers—then he got the cow. The compurgators did not have to swear to knowledge of ownership of the cow, but rather to the "cleanness" of the original oath.

From even such a cursory review, one can sense why the appearance of a jury system, the precursor of which was brought from Norman France by William the Conqueror and his followers, was a welcome change in the direction of justice.

A SHORT HISTORY OF LAW

> Such is the unity of all history that any one who endeavors to tell a piece of it must feel that his first sentence tears a seamless web.[4]
>
> —Maitland (1898)

MESOPOTAMIA

Hammurabi was the greatest ruler in the first Babylonian dynasty. The dates of his life and rule cannot be determined precisely, but estimates place his reign as about 1792–1750 BCE.[5] Hammurabi extended the Babylonian empire northward from the Persian Gulf through the Tigris and Euphrates river valleys and westward to the coast of the Mediterranean Sea.[6] It extended roughly over what are now the modern nation states of Iraq and Syria. After consolidating his territorial gains under a central government in Babylon,[7] Hammurabi devoted most of his energies to fostering domestic prosperity in the empire.

Hammurabi's accomplishments included not only the compilation of the great legal code bearing his name but also language reform. His use of the Akkadian language, in which the code was written, became the model for all future writers of ancient Mesopotamia.[8] The history of Babylonia is considered to begin with Hammurabi.

Although a very able administrator and diplomat and a successful military leader, Hammurabi is mostly remembered for codifying the laws that governed

---

4. Frederic William Maitland, *A Prologue to a History of English Law*, 14 L. QUARTERLY REV. 13 (1898); see also FREDERICK POLLOCK & FREDERIC W. MAITLAND, THE HISTORY OF ENGLISH LAW 1 (2d ed. 1899). As quoted in *Re: Quotation Source? 'Law is a Seamless Web.'* Accessed at http://lawlibrary.ucdavis.edu/LAWLIB/June99/0242.html on December 16, 2002.
5. "Hammurabi," © 1992–1994 Microsoft Corporation. Accessed at http://home.echo-on.net/~smithda/hammurabi.html on December 13, 2002.
6. *Id.*
7. THE WORLD BOOK ENCYCLOPEDIA (1990), vol. 2 at 12. Babylon was located approximately 60 miles south of present-day Baghdad, Iraq. "A great civilization began in this region about 3500 B.C. and lasted until the 500s B.C. It produced the first forms of writing, a set of laws, and studies in mathematics, astronomy, and other sciences." *Id.*
8. THE WORLD BOOK ENCYCLOPEDIA (1990), vol. 9 at 36.

Babylonian life. This set of laws, known as the Code of Hammurabi, is one of the first law codes in history.[9] Hammurabi changed the legal system of his country by revising older legal codes, including one estimated to be 300 years old.[10] Although based on older collections of Sumerian and Akkadian laws, which Hammurabi revised and expanded, the code itself greatly influenced the civilization of all Near Eastern countries.[11] Under the provisions of the code, he set maximum prices and minimum wages, established fair and flexible rules governing sharecropping, and settled rules for inheritance and the division of property during divorce. The main principle of the code was that *"the strong shall not injure the weak."*[12]

An unusually active and capable administrator, Hammurabi also gave his attention to such details as cleaning irrigation canals and the calendar, in which he inserted an extra month.[13] Apparently, he was also an inspiring religious leader because it was during his reign that Marduk, the Babylonian city god, became a recognized leader in the pantheon of deities.[14]

Much of our knowledge of Hammurabi and the Code date from the year 1901 when a stone slab on which the code was carved was discovered in Susa, Iran.[15] Apparently, it had been carried off as a war trophy by an Elamite king after the fall of Babylon. The Code contains some 300 paragraphs or provisions, approximately 60 of which are illegible or have been obliterated.

THE GREEKS

Solon (died 559 BCE) was a great lawgiver and one of the seven wise men of Greece. Athens, unlike Sparta, was a money-mad commercial city. There was much strife between rich and poor. Under Athenian law at that time, if a loan went into default, the creditor could seize the debtor and his family and sell them as slaves to obtain money to pay the debt.[16] The cruelty and arrogance of the rich resulted in the formation of gangs by the poor to save themselves and rescue those who had been sold into slavery, frequently through usury.

The best men of Athens saw Solon as someone who was partial neither to the rich nor the poor. They asked him to lead a reformation of the laws of the city-state. The rich consented because Solon was wealthy and the poor because he was honest. The constitution written by Solon mitigated the class struggle and allowed for the growth of democratic institutions. Initially both sides despised Solon because they did not get all they wanted, but with time came forgiveness.[17]

The laws promulgated by Solon were written on boards. Every one of the leading citizens took a public oath to observe them. This development, along with the creation of a supreme court and establishing an assembly of the poor, was a significant milestone in the development of constitutional law in a democratic setting. Officers and officials of the United States take a similar

---

9. *Id.* at 35.
10. *Id.* at 35–36.
11. *Id.* at 36.
12. *Id.*
13. "Hammurabi," *supra* note 1.
14. *Id.*
15. THE WORLD BOOK, *supra* note 3 at 36.
16. *Solon—The Lawmaker of Athens.* Accessed at http://www.e-classics.com/solon.htm on December 12, 2002. Web site based on PLUTARCH'S LIVES.
17. *Id.*

oath to support and defend the Constitution of the United States against all enemies, both foreign and domestic.

THE ROMANS

In February of the year 528 CE, the Roman Emperor Justinian appointed a commission of 10 to make a new collection of imperial constitutions. The commission was directed to compile one code from those of all previous emperors, as well as his own; to excise unnecessary matters; to add appropriate titles; and to streamline the language. Fourteen months later, the code was completed and declared to be law (April 16, 529) under the title the *Justinianeus Codex*. Thereafter, the sources from which the Code was derived were no longer to have any binding force, and the Code itself alone was to be referred to as legal authority.[18]

The *Digest*, or Pandects, was issued in 533 and was a greater achievement than the Codex. It compiled the writings of the great Roman jurists, such as Ulpian, along with current edicts. The issuance of the Digest marked a turning point in Roman civil law; from then on contradictory case laws of the past were subsumed into an ordered legal system.[19] The *Institutes of Justinian* was intended as a textbook for legal studies and included extracts from the two major works, the Codex and Digest.

The Digest and the Institutes were compiled after the publication of the code; subsequently, 50 decisions and some new constitutions also were promulgated by the emperor. Thus, a new code was required, and accordingly a new commission for that purpose was issued to Tribonianus and four others. The new code was promulgated at Constantinople on the 16th day of November, 534. The first edition was forbidden, and the second edition is the Code of Justinian that is now found in 12 books, each of which is divided into titles. It is unknown how many books the first edition contained.[20]

Some observers have remarked that the inclusion of two heresies as crimes in Justinian's Code also marks a turning point in the attitude of Western law toward established religions.[21] Although enforcing Christianity as the state religion was far from the only concern in the codification of 529, heresy did appear high on the list of crimes incurring severe penalties. Church officials were not slow to invoke these new laws, and the same attitudes endured and were adopted as law in other countries. In the United Kingdom, the last public execution for anti-trinitarianism took place in Edinburgh in 1697.[22]

THE ENGLISH

In 1066, William, Duke of Normandy, defeated Harold the Saxon at the Battle of Hastings. Thus, William the Conqueror, as he was thereafter known, took seisin of all of England and became its king. The battle in which Harold was killed took place on October 14, 1066, and William was crowned on

---

18. George Long, *Codex Justinianeus*, WILLIAM SMITH, A DICTIONARY OF GREEK AND ROMAN ANTIQUITIES (1875). Accessed at http://www.ku.edu/history/index/europe/ancient_rome/E/Roman/Texts/secondary/SMIG on December 16, 2002.
19. *Medieval Sourcebook: The Institutes, 535 CE.* Accessed at http://www.fordham.edu/halsall/basis/535insitutes.html on December 16, 2002.
20. *Id.*
21. *The Justinian Code, 30 June 2001.* Accessed at http://www.aloha.net/~mikesch/jus code.htm on December 12, 2002.
22. *Id.*

Christmas Day of that year. It took about 4 years for William to complete a series of campaigns against the English nobility, most of whom did not accept him. During those campaigns, 90% of them were killed and replaced by new French nobility.[23]

Perhaps the greatest single institution to arise from the Norman Conquest was the development of trial by jury. The initial device was similar to the modern grand jury. However, although the term "trial by jury" appeared in 13th-century materials, its funtioning is much different today. In the Middle Ages, jurors were picked from the neighborhood and were given a fortnight to gain clarity of the facts in dispute. Then, they told under oath what they knew about the matter to the sheriff.[24] Now, members of the jury are selected on the understanding that they have no knowledge of the parties or the dispute. This is done to restrict their decision making to evidence presented in court under the rules of evidence.

***Glanvill's* De Legibus.**   About 1188, a legal treatise, attributed through antiquity to Glanvill, but probably not written by anyone with that name, made its appearance. The treatise itself is organized around various writs and gives details of legal procedure. In some places, the author abandons discussion of the writs and appears to write about law in substantive form, giving details of common customs.[25]

The significance of this treatise is that it is our best look at early English law and the first organized treatise to appear on the subject.[26] Certainly, there are earlier books on English law, preeminent among which is *The Laws of Henry I*; however, they do not reflect anything other than the diversity of law and fail to constitute an organized approach. Glanvill is organized and reflects the law in transition from discretionary justice (pre–1176) to a growing centralized court, from tenures as contract to tenures as property, and from chaos to an emerging rule of law. The early plea rolls (court records) date from about the year 1200, and this treatise sheds light on the beginnings of English common law before that time. Whoever the author of this treatise was, he was both literate and knowledgeable about the law. As with much history, however, Glanvill is not without ambiguity, and consequently, there is still some scholarly debate about its interpretation.[27]

The Great Charter.   As a result of various abuses of law and power by King John, the barons assembled an army and confronted him at a meadow, about 35 miles southwest of London on the South Bank of the Thames, and there presented him with an ultimatum: Sign the charter and restore our rights as Englishmen or else face war. John signed the Great Charter, *The Magna Carta*, on or after June 23, 1215. Four copies of the document still exist; the number of originals has been estimated to be as low as 13.[28] War broke out almost

---

23. *Middle Ages: Age of Feudalism 1066–1485*. Accessed at http://faculty.acu.edu/~appletonl/mb1/ma.htm on December 16, 2002.

24. A. R. HOGUE, ORIGINS OF THE COMMON LAW (1966, Liberty Fund reprint 1985) at 185–186.

25. *Glanvill*. Accessed at http://vi.uh.edu/pages/bob/elhone/glanvill.html on December 17, 2002.

26. *Id.*

27. *Id. See, e.g.*, Palmer, *The Feudal Framework of English Law*, 79 MICH. L. REV. 1130–1140 (1981) as cited in *Glanvill, supra* note 23.

28. *See Magna Carta*. Accessed at http://portico.bl.uk/diglib/magna-carta/overview.html on December 17, 2002. All four surviving documents declare themselves to have been "given by our hand in the meadow which is called Runnymede between Windsor and Staines on the 15th day of June in the 17th year of our reign" (1215). All four survivors differ slightly in size, shape, and text. *Id.*

immediately. King John died in 1216 in the midst of the war, but later kings agreed to the terms of the charter. It came to be recognized as part of the fundamental laws of England.[29] As one author notes,

> It is an error to say that Magna Carta guaranteed individual liberties to all people. In later centuries, it became a model for those who demanded democratic government and individual rights for all. In its own time, however, the greatest value of Magna Carta was that it placed the king under the law, and decisively checked royal power.[30]

Magna Carta contained 63 articles, most of which pledged the king to uphold feudal law. These articles chiefly benefited the barons and other members of the feudal aristocracy. Some of the articles granted the church freedom from royal interference. A few mentioned the rights of a rising middle class in the towns. Ordinary freemen and peasants were hardly mentioned at all, even though they constituted the majority of England's population.[31] The subject of religious freedom would, as we see later, play a more important part in British history in about 400 years. Meanwhile, the Great Charter was undergoing an evolution of its own, according to one observer:

> Magna Carta was largely forgotten during the 1500s. But members of the Parliament brought it to life again during the 1600s. They used it to rally support in their struggle against the despotic rule of the Stuart kings. Members of the Parliament came to view the charter as a constitutional check on royal power. They cited it as legal support for the argument that there could be no laws or taxation without the consent of Parliament. These members of Parliament used the charter to demand guarantees of trial by jury, safeguards against unfair imprisonment, and other rights.
>
> In the 1700s, Sir William Blackstone, a famous lawyer, set down these ideals as legal rights of the people in his famous *Commentaries on the Laws of England*. Also, in the 1700s, colonists carried these English ideals on legal and political rights to America. The ideals eventually became part of the framework of the Constitution of the United States.[32]

***Bracton's* De Legibus.**   The 13th century also produced the work that has been called "incomparably the best English legal work of the Middle Ages"[33] and "the crown and flower of English jurisprudence."[34] This book, *Bracton on the Laws and Customs of England*, is attributed to Henry of Bracton (probably Henricus de Brattona or Bractona); however, research indicates that the bulk of the work was written by persons other than Bracton in the 1220s and 1230s. It seems to have been edited and partially updated in the late 1230s, and various additions were also made to it between that time and the 1250s. The last owner of the manuscript and probably the author of the later additions was Bracton.[35]

---

29. THE WORLD BOOK ENCYCLOPEDIA (1990), vol. 13 at 54.

30. *Id.* at 53.

31. *Id.*

32. *Id.* at 54.

33. *Sir Henry De Bracton* (d. 1268). Accessed at http://www.law.upenn.edu/bll/medallion/bracton/bracton/htm on December 17, 2002.

34. Quote attributed to F. W. Maitland, *Bracton: De Legibus Et Consuetudinibus Angliae*. Accessed at http://bracton.law.cornell.edu/bracton/Common/ on December 17, 2002.

35. *Bracton: De Legibus* etc., *supra* note 24.

His name first appears as a judge of Assizes in Southwest England in records from 1245.[36]

Sir Edward Coke (1552–1634).

Sir Edward Coke is famous for his political activities, as well as his career in the courts and Parliament. His publications are equally renowned, the most famous of them being the *Reports* and his *Institutes*, which include his commentaries on Littleton's *Tenures*.[37] Although Sir Edward Coke had a remarkable political career, besting Sir Francis Bacon for the post of attorney general in 1593 and thereby making a bitter enemy,[38] his contributions to the literature of the law are probably his most outstanding legacy.

Coke earned a reputation as a fierce prosecutor, notably at the trial of Sir Walter Raleigh.[39] He held a favorable position at the court of King James I, and he became chief justice of the common pleas in 1606. In this position and later (1613) as chief justice of the King's Bench, Coke gained a reputation as a champion of the common law against royal encroachments.[40] Although his historical arguments were faulty (as in his interpretation of the Magna Carta), his reasoning was brilliant and his conclusions impressive.

Ultimately, Sir Edward's constant collisions with the king and the growing list of his enemies, especially Thomas Egerton and the chancellor, Baron Ellesmere, brought about his downfall in 1616. Chief among the architects of Coke's fall from grace was his old enemy Francis Bacon.[41] Using all of his political and personal influence, Coke got himself back on the Privy Council and in 1620 was elected to Parliament where he became one of the leaders of the popular faction in opposition to James I and Charles I.[42]

A relatively minor chapter in Sir Edward Coke's life was important for religious freedom in the colonies and later in the United States. A boy named Roger Williams was born in approximately 1603 to a merchant tailor in London.[43] As a youth, he became a scribe for Sir Edward Coke. Coke helped Williams enter Cambridge University, where he took a bachelor's degree in 1627. Williams was a religious nonconformist, even though he held the post of chaplain in the household of a very wealthy family. His disagreements with the official church, the Church of England, made Williams a target for persecution.

In 1631, Williams and his wife, Mary Barnard, moved to Massachusetts Bay Colony.[44] In 1634, Williams became the minister of a church in Salem, Massachusetts. There, many people favored his desire to form a church that was independent of the Church of England and of the colonial government. However, officials of Massachusetts Bay Colony wanted to deport Williams to England.[45] To avoid deportation, Williams fled into the wilderness of New England in January 1636. The Narragansett Indians provided Williams with

---

36. *Sir Henry* etc., *supra* note 23.
37. *Coke, Sir Edward.* Accessed at http://www.infoplease.com/ce6/people/A0812817.html on December 17, 2002.
38. *Coke, Sir Edward*, THE COLUMBIA ENCYCLOPEDIA (6th ed. 2001). Accessed at http://bartleby.com/65/co/Coke-Sir.html on December 17, 2002.
39. *Id.*
40. *Id.*
41. *Id.*
42. *Id.*
43. THE WORLD BOOK ENCYCLOPEDIA (1990), vol. 21, at 312.
44. *Id.*
45. *Id.*

land beyond the boundaries of Massachusetts, and there he founded Providence, later the capital of Rhode Island.[46]

As a result of his experiences and beliefs, Roger Williams led the Rhode Island government to be a champion for religious tolerance. In 1657, Williams contributed to Rhode Island's decision to provide refuge for Quakers who were banished from other colonies, such as Massachusetts, on pain of death if they returned. He also argued for and published a treatise upholding the arguments for the separation of church and state.[47]

In a similar vein of protest against authority and dissent, although removed from the religious realm, Sir Edward Coke spent his last years fighting for common law rights.[48] In 1620, Coke, having returned to Parliament, drafted the Protestation of the Commons, a proclamation declaring that ever since the Magna Carta was signed in 1215, Parliament had been subject *only* to the common law for its liberties, privileges, and jurisdiction. That action, together with his participation in debates about parliamentary liberties in 1621, earned Sir Edward 9 months in prison.[49]

In 1628, after King Charles succeeded James to the throne, Parliament adopted Coke's Petition of Right. This document reinforced the due process clause contained in the Magna Carta and became a charter of liberty limiting the royal prerogative. Sir Edward died in 1634, but his "contributions continued to shape the political forces after his death. The Petition of Right, the Habeas Corpus Act of 1679, the Bill of Rights of 1689, and the limited monarchy established by the Act of Settlement in 1701 all were based on Coke's work."[50]

Early Printed Books on English Laws.   As noted previously, *Littleton's Tenures* was probably the first law book printed in England. It was printed in either 1481 or 1482.[51] Among its most striking features is the language in which it is written. In 15th-century England, the language of law was an archaic tongue known as Law French. For the next 150 years, Law French was the principal language used in law books. It took a civil war and an Act of Parliament (1650) to establish English as the language of law in England.[52]

Twenty-two years before that act passed, however, *Littleton's Tenures* enjoyed a rebirth, in English, when Sir Edward Coke published the first volume

---

46. *Id.*
47. *Id.*
48. *Alternative Rules* etc. Accessed at http://www.thelockeinstitute.org/journals/tortliability.html on December 17, 2002.
49. *Id.*
50. *Id.*
51. *The Earliest Printed Books* etc. Accessed at http://www.geocities.com/Athens/Parthenon/7933/littn.html on December 17, 2002.
52. *Id.* It is worth noting here that after the Battle of Hastings (1066), French became the official language of the government. England, a conquered land, was considered possessed by an inferior culture and was there only to be exploited for the enrichment of the Norman French. The masses spoke English, and it was considered the language of the lower class. *Middle Ages:* etc. Accessed at http://faculty.acu.edu/~appleton1?mbl/ma.htm on December 18, 2002. As a rough timeline, one observer states that the century between 1250 and 1350 was a period of transition from French to English for the nobility. A large influx of French words into English marks this as a time that English was being spoken by people accustomed to speaking French. *Id.* The same observer notes that the 16th century (1400–1500) was also a transitional time for English, with the early period dominated by Chaucer. The publication of Sir Thomas Mallory's *Morte D'Arthur* (1485) by William Caxton, who had introduced movable-type printing to England, is seen as the end of medieval literature.

of his *Institutes*.[53] Subsequent volumes of the *Institutes* were clearly free-standing Coke, but volume one was *Coke on Littleton*. Coke's preface states why he translated Littleton into English and why his comments are in English in these words: that "the nobility and gentry of the realm ... may understand ... seeing that ignorance of the law is no excuse."[54]

This issue of language and accessibility to the general population is still with us as we enter the 21st century. One of the current issues is that the form of English used by many lawyers in the United States is almost as obscure to many Americans as Law French.

An interesting point is the intended audience for *Littleton's Tenures*. Most law books are intended as references for other lawyers and, as such, are usually filled with references to case reports and other sources of authority. Littleton's book offered neither footnotes nor citations. It was written as a teaching volume intended for his son, then preparing for a career in law. As such, it was intended to be read from cover to cover and mastered. The stature of the book came only posthumously—from Coke.[55]

Coke's other publication of note, the *Reports*, was published in 13 volumes from 1600 to 1615, with the last two volumes appearing after Coke's death in 1656 and 1659, respectively. The first 11 volumes were initially published in French and Latin and were republished in English in 1658 and 1659.[56]

In 1713, Sir Matthew Hale, Lord Chief Justice, published his *History of the Common Law of England*. It appears to be based on Justinian's Codex in a number of respects. First, it is in Latin and, second, it is divided into Codex, Digests, and Institutes—apparently along the same lines as Justinian's work 1,200 years earlier. With the exception of some scholarly interest, Hale's work seems to have created little impact.

Blackstone's Commentaries (1765–1769). The work that captured the imagination of lawyers in England and America was the publication in 1765 to 1769 of Sir William Blackstone's *Commentaries on the Laws of England*. Blackstone (1723–1780), an English judge, author, and professor, won wide recognition for his commentaries. This work in four volumes presents a comprehensive picture of the English law of his time. It became the most influential book in the history of English law and was the basis for legal education in England and America for decades.[57]

At first unsuccessful in his law practice, Blackstone turned to scholarship and teaching.[58] On the advice of a friend, he began to deliver lectures on English law at Oxford University. This was a novel undertaking because at that time English law was not considered an appropriate subject for instruction. Instead, Roman civil law and the law of continental Europe were taught at Oxford.[59] Blackstone, however, was a firm proponent of the position that

---

53. *The Earliest Printed* etc., *supra* at note 49.
54. *Id.*
55. *Id.*
56. *AIM 25: University College London: Coke Volume.* Accessed at http://www.aim25.ac.uk/cgi-bin/search2?coll_id=3617&inst_id=13 on December 17, 2002.
57. THE WORLD BANK ENCYCLOPEDIA (1990), vol. 2 at 410.
58. *Blackstone, Sir William,* THE COLUMBIA ENCYCLOPEDIA (6th ed. 2001). Accessed at http://www.bartleby.com/65/bl/BlackstoW.html on December 17, 2002.
59. THE WORLD BOOK, *supra* note 55.

"every gentleman and scholar" should have "a competent knowledge of the laws of that society in which we live."[60]

Blackstone's lectures were so popular and so successful that Charles Viner (1678–1756), author of an abridgment of English law, endowed a chair on the subject. Blackstone became the first Vinerian professor of English law at Oxford in 1758.

It was Blackstone's lectures that were published as the four volumes of *Blackstone's Commentaries on the Laws of England*. His work brought order and lucidity to the formless mass of English law. It ranks with the achievements of Sir Edward Coke and Sir Matthew Hale.[61] Blackstone wrote in an urbane, dignified, and clear style. His *Commentaries* are widely regarded as the most thorough treatment of the whole of English law ever produced by one individual. Among other achievements, it demonstrated that English law as a system of justice ranked equally with Roman civil law and the law of the European continent.[62]

Blackstone's work exerted tremendous, almost immeasurable, influence on the legal profession and on the teaching of law in England and the United States. Of famous American jurists who studied law from *Blackstone's Commentaries*, the names of Abraham Lincoln and Clarence Darrow come speedily to mind; the rest are legion and lesser known. In his later life, Blackstone resumed practice, served in Parliament, was solicitor general to the Queen, and was judge of common pleas.[63]

Jeremy Bentham, the famous philosopher and public intellectual, criticized *Blackstone's Commentaries* because he thought Blackstone presented law in too great a light as being potentially beyond improvement. He also faulted Blackstone for failing to clearly analyze the social and historical factors underlying the legal system. We return to Mr. Bentham in Chapter 3.

A BRIEF LOOK AT U.S. LEGAL HISTORY

THE DECLARATION OF INDEPENDENCE (JULY 4, 1776)

Thomas Jefferson of Virginia, later the third president of the United States, penned the Declaration of Independence. It is an important part of the American Testament,[64] although domestically, it has no force of law. The document was passed by the Second Continental Congress on July 4, 1776, just 2 days after the Congress had approved a resolution introduced by Richard Henry Lee of Virginia nearly a month earlier "that these United Colonies are, and of right ought to be, free and independent states."[65]

One prominent author and scholar used the following words to describe the importance of the Declaration of Independence:

> While the Declaration of Independence, as promulgated on July 4, 1776, did not bring this nation into existence or establish the

---

60. Sir William Blackstone, *Discourse on the Study of Law: Being an Introductory Lecture Read in the Public Schools*, October 25, 1758 (Oxford, 1758) p. 3 as cited in BERMAN & GREINER, THE NATURE AND FUNCTIONS OF LAW (4th ed. 1980) at 1.
61. *Blackstone, Sir William, supra* note 56.
62. *Id.*
63. *Id.*
64. *See* MORTIMER ADLER, WE HOLD THESE TRUTHS (1987) at 6–8.
65. THE WORLD BOOK ENCYCLOPEDIA (1990), vol. 5 at 74.

government of the United States of America, it magnificently enunciated the fundamental principles of republican or constitutional government—principles that are not stated explicitly in the Constitution itself.

The Declaration was, therefore, in the most profound sense, a preface to the Constitution, more fundamental politically than the Constitution's own Preamble. Since the word "preface" lacks the dignity and weight that should be accorded the Declaration in relation to the Constitution, we should perhaps think of it as the architectural blueprint for the government of the United States.[66]

It is appropriate that the original Declaration of Independence, as preserved in the National Archives Building in Washington, DC, stands above the United States Constitution and the Bill of Rights.[67]

Three days after Richard Henry Lee of Virginia introduced his resolution for independence on June 7, 1776, the Congress voted to form a committee to write a formal declaration of independence in the event that Lee's resolution passed. This committee, formed the next day on June 11th, was composed of John Adams, Benjamin Franklin, Thomas Jefferson, Robert R. Livingston, and Roger Sherman. Jefferson's colleagues asked him to draft the Declaration.[68] Thomas Jefferson finished the task in about 2 weeks, and only Franklin and Adams made minor changes in Jefferson's draft.

On July 2, 1776, the Second Continental Congress began debating Jefferson's draft as presented by the committee. A few passages, including one condemning King George III for encouraging the slave trade, were deleted. There is some evidence for the proposition that Thomas Jefferson was actively opposed to slavery as a young man, but that he became silent on the subject in his later years.[69] A few other changes dealing mostly with style were made, and on July 4, 1776, the Congress adopted the final draft of the Declaration of Independence.

"We hold these truths to be self-evident, that all men are created equal, that they are endowed by their Creator with certain unalienable Rights, that among these are Life, Liberty, and the pursuit of Happiness."[70] These words ring down the halls of time. They have inspired countless people. Some question how these concepts came to be written and signed by slaveholders in an era in which women did not vote, the aboriginal people did not count for purposes of the census, and ultimately a slave counted as three fifths of a person for representation in Congress. The answer, I suggest, is that this document represents an IOU made out to future generations of Americans who would have to deliver on the promises and potentials of this great experiment—in the words of Abraham Lincoln, "the Last Best Hope of Mankind."[71]

---

66. MORTIMER ADLER, *supra* note 64, at 7.
67. THE WORLD BOOK ENCYCLOPEDIA, vol. 5, at 75 (caption to illustration).
68. *Id.* at 74.
69. *See* JOSEPH J. ELLIS, AMERICAN SPHINX: THE CHARACTER OF THOMAS JEFFERSON (Vintage ed. 1998) at 5.
70. THE DECLARATION OF INDEPENDENCE [A Declaration of Rights, 2nd part] as quoted in THE WORLD BOOK, *supra* note 63 at 76.
71. MARK E. NEELY, JR., THE LAST BEST HOPE OF EARTH: ABRAHAM LINCOLN AND THE PROMISE OF AMERICA (1993) at v. The title of Neely's book is taken from President Lincoln's address to the Congress in December 1862. Lincoln closed his remarks with this line: "We shall nobly save, or meanly lose, the last best hope of Earth." *Id.*

THE ARTICLES OF CONFEDERATION (1781–1788)

Before there was a Constitution, there were Articles of Confederation. These laws were meant to bind together a loose alliance of 13 colonies. The Revolutionary War began on April 19, 1775, when British troops tried to seize military supplies of the Massachusetts militia.[72] Colonists, first at Lexington and then at Concord, Massachusetts, took up arms to turn back the British troops.[73] The Second Continental Congress met on May 10, 1775, to organize the colonies for war and to form the Continental Army.[74] The Congress named George Washington of Virginia commander in chief of the Army on June 15th. King George III officially declared the colonies in rebellion on August 23, 1775. The war was more than a year old before the Declaration of Independence was issued.

The Revolutionary War dragged on from 1775 until October 19, 1781, when the Americans won a decisive victory over General Cornwallis and the British at Yorktown, Virginia.[75] In that year, the states set up a federal government under laws called the Articles of Confederation. Those Articles gave the federal government the power to declare war and manage international affairs. However, the Articles did *not* give the central government any power to collect taxes, regulate interstate commerce, or otherwise direct or control the activities of the 13 states.[76] The Founding Fathers had just gotten over a bad experience with a strong central government in London and did not wish to risk a similar experience at home.

However, the experience under the Articles of Confederation was not good, and soon, the nation's problems seemed to demand a stronger central government. The United States had piled up a huge national debt during the Revolutionary War, but, since the government could not tax, it was unable to pay those debts and put the nation on a firm financial footing.[77] Moreover, the federal government could not raise money to provide for a national defense, and it lacked the power to regulate commercial disputes among the states. In addition, some states began to issue money, causing sharp fluctuations in the value of currency and threatening economic chaos.[78]

In September 1786,[79] Virginia invited all the states to send delegates to a convention at Annapolis, Maryland, to discuss interstate commerce and the use of waterways.[80] Only 5 of the 13 states—New York, New Jersey, Pennsylvania, Delaware, and Virginia—sent delegates. As a result, Alexander Hamilton, James Madison, and others urged all the states to send delegates to a second, more inclusive convention that was to begin in May 1787 in Philadelphia.[81]

In May 1787, delegates from every state except Rhode Island met in Independence Hall in Philadelphia to consider revisions to the Articles of Confederation. Rhode Island elected not to participate because of resentment it had

---

72. THE WORLD BOOK ENCYCLOPEDIA (1990), vol. 20 at 148.
73. *Id.*
74. *Id.*
75. *Id.* at 149.
76. *Id.* at 150–151.
77. *Id.* at 151.
78. *Id.*
79. THE WORLD BOOK ENCYCLOPEDIA (1990), vol. 1 at 516.
80. *Id.*, vol. 20 at 151.
81. *Id.*, vol. 1 at 516.

toward "outside interference" in its affairs.[82] However, instead of merely revising the articles, the delegates chose to write an entirely new constitution.[83] They chose George Washington to preside over the meeting.[84]

THE CONSTITUTION OF THE UNITED STATES (1788–PRESENT)

On May 13, a Sunday, General Washington arrived in Philadelphia. He was greeted with booming cannons and church bells.[85] His first move was to call on Dr. Benjamin Franklin, who had laid by a cask of port and had his dining room remodeled to seat 24 in anticipation of the Convention.[86] On Monday, May 14, 1787, the Convention began. It was to last until September 17, 1787, also a Monday and the day on which the delegates signed the Constitution with all its compromises, tendering it to the states for ratification.[87] Some of the hardest work now lay ahead; nine states needed to ratify the Constitution for it to become law.[88]

The Constitution, as finally hand written and signed, had seven articles. Against the wishes of Dr. Franklin, it provided for a bicameral legislature (two houses—not the one as in Pennsylvania that Franklin favored). The number of members of the House of Representatives was based on population, a move that the larger states favored. Senators were distributed equally, a move that the smaller states liked. The Constitution, although reserving certain powers to the states, also gave the federal government many powers, including the right to collect taxes and regulate trade. It provided for three coequal branches of government: the executive, led by the president; the legislative, made up of the two houses of Congress; and the judicial, headed by the federal court system. In a masterstroke, the Founders provided for a system of checks and balances among the three branches. Each branch received powers and duties that assured the other branches would not be too powerful. On August 20th and again on September 12th, the delegates looked at and dismissed the idea of a bill of rights[89]; this decision was to have a lingering impact.[90]

Some Americans fiercely opposed the adoption of the Constitution. In fact, Patrick Henry opposed it to the bitter end in the Virginia legislature.[91] Four men who opposed the Constitution were absent on the day of signing, but nine who favored it were also not present. Three prominent members of the Convention—Edmund Randolph (Virginia), George Mason (Virginia), and Elbridge Gerry (Connecticut)—were present, but refused to sign the final document.[92] Only Alexander Hamilton signed for the State of New York. The battle lines were drawn on the matter of a strong central government, still repugnant to many, and the lack of a bill of rights to protect individual freedoms against such a government.

The Federalists argued that the government was one of limited powers, having only those powers expressly dealt it. Consequently, it would be unwise

---

82. *Id.*, vol. 20 at 151.
83. *Id.*
84. *Id.*
85. CATHERINE DRINKER BOWEN, MIRACLE AT PHILADELPHIA at 16 (1966, reissued 1988).
86. *Id.*
87. *Id.* at 254.
88. THE WORLD BOOK ENCYCLOPEDIA (1990), vol. 20 at 150–151.
89. C. D. BOWEN, *supra* note 81, at 244.
90. *Id.* at 245–248.
91. *Id.* at 300–305.
92. *Id.* at 262–63.

to attempt to name all the basic freedoms reserved to free men.[93] The opposition noted that a bill of rights was so elementary, so much a part of what it means to be a free people that no document was acceptable without one. The anti-Federalists argued, "The business went back to the Magna Carta! Blackstone had defined it, and Lord Coke before him in his *Second Institute*."[94] Hamilton, Madison, and John Jay responded to criticisms of the document in a series of letters to the newspapers. Called *The Federalist Papers*, these letters generated much support for the Constitution.[95] On June 21, 1788, New Hampshire became the ninth state to ratify the Constitution, and it became the law of the land.

THE BILL OF RIGHTS (1791–PRESENT)

"In most states, Federalist proponents of the Constitution succeeded in securing ratification *only* by promising that they would seek a bill of rights when the new Congress convened after ratification"[96] [italics is added]. State conventions sent the Congress 210 suggested constitutional amendments. James Madison of Virginia, who took the lead in pursuing a bill of rights, managed to pare that list down to 19.[97] Ultimately, the House of Representatives and the Senate were able to agree on 12 amendments, which were submitted to the states for ratification in September of 1789.[98]

Roger Sherman a founder who had signed both the Declaration of Independence and the Constitution as a representative of Connecticut, unwaveringly opposed a bill of rights. In a letter to a New Haven paper, Sherman—who signed it "A Countryman"—wrote, "No bill of rights ever yet bound the supreme power longer than the honeymoon of a new married couple, unless the rulers were interested in preserving the rights; and in that case they have always been ready enough to declare the rights, and to preserve them when they were declared."[99] The boldest and barest argument against a bill of rights came, somewhat surprisingly, from a noted anti-Federalist, General Charles Cotesworth Pinckney of South Carolina, who declared to the legislature, "Bills of rights generally begin with declaring that all men are by nature born free. Now, we should make that declaration with very bad grace, when a huge part of our property consists in men who are actually born slaves."[100]

Yet, in his First Inaugural Address, George Washington hinted that Congress should promptly add a bill of rights to the Constitution.[101] Madison

---

93. Noah Webster, "stung by the New York convention's arguments for a bill of rights, addressed the members (via the newspapers) in his best free-swinging sarcasm. To complete their list of unalienable rights, Webster suggested a clause 'that everyone shall, in good weather, hunt on his own land, and catch fish in rivers that are public property . . . and that Congress shall never restrain any inhabitant of America from eating and drinking, at seasonable times, or prevent his lying on his left side, in a long winter's night, or even on his back, when he is fatigued by lying on his right.'" *Id.* at 246.

94. *Id.* at 245.

95. THE WORLD BOOK ENCYCLOPEDIA (1990), vol. 20 at 152.

96. JETHRO K. LIEBERMAN, THE EVOLVING CONSTITUTION (1992) at 76.

97. *Id.*

98. *Id.* C. D. BOWEN, *supra* note 81, at 304. In her history, C. D. Bowen suggests in a footnote that the basis for Madison's work can be found in the 20 proposed amendments that accompanied the final vote of 89–79 in the Virginia legislature for ratification.

99. Sherman letter as quoted in C. D. BOWEN, *supra* note 81, at 246.

100. Pinckney's statement to South Carolina legislature as quoted in C. D. BOWEN, *supra* note 81, at 247.

101. SAMUEL ELIOT MORISON, THE OXFORD HISTORY OF THE AMERICAN PEOPLE (1965) at 319.

took the lead in the Congress. Prophetically, Thomas Jefferson wrote Madison from Paris in support of the idea, saying the best argument for it was "the legal check which it puts into the hands of the judiciary."[102] Although several leading anti-Federalists—particularly William Grayson and Patrick Henry—continued to rant against the bill of rights, some prominent historians believe they actually pushed most of those still opposed into the other camp.[103]

On December 15, 1791, Virginia became the 11th state to ratify the Bill of Rights, but 11 were all that were needed to put Amendments I through X into effect.[104] In a small historical irony, the State of Massachusetts that had set the ball rolling for the "ratify-and-then-we'll-add-a-bill-of-rights" movement did not ratify until the 150th anniversary of the Bill of Rights, when someone discovered the oversight.[105]

The Bill of Rights guarantees freedom of speech, freedom of religion, freedom from state-established religion, freedom of the press, the right to trial by jury, the right against unreasonable searches and seizures, and the right to peaceable assembly to petition the government. Initially, the Bill of Rights were limitations on the powers of Congress; however, after passage of the 14th Amendment, the Supreme Court in a period from roughly 1920 to 1970 "selectively incorporated" most, but not all, of the Bill of Rights into the due process clause of the 14th Amendment.[106]

A PRIMER ON JURISPRUDENCE

INTRODUCTION TO JURISPRUDENCE

What is jurisprudence? Jurisprudence is the study of the philosophies of the law.[107] The root words are "juris," meaning law, and "prudence," meaning wisdom of. Thus, we could state that jurisprudence is the study of the wisdom of law; because the word "philosopher" means lover of wisdom, we could conceive of jurisprudence as a study of the wisdom/philosophy of law. There are many philosophies offered to explain the phenomenon of law. One British author suggests, "Jurisprudence is often thought of as a long running battle between two camps: the 'legal positivists' and the 'natural lawyers.'"[108] It is much more complex than that, but it is also true that the debate over legal positivism has occupied center stage for a long time in jurisprudential circles.[109]

This section examines various schools of thought in jurisprudence. The reader should keep in mind two things as we briefly review this area: (a) all forms of condensation involve some distortion, and (b) use care in dealing with this overview because a little bit of knowledge is a dangerous thing.[110]

---

102. *Id.* citing letter from Jefferson at 319.
103. *Id.* at 319.
104. The two amendments that were not ratified determined the size of the House of Representatives and forbade members of Congress from raising their own salaries. Connecticut and Georgia did not ratify until 1941—after the sesquicentennial of the Bill of Rights. *Id* at 319, note 1.
105. *Id.* at 319.
106. J. K. LIEBERMAN, *supra* note 92, at 76.
107. M. BIXBY ET AL., THE LEGAL ENVIRONMENT OF BUSINESS (1996) at 5.
108. N. E. SIMMONDS, CENTRAL ISSUES IN JURISPRUDENCE (1986) at 77.
109. *Id.*
110. Apologies to Alexander Pope. Note that in his Introduction, Simmonds says, The best way of beginning the study of jurisprudence is, therefore, to attack the conception of law that is so firmly rooted in the students' minds. This is not to say that the conception of law is

Steve Benson: © Arizona Republic/Dist. by United Feature Syndicate, Inc.

The review covers an arbitrary assortment of legal philosophies starting with positivism.

LEGAL POSITIVISM (POWER)

Legal positivism holds that law is command. Blackstone argued that law was "a rule of civil conduct, prescribed by the supreme power in a state, commanding what is right and prohibiting what is wrong."[111] In this definition, Blackstone has conflated law and morality. This seems unavoidable because of his belief in the divine right of kings.

The positivist school regards law as a set of rules imposed by a sovereign, such as Parliament in England after about 1700. The root word, *posit*, which means to place or put or lay something down, is the basis for the term "positivism." Thus, Justinian's Institutes define law with a Latin phrase meaning "whatever has pleased the Prince, has the force of law."[112] A similar understanding influenced other lawgivers and writers from Hammurabi to Blackstone.

NATURAL LAW

Natural law was the predominant theory of jurisprudence at the time of the founding of the United States, as one can readily see by reading the Declaration of Independence (1776). It remained the dominant theory until approximately 1900 when it was supplanted by legal positivism. Natural law theory holds that law is a basic system of moral rules that have been developed through

---

wrong and must be eradicated. . . . But the *first* aim must be to get the student worried, to make him see that there are problems with his taken for granted assumptions, puzzles that are hard to resolve and that lead into surprisingly deep intellectual waters." *Id.* at 2.

111. W. BLACKSTONE, I COMMENTARIES ON THE LAW OF ENGLAND 38 (1771) as quoted in J. BLACKBURN ET AL., THE LEGAL ENVIRONMENT OF BUSINESS (1982) at 12.

112. Justinian, 2 INSTITUTES 9 (T. Cooper trans. 1812) as quoted in *id.* at 13.

reason and are grounded in an innate set of rights built by a Supreme Being into every human. These "laws" may or may not coincide with the civil and criminal laws, yet all legal systems should be judged against the laws established by this "Higher Authority." Such philosophers as Socrates, Plato, Aristotle, and Thomas Aquinas have contributed to the development of natural law through their writings and teachings. The modern resurgence of natural law theory was led by John Locke and Rousseau.

LEGAL REALISM

Legal realism holds that law is merely *that* body of rules *enforced* by the courts and the society.[113] A short example may be helpful here. If the posted speed limit is 55 mph, but the state patrol does not stop anyone unless he or she is traveling in excess of 62 mph, then the *real speed limit is 62 mph*. The great jurist, Oliver Wendell Holmes, Jr., son of the illustrious Dr. Oliver Wendell Holmes, Sr., was a proponent of legal realism. Mr. Justice Holmes wrote, "[T]he prophecies of what the courts will do in fact, and nothing more pretentious, are what I mean by the law."[114]

For our purposes, a realist could say that, after examining the sentences of two criminals—one a white-collar criminal who bilked hundreds of victims' life savings and a second who held up a gas station with a pistol for a paltry sum—that U.S. law views white-collar crime as substantially less serious than armed robbery, regardless of harm. Given that the United States has the capacity to audit only about 2% of income tax returns, a realist might say that the Internal Revenue Service involves voluntary compliance, say when compared to the expenses involved in maintaining immigration agents on the Mexican border.

HISTORICAL SCHOOL

The historical school of jurisprudence argues that law is produced and shaped by historical events, such as the Industrial Revolution, the rise of populism, and the civil rights movement. Consequently, to understand the law, one would have to study and understand the historical forces that resulted in the development of the area of law being studied. Mr. Justice Holmes, a complex man with a first-rate mind, contributed to this area with the publication in 1886 of his lectures on *The Common Law*.

SOCIOLOGICAL SCHOOL

Under this philosophy, law is the product of social forces. Sociological "jurisprudes" seek to understand the law from a perspective of its impact on society, and how law is influenced by the needs of different groups within a society. For example, in *Brown v. The Board of Education of Topeka*, 347 U.S. 483 (1954), the U.S. Supreme Court overruled the precedent of *Plessy v. Ferguson* (1896) on the basis of sociological studies that established that separate but equal schools were "inherently unequal" because they created a badge of inferiority for the children of color who were segregated. By a 9–0 vote, the court in an opinion by Mr. Chief Justice Earl Warren held that the social research was sufficient to require a change in the laws of the land. One of the main

---

113. BIXBY, *supra* note 104, at 7.
114. O. W. HOLMES, *The Path of the Law*, 10 HARV. L. REV. 809 (1897) as cited in CHARLES R. MCGUIRE, THE LEGAL ENVIRONMENT OF BUSINESS (2d ed. 1989) at 18.

distinctions between the historical school and the sociological school is that the latter emphasizes values more strongly.

Two subsets of the sociological school are feminist jurisprudence and critical legal studies (CLS) jurisprudence. The feminist school takes the perspective that law can best be understood as a male-dominated social institution and interpreted from that viewpoint. The CLS perspective is that law is an instrument that is used by the powerful to maintain dominance over the rest of society.

What does it mean to have a critical perspective? In the context of critical examination, critical means "characterized by careful and exact evaluation and judgment: *a critical reading.*"[115] However, from a CLS or jurisprudential perspective, critical has a slightly different meaning. CLS proponents rely heavily on such disciplines as sociology and anthropology for their studies of power, position, and wealth.[116] According to one textbook, "CLS advocates are highly critical of the status quo and seek to expose legal doctrines reinforcing the current power structure."[117] Some commentators link CLS to a Marxist class-conflict orientation.[118]

Another important subset of sociological jurisprudence is feminist jurisprudence, which, as a field, began in the 1960s.[119] Feminists believe that male-written history has created a bias in the society's concepts of human nature, gender potential, and social arrangements and that, consequently, law's structure reinforces traditionally masculine values. The result, some feminists argue, is that those characteristics perceived as masculine are seen as the norm and supposedly feminine characteristics are treated as deviant. Thus, law—in its language, logic, and structure—is understood as an instrument for the perpetuation of patriarchal power.[120]

Within the ranks of feminist "jurisprudes," there are divisions. For example, feminists' response to traditional liberal legal thought/jurisprudence (a la Ronald Dworkin) is usually determined by whether or not they believe there is anything in the legal tradition that is worth saving and reforming.[121] Two formulations commonly found in discussions of the schism in American feminist jurisprudence characterize the split as the *"reformist/radical"* debate or as the *"sameness/difference"* debate.[122] Within the former, the reformists argue that there is enough of value in the liberal tradition that it should be saved and reshaped to serve feminist ends. The radicals, in contrast, argue that the traditional liberal system is so bankrupt that all or parts of it must be abandoned and replaced in order to obtain freedom from the existing biases.[123]

The central concern for feminists in the sameness/difference debate is to understand the role of difference and how women's needs must be

---

115. THE AMERICAN HERITAGE DICTIONARY (1985) at 341.
116. BIXBY ET AL., THE LEGAL ENVIRONMENT OF BUSINESS (1996) at 8.
117. *Id.*
118. *See Washington Whispers* (November 2002) at p. 3. The point is made: "President Bush's tax cut provides 52% of the tax relief to families making over $1.5 million per year. Criticizing this tax cut on these grounds is called class warfare by defenders. If this is class warfare, I'm all for it."
119. Legal Information Institute, *Feminist Jurisprudence: An Overview.* Accessed at http://www.law.cornell.edu/topics/feminist_jurisprudence.html on September 3, 2004.
120. *Id.*
121. *Responding to Liberalism: Questions of Perspective* as found in *Feminist Jurisprudence.* Accessed at http://www.iep.utm.edu/j/jurisfem.htm on September 3, 2004.
122. *Id.*
123. *Id.*

characterized before the law. "Sameness" feminists argue that to emphasize differences between men and women is to weaken women's abilities to gain the rights and protections that men have traditionally enjoyed. "Difference" feminists, at least many of them, argue that the differences between men and women are as significant as other types of differences, such as age, race, and sexual orientation. Consequently, what may have been good law for men cannot be simply adapted for women.[124]

These two schools of feminist jurisprudence share some common ground. Those who argue for the sameness position are often able to accommodate their stance, at least to a degree, with the reformist views. Difference feminists are often seen as more comfortable with or sharing some of the views of the radicals. This discussion of gender roles is continued in Chapter 8, "Through the Gender Lens."

THE AMERICAN TESTAMENT

Mortimer Adler (1902–2001), the late distinguished philosopher and prolific writer from Chicago, wrote that the Declaration of Independence (1776), the Constitution of the United States (1787), and Lincoln's Gettysburg Address (1863) together comprise "the American Testament"[125] (see Appendices). He wrote, "To call these three documents 'the American testament' is to say that, together and in relation to one another, they are *like* the sacred scriptures of this nation" [italics in original].[126] In a very real sense, these three documents shape the culture, the society, and the government under which we Americans live. They provide the creed that defines what it means to be an American.

Sociology has been said to be the objective study of human behavior insofar as it is affected by the fact that people live in groups.[127] Rules enable people to live together in groups with a minimum of conflict. Social contract theory holds that individuals are the basic building blocks of society and that at some time in the prehistoric past people got together and negotiated the basic social contract; that is, the ground rules that enable us to live peaceably in proximity to one another. The initial compact might have been as crude as "I'll respect your family, possessions, and cave if you'll do the same for me."

The words of the Declaration of Independence—"We hold these truths to be self-evident: that all men are created equal and they are endowed by their Creator with certain unalienable rights, among these Life, Liberty, and the Pursuit of Happiness"—are the bedrock on which a great society could be founded. Note that this expression is an expression of natural law, a jurisprudential philosophy popular in the 18th century. Natural law holds that rights are embedded in the design of human beings by the Creator and exist whether recognized or not by a society or a legal system.

Do not overlook this point: The pursuit of happiness was not and is not a commitment to hedonism in any way or form. The Founding Fathers were almost all classically educated; most were able to read Greek and Latin, as well as other modern languages. Most studied and were conversant with Aristotle's theory of virtue. Consequently, when Thomas Jefferson penned these words,

---

124. *Id.*
125. MORTIMER ADLER, WE HOLD THESE TRUTHS: UNDERSTANDING THE IDEAS AND IDEALS OF THE CONSTITUTION (1987) at 7–8.
126. *Id* at 7.
127. BARRY SUGARMAN, SOCIOLOGY at 1.

he did so with confidence that they would be understood to mean an Aristotelian pursuit of *eudemonia*—a life lived in balance, a life worth living, a life spent in the pursuit of virtue.[128]

In our American Testament, we find the roots of a moral community with a commitment to a vision of a society that would improve and evolve toward a more just community over time. It is difficult, if not nearly impossible, to understand the promises and ideals in the American Testament as anything other than promissory notes to be paid by future generations of freedom-loving peoples. Western jurisprudence has held for a thousand years that ignorance of the law does not excuse a violation of it. In a system of universal suffrage and mandatory public education, does this create a moral duty for the school systems to do a rigorous job of teaching civics?

---

128. If more argument is needed, one need only look at the end of the Declaration of Independence. The document ends with these words: "We mutually pledge to each other our lives, our fortunes, and *our sacred honor*" [italics added]. MORTIMER ADLER, *supra* note 27, at 169.

CHAPTER

3

A Primer on Ethics

One of the disturbing trends of our times is the tendency of some to equate business ethics with white-collar crime. A recent issue of *The Chronicle of Higher Education* illustrated the pervasive nature of this confusion by advertising a position for a "Director of Business Ethics Center" that stated a major part of the job was to develop techniques for detecting corporate fraud.[1] We do not know whether this is just common run-of-the-mill ignorance or whether the level of conduct in business has fallen so far that whether or not to commit felony fraud is presumed to be a major ethical issue. In this book, I continue to recognize the major distinction between ethical issues and questions of criminal justice. The latter questions are reserved for courses in criminology.

Ethics has long been a concern of human beings. Those of us with an active conscience seek a path through life that will allow us a good night's sleep. Our search for the good, the just, and the beautiful is an expression of our higher nature or perhaps a manifestation of the angels of our better nature. The Manichean heresy was that the forces of light and darkness were at war in the world; similar forces may actually be at war in each of us. Some authors identify four basic drives in human nature: the drive to acquire, the drive to bond, the drive to learn, and the drive to defend.[2] How these human drives are managed and directed by us determines whether we go over to "the dark side" or not.[3]

Various definitions of ethics and morals have been offered, and, in everyday speech, the terms are used interchangeably. In this book, I define these terms separately and use them differently in a correct, if somewhat rigid and technical manner. *Morals are the collections of prima facie,*[4] *black-letter*[5] *principles by which we live; ethics, by contrast, is the cognitive, systematic, and rational application of moral principles to complex or unclear situations.*

In earlier times, the right and the just were defined by secular and ecclesiastical laws, precepts, and dogma. Ethical conduct—at least in its social context—was conduct that conformed to cultural or religious norms. Such structures gave order to society. In many cases, though not all, they also served to maintain the powerful on their thrones or in their estates. Ideology, tradition, and class defined the nature of human relationships, and ethical standards often reflected the given order.

HISTORICAL FRAMEWORK

After the Age of Enlightenment, as Western society evolved toward more open and egalitarian forms, ethical conduct previously confined by religious and

---

1. *The Chronicle of Higher Education* (February 28, 2003) at C12-14. The initial position description is "*Business Ethics*: Director for Social Responsibility and Corporate Reporting." But when we read further, we find that "the Director will develop and coordinate a combined program of management/marketing ethics, *and fraud prevention/detection*" [italics added]. *Id.* at C13.
2. *See* Joseph A. Petrick, *Sustainability, Democracy and Three Challenges to Global Judgment Integrity Capacity*, 6 INNOVATION: MANAGEMENT, POLICY & PRACTICE (no. 2, August 2004) 156–166 and 162–164.
3. *Id.*
4. The term *prima facie* is of legal origin and means "sufficient to establish a case unless disproved" or overridden—as in by the playing of a higher trump in a card game featuring one suit as trump. *See* MERRIAM WEBSTER'S COLLEGIATE DICTIONARY (10th ed. 1995) at 925. Consequently, if principles of behavior conflict, a moral principle will prevail *unless* overridden by a higher moral principle.
5. The term "black letter" comes from law and is a reference to black-letter law, that is, rules of law so well established that they can be stated in summary form in old-fashioned black-letter type in legal horn books (narrative treatises of the law in given areas, such as contracts, agency, or torts). One law dictionary defines a similar phrase, "horn-book law," as "the rudiments or most familiar principles of law." BLACK'S LAW DICTIONARY (4th ed. 1957) at 870.

cultural tradition became defined more broadly. No longer was the individual seen primarily in relation to hierarchical structures that encompassed economic, political, and, often, theological values. Instead, avenues were opened for individual development based on personality, persistence, and achievement in a competitive economic environment. Achievement itself became a goal—one that often was transmuted into acquisitiveness. Although this development—along with its political counterpart, democracy—loosened the strictures of tradition and eroded the power of privilege, it fragmented society. The rule of meritocracy, a democratic ideal, led paradoxically to a diminution of community. The individual became subject to economic forces that had little grounding in ethical or metaphysical values and no link to community other than that represented by what became known as market forces. This process led, in the first half of the 19th century, to the Marxian critique of industrial capitalism: that it had left "no other nexus between man and man than . . . callous cash payment"[6]

ADAM SMITH AND CAPITALISM

Modern economics begins with the publication in 1776 of Adam Smith's *An Inquiry into the Nature and Causes of the Wealth of Nations*. Smith held the Chair in Moral Philosophy at the University of Glasgow in austere, Calvinist Scotland. His *Wealth of Nations*, the often-quoted but seldom-read foundation of classical economics, has become a byword for the approbation of capitalism. Adam Smith is, for many, instantly associated with the profit motive.

It is important to note, however, that Smith did not intend *Wealth of Nations*, largely an analysis of competitive factors, to stand alone as the definitive word on the emerging capitalist society. Rather, *Wealth* is part of a trilogy. In 1759, Smith had published *The Theory of Moral Sentiments*, and shortly before he died in 1790, Smith ordered that several manuscripts be destroyed, including a framework on jurisprudence. (A version of this third work survives in the form of students' lecture notes.) Thus, Adam Smith was not the one-dimensional economist that he is sometimes made out to be. Indeed, *Wealth* contains numerous condemnations of rapacious self-interest and unfair advantage taken by the privileged classes. Adam Smith saw social welfare in terms that went far beyond the economic sphere.

In his works, Smith sought to explain how individual self-interest could be brought into harmony with the general welfare of society. He understood that human beings are motivated also by compassion and a desire for justice. Self-interest, he said, could be restrained by morality, by markets, and by government.

Smith's thought comprises three parts: a moral system, in which sympathy or compassion constrains self-interest; a market system, in which self-interest is channeled into socially desirable directions by competition; and a system of jurisprudence, in which civil government supports and complements the first two.

LIMITS OF CAPITALIST THEORY

Capitalism, however, soon posed seemingly insoluble ethical problems. Experience showed that, however "enlightened" self-interest might be viewed

---

6. KARL MARX & FRIEDRICH ENGELS (eds.), THE COMMUNIST MANIFESTO (1848) at 11.

in theory, its operation led inevitably to inequity and injustice. This occurred most notably during the 19th-century Industrial Revolution, as science transformed economic activity from essentially subsistence to production and consumption on an ever-expanding scale. Those who "had" generally acquired more, whereas people at the bottom rung of the economic ladder often found themselves slipping and falling. The exploitative practices of many industrialists in England, continental Europe, and the United States became subjects for scathing attack by novelists and journalists, the new prophets of morality in a profit-driven industrial world.

In time, the more progressive societies developed limits and guidelines for the operation of self-interest, particularly corporate self-interest. Law and regulation became accepted features of economic life in the industrialized West, if not elsewhere. Although full consensus on what was allowable or desirable never was reached, a trend toward greater societal control and corporate accountability was evident. Such norms and expectations may play the role that tradition and ideology played in former times: that of exercising restraint on self-interest and guiding people toward the ethical conduct that is humankind's highest goal.

VIEW TO THE FUTURE

At the start of the 21st century, Western culture seems to be on the eve of a change in values comparable in magnitude to that of Adam Smith's time. In this century, production of goods and services and the status-conferring consumption of them may be subordinated gradually to other human interests. Such a transformation may occur in conjunction with a global and cosmic vision in which human beings are seen as innately linked elements in a larger, organic whole, rather than as competitive, self-contained units. Current demands for corporate responsibility in employment equity and environmental sensitivity may be harbingers of such a future.

In the near term, the industrial and corporate structures that evolved during the past two centuries will continue to orchestrate economic life. Nevertheless, demands on bosses for managerial and economic decisions that are just, fair, and public spirited—and that ultimately facilitate community (however that may be defined in the future)—will continue and probably increase. People who aspire to achievement in business thus would do well to ground themselves in the Western experience of what is considered ethical.

BASIC CONCEPTS IN BUSINESS ETHICS

The study of business ethics is not a straightforward, easily classified pursuit. Philosophy, psychology, organizational dynamics, and economics all play a role.[7] The complexity of the field means that in ethics, especially in certain applied ethics areas such as business ethics, there are more questions than there are answers. Sometimes, the best we can do is work toward asking the right questions.

Here are some examples of basic questions in ethics. What is the difference between morals and ethics? Can ethics be studied independently of religion? If different people have different ethical systems, does that mean that any system is as good as any other? Why do some ethicists argue that following the law is inadequate as a moral guide? Does business have an obligation to be socially responsible? How does one live an ethical life in the context of a business career?

Four components of moral decision making were identified by James Rest of the University of Minnesota: moral sensitivity, moral judgment, moral will, and moral action. Over the years, the first component has presented great difficulty for many people in business. Some businesspeople tend to assume that any decision in the area of economics is value-free. Such an attitude, sometimes ingrained as part of an ideology, prevents managers from examining the ethical ramifications of business decisions.

To be sure, some choices involve no moral dimension. For example, a decision on which pair of shoes to wear to work normally has no moral significance; likewise, whether an urgent message is faxed or sent by overnight mail has no significance morally. Although choices clearly are morally neutral, it is no more correct to assume that all business decisions are morally neutral than it is to assume that all business decisions have moral significance.

In the contemporary environment, managers should be able to recognize choices that may be ethically significant so that their consequences may be analyzed properly. Good—that is, ethical—decisions generally are good business. Thus, developing the ability to recognize morally significant choices is an important objective of any course in business ethics.

THE MORAL CONTINUUM

One's approach to ethical problem solving depends in large measure on the way one thinks. The modern business world long has been characterized by a manner of thinking depicted as "white male consciousness."[8] In the view of Ann Wilson Schaef, such a mind-set attempts to force decisions into an

---

7. William A. Wines & J. Brooke Hamilton, *Observations on the Need to Redesign Organizations and to Refocus Corporation Law to Promote Ethical Behavior and Discourage Illegal Conduct*, 29 DELAWARE JOURNAL OF CORPORATE LAW, 43–82 (no. 1, August 2004).
8. *See* ANNE WILSON SCHAEF, WOMEN'S REALITY: AN EMERGING SYSTEM IN THE WHITE MALE SOCIETY (1981).

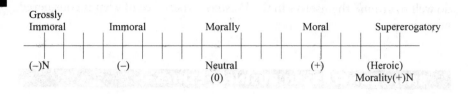

■ FIGURE 3.1

The moral continuum.

either-or, hierarchical mode; thus, anyone operating in such a binary consciousness is likely to see all choices as either moral or immoral.

Morality, however, is not so simple; it proceeds along a continuum from immoral to morally inert to simple morality to supererogatory morality (Fig. 3.1). Supererogatory morality, at the far extreme, is morality of heroic proportions. The term comes from the Latin for "over" and the past participle of the Latin verb for "has been paid out." If what one has been paid for is one's duty and if one does more than what one is paid for, such conduct is "over and above the call of duty." This phrase appears in many military citations for bravery.

Understand that not doing a moral act is thought of as immoral, whereas not doing a supererogatory moral act is not immoral but morally neutral—or merely human. A reasonable moral code cannot require that people, on pain of being judged immoral, act in a manner that can be achieved only by heroic figures.

"Moral" as an adjective means that an act is compatible with a code of conduct—a set of rules for living. When gauging an individual's moral code, watch the person's actions and discount his or her words. Thoughtful people tend continually to examine and adjust their moral codes. This is a way of developing moral sensitivity.

Some people have patently inadequate moral codes, but everyone has one. One prize fighter of an earlier era claimed he lived by just two rules: he never hit anyone from behind, and he never slept with another man's wife. This is an example of a moral code, but an extremely primitive one. Most of us live by much more evolved and complicated sets of moral principles.

The soundness of moral standards depends on the adequacy of the reasons that support or justify them. Morality cannot be divorced from reasoning.

Intelligent application of a set of values to complex, real-life situations requires the use of reasoning (as opposed to rationalization). Ideology is not a good substitute when it comes to reasoning, although ideology is certainly present in the ordering of one's set of values. By the time a value or moral precept is embedded in an ideology—for our purposes, a very closely held value set—that value or moral precept has been placed beyond the reach of reasoned review.

TYPES OF ETHICAL STATEMENTS

In developing a framework for business ethics, note that ethical statements can be classified as descriptive, normative, or meta-ethical. Descriptive ethical statements tend to be qualified and give an indication of the current practices in a community or segment of society. "Thirty-five percent of those surveyed admitted to calling in sick when they were not ill" is an illustration of a descriptive ethical statement. A norm is a standard; normative ethical statements invoke an ethical standard as applied to an activity. Thus, "You should always respect your parents," is a normative ethical statement. Finally, a meta-ethical statement involves an analysis of the underlying good chosen for normative purposes. An example of a meta-ethical statement would be, "Happiness is the ultimate good because it is the only thing human beings seek for its own sake." Most works on business ethics concentrate on the first two kinds of inquiry and do little in the realm of the meta-ethical. This book is no exception.

LEVELS OF STUDY

A thorough study of business ethics requires examination of three levels of questions: (1) the individual, using classical moral philosophy to address the question of how one can live a good life in a business context; (2) the entity or corporate level, asking whether business has an obligation to be socially responsible; and (3) the societal level, asking what a truly just and fair society would look like and how it would formulate its rules. If the second question were answered in the negative, there would be no need to address the third. However, if one accepts that business has social responsibilities, one must evaluate issues of justice and fairness to determine the limits of business obligations.

One of the current problems in higher education is that there is no agreement in academic circles as to how business ethics should be defined. Scholars disagree both about what business ethics is and whether it can even be taught. Much of the disagreement revolves around what goals are appropriate to business ethics courses. Some academics poke fun at business ethics; for example, one author wrote an essay titled "Could an Ethics Course Have Kept Ivan [Boesky] From Going Bad?"[9]

Such cynicism betrays faulty assumptions about the purposes and effects of business ethics courses. First, it commits the intellectual fallacy, the assumption that intellectual knowledge translates directly into action. Socrates made that argument 2,500 years ago, but failed to convince his most illustrious student

---

9. David Vogel, *Could an Ethics Course Have Kept Ivan From Going Bad?*, WALL STREET JOURNAL (April 27, 1987) at 22.

Plato, as well as Plato's student, Aristotle. They held that knowledge had to be filtered through an intervening station of willpower before it could be translated into action. Modern research in moral psychology supports the role of willpower.

As Professor Thomas Lickona noted, some management graduates perform at a lower moral level than their classroom scores would predict because of situational or environmental factors, such as corporate culture. In certain settings, people lack the willpower to act ethically. The basis for understanding this behavior was laid in ground-breaking work on authority by Stanley Milgram at Yale and in such studies as the Stanford Prison experiment by Professor Zimbardo (see Chapter 9). Any study of business ethics **must** address the corporate and business environment.

A second problem inherent in the question, "Would an ethics course have kept Ivan from going bad?" is that it attempts to apply a standard to one type of course that is not generally applied elsewhere in higher education. We do not ask English instructors to document the quality of written work performed by former students. College instruction is designed to improve the quality of students' thought, ability to communicate, knowledge, and skill level—in other words, to give them tools for future development.

Business ethics courses should seek to improve student thinking in identifying business decisions that have a moral dimension and to correctly analyze alternatives from various ethical perspectives; and to develop basic skills in using ethics as an alternative problem-solving technique. These objectives require the student to become familiar with schools of ethical thought and to grapple with problems or cases representative of business ethics conflicts.

As an academic discipline, business ethics is in its infancy. The field is characterized by competing academic approaches to basic issues. Some authorities suggest that any course or module in business ethics should be designed to further moral development along the scale developed by Larry Kohlberg, the late moral psychologist at Harvard.[10] Others argue that ethical questions in business decisions arise only when there is conflict between corporate social responsibility and profit-making.[11] Yet another group of ethicists declares that the study of business ethics requires that business activities be viewed according to some concept of human good, some philosophical system.[12]

Still others have taken multifaceted approaches to the subject. Richard DeGeorge of the University of Kansas (1990) argues that business ethics involves four kinds of activities: (1) the application of general ethical principles to particular cases or practices in business; (2) a meta-ethical inquiry into the appropriateness of applying moral terms generally used for individuals to collectives, such as corporations; (3) an analysis of the presuppositions of business, both moral and economic, from a moral perspective; and (4) an examination of macro-moral issues, such as whether rich countries have any moral obligations to poor ones.[13]

Robert Solomon, in a similar manner, identifies three ethical realms within business ethics: (1) micro-ethics—the realm of the individual; (2) molar

10. Edward J. Conry & Donald R. Nelson, *Business Law and Moral Growth*, 27 AMER. BUS. L. J. (Spring 1989) 1–39 at 1.

11. HOSMER, L R. T., THE ETHICS OF MANAGEMENT (1987).

12. DONALDSON & WERHANE, BUSINESS ETHICS (1983).

13. DEGEORGE, BUSINESS ETHICS (3rd ed. 1990) at 17–19.

	ETHICAL	UNETHICAL
LEGAL	Illus: being kind to children	Illus: not rescuing a drowning person
ILLEGAL	Illus: buying marijiuana for pain relief in terminal case	Illus: perjury, theft, or murder

■ **FIGURE 3.2**

A decision-making grid. Suggested by W. Michael Hoffman and Jennifer Mills Moore, *Business Ethics, Readings and Cases and Corporate Morality* (1984) at 67.

ethics—the realm of business, corporations, and industries; and (3) macro-ethics—the realm of the free enterprise system, capitalism, and the world.[14]

DISTINCTIONS: MORAL, ETHICAL, AND LEGAL

In this book we make a distinction between moral and ethical, even though the terms are frequently used interchangeably in everyday conversation. The term "morals" denotes the application of moral codes—the *prima facie* (i.e., rebuttable rather than absolute) rules of behavior that everyone has. Ethics refers to an activity that is higher and more abstract than the direct application of our personal rules to behavior choices. Ethics, for our purposes, is the cognitive, analytical, systematic, and reflective application of moral codes to complex, conflicting, or unclear situations. These definitions operate at the first, or individual, level of business ethics. As indicated in the previous section, this book also examines the entity level, in which we ask questions about the social responsibility in business, and the societal level, in which we inquire about fairness and justice in our world.

Good laws promote justice, a moral goal for any society. However, even though laws may be related to moral goals, what is legal is not necessarily the same as what is right (Fig. 3.2). Thus, law may be viewed as a minimum standard of behavior in a society. Failure to conform to this minimum results in civil sanctions or criminal penalties. Moral standards at any but the most primitive levels should exceed any legal requirements.

As groundwork, let us explore how law and ethics interact. Edmond Cahn, in his brilliant work, *The Moral Choice: Right and Wrong in Light of American*

---

14. ROBERT SOLOMON & KRISTINE R. HANSON, IT'S GOOD BUSINESS (1985) at 55.

Law,[15] describes this dynamic in "Morals as a Legal Order" (Chapter 1) and "Law as a Moral Order" (Chapter 2).

Cahn asserts that "in every mature society, there is a considerable overlap between legal questions and moral questions." He says the purpose of his book is to draw upon the "supply of moral insight and experience that American courts have gradually developed." We should learn what we can about good and evil and other moral concerns by looking critically at the way American law deals with them.[16] Cahn sees three important stages by which group moral legislation becomes individual moral decision: (1) impressing the group command on the individual; (2) internalizing the commands and fitting them to one's own character; and (3) relegislating the commands by our teaching and life (our moral type).

Cahn claims that moral precepts would remain too abstract if there were not moral types that represent the incarnation and animation of precepts. These moral types are the most potent varieties of moral legislation and come generally in four forms: (1) muscular (humorless and direct, almost ascetic); (2) eupeptic (fully rounded and human); (3) well-adjusted individual (actually a cryptic mimic—one who has decided with Pindar that "custom is king"); and, rarely, (4) prophetic (executes all three stages of moral legislation on an imposing scale—possibly a genius).

Cahn says that prophets are true prophets to the extent that they reflect a moral constitution, possibly of a universal community, in attacking national practice or precept; otherwise, they are false prophets. Thus, Cahn sees a system in which group moral decision progresses into individual moral decisions, that in turn are relegislated into community standards. He argues, "It is impossible, thus, for anyone to escape acting as a moral legislator, for, whether he builds or weakens the total order he inevitably modifies it."[17]

Turning to law as a moral order, Cahn notes that morality, like the self, is not singular but plural—meaning that everyone has many sides to his or her personality. Cahn sees three levels of moral standards: (1) required morality (enforced by the group); (2) desired morality (encouraged by praise); and (3) ideal or revered morality, which exercises an upward pull on the first two. As moral progress occurs, society moves in the direction of revered morality. For example, after the stock market crash of 1929 and during the Great Depression, U.S. responses to unemployment shifted from private sympathy and charity to publicly financed unemployment compensation.

Cahn critiques popular beliefs about law and morals. First, he points out that law does not deal only with minimum standards for moral behavior that are indispensable for community existence. Second, he rejects the notion that law is merely concerned with external conduct, because in many situations intent is critical. Finally, Cahn concludes that "there are moral values in the law and moral values outside the law; the only practical difference between them is in the respective methods by which they are enforced."

Sir William Scott in (Later Lord Stowell) *Evans v. Evans* (1790), explained the relationship between law and ethics this way:

> Courts of justice do not pretend to furnish cures for all the miseries of human life. They redress or punish gross violations of duty but they go no farther; they cannot make men virtuous; and as the happiness

---

15. EDMOND CAHN, THE MORAL CHOICE (1955/1981).
16. *Id.* at 3.
17. *Id.* at 25.

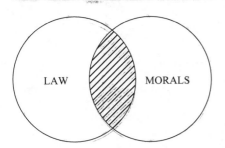

The intersection of law and morals.

of the world depends upon its virtue, there may be much unhappiness in it which human laws cannot undertake to remove.[18]

Americans generally are great believers in laws and our legal system even while they tend to deprecate lawyers.

What is the relationship between law and morals (Fig. 3.3)? Note that the shaded area is not static but dynamic and is under great tension. Law is not, however, coextensive with morals. (An exception might be a theocracy, such as Iran, which under the Ayatollah Ruholla Khomeini [1900–1991] attempted to fashion that country into a model Islamic state.) In fact, in a number of instances, situations may be cited to demonstrate that ethical and lawful behaviors sometimes do not coincide.

While we advance this model for consideration, I caution against concluding that there is no relationship at all between law and morals, or that the two are not related in some ways. Cahn argues that over time our moral standards—in Western civilization, at least—tend to improve or rise. We have, according to Cahn, tripartite moral standards starting with the standards we require, then the standards we desire, and finally the highest standards—those we revere or praise.[19] He contends that the rise in moral standards in turn has pulled the law, seen as the minimum for acceptable behavior, to higher levels.

The model shown in Figure 3.4 tends to support Cahn's observation, which was based on a more detailed and much more complex argument. This business of ethics is a cognitive, thinking matter. Moral decision making should promote choices *that are supported by the best reasons*. It involves such skills as critical thinking and problem solving—hard but ultimately rewarding work of the mind.

THREE PRINCIPAL SCHOOLS OF MORAL PHILOSOPHY

Moral philosophy recognizes three major approaches to ethical problems: **consequential ethics,**[20] **ethics of duty,**[21] **and ethics of virtue.**[22] This

---

18. *Evans v. Evans* (1790) 1 Hag. Con. 35, 161 Eng. Rep. 466 (Consistory Court of London).
19. *Id.* at 40–41.
20. *See, e.g.,* JOHN STUART MILL, ON UTILITARIANISM (1861) as discussed in JAMES RACHELS, THE ELEMENTS OF MORAL PHILOSOPHY (2d ed. 1993) at 90–116.
21. *See, e.g.,* IMMANUEL KANT, THE FUNDAMENTAL PRINCIPLES OF THE METAPHYSIC OF MORALS (1785 orig., Prometheus ed. 1988, transl. by T. K. Abbott).
22. *See, e.g.,* THE NICHOMACHEAN ETHICS (Hugh Tredennick, ed., rev. ed. 1976).

■ **FIGURE 3.4**

Law as the floor for moral code and ethics.

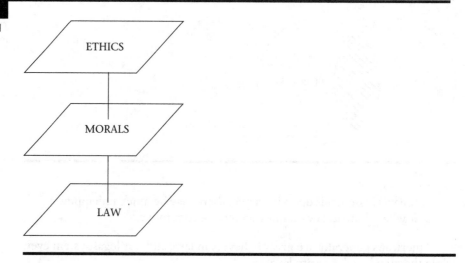

division reflects the central question in moral philosophy: whether the ends justify the means.

"To see life steadily and see it whole"[23] is a challenge for each of us; it is another way of describing the perspective that Aristotle argued was essential to the moral position. In Aristotle's terms, ethics may be defined as the quest for and the understanding of the good life—living well, a life worth living, or, from the Greek, *eudaimonia*. The pursuit of *eudaimonia* is largely a matter of attempting to gain and maintain a balanced *perspective* on life.[24] Aristotle argued that avoiding extremes and hewing to a "golden mean" was the path of virtue.[25] Other commentators phrased it this way:

> *Ethics* [italics in original] is, first of all, the quest for, and the understanding of, the good life, living well, a life worth living. It is largely a matter of *perspective*: putting every activity and goal in its place, knowing what is worth doing and what is not worth doing, knowing what is worth wanting and having and knowing what is not worth wanting and having. It is keeping in mind the place of a business career in our life as a whole, not allowing limited business successes or even business success in general to eclipse our awareness of the rest of life.[26]

This is no small task and a goal not easily reached.

Consequentialists (*teleological* ethicists) and duty or rule-based ethicists (*deontological* ethicists) focus on the acts being considered by the decision maker. Thus, the central question for them is, Does this act meet my moral requirements? The consequentialists, of whom the utilitarians are the best known, argue that an act should be judged by its outcome. Utilitarianism was

---

23. Matthew Arnold, *To a Friend*, as quoted in KENNETH E. GOODPASTOR (ed.), PERSPECTIVES ON MORALITY: ESSAYS OF WILLIAM FRANKENA (1976) at 106.
24. ROBERT C. SOLOMON & KRISTINE R. HANSON, BUSINESS ETHICS (1983) at 9.
25. *See, e.g.*, J.A.K. THOMSON (trans.), THE ETHICS OF ARISTOTLE: THE NICHOMACHEAN ETHICS (rev. ed. 1976) at 101–107 (Hugh Tredennick, ed). At 102, Aristotle declares, "It [virtue] is a mean between two kinds of vice, one of excess and the other of deficiency; . . . virtue discovers the mean and chooses it. Thus from the point of view of its essence and the definition of its real nature, virtue is a mean; but in respect of what is right and best, it is an extreme."
26. ROBERT C. SOLOMON & KRISTINE R. HANSON, ABOVE THE BOTTOM LINE: AN INTRODUCTION TO BUSINESS ETHICS (1983) at 9.

proposed by David Hume (1711–1776), but it was shaped and effectively advocated by Jeremy Bentham (1748–1832) and John Stuart Mill (1806–1873).[27] Jeremy Bentham would argue that a good act is one that produces the greatest amount of utility over disutility.[28] The best-known school of rule-based or deontological ethics is Kantian ethics, founded by Immanuel Kant.

Immanuel Kant believed that the only good thing was a good will. He proceeded to articulate a normative system based on that axiom. Kant (1724–1804) held that the rightness of an action depended on (1) the act's form or character, that is, whether it conformed to certain rules of conduct; and (2) the intentions of the actor. Unlike theologism, which justifies its rules by appeals to Divine authority, Kant made his reference point the *categorical imperative*.

Kant called his principle an imperative because he saw it as a command. It was categorical because Kant believed it applied in all places and at all times to all people, unlike a conditional imperative, such as "If you want to go to the national sales conference in Hawaii this winter, you'd better make your sales quota before year's end." Parental imperatives are also frequently conditional—tying a privilege to a duty by making the permission conditional on performance of the duty. Kant framed his categorical imperative in several different ways, arguing, not always persuasively, that they were interchangeable and represented the same basic moral principle. One way that Kant framed his imperative was "Always treat humanity whether in yourself or in others as an ends and never merely as a means."

Aristotle, whose ethics of virtue (*ontological* ethics) went into decline in the early 20th century only to experience a resurgence at the end of the century, argued from a position that declared, "We tend to become what we do." In short, we are always in a position of defining ourselves by our actions. Our actions declare that we are the kind of person who does those kinds of things. As a result, Aristotle argued that we should pick the kinds of virtues we want to manifest in our lives and then only perform actions that are consistent with our set of selected virtues. By repetition, we will habituate ourselves to act in honest, brave, kind, and munificent ways. Eventually, we will act virtuously out of reflex, without even needing to think about it at a cognitive level.

All three major schools of ethical thought have distinct theoretical approaches to the question of how can we know whether an act is good or bad. The consequential position is that an act is good if it produces good results; it is frequently measured by utility. Duty-based ethics measures the quality of the act by moral yardsticks that are constructed on rules of moral duties. Ontological ethics concentrates on the character of the actor, grounded on the premise that we tend to become what we do. Because we are always in the process of defining ourselves, our goal should be to become a good person, "especially the kind of person who performs right actions by habit and by desire."[29] A good act, then, would be one that complies with the rules, promotes good ends, and most important, moves us in the direction of becoming a good person.[30]

An ethics of care has evolved based on the pioneering work of Carol Gilligan (see Chapter 8). Some see this emerging system as a fourth and separate

---

27. JAMES RACHELS, THE ELEMENTS OF MORAL PHILOSOPHY (3rd ed. 1999) at 96.
28. *Id.* at 97.
29. LISA H. NEWTON, DOING GOOD AND AVOIDING EVIL: PRINCIPLES AND REASONING OF APPLIED ETHICS (1992) at 39.
30. *Id.*

A Matter of Perspective

Ethics, according to Aristotle, involves not only knowledge of the good and of virtues, but also putting such knowledge into practice (Aristotle, *Ethics*, p. 335.) An English professor at Northwestern University used to ask her students, "Do you see life steadily and see it whole?" This is a central question of ethical inquiry. Clearly, gaining and maintaining a proper perspective is what the study of ethics is all about—just as discovering that the world does not revolve around us and our needs is the task of growing up.

Perspective is an interesting word. It comes from the Latin word, *perspectus*, the past participle of *perspicere*, meaning to look through or to see clearly. In *Webster's New Collegiate Dictionary*, perspective is defined at 2b as "the capacity to view things in their true relations or relative importance."

The good life, *eudaimonia*, was the goal of an examined life according to the Greeks. *Eudaimonia* translates as the "good life" or "prosperity" or "the life worth living" or—very roughly—"happiness." The good life involves perspective—that is, knowing what is worth doing and what is not, what is worth knowing and what is not, and what is worth having and what is not. Wisdom was once defined, by Edmund Cahn, as knowing the worthlessness of a bauble before you held it in your hand.

In an effort to gain perspective, let us look at what physics and anthropology tell us about humankind and the cosmos—a harmonious, systematic universe. We know, for instance, that light travels 186,000 miles per second, or seven times around the planet earth. In 8 minutes, light reaches earth from the sun. Thus, we are 8 light-minutes from the sun. If light were to travel 8 billion light-years, it would have traveled only half way across the known universe.

Yet, try gaining perspective another way: The cosmos is between 10 and 20 billion years old, the earth is 4.6 billion years old, and the earliest footprint of a hominid was found in Tanzania by Mary Leakey and is only 3.6 million years old. If we take the last 50,000 years as a sample of time for examination, we have a period of 800 life spans of approximately 62 years each. Of these 800 people, 650 spent their lives in caves or worse; only the last 70 had any truly effective means of communicating with one another; only the last 6 ever saw a printed word or had any real means of measuring heat or cold; only the last 4 could measure time with any precision; only the last 2 used an electric motor; and the vast majority of the items that make up our material world were developed within the life span of the 800th person.

—KENNETH BOULDING, THE MEANING OF THE 20TH CENTURY, (1964) at 7. *See also* ALVIN TOFFLER, FUTURE SHOCK, at p. 15.

system of ethics.[31] I believe that a better reasoned view is that both the ethics of virtue and the ethics of care are examples of ontological ethics as contrasted to deontological and teleological ethics.

One feature shared by these different ethical schools is that all tend to promote human dignity. Utilitarianism strives to produce the greatest good for the greatest number of those affected by the act.[32] Immanuel Kant asserts that we must always treat humanity whether in ourselves or in others as an end and never merely as a mean.[33] Aristotle argues that we should seek to define ourselves as people who habitually and by desire perform right actions—right actions being those that make us better human beings.[34]

---

31. *See, e.g.,* NANCY KUBASEK, DAN HERRON, ET AL., CONTEMPORARY BUSINESS LAW IN A GLOBAL ECONOMY (2003) at 14–15 (listing four theories of ethics). *But cf.* James Rachels, THE ELEMENTS OF MORAL PHILOSOPHY (4th ed. 2003) at 171–172. Rachels argues that "the ethics of care, therefore, turns out to be one part of the ethics of virtue." *Id.* at 172.

32. RICHARD T. DE GEORGE, BUSINESS ETHICS (5th ed. 1999) at 61.

33. WILLIAM SHAW, BUSINESS ETHICS (2nd ed. 1996) at 61.

34. MANUEL G. VELASQUEZ BUSINESS ETHICS: CONCEPTS AND CASES (4th ed. 1998) at 133–138.

Moral Mandates in Terms of Precious and Nonprecious Metals*

THE PLATINUM RULE: *Do unto others as they would have you do unto them.*[1]

THE GOLDEN RULE: *Do unto others as you would have them do unto you.*[2]

THE SILVER RULE: *Whatsoever you do not want men to do unto you, do not do unto them.*[3]

THE BRASS RULE: *Do unto others as they do unto you.*[4]

THE IRON RULE: *Do unto others (as you like) before they do unto you.*[5]

THE COIN OF THE REALM RULE: *Those with the gold make the rules.*[6]

---

*This list was suggested by a similar list compiled by the late Carl Sagan and published in CARL SAGAN, BILLIONS AND BILLIONS: THOUGHTS ON LIFE AND DEATH AT THE BRINK OF THE MILLENNIUM (1997) at 190. Sagan's list was entitled "Table of Proposed Rules to Live By" and listed the Golden Rule, the Silver Rule, the Brazen (Brass) Rule, the Iron Rule, and the Tit-for-Tat Rule. It was based more on game theory research and less on ethics or morality. *Id.*

[1] Mace Vaughn, J. Howard & Associates, at a program on "Managing Inclusion," Miami University, January 24, 2003, Oxford, OH.

[2] Matthew 7:12: "Therefore, whatever you want men to do to you, do also to them."

[3] Rabbi Hillel was the one who made this moral rule famous. Other famous proponents of this rule included Mahatma Ghandi (learned from his wife!), and Martin Luther King, Jr. *See e.g.,* http://www.acsu.buffalo.edu/~reymers/courses/. Accessed on or about January 23, 2003. *See also* http://www.gerzon.com/resources/golden_rule.html and http://maverik. rootsweb.com/mcuz/OscrNich.html. Both accessed on or about January 23, 2003.

[4] Confucius urged this kind of behavior (repay a kindness with kindness), as did Aristotle. It is also found in the *lex talionis* (an eye for an eye and a tooth for a tooth.) This concept of justice is advocated in various places in the books of the Old Testament.

[5] A variation of this rule is sometimes stated, "Might makes right." Iron, which for many centuries was the metal of weapons and armor, seems appropriate to the level of sentiment expressed.

[6] Some see this as a secular and cynical revision of the Golden Rule. Accessed at http://www.gerzon.com/resources/golden_rule.html on or about January 23, 2003.

Typically, so-called value-neutral education in colleges of business turns out confirmed utilitarians. Many business graduates are not familiar with John Stuart Mill or Jeremy Bentham or even the term "utilitarian," but find themselves drawn ineluctably toward utilitarian solutions to moral dilemmas. This may well be the result of years of case analysis and management solutions that pivot on return on investment, portfolio yields, and profit maximization. In that context, best solutions are the ones that produce monetary results. Without raising the utilitarian method to the level of consciousness, many business students find themselves applying the same approaches to moral problems.

CONCLUSION

Moral development is a lifelong task. It often involves wrestling with disquieting issues and uncomfortable topics. Some philosophers and psychologists argue that *elenchus*, a Greek word that is translated roughly as disequilibria, is an indispensable step toward moral growth.[35] An important first step in moral development, as well as in the study of ethics, is to develop sensitivity to the moral dimension. The moral dimension can be understood roughly as the area in which decisions affect either the quality or the quantity of life for any form of sentient creation.

---

35. *See, e.g.,* James E. MacDonald, *Socratic Method and the Teaching of Law and Virtue,* 7 JOURNAL OF LEGAL STUDIES EDUCATION 19–34 at 26–29.

CHAPTER 4

Psychology of Moral Development

My salad days, When I was green in judgement
      —William Shakespeare, *Antony and Cleopatra*, Act I, sc. 5, l. 73[1]

M oral developmental psychology is a relatively new field. The origins of moral development as a subject for psychology can be found in the studies of children done by Jean Piaget in France. Piaget's work was the basis for a breakthrough development in 1958 when Lawrence Kohlberg was able to posit a theory of lifelong moral development with six stages and three levels. The astonishing thing was that Kohlberg had developed a theory that could also empirically measure the development of levels of moral reasoning. In an age that prized scientific, mathematical, and empirical research,[2] his theory brought psychology to the leading edge, so to speak, of the social sciences.

However, the basic concept that people evolve and mature in their moral beliefs is as old as the species; it finds emphasis in the culture of respect for elders common in Asia, in the dialogues of Socrates, and even in the plays of Shakespeare. Industrial psychology was the earliest application of the emerging field of psychology to management and business.

Abraham H. Maslow (1908–1970)[3] developed a general motivational hierarchy: Moving from lower to higher, people are motivated by physiological needs, safety needs, belongingness and love needs, esteem needs, and the need for self-actualization.[4] The term "self-actualization" was coined by Carl Jung, one of Sigmund Freud's followers who developed his own system of psychology. By self-actualization, Jung meant the development of full individuality, with all parts of the personality somehow in harmony. The term "self-actualization," as well as closely related ones (productive orientation, creative becoming), began to be used by psychologists who criticized motivational theory for being too narrow, concerned with short episodic behavior, rather than with more profound and pervasive aspects of individual hopes and aspirations.[5]

Maslow may be understood as saying that human beings are perpetually wanting creatures; that is, as soon as a lower level need is met, it is no longer a motivator and the human moves on to the next higher need. In addition to his general motivational hierarchy, Maslow distinguished between the lower and higher motives in this hierarchy as either deficiency motives (D-motives) or being motives (B-motives).[6] By this, Maslow meant to indicate that the lower motives are aroused by their absence or deficiency; these lower motives are powerful and urgent motivators when unsatisfied. The higher motives come into play when the lower motives have been cared for. Thus, for people to

---

1. THE COMPLETE WORKS OF WILLIAM SHAKESPEARE (Cambridge ed. text, William Aldis Wright [ed.] 1936) at 1066.
2. *See, e.g.,* ALFRED W. CROSBY, THE MEASURE OF REALITY: QUANTIFICATION AND WESTERN SOCIETY, (1997) at 1250–1600.
3. THE WORLD BOOK ENCYCLOPEDIA (1990), vol. 13 at 265. Abraham Harold Maslow was an "American psychologist whom many people consider the founder of a movement called humanistic psychology. The movement developed as a revolt against behaviorism and psychoanalysis, the two most popular psychological views of the mid–1900s. Humanistic psychologists believe individuals are controlled by their own values and choices and not by the environment, as behaviorists think, or by unconscious drives as psychoanalysts believe."
4. ERNEST HILGARD ET AL., INTRODUCTION TO PSYCHOLOGY (5th ed. 1971) at 330–331 citing A. H. MASLOW, TOWARD A PSYCHOLOGY OF BEING (2nd ed. 1968).
5. *Id.* at 330.
6. *Id.*

function at their higher levels, their survival and normal social requirements must first be satisfied.

In a study of college students, self-actualizers were determined to be the healthiest 1% of the students; that is, they were not neurotic or psychotic and they had full use of their talents, capacities, and potentialities. Maslow selected some eminent historical figures as self-actualizers: Abraham Lincoln, Thomas Jefferson, Albert Einstein, Eleanor Roosevelt, and William James.[7] Some empirical studies with a narrower focus also support Maslow's ideas. For example, one study found that people who score high on a dogmatism scale (who would thus be classified as non-self-actualizers) are less perceptive in some respects than other people: Laboratory measures show a correlation of −.61 between dogmatism and sensory acuity.[8]

MOTIVATION ON THE JOB

A management professor from Utah took Maslow's hierarchy, extended it, and applied it with greater specificity to work situations. Frederick Herzberg believed that two sets of needs were involved in motivation on the job: One set deriving from our animal nature and involving dissatisfaction-avoidance he called *hygiene factors*, and the second set involving learned drives related to human growth and achievement he termed *motivator factors*.[9] The growth or motivation factors are achievement, recognition for achievement, the work itself, responsibility, and growth or advancement. The dissatisfaction-avoidance or hygiene factors that are intrinsic to the job itself include company policy and administration, supervision, interpersonal relationships, working conditions, salary, status, and job security.[10]

Empirical studies done on employees involving thousands of job incidences showed that "of all the factors contributing to job satisfaction, 81% were motivators. And of all the factors contributing to the employees' dissatisfaction over their work, 69% involved hygiene elements."[11] Thus, generalizing from these data, it would seem that the absence of hygiene factors creates a job environment that is painful and unsatisfactory for the worker. However, the presence of hygiene factors really does not motivate most workers, but rather removes an unsatisfactory environment and can be seen as mostly neutral. What really "motivates" employees are the motivators: recognition, advancement, satisfying work, and the opportunity for personal growth.

What is the significance of all these findings? *The principal significance is that human beings are not the rational, utility-maximizers of neoclassical economic theory*.[12] Many managers produced by U.S. business schools have bought into neoclassical economic theory; it has become reflexive ideology for many of

---

7. *Id.* at 330–331.

8. *Id.* at 331 citing M. F. Kaplan and E. Singer, *Dogmatism and Sensory Alienation: An Empirical Investigation*, 27 JOURNAL OF CONSULTING PSYCHOLOGY 486–491 (1963).

9. FREDERICK HERZBERG, THE MANAGERIAL CHOICE: TO BE EFFICIENT AND TO BE HUMAN (rev. 2nd ed. 1982) at 58.

10. *Id.*

11. *Id.* at 60.

12. *See, e.g.*, Robert J. Shiller, *How Wall Street Learns to Look the Other Way*, N.Y. TIMES (February 8, 2005). Accessed at http://www.nytdirect@nytimes.com on February 8, 2005. "The view of the world that one gets in a modern business curriculum can lead to an ethical disconnect. The courses often encourage a view of human nature that does not inspire high-mindedness." *Id.*

them. The problem is that it is fundamentally untrue when it comes to motivating a workforce. Thus, when I represented a teachers' union in collective bargaining, the lawyer for the school district wanted to know why the teachers had not done better (performed at a higher level) as a result of the pay raises contained in the last contract. Although I did not know Herzberg's theory at the time, one simple answer would be that pay is not a motivator; rather, it is a hygiene factor. Another way to say the same thing is that good pay will eliminate worker dissatisfaction, but it will hardly ever motivate an employee. To motivate employees, one must structure work so as to embrace Herzberg's motivators: recognition, advancement, satisfying and challenging work, and growth.

Not everyone is enamored with Herzberg's work. For instance, two authors say that, although Herzberg's work is "very popular" and "has been widely received among managers concerned with the problems of human behavior at work," it has been much less well received by organizational researchers.[13] They then include in their textbook an article concluding that Herzberg's research is flawed in that (a) the theory is methodologically bound, (i.e., other methods of research need to be used to verify the conclusions but were not used); (b) the underlying research is faulty because the data need to be interpreted by the rater and inadequate operational definitions were used; and (c) the theory is inconsistent with past evidence concerning satisfaction and motivation.[14]

KOHLBERG AND THE BIRTH OF MORAL PSYCHOLOGY

Lawrence Kohlberg (1927–1987)[15] received his Ph.D. from the University of Chicago in 1958 for his work on stages of moral development; his dissertation extended and expanded the earlier work done by the eminent Swiss psychologist, Jean Piaget (1896–1980).[16] Piaget and his colleagues, who collectively published more than 30 volumes on this subject, studied the development of children's thinking. He believed that children pass through four periods of mental development: (1) a sensorimotor period lasting until age 2; (2) a preoperational period from about 2 to 7 years; (3) a period of concrete operations lasting from about 7 to 11 years; and (4) the formal operations period lasting from about 11 to 15 years.

Kohlberg spent the remainder of his life developing, defending, and polishing the theory of lifelong moral development contained in his dissertation. Unfortunately, his longitudinal study group consisted only of 84 people, all males.[17] This gender exclusion of women opened Kohlberg to the criticism that his work might not be accurate when applied to females or that it may, unintentionally but systematically, underrate the moral development of women.[18]

---

13. RICHARD M. STEERS & LYMAN W. PORTER, MOTIVATION AND WORK BEHAVIOR (1975) at 87.

14. Richard J. House & Lawrence A. Wigdor, *Herzberg's Dual-Factor Theory of Job Satisfaction and Motivation: A Review of the Evidence and a Criticism*, 20 PERSONNEL PSCHOLOGY 369–389 (1967) as cited in STEERS & LYMAN, *supra* note 10, at 104–114.

15. *See e.g., Harvard Professor of Education Reported Missing Since January 17*, N.Y. TIMES (January 31, 1987) at 10; and *Lawrence Kohlberg is Dead*, N.Y. TIMES (April 8, 1987) at D30.

16. THE WORLD BOOK ENCYCLOPEDIA (1990), vol. 15 at 449.

17. CAROL GILLIGAN, IN A DIFFERENT VOICE (1982) at 18.

18. *Id.*

Kohlberg theorized that life-long moral development is possible and that there are six stages of moral development that apply universally to all people in all cultures and all times. His theory emphasizes an ethics of justice and groups the six stages into three levels[19]:

■ Preconventional Morality
1. *Punishment and obedience orientation.* At this stage, the physical consequences of an action determine its goodness or badness, regardless of the human meaning or value of these consequences. Avoidance of punishment and unquestioning deference to power are valued for themselves, without regard to underlying moral issues.
2. *Instrumental relativist orientation.* Right action is seen as that which instrumentally satisfies one's own needs and occasionally the needs of others. Human relations are viewed in terms similar to those of the marketplace. Elements of fairness, reciprocity, and sharing are present, but they are *always* interpreted in a physical, pragmatic way.

■ Conventional Morality
3. *Interpersonal concordance or "good boy/nice girl" orientation.* Good behavior is that which is helpful or pleasing to others and is approved by them. There is much conformity to stereotypical concepts of majority behavior. Behavior is frequently judged by the intention of the actor.
4. *"Law and order" orientation.* There is an orientation toward authority, fixed rules, and the maintenance of the social order. Right behavior consists of doing one's duty, showing respect for authority, and maintaining the given social order for its own sake.

■ Postconventional Morality
5. *Social-contract-legalistic orientation.* Generally, this stage has some utilitarian overtones. Right action tends to be defined in terms of general individual rights and of standards that have been critically examined and accepted by the entire society. There is also an emphasis on changing law in terms of rational considerations of social utility.
6. *Universal ethical principle orientation.* Right is determined by the decision of the conscience in accord with self-chosen *ethical principles* appealing to logical comprehensiveness, universality, and consistency [italics in original]. These principles are abstract and ethical (the Golden Rule, the categorical imperative); they are not concrete moral rules, such as the Ten Commandments. At heart, these are universal moral principles of justice, of the reciprocity and equality of human rights, and of the respect for the dignity of all human beings.

Kohlberg believed that this hierarchy of moral development was universal; in an attempt to obtain data from various cultures, he did field research in

---

19. Lawrence Kohlberg, *Stages of Moral Development as a Basis for Moral Education*, reprinted with permission as Chapter 2 in BRENDA MUNSEY (ed.), MORAL DEVELOPMENT, MORAL EDUCATION, AND KOHLBERG: BASIC ISSUES IN PHILOSOPHY, PSYCHOLOGY, RELIGION, AND EDUCATION (1980) at 91–93.

various Third World locations and contracted a tropical parasite that invaded his major muscle groups. The condition proved incurable, and he took his own life on January 17, 1987, while on medical leave from a Boston-area hospital.

CAROL GILLIGAN'S WORK

Carol Gilligan was a colleague of Lawrence Kohlberg on the Harvard faculty. Making some of the initial and most telling criticisms of his scale for moral development, Gilligan developed another moral system, the ethics of care. She reported, "Psychologists studying moral development have equated morality with justice, characterized the parent-child relationships as relationships of inequality, and contrasted it with the equality of peer relationships."[20] Some research studies of the two moralities, the ethics of justice and the ethics of care, have been cast in terms of inequality and equality, following Piaget's equation of moral development with the development of the idea of justice and Piaget's distinction between relationships of constraint and relationships of cooperation.[21]

Gilligan and Attanucci's work reported on studies that showed that (a) concerns about both justice and care are represented in people's thinking about real-life moral dilemmas, but people tend to focus on one set of concerns and minimally on the other; and (b) there is an association between moral orientation and gender such that men and women use both orientations, but the care-focused dilemmas are most likely to be presented by women and the justice-focused dilemmas by men.[22] The authors concluded, "Consideration of moral orientation transforms the debate over sex differences in moral reasoning into serious questions about moral perspectives that are open to empirical study."[23]

Gilligan and Attanucci raise the concern that the choice of moral standpoint, whether explicit or implicit, may indicate a preferred way of seeing. If so, the implications of such a preference should be explored. Orientation may be a dimension of identity or self-definition, especially when moral decision becomes more reflective or postconventional. Another caution that they raised was that researchers need to inquire not only about the subject's orientation but also must be aware of their own orientation and how it might influence their perspectives on the interview.[24]

GILLIGAN'S CHALLENGE TO THE KOHLBERG SYSTEM

Carol Gilligan, a colleague of Kohlberg's at Harvard, studied boys and girls, who tended to be upper-class, and came forward and proposed the "language of responsibilities that sustains connection" instead of Kohlberg's "language of rights that protects separation."[25] Nona Lyons defined some critical points of comparison between Kohlberg's "morality of justice" and Gilligan's "morality of care." Morality of action in reference to justice is determined by equity

20. Carol Gilligan and Jane Attanucci, *Two Moral Orientations: Gender Differences and Similarities*, 34 MERRILL-PALMER QUARTERLY (July 1988) no. 3, at 223–237, 225.
21. *Id.*
22. *Id* at 223.
23. *Id.* at 235.
24. *Id.*
25. ELLIOT, p. 21.

for the parties, whereas the same morality of action under Gilligan's theory is determined by the maintenance or restoration of relationships.[26]

Gilligan's theory posited a three-tiered foundation for moral development. *The first level concerns an orientation with the powerless self.* At this stage, the person is able to take other's feelings into consideration, but still has the tendency to blame others for his or her actions. *Level two is a stage of self-sacrifice.* The person sacrifices for the self and for the well-being of others. In this level the person grows to include a sense of truth. At this point the person begins to consider the self again. A new sense of the self being deserving of consideration evolves. *Level three is termed nonviolence.* This stage involves no conflict between the care of others and the consideration of the self. The minimization of harm and pain is the ultimate definition of morality.[27]

JANE LOEVINGER'S EIGHT STAGES

Although Gilligan's theory is affiliated with female moral development, there is another psychologist, influenced by Kohlberg, Adler, Piaget, and others, who believed that the broad parameters of her own theory could apply to both sexes. Jane Loevinger developed an eight stage theory of moral development. The presocial infant develops symbiotic relations to caretakers. The result of these attachments leads to impulsiveness. This stage is identified by punishment and reward and the anticipation thereof. Self-protection sets in and concepts of right and wrong develop. There is still confusion with self control. Conformity is the next step, and it compares to Kohlberg's peer approval stage. Conscientiousness develops and is marked by goal attainment and personal decision making. The autonomous stage follows with deeper inner conflict and a heightened sensitivity to and respect for interpersonal relations. Stage eight would represent a very small population. It entails integration of previous dilemmas. This person disregards prejudice, values justice, and manages internal moral dilemmas.[28]

ERIKSON'S EIGHT AGES

In Erik Erikson's theory, spelled out in his book, *Childhood and Society*, people go through eight stages that are characterized by basic psychological conflicts (Table 4.1).[29] If the conflict in a given stage is not resolved, then that person will continue to revisit it until it is resolved or until he or she dies. In the first stage of infancy, the conflict is between basic trust and basic mistrust. Erikson writes, "The infant's first social achievement, then, is his willingness to let the mother out of sight without undue anxiety or rage, because she has become an inner certainty as well as an outer predictability."[30] He adds, "In psychopathology the absence of basic trust can best be studied in infantile schizophrenia, while lifelong underlying weakness in such trust is apparent in

---

26. *Id.* at 22.

27. *Id.* at 22.

28. JOHN MARTIN RICH & JOSEPH L. DEVITIS, THEORIES OF MORAL DEVELOMENT (1985) at 111–116.

29. ERIK H. ERIKSON, CHILDHOOD AND SOCIETY (2d ed. 1993) at 247 ff.

30. *Id.* at 247.

■ TABLE 4.1 Erikson's Eight Stages of Identity

	Infancy	Early childhood	Play age	School age	Adolescence	Young adult	Adulthood	Mature age
I Infancy	Trust vs. Mistrust				Unipolarity vs. Premature Self-Differentiation			
II Early Childhood	HOPE	Autonomy vs. Shame, Doubt WILL			Bipolarity vs. Autism			
III Play Age			Initiative vs. Guilt		Play Identification vs. (Oedipal) Fantasy Identities			
IV School Age			PURPOSE	Industry vs. Inferiority COMPETENCE	Work Identification vs. Identity Foreclosure			
V Adolescence	Time Perspective vs. Time Diffusion	Self-certainty vs. Identity Consciousness	Role Experimentation vs. Negative Identity	Anticipation of Achievement vs. Work Paralysis	Identity vs. Identity Diffusion FIDELITY	Sexual Identity vs. Bisexual Diffusion	Leadership Polarization vs. Authority Diffusion	Ideological Polarization vs. Diffusion of Ideals
VI Young Adult					Solidarity vs. Social Isolation	Intimacy vs. Isolation LOVE		
VII Adulthood							Generativity vs. Self-absorption CARE	
VIII Mature Age								Integrity vs. Disgust, Despair WISDOM
	FAITH	WILLPOWER	PURPOSEFULNESS	EFFICIENCY	DEVOTION	AFFECTION	RESPONSIBILITY	WISDOM

Note. Adapted from *Identity and the Life Cycle* (Erikson, 1959) and *A Way of Looking at Things* (Erikson, 1987).

Cartoon by Rich Rice

Horoscope: You will experience emotional, physical and spiritual hardships in the years to come, and there is nothing you can do about it.

American Psychological Association Journal circa 1991.

adult personalities in whom withdrawal into schizoid and depressive states is habitual."[31]

In early childhood, the next conflict is autonomy versus shame and doubt.[32] Erikson declares,

> Doubt is the brother of shame.... The 'behind' is the small being's dark continent, an area of the body which can be magically dominated and effectively invaded by those who would attack one's power of autonomy and who would designate as evil those products of the bowels which were felt to be all right when they were being passed. This basic sense of doubt in whatever one has left behind forms a substratum [of the psyche] for later [doubting].[33]

Each stage of Erikson's can be understood as having its own goal; the goal for the first stage is "faith" and the goal for autonomy versus shame and doubt is "willpower." The remaining conflicts are as follows:

3. Initiative versus Guilt   Play Age
4. Industry versus Inferiority   School Age
5. Identity versus Identity Diffusion   Adolescence
6. Intimacy versus Isolation   Young Adult
7. Generativity versus Self-absorption   Adulthood
8. Integrity versus Despair   Mature Age

---

31. *Id.* at 248.
32. *Id.* at 251 ff.
33. *Id.* at 253–254.

Erikson's theory is more than just mildly interesting for our purposes be-cause the implications overflow into the individual's expectations and relations with social institutions, government, business, organized religions, employers and the like. As Erikson himself noted,

> Each successive stage and crisis has a special relation to one of the basic elements of society, and this for the simple reason that the hu-man life cycle and man's institutions have evolved together. ... This relation is twofold: man brings to these institutions the remnants of his infantile mentality and his youthful fervor, and he receives from them—as long as they manage to maintain their actuality—a rein-forcement of his infantile gains.[34]

In this vein, Erikson concludes,

> Each society and each age must find the institutionalized form of reverence which derives vitality from its world-image—from predes-tination to indeterminacy. The clinician can only observe that many are proud to be without religion whose children cannot afford their being without it. On the other hand, there are many who seem to derive a vital faith from social action or scientific pursuit. And again, there are many who profess faith, yet in practice breathe mistrust both of life and man.[35]

FOWLER'S THEORY OF STAGES OF FAITH

In his book, *Stages of Faith*, John Fowler posits that moral development has an analog in the area of faith development.[36] Frequently citing Piaget, Kohlberg, Erikson, and Gilligan, Fowler works out a theory of faith development that has the following six stages:

- Infancy and Undifferentiated Faith.
- Stage 1: Intuitive-Projective Faith.
- Stage 2: Mythic-Literal Faith.
- Stage 3: Synthetic-Conventional Faith.
- Stage 4: Individuative-Reflective Faith.
- Stage 5: Conjunctive Faith.
- Stage 6: Universalizing Faith.[37]

In his book *Faith Is a Verb: Dynamics of Adult Faith Development*, Kenneth Stokes took James Fowler's model and made it more accessible.[38] He argued that faith can be understood in the following terms:

> Faith, then, is a quality of human living. At its best, it has taken the form of serenity and courage and loyalty and service; a quiet confi-dence and joy which enable one to feel at home in the universe, and to find meaning in the world and in one's own life, a meaning that is

---

34. *Id.* at 250.
35. *Id.* at 251.
36. JAMES W. FOWLER, STAGES OF FAITH: THE PSYCHOLOGY OF HUMAN DEVELOPMENT AND THE QUEST FOR MEANING (1981).
37. *Id.* at 117–213.
38. CHARLOTTE DAVIS KASL, MANY ROADS, ONE JOURNEY: MOVING BEYOND THE 12 STEPS (1992) at 26 citing KENNETH STOKES, FAITH IS A VERB: THE DYNAMICS OF ADULT FAITH DEVELOPMENT (1989).

profound and ultimate, and is stable no matter what may happen to oneself at the level of the immediate event.[39]

Faith is not fixed; rather, faith grows and changes with age and experience. The stages follow a linear pattern that parallels human development, starting with early childhood. As in all models of human development, it is difficult and inaccurate to portray a steady linear pattern of growth because the phases often overlap and there is also a tendency to return to earlier stages under stress or changing conditions. These stages are cumulative; each new stage builds on its predecessor(s).[40]

Note that in the summary that follows, I do not delve into male-female differences.[41] The first stage is essentially *the Innocent*, between age 1 to 6 years. This is primarily the level of faith found in preschool children who echo what their parents say and do; for example, "I go to Hebrew School because Mommy and Daddy go to synagogue and want me to learn Hebrew." The child has no personal grasp of concepts. Thus, family practices, such as prayer before meals, reading the Nativity story, or celebrating Passover, are filled with fantasy and imagination.

Stage two, *the Literalist*, usually occurs between ages 6 and 12. This stage is characterized by concrete, literal thinking. When the child hears that the earth was created in 7 days, he or she takes that to mean seven 24-hour days. If challenged, the child will respond, "My Sunday School teacher told me so" or "The Bible says exactly that." The authority still resides outside the child, but the reference group has expanded far beyond the parents. As Dr. Kasl says, "There is security in this phase because one believes, so simply, that this is the only way and the right way.[42]

Stage three, *the Loyalist*, usually develops between ages 12 and 15 or 16. In this adolescent phase, the key words are *belonging, loyalty, harmony,* and *conformity*. This mirrors the stage in Kohlberg during which children look to their peers for clues as to what is right and wrong and move away from the influence of parents. According to Fowler's study, a majority of church members in the United States fit this level of faith. They are most comfortable with groups of like-minded believers, and they say things such as "We Methodists believe" or "We Muslims believe." There is a strong emphasis on creeds, doctrines, and traditions, yet, authority still rests outside the individual. People in the first three stages have a sense of "rightness" that they may be convinced gives them the right, almost a duty, to impose their beliefs on others, who are obviously wrong if they disagree.

Stage four, *the Critic*, may develop, if at all, at any time between age 16 and the decade of one's thirties. This phase involves observations, experimentation, and growing inner awareness that often lead to disillusionment, struggle, doubt, and difficult questions that go against the established order. It can be a most difficult and even shattering stage. At this level, people start paying more attention to inner experience and their own observations. They start developing the ability to reflect, understand paradox, and look inside themselves. The central question shifts from What do they think? to What do I think? and How do I fit into the bigger picture?

---

39. KASL, *supra* note 38, citing WILFRED CANTELL SMITH, THE MEANING AND END OF RELIGION (1976).
40. KASL, *supra* note 38, at 27.
41. Those readers who are interested in pursuing the male-female differences in faith development stages are referred to KASL, *supra* note 38, at 27–34.
42. KASL, *supra* note 38, at 29.

Stage five, *the Seer*, reflects an integration of the four previous stages and does not appear until at least the age of 30, if at all. People at this stage have taken their experiences, mulled them over, questioned and synthesized them, and integrated them until they have arrived at values that ring true for them. There is a deep sense of internal rightness or what Quakers call "clearness" when they reach their inner truths. They are able to go beneath external forms to underlying truths, which many believe often have common threads. With an integrated faith common to both stages five and six, the principle of treating others as you would treat yourself and vice versa is deeply felt. A person at this stage cannot stand by passively in the face of starvation and pain. The quality of one's life is experienced in the context of the quality of life as a community.

Only a small group of people reach the sixth stage, *Wisdom or Universalizing Faith*. People at this stage experience a total commitment to the ongoing, guiding presence of God or whatever term one uses for the Ultimate Authority. Values, beliefs, and one's actions merge into a single whole or unity. They do not so much think about their faith or values as they work to live them. At this stage they are deeply connected to all of humanity and often cease to experience themselves as separate. Illustrations are scarce, but Mother Teresa and Gandhi come to mind, as well as a few extraordinary people I have known.

CONCLUDING OBSERVATIONS

"Life is not an easy game, Sister," Rooster Cogburn [John Wayne] says to Miss Eula Goodnight [Katherine Hepburn] in one of his later movies.[43] Life is also dynamic, not static. That is one of the reasons why developmental linear theories have such an innate appeal. We know, if we pay attention, that we change over time and that those we care about do too. The theories described in this chapter are attempts to explain those observations in ways that can be generalized and that can help us understand the people around us.

---

43. *Rooster Cogburn (. . . and the Lady)* (Universal Pictures 1975).

CHAPTER 5

Theories of Distributive Justice

Injustice is relatively easy to bear; what stings is justice.

—H. L. Mencken[1] (1922)

What does the Lord require of thee, but to do justly, and to love mercy, and to walk humbly with thy God.

—Micah[2] 6:8

Life is never fair, and perhaps it is a good thing for most of us that it is not.

—Oscar Wilde[3] (1895)

The issue of justice has been the subject of discussion and debate for millennia. It is a perennial quest of humanity; we seek to achieve the just society. Justice, of course, can be analyzed by its various forms: (1) criminal justice and civil justice, (2) substantive justice and procedural justice, or (3) retributive justice and distributive justice. In this chapter, we explore distributive justice.

Distributive justice asks how a just society would fairly distribute the benefits and burdens of citizenship. The debate on this matter has been ongoing since before the time of Aristotle (384–322 BCE).

Aristotle declared the first (sometime referred to as the formal) principle of justice: *"Treat like cases alike and unlike cases differently"*; some add the phrase, *"in proportion to their inequality."* That seems intuitively correct, at least to most people. The problem arises when we attempt to measure what makes cases alike.

What is the quality that we shall use to determine "alikeness"? Is it humanity—in which case everyone gets an equal share? Or should we use merit, effort, social contribution, or need? Let us examine each quality in turn.

HYPOTHETICAL PROBLEM IN DISTRIBUTIVE JUSTICE: WHICH Q?

Suppose we have a small island society made up of five people, and that we wish to distribute eight coconuts and four fishes. How would we do so? Should we simply give everyone an equal share: 1.6 coconuts and 0.8 fish? Suppose the five people include a fisherman, a male doctor, a 10-year-old boy, a female basket weaver, and a female CPA. Suppose further that the fisherman caught all four fish and that the boy found all eight ripe coconuts.

Now, if we use, *equality* or an egalitarian distribution, then everyone gets an equal share. Yet, the boy does not burn as much energy or need as much food as the men; neither do the two women. Thus, an equal distribution may give some more than they need and others less than they need. In addition, if we start distributing chores on our island, we will find that an equal distribution will overburden the boy, but will probably be too easy for the adults. Moreover, some of the people are better equipped by skill and experience for certain chores, whereas others are better suited for others. Thus, an equal distribution of benefits will be ill suited to a happy state.

---

1. H. L. MENCKEN, PREJUDICES, THIRD SERIES (1922), Chapter 3 as quoted in BARTLETT'S FAMILIAR QUOTATIONS (16th ed. 1992) at 642.
2. Micah 6:8 (King James).
3. Oscar Wilde, "An Ideal Husband" (1895).

DILBERT® by Scott Adams

5/30/95 DILBERT © United Feature Syndicate, Inc.

©DILBERT reprinted by permission of United Feature Syndicate, Inc.

Suppose we use need as a basis, thus adopting a Marxist distribution: "From each according to his abilities, to each according to his *need*."[4] If we use this rule for distribution, we run the risk that the fisherman and the boy will feel ill used because they will be feeding five people and not getting much in return. The doctor is of little use unless one is sick or injured, and the CPA is of no use at all in our micro-society. After time, the boy and the fisherman may slack off in their efforts as their resentment of the others increases. The basket weaver may be able to contribute mats for sleeping and baskets for keeping fish and coconuts, but after a while her services may also be of little benefit to the group.

Suppose we use *merit (individual)* as the basis for distribution. First, merit may prove difficult to measure. The boy and the fisherman may feel quite meritorious because they are providing most, if not all, of the food. Yet, the basket weaver will also have made a contribution. Moreover, the physician will argue that having spent most of his adult life studying medicine is meritorious because he may be able to save a life in an accident or illness situation. The CPA will have the hardest time making a case for merit until the complexity of the society becomes such that a market is generated and people need auditing services or cost accounting systems. Finally, distributing burdens on the basis of merit would be even more fraught with difficulty. Do meritorious people get out of guard duty? Kitchen police? Do they pay less in taxes? Do they pay more?

Suppose we were to use *effort* as the basis of distribution. If it is purely effort that is to be the basis, what would stop the fisherman from attempting to build a sailboat or the boy from working at becoming a baseball player? If they were to work hard at these goals, would they not be entitled to a fair distribution, even though their efforts contributed nothing to the well-being of the island society? Moreover, could one not effectively fake effort by acting busy while in reality goofing off? Effort would be a poor basis on which to build a distribution system.

Finally, there is the criterion of *social contribution*. This is almost impossible to measure, and thus, it, like need and effort, is mostly theoretical. For instance,

---

4. This is "one of the best-known slogans from Marx." ROBERT C. SOLOMON & KRISTINE HANSON, ABOVE THE BOTTOM LINE: AN INTRODUCTION TO BUSINESS ETHICS (1983) at 267.

what, if the CPA, having nothing to take up her time, turns to painting and manages to paint what everyone agrees is a magnificent painting of a sunset? Does that count as a social contribution on our island where survival is at stake and there are no art critics or museums? Yet, it might be that after all the island's inhabitants have died, explorers find the island and discover that the only thing of value left is that painting. How would we make amends?

FRANKENA'S QUANTIFICATION OF ARISTOTLE'S PRINCIPLE

William Frankena, professor emeritus of philosophy at University of Michigan, managed to quantify Aristotle's Principle as follows:

$$\frac{\text{A's share of P}}{\text{B's share of P}} = \frac{\text{A's share of Q}}{\text{B's share of Q}}[5]$$

where P is the sum total of the benefits and burdens to be divided by society and Q is the quality used for the distribution. Thus, according to Frankena, A's share of society's benefits and burdens would bear the same proportion to B's share of society's benefits and burdens as A's share of Q (the quality used as the basis, say merit) bears to B's share of Q. Frankena states,

> Aristotle's discussions of distributive justice in the *Ethics and Politics* will serve as a useful basis for our inquiry. Following his lead we may say that the typical case of distributive justice involves (1) at least two persons, A and B, (2) something to be distributed, P, (3) some basis of distribution, Q, and (4) a geometrical proportion or ratio.

According to Frankena, Aristotle saw three main theories of distribution: oligarchical, aristocratic, and democratic. The oligarchical distribution is based on wealth or property as the Q. The aristocratic distribution is based on merit, and the democratic is based, as Aristotle conceived of it, on free birth. (In this last criterion, Aristotle was making an allowance for slavery; a contemporary democrat would say Q is simply the fact of being human.[6])

RAWLS'S THEORY OF JUSTICE

John Rawls's most famous work is his *Theory of Justice*. In fact, it is Rawls's masterpiece and "is widely regarded as the most important book produced by an American political theorist in this century."[7] In addition to eliciting high praise (and vigorous critiques) from fellow scholars, Rawls has accomplished a truly remarkable feat. He has caused philosophers, political scientists, economists, sociologists, and law professors to engage in an ongoing discussion of exceptional depth and vigor.[8] *Theory of Justice* was first published in 1971.[9]

---

5. KENNETH E. GOODPASTER (ed.), PERSPECTIVES ON MORALITY: ESSAYS OF WILLIAM K. FRANKENA (1976) at 95.

6. *Id.* at 95–96.

7. RICHARD H. POPKIN & AVRUM STROLL, PHILOSOPHY MADE SIMPLE (2nd ed. 1993) at 93.

8. H. GENE BLOCKER & ELIZABETH H. SMITH, JOHN RAWL'S THEORY OF SOCIAL JUSTICE: AN INTRODUCTION (1980) at 5.

9. JOHN RAWLS, A THEORY OF JUSTICE was published in 1971 by the Harvard University Press. The copyright is held by the President and the Fellows of Harvard College.

The significance for us is that John Rawls managed to integrate two popular Q's: equality and merit. This is the *first synthesis* of two bases for distribution since Aristotle laid out his formal principle of justice over 2,500 years ago. In his two principles of justice, Rawls says we start with an equal distribution and then we *tolerate* inequalities *only* so long as the inequality benefits everyone in the society—but especially the worst off.

Rex Martin critiqued Rawls's theory and explained that it can be separated into a four-part structure: (1) primary goods, (2) two principles of justice, (3) basic structure of a society, and (4) workings of a society.[10] In the first component are the primary goods that would be desired by any rational person, whatever his or her value in life might be. The two principles of justice, as explained by Rawls, are as follows:

> [1] Each person is to have an equal right to the most extensive total system of equal basic liberties compatible with a similar system of liberty for all. [2] Social and economic inequalities are to be arranged so that they are both: (a) to the greatest benefit of the least advantaged ... and (b) attached to offices and positions open to all under conditions of fair equality of opportunity.[11]

Martin critiqued the above principles as being abstract in that Rawls usually refers to the first principle as a right, whereas the second principle is not formulated by Rawls as a right.

Continuing with Rawls's formulation, the basic structure of society, or "Rawls' primary subject of justice,"[12] is designed to distribute among the members of society certain burdens and benefits of social cooperation. (This "primary subject of justice" is explained in more detail in the following paragraphs.) The fourth piece of the structure, workings of a society, deals with concerns for the expectations of individuals in society.

Rawls's *Theory of Justice* has two basic goals. The first is to express a set of basic principles of justice that make up for the "various considered moral judgments we make in particular cases."[13] These "considered moral judgments" Rawls is speaking of are rather moral actions we may choose pertaining to laws, beliefs, rules, or any other governing nature. Blocker illustrates these "considered moral judgments" with these examples. The judgment that racial discrimination is unjust is one of our most basic, firmly held considered moral judgments concerning justice. An example of a more particular considered moral judgment is the judgment that it would be unjust for a certain employer, Mr. Smith, to refuse to hire a certain job applicant, Mr. Jones, simply because Mr. Jones is Black.[14]

Rawls's second goal is to develop a theory of social justice that is superior to one based on utilitarianism. Although there are multiple versions of utilitarianism, Rawls concentrates on merely two: average and classical utilitarianism. Let me clarify the two versions of utilitarianism. Classical is the view that social institutions are "just" when and only when they serve to maximize the *aggregate* utility. Average utilitarianism can be defined as a view that social

---

10. REX MARTIN, RAWLS AND RIGHTS (1985).

11. JOHN RAWLS, *supra* note 9, at 302.

12. BLOCKER, *supra* note 8, at 7.

13. *Id.* at 6.

14. *Id.*

institutions are "just" when and only when they serve to maximize the *average* utility per capita. Rawls states,[15]

> Many different kinds of things are said to be just and unjust: not only laws, institutions, and social systems, but also particular actions of many kinds, including decisions, judgments, and imputations. We also call the attitudes and dispositions of persons, and persons themselves just or unjust. *Our topic, however, is that of social justice. For us the primary subject of justice is the basic structure of society*, or more exactly, the way in which the major social institutions distribute fundamental rights and duties and determine the division of advantages from social cooperation.[16] [italics added]

This leads us into Rawls's primary component of justice or his "basic structure of society." A few examples of this structure of society are a constitution, private ownership of the means of production, competitive markets, and the family. In general, the basic structure of society should be able to satisfy the requirement of a just distribution of two items: the burdens of social cooperation (liabilities, duties, obligations—paying taxes) and the benefits of social cooperation (wealth and income, food and shelter, authority and power, rights and liberties). Rawls argues that the two principles of justice should govern distribution of and that the rules of the society should be negotiated behind a "veil of ignorance" so as to guarantee fairness.[17]

Rawls has been criticized by those holding different views of society. Philosophers holding the Platonic view criticize Rawls because they believe a person who contributes in a more valuable way to society as a whole should be compensated differently from one who merely contributes to the average (or mean of society at any given time). The next section focuses on a libertarian critique of Rawls.

NOZICK'S DEVASTATING CRITIQUE

Robert Nozick wrote *Anarchy, State, and Utopia* as an argument against John Rawls's *Theory of Justice*. Nozick's main argument is that "the state should have no large role in economy and society if the libertarian rights of the individuals are to prevail."[18] This belief follows the political line of libertarianism and is the reason Nozick has been called a radical libertarian. Reviews of Nozick's work range from "outstanding"[19] to the following less enthusiastic review by Jeffrey Paul:

> Robert Nozick attempts to set forth the libertarian position in a way that will persuade some of those who do not already accept it. Despite its ingenuity of detail, the effort is entirely unsuccessful as an attempt to convince, and far less successful than it might be as an attempt to

---

15. *Id.* at 8.
16. RAWLS, *supra* note 9, at 7.
17. *Id.* at 12. Rawls explains that "no one knows his place in society, his class position or social status, nor does anyone know his fortune in the distribution of natural assets and abilities, his intelligence, strength, and the like." *Id.* Rules negotiated under such conditions would, by definition, be fair.
18. TED HONDERICH, OXFORD COMPANION TO PHILOSOPHY (1995) at 269.
19. ROBERT E. GOODIN & PHILIP PETTIT, A COMPANION TO CONTEMPORARY POLITICAL PHILOSOPHY (1995) at 16.

explain to someone who does not hold the position why anyone else does hold it. The book may come to occupy the position of an official text of libertarian political theory, but it is unlikely to add to the ranks of believers in that view unless it converts a few unwary philosophical anarchists by persuading them that the minimal state need not after all violate their austere moral requirements.[20]

According to Nozick's theory, people can gain possession of certain properties by historical processes and by acquiring property that did not belong to any individual. In the area of distributive justice, Nozick's view can be summed up under a notion called "entitlement"; that is, a person is entitled to what he or she came by fairly.

What is radical about this approach is that it does not provide for a static distribution as Aristotle's formal principle would. Rather, Nozick is talking about a dynamic process in which justice lies in the process, *not* in the result. Nozick uses the Wilt Chamberlain basketball exhibition game to make his point. After time is stopped and we all get behind Rawls's curtain of ignorance, assume the original position and negotiate a set of rules that are fair. Then distribute the benefits and burdens of society and redistribute as long as the inequality redounds to the benefit of everyone. What we end up with is a set-piece. Nozick makes the devastating point that no one can spend a quarter without destroying this seemingly perfect distribution.[21] Rather, his work emphasizes that a dynamic process is required.

One concept that is extremely different from Rawls in context but that may seem superficially similar in description is *Nozick's legitimacy of redistribution* in the direction of equality. Rawls believes we should share the wealth with those less fortunate. Nozick takes the idea toward the libertarian end of the political spectrum.

Yet, Nozick's legitimizing of inequality in distribution through his endorsement of "entitlement" to wealth or property that one created or acquired fairly bears only a superficial resemblance to Rawls's principle of inequality. Some authors are careful to point out that entitlement is not the same as morally deserving.[22] Rawls argues that we should tolerate inequalities only so long as they benefit all of society and especially those who are less well off.[23] Nozick takes the idea of inequality and blesses it with libertarian legitimacy.

The legitimacy of redistribution in the direction of equality is, as Nozick says, more often assumed than advocated. We discover that, say, the wealthiest 5% of the population holds 40% of the national wealth, and then we ask, "What can be done about it?" Using the criterion of entitlement, such facts do not in themselves suggest that we ought to do anything. It all depends on how the present distribution came about.[24]

Nozick, and the libertarians before him, tend to base much of their philosophical emphasis on the right of property. Nozick calls his form of private property "entitlement." The rights of each individual to his or her own person and abilities, as well as to that property that was acquired by legitimate means, are the backbone of Nozick's viewpoint. No one should deprive another

---

20. JEFFREY PAUL, READING NOZICK (1981) at 192–193.
21. WILLIAM H. SHAW, BUSINESS ETHICS (3rd ed. 1999) at 97–99 citing ROBERT NOZICK, ANARCHY, STATE, AND UTOPIA (1974).
22. SOLOMON & HANSON, *supra* note 4, at 271.
23. RAWLS, *supra* note 9, at 14–15.
24. PAUL, *supra* note 20, at 42.

individual of property by the use of force (if the individual has not committed a crime), and neither should the state.[25]

LIBERTARIAN APPROACHES

"The history of civilized man is the history of the incessant conflict between liberty and authority."[26] From the conflicts of libertarians and authoritarians to the views of John Rawls and Robert Nozick, these 16 words provide one possible perspective to help illuminate the great debate. John Rawls, of course, comes out of the social contract school.[27] In contrast, a libertarian can be defined as "a person who believes in freedom of action and thought."[28] This definition casts such a wide net that practically all of us are libertarians. In practice, the politics of libertarians tends to be on the conservative end of the spectrum and places a heavy emphasis on personal freedom of choice, private property, contracts, and vigilance against the usurping of liberty by government.[29]

The philosophy called libertarianism (from the Latin *libertas*, liberty) promotes the view that everyone is in charge of his or her own life and of no one else's life. From this view, it also follows that a person has a right to make his or her own choices as long as those choices do not trespass on the lives (and possibly choices) of other people. This viewpoint can be stated in several ways:

- No one is anyone else's master, and no one is anyone else's slave.
- Other people's lives are not yours to dispose of.
- No human being should have a nonvoluntary mortgage on the life of another.[30]

Libertarianism's heritage can be traced to the age of Aristotle. Some argue that the concept of libertarianism began when Aristotle acknowledged moral significance.[31] Since that time, there has been a constant and (usually) uphill struggle for libertarians in all corners of the earth. The struggle is, of course, seen by most libertarians as the clash between liberty and authority and has five components.

The first great struggle is for freedom of thought. Libertarians believe that if an individual is able to have freedom of thought he or she would gain more knowledge, which in turn would aid in the advancement of civilization. In contrast, authoritarians believe that if people are given freedom of thought they may think wrongly and follow this wrongful thought with actions. Therefore, authoritarians believe that those people who have been divinely chosen to rule the people should remain in power. *The second struggle is for the freedom to speak freely.* The State believes that this freedom could cause severe damage by permitting

---

25. GOODIN, *supra* note 19, at 296.
26. CHARLES T. SPRADING, LIBERTY AND THE GREAT LIBERTARIANS (1972) at 11.
27. RAWLS, *supra* note 9, at viii. "What I have attempted to do is to generalize and carry to a higher level of abstraction the traditional theory of the social contract as represented by Locke, Rousseau, and Kant." *Id.*
28. AMERICAN HERITAGE DICTIONARY (1995) at 395.
29. FREDERICK D. STURDIVANT, BUSINESS AND SOCIETY: A MANAGERIAL APPROACH (1981) at 48. "Quite simply, [for Libertarians] the state traditionally had been something to fear." Professor Sturdivant goes on to quote R. M. MacIver for the proposition that "the state, conceived in violence, was born to power." *Id.*
30. TIBOR R. MACHAN, THE LIBERTARIAN ALTERNATIVE (1974) at 3–5.
31. *Id.* at xi.

citizens to converse openly about areas that should not even be considered—perhaps because truth might be told. Currently, the Chinese, Cuban, Libyan, North Korean, and Vietnamese governments still place limitations on freedom of thought and speech. For that matter, so does the U.S. Armed Forces, but then the military makes no pretense about being democratic. *The third trial is freedom of the press.* Once again, individuals, corporations, and political states that have many things to hide oppose this liberty. Sometimes, opponents of a free press hide behind the veil of patriotism or national security. *The fourth struggle is for the freedom to assemble.* Authoritarians prohibit this request for fear of citizens assembling and planning acts of treason or revolution. *The fifth important struggle is over the issue of religion.* Libertarians argue that a person should be free to worship at any shrine or at no shrine whatsoever. Throughout history, civilizations have successfully gained certain freedoms, such as these; however, as many civilizations have also lost such freedoms.[32]

THE RICH AND POOR

If the entire world (1971 era) were a village of 1,000 people,

> Imagine that we could compress the world's population of close to four billion persons into one town of 1,000 persons, in exactly the same proportions. In such a town of 1,000 persons there would be only 70 (United States) Americans. These 70 Americans—a mere 7% of the town's population—would receive half of the town's income. This would be the direct result of their monopolizing over half of the town's available material resources. Correspondingly, the 70 Americans would have 15 times as many possessions per person as the remainder of the townspeople.
>
> The 7% Americans would have an average life expectancy of 70 years. The other 930 would average less than 40 years. The lowest income group among the Americans, even though it included a few people who were hungry much of the time, would be better off by far than the other townspeople. The 70 Americans and about 200 others representing Western Europe and a few classes of South America, South Africa, Australia, and Japan, would be well off by comparison with the rest.
>
> Could such a town, in which the 930 non-Americans were quite aware of both the fact and means of the Americans' advantages, survive? Could the 70 Americans continue to extract the majority of the raw materials essential to their standard of living from the property of the other 930 inhabitants? While doing so, could they convince the other 930 inhabitants to limit their population growth on the thesis that resources are limited? How many of the 70 Americans would have to become soldiers? How much of their material and human resources would have to be devoted to military efforts in order to keep the rest of the town at its present disadvantage?[33]

The earth is like a large, enclosed system; this image suggests the earth's limited resources; the interrelationships among its ecological, political,

---

32. SPRADING, *supra* note 26, at 11–14.
33. RICHARD L. HEISS & NOEL F. MCINNIS, CAN MAN CARE FOR THE EARTH? (1971) at 31–32.

economic, and other systems; and the increasing links and confrontations among its people. In an interdependent world, the domestic problems of one nation frequently become a challenge to the resources and ingenuity of the global community of nations. Imbalances in the distribution of wealth, population, jobs, and food affect both the rich and the poor. These are realities of an increasingly interdependent world. Yet, today there are many gross inequalities in the distribution of wealth and resources among the people of the earth.[34]

The disparity in material conditions between rich and poor countries is exacerbated by the rapid population growth in the less well-developed nations. The rich are becoming richer, and the poor are becoming not only poorer but more numerous as well. Starvation is becoming epidemic. As of 1995, the U.S. population was 263,437,000 and growing at a rate of about 9% per year.[35] Poorer countries are growing at a rate more than three times that of the United States. The population of the planet earth hit 6 billion on October 12, 1999—ahead of estimates,[36] after doubling in about 40 years.[37] Whereas the U.S. population will double in approximately 80 years, some less well-developed nations will double their populations in as little as 15 years.[38] Some projections estimate that the planet will have 9.3 billion people by the year 2050.[39]

Overly rapid population growth in a poor country siphons away resources that are desperately required for reducing economic and social deprivation. At the national level, governments must devote a greater and greater amount of investment simply to provide minimal services for an ever-increasing number of poor children.[40] As children reach adulthood, the poverty problem is compounded by rising unemployment. There are not enough jobs to go around for the increasing population, thus, the cycle of poverty tightens, and the economic framework of the nation weakens under the massive weight of population. Social tensions, political problems, and violence are the final products of such unmanageable population pressures.

The crucial question, therefore, is how can the great majority of families break out of this vicious circle. Recognizing the fact that their social and economic difficulties worsen every day that population growth continues unrestrained, many developing countries look to the United States, "the rich," for support. The United States has been looked on for a century as one of the strongest and richest nations in the world. However, as Kevin Phillips wrote, "America's loss of economic power accelerated during the 1980s and was reflected in rising U.S. international debt and asset sales. By 1989, wealth was on the move globally, and the domestic consequences were profound."[41] Americans tremble to think that the United States is not the richest and most

---

34. DAVID KING, INTERNATIONAL EDUCATION FOR SPACESHIP EARTH (1970).
35. Microsoft Encarta, 1993–1995.
36. See *infra* Chapter 19, Environmental Issues, section A, especially notes 1 and 2.
37. *Id.*
38. For instance, the population of Kenya quadrupled in the 40 years between 1950 and 1990. *See* Paul R. Ehrlich & Anne H. Ehrlich, *Population, Plenty, and Poverty*, 174 NATIONAL GEOGRAPHIC MAGAZINE (no. 6, Dec. 1988) at 914–945, 942. Kenya's population was 6,100,000 in 1950 and had reached 23,300,000 in 1988 and was projected to hit 79,200,000 by 2020. *Id.*
39. Refer to Chapter 19, *supra* note 39.
40. Robert McNamara, *A Burden on Development in Population: The U.S. Problem, The World Crisis*, N.Y. TIMES SPECIAL MAGAZINE (April 30, 1972).
41. KEVIN PHILLIPS, THE POLITICS OF RICH AND POOR: WEALTH AND THE AMERICAN ELECTORATE IN THE REAGAN AFTERMATH (1990) at 116.

powerful nation in the world; but, on the other hand, losing this position takes some of the burden off of us as a country when underdeveloped nations look for financial support.

What can be done to solve the problems of overpopulation and the resulting death and starvation? The geography of hunger clearly indicates that widespread malnutrition is inextricably linked to global poverty. In every country in which the average national diet is nutritionally inadequate, the income per person is less than $400 yearly.[42] Likewise, in the United States, the poorer groups in society tend to suffer from malnutrition and disease. As a report titled *Hunger USA Revised* states, "There are still 26 million Americans living at or below federally defined poverty levels and who, therefore, cannot afford to purchase an adequate diet; and over 11. 2 million of them receive no help whatever from any federal food program."[43]

Kevin Phillips's book, *The Politics of Rich and Poor*, is about a weakness in American politics and governance–the frightening inability of the nation's leaders to face, much less define and debate, the unprecedented problems and opportunities facing the country. Phillips skillfully demonstrates how in 1990 the U.S. government was unsure whether the economy was strong or weak or where the United States stood globally. He argues that both political parties were out of step with a profoundly changing world. Phillips observed American political economy in these terms:

> *Liberty and equality are like buckets in a well. When one goes up, the other goes down, and in the 1980s the bucket of liberty and economic freedom rose, while the bucket of income equality fell.* Upper-tier Americans significantly expanded their share of national wealth while low-income citizens lost ground, and Reagan policies were critical to this shift [italics added].[44]

The gap between the wealthy states and metropolitan areas and the poorer areas—mostly rural, low-income urban, or small towns—grew sharply in the 1980s. The most prosperous sections of the country were New England, the Mid Atlantic States, and the Far West. The poorer areas were the Great Lakes, Plains, Southwest, Rocky Mountain, and the Southeast regions. In 1985, the Atlantic coastal states and California had the largest personal income average at $14,588 and all the others were at $12,580. Unemployment in the coastal areas registered low at 5.6% and the other states at 7.8%. In 1985, there were 832,700 millionaires and 13 billionaires in the United States. By 1988, those numbers rose to 1,601,200 and 51, respectively. During the same time period, per capita income only rose by $600.[45] As the cliché goes, "The rich are getting richer and the poor are getting poorer."

These statistics should raise questions of distributive justice. What is right and what is wrong? Can we solve this problem? Should we try to stop this increase in the gap between rich and poor? Is it really a problem or just a sign of another swing of the political pendulum? Is it right for many of the poor to try to live on welfare? Is it morally defensible that many millionaires and billionaires in this world have so much money that they will never be able to spend it all?

---

42. Microsoft Encarta 1993–1995.
43. Robert E. Anderson & John Kramer, *Hunger USA Revisited* (1972), a report written for the Citizens' Board of Inquiry into Hunger and Malnutrition in the U.S. (Washington, D.C.).
44. KEVIN PHILLIPS, *supra* note 44.
45. *Id.* at 185–188.

LIFEBOAT ETHICS

A review of lifeboat ethics may help us begin to answer these questions. There is a considerable amount of literature written on the lifeboat ethics problem, and each author has a little different perspective, ranging from biblical theology and situation ethics to social biology, economics, and analytical philosophy. Key issues include the following:

- the nature and validity of the lifeboat metaphor itself
- the use of triage in determining food allocation
- the responsibility of developing nations to themselves
- the reality of the Third World's plight
- the real implications of feeding the hungry

Lifeboat ethics is a relatively young and controversial concept that moves the discussion of global hunger beyond simple solutions into realistic appraisals and practical judgments. Some see lifeboat ethics as merely a special application of the logic of the commons. The classic paradigm is that of a pasture held as common property by a community and governed by the following two rules: first, each herdsman may pasture as many cattle as he wishes on the commons, and second, the gain from the growth in the number of cattle accrues to the individual owners of the cattle. In an underpopulated world, the system of the commons may do no harm and may even be the most economic way to manage, because management costs are kept to a minimum. However, an overpopulated (or overexploited) world, the system of the commons leads to ruin because each herdsman has more to gain individually by increasing the size of his herd than he has to lose as a single member of the community by lowering the carrying capacity of the general environment. Consequently the herdsman, along with others, overloads the commons.[46] The tragedy of the commons is that in a crowded world of less-than-perfect human beings, mutual ruin is inevitable if there are no controls over the pursuit of self-interest.

Garrett Hardin believes that one of the major tasks of education today should be the creation of such an acute awareness of the dangers of the commons that people will recognize their many varieties. For example, air and water have become polluted because they are treated as commons. Further growth in the population or in the per capita conversion of natural resources into pollutants will only make the problem worse. The same holds true for the fish in the oceans. Fishing fleets have nearly disappeared in many parts of the world, and technological improvements in the art of fishing are hastening the day of utter depletion. Only the replacement of the system of the commons with a responsible system of control will save the land, air, water, and oceanic fisheries.[47]

Hardin states the lifeboat problem in this way:

> If we divide the world into rich nations and poor nations, two thirds of them are desperately poor, and only one third comparatively rich, with the U.S. the wealthiest of all. Metaphorically each rich nation can be seen as a lifeboat full of comparatively rich people. In the ocean

---

46. Garrett Hardin, *Lifeboat Ethics: The Case against Helping the Poor*, reprinted from PSYCHOLOGY TODAY (1974) in RAZIEL ABELSON & MARIE-LOUISE FRIQUEGNON, ETHICS FOR MODERN LIFE (4th ed. 1991) at 302–311.
47. *Id.*

outside each lifeboat swim the poor of the world, who would like to get in, or at least share some wealth.[48]

He continues the scenario, putting 50 people in a lifeboat. It has room for 10 more people, but there are 100 people floating in the water begging to come aboard. What should the lifeboat passengers do? If they let people board, who should board? There are several options: one of them being the Christian ideal of being "our brother's keeper" and another being the Marxist ideal of "to each according to his needs."[49] Yet, perhaps it is not that simple.

Responses based on Christian ethics, even if one were to start with "being my brother's keeper," might be as varied as the sects and multiple traditions in the Christian faith. One can find a large variety of texts in the New Testament to use (or "proof-text" from) for support of a large number of positions. "Take no thought for what you are to wear or eat" might be one.[50] Another might be a reference to the pure form of socialism practiced in the first century and administered by the Apostles.[51] Under such an approach, we might have everyone take 20 minutes of rest in the lifeboat every hour.[52]

Another view is presented by Peter Singer in *Famine, Affluence, and Morality*.[53] He believes that suffering and death from lack of food, shelter, and medical care are bad. His main point is that, if it is in our power to prevent something bad from happening, without thereby sacrificing anything of comparable moral importance, we ought to do it. By not sacrificing anything of comparable moral importance, he means without causing anything else comparably bad to happen, or doing something that is wrong in itself, or failing to promote some moral good comparable in significance to the bad thing that can be prevented.[54] Singer understands that this type of behavior will probably not take place in our society because (a) it abolishes the traditional line between moral duty and charity; (b) many assume that governments have the responsibility, not individuals; and (c) it will only postpone suffering unless we can control world population growth.[55]

CONCLUSIONS

To be generous with one's own possessions is quite different from being generous with those of our posterity. We should call this point to the attention of those who, from a commendable love of justice and equality, would institute a system of the commons, either in the form of a world food bank or

---

48. *Id.* at 302.
49. *Id.* at 302–303.
50. *See* Matthew 6:25–34 (New King James version). "'Therefore I say to you, do not worry about your life, what you will eat or what you will drink; nor about your body, what you will put on. Is not life more than food and the body more than clothing? Look at the birds of the air.... Consider the lilies of the field.... Therefore do not worry about tomorrow, for tomorrow will worry about its own things. Sufficient for the day is its own trouble."
51. Acts of the Apostles 4:32–37.
52. *See, e.g.,* JIM WALLIS, GOD'S POLITICS: WHY THE RIGHT GETS IT WRONG AND THE LEFT DOESN'T GET IT (2005) at 212 wherein Wallis says that there are several thousand verses in the HOLY BIBLE addressing the poor and God's response to injustice.
53. Peter Singer, *Famine, Affluence and Morality*, reprinted with permission from 1 PHILOSOPHY AND PUBLIC AFFAIRS (no. 3, 1972) in RAZIEL ABELSON & MARIE-LOUISE FRIQUEGNON, ETHICS FOR MODERN LIFE (4th ed. 1991) at 292–301.
54. *Id.* at 293–294.
55. *Id.* at 297–300.

of unrestricted immigration. We must convince them if we wish to save at least some parts of the world from environmental ruin. Without control of human reproduction and the limiting of consumption to the use of sustainable resources, the peaceful sharing of the earth seems an impossible dream. For the foreseeable future, human survival seems to demand that we govern our actions by the ethics of the lifeboat, harsh though it may be. Posterity, Hardin argues, may be satisfied with nothing less.[56]

---

56. Garrett Hardin, *supra* note 49.

PART

2

Social Justice Concerns

Quebec's profound distinctness on this continent, its continued—though increasingly diluted—defiance of the Anglo-American notion of individualism at all costs, means that Canada has available to it a different way of looking at society, an original blueprint. In other words, English Canada has a significant other, and its lifelong dialogue with Quebec has made it a richer place. (The United States, in contrast, seems to be engaged in a narcissistic monologue, gazing at itself in a mirror as an increasingly disgusted world looks on.) The continuing dynamic with significant others—francophone Québécois and natives—is what makes English Canadians more than just unarmed Americans with health cards.

—Taras Grescoe (2000)[1]

Adam Smith (1723–1790) attempted to reconcile the individual welfare with the common good, at least in economics, by the device of the "invisible hand." Somehow, mystically, individuals pursuing their own self-interest in the marketplace would be led by an invisible hand to promote the general welfare. Smith, a keen observer of society, watched this drama play out in the markets of pre–Industrial Revolution Scotland and Europe. Smith was cautious about the limits of this system of political economy.

Karl Marx (1818–1883) took a more optimistic view of human nature. Writing his masterpiece, *Das Kapital* (1867), in the reading room of the British Museum, Marx believed that altruism and the spirit of community would lead workers to produce goods and services for the common welfare, independent of what was in it for them. Marx was an enormous intellectual influence on Western thought, but in his optimism, he appears to have been mistaken. Agricultural workers in the former Soviet Union who worked in collective farms (*kolkhoz*) or state farms (*sovkhoz*) that had checkered records in meeting their quotas seemed to become almost gifted in farming when they were allowed to develop small truck gardens for their own accounts.[2]

SOME CULTURAL ORIGINS OF COMMUNITY AND INDIVIDUALITY

Nor was there anyone among them who lacked; for all who were possessors of land or houses sold them, and brought the proceeds of the things that were sold, And laid them at the apostles' feet; and they distributed to each as anyone had need.

—The Acts of the Apostles 4:34–35.[3]

---

1. TARAS GRESCOE, SACRÉ BLUES: AN UNSENTIMENTAL JOURNEY THROUGH QUEBEC (2001) at 301.
2. *See, e.g.*, GREGORY & STUART, RUSSIAN & SOVIET ECONOMIC PERFORMANCE & STRUCTURE (7th ed. 2001) at 156–159. The authors state, "Finally, although the private sector played an important role in providing food for Soviet citizens, its efficiency was difficult to assess because data on inputs such as labor and capital was generally not available." *Id.* at 158–159. The fact remains, however, that the 33 million private plots were significant contributors to the agricultural market and to the documented improvement in the diet of the average citizen.
3. *See also* Acts 2:44–45, wherein it states, "Now all who believed were together, and held all things in common, And sold their possessions and goods, and divided among them all, as anyone had need." THE INTERPRETER'S ONE-VOLUME COMMENTARY ON THE BIBLE (1971) at 734 says that the sharing described above was voluntary unlike the required communalism at Qumran and that the "laying at the feet" was "reminiscent of ancient customs in transfer of possessions or of religious dedication of an offering to the gods."

Tocqueville described the mores—which he on occasion called 'habits of the heart'—of the American people and showed how they helped to form the American character.... He also warned that some aspects of our character—which he was the first to call 'individualism'—might eventually isolate Americans one from another and thereby undermine the conditions of freedom.

—Robert Bellah[4]

American culture is awash in messages of praise for rugged individualists,[5] personal independence,[6] and self-reliance.[7] In the upscale stock market craze, some scholars have taken to writing papers in praise, not of free markets, but of the inherent so-called morality of the market.[8]

THE "CULT" OF INDIVIDUALISM

The use of the term "cult" to describe individualism may seem harsh or hyperbolic. Yet, one definition of a cult is "a devoted attachment to or extravagant admiration for a person, principle, or lifestyle, especially when regarded as a fad."[9] If we were to add to the series in the above definition the word "theory," then we could see from one perspective how both individualism and capitalism could be considered to be cults. Many Americans have become so acculturated to the notion of self-reliance and the myth of the self-made man that they seem oblivious to their own needs for healthy communities or for their need for a meaningful public life.[10]

One of the most obvious characteristics of modern life is how interdependent we are. The development of specialization, as foreseen by Adam Smith in *The Wealth of Nations*, has contributed hugely to our mutual interdependence. We are not tillers of the soil who wield a few iron implements and generate the rest of what we need from the land and our toil. A person can hardly do anything in the 21st century that does not have implications for the lives of others. Yet, especially but not exclusively in the United States, the myth of individualism continues to run strong, occasionally blinding us to various aspects of reality.

DE TOCQUEVILLE'S WARNING

The first warning that Americans might be tempted to carry individualism to excess came from that brilliant social observer, Alexis de Tocqueville, in his masterpiece *Democracy in America*, which was initially published

---

4. ROBERT BELLAH et al., HABITS OF THE HEART: INDIVIDUALISM AND COMMITMENT IN AMERICAN LIFE (1985) at viii [hereinafter cited as HABITS OF THE HEART].

5. *See, e.g.*, the continued support for the movies of John Wayne, who consistently ranks in the top ten male box office attractions more than 20 years after his death.

6. This devotion to independence manifests itself in both the continuing fiction of the so-called self-made man and in ads pitched to women subliminally suggesting that they will be independent if they smoke certain cigarettes or drive certain automobiles. *See, e.g.*, "Advertising and the First Amendment" (Boston University, 1987).

7. The praise for self-reliance dates back to, at least, the year 1841 when Ralph Waldo Emerson's essay "On Self-Reliance" first appeared.

8. *See, e.g.*, "Markets and the Force for Good," a paper presented to Hurst Seminar at U of Florida by Thomas Dunfee, Kolodney Professor of Business Law & Ethics, Wharton School, University of Pennsylvania in February 1999. *But cf.* Harvey Cox, *The Market as God: Living in the New Dispensation*, THE ATLANTIC MONTHLY (March 1999) at 18–23.

9. WEBSTER'S NEW WORLD DICTIONARY (3rd college ed. 1994).

10. *See, e.g.*, HABITS OF THE HEART (1985).

in 1835–1839. De Tocqueville first acknowledged the power of materialism in these words:

> What we call love of gain is praise-worthy industry to the Americans, and they see something of a cowardly spirit in what we consider moderation of desires.
>
> One must go to America to understand the power of material prosperity over political behavior, and even over opinions too, though these should be subject to reason alone.[11]

De Tocqueville proceeds later in his treatise to warn of the dangers of self-interest, improperly understood, that is, the combination of self-interest and general ignorance as the cause of "shameful troubles":

> So the doctrine of self-interest properly understood is not new, but it is among the Americans of our time that it has come to be universally accepted. It has become popular. One finds it at the root of all actions. It is interwoven in all they say. You hear it as much from the poor as from the rich....
>
> I might drop the argument at this point without attempting to pass judgment on what I have described. The extreme difficulty of the subject would be my excuse. But I do not want to plead that. I would rather that my readers, seeing clearly what I mean, refuse to agree with me than that I should leave them in suspense....
>
> Self-interest properly understood is not at all a subtle doctrine.... Being within the scope of everybody's understanding, everyone grasps it and has no trouble in bearing it in mind. It is wonderfully agreeable to human weaknesses, and so easily wins great sway. It has no difficulty in keeping power, for it turns private interest against itself and uses the same goad which excites them to direct passions....
>
> I see around me nothing but people bent publicly on proving, by word and deed, that what is useful is never wrong. Is there no chance of finding some who will make the public understand that what is right may be useful?
>
> No power on earth can prevent increasing equality from turning men's minds to look for the useful or disposing each citizen to get wrapped up in himself....
>
> If citizens, attaining equality, were to remain ignorant and coarse, it would be difficult to foresee any limit to the stupid excesses into which their selfishness might lead them, and no one could foretell what shameful troubles they might plunge themselves for fear of sacrificing some of their own well-being for the prosperity of their fellow men....
>
> Hence it is all-important for them to be educated, for the age of blind sacrifice and instinctive virtues is already long past, and I see a time approaching in which freedom, public peace, and social stability will not be able to last without education.[12]

---

11. De TOCQUEVILLE, DEMOCRACY IN AMERICA (trans. GEO. LAWRENCE, ED. J.P. MAYER, Anchor Books edition 1969) at 284–285.
12. *Id.* at 526–528.

Bellah seems to capsulate these sentiments as follows. "He also warned that some aspects of our character—what he was one of the first to call 'individualism'—might eventually isolate Americans one from another and thereby undermine the conditions of freedom."[13]

EVOLUTION OF INDIVIDUALISM

The evolution of individualism to its modern and radical state in America is a process that has extended over centuries. The impetus for this evolution as well as moral license for it can be derived from the works of Jeremy Bentham[14] and Adam Smith.[15] However, their push for individualism had its roots in the work of Sir Isaac Newton and Descartes.[16]

Some have argued that the entire process of civilization has been the building of community, in that it has been characterized as a movement from family to clan to tribe to nation state to attempts at cooperative global government. Others have argued that the process of evolution has been toward the development of cooperation among *Homo sapiens*.[17]

Assuming, without argument, that both premises can be sustained, one would conclude that cooperation and community were the *status ante quo*. In short, human community was the given in the Middle Ages and in the period just before the Enlightenment.[18] Consequently, it may be a misplaced question to ask "who argues for community" in the contemporary Western world or specifically in the United States. Rather, the conditions of community were so solidly in place by the late Middle Ages that no one argued for it; rather, the only proponents were those for individualism because community, to a large extent, was a given. If this is an accurate description of the situation, then modern individualism, even radical individualism, in the United States today rules in a vacuum; there is no loyal opposition. That lack of dynamic, healthy social tension may be contributing to our current social malaise.

Individualism did not come full blown from the forehead of Minerva. Rather, modern individualism and radical individualism evolved gradually over a period of several hundred years, as Robert Bellah and others have pointed out. In 17th-century England, John Locke presented a radical philosophical defense of individual rights owing little to either classical or biblical sources. Locke professed an almost ontological individualism[19] in which the individual is prior to society and society comes into being only through the voluntary contract of individuals seeking to maximize their own self-interest.

---

13. HABITS OF THE HEART, *supra* note 3, at viii.
14. *See, e.g.*, JEREMY BENTHAM, THE PRINCIPLES OF MORALS AND LEGISLATION (1789, Prometheus Books Great Books ed. 1988).
15. *See, e.g.*, ADAM SMITH, AN INQUIRY INTO THE NATURE AND CAUSES OF THE WEALTH OF NATIONS (orig. 1776, Random House Modern Library ed. 1937).
16. Interview with Professor of Economics R. Larry Reynolds, Boise State University, Boise, Idaho, on April 13, 2000. Professor Reynolds pointed out, for instance, that Adam Smith was a fan of science and actually published a history of astronomy. Newtonian mechanics and Decartes' philosophy laid the mechanistic, atomistic groundwork for the later economics and moral philosophy of Bentham and Smith.
17. *See, e.g.*, G. ALLMAN, STONE AGE PRESENT (1995).
18. The Enlightenment can be defined as "a philosophic movement of the 18th century marked by a rejection of traditional social, religious, and political ideas and an emphasis on rationalism." MERRIAM WEBSTER'S COLLEGIATE DICTIONARY (10th ed. 1995) at 384.
19. Ontology is the science of being or reality. Derivation is from the Greek *onto*, meaning "being," plus *logia*, meaning "science of."

"Individualism lies at the very heart of American culture."[20] So assert Bellah et al., at the start of Chapter 6 on Individualism, "Our highest aspirations not only for ourselves, but for those we care about, for our society and for the world are closely linked to our individualism."[21] Yet, some of our deepest problems are also linked to individualism.

Contrast classical republicanism, evoking an image of the individual as an active citizen contributing to the public good; Reformation Christianity, inspiring a notion of government based on voluntary participation of individuals; and modern individualism in which the self has become "the only or main form of reality."[22] We have moved in the space of 500 years from an ordered society governed by the institutions of State and Church to the most powerful country on earth asserting that the individual is the primary building block of society.

The issue is whether modern individualism in which the self has become the main form of reality can be sustained. This is not an issue of whether self-contained individuals might withdraw from the public sphere to seek their private ends, but "whether such individuals are capable of sustaining either a public *or* a private life."[23] In undermining these traditions, as de Tocqueville warned, individualism also weakens the very meanings that gave content and substance to the ideal of individual dignity.[24]

What are "themes"? A theme is a subject of discourse, discussion, or meditation—hence a topic. In music, a theme is a principal subject in a composition. In a sense, a theme might be seen as recurring topic in the chapters that make up the volume of culture. Yet, the themes might have different emphases as played in the different strands of culture. The Puritans—although prone to see material prosperity as a sign of God's approval—embraced as the fundamental criterion of success the creation of a community in which a genuinely ethical and spiritual life could be lived.[25]

Themes of success, freedom, and justice are found in all three central strands of culture: biblical, republican, and modern individualism.[26] Sturdivant writes that the classic definition of culture is "that complex whole which includes knowledge, belief, art, morals, law, custom, and any other capabilities and habits acquired by a man *as a member of society*" [emphasis supplied].[27] Ralph Ross says that culture as a social-bonds metaphor may ultimately sustain like a climber's rope and restrain like the chains on a slave. Solomon and Hanson argued that culture is an essential element of the good life because it adds the dimension of time and genius to our lives.[28] "So long as it is vital, the cultural tradition of a people—its symbols, ideals, and ways of feeling—is always an argument about the meaning of the destiny its members share. Cultures are dramatic conversations about things that matter to their participants, and American culture is no exception."[29]

---

20. BELLAH ET AL., HABITS OF THE HEART at 142.
21. *Id.*
22. Robert Coles, *Civility and Psychology*, DAEDALUS (Summer 1980) at 137 as cited in HABITS OF THE HEART, *supra* note 3, at 143.
23. HABITS OF THE HEART at 143.
24. *Id.* at 144.
25. *Id.* HABITS OF THE HEART at 28–29.
26. *Id.* at 28.
27. FREDERICK W. STURDIVANT, BUSINESS AND SOCIETY: A MANAGEMENT PERSPECTIVE (rev. ed. 1981) at 27.
28. R. SOLOMON & K. HANSON, ABOVE THE BOTTOM LINE: AN INTRODUCTION TO BUSINESS ETHICS (1983) at 409.
29. *Id.* at 27.

This argument has its reflection in the inner tensions of modern American individualism[30]: the deep desire for autonomy and self-reliance combined with an equally deep conviction that life has no meaning unless shared with others in the context of community. This adds up to a classic case of ambivalence.

STAGES OF INDIVIDUALISM A LA BELLAH

Look at five stages of individualism in the U.S. tradition and the famous individuals who exemplified each stage:

1. *Biblical individualism* has the goal of a just and compassionate society. Illustrative prototype: John Winthrop, governor of the Massachusetts Bay Colony.
2. *Republican individualism* has, for its goal, participatory government. Illustrative prototype: Thomas Jefferson, third president of the United States.
3. *Utilitarian individualism* has a goal of wealth and material or worldly success. Illustrative prototype: Benjamin Franklin.
4. *Expressive individualism* has as its goal a richer and deeper life experience, both sensual and intellectual. This fourth type can be understood both as a reaction against #3 *and* as a transitional stage to #5. Illustrative prototype: Walt Whitman.
5. *Radical individualism* has as its goal isolation. The refusal or inability to support any demands from others characterizes this type. Illustrative prototype: Howard Hughes, at one time the richest American and founder of Hughes Aerospace.

Bentham and Mill's advocacy of utilitarianism gave individualism a boost by providing a moral defense of the pursuit of individual utility. That is, disconnecting morality from its centuries-old basis in Catholic teaching, Bentham made the radical argument that the "good" was an existence as rich as possible in enjoyments and as exempt as possible from pain. Furthermore—and on this point, Bentham lost the support of his disciple, John Stuart Mill—the welfare of society could be determined simply by adding together the utility of the society minus the disutility. This was the basis of Bentham's famous utilitarian calculus.

THE FALLACY OF BENTHAM'S UTILITARIAN CALCULUS

I believe that the fallacy of Bentham's utilitarian calculus, in specific instances, can be demonstrated. For instance, take the case of gender-selection abortions in certain hospitals in Seoul, Korea. As each couple moved to maximize its utility by having a baby boy, the ratio of baby boys to baby girls soared from 102:100 to 117:100 before government steps were taken in an attempt to abate the process.[31] As the author noted, a change of 15 to 20% in the gender ratio on a sustained basis would be a social disaster in this era of AIDS. Thus, couples pursuing their own self-interest could easily put the fate of the entire nation state at risk.

---

30. *Id.* at 150–151.
31. *See* John Leo, *Baby Boys to Order*, WINES, READINGS IN BUSINESS ETHICS AND SOCIAL RESPONSIBILITY (1999) at 13.

In rural China, many families violate the rules that were established by the government in an effort to limit population. They reason that having more children, especially sons, will make for more farm labor and a more comfortable old age. This is rational utility pursuit on the part of the families that can hide their violation from law enforcement. However, China and the planet do not need the extra people. In addition, in China, the pressure to limit families may produce a potentially explosive high number of sons.[32]

Take another example closer to home. In the military budgeting process and in some state government processes, departments that do not spend all of their appropriations by the end of the fiscal year not only lose those monies but also risk having next year's appropriation cut. The argument given is that they did not "need" all the money they were budgeted last year. To avoid these consequences, many military departments and installations burn the midnight oil cutting requisitions on the last day of the fiscal year to "spend up" their full appropriation. Yet, this behavior seen from the viewpoint of American society is both wasteful and irrational. Individuals building their careers and expanding their empires maximize their utility at a huge cost every year to our society.

Finally, look at the centrality of the automobile in U.S. society. We know that petroleum reserves are finite and that automobile fumes contribute to air pollution. Yet, many of us seem to be addicted to having an automobile. There are as many automobiles in the United States as there are men, women, and children. Planning and zoning commissions approve suburban developments beyond the reach of mass transit regularly on the implicit assumption that Americans will always have cheap gas and a desire for individual conveyances. The collective results are not healthy for the society or its future.[33]

WHENCE COMES THE MANDATE FOR THE COMMON WELFARE?

Some invariably ask the question, Where is the mandate for the common welfare to override my individual preferences? A warrant for the government to be the agent of the common good can be found in the U.S. Constitution, the police power of the state, and in the theory of social contract.

Yet, reasonable people can and do disagree about the proper extent of police power. Similarly, people disagree about how active a role the government should play in promoting the commonweal. The reader may recall that we discussed theories of government at length in Chapter 1.[34] Five major theories of government were given as Marxist, libertarian, pluralist, welfare, and modern cynic.[35] One who believed in a welfare theory of the state would hold that the government should do those things necessary to the welfare of the society that

---

32. VALERIE M. HUDSON & ANDREA M. DEN BOER, BARE BRANCHES: SECURITY IMPLICATIONS OF ASIA'S SURPLUS MALE POPULATION (2004).

33. This was brought forcibly home to me at a Quaker gathering where several "Friends" were arguing that a "good Quaker" should not own an automobile. They lived in an urban area with mass transit. I reminded them gently that some states (e.g., Alaska, Idaho, Montana, and Wyoming) have virtually no mass transit and miles between essential services.

34. See, *supra*, pp. 1–7 to 1–12.

35. *See* FREDERICK D. STURDIVANT, BUSINESS AND SOCIETY: A MANAGERIAL PERSPECTIVE (rev. ed. 1981) at 47–60.

people cannot do for themselves. Yet, even here we find disagreement about the nature of things that people really cannot do for themselves.

Amitai Etzioni, formally trained as an economist, has generated papers and books advocating a brand of communitarianism. Etzioni argues that "a moral revival in these United States is possible without Puritanism"[36]—that is, without either a loss of personal privacy or the presence of thought police for our intellectual life. In his view, "Communitarians are dedicated to working with our fellow citizens to bring about the changes in values, habits, and public policies that will allow us to do for society what the environmental movement seeks to do for nature: to safeguard and enhance our future."[37] In his book, Professor Etzioni argues that we need a resurgence of moral foundations and a renewed commitment toward meeting our civic responsibilities, but yet each community must be allowed to find its own way.

His book, *The Spirit of Community*, although interesting and in places provocative, is not entirely persuasive. My biggest difficulty with it was not with what it proposed, but rather with its vagueness about how all 285 million Americans are going to be mobilized to engage in the political activism that will be needed. Much of what he calls for had already been discarded when we embraced radical individualism. Yet, I did not find any antidote for the virulent individualism that has sapped Americans' desire to be involved in community and public life. Without such an antidote, many will respond ignorantly that they are promoting the public interest simply by pursuing their own preferences.

A further problem is that studies have indicated we tend to underestimate the value of common goods and of our fair share required to maintain the common good. One of the reasons, I believe, that so many Americans complain about high taxes is that we chronically underestimate the real costs of maintaining state parks, highways, schools, and prisons and what should be our share of those costs.

A few years ago, students in my senior classes in Business, Government, & Society responded to hypothetical problems in a manner that indicated a decided preference for individual choice and freedom, even at the expense of the welfare of society generally. The 70 to 80 students were placed in groups of three and asked whether the federal government should implement mandatory technical devices that would guarantee seatbelt use and eliminate drunk driving. Approximately 75% of the groups rejected the seatbelt device mandate, and almost all the groups rejected the interlock Breathalyzer mandates. I have further work to do analyzing these results, but they suggest a strong bias toward individualism, rather than community welfare.

In 2000, Robert Putnam wrote a book, *Bowling Alone*, documenting the decline of social capital in the United States.[38] He notes that the "core idea of social capital theory is that social networks have value."[39] Putnam also observes, " 'Social Capital' is to some extent merely new language for a very old debate in American intellectual circles. Community has warred incessantly with individualism for preeminence in our political hagiology."[40]

---

36. AMITAI ETZIONI, THE SPIRIT OF COMMUNITY: RIGHTS, RESPONSIBILITIES, AND THE COMMUNITAR-
    IAN AGENDA (1993) at 1.
37. *Id.* at 3.
38. ROBERT D. PUTNAM, BOWLING ALONE: THE COLLAPSE AND REVIVAL OF AMERICAN COMMUNITY
    (2000).
39. *Id.* at 18–19.
40. *Id.* at 24.

In graph after graph and table after table, Putnam documents that social capital in the United States has experienced a massive decline since about 1965. In one table, Putnam shows that measures of "civic disengagement" have declined across the board for all age groups since 1975, but that, most significantly, civic disengagement is concentrated in the younger cohorts, those 18–29 and 30–44 years of age.[41]

CONCLUDING OBSERVATIONS

Lack of interest in public life and an inability to come together to deal with common problems are what Alexis de Tocqueville warned about in the 1830s.[42] This is the problem that Etzioni and the other communitarians hope to address. A campaign for moral standards, family life, and ethical responsibilities concomitant with legal rights will not be effective alone. First, we need to bring into the sunshine, up to the level of consciousness, the ideology that protects individualism from direct intellectual scrutiny. How that can be accomplished is beyond the scope of this chapter, but would be a fruitful topic for future research.[43] Next, we need to address ways in which American social capital can be enhanced and rebuilt.[44] Finally, we should avoid despair because, as Putnam emphasizes, social capital in the United States has not experienced anything resembling a steady decline, but rather has displayed a cyclical property of rising and falling—like a *sine* curve.[45]

---

41. *Id.* at 252, Table 3.
42. HABITS OF THE HEART at viii.
43. The January 2001 electrical crisis in California, from one perspective, might be understood as an illustration of how ideology (unthinking, reflexive values application) can wreak social havoc. The California legislature, being dominated apparently by free-market zealots in the form of lobbyists with almost unlimited cash, deregulated the supply-side (wholesale) electrical production part of the industry and left the retail side regulated. The retailers were caught in a crunch when the suppliers produced fewer kilowatt hours for substantially (in one case 300%) higher prices. *See* Jim Lehrer Newshour, PBS, on January 23, 2001.
44. Putnam addressed this topic at the end of his book. See BOWLING ALONE, *supra* note 38, at 367–414.
45. BOWLING ALONE, *supra* note 38, at 25.

CHAPTER 7

The Role of Higher Education in a Free Society

When asked how educated men compared to uneducated, Aristotle replied as the living do to the dead.

— Attributed to Diogenes Laertes[1]

The presidential campaign of 2000 raised issues of educational reform, and almost every politician has some ideas about changes that need to be made to public education (mostly K through 12). The media cover test scores made by schoolchildren with intense interest, as if the Iowa Basic Test Scores were the last word about learning and quality of education. State legislatures have become involved in setting outcomes standards for public-school students.[2] With the passage of the so-called No Child Left Behind Act signed by President George W. Bush on January 8, 2002, emphasis on passing scores on standardized tests have taken on greater significance.[3] States must now participate in National Assessment of Educational Progress (NAEP) reading and mathematics tests.[4]

In kindergarten through 12th grade, school voucher programs have been a bone of much contention. Under a voucher program, the parents of a child who does not want to attend public school can request and get a voucher for a certain amount of money, representing all or only a portion of the state expenditure per child on public education, to use at a nonpublic school. Voucher programs are not uniform[5] and have been tried in Cleveland, Ohio, and in Milwaukee, Wisconsin. Some advocates of vouchers assert that competition will help failing public schools. Yet, such groups as the National Education Association, a large teachers' union, are generally opposed to vouchers because they contribute to further underfunding of needy public schools. Another objection to vouchers is that "choice" schools are not subject to the same testing as is mandated for public schools in the No Child Left Behind law.

In the higher education arena, there is a national debate about how much distance or on-line education is appropriate in a college degree and whether a

---

1. Diogenes Laertes, Aristotle 11 as cited in JOHN BARTLETT, FAMILIAR QUOTATIONS (13th ed. 1955) at 71.
2. *See, e.g.,* Bill Roberts, *Legislators to Set Educational Standards,* ID. STATESMAN (January 8, 2001) at 1B.
3. Pub. Law 107-110 of 107th Congress, 115 STAT 1425 (2002).
4. *See, e.g.,* National Education Association (NEA), *NAEP and ESEA Testing: Confirming State Test Results.* Accessed at http://nea.org/accountability/naep-accountability.html?mode=print on February 11, 2005.
5. For instance, Ohio Governor Bob Taft has proposed a state initiative on vouchers that would provide 2,600 vouchers statewide for the amount of about $3,500 per student. The current base per pupil aid would be increased by 3% to $5,328 in 2006 and increased another 3% in 2007 to $5,489. Governor Taft's plan would not start until 2007—if it is approved by the legislature. *See* Reginald Fields, *Taft School Budget Gives Boost to Low-Income Districts,* CLEVELAND PLAIN DEALER (February 11, 2005). Accessed at http://www.cleveland.com/printer/printer.ssf?/base/news/1108118007274001.xml on February 13, 2005. Opponents of the governor's plan argue that the Cleveland voucher plan is a failure because students who participated in the Cleveland pilot plan did not achieve at the levels of their counterparts in the Cleveland Public Schools. *Id.* In Milwaukee, the mayor praised the voucher plan as a success, whereas the opponents produced figures suggesting that an expansion of the plan coupled with a new (2003) proposed state-revised funding formula amounts to "war" on the Milwaukee Public Schools. *See, e.g., Letter from Mayor John O. Norquist* in MILWAUKEE JOURNAL SENTINEL (October 12, 2002). Accessed at http://www.adti.net.mjs_10_12_2002.htm on February 11, 2005, and Dennis W. Redovich, *A Brief Synopsis of The War Against the Milwaukee Public Schools,* Center for the Study of Jobs & Education in Wisconsin. Accessed at www.jobseducationwis.org on February 11, 2005.

PEANUTS

© PEANUTS reprinted by permission of United Feature Syndicate, Inc.

degree obtained exclusively through cyberspace is equal to one obtained at a traditional campus.[6]

The president of a state university in the inter-mountain West raised another issue in his annual "State of the University" address given in 2001. In addition to other materials related to campus news, appropriations, and athletics, he disclosed that his "pitch" to the legislature for funding was that "higher education is the engine that drives the 'new economy.'"[7] I have some difficulties with such an emphasis. First, it allows legislators to continue to view all higher education as vocational training, a view with numerous supporters. Second, it ignores the task of a liberal education in preparing citizens to take a meaningful role in our society. Third, purely from a political or tactical perspective, it ties higher education's fortunes to a state's economy, a coupling that has not always benefited education in the past. In my view, higher education is not about vocational training. Vocational training is a fancy term for job training. Job training has an important place in our economy, but that place is not in a university.

Vocational training prepares someone to do a job, a task, or series of tasks. We might, for example, train someone to do word processing, or to operate a forklift, or to drive an 18-wheeler. Certainty, that training has value; all honest labor has dignity. Yet, such training is not education because it misses some essential ingredients: (a) instilling a love of learning so as to make the person a life-long learner, (b) starting the person on the road to self-actualization, a la Abraham Maslow, (c) developing habits of critical (independent) thinking, and (d) putting the student in control of his or her intellect. Admittedly, no university does this job perfectly; we all know college graduates who are deficient in one or more of these skills. However, that does not justify downgrading the entire enterprise.

A national debate is under way on the purpose of education. Some argue that the public schools and universities have a duty to respond to the dictates of Corporate America and to turn out job-ready graduates. These advocates urge schools to "partner" with business. Apparently, they do not believe that educators are fully competent to make curricular or skills decisions by themselves. Funny, almost everyone who has gone to school in this country seems

6. *See, e.g.*, Eyal Press & Jennifer Washburn, *Digital Diplomas: Welcome to the Brave New World of Higher Education* ..., MOTHER JONES (January/February, 2001) at 34–83.
7. Personal recollection, January 16, 2001.

Nature of Education

Education is a social process.... Education is growth.... Education is not preparation for life; education is life itself.

— John Dewey, as quoted in JAMES T. WEBB ET AL., GUIDING THE GIFTED CHILD (1982) AT 220

to think he or she is an expert in education. If that is true, why is everyone who has a checking account not qualified to tell bankers how to run their businesses?

Other voices in this debate argue that the true purpose of education is to enable individuals to take control of their own intellects,[8] to become life-long learners, and to be prepared to assume meaningful roles in our governments and society. One author puts the dilemma in these words:

> At the root of every discipline there are a few apparently simple questions which regularly deflate its experts because they cannot answer them in unison. In education these questions all swirl around one which is absolutely basic:
>
> *What are we trying to do when we teach* [italics in original]?
>
> This is the most important question any educator can ask. It is also the one which is today being fumbled more than any other. What is the basic purpose of an education? To transmit the past or to control the present? To nurture an elite or to make all men equal? To impart information or to elicit criticism? To cultivate minds alone or men as well? Should it take as its object man universal, stripped of all irrelevancies of time, fortune, and motivational intent, or man particular, shaped by the crucial variables of culture and idiosyncrasy?... The most obvious fact about twentieth-century America is its inability to turn up with a single answer to these truly first-class questions.[9]

The last 45 years, in my opinion, have not produced any more clarity on these basic issues than the first 55; if anything, we are more confused than ever.

TEACHING VALUES AT SCHOOL

Some experts on public education contend that all education should be value-neutral. I disagree because I do not believe that instruction either can be or should be value-neutral. Edmond Cahn wrote, "It is impossible, thus, for anyone to escape acting as a moral legislator, for, whether he builds or weakens the total order, he inevitably modifies it."[10] By that, he meant that, whenever we act, others are watching and are influenced—even when we think otherwise. Thus, Cahn sees us assimilating the moral values of our culture and relegislating them to other generations through our behavior, a behavior that models and reinforces.[11]

---

8. *See, e.g.,* ALLAN BLOOM, THE CLOSING OF THE AMERICAN MIND (1987).
9. HUSTON SMITH, THE PURPOSES OF HIGHER EDUCATION (1955) at 1–2.
10. EDMOND CAHN, THE MORAL CHOICE: RIGHT AND WRONG IN LIGHT OF AMERICAN LAW (Midland ed. 1981) at 25 .
11. *Id.* at 24–25.

Children Learn What They Live

If children live with criticism,
They learn to condemn.
If children live with hostility,
They learn to fight.
If children live with fear,
They learn to be apprehensive.
If children live with pity,
They learn to feel sorry for themselves.
If children live with ridicule,
They learn to feel shy.
If children live with jealousy,
They learn to feel envy.
If children live with shame,
They learn to feel guilty.
If children live with encouragement,
They learn confidence.
If children live with tolerance,
They learn patience.
If children live with praise,
They learn appreciation.
If children live with acceptance,
They learn to love.
If children live with approval,
They learn to like themselves.
If children live with recognition,
They learn it is good to have a goal.
If children live with sharing,
They learn generosity.
If children live with honesty,
They learn truthfulness.
If children live with fairness,
They learn justice.
If children live with kindness and consideration,
They learn respect.
If children live with security,
They learn to have faith in themselves and in those
about them.
If children live with friendliness,
They learn the world is a nice place in which to live.
— Dorothy Law Nolte

To take a classroom example, a teacher in the lower grades who carries a paddle and uses it on the buttocks of students for disciplinary purposes is modeling violence and the use of violence as a "solution" to social conflict. This behavior is roughly akin to the illogical parent who spanks his children to teach them not to fight. A positive example would be a professor who persists in treating students with respect and dignity and who endeavors to be fair in his or her dealings with them. Thus, those who teach, whether they wish to or not, model values in deportment for their students. There has been a national decline in civility.[12] Teachers and professors should be in the front ranks of those seeking to reinstill civility as a national value.

I grew up with a now distinguished and nationally renowned mathematics professor who teaches at Temple University in Philadelphia. In one of his books, he describes the following classroom situation that helped start him on the road to being a mathematician:

> The earliest memory I have of wanting to be a mathematician was at age ten, when I calculated that a certain relief pitcher for the then Milwaukee Braves had an earned run average (ERA) of 135. (For baseball fans: He allowed five runs to score and retired only one batter.) Impressed by this extraordinarily bad ERA, I diffidently informed my teacher, who told me to explain this fact to the class. Being quite shy, I did so with a quavering voice and a reddened face. When I finished,

---

12. *See, e.g.,* MARK CALDWELL, A SHORT HISTORY OF RUDENESS (1999).

he announced that I was wrong and that I should sit down. ERAs, he asserted authoritatively, could never be higher than 27.

At the end of the season, *The Milwaukee Journal* published the averages of all Major League players, and since this pitcher hadn't played again, his ERA was 135, as I had calculated. I remembered thinking of mathematics as a kind of omnipotent protector. You could prove things to people and they would have to believe you whether they liked you or not.[13]

In my elementary school, I remember a sixth-grade teacher who announced that I had been selected for All-City Band, a minor but not completely insignificant honor in a city of almost 1 million people. She then said, "It's a good thing you can play an instrument, because you'll never be able to sing in tune." To this day (over 40 years later), I do not sing in public, in large part because of her cruel and unnecessary remark.[14]

A professor who does not show respect for opposing viewpoints when he or she lectures does a disservice to the profession. There are few areas in higher education in which dissenting or radical voices have not been raised. College students do not deserve to be spoon-fed; rather, they deserve to be exposed to an honest and an as humanly as possible balanced assessment of the discipline they are studying. To fall below this standard is to engage in the dissemination of propaganda or, more bluntly, mind-washing. Honest scholarship is what we should strive to model, even if we must occasionally, because of our passions, declaim, "However, I believe the better reasoned view to be. . . ." Sometimes the best answer a teacher can give is, "I do not know." The false and prideful façade of being the "answer man" or "answer woman" misleads students into corrupt notions of what the life of the mind is about and ultimately is self-destructive.

VALUES ONCE MORE: RELATIVE OR ABSOLUTE

Are there any values that are true for all times, for all people, and in all situations? In an exceptionally thoughtful book, Professor Huston Smith asserts, "If there is no medicine which a reputable doctor would prescribe without diagnosis, neither are there specific values which can be confidently prescribed without consideration of the situations for which they are intended."[15] Yet, as soon as he finishes this sentence, Smith wisely adds a footnote: "Whether there are general values, analogous to doctors' standing orders for adequate nourishment and good sanitation, will be considered later."[16]

After considerable analysis and consideration, Professor Smith returns to answer the question posed in his footnote. Smith embraces a third position he calls "objective relativism."[17] He explains it as follows:

> With relativism it acknowledges that there are no values that are unaffected by their contexts: given a relative difference in situation, what

---

13. JOHN ALLEN PAULOS, INNUMERACY: MATHEMATICAL ILLITERACY AND ITS CONSEQUENCES (1988) at 73.
14. This incident brings to mind the advice of the writer of the Epistle of James: "My brethren, let not many of you become teachers, knowing that we shall receive a stricter judgment," JAMES 3:1 (New King James Version, 1985).
15. HUSTON SMITH, *supra* note 5, at 13.
16. *Id.* at note 1.
17. *Id.* at 28.

is of value for that situation will also be different. But having granted this, objective relativism then goes on to agree with absolutism (1) that the question of what *is* good in any given situation is a question of objective fact to be determined by the character of the situation as a whole and never simply by personal preference or opinion, and (2) that contexts are sufficiently similar to warrant value generalizations concerning individuals, societies, and mankind as a whole....

Practically speaking, wisdom depends on the ability to define the range of the context for which the value in question is both relative and absolute.[18]

The issue of cultural relativism is a more concrete arena in which to explore the issues of relativism/absolutism. The slogan for cultural relativism might well be, "When in Rome, do as the Romans do."[19] Many people believe that the idea of universal truth in ethics is a myth. To them, the concept that different cultures have different moral codes seems to be the key to unlocking the mystery of morality.[20]

As Professor James Rachels explains, the cultural differences argument is usually a variation of the following general argument: "Different cultures have different moral codes. Therefore, there is no objective 'truth' in morality. Right and wrong are only matters of opinion, and opinions vary from culture to culture."[21]

To many, this argument is persuasive; however, it is logically unsound. The conclusion does not follow from the premise because it moves from a statement about human belief to a statement about objective reality. To illustrate, if we said: "Many people believe the moon is made of green cheese and others do not; therefore, we can never actually know what the moon is made of," we immediately recognize the fallacy of the argument.

Although the argument is invalid, the conclusion might be true. Let us assume for purposes of discussion that it is true. The consequences of such a truth would be heavy. First, we could no longer say that the moral customs of other societies are morally inferior to our own. Thus, a society that made war on another society for the purpose of taking slaves would be above moral condemnation. Second, questions of right and wrong could be disposed of merely by reference to existing moral standards. Third, there would be no such thing as moral progress.[22] The three consequences of cultural relativism have caused many philosophers to reject it outright.

Finally, we can point to values that all cultures have in common. All societies, even those that permit infanticide, value and protect their young. Without that practice, the young in the human race would not survive, and the society would die out. Next, all societies promote truth telling; not to do so would make all discourse inane. Finally, all societies have rules protecting their members against violence to enable people to live together in proximity

---

18. *Id.* at 28–29.
19. The basis for this aphorism is probably lost in history, although one scholar suggests an origin dating to the fourth century. "When I am at Rome I fast as the Romans do; when I am at Milan I do not fast. So likewise you, whatever church you come to, observe the custom of the place." St. Ambrose (337–397 AD): *Advice to St. Augustine on Sabbath Keeping.* As quoted in BERGEN EVANS, DICTIONARY OF QUOTATIONS (1968) at 597–598.
20. *See* JAMES RACHELS, THE ELEMENTS OF MORAL PHILOSOPHY (3rd ed. 1999) at 22–27 for an excellent and succinct discussion of cultural relativism, to which this author is indebted.
21. *Id.* at 24.
22. *Id.* at 25–26.

to one another, in short, to live in community. Any other rule would promote anarchy and destroy the society.[23]

THE UNITED STATES MOVES TOWARD UNIVERSAL SUFFRAGE

When the U.S. Constitution was ratified by the states in 1788,[24] only certain white men could vote in elections. Women, slaves, and the indigenous people could not vote; they were disenfranchised. Actually, the U.S. Constitution itself is silent on voting rights; nowhere in the body of the Constitution is there an explicit declaration of the right to vote. It is, instead, found implicitly in the guarantee that every state will have a republican form of government (Art. IV, sec. 6), in the description of the House of Representatives as chosen by the people (Art. 1, sec. 2), and in the references to the election of senators and the president.[25]

The task of setting electoral qualifications for both state and national elections was initially left exclusively to the states. The states initially excluded all men without property and all women from voting. This exclusion did not change until the 15th Amendment was passed in 1870, 5 years after the end of the Civil War. The 15th Amendment prohibited states from denying the right to vote on account of "race, color, or previous condition of servitude." Despite its clear language and intent, the 15th Amendment did not enfranchise Black voters in the South for another 95 years. Most Southern Blacks were denied the right to vote by the use of poll taxes, fraudulently administered literacy tests, White primaries, and violence.[26]

The roots of the women's suffrage movement can be traced to the expansionist period of U.S. history (1820–1850). Early American women enjoyed few rights. There were no colleges for women, and most professional careers were closed to them. A married woman could not own property; instead, her husband was conclusively presumed to be the manager of the marital estate, including property that the wife brought with her into the marriage. Finally, American women were barred from voting in all elections.[27]

In 1835, Oberlin College became the first men's school in the United States to admit women. Other men's colleges soon followed, and new colleges for women were built. Mount Holyoke College for women opened in 1836; Wesleyan College for women opened in Macon, Georgia, in 1836; and Massachusetts State Teachers College in Framingham, Massachusetts, opened in 1839. In 1848, New York became the first state to allow women to own real estate (land). That same year, Lucretia Mott and Elisabeth Cady Stanton organized a Woman's Rights Convention in Seneca Falls, New York. That convention issued the first formal demand that women be given the right to vote. The fight for women's suffrage was to be a long campaign, lasting 72 years.[28] In

23. *Id.* at 29–31.
24. By July 26, 1788, 11 states had ratified the Constitution; the remaining 2, North Carolina and Rhode Island, ratified on November 21, 1789 and May 29, 1790, respectively. GUNTHER & DOWLING, CONSTITUTIONAL LAW: CASES AND MATERIALS (8th ed. 1970) at note, lxxxiv.
25. KERMIT L. HALL (ed), THE OXFORD COMPANION TO THE SUPREME COURT OF THE UNITED STATES (1992) at 899 .
26. *Id.* at 900. "White primaries" were primary elections in which only "White" voters were allowed to vote.
27. THE WORLD BOOK ENCYCLOPEDIA (1990), vol. 20 at 161.
28. In 1869, Susan B. Anthony and Elizabeth Cady Stanton founded the National Woman Suffrage Association. The Territory of Wyoming gave women the right to vote the same

1920, the 19th Amendment was enacted, declaring that the right to vote "shall not be denied or abridged by the United States or by any State on account of sex."[29]

The only longer wait for the right to vote was reserved for African Americans. In 1953, the U.S. Supreme Court voted to end White-only primaries, arguing that they violated equal protection rights guaranteed by the 14th Amendment. Before passage of the 1965 Voting Rights Act, the federal government had responded to racial discrimination in voting in the South in a lukewarm and haphazard way that relied on litigation. After the outrageous police-state violence against nonviolent civil rights marchers in Selma, Alabama,[30] the Johnson Administration pushed through the Voting Rights Act of 1965. It was based on Congress' power to enforce the 15th Amendment and broadly restated the Amendment's prohibitions against voting discrimination. However, it was specifically directed against seven Southern states that used literacy tests, spurious educational norms, and so-called good character tests to obstruct Black voter registration.[31]

Even with the passage of the 1965 Voting Rights Act and with the lowering of voter age requirements from 21 years to 18 years in national elections starting in the 1972 elections, voter turnout has not been very high in the United States. In all the presidential elections from 1932 through 1996, the highest turnout was 62.8% in 1960 for the Kennedy-Nixon campaign. In 1996, for the Clinton-Dole-Perot contest, only 49.0% of the eligible voters participated.[32] It was the lowest turnout on record since the Federal Election Commission Study was begun.[33]

MOVING TOWARD UNIVERSAL EDUCATION

In the same expansionist era of 1820–1850, most of the good schools in the United States were expensive private schools. Poor children went to second-rate "charity" schools or did not go at all. During the 1830s, Horace Mann of Massachusetts along with other reformers began demanding education and better schools for all American children. States began establishing public school systems, and more children were exposed to formal education. Keep in mind, however, that there were no child labor laws, so, children of the poor almost without exception went to work to help the family survive. This was true until child labor laws were finally upheld as constitutional in 1941.[34]

---

year. A few states followed, but only for local elections. *See* WORLD BOOK ENCYCLOPEDIA (1990), vol. 20 at 171.

29. GUNTHER & DOWLING, *supra* note 20, at lxxxviii.

30. Two marchers were killed, one Black and one White. The events before and after "Bloody Sunday," March 7, 1965, are well described in JUAN WILLIAMS, EYES ON THE PRIZE (1987) at 262–285.

31. KERMIT L. HALL (ed), *supra* note 21, at 902–903. The states most directly involved were Alabama, Georgia, Louisiana, Mississippi, North Carolina (partial), South Carolina, Virginia, and, additionally, Alaska.

32. THE WORLD ALMANAC AND BOOK OF FACTS, 2000 (1999) at 500.

33. *Id.*

34. *United States v. Darby Lumber Co.* 312 U.S. 100 (1941) upheld the child labor provisions contained in the Fair Labor Standards Act of 1938. In *Hammer v. Dagenhart*, 247 U.S. 251 (1918), the U.S. Supreme Court in a 5–4 decision overturned the Keating-Owen Child Labor Act, which had used the commerce power to bar goods made by children from interstate commerce. This Act was viewed by some as the high-watermark of the Progressive movement. The dissent was led by Justice O. W. Holmes, Jr., in what has been called one of his greatest dissents.

To a certain extent, it is still true among migrant farm workers whose poverty necessitates child labor and whose mobility facilitates it.

Horace Mann (1796–1859) has been called the "Father of the Common Schools."[35] In 1837, Mann gave up his law practice to become the secretary of the newly established Massachusetts State Board of Education. He founded the first state normal school (teacher's college) in Lexington, Massachusetts, in 1839. He strengthened education in his own state through a series of laws that improved financial support and public control of schools. Mann studied European educational methods and included his findings in one of his 12 annual reports for the State Board of Education. These reports covered almost every aspect of the problems facing U.S. education. As a result of his efforts, Mann's influence benefited education in nearly every other state. In 1848, he resigned from the State Board of Education to take a seat in the U.S. House of Representatives.[36]

Between 1840 and 1916, most states began to establish state normal schools. These colleges trained teachers for a system of public education based on standardized courses of study. As a result, children throughout the entire country began to receive much the same lessons out of the same or similar texts. In the mid-1850s, children learned how to read by studying the *McGuffey* or *Eclectic Readers*.[37] These books taught patriotism and morality as well as reading.

SOME CONCLUDING OBSERVATIONS

Thomas Jefferson, author of the Declaration of Independence and the third president of the United States, wrote, "If a nation expects to be ignorant and free, in a state of civilization, it expects what never was and never will be."[38] James Madison, Jefferson's successor in the White House, reportedly said in a similar vein, "A people who mean to be their own governors must arm themselves with the power that knowledge gives."

In the spirit of Jefferson and Madison, we should note that the move to universal suffrage had to be accompanied by a movement toward universal public education, unless we were to imperil this great experiment in republican democracy. In general, our history supports that observation. Thus, the most important task of education, which is to turn out people prepared for informed participation in our government and for civic leadership, should be acknowledged as pervasive in our history and neglected in our present.

We expect our public schools to perform many social tasks that are not at all related to education per se. For instance, many states require schools and their employees to report instances of child abuse. The public schools are charged with administration of vaccination programs in some states; in all states, the schools are also required to provide various supplemental nutrition programs for children of poverty. Many school administrators are bound by local precedent and social pressure to cooperate with various religion programs that conflict with school hours. In some cities, fancy concerts are required by

---

35. WORLD BOOK ENCYCLOPEDIA (1990), vol. 13 at 164.
36. *Id.*
37. THE WORLD BOOK ENCYCLOPEDIA (1990), vol. 20 at 161.
38. Jefferson in a letter to Colonel Charles Yancy (January 6, 1816) as quoted in BARTLETT'S FAMILIAR QUOTATIONS (13th ed. 1955) at 375b.

music administrators that pull children out of the classrooms for numerous hours. Children with special needs are also mandated by state and federal laws to receive labor-intensive special services. Because of the huge number of families with two working parents, in some states, the schools are mandated to provide after-school recreation programs for students. The list could be extended.

The point, however, is that we as a society have placed extensive requirements on schools that go way beyond education. Even in the area of student discipline, the courts and legislatures have required record keeping and due process hearings. All of these additional requirements drain energy and resources from the primary task of educating children to be meaningful participants in this republic. Moreover, as long as education is seen as an entitlement rather than a privilege, the attitudes of students and their parents will be less than ideally suited for the primary task.

No approach to educational reform will succeed unless it provides a focus for resolving most, if not all, of the issues confronting public schools in our society.[39] For instance, do we want our public schools to be a major social agency? If not, then how far do we retreat on the use of schools for implementing social agendas? Is higher education for everyone? Should we provide vocational tracks in grades K–12? Where do vocational/technical schools and community colleges fit? Are we prepared to address the issue of whether higher education has to get smaller to get better? Should we reexamine whether education is an entitlement? Do school vouchers help or hurt the overall quality of public schooling? Perhaps, should education, beyond the basics, be viewed as a privilege?

---

39. For example, the U.S. Census Bureau on August 11, 2003 issued a statistical summary of American schools that said that only 72% of American children "are academically on track for their age. The rate is higher for girls than for boys (79 versus 69 percent)." U.S. Census Bureau, *Facts for Features: Back to School.* Accessed at http://www.census.gov/Press-Release/www/releases/archives/facts_for_features/001286.ht on February 13, 2005.

CHAPTER

8

Through the Gender Lens

A human being's sex is determined by whether the father contributes an x or a y chromosome at the time of conception.[1] This random event has far-reaching consequences on the life of the fertilized ovum, if it is carried to term and survives. This chapter discusses some of the cultural and social impacts of sexual identity. In some societies, the child's sex will help determine whether the child receives an education, and in other societies, it will determine the amount and type of education the child receives. Sex, in some societies, will determine whether the child needs a dowry when it marries. It will determine, to a large extent, the career opportunities open to the child and his or her lifetime earnings. In the United States, the sex of the child may also be the basis for legal protections on the job and determine the choices of assignment in military service.

In the United States, unreasoning gender bias costs Americans billions of dollars each year.[2] Yet, the roots of such irrational prejudices defy easy identification. Some types of mild gender bias emerge spontaneously without being noticed by the speaker unless pointed out by a listener. For instance, students in a College of Business class discussing an ethics problem fell into the pattern of describing the bank supervisor as "he" and the bank teller as "she," even though sex was not given in the problem. When the instructor pointed at the pronoun usage and its implication, one student argued that the sex was given in the problem; in fact, it was not, but a rereading was necessary to convince some students.[3] In the actual situation on which the ethics problem was based, the supervisor was female.

This chapter provides useful information for extending our understanding of gender bias and for applying basic issues raised in Chapters 4 (moral development), 5 (distributive justice), 11 (affirmative action), 17 (designing a better organization), and 19 (consumption and modern advertising). For instance, *should* (a moral question) a child be held back educationally or restrained economically because the father contributed one chromosome, rather than the other? Is sex a relevant criterion on which to base the distribution of society's goods and services, burdens, and duties? Would it be rational to pay one set of offspring 70 cents on the dollar for their work and the other set a full dollar for theirs based on their sex? Finally, is a beer advertising campaign that uses scantily clad, voluptuous women for Pavlovian-style programming of young male consumers a causative factor in sexual harassment?[4] Does such advertising demean both men and women? *Should* socially responsible producers use such advertising techniques?

SOCIALLY ASSIGNED GENDER ROLES VERSUS SEXUAL IDENTITY

How we see and what we see are governed to a large extent by what we look for and by what we expect to see.[5] We refer to this phenomenon as a "lens"

---

1. *See, e.g.*, LENNART NILSSON, A CHILD IS BORN (CLARE JAMES, TRANS. 1990) at 55. Modern medicine has followed the development of human embryos and has discovered that male external genitalia do not begin to develop until the 8th week of pregnancy. Moreover, at 6 weeks the embryo has a pair of indifferent sex accessory ducts that can develop into either female or male external genitalia. One perspective is that because the external genitalia evolve into female organs in the absence of testosterone the neutral or natural condition of human embryos is female.

2. WILLIAM H. SHAW, BUSINESS ETHICS (1991) at 304.

3. See WILLIAM A. WINES, READINGS IN BUSINESS ETHICS AND SOCIAL RESPONSIBILITY (rev. printing 1999) at 267, problem #4. "A Frank Problem in Foreign Exchange." *See also* INSTRUCTOR'S MANUAL, problem 8.a.

4. Joyce Hollyday, *Selling Sex and Beer*, SOJOURNERS (February–March 1992) at 4.

5. C. ROLAND CHRISTENSEN WITH ABBY J. HANSEN, TEACHING AND THE CASE METHOD (1981, 1987) at 79–82. The portion of the book entitled "Louis Agassiz as a Teacher" by Lane Cooper recounts

that filters information in the same way that various color lenses filter white light. Each of us has a gender lens through which we see the world.

Our observations are filtered in much the same way that our values are filtered—through the screens of our education, upbringing, and experience.[6] In some systems of theology, for instance, gender is an eternal characteristic[7]; in others, the Godhead is both male and female.[8] In still other systems of religion, the Godhead is feminine,[9] and in many religions and theologies, the Godhead is male and is addressed specifically as "Father."[10] How can the childhood induction into such profound, personal, and powerful value beliefs fail to influence how a child perceives his or her gender and the appropriateness of socially assigned gender roles within its community?

Classification by sex refers to the distinction between male and female based on physiological characteristics[11]; classification by gender refers to the psychological and cultural definitions of the dimensions "masculine" and "feminine" and only tends to a dichotomous distinction between groups. When speaking of learned roles, some suggest that the proper term is "gender role."[12] Despite the wealth of literature in which the terms "sex" and "gender" are assumed to be interchangeable, the primatologists (those who study primates) insist that the term "sex role" used correctly describes positions during sexual intercourse.

Biological sexual identity is different from *socially assigned gender roles* that also vary among cultures. Margaret Mead suggested that status and power (and, hence, wealth,[13] at least in Western civilization) tend to flow to male-dominated activities.[14] Examine, if you will, the rather simple matter of "air time" in a graduate law class for a simple illustration of the different lenses that males and females have that alter their views of the world. Bert Neuborne taught a class on constitutional law at New York University in which he tried to equalize the amount of time male and female students spoke, for our purposes

---

Professor Agassiz's initiation of graduate students whom he routinely sat down and instructed to study a specimen fish for days to "find out what you can!"

6. *See* William A. Wines and Nancy K. Napier, *Cross-Cultural Ethics: Towards a Tentative Model*, J. OF BUS. ETHICS (November 1992) at 831–841. Note especially Figure 6 that shows that education, life experience, and gender filter the manager's perception of the environment in developing a value set.

7. *See, e.g.,* "The Family: A Proclamation to the World from the LDS Church." Accessed at http://www.lds-mormom.com/potf.shtml (on January 6, 2005) wherein it states, "Gender is an essential characteristic of individual premortal, mortal, and eternal identity and purpose."

8. *See* CHERYL BAUER & ROB PORTMAN, WISDOM'S PARADISE: THE FORGOTTEN SHAKERS OF UNION VILLAGE (2004) at 15.

9. *See, e.g.,* LEONARD SHLAIN, THE ALPHABET VERSUS THE GODDESS: THE CONFLICT BETWEEN WORD AND IMAGE (1998) at vii to ix, wherein Dr. Shlain refers to Minoan Bronze Age cultures in which women were priestesses and the religion worshiped a female deity.

10. *See, e.g.,* Mark 14:36 and Luke 11:2 (New King James, 1980).

11. Significantly, it should be noted here before preceding that, with the 6 billion plus human beings on the planet, we do not, in reality, all fit neatly into male and female dichotomous genital-based categories. There are people with mixed sexual organs (so-called transgendered) and other anomalous sexual identities that I do not address in this book. This failure to address the ethical and moral issues faced by these people should in no way be taken as denying or dismissing the seriousness of the issues or the pain encountered by these people. It does reflect the limitations of this project.

12. TRESEMER, *supra* note 19, at 309.

13. *See, e.g.,* ROBERT HEILBRONER, THE MAKING OF ECONOMIC SOCIETY (10th ed. 1992).

14. *See, e.g.,* MARGARET MEAD, SEX AND TEMPERMENT IN THREE PRIMITIVE SOCIETIES (orig. 1935, 1963 Morrow-Quill ed.).

DOONESBURY/Garry Trudeau

©DOONESBURY reprinted with permission of Universal Press Syndicate, Inc.

loosely termed "air time."[15] Professor Neuborne kept a log of the speaking time in class by sex and found that with encouragement females spoke between 40 and 45% of the time. In "normal" sex-mixed conversation, females speak only about one third of the time.

The male students in Professor Neuborne's class met with him at the end of the semester and expressed anger that the female law students had "dominated" the entire class. When asked how much time the females had used, the males estimated female air time to be 80%![16] This is but one example of how our view of reality can be warped by the gender lenses through which we view the world.

GENDER SOCIALIZATION AND MYTHOLOGY

The myths that a culture perpetuates are analogous to the strands of DNA in a human and may be understood as the cultural DNA programming of the software of the brain. Every society develops a sex/gender system in which biological sex differences are invested with culturally determined significance. Biological sex differences are moderated and altered by cultural myths so that they reappear as socially constructed gender roles.[17] Ideological processes— that is, deeply entrenched and often subconscious principles for decision making—are established for gendered social relations.[18]

STEREOTYPES OF MALES AND FEMALES

Stereotypes describe a standardized conception or common image of groups of people that ignores normal individual human differences and the complex set of characteristics, motives, values, and behaviors that are a part of each person. Real physical differences and imagined psychological differences have been used to establish a system of stereotypically defined gender roles that

---

15. BERNICE RESNICK SANDLIER ET AL., THE CHILLY CLASSROOM CLIMATE: A GUIDE TO IMPROVE THE EDUCATION OF WOMEN (1996) at 21–22.
16. *Id.* at 22.
17. "Sex roles" are defined by primatologists as the positions assumed during the act of sexual intercourse. See discussion, *infra* under subheading "Gender Roles."
18. CLARE ROSE, MEETING WOMEN'S NEW EDUCATIONAL NEEDS (1975) at 2.

restrict and limit the life choices, contributions, and happiness of both men and women.[19]

The dominant stereotype of men represents them as being tough, strong, aggressive, independent, brave, sexually active, and rational. The corresponding view of women is that they are vulnerable, weak, nonaggressive, kind, caring, passive, easily frightened, and dependent. The descriptive words used for women and men are indicative of the descriptors that are used for boys and girls. Baby boys and girls are treated very differently from birth. They are spoken to differently, dressed differently, and played with differently. Most societies entertain different expectations for boys and for girls.

Take a baby out into the street, stop the first 20 people you meet, ask them to hold "Mark," and tell you what sort of baby he is. Repeat the procedure, but this time ask them what they think of "Mary." The baby is the same in both cases, but "Mark" will undoubtedly be described as bouncing, cheeky, mischievous, and strong; whereas "Mary" will be seen as lovely, sweet, gorgeous, and cute.[20]

PARENTING BY SEX AND ESTABLISHING GENDER

Sussex University investigators invited 32 mothers to play with a baby they had never seen before and then filmed the result.[21] The same baby was presented to the mothers as either a boy or a girl. As you might guess, the toys and the color of blanket that the women chose for the baby were very different, depending on whether the baby was presented as a girl or a boy: a doll and pink color blanket for a girl, a hammer and blue blanket for a boy. More interestingly, the mothers interpreted the same behavior differently, depending on whether they thought the baby was a girl or a boy. When the baby became restless and they thought it was a boy, that behavior was interpreted as a wish to play, so the women played with "him." When they thought it was a girl and she started to wiggle, the same behavior was interpreted as an indication that "she" was upset and she was soothed.[22]

Such typical behavior teaches boys and girls powerful messages about the way to manipulate and control their environment. Boys are taught to demand attention and to control situations to get what they want, whereas girls are taught to be passive and wait before reacting. If this is true, it has far-reaching consequences for understanding adult behavior.

The stereotype of active men and passive women can be applied to many situations. For example, men are expected to be better at sports; women are expected to assume supportive roles. If boys do learn to negotiate their environment more actively, then this has enormous implications for learning, particularly for learning that involves experiment and investigation. We do not desire to perpetuate sexual stereotypes. It is important to raise questions about how socialization of children affects their learning.[23]

Parents are clearly powerful role models for young children, and mothers still do most of the nurturing. Evidence suggests that fathers tend to be more physical when playing, particularly so with boys.[24] If so, that would fit with a

19. DAVID TRESEMER, ANOTHER VOICE: FEMINIST PERSPECTIVES ON SOCIAL LIFE AND SOCIAL SCIENCE (1975) at 136–151.
20. I. NICHOLSON, MEN AND WOMEN: HOW DIFFERENT ARE THEY? (1984) at 86.
21. C. Smith & B.B. Lloyd, *Maternal Behaviour and Perceived Sex of Infant*, 49 INFANT DEVELOPMENT, at 1263–1265.
22. *Id.*
23. SUE ASKEW & CAROL ROSS, BOYS DON'T CRY: BOYS AND SEXISM IN EDUCATION (1988).
24. NICHOLSON, *supra* note 20.

suggestion that boys and men do learn to value action, rather than emotional closeness and communication in relationships. The same author also argues that evidence suggests that men are more concerned than women that their sons be masculine and their daughters feminine.[25]

MEDIA AND OTHER CULTURAL SUPPORTS FOR GENDER ROLE STEREOTYPES

Most books and media images that children of all ages encounter support very stereotyped gender roles. The majority of television programs watched by young children show male heroes in a variety of violent postures. Most cartoons for children are a variant of this theme and involve fairly horrific incidents.[26] Television advertisements for toys for young children are extremely stereotypical. Girls are shown playing either with toys that copy adult women's roles, such as toy cookers or tea sets, or they are shown with soft cuddly animals. Boys, in contrast, quite predictably are shown playing with games, cars, mechanical toys, or space monsters.

Even when boys and girls play with the same toy they often play with it differently. When a little girl plays with a doll, she often plays at being "mother." She feeds the doll, takes it for walks, bathes, and dresses it. Boys, in contrast, play differently with dolls. A boy may sometimes "become" the doll and take part through the doll (now "action figure") in elaborate fantasies about fighting and killing. Girls' play revolves around relating to a second person (the doll); boys, through the "action figures" (formerly "dolls"), become the heroes of their own plays.

GENDER ROLES AS LEARNED ROLES

Even though extensive similarities do exist between the sexes, deeply held beliefs—although highly controversial in some areas—are pervasive among social scientists, biologists, and physicians that physiological differences between the sexes (more extensive than genital and hormonal differences) are strong and really do exist, independent of socialization factors.[27] The global qualities or capabilities of being and feeling and social-emotional orientation are associated with the feminine principle; the qualities of doing, thinking, and task orientation are associated with the masculine principle. Many psychologists and sociologists believe that the healthiest, most effective personality requires an integration of both of these conceptual poles: "feminine" warmth

---

25. *Id.*
26. ASKEW, *supra* note 23.
27. Lawrence H. Summers, president of Harvard University and formally trained as an economist, participated in a conference on women and science, hosted by the National Bureau of Economic Research on Friday, January 14, 2005. He made some "reference to innate differences" between the sexes, and he added that people would prefer to write them off to socialization factors but that much research still needed to be done to support such conclusions. About then, the M.I.T. biologist Nancy Hopkins walked out, according to reports in the *Boston Globe*. *See, e.g.*, Associated Press, *Gender Comments Draw Fire: Harvard President's Remarks Criticized*, CINC. ENQUIRER (January 18, 2005) at A5. Five other conference participants said they were offended; and four—contacted by the *Boston Globe*—said they were not. *Id.* The tempest grew over the next several days. *See, e.g.*, Justin Pope, *Tempest Over Remarks Rages On*, CINC. ENQUIRER (January 21, 2005) at A10. President Summers posted a letter with an apology on the Harvard University's web site. He said, "I was wrong to have spoken in a way that has resulted in an unintended signal of discouragement to talented girls and women." Accessed at http://www. President.harvard.edu/speeches/2005/womensci.html on February 2, 2005.

and interpersonal sensitivity with "masculine" leadership and goal-oriented striving.

An increasing number of studies claim that gender-role boundaries are narrower and more restrictive for the male, especially in adolescence.[28] It is beyond the scope of this chapter to explore which group has it "worse"; change in the structural limitations placed on one gender role will require changes in the other gender role, and these processes cannot be considered apart from each other. Broad generalizations comparing huge groups of people by gender ignore the numerous exceptions in which many individuals have integrated achievement, expression, intellect, and emotion in many meaningful ways.

Oversimplifications of divisions between the sexes are characteristic of, and perhaps necessary for, early stages of development in the human life cycle. However, it is important to place more emphasis on the potentialities of maturing beyond those models. More comprehensive ways of understanding the complex matters of styles of thinking and patterns of living are implicit in the new models of androgyny. They require a shift, at least, of some of the focus on neonatal learning and early childhood socialization to the possibilities of adult socialization and change.

Differences between the biological sexes clearly exist, but we do not yet have a clear sense of the relative importance of various differences. In addition, how often the biological differences are used as the basis for gross exaggerations about the classes "male" and "female" has certainly not been established. Such judgments are often made within the context of an unstated set of values. Rather than documenting or bewailing the inhibitions and inequities imposed early in life on the basis of sex, attention and energy would be better directed to the future. One authority suggests that an existential confrontation with the inevitability of death may lead to the choice of more meaningful behavior and more meaningful enactment of roles.[29]

BRAIN PHYSIOLOGY

Some authors argue that the differences between the sexes are significant, and they emphasize that males are neurologically different from females. Females, these authors claim, are equal to men *only* in their common membership in the same species, humankind. "To maintain that they are the same in aptitude, skill or behavior is to build a society based on a biological and scientific lie," declared Anne Moir and David Jessel.[30] They state that the sexes are different because their brains are different. The brain processes information differently in males than in females, which results in different perceptions, priorities, and behavior. These differences can no longer be explained away entirely by social conditioning. Today, there is too much new biological evidence for the sociological argument to prevail.[31] The brain specialists, in short, say males and females are "hardwired differently."

We need to examine the general structure of the human brain before we can look at the differences. It is now known that the left side of the brain deals predominantly with verbal abilities and the detailed, orderly processing

---

28. *Id.* at 324.
29. NICHOLSON, *supra* note 19, at 196.
30. ANNE MOIR & DAVID JESSEL, BRAIN SEX (1991) at 5.
31. *Id.*

Shoe/Jeff MacNelly

of information. Speaking, writing, and reading are all largely under the control of the left side of the brain. The right side of the brain is the headquarters for visual information. It deals with spatial relations and is responsible for taking in "the big picture" (i.e., basic shapes and patterns). It controls abstract thought processes, as well as some of our emotional responses.[32]

The socially conditioned argument of sex differences asserts that "[m]en are dominant . . . because women are less disposed to achieve, or 'dominate,' because of the sexual role with which they are endowed: giving birth to children of itself leads to a greater emphasis on defensive, compliant, nurturing virtues."[33] However, studies of the left and right brain tell us that males are better at the skills that require spatial ability. They are more aggressive, competitive, and self-assertive. They need the hierarchy and the rules, for without them they would be unable to tell how they ranked—and that ranking is important to most men. Although females are more sensitive to the social and personal context, men are more adept at tuning in to peripheral information contained in expression and gesture and can process sensory and verbal information faster. Women seem to be less rule-bound than men.[34]

Some research has also suggested that a thicker corpus callosum in the brains of females equips them to have readier access to their emotions than do men who generally have a thinner corpus callosum, which is the part of the brain that connects the left and right hemispheres.[35] According to scientists who study brain differences, men tend to be preoccupied with things, theories, and power, and women tend to be more concerned with people, morality, and relationships. With such different priorities, the potential for misunderstanding is great, which is part of what makes the relationship between the sexes at once fascinating and frustrating, complicated and compelling.

---

32. *Id.* at 20.
33. MOIR & JESSEL, *supra* note 39, at 86.
34. *Id.* at 84–85.
35. *See, e.g.,* discussion of this by Robert Bly in the video, *Men and Women Talking Together,* (MFIRE, 1993). *See also* L. S. Allen, *et al., Sex Differences in the Corpus Callosum of the Living Human Being,* 11, J. OF NEUROSCIENCE (1991) at 933–942. The reported sexual dimorphism of the corpus callosum has stayed controversial since the original report in 1982. This article is part of a growing literature on the subject and reports some shape differences between sexes. *Id.* at 933.

A SHORT HISTORY OF EMPLOYMENT FOR U.S. WOMEN

An historic overview of work performed by women in the United States shows an evolution from strenuous labor in an agricultural economy (childrearing, animal care, food gathering, baking, cooking, canning, weaving, sewing, producing vast amounts of household goods for barter and sale) to factory work as the United States moved into a manufacturing economy; in this industrialized economy, contrary to a popular misconception, women (not men) were the first to enter in significant numbers.[36] Young girls often toiled in the early textile mills because "men's work" in the mines and fields was considered too valuable.[37]

WORLD WAR II WATERSHED

The origins of World War II can be found not only in the war reparations exacted from Germany after World War I but also in the resolution of the Franco-Prussian War of 1871, in rampant nationalism around the globe, in the rise of fascism, and in the European colonial system. World War II differed from the two previous wars in that racism played such a strong role in precipitating the conflict. Wars fought to secure hegemony of one race or ethnic group over another were surely nothing new, but never before had so many lives been lost in a savage and brutal struggle for dominance by one group over another. Such mass destruction[38] required unprecedented cooperation.

While Germans were trying to establish Aryan supremacy by conquering Europe and by killing Jews and others they considered inferior, a cooperation of another kind was occurring in America. Women were called from their traditional roles as wives, mothers, and nurses to fill wartime positions in the burgeoning industrial sector and in businesses from which men had been called up to fight. In factories, offices, and farms, women took over the management of small businesses and farms, taught college, and built tanks—and they did it well. Jobs that had once been reserved for men only were performed effectively by women, and many learned an unforgettable lesson: There are no masculine or feminine occupations.

From 1945 on—despite the fact that immediately after the war women lost their jobs to returning veterans pursuant to a new federal law—the number and percentage of working women of all kinds—married and unmarried,

---

36. *See, e.g.* ROBERT L. HEILBRONNER & WILLIAM MILBERG, THE MAKING OF ECONOMIC SOCIETY (11th ed. 2002) at 67–68 in which the manufacturing work of girls in early 18th-century England was described as including 19-hour work days with only three breaks totaling 1 hour, some of which was routinely forfeited for cleaning of the machines. Life expectancy in Manchester, England, circa 1840 was 17 years at birth; and infant mortality rates were over 50%. *Id.*

37. LINDA M. BLUM, BETWEEN FEMINISM AND LABOR (1991).

38. "World War II (1939–1945) killed more people, destroyed more property, disrupted more lives, and probably had more far-reaching consequences than any other war in history." THE WORLD BOOK ENCYCLOPEDIA (1990), vol. 21 at 470. In the war, about 70 million men and women served in the armed forces of the Allied and Axis nations; about 17 million of them died. No one knows how many civilians lost their lives as a direct result of the hostilities. The Soviet Union and China suffered the highest civilian losses; as many as 20 million Soviet citizens and 10 million Chinese civilians are thought to have perished. *Id.* at 498. Additionally, the Holocaust killed approximately 11 million men, women, and children; although no one knows the exact number. By May 8, 1945 (V-E Day), the Nazis had killed about 6 million Jewish men, women, and children. That number represented more than two thirds of the Jews living in Europe. The 11 million total is reached by adding in the other groups marked for extinction in the death camps, especially Gypsies, Poles, and Slavs. *Id.*, vol. 9 at 282.

young and mature, parent and nonparent—increased dramatically. The number of working women grew, and the realities of women's lives changed. What changed very little and what eventually caused much of the conflict that crystallized in the fifties and exploded in the sixties were the projected ideals of femininity and the "place" of women. Except for the brief wartime cameo of Wanda the Welder and Rosie the Riveter, America's dream girl image never adjusted to women's new realities and changing needs.[39]

THE SO-CALLED PINK-COLLAR GHETTO CONTINUED AFTER WORLD WAR II

A number of writers in the area of gender-based employment discrimination have referred to the concentration of women in five occupation groups as the "pink-collar" ghetto.[40] They have done this to dramatize the occupational segregation of work by gender. Occupations considered part of the traditional "pink-collar" (female) employment ghetto are clerical, secretarial, nursing, waiting tables, and teaching school.[41]

One study compared men and women clerical-secretarial workers in a public-sector institution.[42] Just 7% of the workforce was male, and they were concentrated mainly in clerical jobs. Men were less committed to the occupation than women and reported a greater sense of occupational choice. Women tended to find the work more personally meaningful than men, and the men were somewhat more likely to find the work trivial and tedious. Both sexes were extremely dissatisfied with their developmental and promotional opportunities. One hopeful sign was that younger workers as a group seemed less willing to accept the restraints that have been part of pink-collar work.

In the present service economy, women once again are dominant, holding 60% of all jobs in the service sector, whereas men now retain the largest share in the manufacturing sector.[43] As technology progressed, some occupations formerly held by men were broken into smaller components and then transferred to women. Some more lucrative jobs (such as teaching stenography, typing, and office skills in voc-tech schools and higher education) that were formerly open to and dominated by women were taken away (and replaced by "computer science" courses taught by men).[44]

Between 1962 and 1974, the number of employed women increased by 10 million or 45%, and their proportion of the workforce increased from 34 to 39%. The largest employment gains for women occurred in those pink-collar occupations in which women had been more likely to be employed previously. The largest gain, 4.8 million, occurred in clerical occupations in which women accounted for almost 70% of all employees in 1962. By 1974, women held almost four out of five jobs in this category, and the rapid rate of growth of women's employment in this occupation helped account for a

---

39. *See, e.g.,* SHERMA GLUCK, ROSIE THE RIVETER REVISITED (1987).
40. *See, e.g.,* Ruth G. Blumrosen, *Wage Discrimination, Job Segregation, and Title VII of the Civil Rights Act of 1964,* 12 U. MICH. J. L. REF. 397 (1979).
41. For an updated attempt to explain and define the pink-collar ghetto, *see Ask Liz,* THINKING ALOUD: YOUR WORLD WIT NEWSLETTER (May 3, 2004.) Accessed at http://www.imakenews.com/worldwit/e_article000255294.cfm on September 2, 2004. *See also* SHARON MASTRACCI, BREAKING OUT OF THE PINK COLLAR GHETTO: POLICY SOLUTIONS FOR NON-COLLEGE WOMEN (2004).
42. Gerald Hunt, *Sex Differences in a Pink-Collar Occupation,* BUS. WEEK (February 24, 1993) at 116–134.
43. *Id.*
44. *Id.*

substantial portion of the overall increase in the number of women in the workforce.[45]

HISTORY AFTER 1980

As pink-collar women came to make up a large proportion of the constituency for organized labor, organizing efforts directed at women in service sector jobs began to show positive, although clearly not overwhelming, results. In public sector unions, such as AFSCME and SEIU, in which pink-collar workers made up about half the membership, comparable worth was a priority issue in the mid-1980s.[46]

Occupational gender-based segregation in the United States has declined over the years since 1980 and is also a bit lower for new entrants to the workplace compared to older workers. The boundaries between male and female occupations are somewhat porous.

Society may be nearing a turning point. The relationship between men and women permeates our lives through gender-role assignments, through life choices, and through all our social institutions—from family and religion to politics and economics. The possibility of continuing on the same path for much longer seems headed to a natural end. "At our level of technological development, it's basically going to self-destruct," warns Riane Eisler.[47] Man's conquest of women and other men and man's attempt to dominate nature will self-destruct if humankind does not heed the warnings.[48]

THE WHITE MALE SYSTEM AND THE FEMALE SYSTEMS

In *Women's Reality*, Anne Wilson Schaef defines the *the White male system* as "the system in which we live, and in it, the power and influence are held by White males."[49] The system, as she is careful to call it, "permeates our lives. Its myths, beliefs, rituals, procedures, and outcomes affect everything we think, feel and do."[50] The female system is one other reality.[51] It exists in two forms. One is a reactive system that has been developed to cope with and stay safe within the White male system. It would be helpful if women shared their insights about themselves and men gained from the reactive system. If women

---

45. LOUISE K. HOWE, PINK COLLAR WORKERS: INSIDE THE WORLD OF WOMEN'S WORK (1977).

46. Michael A. Pollock, *Pink-Collar Workers: The Next Rank and File?* BUS. WEEK (February 24, 1986) at 116–118.

47. RIANE EISLER, THE CHALICE AND THE BLADE (1987) at xvii.

48. WILLIAM F. ALLMAN, THE STONE AGE PRESENT (1995) at 247 in which Allman, a social anthropologist, declares,

> Ironically, if we are going to surpass the tenure of our ancestor species on Earth, we will have to overcome the same fundamental challenge that they faced on the savanna eons ago: each other. It is not the threat of nuclear annihilation, the prospect of vast climate change, or the spread of deadly diseases that endanger our existence in the future, but the very thing that brought our species into the twentieth century in the first place—our evolved psychology, with its amazing abilities to cooperate. Our ancestors evolved brains that were custom-designed for helping them get along with each other, cooperating to do together what would be difficult, if not impossible, to do alone.

49. A. W. SCHAEF, WOMEN'S REALITY (1981) at 2.

50. *Id.*

51. *Id.* at 20.

did so, a second female system could emerge in which women were clear and trusting of their own perceptions.[52]

Schaef explains the dynamics of the White male system. "This system did not spring up overnight, nor was it the result of the machinations of only a few individuals; we all not only let it occur, but participated in its development."[53] She goes on to say that it is a system of consciousness and *not* a reality.[54] However, this system "controls almost every aspect of our culture."[55]

Schaef draws a powerful analogy between the White male system and air pollution. She asserts,

> [W]hen you are in the middle of pollution, you are usually unaware of it (unless it is especially bad.) You eat in it, sleep in it, work in it, and sooner or later start believing that that is just the way the air is. You are unaware of the fact that pollution is not natural until you remove yourself from it and experience non-pollution.[56]

The White male system, unlike air pollution, is not something you can get away from by moving to another city or state. It is what we live in.

THE FOUR (MAYBE FIVE) MYTHS OF THE WHITE MALE SYSTEM

Schaef is careful to explain that she has described the White male system as it is perceived by female system women and that it behooves everyone to understand other systems and be able to make different choices.[57] There are four myths that govern the White male system according to Schaef:

1. The White male system is the only thing that exists.
2. The White male system is innately superior.
3. The White male system knows and understands everything.
4. It is possible to be totally logical, rational, and objective.[58]

What we see in the White male system is that men are so convinced their way is the only way that they believe other ideas or perceptions actually threaten their system. So that their existence and system will not be jeopardized, men spend a lot of energy and time keeping everyone else in their proper place. The first and second myths are clearly contradictory: If the White male system is the only thing that exists, then to what is it superior? Apparently, at some level of consciousness, men must have some sense that theirs is not the only system. The third myth supports the second as does American society generally.

Schaef summarizes the four myths of the White male system like this:

> [T]his final myth is that it is possible for one to be God. If the White Male System is the only system that exists, if white males are innately superior, if they know and understand everything, and if they can be totally logical, rational, and objective, then they can be God—at least,

---

52. *Id.*
53. A. W. SCHAEF, WOMEN'S REALITY (1981) at 2.
54. *Id.*
55. *Id.*
56. *Id.* at 4.
57. *Id.* at 7.
58. A. W. SCHAEF, WOMEN'S REALITY (1981) at 24.

the way the White Male System defines God.[59] Schaef concludes by declaring "This final myth is that *it is possible for one to be God*" [italics in original].[60]

Our culture is set up according to this basic hierarchical structure:

God
Men
Women
Children
Animal
Earth

There are numerous social and cultural difficulties associated with such a hierarchical system. One problem is that along with dominance, there is a tendency to control, exploit, or rape lower rungs of the hierarchy. Such behavior may be accompanied by feelings of inadequacies combined with a desire to move up the ladder. This hierarchy may also be a significant contributing cause to the epidemic of violence (both physical and economic) that is sweeping this country and the world.[61]

TWO FEMALE SYSTEMS

Two female systems occur in American society, according to Schaef. The first is a reactive system, a way of coping with role assignments under the White male system. The second female system emerges when women are free to express their values and perceptions. This female system is much more coherent and cohesive than the reactive female system.[62] What Schaef communicates effectively are the differences associated with each system. When men do not understand the culture of women and when women do not understand the culture of men, both groups make negative value judgments about behaviors they consider alien.

Significantly, our disparate approaches are not primarily intentional choices, but rather are ways of perceiving reality instilled by our culture since earliest childhood. Women may need to cultivate an understanding of the "foreign" male culture so that they can make better choices that will open the door to healthier relationships and greater happiness at home and at work; men likewise need to work on becoming conscious of another system of understanding, the female system, for the same reasons.

Deborah Tannen in *You Just Don't Understand*, makes the case that little girls playing in groups learn to blend in, be sensitive to one another's feelings, and avoid boasting, because they are punished by exclusion when they are bossy. Little boys, she observed, are primarily concerned with dominance and are rewarded for being the boss—whether in Little League or in a gang selling lemonade on the corner. Boy groups are about who's up and who's down. Girl groups are about including everyone and at least feigning niceness. Men are the people of the ladder and women are the people of the circle.[63] These differences in styles follow us to the workplace. Consequently, women end up

---

59. *Id*. at 15.
60. *Id*.
61. *See infra*. Chap. 9 on "The Ethos of Violence."
62. *Id*. at 24.
63. DEBORAH TANNEN, YOU JUST DON'T UNDERSTAND (1990) at 43–44.

bumping their heads on the glass ceiling.[64] To smash through the glass ceiling, women have to learn how to "play hardball."

Pat Helm agrees with Tannen that society teaches us how to be successful men and women. These lessons are profound and stay with us for the rest of our lives. Boys learn to be competitors on the field of life, whereas girls learn to be warm, nurturing mothers. Helm contends, "[O]ur training is crucial in helping women fulfill our biological roles, but it may work against us in the business world. Think of it this way: If you put a great basketball player into a baseball game, it's likely that his strengths won't be valued—or even evident."[65]

Boys learn to resist aggression, to conquer fear, to stand up for themselves. They are taught not to offer alibis for poor performance, not to ask for help, and not to talk about their uncertainties. Girls do not learn these lessons. While boys play cops and robbers, superheroes, and war, girls play intensely with one or two best friends, thoroughly engaged in make-believe and dolls, or playing house, safe in their homes and backyards.[66]

Helm contends that when boys and girls grow up, they "play" business in much the same way they played as children: Men continue to see business as a team sport, whereas women perceive business as a series of separate personal encounters; they seek out cooperation and intimacy. Girls learn to master interpersonal relationships and deal with flat (nonhierarchical) organizations; in contrast, boys play games that teach competition, aggression, how to accept praise and criticism, and—since time immemorial—that winning is the only thing that counts.

Helm concludes, "The truth is, since business has been overwhelmingly dominated by men until only recently, masculine culture permeates corporate life today. Men have simply transposed the rules of their childhood games onto their jobs as CEOs, managers, salesmen, supervisor, and entrepreneurs."[67] Tannen, when asked why men do not ask for directions, responded that she believed asking for directions or for any kind of help in the minds of men puts them in the one-down position; this analysis squares directly with Schaef.[68]

MEN AND WOMEN: CROSS-CULTURAL COMMUNICATION

Pat Helm and Deborah Tannen teach us that many difficulties between men and women arise because boys and girls grow up in essentially different cultures. Thus, talk between men and women is a form of cross-cultural communication. Men as a class are dominant in our society's culture, and many individual men seek to dominate the women in their lives. Yet, male dominance is not the whole story. It does not account for everything that happens to men and women in conversations—especially conversations in which both are genuinely trying to relate to each other with attention and respect. Dominance is not always intentional, that is to say, conscious.

---

64. The glass ceiling is "an intangible barrier within the hierarchy of a company that prevents women or minorities from obtaining upper-level positions." MERRIAM WEBSTER'S COLLEGIATE DICTIONARY (10th ed. 1995) at 495.

65. PAT HEIM, HARDBALL FOR WOMEN (1992) at 25.

66. *Id.* at 15.

67. *Id.* at 20–21.

68. DEBORAH TANNEN, TALKING FROM 9 TO 5 (1994) at 24.

There are 3 billion women
who don't look like supermodels
and only 8 who do.

THE BODY SHOP
KNOW YOUR MIND LOVE YOUR BODY

Reproduced with the kind permission of The Body Shop International pic.

Except for the mystical (and not insignificant) impact of culture, there is no reason why the work of men and women cannot be valued equally. It has been argued that if men are paid for their ability to elaborate their mechanical expertise into complex edifices and machines, then women should be paid fairly for their skill in understanding and predicting human action and their ability to sense motives and emotions. All types of intellectual skills and abilities are necessary for the preservation and advancement of civilization.

WOMEN THROUGH THE LANGUAGE LENS

Psychoneurolinguistics is a relatively new field. Yet, even before the advent of that field, a philosopher, Robert Baker, illustrated the male conception of women through the use of descriptive language.[69] The English language designates gender through proper noun and pronoun usage. Baker ascertains from this that our society thinks "the most important thing one can know about a person is that person's sex."[70]

---

69. Robert Baker, *A Plea for 'Persons,'* (1975, 1984) reprinted in WILLIAM A. WINES, READINGS IN BUSINESS ETHICS AND SOCIAL RESPONSIBILITIES (rev. printing 1999) at 82–86.
70. *Id.* at 82.

Baker then demonstrates the interchangeability of the words "man," "mankind," and "humanity." "Woman," however, is not synonymous with any of these other words. In the *American Heritage Dictionary*, womankind is defined as "female human beings, collectively." Mankind, in contrast, has two definitions. The first is "the human race," and the second refers to "male human beings, collectively."

Baker analyzes the different terms used to describe women, typically terms used by men. The words fall into these categories—neutral, animal, plaything, gender, and sexual terms—including the use of pet names and other terms supposedly of endearment. Baker's analysis may well explain such usage both at a conscious and a subconscious level. Not only are there words that directly identify women, frequently in vulgar and obscene slang, but there are also words that indirectly indicate gender. For example, the following terminology suggests that the subject of the sentence is a woman: "After delivering the acceptance speech, the candidate fainted." A man would have been described as having "passed out."[71]

Tannen argues that journalists, writers, and speakers use a language that has an established means of gender identification. She states that by simply "understanding and using the words of our language, we all absorb and pass on different, asymmetrical assumptions about men and women"[72]

CAN THE FEMALE SYSTEM AND MALE SYSTEM FIND ROMANCE?

Anne Wilson Schaef addresses the way the female system and the White male system tend to influence romantic relationships. The center of the White male's universe is work and the self (morality of justice—individuals are defined as separate in relation to others), whereas the center of the female system is grounded in relationship (morality of care—individuals are defined as connected in relation to others[73]; see Chapter 4).

According to Schaef, women operate from the standpoint that the relationship is paramount. The relationship defines one's self and work. Men, White men to be specific, are the antithesis. Their work and self define all else. Men are task oriented, and they approach relationships as tasks to be carried out and accomplished. Women think that men during courtship have adjusted their ideologies of relationships, but then men revert to their familiar system with work and self as center of their universe. Understandably, women feel cheated.[74]

Schaef notes that many women recognize the existence of the two systems and try to adapt to the White male system. The self and work become important. Women then desire to make it in the White male system. Relationships fall by the wayside as work, creativity, and contribution take precedence. Yet, moving into the White male system has disadvantages. A woman executive told of her experience entering the corporate world: The more she behaved less like a woman, as perceived by men (being yielding and submissive), the less she was perceived as a woman. The day she most successfully impersonated a man, the CEO turned to her, seeing the familiar suit and briefcase, and

---

71. TANNEN, YOU JUST DON'T UNDERSTAND (1990) at 241.
72. *Id.* at 243.
73. A. W. SCHAEF, WOMEN'S REALITY (1981) at 108.
74. *Id.*

uttered a vulgar and sexist boy's locker room slogan.[75] This woman was left asking herself whether her successful commercial transformation had been worth the loss of her integrity.[76] A former MBA student received a mixed compliment when her boss at a large, local electronics firm told her, "I've always admired your intellect; you think just like a man."[77] Schaef theorizes that women get bored with the White male system and tend to return to a nonreactionary female system in which they are then no longer defined by their relationships with men.[78]

SEX AND VIOLENCE—U.S. STYLE

Violence, as we establish in an extended discussion in the next chapter, is usually thought of as a physical act, but it can also take economic form or be expressed as psychological/emotional abuse or damage. Surprisingly, there are several links between sex and violence. One is the damage done to adolescent girls' self-esteem by U.S. culture; another is the manner in which various cultures, including ours, have over the centuries devalued women's worth and contributions. In China, there is even a history of rebellion (circa 1850) caused by the shortage of women brought about by the culture's prizing of male heirs.

TEEN GIRL SELF-ESTEEM ROBBERY

In the reactionary female system, women try to absolve themselves from the Original Sin of Being Born Female by finding their identity through relationships with men.[79] This search starts young for many because of lapses in self-esteem during adolescence.

Research has shown that girls who were outspoken tend to have a greater loss of confidence when entering their teens than do boys. "[G]irls at puberty still get the message that the culture doesn't value their experience; it literally doesn't want to listen to what they have to say. Girls adjust by stifling themselves."[80]

This self-induced stifling probably causes intelligent girls to be less demanding and to be silent; consequently, bright girls are the most neglected group in the American educational system. Boys tend to demand more attention in class by calling out. Girls "learn that sounding too sure of themselves will make them unpopular with their peers," whereas boys "learn to use language to negotiate their status in the group by displaying their abilities and knowledge, and by challenging others and resisting challenges."[81] Educators tend to show boys how to do something; but when asked a question by a girl,

75. LEA P. STEWART & STELLA TING-TOOMEY, COMMUNICATION, GENDER, AND SEX ROLES IN DIVERSE INTERACTION CONTEXTS (1987) at 116.

76. *Id.*

77. Author's interview with C. Kay Henry, M.B.A., in Boise, Idaho, on April 15, 1997. Ms. Henry has since changed employers.

78. A. W. SCHAEF, WOMEN'S REALITY (1981) at 111.

79. *Id.* at 37.

80. Elizabeth Larsen, *The Great Teen Girl Self-Esteem Robbery*, UTNE READER (January/February 1992) at 20–21.

81. *The Power of Talk: Who Gets Heard and Why*, 73 HARVARD BUS. REV. (no. 5, 1995), 138–148 at 140.

they often merely finish the problem themselves. For many of us, the patterns set in adolescence follow us into our adult lives.[82]

THE RESULTS OF GENDER SELECTION

In Belgium, a fertility center in Ghent run by a medical school professor has come up with a controversial technique that promises to allow couples to choose the sex of their offspring.[83] This procedure raises serious issues in both medical ethics and business ethics.[84] The U.S. Food and Drug Administration is currently conducting a full study of the sperm selection technology, and in Great Britain, the government authority with jurisdiction recently launched a nationwide consultation over the matter.[85]

The People's Republic of China is currently facing a potentially disastrous shortage of girls because of cultural preferences for boys.[86] According to one report, in China, the boy-girl birth ratio is 120:100, and in conservative Hainan Island, the ratio is more than 130 boys per 100 girls.[87] Some of the elementary-school classes up through third grade on the Island have boy–girl ratios of 3:1.[88] Chinese leaders are now taking steps to discourage birth-selection abortions. In India, some districts have boy to girl ratios of 129:100.[89] Indian government officials are working to halt this trend, but see their efforts as "putting drops in the ocean."[90]

One recent book on the subject of Chinese cultural preferences for male offspring points out an intriguing historical precedent.[91] In northern China in the 1850s, after decades of drought, flood, and starvation, the practice of female infanticide led to as many as 25% of the men being unable to marry. Some of these men formed into gangs and then into small armies. At the peak of the Nien Rebellion, about 100,000 of these men nominally controlled a part of China in which 2 to 6 million Chinese lived. It took years for the Qing Dynasty to put down the rebellion.[92]

CONCLUDING OBSERVATIONS

Few, if any, books on business ethics address the topic of the gender lens. Most courses in business ethics ignore the different value perceptions held by women and men, fail to address differences in communications styles between the sexes, and ignore the debate about potential differences in moral development

82. *See, e.g.,* DEBORAH TANNEN, YOU JUST DON'T UNDERSTAND (1990) at 76.
83. *Belgian Clinic Offers Baby Gender [sic] Selection.* Accessed at http:www.dw-world.de/dw/article/0,,639046,00.html on February 2, 2005.
84. The Italian, German, and Dutch governments have publicly opposed the use of human genetic material in commercial ventures that have no medical advantage, such as this one. *Id.*
85. *Id.*
86. *See* Michael A. Lev, *In China, it's a boy-boy-boy-girl world,* CHICAGO TRIBUNE (January 30, 2005). Accessed at http://www.chicagotribune.com/news/nationworld/chi-0501300336j on February 7, 2005.
87. *Id.*
88. *Id.*
89. David Rohde (N.Y. Times), *India Attempting to Halt Aborting of Female Fetuses,* CINC. ENQUIRER (October 26, 2003) at A17.
90. *Id.*
91. *Id.* citing VALERIE HUDSON & ANDREA M. DEN BOER, BARE BRANCHES: THE SECURITY IMPLICATIONS OF ASIA'S SURPLUS MALE POPULATION (2004).
92. *Id.*

between men and women.[93] The omission is even more startling than the failure to address cross-cultural ethics that we documented in an earlier article.[94] It is more startling because the tendency is to endorse, by default, the unstated assumption that the White male perspective of business does not need to be examined.

---

93. It is impossible to make a citation to a void, but *see, e.g.*, popular textbooks by well-known authors, such as Vincent Shaw, Donaldson and Werhane, Norman Bowie, and Manuel Valezquez.
94. *See* Wines & Napier, *supra* note 6.

CHAPTER

9

The Ethos of Violence

Nonviolence is no longer in fashion.

—New York Times[1] (2002)

[Without compassion,] economics becomes merely a highly developed form of violence.

—Matthew Fox[2]

INTRODUCTION

When reflecting on the amount of violence presented in our popular culture, one is tempted to ask whether American capitalism wears a white hat[3] or rides a pale horse.[4] U.S. businesses make enormous amounts of money selling violent video games,[5] violent movies,[6] and rap music[7] that promote

---

1. Barbara Crossette, *A Tough Time to Talk of Peace: Buddhists Find Nonviolence Out of Fashion After Sept. 11*, N.Y. TIMES (February 12, 2002, Late ed.) at B1.
2. MATTHEW FOX, A SPIRITUALITY NAMED COMPASSION AND THE HEALING OF THE GLOBAL VILLAGE, HUMPTY DUMPTY AND US (1979) at 177.
3. It is a cinema cliché that the "good guys" wear white hats. This is part of the Western movie as a descendant of the medieval morality play. In addition to the white hat, in certain Westerns, the white horse is another symbol of the virtue of the "good guy." For instance, the Lone Ranger rides a famous white horse named Silver. For a brief discussion of "white" as a symbol in Westerns, *see* RICHARD SLOTKIN, GUNFIGHTER NATION: THE MYTH OF THE FRONTIER IN TWENTIETH-CENTURY AMERICA (1998) at 375–376. *See also* THE OXFORD HISTORY OF THE AMERICAN WEST (Clyde A. Milner II, et al., eds., 1994); WANTED DEAD OR ALIVE: THE AMERICAN WEST IN POPULAR CULTURE (Richard Aquila, ed., 1996); RICHARD WHITE, "IT'S YOUR MISFORTUNE AND NONE OF MY OWN": A NEW HISTORY OF THE AMERICAN WEST (1991); and BENET'S READER'S ENCYCLOPEDIA (3rd ed. 1987) at 1059 wherein the entry under "white" reads, "A color symbolically denoting purity, simplicity, and candor; innocence, truth, and hope. The ancient Druids and indeed the priests generally in antiquity used to wear white vestments, as does the clergy of the Church of England. . . . In MOBY DICK, [Herman] Melville, in discussing the significance of the whale's unusual color, includes a long essay on white."
4. The "pale horse" reference is in the apocalyptic sense from Revelation 6:7–8 (King James): "And when he had opened the fourth seal, I heard the voice of the fourth beast say, 'Come and see'". And I looked, and behold a pale horse: and his name that sat on him was Death, and Hell followed with him."
5. Video games led the industry (toys and games) in CY 2002 with U.S. $10.4 billion. That represented a 65% growth rate over the prior 5 years. In CY 2002, video games had 28.3% of the market for toys and games. Accessed at www.euromonitor.com/Toys_and_games_in_USA_(mmp) on September 10, 2003.
6. For illustration, as of 2003, *The Matrix Reloaded* (2003) (#19) grossed $280 million as of September 3, 2003; also in the top 50 all time highest-grossing movies were #29 *Raiders of the Lost Ark* (1981), which grossed $242 million; #43 *Saving Private Ryan* (1998), which grossed $216 million; and #49 *Terminator 2: Judgment Day* (1991), which grossed $205 million. *Top 50+ All Time Highest Grossing Movies*. Accessed at http://www.cowetaok.com/ videonetwork/topgrossmovies.htm on September 10, 2003.
7. Although rap music sales were down in CY 2002 by a significant 6.3%, other areas such as country (down 7%) and rhythm and blues (down 11%) were also hurting. Edna Gundersen, *Record Sales Hit the Lower Octaves*, USA TODAY accessed at http://usatoday.printthis. clickability.com/pt/cpt?action=cpt&expire=&urlID=6971852&fb on September 10, 2003. Still, the music industry took in a huge amount of money in CY 2002. The industry recorded revenues of $5.2 billion in the first 6 months of 2002 alone, even though that represented a drop of a little over 5% from the previous year. Jane Black, *Big Music's Broken Record*, BUSINESS WEEK ONLINE (February 13, 2003). Accessed at http://www.businessweek.com:/print/technology/content/feb2003/tc20030213_9095_tc078 on September 15, 2003. In CY 2000, approximately 12.9% of industry income was generated by rap/hip hop. *See Are You My Type?* Accessed at http://my.nctm.org/eresources/view_ article.asp?article_id=6221 on September 15, 2003. Based on the above statistics, it is probably safe to estimate that rap music generated over a billion dollars in CD sales alone in CY 2002.

violent images—not to mention our country's role as the earth's biggest arms dealer.[8] Critics may say we ride the pale horse ridden by Death in St. John's vision of the Apocalypse and that hell follows after.[9] Defenders of so-called free market capitalism would say instead that we wear the white hats, that we are the good guys.[10] This chapter attempts to develop some theoretical grounds for exploring attitudes toward violence in American society.

VIOLENCE—AMERICAN STYLE

"Violence is as American as cherry pie." So spoke H. Rap Brown in 1969 in Baltimore on the occasion that resulted in his conviction for inciting to riot.[11] An older adage says that nations are conceived in violence and born to power.[12] In a periodical published shortly after the end of World War I, A. Phillip Randolph, the father of the modern Black civil rights movement, declared, "Make wars unprofitable and you make them impossible."[13] Yet, organized warfare is only one aspect of violence in American society and an increasingly small part of it over the past 40 years. What we now face is an epidemic of violence sweeping across the landscape of this great country[14] in which young and old, rich and poor, are perpetrators and victims.

To support such a sweeping conclusion, I argue that the term "violence" needs to be understood in a much broader way than it has historically been understood. Violence is, of course, the use of physical force so as to injure or abuse.[15] Violence can be organized on a grand scale; then it goes by the name of "war." However, violence is so much more. We need to expand our definition to encompass such concepts as "unnecessary harm" and "sentient creation" and to include economics as a potential source of organized violence against communities and societies. Is it not an act of violence when a corporation, as one recently did in the Cincinnati area, callously waits until the morning shift arrives for work to tell the workers that the plant has closed down permanently?[16] Is it not an act of violence when a plant relocates out of the country and leaves a town desolate, with roads, schools, sewers, streets, and sidewalks that cannot simply be relocated and workers with their main investments tied up in houses that suddenly have no market?

---

8. *See infra* material accompanying notes 53–57 (2d paragraph after 1. D. Theoretical Causes).

9. *See supra* note 1. [Revelation 6:7-8]

10. *See supra* note 2.

11. *See also* QUOTATIONS IN BLACK (Anita King, ed.,1981) at quotation # 1146 citing H. RAP BROWN, DIE, NIGGER, DIE (1969).

12. R. M. MCIVER, THE MODERN STATE (1929) at 221 as quoted in STURDIVANT, BUSINESS AND SOCIETY (rev. ed. 1981) at 48.

13. QUOTATIONS IN BLACK, *supra* note 1, citing Asa Phillip Randolph, *The Cause and Remedy of Race Riots*, THE MESSENGER (September 1919).

14. Psychologist Dave Grossman reaches this conclusion after a book-length analysis of killing and violence in American society. He states, "Between 1985 and 1991 the homicide rate for males fifteen to nineteen increased 154 percent.... In Vietnam a systematic process of desensitization, conditioning, and training increased the individual firing rate from a World War II baseline of 15 to 20 percent to an all-time high of up to 95 percent. Today a similar process of systematic desensitization, conditioning, and vicarious learning is *unleashing an epidemic, a virus of violence in America*." DAVE GROSSMAN, ON KILLING: THE PSYCHOLOGICAL COST OF LEARNING TO KILL IN WAR AND SOCIETY (1995) at 304.

15. MERRIAM WEBSTER'S COLLEGIATE DICTIONARY (10th ed. 1995) at 1319.

16. Announced on ABC local news, Tuesday, October 22, 2002, Channel 9 at 6 p.m.

VIOLENCE—ENVIRONMENTAL STYLE

The concept of sentient creation was raised to the level of an entity with moral standing by the utilitarianism of Bentham and Mill.[17] When I was attending law school, some of the more cynical bright lights laughed at the notion that trees and whales might be entitled to legal standing and representation. Thirty years later, it may not be so humorous. Global capitalism has raised the specter of decimation of forests and mountains and even aquaculture in its relentless pursuit of profit. Many of the countries where the greatest harm has been done are also among the poorest. Consequently, some of us may argue that global capitalism, in certain times and places, has treated the ecosystem of this planet in the same manner that Buffalo Soldiers treated the indigenous people of the United States less than 250 years ago.

PASSIVE VIOLENCE—COSTS OF LOCKUP

The United States had over 2 million inmates in its prisons in April 2003, a number that makes this country first in the world in rate of incarceration.[18] The number of prisoners in the United States rose 60% between 1990 and 1998.[19] In the rate of incarceration, the United States was second only to Russia in 1998,[20] but in 2003 the United States rose to first place.[21] Homicide became the second leading cause of workplace death in this country in 1995; for women, homicide continues to rise and accounted for almost half the workplace fatalities.[22] The "fallout" of our violent society is evident in many places; for instance, the portion of the Idaho State budget going to prisons has risen from 3.4% to 7.3% between 1989 and 1999.[23] During the same time, the share of the general fund budget appropriated for higher education dropped from 19.3% to 15.6%, and over 4 fiscal years, education received a 19.52% increase in finding, in contrast to a 125.46% increase for prisons.[24]

Most of us think reflexively about violence as physical violence. Similarly, the tenth edition of Webster's Collegiate Dictionary defines "violence" as "exertion of physical force so as to injure or abuse" (as in effecting illegal entry into a house).[25] In the second definition, violence is "injury by or as if by distortion, infringement, or profanation: outrage."[26] The third definition of "violence" is "intense, turbulent, or furious and often destructive action or force <the ~ of the storm>."[27] Thus, it would be correct usage to talk about the violence of global capitalism in the third sense; global capitalism can be

---

17. *See, e.g.,* JAMES RACHELS, THE ELEMENTS OF MORAL PHILOSOPHY (4th ed. 2003) at 97–101.
18. *U.S. Prison Population Largest in World* (THE BALTIMORE SUN, June 1, 2003). Accessed at http://www.charleston.net/stories/060103/wor_01jailbirds.shtml on August 27, 2003. The United States has overtaken Russia and now has a higher percentage of its citizens locked in jails and prisons than any other country. *Id.* The United States has 2,019,234 prisoners according to an announcement by the Justice Department reflecting prisoners as of April 2003. That equates to a rate of 702 prisoners per 100,000 population. Russia has 665 prisoners per 100,000. *Id.*
19. Ted Koppel, *Nightline*, ABC Television Network, August 13, 1998.
20. *Id.*
21. *See supra* note 23.
22. *Credibility Gaps*, JOURNAL OF BUSINESS STRATEGY (July/August 1997) at 6–7.
23. Brenda Miller, *Budgets Help Convicts, Not Kids*, ID. STATESMAN (February 22, 1998) at 12A.
24. *Id.* See also M. Flagg and B. Roberts, *Uncertain Budget Needs Drove Session: Correction Funding Rises as Most Other Agencies Take a Hit*, ID. STATESMAN (March 16, 1997) at 1A.
25. MERRIAM WEBSTER'S COLLEGIATE DICTIONARY (10th ed. 1995) at 1319.
26. *Id.*
27. *Id.*

understood as a very destructive force that is causing damage to established economies and to social structures worldwide.[28]

Therefore, violence can include the abuse of economic power to achieve corporate objectives when the results involve diminution of the quality or quantity of life for sentient creation. For instance, Northwest Airlines laid off 27,000 workers on September 1, 1998, in response to the pilots' strike that was 5 days old.[29] One commentator's analysis of this decision was that it kept corporate losses down by cutting employment in half while simultaneously putting pressure on the Clinton Administration to use the 80-day "cooling off" provision of the Taft-Hartley Act.[30] If the layoff is a ploy to force the pilots back to work under Taft-Hartley, it is a violent act that is morally unjustified, at least by Kantian standards.[31]

This chapter explores a wide variety of expressions of violence in U.S. culture as well as looks for causes of violence in the fabric of American society.

GENERAL OBSERVATIONS ON VIOLENCE

"Just as religion rests on intangible assumptions, nations rely on hypostatized principles to determine policy. The principles, the ideas, the myths, the value-impregnated assumptions—all rather fantastically 'create' reality.... Most myths have become habits of mind that intrude on our actions yet are rarely discernible."[32] Many of the values that are passed onto our children are transmitted in folk stories and literature and popular culture, such as movies and television. We share the myths that determine our family identities, as well as our national identities. Many of these value transmissions take place before children even start school. Sexual identities and stereotypes are part of the package.

One of the most powerful teachers in American society is the television set. Infants and young children are good observers, but bad interpreters. Therefore, "parking" Junior in front of the "boob tube" is not a very good substitute for human care. For one thing, Junior is taking in all the sexism and violence that this electronic babysitter is spewing out. Studies have shown that television viewing increases inappropriate acts of aggression on the part of children.[33]

Furthermore, our popular culture glorifies violence. Take a look at what's playing at the movies. *Lethal Force I, II, III,* and *IV* can be seen along with *Die Hard I, II, III* and four segments of *Dirty Harry* from Clint Eastwood. Is it any wonder that one military officer said the most violent creature on the face of the earth is an 18-year-old American young man? John Wayne has

---

28. *See, e.g.,* WILLIAM GREIDER, ONE WORLD READY OR NOT: THE MANIC LOGIC OF GLOBAL CAPITALISM (1997) and DAVID KORTEN, WHEN CORPORATIONS RULE THE WORLD (1995).

29. *All Things Considered,* NPR, September 2, 1998.

30. *Id.*

31. *See, e.g.,* N. BOWIE & R. DUSKA, BUSINESS ETHICS (2nd ed. 1990) at 46, 50–53. Kant's categorical imperative can be stated, "Always treat humanity whether in yourself or in others as an end and never merely as a means." Here the central economic support of 27,000 people and their dependents is being used only as a means to get the pilots back in the cockpit. If such is the intent of Northwest's management, the action is despicable.

32. H. I. LONDON & A. L. WEEKS, MYTHS THAT RULE AMERICA (1981) at x.

33. *See, e.g.* George Will, *Experts Link TV Violence to Children's Behavior,* as cited in W. A. WINES, READINGS IN BUSINESS ETHICS AND SOCIAL RESPONSIBILITY (rev. ed. 1999) at 129–130.

been dead for over 20 years,[34] yet, he continues to rank in the top ten male box-office performers every year. Most years, he is in the top three. No other dead American shares this distinction.[35] John Wayne is an American cultural icon. He only died in 9 of his over 200 movies.[36] When he actually died of lung cancer, scores of fans did not believe that Wayne was mortal.

The icon of John Wayne rides on in strong national story/myths. He represents the concept of manifest destiny and the taming of the West. Even though Jackson Turner declared that the frontier had "closed" in 1890, the American frontier is alive and well. Look at how President Kennedy used the concept both for his political campaign and to line up popular support for the space race. Even deeper in the Western European psyche lies the powerful myth that might makes right. On this folk notion, English justice used to allow disputes to be settled by trial by battle before the antecedent of the modern jury came into widespread use.[37] John Wayne embodies that notion of what makes right because he never loses; the medieval morality play is there as well: Note that the fellow in the white hat (John Wayne) always wins, and even in the films where his character dies, the villains almost always die first, brought down by Wayne's bullets. Frequently, maudlin notions of patriotism are invoked to help the viewer understand that John Wayne personifies the American way.[38] Eventually, however, the legend drove out the reality of the man/actor. In the end, Wayne's Gold Medal from Congress did not honor the real actor or even a real man; instead, it memorialized the myth of John Wayne, a screen persona and Western hero.[39]

Walter Wink alerts readers to the inherently un-Christian attitudes at work in the popular heroes of violence, such as John Wayne, Clint Eastwood, and Bruce Willis. He focuses on the "myth of redemptive violence."[40] In Wink's analysis, the Babylonian creation myth is the creation story that is most accurately reflected in American society. The Babylonian myth declares that order is created out of chaos by an act of violence—deicide, specifically the killing of Tiamat, the female goddess. According to Wink, the notion of order arising out of violence, and specifically violence against women, reflects U.S. society. In American Westerns and detective stories, the hero is the one who inflicts greater damage on the villains until order is restored. The Garden of Eden in Genesis is a story of order being created by a loving Creator and of violence (murder by Cain) being part of human kind's fallen nature.

---

34. John Wayne, whose original name was Marion Robert Morrison, later had his name changed at age 5 by his parents to Marion Mitchell Morrison. He was born on May 26, 1907, in Winterset, Iowa; he died in the UCLA Medical Center, Los Angeles, California, on June 11, 1979. *See, e.g.*, RANDY ROBERTS & JAMES S. OLSON, JOHN WAYNE: AMERICAN (1995).

35. *See, e.g.*, G. WILLS, JOHN WAYNE'S AMERICA: THE POLITICS OF CELEBRITY (1997) and Audrey Williams, *Influences of the Myths of the American West on Business Culture in the United States* (unpublished Masters Thesis, 1997, on file at BSU Library).

36. "Wayne was not invincible. Wayne's movie character died in nine movies, and four of those were Westerns *(The Alamo, The Man Who Shot Liberty Valence, The Cowboys, The Shootist)*. The man who 'never dies' in Westerns is Clint Eastwood." GARRY WILLS, JOHN WAYNE'S AMERICA: THE POLITICS OF CELEBRITY (1997) at 313.

37. *See, e.g.*, O. W. HOLMES, THE COMMON LAW (Mark DeWolfe Howe ed., 1963) at 206–207.

38. *See, e.g.*, "The Green Berets," "She Wore A Yellow Ribbon," and "Rio Grande."

39. *House Panel Backs Gold Medal for John Wayne*, N.Y. TIMES (May 22, 1979) at C6 and Audrey Williams, *supra* note 18, at 52–53 citing A. P. McDonald, *John Wayne: Hero of the Western*, in RICHARD W. ETULAIN (ed.), WESTERN FILMS: A BRIEF HISTORY (1987) at 60.

40. *See* Walter Wink, *The Myth of Redemptive Violence*, as quoted in W. A. WINES, READINGS IN BUSINESS ETHICS AND SOCIAL RESPONSIBILITY (rev. ed., 1999) at 36–46.

Shylock's Soliloquy

Shylock: Let him look to his bond.

Salarino: Why, I am sure, if he forfeit, thou wilt not take his flesh: what's that good for?

Shylock: To bait fish withal: if it will feed nothing else, it will feed my revenge. He hath disgraced me, and hindered me half a million; laughed at my losses, mocked my gains, scorned my nation, thwarted my bargains, cooled my friends, heated mine enemies; and what's his reason? I am a Jew. Hath not a Jew eyes? Hath not a Jew hands, organs, dimensions, senses, affections, passions? Fed with the same food, hurt with the same weapons, subject to the same diseases, healed by the same means, warmed and cooled by the same winter and summer, as a Christian is? If you prick us, do we not bleed? If you tickle us, do we not laugh? If you poison us, do we not die? And if you wrong us, shall we not revenge? If we are like you in the rest, we will resemble you in that. If a Jew wrong a Christian, what is his humility? Revenge. If a Christian wrong a Jew, what should his sufferance be by Christian example? Why, revenge. The villany you teach me, I will execute; and it shall go hard but I will better the instruction.

—*The Merchant of Venice* by William Shakespeare (1598), Act 111, Scene 1, lines 46–69.

Children develop beliefs and display behaviors based on observations of others. "Past research has shown that as early as 12 months of age, children display behavioral styles that are more or less aggressive across a variety of situations. By the age of 8, aggressiveness becomes a relatively stable personality characteristic."[41] By the time children are in high school, many are engaged in violent and abusive relationships. Adolescents' understanding of what is normal or accepted roles for men and women often includes violence. "[R]esearch has found that children do not understand pro-social messages when the messages are embedded in violence."[42]

Both heroes and villains commit violent acts on television (and on the streets); when a hero figure is violent, he or she is frequently acclaimed or rewarded. Thus, children are baptized into the culture of redemptive violence. Between 1980 and 1990, the average number of violent acts on television increased from 18.6 per hour to 26.4 per hour.[43] On average, American children watch more than 25 hours of television per week. One study indicated that 10% of their viewing time is spent watching programs *not* suitable for children. Children who watch violence on television become desensitized to violence and its consequences.

The 1996 National Television Violence Study confirmed some key findings that violence, as portrayed on television, has few consequences:

- Children's programs portray violence in humorous contexts 67% of the time.
- Perpetrators go unpunished or do not suffer 73% of the time.
- Programs fail to show harm and injury to victims 47% of the time.

---

41. Huesman, L. Rowell, Nancy G. Guerra, *Children's Normative Beliefs About Aggression and Aggressive Behavior*, 72 JOURNAL OF PERSONALITY AND SOCIAL PSYCHOLOGY (no. 2, February 1997) at 408–419.

42. Chris J. Boyatzis, *Power Rangers and V-Chips*, 52 YOUNG CHILDREN (no. 2, November 1997) at 74–79.

43. National Association for the Education of Young Children, NAEYC *Position Statement on Media Violence in Children's Lives*, 45 YOUNG CHILDREN (no. 5, July 1990) at 18–21.

■ In 58% of the incidents no pain is displayed.

■ Only 16% of the programs indicated the long-term consequences of violence, such as financial or emotional damage.[44]

An old adage states that "children are good observers but bad interpreters." Experience with the "Power Rangers" program tends to bear this out. The National Coalition on Television proclaimed the "Power Rangers" program the most violent children's program ever. Each program had over 200 violent acts per hour.[45] Some primary teachers reported that they were spending more time trying to discipline children because of Power Ranger problems than they were actually spending teaching. Similarly, teachers reported that children who watched "Power Rangers" had a lower altruism rate than nonviewers.[46] One study showed that aggression increased steadily with each school grade, but the greatest single increase occurred between first and second grade.[47] Both teachers and parents reported that when they tried to discipline children for Power-Ranger-type problems a common response was, "If the Power Rangers do it, why can't we?"[48] Both parents and teachers concluded that children learned nothing positive from the show.[49] The Fox Television Network defended the "Power Rangers" show, arguing that it brought positive social messages and positive role models to children, comparing the show to "Teenage Mutant Ninja Turtles" and "The Lone Ranger." Yet, 75% of parents who had children who watched the show reported that they had never viewed one episode of the program.[50]

ORGANIZED VIOLENCE: WAR AND ITS HISTORY

Saving Private Ryan starring Tom Hanks was a big hit at the box offices. Even the American Legion was among its fans; it created a new award to bestow on director Steven Spielberg for realism in depicting the invasion of Normandy in 1944. A high-school acquaintance of mine told me that her father was a corpsman on Omaha Beach and thought the only major thing missing from the movie was the smell of fresh blood and saltwater. Yet, my limited experience in the Army during Vietnam convinces me otherwise. I worked on survivor assistance and headed military funerals in the Chicago area for $2^1/_2$ years as a staff officer; the agony and grief of the mothers, fathers, widows, and siblings has never been much of a hit on the silver screen. It goes on too long, has no easy resolution, and lacks the action that sells war movies.

One of the surprising findings highlighted by recent research is that American soldiers are more bloodthirsty now than in prior combat.[51] Grossman's thesis "is that there is a powerful natural disinclination, even among soldiers, to the taking of a human life, an in-built taboo against intraspecies destruction.

---

44. Mediascope, Inc. *The National Television Violence Study: Key Findings and Recommendations*, 51 YOUNG CHILDREN (no. 3, March 1996) at 54–55.

45. Boyatzis, *supra* note 22.

46. *Id.*

47. Huesman, *supra* note 21.

48. *Id.*

49. *Id.*

50. *Id.*

51. *See, e.g.*, D. GROSSMAN, ON KILLING: THE PSYCHOLOGICAL COST OF LEARNING TO KILL IN WAR AND SOCIETY (1995), B. EHRENREICH, BLOOD RITES (1997), and J. Bourke, AN INTIMATE HISTORY OF KILLING: FACE-TO-FACE KILLING IN TWENTIETH CENTURY (1999).

But the taboo has been breaking down both in battle and in society, with results that any reader of a newspaper or viewer of the late-night local news understands all too well."[52] He continues, "We are reaching that stage of desensitization at which the inflicting of pain and suffering has become a source of entertainment: vicarious pleasure rather than revulsion."[53] Grossman writes, "We are learning to kill, and we are learning to like it."[54]

In the Civil War after the battle of Gettysburg, about 90% of the over 27,000 muskets recovered from the battlefield were loaded. One musket had 19 rounds loaded. In that war, 95% of the time was spent loading and only 5% was spent firing; Grossman's conclusion from this fact is that most of the soldiers were not trying to kill the enemy. During World War II, firing rates increased from to 15 to 20% and in Vietnam soared to over 90%. Grossman theorizes that this dramatic increase was due to the training methods employed. The American GI in Vietnam had been intentionally desensitized and conditioned to overcome his normal reluctance to killing. Vietnam-era boot camps simulated actual battle conditions and substituted pop-up human silhouettes for the circular targets (originally competition targets from the National Rifle Association) that were used previously. The pop-ups dropped when the trainee made a "hit." Combined with the breakdown of the American family, the rise of gangs, and the media violence, Grossman states that "an epidemic, a virus of violence" has been unleashed in America.[55]

THEORIES ON THE CAUSES OF VIOLENCE IN AMERICAN SOCIETY

Why is our society saturated with violence? Responses to this question center on at least five themes:

1. violence being good for business (capitalism and materialism)
2. modern Narcissistic Personality and breakdown of family/community
3. isolation in American society and maternal overload in family model
4. Western values and cultural myths
5. sexual stereotypes in American society

Let us briefly review each of these thematic groupings in turn.

War is good for the American economy; rumors of war usually push prices higher on the New York Stock Exchange. The United States accounts for over one third of the arms expenditures made on this planet.[56] Based on so-called rough estimates for 1996, the United States manufactured almost half of the arms produced in the world.[57] In 1997, the top 100 arms-producing companies

---

52. Richard Bernstein, *Book Studies the Psychology of Killing* [New York Times News Service], ID. STATESMAN (October 15, 1995) at 3D.
53. GROSSMAN, *supra*, note 31, at 311.
54. *Id.* A three-star general in the U.S. Marine Corps recently said, "It's a hell of a lot of fun to shoot" Taliban members in Afghanistan. See *Rumsfeld: Case Closed on General's Shooting Remark*, U.S.A. TODAY (February 7, 2005) at 11A.
55. *Id.*
56. "Global Action to Prevent War: A Coalition-Building Effort to Stop War, Genocide, & Internal Armed Conflict" (May 2000, Rev. 14). Accessed at www.globalactionpw.org on October 31, 2000.
57. "SIPRI Yearbook 1999: Armaments, Disarmament and International Security." Accessed at http://www.reliefweb.int/library/documents/sipri99.html on October 31, 2000, at p. 12 of 20.

©Cagle Cartoons, Inc.

in the world (excluding China) produced $156 billion worth of armaments, representing three quarters of the total arms produced in the world.[58] After the United States, the next two countries in arms production, France and the United Kingdom, accounted for only 10% of the world's production each.[59] Russia produced only 4% of the world's arms.[60] From the standpoints of both expenditure and production, the United States literally dwarfs the rest of the planet in the business of preparing people to kill one another.

Materialism abounds in American society, whether we look at commercials on television, advertisements in the print media, or store windows. The message of Madison Avenue is that you will be happy or you will have more status if you were to buy *one more thing*. Inevitably, the next purchase does not do it. Humans are, as Abraham Maslow noted, perpetually wanting creatures. As soon as a need or want is met, it no longer serves to motivate.[61] Those who feel left out in a society of riches may be tempted to turn to violence to deal with inner rages arising from feelings of inadequacy, jealousy, or discrimination. Violence may be directed anonymously, randomly, at family, or at supervisors. It may be directed at victims of crime who resist or present a threat of identification.

Christopher Lasch argues that an analogy to psychological pathology may be necessary to understand American society at the end of the twentieth century.[62] Lasch argues, "The American cult of friendliness conceals but does not eradicate a murderous competition for goods and position; indeed this

---

58. *Id.*
59. *Id.*
60. *Id.*
61. ABRAHAM MASLOW, MOTIVATION AND PERSONALITY (1970) at 24.
62. C. LASCH, THE CULTURE OF NARCISSISM: AMERICAN LIFE IN AN AGE OF DIMINISHING EXPECTATIONS (1979, 1990) at 38.

competition has grown more savage in an age of diminishing expectations."[63] Indeed, Lasch characterizes his 1979 book, *The Culture of Narcissism*, in these words: "This book, however, describes a way of life that is dying—the culture of competitive individualism, which in its decadence has carried the logic of individualism to the extreme of a war of all against all, the pursuit of happiness to the dead end of a narcissistic preoccupation with the self."[64] Note the echo of the Hobbesian state of nature in which life is "brutish, nasty, solitary and short." Thus, Lasch sees us in our extreme individualism engaging in a war of all against all. Violence inheres in that conclusion.

In his book *The Pursuit of Loneliness*, Phillip Slater argues that our destruction of family and community bonds has led to an isolation of individuals and an inherent overload on the middle-class housewife and mother, who produces sons innately drawn to violence and sadism.[65] His analysis seems to fit the condition of single mothers of the 1990s, as well as of suburban soccer moms. Slater theorizes, "In most societies the impact of the mother's character defects is diluted by the presence of many other nurturing agents. In middle-class America the mother not only tends to be the exclusive daytime adult contact of the child, but also has a mission to create a near-perfect being."[66] "Societies in which deprived mothers turn to their sons," Slater concludes, "for what they cannot obtain from male adults tend to produce men who are vain, warlike, boastful, competitive and skittish toward women. . . . They often huddle together in male gangs."[67]

The study findings showing that violence on television increases inappropriate aggression in children and desensitizes children toward violence, when coupled with Grossman's research on conditioning GIs to kill in battle, present a fairly compelling argument that our entertainment sources are contributing significantly to violence in our society. Moreover, the myths of the American West—personified best but not exclusively by any means, in John Wayne, the actor and cultural icon—are very violent. Six dominant values characterize the culture and history of the American West: the doctrine of no retreat, the imperative of personal self-redress, the homestead ethic, the ethic of individual enterprise, the Code of the West, and the ideology of vigilantism.[68] Four of the six—no retreat, self-redress, the Code of the West, and vigilantism—frequently lead directly to violence and sudden death.

American sexual stereotypes have an unfortunate impact. "Boys will be boys" and "big boys don't cry" typify two of the most damaging. When it is used to raise young boys, this kind of thinking produces men who are emotionally constipated. As Susan Faludi notes, "The veterans of World War II were eager to embrace a masculine ideal that revolved around providing rather than dominating."[69] Yet, when NBC produced a documentary based on Tom Brokaw's book *The Greatest Generation*, the "troubling subtext" according to Susan Faludi, "was how devastatingly unfathered those sons [of WW II veterans]

---

63. *Id* at 64.
64. *Id*. at xv.
65. P. SLATER, THE PURSUIT OF LONELINESS (1970, 1976, 1990) at 63–64.
66. *Id*. at 63.
67. *Id*. at 63–64.
68. R. M. BROWN, OXFORD HISTORY OF THE AMERICAN WEST (1994).
69. Susan Faludi, "The Betrayal of the American Man," NEWSWEEK (September 13, 1999) at 48, 52. This article appears as a "book excerpt" from SUSAN FALUDI, STIFFED: THE BETRAYAL OF THE AMERICAN MAN (1999).

were, how inadequately they'd been prepared for manhood by their 'heroic' fathers."[70] Finally she notes that the "critical paradox for our society is that "the model [of the male paradigm of confrontation in which an enemy is identified, contested, and defeated] women have used to revolt [against] is the exact one men not only can't use but are trapped in."[71]

As Slater notes, American women are progressively desexualized as they move from young unmarried girls, who are permitted to be fully female, through the married state to the matronly state.[72] No wonder that disenchantment sets in for many American men, whose three pillars of identity are work, sex, and war,[73] when the "missus," following societal dictates, focuses on the children and has less energy and time for him. If divorce is not an option, then we can see that work and war—both places of intense violence to body and soul—are the only avenues available for a "real man" to prove himself. Moreover, even the notion of a real man comes with baggage in certain levels of American society. As one authority sardonically noted, "If you're going to be a real man, you've got to [sexually] harass your secretary."[74]

ECONOMIC/ENVIRONMENTAL VIOLENCE

In 1979, Matthew Fox wrote, "[Without compassion,] economics becomes merely a highly developed form of violence."[75] What did the former Dominican priest and the director of the Institute for Creation-Centered Spirituality mean by that statement? I suspect that he meant it literally and exactly as he wrote it. Without compassion, the idea of a market-driven economics is merely a theoretical excuse for greed to rule the world, nominally under the banner of Adam Smith but without his moral grounding. Adam Smith was first and foremost a moral philosopher. As E. F. Schumacker reportedly once observed, "The market is the institutionalization of nonresponsibility."

ECONOMICS AS A FORM OF VIOLENCE AGAINST THE POOR

The poor do not have any votes in the marketplace where the consumer is sovereign, and Third World countries are on the verge of becoming meaningless nation-states that are in thrall to the World Bank and the World Trade Organization (WTO). They may be destined to be subject to an endless form of colonialism that allows their resources to be stripped and shipped to the developed nations without creating any significant economic infrastructure for them. The high-minded theories of Adam Smith have, in some respects, devolved into a code word under which economic and environmental rapine rule.

Let us not leave the subject at such a high level of abstraction; we can bring it down closer to the ground. Look at Vietnam since it moved toward opening

---

70. *Id* at 54.
71. *Id* at 58.
72. SLATER, *supra* note 43, at 64.
73. S. KEEN, FIRE IN THE BELLY (1991) at 34.
74. Lin Farley as featured in movie "The Workplace Hustle" (1980).
75. MATTHEW FOX, A SPIRITUALITY NAMED COMPASSION AND THE HEALING OF THE GLOBAL VILLAGE, HUMPTY DUMPTY AND US (1979) at 177.

its markets to the West.[76] Look at Nigeria.[77] Look at Chile.[78] In Saudi Arabia, oil is gold, and the family of Saud is king. The poor are no better off, and when the oil is gone, they will be worse off.[79] In Vietnam before capitalism, under a planned economy, the rice farmers made approximately $25 per year.

76. Vietnam has a population of over 81 million people living in a land area slightly larger than New Mexico. The population is young; the median age is 24.5 years. Yet, 37% of the people live below the official poverty line. Unemployment is officially 25%. Only 17.41% of the land area is arable. Current environmental issues include the following: "logging and slash and burn agricultural practices that contribute to deforestation and soil degradation; water pollution and overfishing threaten marine life populations; groundwater contamination limits potable water supply; growing urban industrialization and population migration are rapidly degrading environment" in the urban areas of the North. Vietnam has yet to recover from the ravages of war. It is a poor, densely populated country that badly needs an overhaul of its administrative structure; a new and predictable legal system, and a thorough reform of its banking sector, considered one of the riskiest on the planet. Accessed at http://www.abacci.com/atlas/economy2.asp?misspellID=531 and http://www.cia.gov/cia/publications/factbook/geos/vm.html on September 20, 2003.

77. Nigeria has experienced the first peaceful transition of civilian governments under its new Constitution (1999) following the elections of April 2003. The president faces the "daunting task of rebuilding a petroleum-based economy, whose revenues have been squandered through corruption and mismanagement." He also needs to institutionalize democracy—a difficult task given Nigeria's history. Nigeria has a population of over 133 million people occupying a land mass approximately twice the size of California. The people are poor; per capita GDP is only two-thirds of what it is for the people of Vietnam. Only 31% of the land is arable. Life expectancy is 51 years, and literacy rates are about 68%. The population is very young; the median age is 18 years. The official poverty rate is set at 60%. Unemployment is estimated at 28%, but may be higher. For the population of over 133 million people, there are three television stations broadcasting to less than 7 million sets, 700,000 telephones, and 23.5 million radios. Drug trafficking is a big activity, and Nigeria is a major money-laundering center for the world. Nigeria is also a transit point for drugs headed for European, East Asian, and North American markets. Ethnic and religious tensions continue to pose threats to long-term national stability. Finally, Nigeria has a HIV/AIDS prevalence rate among adults at just under 6% of the population. This is a potentially disastrous public health issue. Accessed at http://www.cia.gov/cia/publications/factbook/print/ni.html on September 20, 2003.

78. Chile has a population of over 15.6 million people living on a land mass slightly smaller than twice the size of Montana. The arable land is 2.65% of the total. Current environmental issues include "widespread deforestation and mining" threatening the country's natural resource base; air pollution from industry and vehicles; and water pollution from raw sewage. Although Chile experienced "unprecedented growth in 1991–97," the GDP rate was 1.8% in real terms (2002 est.). An estimated 9.2% (2002) of workers are unemployed, and the poverty rate is officially 21% (based on 1998 est.). Chile has large proven reserves of natural gas and oil, but exports of the same are not available. Exports are mainly agricultural products, copper, fish, and pulp and paper. Imports include mostly finished goods, such as consumer goods, motor vehicles, fuels, and machinery. The gap between haves and have-nots is high; the top 10% of the households receives 45.6% of the national income, whereas the bottom 10% of households gets 1.3% of the national income. Chile is a growing trans-shipment country for cocaine destined for the United States and Europe. With prosperity for the upper class, domestic cocaine consumption is rising. Accessed at http://www.cia.gov/cia/publications/factbook/print/ci.html on September 20, 2003.

79. Saudi Arabia became a country when it was united by Abd Al-Aziz bin Abd al-Rahman Al Saud in 1932 after a 30-year campaign to unify the Arabian Peninsula. Major governmental concerns include a burgeoning population, aquifer depletion, and an economy largely dependent on petroleum output and prices. Furthermore, there is unrest and division among Muslim extremists, which concerns Saudi Arabia as the site of the two holiest places in Islam, Mecca and Medina. The population of over 24 million people lives on a land mass slightly greater than 20% (one fifth) of the United States. Only 1.72% of the land is arable, and natural hazards include frequent sand and dust storms. The population is very young with a median age of 18.8 years. The literacy rate (defined as 15 and over, can read and write) is 78.8%. The government and the legal system are based on Islamic law (Shari'a). There is no suffrage. The real growth rate of GDP in 2002 was 0.6%. Unemployment is officially 25%. The poverty

Then, when allowed to export, the rice farmers temporarily made more money, and rice exports grew. Unfortunately, the resulting drop in rice prices on the world market left the rice farmers of Vietnam producing much more rice, but ultimately no better off, because their income fell to $25 per year, again. Meanwhile, courtesy of unending war from 1939 to 1975, Vietnam's lands have been stripped of timber; the tree cover in Vietnam is 60% smaller than it was before World War II. The natives are eating endangered species. At the same time, Honda sells motor scooters (the Dream II is tops) to Vietnamese who have now become part of the fossil fuel economy. There are unprecedented traffic jams in Hanoi, but it seems to me that the people are no better off than they were with "cyclos"[80] and water buffalo carts; in fact, they may be worse off.

CYCLES OF ECONOMIC VIOLENCE IN THE UNITED STATES

We do not have to go overseas to find evidence of economic violence. Look at the response of the populist legislature of Minnesota to the Great Depression: They passed a mortgage foreclosure moratorium act in April 1933 to alleviate the suffering caused by massive mortgage foreclosure.[81] The U.S. Supreme Court upheld it by the slimmest of margins as not an infringement of contract and declared it did not violate the due process clause. Other state laws passed during the Depression to provide relief to debtors did not fare as well.[82]

Listen to the emotions revealed by this excerpt from Robert Bly's memoirs of his rural Minnesota boyhood about 1940:

> We always had some suspicion of men from the town, who did not work with their hands. In town, they thought themselves better, but my father did not share that view, and he shielded us from its destructive radiation. He ran a threshing rig, and stood on it, respecting a number of grown men and even horses who worked with their hands, shoulders, and hooves all day. At times if we were threshing a field that the bank owned, having foreclosed during the late disastrous thirties—perhaps six or seven years before we were threshing—then the bank, to make sure the grain was divided properly, would send a cashier or teller out to watch the wagon boxes being pulled up to the thresher, and pulled away full, and where they went—from their cars—the bank often accepting their loads at a different elevator than the renter was using. How we pitied these creatures! Getting out of the car with a white shirt and necktie, stepping over the stubble like a cat so as to not get too much chaff in his black oxfords, how weak and feeble! What a poor model of a human being! It was clear the teller was incapable of any boisterous joy, and nothing but a small zoo animal of some sort that locked the doors on itself, pale from the

---

rate is not available. A total of 6.8 million phones serve the population of over 24 million. Statistics on the haves and the have-nots are also not available.

80. "Cyclo" was the term I was introduced to in Vietnam in 1994. It meant a three-wheeled, pedal-driven cycle that had room for two passengers and was powered by a rider who operated the pedals and charged for carriage.

81. Chap. 339 of the Laws of Minnesota, popularly called the "Minnesota Mortgage Moratorium Law," as cited in *Home Building & Loan Ass'n v. Blaisdell* 290 U.S. 398, 54 S. Ct. 231, 78 L. Ed. 413 (1934) (5–4), which upheld the Minnesota law.

82. *See, e.g.,* cases cited in commentary in GUNTHER & DOWLING, CONSTITUTIONAL LAW: CASES AND MATERIALS (1970) at 934–935.

reflected light off the zoo walls, light as salt in a shaker, clearly obsessed with money – you could see greed all over him. How ignoble! How sordid and ignoble! What ignobility![83]

The scars of the experience seared an entire generation, who never completely healed from the shame of losing the family farm or home.

I had a favorite aunt, a chemist with a Ph.D., who was married to a Yankee, a Swede from Duluth, Minnesota, and who worked as a researcher up North; she spent much of her adult life buying back pieces of the family farm we lost in 1937 in Bibb County, Georgia. In retrospect, it seems that she was redeeming the family honor paycheck by paycheck and acre by acre. At least one generation of Americans believed that losing the family farm was the only unforgivable sin in America.

Of course, we do not have to go back to the Great Depression to experience economic violence. In the so-called farm crisis of the early 1980s, mobs in Iowa stood down sheriff's sales. Family farms were being foreclosed in part because of the unanticipated elimination of farm price supports and in part because of the drop in farm prices that occurred after many families had expanded their farms in times of high interest rates and high land prices in the late 1970s. In the town where I lived, North Liberty, a farmer came into town with his shotgun and shot his banker to death before turning the gun on himself. Later, the farmer's wife was found shot dead on the floor of the farmhouse kitchen. A survey that year at Iowa State, an agriculture college, found that over 24% of the students did not believe that life was worth living.[84] I do not know a way to measure the injury to their young psyches caused by watching the farms being foreclosed.

A NATIONAL BUDGET WITHOUT COMPASSION

In the presidential election of 2000, George W. Bush ran as a "compassionate conservative." Where does that compassion show in the federal budget? Is it in the "No Child Left Behind" program? Can we find compassion for any but the super-rich in the federal income tax cut that President Bush championed? How much violence will result from the loss of 3 million jobs when the average time to find a new one is now about 5 months? Indeed, it seems that Matthew Fox was right; without compassion, economics is merely a highly developed form of violence.

The federal government under a succession of presidents, but mainly in the two-term presidency of William Clinton, moved more and more federal programs down to the state level. Indeed, that was one of the primary ways in which the federal budget was balanced, at least for a brief time. The states, however, did not always accept their responsibility for former federal programs, especially when the mandate came to them with no federal monies. For example, the Aid for Families with Dependent Children Program (AFDC) was pushed onto the states. On the effective date of the transfer, the program ceased to exist in the State of Idaho. For some states, keeping the budget balanced and not raising taxes, the GOP battle cry since 1980, were more important than helping hungry children.

---

83. Robert Bly, *Being a Lutheran Boy-God in Minnesota*, in GROWING UP IN MINNESOTA: TEN WRITERS REMEMBER THEIR CHILDHOODS (ed. Chester G. Anderson, 1976) 205–219 at 213.
84. *See* Timothy Chanand, *Validity of Stress Poll Questionable*, IOWA STATE DAILY (May 7, 1985) at 1. A stress poll of I.S.U. students was run by the Office of Student Life at Iowa State University. *Id.*

©Reprinted with permission of PictureHistory.com.

CONCLUSIONS

Clearly, more research needs to be done on violence and its causes in American society. This chapter barely scratches the surface. However, let me offer some suggestions for future research:

- It should be based on more comprehensive notions of violence.
- It should look at the impact that economic decisions have on the lives of working people.
- It should address the violent impact that economic decisions have on other sentient forms of life that share this planet with humankind.

We can no longer afford to ignore the effects of unemployment when we know that it leads to increased coronary heart disease, increased alcohol and drug abuse, increased spousal and child abuse, and increased suicides and homicides.[85] We know that global capitalism will only lead to a downward spiral of violence against workers and the environment unless law reform is urgently addressed.[86] Nonviolent methods of dispute resolution need to be initiated whenever possible. Sustainability needs to become not only a watchword but also the standard by which environmental impact is governed.

85. Angelo Kinicki et al., *Socially Responsible Plant Closings*, PERSONNEL ADMINISTRATOR (June 1987) at 116.
86. *See, e.g.*, William A. Wines et al., *The Critical Need for Law Reform to Regulate the Abusive Practices of Transnational Corporations: The Illustrative Case of Boise Cascade Corporation in Mexico's Costa Grande and Elsewhere*, an unpublished paper presented to the Rocky Mountain Academy of Legal Studies in Business on September 20, 1997 in Vail Village, Colorado. (Copy in possession of author.)

Finally, we need to find a way to make warfare unprofitable so that we may "practice war no more." As President Dwight Eisenhower said so well more than four decades ago,

> Every gun that is made, every warship launched, every rocket fired signifies, in the final sense, a theft from those who hunger and are not fed, those who are cold and are not clothed. This world in arms is not spending money alone. It is spending the sweat of its laborers, the genius of its scientists, and the hopes of its children. The cost of one modern heavy bomber is this: a modern brick school in more than 30 cities. It is two electric plants, each serving a town with a population of 60,000. It is two fine, fully equipped hospitals. It is some 50 miles of concrete highway. We pay for a single fighter plane with a half million bushels of wheat.... This is not a way of life at all, in any true sense. Under the cloud of threatening war, it is humanity hanging from a cross of iron.[87]

---

87. Dwight D. Eisenhower, 34th President, Speech in Washington, D.C., April 16, 1953, in J. PODELL & S. ANZOVIN (ed.), SPEECHES OF THE AMERICAN PRESIDENTS (1988) at 570.

PART
3

Civil Rights

CHAPTER 10

U.S. CIVIL RIGHTS YEARS

Robert E. Lee's surrender of the Army of Virginia at Appomattox ended the U.S. Civil War in April 1865 and offered Black Americans hope for renewal of life and for the opportunities of freedom. The 13th, 14th, and 15th Amendments to the Constitution were ratified between 1865 and 1870. These amendments outlawed slavery, guaranteed federal and state citizenship to Blacks, and stated that the right to vote could not be denied by the federal government or any state. Between 1870 and 1910, Congress enacted several civil rights and Reconstruction acts. However, by 1910, the laws and acts had been so modified by other statutes that they had very little impact. From 1910 to the early 1940s, the federal government played a very limited role in the protection and enforcement of civil rights. It was not until after the Depression that the civil rights movement began its triumphant struggle to "make America be America for all its citizens."[1]

A. PHILIP RANDOLPH

One of the men responsible for the civil rights movement in the middle of the 20th century was A. Philip Randolph. He was dedicated to and preached civil rights for more than 50 years. He first began his triumphant quest for civil rights by establishing the Brotherhood of Sleeping Car Porters (BSCP) in 1925. The BSCP was a union of Black porters who worked on the country's trains. Before 1925, no railroad unions were open to Black workers.[2] The union represented not only the laborers but also spoke out for civil rights to help improve the lives of African Americans. After the March on Washington in 1963, Randolph went on to become the president of the Negro American Labor Council. In addition, he founded the A. Philip Randolph Institute of New York, which sponsored educational projects and helped Black Americans obtain skilled-trades jobs.

FIRST BLACK MEN'S MARCH ON WASHINGTON, D.C. (1941)

Mr. Randolph helped ignite the modern Black civil rights movement by threatening to stage a march on Washington, D.C., in 1941 if President Franklin Delano Roosevelt did not help Black Americans get more jobs in defense work. In 1941, the United States was engaged in the Lend-Lease program in which it was loaning military supplies to Great Britian, and it was facing involvement in another world war. There were many jobs open in the defense industries, but those jobs were off limits to Blacks. After his bitter experience in World War I, Mr. Randolph believed that the time for getting equal employment opportunity in defense production facilities was before the war and not after it had been won. He knew that Whites were getting most of the jobs, and further, that big defense contractors were complaining about a shortage of workers while denying jobs to qualified Blacks.

The march on Washington was scheduled. Mr. Randolph planned to have 100,000 Black men march if President Roosevelt did not issue an executive order prohibiting employment discrimination. This protest march was intended to demonstrate not only to other African Americans that they should

---

1. JUAN WILLIAMS, EYES ON THE PRIZE: AMERICA'S CIVIL RIGHTS YEARS, 1954–1965 (1987) first series, part one, "Awakenings: 1954–1956."
2. EYES ON THE PRIZE at 197. [The book is a companion volume to the PBS television series.]

object to the inequalities in the workplace but also to create awareness among members of Congress of the need for governmental action to remove discriminatory barriers in government contracting.

FRANKLIN DELANO ROOSEVELT AND CIVIL RIGHTS

Prior to the march, President Franklin Delano Roosevelt (popularly known as FDR) met with A. Philip Randolph on several occasions to attempt to prevent the march and demonstrations from occurring. FDR objected to the march as demonstrating national divisions on the eve of war, and he was also seriously concerned that Washington, D.C., a segregated backwater town with a racist police force, might be the scene of a police riot if 100,000 Black men attempted a protest march.

Eventually, FDR capitulated to Randolph's demands, and he issued an executive order that stated, "There shall be no discrimination in the employment of workers in defense industries or government because of race, creed, color or national origin."[3] In addition, he established the Fair Employment Practices Committee. This agreement was a huge step for Americans in the United States work force, and it represented one of the most powerful acts taken by the federal government in support of civil rights since the Civil War. Randolph was satisfied with FDR's executive order, and the proposed march was canceled.

To be sure, President Roosevelt, in taking those two actions, was not a heroic figure. In fact, FDR did not want anything to do with racial problems in 1941. The U.S. economy was booming because of the manufacturing of defense materials. The majority of FDR's Democrats, not just those from the southern states, were White segregationists. So were most of the Congressional leaders. If FDR were to support Black civil rights, he might antagonize southern Democrats and jeopardize what he considered his more important programs in Congress.[4] Roosevelt also feared that the march would not be in the best interest of the nation under the current circumstances. "It would make the country look bad in war time," he told Mr. Randolph at another White House meeting, this time before the entire cabinet. "It would help the Germans."[5]

The Roosevelt administration did not recommend any civil rights legislation, nor was any enacted by Congress during his terms.[6] The Roosevelt administration deserves credit for ordering nondiscrimination in defense industry employment (Executive Order 8802) in 1941. However, this order did very little to eliminate the ordinary, run-of-the-mill, daily discriminatory practices against African Americans.

JOSEPH RAUH'S IMMORTAL PHRASE

Joseph L. Rauh, Jr., was a lawyer on President Roosevelt's staff in 1941. He was assigned the job of creating the Executive Order for the Fair Employment Practices Commission. He was not given a week or even days to create this executive order, but just hours. Within these few hours, Rauh established not

---

3. *Id.* at 197.
4. DAVID BRINKLEY, WASHINGTON GOES TO WAR (1988) at 78.
5. *Id.* at 83.
6. CONGRESSIONAL QUARTERLY SERVICE (1968) at 2.

only an executive order that would be the first of many to deal with racial discrimination but also uttered an immortal phrase that would be embedded in the minds of most Americans for decades to come. The phrase read, "No discrimination on the grounds of race, color, creed, or national origin." He would later become the counsel for the Mississippi Freedom Democratic party. Rauh also was the counsel for the Leadership Conference on Civil Rights and worked with Clarence Mitchell in lobbying for the Voting Rights Acts of 1965, 1970, and 1975; the Fair Housing Act of 1968; and other civil rights legislation.[7] Joseph Rauh was a stalwart in the fight for civil rights.

WATERSHED: *BROWN V. BOARD OF EDUCATION* (1954)

The unanimous decision of the U.S. Supreme Court in *Brown vs. Board of Education* (Brown I) was announced on May 17, 1954. In an opinion written by Chief Justice Earl Warren (R. Ca.), the court ruled that "separate but equal"—the doctrine promulgated in 1896 in *Plessy v. Ferguson*—had no place in public education. The decision sent shock waves through American society. Students in the South marched in protest.

Thurgood Marshall (1908–1993) and other lawyers on the staff of the National Association for the Advancement of Colored People (NAACP) had worked for decades to overturn the "separate but equal" doctrine. First, Marshall and the NAACP Legal Defense Fund took on with litigation to get highly qualified African Americans admitted into graduate schools in states with segregation but no graduate schools for "coloreds."[8] In 1937, Chief Justice Hughes, in what has been called the "first of the 'modern' school desegregation cases,"[9] ruled that Missouri could not satisfy the Constitutional requirements of "separate but equal" by paying out of state tuition for a Negro plaintiff refused admission to the Missouri School of Law because of his race.[10]

Other cases followed, using the same arguments; and many produced similar results. In January 1948, *per curiam*, the U.S Supreme Court reversed an order by the Oklahoma Supreme Court and ordered a Negro women admitted to the University of Oklahoma Law School because it was the only state institution for legal education.[11] On June 5, 1950, the U.S. Supreme Court handed down two decisions: The first integrated the University of Texas Law School,[12] and the other removed racial segregation restraints for the sole Negro seeking an Ed.D. at the University of Oklahoma graduate school where

---

7. WILLIAMS, EYES ON THE PRIZE, *supra* note 2, at 292.
8. As NAACP counsel, Thurgood Marshall implemented the strategy of integrating graduate schools first because there was less resistance at that level. Marshall could not help commenting on the lack of logic involved. He said, "Those racial supremacy boys somehow think that little kids of six or seven are going to get funny ideas about sex and marriage just from going to school together, but for some equally funny reason, youngsters in law school aren't supposed to feel that way. We didn't get it, but we decided if that was what the South believed, then the best thing for the moment was to go along." MICHAEL D. DAVIS & HUNTER R. CLARK, THURGOOD MARSHALL: WARRIOR AT THE BAR, REBEL ON THE BENCH (1992) at 12.
9. GERALD GUNTHER & NOEL T. DOWLING, CONSTITUTIONAL LAW: CASES AND MATERIALS (8th ed. 1970) at 1422.
10. *Missouri ex rel. Gaines v. Canada* 305 U.S. 337 (1938). With Justices McReynolds and Butler dissenting, the Court (6–2) voted to essentially integrate or close the Missouri Law School by finding that sending plaintiff out of state was a denial of equal protection.
11. *Sipuel v. Board of Regents* 332 U.S. 631 (1948). Thurgood Marshall and Amos T. Hall argued for petitioner.
12. *Sweatt v. Painter* 339 U.S. 629 (1950).

he had been required to eat at a separate table and sit in a row of classroom seats designated for Negroes.

In the fall of 1952, the NAACP brought four cases to the U.S. Supreme Court: one each from Kansas, South Carolina, Virginia, and Delaware. These cases argued for overturning the "separate but equal" standard in K–12 public schools. The cases were combined at the high court, and oral argument was held on December 9, 1952. The Court was divided 5–4 in favor of overruling Plessy; but Chief Justice Fred Vinson, a Truman appointee, was opposed to the decision because he envisioned it shutting down public education in the South.[13] No one was pushing to announce a decision in the spring of 1953 because the chief justice knew he would lose and no one in the majority was comfortable with such a close vote. Justice Felix Frankfurter managed to postpone a fragmented decision by finding three major questions that needed to be addressed on reargument.[14]

In September, 1953, just 3 months before reargument, Chief Justice Vinson, aged 63, died of a heart attack.[15] President Eisenhower, reluctantly keeping a campaign promise, appointed Governor Earl Warren of California to be the new chief justice.[16] On May 17, 1954, the Court ruled (9–0) that the "separate but equal" doctrine had "no place" in public education.[17] Constance Baker Motley, the first Black women ever appointed to the federal bench (1966) and a protégé of Thurgood Marshall,[18] would remark years later that the Brown decision "emboldened" the Black community because they saw it as a sign they had a "friend, so to speak" in the U.S. Supreme Court.[19]

PORTRAIT OF A LYNCHING: EMMETT TILL IN MISSISSIPPI (1955)

In 1955, White men killed several African Americans in Mississippi. The reasons that were usually given when murder was committed varied from stealing food to talking back to a White person. Although murder motivated by racial differences was not new to Mississippi, the three murders in 1955 were different. Two of the victims, the Reverend George W. Lee and Lamar Smith, were NAACP organizers who were trying to register Black voters.[20] The third victim was a 14-year-old boy from the South Side of Chicago. Emmett Till's death was so ghastly that it made the front page of almost every Black newspaper in the nation.[21]

In August of 1955, Emmett and his cousin, Curtis Jones, were visiting some relatives near the town of Money, Mississippi. They were staying with Jones's grandfather and Till's uncle, Mose Wright. Emmett, an only child, was known to his family and friends as a prank-loving eighth grader who did well in school, even with the speech defect he had acquired at age 3 from nonparalytic polio.

---

13. *See, e.g.,* BERNARD SCHWARTZ WITH STEPHAN LESHER, INSIDE THE WARREN COURT 1953–1969 (1983) at 25–27.
14. *Id.* at 27.
15. *Id.*
16. *Id.*
17. 347 U.S. 483 at 495.
18. MICHAEL D. DAVIS & HUNTER R. CLARK, THURGOOD MARSHALL: WARRIOR AT THE BAR, REBEL ON THE BENCH (1992) at 339.
19. EYES ON THE PRIZE, first series, part one, "Awakenings: 1954–1956" (1986).
20. WILLIAMS, EYES ON THE PRIZE, *supra* note 2, at 39.
21. *Id.*

According to the kids in his neighborhood, Emmett's stutter did not make him shy; on the contrary, he liked to talk smart and dress smart. Emmett had lived in Chicago all his life. His mother, Mamie Bradley, had moved there with her family when she was 2 years old. The segregation that Emmett was exposed to in the North was a far cry from what he was to experience in Money (Leflore County) Mississippi. His only warning came from his mother, who said, "If you have to get on your knees and bow when a White person goes past, do it willingly."[22]

One Wednesday evening in August, 1955, Emmett and Curtis drove their grandfather's '41 Ford to Bryant's Grocery and Meat Market, a small country store. The two teenagers met up with some other Black children, and Emmett began showing off a picture of a White girl who was a friend of his in Chicago. Before long, Emmett, who enjoyed playing pranks, was bragging that the girl in the picture was his girlfriend. Curtis Jones was playing a game of checkers with a 70-year-old man outside the little store. He remembered one of the boys telling Emmett that there was a White girl [actually a young White woman, Carolyn Bryant] inside the store, and he bet that Emmett wouldn't go in and talk to her. Emmett immediately went in the store to get some candy. While he was leaving, he told the lady, "Bye, Baby." The older man playing checkers then warned the boys that the woman would come out, get her pistol out of her car, and shoot Emmett. As Carolyn Bryant walked out of the store, Emmett and Curtis jumped in their grandfather's truck and sped out of town. After a day or so, the store incident had become just a good story to the two northern boys.[23]

However, the story had spread beyond the boys. One girl warned them that there would be trouble once Carolyn's husband, Roy Bryant, came back into town. Roy was trucking shrimp from Louisiana to Texas at the time. Both Emmett and Curtis kept the incident a secret from Curtis's grandfather, Mose Wright, and hoped that it would just blow over. However, some time after midnight on Saturday, 3 days later, a car headed through the cotton field to Mose Wright's cabin. Roy Bryant and his brother-in-law, J. W. Milam, had come for Emmett. Mose tried to explain to the men that the boys were from up North and did not know how to act with Whites in the South. He also told them that Emmett was only 14 and that this was only his second time visiting Mississippi. The two men did not listen to Mose, and as they dragged Emmett outside and pushed him into the back seat of their car, they told Mose that if he caused any trouble, he wouldn't live to see his next birthday.[24]

---

22. *Id.* at 41.
23. *Id.*
24. *Id.* at 42. Two months after the trial, a White Alabama journalist, William Bradford Huie, paid Bryant and Milam $4,000 to tell their story. The two men claimed that they had only wanted to scare Emmett and had not intended to kill him. However, when the young boy had refused to beg for mercy or repent, they stated that they were forced to kill him. According to the account written by William Huie, J. W. Milam drove Emmett to the Tallahatchie River and then made him carry a 75-pound cotton-gin fan to the bank of the river. After Emmett was ordered to strip, Milam shot him in the head. The story that Milam and Bryant told the journalist left numerous questions unanswered. *Id.* at 25. Most of those questions are still unanswered after almost 50 years. *See, e.g.,* Bob Longine, *Unfinished Story of Emmitt Till,* CINC. ENQUIRER (January 6, 2003) at C2. A novice filmmaker, Keith Beauchamp, has been criss-crossing the country for 7 years documenting never-before-published eyewitness accounts of the Till case for an unfinished movie. Another documentary film and two books have also come out recently. *Id.* Mamie Till Mobley died on January 6, 2003 at the age of 81 in Chicago. Accessed at http://www.msu.edu/~daggy/cop/bkofdead/obits-0.htm on May 27,

Mose Wright, at least initially, heeded the threat by not calling the police. However, the next morning, Curtis Jones called the sheriff and told him that Emmett Till was missing. The body of 14-year-old Emmett Till was found 3 days later when the barbed wire that was wound around a cotton gin fan and tied to his neck snagged on a river root. One eye had been gouged out, his forehead was crushed in, and there was a bullet in his head. Milam and Bryant, who had only been charged with kidnapping up to this point, were now charged with murder, and the speed of the indictment surprised many. White Mississippi newspapers and officials were stating that all "decent" people were outraged by what had happened and swore that justice would be done. Initially, not a single local lawyer was willing to defend Milam and Bryant.[25]

Emmett's body was so distended and so badly mangled that Mose Wright could only identify the boy by his initialed ring. The sheriff in Money wanted to bury the body immediately, but Curtis Jones was able to get word to Emmett's mother of her son's death and imminent burial. Mamie Bradley immediately ordered her son's body to be sent to Chicago; the sheriff's office conceded, but had the mortician sign an order that the casket was not to be opened.

When the casket arrived in Chicago, Mamie Bradley immediately had it opened. She wanted to be sure that the body inside was indeed her young son. After studying the teeth and the hairline, Mamie proclaimed that the entire world would see what had been done to her son. The funeral would be with an open casket. The mutilated body of Emmett Till shocked the city of Chicago, and after a picture was published in *Jet*, a weekly Black magazine, all of Black America saw the mangled corpse. Viewing Emmett Till's body moved African Americans in a way that the NAACP had been unable to do only weeks before as it was trying to pay off debts incurred by its desegregation litigation. Contributions soared to record levels.[26]

However, White Mississippians did not respond in the same manner. The state's White press did not appreciate the NAACP's labeling of the killing as a lynching; one Southern writer called the "condemnation of Mississippi a 'Communist ploy' to destroy southern society."[27] Scores of lawyers now lined up to defend Roy Bryant and J. W. Milam, and a fund for their defense raised $10,000. The trial date was set for September 19, just 2 weeks after Emmett Till was buried in Chicago.

Without any witnesses, the prosecution would not have a case.[28] For a Black man to accuse a White man of murder in 1955 in Mississippi was

---

2003. As a result of the work of two filmmakers, Keith Beauchamp and Stanley Nelson (who had aired a documentary on PBS in 2003), the U.S. Justice Department announced on May 10, 2004 that it was reopening the case of Emmett Louis Till. "Emmett Till" as found at http://en.wikipedia.org/wiki/Emmett_Till (last visited on 4/30/2005). Research by those two filmmakers indicated that as many as 10 people may have been involved in the killing of Till. *Id.* The federal statutes of limitation have run out, but the State of Mississippi could still bring charges. *Id.* Milam died in 1980, and Bryan in 1990. *Id.*

On Wednesday, May 4, 2005, the Federal Bureau of Investigation announced that it planned to exhume Till's body and have an autopsy performed. Don Babwin (AP), *Autopsy Slated for Emmett Till*, CINC. ENQUIRER (May 5, 2005) at A7.

25. WILLIAMS, *supra* note 2, at 42.
26. *Id.* at 43–44.
27. *Id.* at 44.
28. *Id.* at 44–45.

essentially to commit suicide. Curtis Jones, who went on to become a Chicago policeman, recalled that his mother would not let him return to Mississippi to testify for fear of his life. The word was spreading through this southern Black area to keep your mouth shut. Emmett's grandfather, Mose, had not slept at his house since the night Emmett disappeared for fear of the men returning. He received numerous warnings to leave Mississippi before the trial began, but 64-year-old Mose Wright put away his fears and committed himself to testify. No one knew what might happen when Mose took the stand. In a courthouse 20 years earlier, a White man pulled out a pistol and began shooting when a Black boy got up to testify. Michigan Congressman Charles Diggs attended the trial and stated, "it was the first time in the history of Mississippi that a Negro had stood in court and pointed his finger at a white man as a killer of a Negro."[29]

Mose Wright's testimony encouraged others to come forward, including Willie Reed, who said he had seen Emmett in the back of a passing pickup truck. Reed said that there were four White men and two other Black men in the truck. He recognized only Emmett and J. W. Milam. Reed said that the truck backed up to a shed on the plantation, and then he heard desperate cries coming from inside the shed.[30] Reed's aunt, Amanda Bradley, also testified that she too heard the sound of a beating coming from the shed.[31] Reed testified that the three Black men helped the others put something in a tarp into the back of the pickup truck. Emmett's own mother testified that the body was indeed her son. One of the continuing questions has been why it would take six men to intimidate a 14-year-old boy, assuming that "scaring" him was the object of the abduction. Another unanswered question is the identity of the other men Reed saw with Milam and Till.

The trial lasted for 5 days, and the two defendants never took the stand. The jury was gone about 75 minutes. On their return, the judge read their verdict, "Not guilty." Later, the jury foreman stated that the state had failed to prove that the identity of the body was Emmett Till. The reaction to the verdict was evident in the major rallies staged in Chicago, Cleveland, Baltimore, New York, Detroit, Youngstown, and Los Angeles. Even some of the major White dailies compared the events in Mississippi to the Holocaust of Nazi Germany. When a second grand jury refused to indict Bryant and Milam on charges of kidnapping, the fury rose even more.

Emmett Till's murder had a huge impact on young African Americans. This new generation would soon demand freedom and justice as none had done before. In Montgomery, Alabama, the *Montgomery Advisor* ran the Till story. Three months later, the historic boycott of the Montgomery bus system would begin.

MONTGOMERY BUS BOYCOTT AND THE RISE OF MARTIN LUTHER KING, JR.

On December 5, 1955, in Montgomery, Alabama, Black Americans started a year-long boycott of the city buses in protest against segregation, after

---

29. *Id.* at 48. "Actually, Wright's testimony was not literally the first such instance, but it was a rare and courageous act for that time and place." *Id.*
30. *Id.*
31. *Id.*

©AP/Wide World Photos.

Mrs. Rosa Parks, a seamstress who was also active in the NAACP, refused to give up her seat to a White person.[32] She was promptly arrested, tried, convicted, and fined $10. Segregation of public transportation even affected Black Washingtonians, who had to move to the rear once the Capital Transit bus crossed the river into Virginia.[33]

In Montgomery, even though the Black riders accounted for over 75% of all bus passengers, they were frequently requested to surrender their seats to the Whites. The boycott was sparked by the distribution of 35,000 handbills run off by Jo Ann Robinson of the Women's Political Council. She called for a successful 1-day boycott of the buses to support Mrs. Parks.[34] Montgomery's 18 Black-owned taxi companies agreed to transport Blacks for the same fare they would pay on the bus, ten cents.[35]

When the 1-day boycott was successful, E. D. Nixon, local head of the NAACP, and others pushed to have it extended. Some of the boycott organizers were skeptical whether such a boycott would actually be successful because they worried that threats of retaliation from White folks might deter supporters. However, the following day the empty buses roared through the city and side streets as the Black Americans stuck to their boycott. The one-day boycott had turned out to be a success. Now the organizers were faced with the problem of continuing and maintaining it.

Dr. Martin Luther King, Jr., just 26 years old and the newly appointed president of the Montgomery Improvement Association (MIA), preached to the community on the day of the boycott. He outlined MIA's three demands: (1) courteous treatment on the buses; (2) first-come, first-served seating, with Whites in the front and the Blacks in the back; and (3) the hiring of Black drivers on Black bus routes.[36] Days turned into weeks as the boycott continued. On January 30, 1956, both King's and E. D. Nixon's homes were bombed. Meanwhile, Montgomery Whites continued to use the law as a hammer to stop the boycott. Some of the prominent White lawyers in Montgomery suggested that the protest could be stopped by prosecuting the leader of the MIA under an old, seldom-used law prohibiting boycotts. On

---

32. CONGRESSIONAL QUARTERLY SERVICE (1968) at 10.

33. DAVID BRINKLEY, WASHINGTON GOES TO WAR (1988) at 21.

34. WILLIAMS, *supra* note 2, at 67–69.

35. WILLIAMS, *supra* note 2, at 72.

36. *Id.* at 76.

The Woman from Tuskegee, Alabama

On February 4, 1913, Rosa Louise McCauley was born in Tuskegee, Alabama. She was the daughter of a carpenter and a schoolteacher. She was home-schooled by her mother until the age of 11 when she enrolled in the Montgomery Industrial School for Girls, a private school founded by some Northern liberal-minded women.[1] The school's philosophy was consistent with her mama's advice to "take advantage of the opportunities, no matter how few they were."[2]

As a girl, Rosa remembered going to sleep listening to the Ku Klux Klan ride at night and once hearing the sounds of a lynching and wondering if her house would burn down. Later, she attended the Booker T. Washington High School in Montgomery, but had to quit school to care for her sick mother. She married at 19, and with the support of her husband was able to finish high school and get her diploma in 1934.

Rosa Louise and her husband lived in Montgomery, and she worked as a seamstress in a Montgomery department store. When she was 42 years old, she was arrested and convicted of violating a local ordinance. Other than that, she had no run-ins with the law. She and her husband joined the local chapter of the NAACP. She remembered, years later, working on cases involving beatings, rape, and murder, as well as floggings and peonage (forced labor as a result of debt).[3]

In 1957, Rosa Louise, her husband, and her mother moved to Detroit after she lost her job at the department store and could not find other work and her family was threatened and harassed. Rosa Louise found a job in the office of U.S. Representative John Conyers, for whom she worked until she retired. Her husband died in 1977. She continues to live quietly in Detroit at the time of this writing.

The Rest of the Story: Rosa Louise's one run-in with the Montgomery Police Department stemmed from her refusal on December 1, 1955, to give up her seat on the bus. This act of courage led to a 382-day boycott of the Montgomery bus system and a U.S. Supreme Court decision that ended segregated buses in Montgomery.[4] The name of the young minister who headed the Montgomery Improvement Association, a civil rights umbrella group that coordinated the boycott, was Martin Luther King, Jr.; and Rosa's husband's name was Raymond Parks.

---

[1] *Rosa Parks: A Pioneer in Civil Rights.* Accessed at http://www.achievement.org/autodoc/page/par0bio-1?rand=18138 on May 1, 2003.
[2] *Id.*
[3] *Id.*
[4] *Id.*

February 23, the grand jury indicted more than 100 Blacks[37] including King as well as 24 other ministers, for conspiring to boycott. A few days later, the U.S. Supreme Court held that segregation in public transportation violated the equal protection clause of the 14th Amendment and so ended the year-long boycott.[38] The boycott and injunction set the stage for demonstrations in other cities and contributed to the progress of the Black civil rights movement, as well as the rise to national prominence of Martin Luther King, Jr.

King was born in 1929. He graduated from Morehouse College in Atlanta in 1948 with a bachelor's degree and from Crozer Theological Seminary in Chester, Pennsylvania, with a B.D. in 1951. After taking a doctorate in divinity in Boston, King moved to Montgomery to preach at Dexter Avenue Baptist Church in 1954.[39] Martin Luther King, Jr., believed in nonviolent demonstrations as a tool to force negotiations on civil rights issues. Nonviolent direct action seeks to generate a creative tension so that a community that has refused

---

37. RALPH DAVID ABERNATHY, AND THE WALLS CAME TUMBLING DOWN (1989) at 169.
38. *Id.* at 175.
39. *Id.* at 89.

A Baptist Preacher from Rural Georgia

Mike was born on December 19, 1899, to Jim and Linsey King, the eldest of nine children.[1] His parents were sharecroppers near Stockbridge, Georgia.[2] Mike's father was a "troubled" man, "an alcoholic who beat Mike's mother after Saturday-night binges."[3] When his papa abused Mike's mother one awful Saturday night, Mike wrestled him to the floor and finally pinned him down with his arm around his father's neck. The next day, his father apologized and promised never to hurt Mama again, but Mike had had enough of share-cropping and left for Atlanta, walking with only an extra pair of boots slung over his shoulder.[4]

As a member of Floyd Chapel Baptist Church in atlantas, Mike was attracted to the few ministers who risked speaking out against racial injustice. In 1917, at the age of 18, he decided to become a minister. Despite his educational deficiencies, the ministers from his church trained and licensed him.[5] On Thanksgiving Day in 1926, Mike married Alberta Williams, the daughter of a prominent Baptist minister who had started Ebenezer Baptist Church in Atlanta. Together, they had three children, a daughter and two sons.

All his life, Mike worked and preached against racial injustice. Some people thought that Mike was always "straightening out the White folks."[6] He would not ride the city buses and sit in the back, and he would not allow White agents to make col-lections at his house. One day, with his older son riding with him in the family car, Mike was stopped by a white patrolman. He spat out, "Boy, show me your license." Mike relied, "Do you see this child here?" He pointed at his son. "That's a boy there. I'm a man. I'm Reverend King."[7]

When Mike was 68 years old, his oldest son was murdered. The next year, his second son drowned. Then on Sunday, June 30, 1974, Mike's wife of 48 years, Alberta, was shot and killed as she sat at the organ in his church. Ten years later, Mike died of heart disease at a local hospital.

The Rest of the Story: Mike is probably best known because of his older son. In 1934, Mike officially changed both of their names from Michael King to Martin Luther King, Sr. and Jr. His son won the Nobel Peace Prize in 1964 at age 35, the youngest person to be so honored.

---

[1] MLK Papers Project, *King Sr., Martin Luther (1897–1984).* Accessed at http://www.stanford.edu/group/King/about_king/encyclopedia/King_Sr_Martin_Luther_King on April 29, 2003.
[2] *Biographical Outline.* Accessed at http://www.the_kingcenter.com/mlk/bio.html on April 29, 2003.
[3] STEPHEN B. OATES, LET THE TRUMPET SOUND: THE LIFE OF MARTIN LUTHER KING, JR. (1982) at 6.
[4] *Id.*
[5] MLK Papers Project, *supra* note 1.
[6] OATES, *supra* note 3, at 12.
[7] *Id.*

---

to negotiate is forced to confront the issue. It seeks to dramatize the issue so that it can no longer be ignored.[40] His philosophy would later affect the entire civil rights movement. He was a leader of the March on Washington, D.C., in 1963 and was awarded the Nobel Peace Prize in 1964.[41]

PRESIDENTIAL POLITICS—1960S STYLE

By 1960, some White politicians began to wonder whether the older civil rights leaders, those who had sought change through the courts and Congress, might be losing their preeminent status in the movement. Blacks too sensed a power shift.[42] However, both presidential candidates, John F. Kennedy and Richard Nixon, tried to avoid addressing civil rights issues. The issue was seen as a lose/lose proposition. If they were to support segregationists, they

---

40. Martin Luther King, Jr., *Letter From Birmingham Jail* (1963) as reprinted in WILLIAM A. WINES (ED.), READINGS IN BUSINESS ETHICS AND SOCIAL RESPONSIBILITY (rev. ed., 1999) at 25–35.
41. CORETTA SCOTT KING, THE WORDS OF MARTIN LUTHER KING, JR. (1983) at 12.
42. WILLIAMS, *supra* note 2, at 136.

feared they would lose most of the Black votes; however, if they spoke out for civil rights for Blacks, then they would risk losing the backing of the White segregationists who controlled southern politics.

John F. Kennedy had little experience with civil rights issues. In fact, many observers thought that the Republican candidate, Richard Nixon, was more of a supporter of civil rights than the unknown Kennedy. Kennedy had to learn fast about the civil rights issues and concerns if he were going to win the presidential election. He even went to the extreme of supporting and encouraging student sit-ins across America. This represented the first time a presidential candidate addressed a civil rights issue during a campaign.

Martin Luther King, Jr., agreed with this type of demonstration because it was nonviolent. King actually participated in a sit-in, but not as a leader. King had been arrested earlier for driving without a Georgia license, and his arrest at the sit-in turned out to be a violation of his probation.[43] Kennedy, on the recommendation from an aide, made the limited gesture of telephoning Mrs. King to express his sympathy. However, Kennedy's other aides were furious when they heard about the call. They were afraid that this type of action would be damaging to the presidential candidate. However, John Kennedy's younger brother, Robert F. "Bobby" Kennedy, actually called the judge in Atlanta to help expedite King's release. Martin Luther King, Sr., then made the statement, "It's time for all of us to take off our Nixon button."[44]

The Kennedy campaign immediately distributed pamphlets that read, "NO COMMENT NIXON VS. A CANDIDATE WITH A HEART—SEN. KENNEDY: The case of Martin Luther King, Jr." The Gallop Poll showed that Kennedy received 68% of the Black votes in the 1960 election. Blacks had helped elect a president who would advance the civil rights movement.[45] Until this time, the White Democrats had controlled the South as a one-party system that excluded Blacks. Supporting the Democratic candidate was a huge and positive move for the civil rights movement.

However, Kennedy initially introduced no new civil rights legislation and he did not fulfill his campaign promise to wipe out housing discrimination. Kennedy was also reluctant, after his narrow presidential victory, to endorse the civil rights movement because it might hurt him on some of his more important issues.

AUGUST 1963: THE CIVIL RIGHTS MARCH ON WASHINGTON, D.C.

In 1963, the unemployment rate for African Americans was over twice that of White Americans. Martin Luther King, Jr., his staff at the Southern Christian Leadership Conferences, and A. Philip Randolph decided to organize a march on Washington to show America, the president, and Congress that Black Americans were tired of being treated unfairly. Unrest had been building for several years. Black Americans were being brutalized, and some were murdered in the South. There had been bombings, beatings, and several attempts by White Americans to prevent civil rights legislation. Medgar Evers, the NAACP field representative in Mississippi, was murdered in an ambush as he walked

---

43. WILLIAMS (1987) at 142.
44. *Id.* at 143.
45. MIZELL (1992) at 120.

from his car to his front door just after midnight in the early morning hours of June 12, 1963. Meanwhile, President Kennedy had just presented a newer and stronger civil rights bill to Congress.

This time, unlike in 1941, the March on Washington was not canceled. On August 28, 1963, Mr. Randolph, Dr. Martin Luther King, Jr., several speakers from other civil rights groups, and nearly a quarter-million people attended the symbolic march from the Washington Monument to the Lincoln Memorial. No violence marred the day. President Kennedy took the march as support for his pending civil rights bill.

HISTORY OF THE CIVIL RIGHTS ACT OF 1965

In 1962, the Kennedy Administration endorsed two measures: the perennial anti-poll tax proposal and a bill to make anyone with a sixth-grade education eligible to pass a literacy test for voting in federal elections. A Constitutional amendment outlawing the poll tax was approved in 1962, but the literacy test bill died in a filibuster. In the fall of 1962, the Kennedy Administration focused its efforts on executive action in support of voting rights, employment, transportation, and education. In early 1963, Kennedy submitted to Congress another rights package, this also focusing on voting rights, technical assistance to communities that were desegregating schools, and the extension of the Civil Rights Commission. Republicans depicted it as a "thin" package, and it died in committee.

On June 11, 1963, after a confrontation during the day between the Justice Department and Alabama Governor George C. Wallace over admitting Black students to the University of Alabama, President Kennedy addressed the nation on television that night. Taking the strongest stand of any president since Lincoln, he called segregation a "moral crisis" and declared that race had no place in American life or law.[46] On June 19, 1963, President Kennedy submitted a new, stronger, and more extensive civil rights bill Congress.[47] The new proposal included his prior proposals, as well as authority for the federal government to file suit to desegregate public accommodation, to aid school desegregation, and to cut off the flow of federal funds to programs and areas that did not spread their benefits equally between Negroes and Whites. This time, the SCLC, Congress of Racial Equality, Students Nonviolent Coordinating Committee, NAACP, and other were determined not to allow the bill to die in Congress. On August 28, 1963, more than 250,000 people, over 25% of them White, marched on Washington, D.C., in support of President Kennedy's civil rights program.[48]

On November 22, 1963, John F. Kennedy was killed in Dallas, Texas. His successor, President Lyndon Baines Johnson, was determined to push Kennedy's civil rights package through Congress as a memorial to his fallen predecessor. President Johnson signed the Civil Rights Bill of 1964 into law on July 2, 1964, to take effect 1 year later. He also pushed through and then signed the Voting Rights Act of 1965, the most comprehensive voting rights legislation ever to gain Congressional approval.

---

46. WILLIAMS, EYES ON THE PRIZE, *supra* note 2, at 195.
47. WILLIAMS, *supra* note 2, at 195.
48. *Id.* at 195–199.

STUDENT NONVIOLENT COORDINATING COMMITTEE

Black students who attended a meeting held at Shaw University in Raleigh, North Carolina, on Easter weekend, 1960, founded the Student Nonviolent Coordinating Committee (SNCC).[49] With approximately 300 people, both White and Black, SNCC pursued civil rights and desegregation for Blacks. It initiated intensive and dangerous grassroots organizing voter registration projects in several areas in the rural Deep South.

SNCC played a critical role in the Freedom Ride that took place in May 1961. The Freedom Ride was an attempt to promote desegregation of buses and transportation terminals. Two buses left Washington D.C., taking separate routes—one carrying SNCC supporters and the other carrying civil rights leaders—with the hopes of meeting safely in New Orleans. However, the first bus carrying the SNCC supporters was burned by White segregationists in Anniston, Alabama, and the second bus carrying the civil rights leaders was attacked by a mob in Birmingham, Alabama. The hopes of meeting safely in New Orleans went up in flames along with the first bus.

In November of that same year, a federal law was passed mandating the desegregation of public transportation. SNCC, on hearing of the law, attempted to ride buses, in Albany, Georgia, but all who participated were arrested. This proved to many in SNCC that federal laws did not matter to local law enforcement. SNCC continued to face the ever-present shadow of White violence. The continual beatings, frequent jailings, and even occasional murders became almost an everyday fact of life. Going to jail was scary because some SNCC members who were jailed were never heard from again.[50]

VIETNAM: SNCC COMES OUT AGAINST U.S. POLICY

Before the escalation of the Vietnam War in early 1965, SNCC was not concerned much with U.S. foreign policy. However, after the rapid escalation of the war, the students quickly began to see themselves as one of the many victims of U.S. power all over the world. Howard Zinn, a SNCC adviser, had this to say in 1965:

> Events in Vietnam became easier to understand in the light of recent experience in the South. . . . Just as the white South finds it hard

---

49. WILLIAMS, *supra* note 2, at 136–137.

50. The summer of 1964 was designated "Freedom Summer," a project organized under the banner of an umbrella civil rights group called the Council of Federated Organizations (COFO). Its goals included voter registration, freedom schools, and the establishment of a Freedom Democratic Party to challenge the Mississippi State democrats who were rabid segregationists for seats at the Democratic National Convention. On Sunday, June 21, 1964, three civil rights workers engaged in Freedom Summer (two from CORE and one from SNCC) were reported missing after they were arrested near the town of Philadelphia, Mississippi. They were Michael Schwerner, 24 years old from Brooklyn, New York; Andrew Goodman, a 20-year-old Queens College (NY) student; and James Chaney, a 21-year-old Black Mississippian who worked for CORE. Their bodies were found buried in an earthen dam on a farm near Philadelphia on August 4, 1964. Twenty-one White Mississippians, including the deputy sheriff who arrested them for speeding, were charged in state court; eventually all the charges were dropped. Six of the group later were convicted and served time for federal civil rights violations. See WILLIAMS, *supra* note 2, at 226–235. *See also* SETH CAGIN & PHILIP DRAY, WE ARE NOT AFRAID: THE STORY OF GOODMAN, SCHWERNER AND CHANEY AND THE CIVIL RIGHTS CAMPAIGN FOR MISSISSIPPI (Bantam ed. 1989) for an authoritative and very thorough account of the murders. For recent prosecutions, *see* note 114 *infra*.

to believe that Southern Negroes are genuinely dissatisfied, and so attributes the Negro revolt to "outsiders," the U.S. finds it hard to believe that the Vietnamese peasant really is in revolt against the old way of life, and so blames the rebellion on "outsiders" from the Communist nations. . . . in both cases there is a home-made uprising against an oppressive system. . . . In both situations there is the use of special words that arouse hatred and distort reality . . . "nigger" [and] "Communist." The word is a blanket which smothers the true complexity of the world and the individuality of human beings.[51]

In an abstract way, SNCC members identified with the poor, non-White people of Vietnam in their struggle against White Americans who showed little respect for their lives (the bombing of civilians seemed compatible with the lack of punishment given to murderers of Negroes) and their social order (the destruction of village life through "pacification" seemed compatible with the destruction of African slave culture.[52]

SOUTHERN CHRISTIAN LEADERSHIP CONFERENCE

The Southern Christian Leadership Conference (SCLC) was a southern Black ministerial association striving for many of the same civil rights goals as the SNCC. Martin Luther King, Jr., as president of the SCLC, was a dominant force in the organization. SCLC held training workshops for SNCC members and helped SNCC financially. Some in the SCLC hoped that SNCC would become a student wing, but this never happened. SNCC was made up of younger college students who enjoyed freedom from adult domination; its members resisted guidance, much less any control, from the SCLC, an organization made up of adults, most of whom were old enough to be their fathers. The fact that the SNCC had no adult direction was a quality many found attractive on choosing to join the organization.

The SCLC sought nonviolent reconciliation as part of its religious vision, whereas SNCC was willing to sacrifice reconciliation and dispense with religious visions. This conflict of belief was an important reason why the two organizations did not join together. SNCC resented older adult authority, which they felt included Dr. King, thereby causing additional conflict. Furthermore, the SNCC felt that the SCLC was frequently butting in where it did not belong. SNCC strived to solve its own problems, even if it took months or years. King would then arrive with the SCLC, causing the SNCC to feel as though its territory was being invaded and that the SCLC was reinforcing in community members a tendency to wait for older leaders to solve their problems. SNCC would begin protest movements and contribute most of the blood, sweat, and tears in starting the movement; then Dr. King and the SCLC would show up to finish the protest, receive most of the credit, and get most of the national recognition. Yet, SNCC had an easy time gathering protestors and marchers when Martin Luther King, Jr., was present, but SNCC organizing was much more difficult when Dr. King was not available. This fact of life further frustrated SNCC leadership.

---

51. Howard Zinn, excerpt from a public speech to an antiwar teach-in, Boston Commons, Boston, MA (June 15, 1965).
52. EMILY STOPER, THE STUDENT NONVIOLENT COORDINATING COMMITTEE: THE GROWTH OF RADICALISM IN A CIVIL RIGHTS ORGANIZATION (1989).

Robert M. Shelton (1929–2003)

Robert M. Shelton, aged 73, died of a heart attack on Monday, March 17, 2003, at the DCH Regional Medical Center in Tuscaloosa, Alabama. Shelton had been the long-time head of a powerful Ku Klux Klan (KKK) faction, the United Klans of America. Under his leadership, the Klan "spread violence and terror across Alabama in the 1960's and 1970's."[1] Shelton was survived by his wife Betty Lou, a son, and a daughter.

Shelton was born in Tuscaloosa, the son of a grocer who was also a KKK member. After a brief stint at the state university, Shelton dropped out and joined the U.S. Air Force in 1947. He was stationed in Germany where "he was outraged at the spectacle of black servicemen dating white women."[2] Once out of the service, Shelton went back to Tuscaloosa, got a job at the B.F. Goodrich plant, and joined the Klan.[3] He rose through its ranks until a conflict with the Grand Dragon caused him to defect and organize his own Alabama Knights.[4]

In 1958, Shelton threw his support behind an Alabama gubernatorial candidate, John Patterson. According to the Klan's history of that time, a grateful Patterson helped B.F. Goodrich land a $1.6 million contract with the state, and Shelton was promoted to a traveling sales job that "covered the South."[5] However, he was fired in 1961 for devoting too much time to the Klan.[6] In May 1961, Shelton was one of four Klan leaders personally named in Judge Frank Johnson's injunction restraining them from inciting or participating in violent interference with the Freedom Rides. Two months later, Shelton merged his Alabama Knights with the Georgia Klansmen led by Calvin Craig and the Carolina Units under Robert Scoggin, creating the United Klans of America.[7]

The United Klans of America (UKA) and its members were linked to numerous racial hate crimes over the years. Two of its highest-profile acts were the 1963 bombing of the Sixteenth Street Baptist Church in Birmingham that killed four Black girls[8] and the 1965 murder of Viola Liuzzo of Detroit, a White civil rights worker, during the 1965 Selma-to-Montgomery voting rights march in Alabama.[9] "Meanwhile, "the high-profile Mr. Shelton—a small, thin man who wore a gold Klan ring with a tear-shaped blood drop on its stone—stumped the South in a large black Cadillac and appeared at Klan rallies and meetings variously attired in a purple satin robe or a business suit."[10]

Shelton appeared at a Klan rally on the night that Dr. King announced the historic 1963 settlement that integrated department stores in Birmingham, Alabama. On camera, Shelton declared that "Martin Luther King's epitaph, in my opinion, can be written here in Birmingham."[11] A few hours later, a bomb ripped through the walls of the room at the Gaston Motel where King had been staying. No one was hurt because Dr. King and his staff had left for Atlanta before the blast.[12]

In 1966, Shelton was sentenced to the maximum 1 year in jail and fined $1,000 for contempt of Congress after being convicted by a federal grand jury of refusing to deliver subpoenaed Klan membership lists to a subcommittee of the House Committee on Un-American Activities.[13] He served 9 months at a federal prison in Texas. On his release in January 1970, he declared, "'We're going to kick the enemies of White people from one end of the country to the other.'"[14]

In 1979, 13 UKA members were convicted of or pleaded guilty to various acts of violence in Alabama, including firing into the homes of officers of the NAACP. In 1987, a federal jury awarded $7 million in damages to Beaulah Mae Donald, the mother of a Black teenager who had been beaten to death by two UKA members.[15] The body of her son Michael was found hanging from a tree in Mobile, Alabama in 1981.[16] Lead counsel for the plaintiff was Morris Dees, founder of the Southern Poverty Law Center in Montgomery.[17] A few weeks after the trial, the United Klans of America surrendered its headquarters building to Mrs. Donald without a fight.[18]

Virginia v. Black 123 S. Ct. 1536 (April 7, 2003) involved the constitutionality of a Virginia criminal statute that proscribed cross-burning with an intent to discriminate. A badly fragmented court affirmed in part, vacated in part, and remanded three convictions. In dissent, Justice Clarence Thomas quoted with approval the following passage: The world's oldest, most persistent terrorist organization is not European or even Middle Eastern in origin. Fifty years before the Irish Republican Army was organized, a century before Al Fatah declared its holy war on Israel, the Ku Klux Klan was actively harassing, torturing, and murdering in the United States. Today . . . its members remain fanatically committed to a course of violent opposition to social progress and racial equality in the United States.[19]

[1] *Robert M. Shelton Dead in Alabama* (AP). Accessed at http://www.miami.com/mld/miamiherald/news/local/5432716.htm on May 1, 2003.
[2] *Welcome to the Mystic Knights of the KKK Cyber Museum.* Accessed at http://www.mysticknights.org/Museum.htm on May 1, 2003.
[3] *Id.*
[4] *Id.*
[5] *Id.*
[6] *Id.*
[7] *Id.*
[8] On September 15, 1963, just 18 days after the March on Washington, someone threw dynamite into the Baptist Church where children were attending a Bible school class. Denise McNair, age 11, and Cynthia Wesley, Carole Robertson, and Addie Mae Collins, all age 14, were killed. JUAN WILLIAMS, EYES ON THE PRIZE (1987) at 202.
[9] Dennis McLellan (LA Times), *Robert Shelton, 73, who Once Headed United Klans Group,* THE SEATTLE TIMES

obituaries. Accessed at http://seattletimes.nwsource.com/html/obituaries/134660009_sheltonobit23.html on May 1, 2003.
[10] *Id.*
[11] JUAN WILLIAMS, EYES ON THE PRIZE: AMERICA'S CIVIL RIGHTS YEARS, 1954–1965 (1987) at 193–94.
[12] *Id.* at 194.
[13] Dennis McLellan, *supra* note 8.
[14] *Id.*
[15] *Id.*
[16] *Id.*
[17] BILL STANTON, KLANWATCH: BRINGING THE KU KLUX KLAN TO JUSTICE (1991) at 201–248.
[18] *Id.* at 247.
[19] *Virginia v. Black* 123 S. Ct. 1536, 2003 U.S. LEXIS 2715 (2003) at p.12. Accessed at http://web.lexis-nexis.com/universe/document?_m=47be239de488541c8594708f544c1bf8& on May 1, 2003, quoting M. NEWTON & J. NEWTON, THE KU KLUX KLAN: AN ENCYCLOPEDIA (1991) at vii.

Stokely Carmichael,[53] one of the dominant leaders of SNCC, became more and more inclined to suggest that at some point, perhaps in the near future, Blacks would have to abandon nonviolence and fight back against White oppression with all available weapons.[54]

SOME ALTERNATIVES TO NONVIOLENCE

1. Malcolm X and the Nation of Islam. Malcolm Little was born in 1925 in Omaha, Nebraska.[55] His father, Earl Little, a Baptist pastor from Georgia, was run over by a street car—some say murdered by White supremacists—when Malcolm was six years old.[56] His mother, Louise Little, was declared legally insane when Malcolm was 13 years old. Malcolm dropped out of school[57] and took to the streets of Boston. Known as "Boston Red," Malcolm lived (before and after flunking his draft physical for WWII) on his street smarts—running numbers, selling dope, selling bootleg whiskey, and stealing. He also worked as an entertainer in bars, waited tables, tended bar, and worked for the New Haven Railroad.[58]

In 1946, Malcolm was sentenced to 8 to 10 years in prison for burglary in Massachusetts. At the urging of his brother Reginald, Malcolm (sometime in 1948) became acquainted with the teachings of the Nation of Islam led by the Honorable Elijah Mohammed. Malcolm was released from prison on August 7,

---

53. Stokely Carmichael (1941–1998) joined SNCC while he was attending Howard University. He was arrested for participating in CORE's Freedom Rides and was jailed. In 1966, after the sniper shooting of James Meredith, Carmichael continued Meredith's March Against Fear With Martin Luther King, Jr., Floyd McKissick, and others. Arrested on that march, he gave his famous "Black Power" speech on his release. In 1967, Carmichael joined the Black Panther Party where he quarreled with the leadership. In 1969, he moved with his then wife, Mariam Makeba, to Guinea, West Africa, where he lived until his death at 57 from cancer. *Stokely Carmichael,* found at http://en.wikipedia.org/wiki/Stokely_Carmichael (last visited on May 4, 2005).
54. RALPH DAVID ABERNATHY, AND THE WALLS CAME TUMBLING DOWN (1989) at 301.
55. THE WORLD BOOK ENCYCLOPEDIA (1990), vol. 13 at 103.
56. *A Chronology of the Life and Activities of Malcolm X,* found at http://www.brothermalcolm.net/mxtimeline.html (last visited on April 30, 2005).
57. In the spring of 1939, Malcolm told his favorite teacher about his desire to become a lawyer. He was told, "That's no realistic goal for a nigger." *Id.*
58. *Id.*

1952, after serving about 6.5 years. After being paroled from the Massachusetts State Prison, Malcolm traveled to Detroit and took a job working as a furniture salesman in a store managed by his brother Wilfred. In January 1953, the FBI opened a surveillance file on him.[59]

Malcolm dropped his last name of Little, a slave name, and took the letter X to indicate the loss of all African family and tribal identity. He moved to Chicago in spring of 1953 and studied for the ministry with Elijah Mohammed.[60] In June 1953, Malcolm X was named assistant minister of the Detroit Temple No. 1. Three months later, Malcolm X was named first minister of Boston Temple No. 11. Over the next 10 years or so, Malcolm X represented the Nation of Islam and Elijah Mohammed in progressively more important and visible assignments including traveling as Elijah's emissary to the heads of state in the Arab world.[61]

Between December 1962, when Malcolm confirmed rumors of Elijah Mohammed's multiple adulteries with various young secretaries at NOI offices and December of 1963 when Elijah suspended Malcolm X's ministry and ordered him silenced for commenting on President Kennedy's assassination, the rift between the two men grew quite serious. By the end of 1963, Malcolm X had organized the Afro-American Unity-Muslim Mosque, Inc., which he served as chairman and director of until his death.[62]

In April 1964, Malcolm took the name "Malik El-Shabazz" and left on a life-changing trip to Mecca by way of Germany. In a letter about his pilgrimage to Mecca, Malcolm wrote that he met many White people who displayed a spirit of unity and brotherhood; that he now had new and positive insights into race relations; and that in true Islam lay the power to overcome racial hatred and to obliterate it from the heart of White America.[63]

The FBI sought to bribe Malcolm to reveal what he knew about Elijah Mohammed's infidelities, but Malcolm refused.[64] In early 1963, Malcolm first met with Alex Haley to plan his autobiography[65]—although Malcolm retained the right to approve every word and every deletion.[66] He also worried about the FBI "bugging" his conversations with Haley.[67] Malcolm was convinced he would not live to read the finished book.[68]

On February 21, 1965, just after 3 p.m. when Malcolm had begun to address a rally of the Organization of Afro-American Unity at the Audubon Ballroom in NYC, a disturbance broke out; security rushed to quell the disturbance.[69] Three black men rushed forward and shot Malcolm to

---

59. *Id.*
60. *Id.*
61. *Id.*
62. *Id.*
63. *Id.*
64. ALEX HALEY, THE AUTOBIOGRAPHY OF MALCOLM X (1965) at 397.
65. *Id.* at 385.
66. *Id.* at 387.
67. *Id.* at 388.
68. *Id.* at 378 and 381 and frontispiece.
69. One source describes the scene at the Audubon ballroom in Manhattan in these terms, "A man yelled, 'Get your hand outta my pocket! Don't be messin' with my pockets!' As Malcolm's bodyguards rushed forward to attend to the disturbance, a black man rushed forward and shot Malcolm in the chest with a sawed-off shotgun. Two other men quickly charged towards the stage and fired handguns at Malcolm." *Malcolm X: Biography and Much More From Answers.com* found at http://answers.com/topic/malcolm-x (last visited on May 3, 2005). Three men, Talmadge Hayer, Norman 3X Butler, and Thomas 15X Johnson, were convicted of first-degree murder in March 1966. Some independent investigators have accused current Nation of Islam

death.[70] On November 5, 1965, the New York Times heralded the publication of *The Autobiography of Malcolm X*, and Betty Shabazz gave birth to twin daughters.[71]

2. Huey P. Newton, Bobby Seale, and the Black Panthers. The Black Panther Party for Self Defense, a radical political organization, was founded in 1966 by Huey P. Newton and Bobby Seale.[72] A chief goal of the group was to protect the Black community from police actions that many Blacks considered brutality. In time, the Panthers dropped the "self-defense" label. The organization shifted into more of a Marxist-Communist mode that favored violent revolution.[73]

During the mid-1960s, the Black Panthers called for neighborhood control of such services as education and the police. They supported the use of guns—both for self defense and for retaliating against those they believed oppressed the poor.[74] During the late 1960s, the Black Panthers began to work with White radical and revolutionary groups that shared their goals. This brought about conflict with some Black groups who saw the struggle of Black people as chiefly a racial issue.[75] According to the Panthers, the basic problem was economic exploitation of both Blacks and Whites by profit-seeking capitalists. The Black Panthers called for fairer distribution of jobs and other economic resources.

In May 1967, 30 armed Black Panthers marched on the California State capital in protest of the state's attempt to outlaw carrying loaded weapons in public. Bobby Seale read a statement of protest, and the police responded by arresting all 30 Panthers.[76] On April 6, 1968, Bobby Hutton, 17-year-old Black Panther Treasurer and one of the six original Panthers, ran unarmed from his blazing house and was shot dead—10 rounds from the Oakland P.D.[77] On December 4, 1969, Fred Hampton, deputy chairman of the Illinois chapter of the Black Panthers, was shot to death in an early morning raid of his apartment where he was asleep.[78] Hampton, wounded in the shoulder, was dragged into the hallway where he was shot twice in the head at point-blank range.[79] The raid was conducted by an elite tactical unit of the Cook County State's Attorney's Office (SAO), facilitated by the Chicago Police Department and the FBI.[80]

---

leader Louis Farrakhan of having planned the assassination. Farrakhan has denied it. Hayer himself later named an additional four accomplices. *Id.* Unsubstantiated rumors continue to circulate about FBI involvement. *See, e.g., Malcolm X—An Islamic Perspective* as found at http://www.colostate.edu/Orgs/MSA/find_more/m_x.html (last visited on May 3, 2005).

70. *A Chronology of the Life…, supra* note 2.

71. *Id.*

72. THE WORLD BOOK ENCYCLOPEDIA (1990), vol. 2 at 406.

73. *Id.*

74. *Id.*

75. *Id.*

76. *Black Panther Party* found at http://www.marxists.org/history/usa/workers/black-panthers/ (last visited on May 3, 2005).

77. *Id.*

78. *Fred Hampton: Information From Answers.com* found at http://www.answers.com/topic/ fred-hampton (last visited on May 3, 2005). For a detailed and controversial look at the FBI's involvement in the nation's struggles with the Black Panthers and American Indian Movement (AIM), *see* WARD CHURCHILL AND JIM VANDER WALL, AGENTS OF REPRESSION: THE FBI'S SECRET WARS AGAINST THE BLACK PANTHER PARTY AND THE AMERICAN INDIAN MOVEMENT (Corrected ed. 1990).

79. *Id.*

80. *Id.* "A hasty internal investigation was undertaken, exonerating the assault team." *Id.*

In 1973, Seale ran for mayor of Oakland, California. Although he lost, Bobby Seale won over a third of the votes.[81] This campaign signaled a turn to more traditional measures for achieving Panther ends, at least for Bobby Seale, who resigned from the Party in 1974. By the mid-1970s, the Black Panther Party had ceased to exist.[82] Bobby Seale was still alive (at this writing) and had his own website featuring his books, including *Barbeque'n with Bobby*.[83] The stories of the rest of the leading Black Panthers are not nearly as peaceful.

Former Information Minister Eldridge Cleaver died in Pomona, California, in 1998 after living in exile from 1968 to 1975, renouncing the Black Panthers, embracing fundamentalist Christianity, and battling a cocaine addiction in his later years.[84] Co-founder and first Defense Minister Huey P. Newton, after being convicted of embezzling funds [to support his drug and alcohol addictions] from a school run by Black Panthers, was gunned down on the streets of Oakland by a drug dealer on August 22, 1989.[85] H. Rap Brown (b. 1943), former justice minister of the Black Panther Party, was convicted in 2002 of murdering a Fulton County sheriff's deputy in 2000 and is now serving a sentence of life without parole plus 35 years.[86]

3. The American Indian Movement (AIM). The American Indian Movement is a civil rights movement that works in the United States and Canada seeking to improve living conditions for American Indians.[87] It was founded in Minneapolis in 1968 by Dennis Banks, George Mitchell, and Clyde Bellecourt.[88] The original goal of AIM was to improve the lives of urban Indians in the Twin Cities and to protect them from police brutality. By 1970, the goals had expanded. On January 2, 1970, Dennis Banks called Russell Means, then a director of the Cleveland American Indian Center, and asked him to help AIM confront the National Council of Churches at its meeting in Detroit.[89]

In 1972, AIM members occupied the headquarters of the Bureau of Indian Affairs in Washington, D.C., for 7 days.[90] The following year, AIM members and other Indians seized the village of Wounded Knee, South Dakota where the U.S. Cavalry had massacred more than 200 unarmed Sioux Indians (mostly women, children, and old men) in 1890.[91] In retaliation for the occupation, the administration of President Nixon began an armed siege of Wounded Knee. As a result of that conflict, on June 26, 1975, two FBI agents were killed and one of the American Indians, Joseph Stuntz, was murdered by an FBI sniper. Three AIM members were tried for the deaths of the FBI agents;

---

81. THE WORLD BOOK ENCYCLOPEDIA (1990), vol. 2 at 406.

82. *Id.*

83. See http://www.bobbyseale.com/mainindex.htm (last visited on May 3, 2005).

84. *Eldridge Cleaver* found at http://en.wikipedia.org/wiki/Eldridge_Cleaver (last visited on May 2, 2005).

85. *Huey P. Newton (1942–1989)* found at http://www.africawithin.com/bios/huey_newton.htm (last visited on May 2, 2005).

86. *Life for 60s Radical H. Rap Brown* found at http://www.cbsnews.com/stories/2002/03/13/national/printable503687.shtml (last visited on May 3, 2005).

87. THE WORLD BOOK ENCYCLOPEDIA (1990), vol. 1 at 411.

88. *Id.* at 412.

89. RUSSELL MEANS, WHERE WHITE MEN FEAR TO TREAD: THE AUTOBIOGRAPHY OF RUSSELL MEANS (1995) at 149.

90. *Id.*

91. For a detailed history of the 1890 massacre and for its spiritual significance for the Sioux Nation, *see* DEE BROWN, BURY MY HEART AT WOUNDED KNEE: AN INDIAN HISTORY OF THE AMERICAN WEST (1970) at 300–313 [1877 murder of Crazy Horse] and 440–445 [1890 Massacre of Big Foot and his band of Minneconjou Sioux].

only Leonard Peltier was convicted. No one was ever tried for the death of Joe Stuntz, a 19-year-old AIM member. Allegedly, over 60 AIM supporters or members were murdered during the so-called "reign of terror" on the Pine Ridge Reservation,[92] a period that lasted approximately 2 years in the mid-1970s, while Richard "Dick" Wilson was President of the Ogallala Sioux tribe at Pine Ridge.[93]

Many of the "facts" about what happened on the Pine Ridge Reservation including the trial and appeals of Leonard Peltier are contested down to the present,[94] and the continued incarceration of Peltier after 27 years is a matter that has raised international civil rights concerns.[95] Dennis Banks, Clyde Bellecourt, and Russell Means were alive at this time of this writing, and both Banks and Means had "home pages" on the World Wide Web from which they peddled various goods. Clyde H. Bellecourt apparently was providing leadership and direction for the American Indian Movement.[96]

SPLIT AT SELMA AND THE EDMUND PETTUS BRIDGE

Selma is a small city located in Alabama. It was the site of movement activity by SNCC, which had started in February 1963 to promote voter education and registration for Blacks. In January 1965, after a state court injunction banning any activity by civil rights groups was lifted, SCLC began a voter registration drive in Selma. This once again caused some friction between the SNCC and SCLC.

---

92. *See*, e.g., Russell Means' account in *Id.* at 304 for a summary. Means declared that "While Wilson reigned, Pine Ridge became the world's homicide capital… Sixty-nine AIM people were killed, and more than 350 others were shot, stabbed, stomped, burned by arson fires, beaten with tire irons or baseball bats, or seriously injured when their cars were run off the road." *Id.* Other sources list similar numbers.

93. The election in February 1974 was hotly contested. *See Means v. Wilson*, 383 F. Supp. 378 (D.S.D. 1974), 522 F.2d 833 (8th Cir. 1975). Russell Means never abandoned his claim that Dick Wilson stole the election by stuffing ballot boxes. By the time, Means got his appeal upheld by the 8th Circuit; the election was moot because a new one had been held. MEANS, WHERE WHITE MEN FEAR TO TREAD, *supra*, note 35, at 206–207, and 304–305.

94. For example, there is a website for No Parole Peltier Association (NPPA). *See* http://www.noparolepeltier.com/response.html (last visited on May 3, 2005). The NPPA describes itself as "made up of those who have a personal connection to the vicious death [sic] of two FBI Special Agents. Secondly, men and women who carry a badge and gun and are willing to place their lives on the line to protect the safety and rights of every citizen, the families of those who have made the ultimate sacrifice in the line of duty, Parents of Murdered Children, those who believe in justice, and, finally, concerned people who are willing to consider all sides of an issue." *Id.* This website appeared to have been last updated sometime in 2001. It listed for an address P.O. Box 54667 in Cincinnati, Ohio 45254-0667—a hotbed for Conservative Republicans, not terribly close to any Indian Country. The Leonard Peltier Defense Committee also gave a P.O. Box for an address in Lawrence, Kansas: P.O. Box 583, Lawrence, KS 66044, as well as a telephone and FAX number. Its website appeared to have been updated in 2004. See http://www.freepeltier.org/story.htm (last visited on May 4, 2005).

95. Amnesty International considers Leonard Peltier to be a political prisoner and supports his immediate and unconditional release (April 6, 1999, statement). Archbishop Desmond Tutu supports the campaign to have Leonard Peltier (April 18, 1999, statement). "The Case of Leonard Peltier: Statement of Fact" by attorney Jennifer Harbury found at http://www.freepeltier.org/peltier_faq.htm (last visited on May 4, 2005).

96. Laura Waterman Wittstock and Elaine J. Salinas, *A Brief History of the American Indian Movement*, accessed at http://www.aimovement.org/ggc/history.html (last visited on May 3, 2005).

SCLC decided to sponsor a march from Selma to the state capital of Montgomery to demand voting rights for Black people. SNCC was suspicious of Dr. King's motives and refused to participate as an organization, but allowed members to participate as individuals. Approximately 500 to 600 Black people began the march on what would be known as "Bloody Sunday," March 7, 1965, without the participation of Dr. King because of the fear of violence and his possible assassination. The head of the march had reached the crest of the Edmund Pettus Bridge when the Alabama State Troopers and some posse members led by Sheriff James Clark rushed the group. Onlookers said the troopers looked as though they swept over the top of the marchers, instead of meeting them head on.

The troopers and posse used whips, clubs, horses, and tear gas to push the marchers back across the bridge. Many Blacks suffered broken bones and multiple bruises, but fortunately no one was killed. People could not believe how violently the marchers were treated when they were demonstrating peacefully for voting rights for Blacks. Martin Luther King, Jr., issued a statement that evening:

> I am shocked at the terrible reign of terror that took place in Alabama today. Negro citizens engaged in a peaceful and orderly march to protest racial injustice were beaten, brutalized and harassed by state troopers, and Alabama revealed its law enforcement agents have no respect for democracy nor the rights of its Negro citizens.... When I made a last-minute agreement not to lead the march and appointed my able and courageous associate, Hosea Williams, for this responsibility, I must confess that I had no idea that the kind of brutality and tragic expression of man's inhumanity to man as existed today would take place. Alabama's state troopers, under the sanction and authorization of Governor Wallace, allowed themselves to degenerate to the lowest state of barbarity.... We will go into federal court immediately to seek to restrain Governor Wallace and his state troopers from the unconstitutional and unjust attempt to block Negro citizens in their quest for the right to vote.[97]

King also announced in this statement that he and Reverend Ralph David Abernathy would lead a march the following Tuesday (March 9, 1965) "in an attempt to arouse a deeper concern of this nation over the ills that are perpetrated against Negro citizens in Alabama."[98]

The second march began in Selma and continued to the same spot on the Edmond Pettus Bridge where the previous march had come to a violent end. Dr. King led the marchers to the bridge and back without violence. SNCC was angry with King because some of the SNCC members suspected that he had cut a secret deal with Sheriff Clark to allow him to march without violence. If this were true, they reasoned, then why did he not do this for the first set of marchers? In fact, King had cut a deal with the U.S. Justice Department representatives in the early hours of Tuesday morning to get protection for the length of the march and also so as to not violate an injunction issued by Federal District Judge Frank Johnson.[99]

---

97. *Id.* at 334.
98. RALPH DAVID ABERNATHY, AND THE WALLS CAME TUMBLING DOWN (1989) at 334.
99. *Id.* at 336–343. The move enraged John Lewis and the leaders of SNCC. As Abernathy recalled, "Once again, the very philosophy of nonviolence was on trial in Selma. Lewis and

The leaders of the SCLC were not interested in provoking a split with the SNCC, despite all their disagreements. The rift between SCLC and SNCC had begun years before and had widened over time. One can almost hear a pained Martin Luther King, Jr., saying something like "SNCC is like a younger brother, you love 'em and you work with 'em but they sure can be a pain in the neck."[100]

KING'S RELATIONS WITH PRESIDENT LYNDON B. JOHNSON

King became impressed with President Johnson when the president issued this February 1965 statement concerning the voting-rights campaign in Selma, Alabama.

> All Americans should be indignant when one American is denied the right to vote. The loss of that right to a single citizen undermines the freedom of every citizen. This is why all of us should be concerned with the efforts of our fellow Americans to register to vote in Alabama. The basic problem in Selma is the slow pace of voter registration for Negroes who are qualified to vote.... I hope that all Americans will join me in expressing their concern over the loss of any Americans right to vote.... I intend to see that that right is secured for all our citizens.[101]

President Johnson provided strong support at a time when his popularity among the SCLC membership had not yet taken the downturn it would as a result of the Vietnam War.[102]

President Johnson used tragic episodes and public sentiment to introduce his tough voting rights act and to press Congress to pass it. Some episodes that he cited included the following:

- February 26, 1965—A young Selma Black (Jimmie Lee Jackson, aged 26) was shot and clubbed to death after protesting voter registration policy.
- March 7, 1965—Alabama state troopers used tear gas, clubs, and whips to halt a march from Selma to the state capital of Montgomery ("Bloody Sunday").
- March 9, 1965—A White Unitarian minister (James Reeb, aged 38) from Boston was clubbed during the march and died 2 days later.[103]

Dr. King, who had been moved to tears by LBJ's nationally televised speech on March 15th urging support of his voting rights bill, was even more impressed with President Johnson's announcement in June that the next, more profound goal in the civil rights struggle was "not just legal equity but human

---

the other members of the SNCC, though theoretically committed to nonviolence, were moving ever closer to fighting back." *Id.* at 343.

100. DAVID J. GARROW, BEARING THE CROSS: MARTIN LUTHER KING, JR. AND THE SOUTHERN LEADERSHIP CONFERENCE (Vintage ed. 1988) at 132–134, 166–167, 409–410, and 423–424.

101. Public Statement of President Johnson on Selma, Alabama Protests, Feb. 4, 1965, at White House Press Conference as quoted in RALPH DAVID ABERNATHY, AND THE WALLS CAME TUMBLING DOWN (1989) at 321.

102. ABERNATHY, *supra* note 298, at 321–322.

103. JOSEPH A. CALIFANO, JR., THE TRIIUMPH & TRAGEDY OF LYNDON JOHNSON: THE WHITE HOUSE YEARS (1991) at 55–56.

equity—not just equality as a right and a theory but equality as a fact and a result."[104] King sent a telegram to Johnson saying how impressed he was, and this gesture aided their public friendship. King was then provided direct phone access to President Johnson.

King became increasingly concerned about America's involvement in Vietnam after August 1965, and he knew, as all of us did at the time, that President Johnson was behind it. Dr. King began to become wary of his so-called friendship with President Johnson. Each of the men had a very different view on Vietnam, and Dr. King was being pressured by his young associates as well as his own conscience to come out against the war. Johnson sent waves of U.S. warplanes over North Vietnam in bombing attacks called Operation Rolling Thunder. He then sent combat troops into South Vietnam. President Johnson thought his enemies would call him a coward, unmanly, and a weakling if he did not take decisive action in Vietnam. King worried that he would lose an important ally if he were to come out publicly against the war.

Yet, Dr. King could not stand to see brown-skinned people being treating this way, and he took the war as a setback in his movement for civil rights. He considered the civil rights movement to be for all brown-skinned people and not only for Black people. King vowed not to sit by and watch the war escalate without saying anything. He said he could not be silent and would never again be silent.

Ultimately, Dr. King spoke out at a rally in New York City in April 1967. The rally attracted between 100,000 and 400,000 people. During his speech King said, "I could never again raise my voice against the violence of the oppressed in the ghettos without having first spoken clearly to the greatest purveyor of violence in the world today—my own government."[105] King also spoke openly at a press conference that was carried on national television about his feelings on Vietnam.[106] These public declarations made President Johnson upset with King; the president demanded to know who in the hell King thought he was and began a behind-the-scenes movement to shut King up.

Some believe President Johnson had had enough of King and his speaking out against Vietnam. They felt that he simply wrote King off, refused to speak to him, and no longer welcomed him to the White House. Others argue that President Johnson continued to invite King to White House events and that it was King who refused to associate with Johnson.

J. EDGAR HOOVER AND THE FBI'S BAG OF DIRTY TRICKS

Jim Harrison was working at the SCLC Atlanta headquarters in a low-visibility finance office. Two FBI agents arranged to meet with him about becoming the informant the FBI needed. The FBI needed someone on the inside of the SCLC who would not be obvious, and Harrison was the perfect insider for the job. He was a young Black man, he held an important position in the SCLC, and he was quiet, keeping to himself. Harrison accepted the offer in less than a week's time and began informing the FBI almost immediately; he received payments for his duties. However, the phone tapings of King had begun in the

---

104. President Lyndon B. Johnson, *To Fulfil These Rights*, Commencement Address at Howard University on June 4, 1963.

105. LLOYD C. GARDNER, PAY ANY PRICE: LYNDON JOHNSON AND THE WARS FOR VIETNAM (1995) at 359.

106. DAVID GARROW, *supra* note 100, at 552–553.

1950s because of J. Edgar Hoover's fears that the Black civil rights movement might be a communist front.

The previous August, in 1963, Dr. King was staying at the Willard Hotel in Washington, D.C., after leading the march on Washington. King was unaware of the many microphones hidden in the lampshades, walls, and telephones of his suite.[107] Martin King's celebration at the Willard Hotel included friends of both sexes and became known in the FBI as "the two-day orgy."

Hoover prided himself on the knowledge that this tape plus other surveillance information proved King was a philanderer who committed adultery with White and Black women.[108] Hoover was known to be obsessed with the sexual behavior of those in the public eye. He was a racist and a confirmed bachelor who often dined alone with his lieutenant, Clyde Tolson. He was rumored to be a closet homosexual, but those rumors were vigorously denied by both Hoover and Tolson.[109]

Hoover distributed copies of the tapes from the Willard Hotel to reporters, law officials, and those in positions who could hurt King. Someone in the FBI put together a tape of highly intimate moments and sent it to King's office. Unfortunately, King's wife, Coretta Scott King, received the tape first. Hoover had hoped to destroy King's marriage, but this ploy did not work. Coretta rose above the pain and continued to stand beside and support her husband. At the end of the tape was a message to Dr. King saying he had 34 days in which to kill himself or he would be exposed.[110] After King's death, both Coretta and Andrew Young claimed publicly that the sounds on the tape were not distinguishable as being made by any one person; some dismissed their claims as attempts to preserve Martin's legacy.[111]

JAMES EARL RAY, MARTIN LUTHER KING, JR.'S, ASSASSIN

James Earl Ray killed Martin Luther King, Jr., on April 4, 1968, at the Lorraine Motel in Memphis where King had gone to support a garbage men's strike. There are many unanswered questions about the events leading up to King's assassination. Two Black Memphis firemen, who had been stationed across the street at the fire station and had a good view of the Lorraine Motel, were later transferred without explanation. Memphis Detective Ed Redditt, also Black, was operating out of the same fire station for the city police. Four hours before

---

107. ABERNATHY, *supra* note 98, at 309–311 and 472–475.

108. STEPHEN B. OATES, LET THE TRUMPET SOUND: THE LIFE OF MARTIN LUTHER KING, JR. (1982) at 265–267.

109. RICHARD GIO POWERS, SECRECY AND POWERS: THE LIFE OF J. EDGAR HOOVER (1987) at 171–172 and 185. Hoover and Tolson, according to Powers, spent 42 years together. They traveled to work together, had lunch together, and vacationed together. Tolson was automatically included on any guest list in Washington D.C. that included the Director of the FBI. Tolson, whose last title was Associate Director, retired from the Bureau the day after J. Edgar died. *Id.*

110. ABERNATHY, *supra* note 98, at 309–311; STEPHEN B. OATES, LET THE TRUMPETS SOUND: THE LIFE OF MARTIN LUTHER KING, JR. (1982) at 331–333. Oates wrote, "The tape was a composite recording that Hoover had authorized Sullivan to compile and send to King in November, 1964." The tape was mailed from Miami by an agent on Sullivan's orders just 34 days before Christmas. *Id.* at 331. It had apparently arrived at SCLC headquarters just before the trip to Oslo for the Nobel Prize and was shipped with other tapes to the King residence where Coretta opened it, read the note, listened to part of the tape, and called her husband on January 5, 1965. OATES at 331.

111. OATES, *supra*, at 332.

the assassination, Redditt was summoned from his post monitoring King to a meeting. Redditt learned of King's death over the radio while sitting in an unmarked car.[112]

Some of the FBI's actions after the assassination are also curious. The 30-minute delay before the FBI became involved in the case has never been explained. James Earl Ray believed that if the FBI had reacted sooner it could have closed all highway exits from Memphis. It also took J. Edgar Hoover and the FBI 2 weeks to link the murder to James Earl Ray. The first batch of "Wanted" posters for Ray were published using the name Eric Stavro Gault, however. Ray left behind fingerprints on the murder weapon, which should have tipped the FBI to his real identity almost immediately.[113]

Who Killed Martin Luther King, Jr.? is the title of a book written by James Earl Ray in 1993. Ray, a small-time career criminal, never came right out and admitted that he assassinated King, but neither did he blame anyone else. Ray died in federal prison without fully divulging what he knew about the murder. Only Ray was convicted for the murder, and the identity of anyone else with complicity in the killing of Dr. King may stay unknown for years to come.[114]

One White supremacist, for instance, had offered a reward of $50,000 to anyone who killed King. This offer was made before King's murder and was probably known to James Earl Ray.[115] Ray, a four-time loser whose usual idea of high crime was a Saturday night stickup of a gas station, seemed unlikely to have accomplished the assassination and his escape to Europe without help. A further complication arose on December 16, 1993, when 67-year-old Lloyd Jowers appeared on ABC and confessed to hiring a professional killer to murder King in Memphis.[116] However, as one authority describes it, "Jowers' confession is not nearly as straight forward" as the conspiracy advocates make it out to be.[117]

CONCLUSION

Mahatma Gandhi and Martin Luther King both believed that it was morally right to break laws that were unjust.[118] They both put into operation the

---

112. GERALD POSNER, KILLING THE DREAM: JAMES EARL RAY AND THE ASSASSINATION OF MARTIN LUTHER KING, JR. (1998) footnote at 24–25.

113. *Id.* at 331–332 (Posner).

114. Yet, recent arrests and prosecutions for civil rights murders in the 1960s raises hopes slightly that some progress may be made on the King case. In 1994, Byron De La Beckwith, who had twice been tried for the murder of Medgar Evers, with both cases ending in hung juries, was convicted of the murder. In 2001 and in 2003, the last two living men involved in the bombing of the Sixteenth Street Baptist Church in Birmingham, Alabama on September 15, 1963 that killed 4 young girls and wounded 20 others were convicted of murder. On Thursday night, January 6, 2005, Edgar Ray Killen, a 79-year old sawmill operator and part-time Baptist minister who organized the killings of Michael Schwerner, Andrew Goodman, and James Chaney, was arrested without incident at his Philadelphia, Mississippi, home. *See, e.g.,* Robert D. McFadden (N.Y. Times), *Klansman Arrested in 1964 Slayings: Preacher Charged in Notorious Murders of 3 Rights Workers.* Accessed at http://www.sfgate.com/cgi-bin/article.cgi?file=/chronicle/archive/2005/01/07/MNGFDAM on February 14, 2005.

115. Gerald Posner, *Killing the Dream: James Earl Ray and the Assassination of Martin Luther King, Jr.* (1998) at 334–335.

116. Posner, *supra* note 68, at 275–280.

117. *Id.* at 277 (Posner).

118. Those who have investigated the murder of Martin Luther King, Jr., in Memphis on April 4, 1968, seem to fall loosely into two camps: those who believe James Earl Ray killed King while acting alone; and those who believe there was a conspiracy that resulted in King's assassination. William Bradford Huie, who wrote for *Look* magazine, came to the conclusion that Ray killed King acting alone. *Id.* at 253. Others, such as lawyers Mark Lane and William

concepts in Thoreau's essay "On the Duty of Civil Disobedience,"[119] linking both of them with the 19th-century moral philosopher. The world has come a long way in terms of desegregation and working toward nonviolence, but still has a long way to go. Segregation by law no longer exists in this country as it once did, but ultimately the most important question is not how the law treats people of different races or different colors, but how we treat one another.

A minimalist moral code would include three principles: noninjury; truth telling, and fairness.[120] The Jim Crow segregation laws fail even these minimalist standards. First, segregation imposes a "badge of inferiority" on the group segregated. Moreover, in addition to psychic trauma, there is the economic[121] and physical violence that accompanies the enforcement of any system of segregation or apartheid. Finally, promise keeping is central to what it means to be fair or just. The American Testament declared that "all men are created equal and endowed by their Creator with the right to life, liberty, and the pursuit of happiness." We—as a people—did not deliver on these promises and consequently failed our basic moral obligations to our brothers and sisters of color. America's civil rights years were a call to renewal of the American spirit.

F. Pepper, believed that Ray was a "fall guy" for a large conspiracy. *Id.* at 226, 267–274. Gerald Posner may have come up with an attractive, almost a commonsense conclusion: "There is no doubt that James Earl Ray shot and killed Martin Luther King, Jr. The more puzzling questions are what motivated him and whether he acted alone or as part of a conspiracy." *Id.* at 333. Posner then eliminates a vast, organized conspiracy involving the Mafia or a government agency with the observation that they would not have let Ray live behind bars for 30 years. Such an organization would have "disposed" of him. *Id.* at 335. Most likely, Posner seems to conclude, the only conspiracy (if there were one) would have been a "crude" family plot and the strong ties Ray felt to his family kept him silent about it to the end. *Id.* James Earl Ray died inside Brushy Mountain State Prison in April, 1998 at age 70.

119. Henry David Thoreau, *On the Duty of Civil Disobedience* (first published in 1849) as reprinted in HENRY DAVID THOREAU, WALDEN (Signet ed. 1960) at 222–240.

120. WILLIAM H. SHAW, BUSINESS ETHICS (3rd ed. 1999) at 296.

121. For an extended treatment of violence, particularly economic violence, *see* William A. Wines, *Does Capitalism Wear a White Hat or Ride a Pale Horse? Physical and Economic Violence in America and a Survey of Attitudes Toward Violence Held by U.S. Undergraduate Business Majors Compared to Ohio Valley Quakers*, in SOUTHERN UNIVERSITY LAW REVIEW (Fall 2005).

CHAPTER 11

The Affirmative Action Debate

"We hold these truths to be self-evident, that all men are created equal, that they are endowed by their Creator with certain unalienable Rights that among these are Life, Liberty and the pursuit of Happiness."[1] Thomas Jefferson (1743–1826) of Virginia, who was to become the third president of the United States,[2] penned these words into the Declaration of Independence on behalf of the committee[3] appointed to do so, even though he owned "numerous slaves"[4] and most likely fathered children by his young slave girl, Sally Hemings.[5] In fact, he was to later write, "Nothing is more certainly written in the book of fate than that these people [slaves] are to be free."[6] The contradictions contained within the heart of Thomas Jefferson reflected the larger contradictions contained within the soul of the new nation that he helped establish.[7]

How could Jefferson, the most gifted of all U.S. presidents, write that "All men are created equal" when only White male landowners could vote? Were women not human? Were African Americans not human? Were the aboriginal peoples not human? Yet, in 1776, women were disenfranchised, African Americans were held in slavery, and the native peoples were subject to genocide. This contradiction is answered by the famous scholar and author Mortimer Adler (1902–2001), who declared that the Declaration and its idealism were and can only be understood as promises to the future that future generations of Americans would have to fulfill.[8]

The tension between practice and policy has lingered throughout American history. We fought the Civil War in part because of this gulf between life and language, between ideals and reality. The divisions continued and were exacerbated after the Civil War. More than 100 years after President Abraham Lincoln's Emancipation Proclamation in 1863, Congress wrestled with and finally passed a comprehensive Civil Rights Act, designed to deliver on the promises of the Founders. And still, the divisions continued.

The national debate over affirmative action can be understood as one thread in these continuing divisions. Yet, this debate has a strange twist of its own. Those who cling to the status quo now claim the moral high ground on the basis that they wear the mantle of the generations of Americans who fought for equal rights and equal opportunity. Those who argue for affirmative action or race-conscious admissions policies in American colleges are now confronted by arguments that they are sexist and racist because they insist on using race and gender as a way of eliminating the remnants of a race-divided,

---

1. "The Unanimous Declaration of the Thirteen United States of America, In Congress, July 4, 1776."

2. THE WORLD BOOK ENCYCLOPEDIA (1990), vol. 11 at 80.

3. *Id.* at 77. The other committee members, John Adams, Benjamin Franklin, Robert R. Livingston, and Roger Sherman, unanimously asked Jefferson to draft the document.

4. *Id.* at 78.

5. "The Thomas Jefferson Foundation stands by its original findings—that the weight of evidence suggests that Jefferson probably was the father of Eston Hemings and perhaps the father of all of Sally Hemings' children." *Monticello: The Plantation: Thomas Jefferson and Sally Hemings: A Brief Account.* Accessed at http://www.monticello.org/plantation/hemings-jefferson_contro.html on February 6, 2003.

6. THE WORLD BOOK ENCYCLOPEDIA, vol. 11 at 78.

7. *See generally, e.g.,* CHRISTOPHER HITCHENS, THOMAS JEFFERSON: AUTHOR OF AMERICA (2005). At one point, Hitchens, the author of this marvelously well crafted and brief study of the third U.S. president, declares: "Jefferson did not embody contradictions. Jefferson *was* a contradiction, and this will be found at every step of the narrative that goes to make up his life" [italics in original]. *Id.* at 5.

8. MORTIMER ADLER, WE HOLD THESE TRUTHS (1987).

gender-segregated society. The moral dilemma, if one is willing to engage it with an open mind, is staggeringly difficult.

Let us eliminate some of the easy issues at the outset. Some arguments seem to be beyond redemption, at least from the perspective of rational and moral justification. For instance, if this nation-state and society were to be almost entirely color-blind and gender-neutral, arguing for the use of racial- or gender-based affirmative action would be morally unjustified and probably unjustifiable. Similarly, in the absence of a generally enforced universal emancipation extending to jobs, education, accommodations, religion, and other civil rights, one who did not argue for such legislation would be in violation of the Spirit of '76 and not likely to find any moral justification for the continuation of irrational discrimination on the basis of irrelevant characteristics. Almost every rational person can agree on these two propositions. We may think of these propositions as the metaphorical bookends of the affirmative action debate.

The remaining issues can be stated a number of different ways. Perhaps, a middle of the road (neutral) statement of the issue might be framed as follows:

> How should we approach the issues of distributive justice in a society that is committed by the law and Constitution to the ideals of gender neutrality and color-blindness but that has not in real terms (social data on education opportunity, law enforcement, and wealth distribution) yet achieved such goals?

Positions vary. The two extreme positions seem to be (a) declare that affirmative action is more a hindrance than an aid to goal achievement and should be discontinued entirely; (b) admit that the goals have not been substantially achieved and we should use color and gender to achieve a more balanced distribution of outcomes such as college admissions and employment until such time as society can be declared to have generally achieved its goals. Note that both positions share one area of near-unanimity: Both sides agree that affirmative action should be a temporary part of the social landscape. One of the disagreements clearly centers on how temporary it should be.

With regard to timing, should we discontinue affirmative action

- when the costs outweigh the benefits?
- when the percentage of African Americans and Latinos who graduate from college approximates the percentage of Whites who graduate from college?
- when the gross per capita wages of African American women approximate the gross per capita wages of White women?
- when the crime rates among inner-city adolescent minorities approximate the crime rates of suburban private high-school adolescents?
- when the per capita level of majority culture volunteers for the all-volunteer Army reaches the same per-capita level of African American volunteers?
- when the unofficial unemployment rates on Native American reservations fall to the levels of unemployment in suburban areas?
- when the percentage of White families below the federal poverty line equals the same percentage of minority families below the poverty line?

It does not take long to see that we cannot reasonably or soon exhaust all the possibilities.

Let us return to the question of distributive justice. What are we distributing when we make admissions decisions at highly selective colleges and universities? There are approximately 3,600 colleges and universities in the United States; it has been estimated that less than 10% are highly selective.[9] By admitting students to these universities, we are distributing, in one sense, tickets of admission to the "American Dream"—at least, the materialistic aspects of it. These highly selective schools are the gateways to graduate schools, good-paying jobs, and material success. It would be helpful at this juncture to review the road we have taken on affirmative action or, if you prefer, affirmative discrimination, or, for the most hardened opponents the most pejorative choice of labels, reverse discrimination.

ROAD TO *GRIGGS V. DUKE POWER* (1971)

On July 2, 1965, the Civil Rights Act of 1964 took effect. That Congress chose to delay implementation of the new law for a full year, an unusually long delay, indicated that big changes were in the wind. The operative sections of the law forbade discrimination in public accommodations, education, and employment on the basis of "race, color, religion, or national origin." This term was coined by Joseph L. Rauh, Jr., a New Deal lawyer (1911–1992), who drafted the first affirmative action executive order [#8802] for Franklin D. Roosevelt in June 1941.[10]

In an effort to scuttle the entire Civil Rights Act, a motion to amend the operative section to include "or sex [meaning gender]" was made from the floor of the House of Representatives. This motion presented a serious Machiavellian challenge to the main bill. If it passed, the conventional wisdom was that Black civil rights leaders would not call in their markers to push the bill over the top because White women might be seen as free riders on the blood and the dues paid by Black activists. If, on the other hand, the motion to amend were defeated, then conventional wisdom was that the women's movement leaders and their representatives might not work their hardest to pass the legislation. President Johnson and his advisors decided to accept the amendment and were able push the package through. However, some studies indicate that white Women may have been disproportionate beneficiaries of the Act.[11]

The first litigation to reach the U.S. Supreme Court on the topic of the Civil Rights Act of 1964 was *Griggs v. Duke Power Co.*[12] Black employees

---

9. *See, e.g.*, U.S. NEWS & WORLD REPORT annual edition on best colleges in the United States. There are approximately 3,600 colleges in the United States. *See also Miami University: About Miami: Recognition.* Accessed at http://www.miami.muohio.edu/about_miami/recognition/index.cfm on May 28, 2003.

10. JUAN WILLIAMS, EYES ON THE PRIZE: AMERICA'S CIVIL RIGHTS YEARS, 1954–1965 (1987) at 197 and 292; *Milestones in the History of the U.S. EEOC: The Early Years*, accessed at http://www.eeoc.gov/35th/milestones/early.html and *Ending Racism in the Military and Sports*, accessed at http://www.geocities.com/wmaxwell/racism1.html at material accompanying note 18 on May 28, 2003.

11. *See, e.g.*, Ellis Close, *The Black Gender Gap*, NEWSWEEK (March 3, 2003) at 47–51. Although the focus of the article is the gap between Black men and Black women, it shows that Black women's median income did not reach that of White women until 2001. *Id.* at 49. Also, 56% of college students in the United States are female; the majority are White women. *Id.* A recent article in the *Wall Street Journal* indicated that at many U.S. colleges the number of men would be much smaller because gender is used to keep the schools closer to parity than they would otherwise be.

12. *Griggs v. Duke Power Co.* 401 U.S. 424 (1971).

of Duke Power Company brought a class action against the company under Title VII, challenging its hiring requirements of a high-school diploma and passing scores on two standardized tests, the Wonderlic Personnel Test, which supposedly measured general intelligence, and the Bennett Mechanical Comprehension Test.[13] The U.S. District Court for the Middle District of North Carolina found that, prior to July 2, 1965, the effective date of the 1964 Act, the "Company openly discriminated on the basis of race in hiring and assigning of employees at its Dan River plant."[14] However, the District Court found that the 1964 Civil Rights Act was prospective only in application and did not reach this behavior. Accordingly, the court dismissed the complaint (292 F. Supp. 243).

The Court of Appeals for the Fourth Circuit (420 F. 2d 1225) reversed the District Court's ruling that residual discrimination arising from past employment practices was insulated from remedial action, but it affirmed the ruling that, absent a discriminatory intent, the diploma and test requirements were proper. On *certiorari*, the Supreme Court in a unanimous opinion (8–0 with Justice Brennan abstaining) by Chief Justice Burger reversed on the issue of intent.

In its 1971 decision, the U.S. Supreme Court held that the Civil Rights Act prohibits an employer from requiring a high-school diploma or passing a standardized test as a condition of employment or promotion when (1) neither standard is shown to be significantly job related, (2) both requirements operate to disqualify Blacks at a substantially higher rate than Whites, and (3) the jobs in question formerly had been filled only with White employees as part of a long-standing practice of discrimination.

THE DUALITY IN THE *GRIGGS* DECISION

Later splits in Supreme Court decisions had their origin in a subtle duality in the Griggs decision.[15] On the one hand, the *Griggs* court declared itself for merit by asserting that "[d]iscriminatory preference for any group, minority or majority, is precisely and only what Congress had proscribed."[16] However, it also endorsed remediation of the legacy of discrimination arguments advanced by Justice Blackmun when it held that racially neutral practices adopted without discriminatory intent may violate Title VII "if they operate to 'freeze' the status quo of prior discriminatory employment practices."[17]

In the same opinion by the chief justice, the unanimous court also noted that if Blacks "have been denied educational opportunities in segregated schools, then literacy tests that deny many the right to vote and written exams that deny others the chance to earn a living handling coal tend to perpetuate past discrimination by assuring that those intentionally denied educational opportunities also lose political and economic opportunities."[18] This passage makes a clear link between prior discrimination and the need for action to

---

13. *Id.* at 425–26 and 429.
14. *Id.* at 428.
15. *See, e.g.*, WINES, *Title VII Interpretation and Enforcement in the Reagan Years (1980–1989): The Winding Road to the Civil Rights Act of 1991*, 77 MARQ. L. REV. 645, 707–708 (1994).
16. 401 U.S. 424, 431 (1971), opinion by Chief Justice Burger.
17. 401 U.S. 424, 430 (1971).
18. 401 U.S. 424, 430 (1971) as cited in WINES, *Title VII Interpretation and Enforcement in the Reagan Years (1980–89): The Winding Road to the Civil Rights Act of 1991*, 77 MARQ. L. REV. 645–718 (1994) at 708.

remedy its lingering effects. This is the heart of the affirmative action argument. It underlies the *Griggs* decision just as surely as the later argument of "identified discriminatee" does the meritocracy passage of the same opinion. The divisions, innocuous at first, have become both profound and bitter in the courts, the legislatures, and now in U.S. society itself.

QUOTAS AND PREFERENCES: BRIAN WEBER AND ALLAN BAKKE

On June 28, 1978, the U.S. Supreme Court ruled on the case brought by Allan Bakke against the Regents of the University of California for denying him admission to the UC-Davis Medical School. In one of the most fragmented decisions in U.S. judicial history, six separate opinions were filed, and the Supreme Court itself split 4–1–4.[19] The result was that Allan Bakke was ordered admitted to the medical school, but the reasons and the holding have been the subject of intense legal debate ever since.

In a book ambitiously titled *Toward an Understanding of Bakke*, the U.S. Civil Rights Commission (1979) wrote a three-and-one-half page "Introduction" and then simply, as if in resignation, reprinted the court's opinions.[20] However, some things can be agreed on and objectively verified. The Bakke decision was the first Supreme Court decision to address voluntary measures designed to remedy the present effects of historical racial discrimination through race-based measures.[21] No single opinion represented the views of any of the five justices. Of the six published opinions, two were supported by four justices apiece, and the swing vote was cast by Justice Powell who agreed with certain results of the two four-vote opinions, but used entirely different reasoning to reach his conclusions.[22]

The result of the divisions between the justices was *one* 5–4 majority that ordered Allan Bakke admitted to the medical school at UC-Davis and found its rigid set-aside policy of affirmative action a violation of Title VI. By *another* 5–4 majority, however, the Court ruled that some forms of race-conscious affirmative action admissions procedures were constitutional. Clearly, however, five justices held that UC-Davis Medical School could *not* reserve 16 of 100 seats for incoming medical students for minorities nor run a two-track admissions program keyed to such a set-aside.

The next Supreme Court term brought another voluntary, race-based, remedial affirmative action plan. This time, the setting was a steel mill in Gramercy, Louisiana.[23] Until 1974, Kaiser hired as craft workers only those with prior craft experience. Because Blacks had long been excluded from the craft unions, before 1974 only 5 of 273 skilled craft workers (1.83%) were Black, even though the labor pool in the area was 39% Black.[24] Pursuant to its national labor contract with the United Steelworkers of America (USWA) AFL-CIO-CLC, Kaiser altered its hiring pattern at the plant. Rather than hire outsiders, Kaiser established a training program to train its production workers for skilled trade slots. Selection of craft trainees was made on the basis

19. *Regents of the University of California v. Bakke* 483 U.S. 265 (1978).
20. U.S. COMMISSION ON CIVIL RIGHTS, TOWARD AN UNDERSTANDING OF BAKKE (May 1979).
21. *Id.* at 1.
22. *Id.*
23. *Weber v. Kaiser Aluminum and Chemical Corp.* 443 U.S. 193 (1979).
24. *Id* at 198–199.

of seniority, with the proviso that "at least 50% of the new trainees were to be black until the percentage of black skilled craft workers in the Gramercy plant approximated the number of blacks in the local labor force."[25]

In 1974, the most junior Black selected into the program had less seniority than several White applicants who were rejected. Brian Weber, one of those rejected applicants, brought a class action suit in federal court alleging reverse discrimination in the apprenticeship training program and charging his employer and union with violating the terms of Title VII of the 1964 Civil Rights Act. The District Court (E.D. La.) held that the plan violated Title VII and entered a permanent injunction against the continuance of it by Kaiser and the USWA.[26] A divided panel of the Court of Appeals for the Fifth Circuit affirmed that all employment preferences based on race, including good-faith affirmative action plans, violated Title VII.[27] A divided U.S. Supreme Court, in an opinion by Justice Brennan, reversed this ruling in a 5–2 decision. Justices Powell and Stevens did not participate in the case.

At the outset, Justice Brennan emphasized the "narrowness" of the issue presented[28]: "The only question before us is the narrow statutory issue of whether Title VII *forbids* private employers and unions from voluntarily agreeing on bona fide affirmative action plans that accord racial preferences in the manner and for the purpose provided in the Kaiser-USWA plan" [italics in original].[29] According to briefs filed on behalf of Brian Weber, two obstacles stood in the path of anyone seeking to hold the negotiated remedial agreement legal: (1) the decision in *McDonald v. Santa Fe Trail Trans. Co.*[30] that held, in a case not involving affirmative action, that Title VII protects both Whites and Blacks from certain forms of racial discrimination and (2) sections 703 (a) and (d) of the 1964 Civil Rights Act. Those sections make it unlawful to "discriminate . . . because of . . . race" in hiring and in the selection of applicants for apprenticeship training programs.

Justice Brennan, writing for the majority, noted,

> Respondent's argument is not without force. But it overlooks the significance of the fact that the Kaiser-USWA plan is an affirmative action plan voluntarily adopted by private parties to eliminate traditional patterns of racial segregation. In this context respondent's reliance upon a literal construction of section 703 (a) and (d) and upon *McDonald* is misplaced [citation omitted]. It is a "familiar rule that a thing may be within the letter of the statute and yet not within the statute, because not within its spirit, nor within the intention of its makers" [citations omitted]. The prohibition against racial discrimination in sections 703 (a) and (d) of Title VII must therefore be read against the background of the legislative history of Title VII and the historical context from which the Act arose [citations omitted]. Examination of those sources makes clear that an interpretation of the sections that forbade all race-conscious affirmative action would "bring about an end completely at variance with the purpose of the statute" and must be rejected [citations omitted].

---

25. *Id.* at 199 citing 415 F. Supp. 761, 764.
26. 415 F. Supp 761 (1976).
27. 563 F. 2d 216 (1978).
28. 443 U.S. 193, 200.
29. *Id.*
30. 427 U.S. 273, 281 n. 8 (1976).

Congress' primary concern in enacting the prohibition against racial discrimination in Title VII of the Civil Rights Act of 1964 was with "the plight of the Negro in our economy" [citation omitted].

Had Congress meant to prohibit all race-conscious affirmative action, as respondent urges, it easily could have answered both objections by providing that Title VII would not require or *permit* racially preferential integration efforts. But Congress did not choose such a course. Rather Congress added section 703 (j) which addresses only the first objection. [italics in original]

Both Chief Justice Burger and then Justice William Rehnquist dissented, and each wrote an opinion. Chief Justice Burger wrote, "Until today, I had thought that the Court was of the unanimous view that 'discriminatory preference for any group, minority or majority, is precisely and only what Congress has proscribed' in Title VII. *Griggs v. Duke Power Co.*, 401 U.S. 424, 431 (1971)." Later, Burger wrote, "It is often said that hard cases make bad law"; he went on to say that hard cases tempt judges to exceed the limits of their authority "as the Court does today by totally rewriting a crucial part of Title VII to reach *a desirable result*" [italics added].

Justice Rehnquist was vitriolic in dissent and not nearly as sympathetic to the result as Burger. He wrote, "Thus, by a *tour de force* reminiscent not of jurists such as Hale, Holmes, and Hughes, but of escape artists, such as Houdini, the Court eludes clear statutory language, 'uncontradicted' legislative history, and uniform precedent in concluding that employers are, after all, permitted to consider race in making employment decisions."

In fairness, it is easier to write glittering prose, even purple prose such as in the previous paragraph, when writing in dissent than when writing an opinion that will be the law of the land. In addition, neither Burger nor Rehnquist pointed out the most serious practical obstacle that would face a court ruling for Brian Weber: Such a ruling would have forced both Kaiser and the USWA to remain vulnerable to a class action suit for illegal discrimination under Title VII by *forbidding* (ironically Justice Brennan's word) them from voluntarily remedying their own historic race-based discrimination against Blacks. Would such a result have served justice better than the one the majority reached?

Notwithstanding the vigorous dissents, the Court's decisions in Bakke and in the Weber case have withstood the test of time and have remained the law of the land for over 25 years. This is despite the fact that in the late 1980s the conservative wing of the U.S. Supreme Court started a case-by-case movement to repeal parts of the judicial gloss on the 1964 Civil Rights Act.[31] This judicial attempt at repeal was firmly stopped by Congress when it passed the 1991 Civil Rights Act that, in essence, restored Griggs and all its progeny.[32]

THE UNIVERSITY OF MICHIGAN CASES

RESULTS AT THE DISTRICT COURT AND SIXTH CIRCUIT

Barbara Grutter, an unsuccessful applicant to the University of Michigan Law School, brought suit against the university on behalf of herself and others

---

31. *See* Wines, *Title VII Interpretation and Enforcement, supra* note 14.
32. *Id.*

similarly situated, alleging that its affirmative action admissions program violated the equal protection clause of the 14th Amendment and Title VI of the Civil Rights Act of 1964. The U.S. District Court (E.D. Mich.) ruled for the plaintiff.[33] On appeal, a sharply divided panel of the Sixth Circuit reversed in part and vacated in part.[34] The Court left for another day its decision in *Gratz v. Bollinger*, nos. 01-1333, 01-1416, 01-1418, 01-1438, a case involving a similar challenge to the undergraduate admissions program at Michigan. The Supreme Court issued a writ of *certiorari* and took jurisdiction on December 2, 2002.[35]

In an opinion written by Chief Circuit Judge Boyce F. Martin, Jr., five judges of the Sixth Circuit held that Justice Powell's opinion constituted Bakke's holding and provided the governing standard for Michigan's admissions policies. Thus, Powell's use of a strict scrutiny standard was viewed by the majority as the narrowest or most limited consideration of race in the various Bakke opinions. Accordingly, it became the opinion of the court.

Next, the majority held that the University of Michigan Law School had a "compelling state interest in achieving a diverse student body." The Sixth Circuit held that "our determination that Justice Powell's diversity conclusion binds this court also finds some support in the Brennan concurrence's qualified approval of the Harvard plan in the first footnote of its opinion."[36] In a note, the majority took this point further by arguing, "Unless one assumes that the Brennan concurrence would have approved the use of race to further an unconstitutional goal, the dissent's aprioristic assertion that the Brennan concurrence 'certainly did not endorse [Justice Powell's diversity rationale]' flouts logic."[37]

Four judges dissented and filed four separate dissenting opinions. Judge Batchelder joined Judge Boggs' dissenting opinion, and Judge Siler joined it in part. Boggs wrote, "This case involves a straightforward instance of racial discrimination by a state institution.... [T]he constitutional justifications offered for this practice would not pass even the slightest scrutiny."[38] Warming to his subject, Judge Boggs continued,

> The Law School absolutely insists that it does *not* consider applicants "without regard to" their race [emphasis in original, citations omitted]. Instead, as is discussed by the majority..., Michigan considers all applicants with exquisite regard for their race and national origin. As I put it to counsel for the Law School in oral argument, if Herman Sweatt, the plaintiff in the famous case of *Sweatt v. Painter*, [citation omitted] (1950), had been able to ask the Dean of the University of Texas Law School, "Dean, would you let me in if I were white," the dean, if he were honest, would surely have said "Yes." I then asked counsel, "If Barbara Grutter walked in to whoever the current Dean of the Law School is and said, 'Dean, would you let me in if I were black?' wouldn't he have to honestly say either 'Yes' or 'pretty darn almost certainly?'" Counsel agreed, but responded that a "black woman

33. *Grutter v. Bollinger* 137 F. Supp. 2d 821, 2001 U.S. Dist. LEXIS 3256 (E.D. Mich. 2001).
34. *Grutter v. Bollinger* 288 F. 3d 732, 2002 U.S. App. LEXIS 9126; 2002 FED App. 0170P (6th Cir.).
35. *Grutter v. Bollinger* 2002 U.S. LEXIS 8677 (U.S. December 2, 2002).
36. Note 34, *supra*, at 742.
37. *Id.*, n. 7.
38. *Id.*, 774.

who had otherwise an application that looked like Barbara Grutter, that *would be a different person*." Tr. At 38 [italics added].

That answer puts starkly the policy of discrimination practiced throughout the ages.

Throughout this discussion, my quarrel is with the constitutionality of the policy, not its proponents....I have no doubt that the proponents of this discriminatory policy act with the most tender of motives. However, the noble motives of those propounding unconstitutional policies should not save those policies, just as some segregationists' genuine belief that segregated education provided better education for both races was inadequate to justify those policies.[39]

Judge Boggs admitted that race and national origin "still matter" in the United States, but contended that we cannot suspend the equal protection clause until they no longer matter. Finally, he argued that there is no "holding" in the Bakke decision on the matter of diversity because that part of Justice Powell and Justice Brennan's decisions went beyond anything required to resolve the issues presented in the case; consequently, the discussion of diversity was mere *obiter dicta*.

THE U.S. SUPREME COURT DECISIONS

On April 1, 2003, the U.S. Supreme Court heard oral arguments in the affirmative action cases involving the University of Michigan admissions programs, both undergraduate and law school. Initial impressions in the press from the give-and-take of oral argument were that Justice O'Connor seemed to be "on the fence," but that the conservative wing (made up of Justices Rehnquist, Thomas, Kennedy, and Scalia) were hostile in its questions and that the liberal wing (Justices Ginsberg, Souter, Stevens, and Breyer) seemed friendlier to the university's position.[40]

The results were announced on June 23, 2003. The Supreme Court found that the Michigan Law School admissions program (5–4) passed Constitutional muster,[41] but a majority (6–3) ruled that the University of Michigan's undergraduate admissions program that "automatically distributed 20 points to every applicant" who was a member of an underrepresented racial or ethnic minority group violated the 14th Amendment and Title VI of the U.S. Civil Rights Act.[42]

In the Grutter decision, Justice O'Connor wrote for the majority. She noted that the University of Michigan Law School ranked "among the Nation's top law schools" and that it received more than 3,500 applications each year for a class of about 350 students.[43] She held that the law school's narrowly tailored use of race in admissions decisions furthered a compelling state interest in obtaining the educational benefits that flow from a diverse student body. Further, she ruled that such a narrowly tailored plan that was "holistic" and did not make race or ethnicity the determining factor did not violate the 14th Amendment's equal protection clause, Title VI, or Section 1981. To be narrowly tailored, the majority said that the admissions program must

---

39. *Id.*, 775.
40. USA TODAY (April 4, 2003) at A-1.
41. *Grutter v. Bollinger* 2003 U.S. LEXIS 4800; 71 U.S.L.W. 4498 (2003).
42. *Gratz v. Bollinger* 123 S. Ct. 2411; 156 L. Ed. 2d 257; 2003 U.S. LEXIS 4801; 71 U.S. L.W. 4480 (2003).
43. *Grutter v. Bollinger* 2003 U.S. LEXIS 4812.

ensure that each applicant is evaluated as an individual. Justices Stevens, Souter, Ginsberg, and Breyer joined in the opinion.

In the Gratz decision, the Court confronted an undergraduate admissions program at the University of Michigan's College of Literature, Science and Arts that used a point system. Plaintiff Gratz had applied in the fall of 1995 and was denied admission; subsequently, she attended the University of Michigan at Dearborn and graduated. Plaintiff Hamacher applied in the fall of 1997 and was denied admission. He subsequently attended Michigan State University.

Beginning in 1998, the college used a point system to determine admissions. An applicant could be awarded a maximum of 150 points, and usually admission was automatic for any applicant awarded at least 100 points. Points were awarded based on high-school grades, standardized test scores, high-school quality, strength of the high-school curriculum, in-state residency, alumni relations, a personal essay, and personal achievement or leadership. None of those criteria was challenged. However, in addition the university awarded 20 points for membership in what it considered to be underrepresented racial or ethnic minority groups: African Americans, Hispanics, and Native Americans. In 1999, the university added a committee to provide an additional level of review for some applicants. Virtually every qualified applicant from an underrepresented group was admitted.[44]

Writing for the majority, Chief Justice Rehnquist held that the automatic award of 20 points to members of underrepresented groups violated the equal protection clause because it did not provide for individualized consideration and was not saved by the addition of a review committee, which in the majority's opinion only emphasized the flaws of the program as a whole. This system was also held to violate Section 1891 of the U.S.C. (United States Code) and Title VI of the U.S. Civil Rights Act. Justices O'Connor, Scalia, Kennedy, and Thomas concurred in Rehnquist's opinion. Justice Breyer concurred in the judgment. For the majority, the automatic award of 20 points seemed too much like the set-aside of 16 of the 100 seats at the Cal-Davis medical school that was struck down in the Bakke decision.

In dissent, Justice Stevens raised the question of whether there was a plaintiff with standing to sue the University of Michigan in Gratz under Article III's requirement for "a real case and controversy" (i.e., that the court not engage in issuing advisory opinions). Stevens argued that neither plaintiff sought continuing admission nor admission as a transfer student to the University of Michigan, and therefore neither had any continuing interest in the admissions policy or whether it changed.

CONCLUDING OBSERVATIONS

As I stated in the beginning of this chapter, affirmative action is a most difficult issue. On one hand, we have the duty-based arguments that we should be gender-neutral and color-blind. These arguments are driven by the laws—both the 14th Amendment and portions of the 1964 Civil Rights Act. On the other hand, we have the outcome-based arguments that we "owe" historically repressed people a chance to get up on the playing field before starting the

---

44. *Gratz v. Bollinger* 156 L. Ed. 2d 257.

"game." This is a classic example of a moral duty versus positive outcome ethical dilemma. As a society, many of us have some sense of urgency to "do" affirmative action until we have achieved a rough economic and social parity and then dismantle it. The Court's decisions in Gratz and Grutter seem to signal the final round of affirmative action—at a minimum—in the area of college admissions.

CHAPTER 12

Media and Free Speech Issues

The basis of our government being the opinion of the people, the very object should be to keep that right; and were it left to me to decide whether we should have government without newspapers, or newspapers without government, I should not hesitate a moment to prefer the latter.

—Thomas Jefferson (1787)[1]

The First Amendment to the Constitution of the United States declares, "Congress shall make no law...abridging the freedom of speech, or of the press."[2] Yet, freedom of the press in the United States dates from a much earlier period in our history. The American heritage of a free press can be traced back to the year 1735 in New York when a printer named John Peter Zenger was tried for libel based on his criticism of the king's colonial governor, William Cosby.[3]

THE TRIAL OF JOHN PETER ZENGER

Understanding the story of Zenger requires some background on the subject of seditious libel. Seditious libel was a felony under English law; criticism of the government was considered defamation and punished as a crime.[4] Truth was no defense to the charge "because the criminal harm lay in lowering esteem— and truth might do that most effectively. The greater the truth, the greater the libel, as the saying went."[5]

The history of the John Peter Zenger trial in 1735 would make a modern reader blanch. Andrew Hamilton of Pennsylvania (no relation to Alexander Hamilton of *Federalist* fame) appeared with local counsel to defend Zenger against charges that he seditiously libeled the Crown's governor of New York, William Cosby, a colonel in the Royal Irish Regiment and a man much despised by the colonists for his greed and corruption. When a grand jury refused to indict Zenger, he was charged on information and refused reasonable bail—the hope being that doing so would cause his newspaper to cease publication.[6]

Hamilton, in a courageous move, admitted that Zenger had printed and published the papers alleged to be libelous,[7] and he stated his intention to defend on the ground of truth.[8] The attorney for the Crown then moved for judgment against Zenger on the ground that not only was truth no defense but it was an aggravation of the offense.[9] Hamilton demurred to this, arguing that words to be libelous must either be false, scandalous, or seditious.

---

1. Thomas Jefferson, *Letter to Colonel Edward Carrington* (January 16, 1787) as quoted in BARTLETT'S FAMILIAR QUOTATIONS (16th ed. 1992) at 343.
2. GUNTHER & DOWLING, CONSTITUTIONAL LAW: TEXT AND CASES (8th ed. 1970) at lxxxiv.
3. JETHRO K. LIEBERMAN, THE EVOLVING CONSTITUTION (1992) at 580–581. Lieberman writes, "Zenger's acquittal...was an important part of the intellectual background of the First Amendment. It also helped establish the principle in American law that truth is a defense to any libel action, although that principle was codified only in 1798 in the Sedition Act." *Id.* at 581.
4. *Id.* (Kalven) at 63.
5. ANTHONY LEWIS, MAKE NO LAW: THE SULLIVAN CASE AND THE FIRST AMENDMENT (1991) at 52.
6. LIVINGSTON RUTHERFURD, JOHN PETER ZENGER: HIS PRESS, HIS TRIAL, AND A BIBLIOGRAPHY OF ZENGER IMPRINTS (1970 reprint of 1904 issue) at 47–48. In fact, Zenger's wife continued the operation of the weekly paper, the *New York Weekly Journal*, during his imprisonment coordinating its publication with him through visits at the jail. *See* Rutherford at 60.
7. *Id.* at 69.
8. *Id.* at 69–70.
9. *Id.* at 70.

Andrew Hamilton, then nearly 80 years old and suffering from gout,[10] paraphrased the information and the arguments of the Crown. He observed "[t]hat by Government we were protected in our lives, religion, and properties; and that for these reasons, great care had always been taken to prevent everything that might tend to scandalize Magistrates, and others concerned in the administration of Government."[11] Further, a libel against a magistrate or other public person is a greater offense because "this concerns not only the Breach of the Peace, but the scandal of the Government; for what greater scandal of Government can there be, than to have corrupt or wicked Magistrates."[12]

The Crown had also noted that Zenger had offended against the "Law of God," citing Acts XXIII.5, to wit: "Thou shalt not speak evil of the ruler of the People." Hamilton, sage and still sharp at trial, responded, "I agree with the Attorney General that Government is a Sacred Thing, but I differ very widely from him when he would insinuate that the just Complaints of a Number of Men, who suffer under a bad Administration, is libeling that Administration."[13]

Further, Mr. Hamilton pointed out that the Crown was citing Star Chamber[14] cases—and cases that dealt with an affront to the sovereign, not a governor of the plantations.[15] "No, the falsehood makes the Scandal, and both make the Libel. And to show the Court that I am in Good Earnest, . . . I will agree, that if he (Attorney General) can prove the Facts charged upon us to be *false*, I'll own them to be *scandalous*, *seditious*, and *a Libel*" [italics added].[16] When the Crown declined his offer, stating rather lamely that it could not prove a negative, Hamilton offered to prove the truth of alleged libels.

At that, the chief justice interrupted, asserting, "You cannot be admitted, Mr. Hamilton, to give the truth of a Libel in Evidence."[17] The court then asserted that it believed the rule that truth was no defense to seditious libel that predated the Star Chamber. Hamilton reviewed the cases from Sir Edward Coke and argued that all the cases that predated the Star Chamber were on indictment rather than information and that truth was an issue. Hamilton argued again that, because the Star Chamber was abolished, then the rulings it made that were cited by the Crown should die with it.[18]

---

10. *Id.* at 58.
11. *Id.* at 71.
12. *Id.* at 71.
13. *Id.* at 74.
14. The Court of the Star Chamber, 1487–1641, had powers that grew considerably under the Stuarts. By the time of Charles I, it had become a byword for misuse and abuse of power by the king and his circle. Under James I and his son, the court operated to suppress criticism and opposition to royal policies. It was also used to try nobles too powerful to be brought to trial in the lower courts. The court could and did order defendants fined, imprisoned, and tortured, but it did not have the power to decree death sentences. The hated Star Chamber was abolished by the long Parliament in 1641. See *The Court of the Star Chamber*. Accessed at http://www.britainexpress.com/History/tudor/star-chamber.htm on September 23, 2004. The name came from the star painted on the ceiling of the room at Westminster Palace where the king's council met; the Court of the Star Chamber developed from the judicial proceedings traditionally carried out by the king and his council. It was entirely separate from the common-law courts of the day. *Star Chamber*. Accessed at http://www.bartleby.com/65/st/StarCham.html on September 23, 2004.
15. RUTHERFURD at 75–76.
16. *Id.* at 80.
17. *Id.* at 81.
18. *Id.* at 80–88.

When the Bench ruled against him on this issue, Hamilton began his arguments to the 12 men of the jury.[19] Hamilton was rebuffed by the chief justice at the close of his argument for citing Bushel's case to the jury, a case in which the jury refused to accept the justice's instruction in a prosecution against William Penn for causing an alleged riot at a Quaker meeting.[20] Zenger reported later that the chief justice was no match for Andrew Hamilton and that "the Jury withdrew and in a small Time returned" with a not guilty verdict. There were three "huzzas" in the crowded hall for the verdict, and Governor Cosby had Zenger released the next day. Hamilton left New York to the salute of several guns in the harbor.

Governor Morris, one of the founders of the Republic, said this of the trial: "The trial of Zenger in 1735 was the germ of American freedom, the morning star of that liberty which subsequently revolutionized America."[21] Although some dispute this analysis, the Zenger case established the right of American juries to declare both the law and the facts almost 60 years before English juries enjoyed that freedom and also freed Americans from punishment for truthful statements that bring government into disrepute.[22] Our country, however, was not yet done with issues of seditious libel.

HISTORY OF THE SEDITION ACT OF 1798

Seditious libel has a long and dishonorable history in the United States.[23] In an atmosphere of bitterness and suspicion, the Federalists, led by John Adams, and the Democratic Republicans, led by Thomas Jefferson, passed the Sedition Act of 1798 on straight party-line votes in both houses of Congress. Federalists saw the Jeffersonian Republicans gaining ground politically and sought to arrest that trend by silencing critics of the government, especially the Republican press. The Sedition Act made it a felony to "write, print, utter or publish . . . any false, scandalous and malicious writing or writings" against the government of the United States, either house of Congress, or the president with "intent to defame" or to "bring them . . . into contempt or disrepute." President Adams and both houses of Congress were protected; curiously, Vice President Thomas Jefferson was not protected under the Act. So sure were the Federalists that such protection would not be long needed that they allowed the Democratic Republicans to amend the Act to have it expire on March 3, 1801, Adams' last day in office.

---

19. At least 7 of the 12 men on the jury were of Dutch ancestry, and one of them had served on the grand jury that had refused to indict John Peter Zenger. The Dutch had settled this part of the New World generations before the English became inclined to govern it and had fought the British for control of the province between 1673 and 1674 when Holland handed control to the British. *See* JOHN M. BLUM ET AL., THE NATIONAL EXPERIENCE: A HISTORY OF THE UNITED STATES (7th ed. 1989) at 34–35. The Dutch seemed to have retained some lingering animosity toward the British; entertained an intense dislike for Cosby, the king's governor; and displayed a fair amount of independence for the instructions of the king's court. *See* RUTHERFURD, *supra* note 6, at 62 and 193.
20. RUTHERFURD at 113–114.
21. RUTHERFURD at 131 quotes Governor Morris, one of the founders of this republic, for this judgment.
22. IRVING BRANT, THE BILL OF RIGHTS: ITS ORIGIN AND MEANING (1965) at 179–181.
23. Lewis devotes all of Chapter 7 to explaining the origins and history of the Sedition Act. *Id.* at 56–66. Much of the material that follows is from that chapter.

Fourteen prosecutions were brought under the Sedition Act; the defendants included leading Republican newspapers, as well as one Republican member of the House of Representatives. At least two newspapers ceased publication because of Sedition Act prosecutions. Most of the prosecutions were brought in the year 1800 and not by accident. Adams's secretary of state, Timothy Pickering, "encouraged Sedition Act prosecutions, and he planned cases to silence the important Jeffersonian newspapers during the election contest of 1800 between Adams and Jefferson."[24]

The Act was worded to catch only "false" and "scandalous and malicious" statements made with the intention to defame, and these provisions had been praised as a liberalizing of the common law of seditious libel under which truth was no defense. However, in practice, these provisions were of little or no help to those charged with sedition because of the way the Act was administered. The federal courts, in which all the judges had been appointed by Federalist presidents, interpreted the requirement of falsity so as to make the defendant bear the burden of proving the truth; a critical statement was presumed to be false unless proven true in all respects. This standard was applied even to statements of opinion and predictions.

Malice was also presumed, and the intent to defame was inferred from publication of words that "had a bad tendency"—the ancient test of seditious libel in common law. Although juries were allowed to decide issues of fact, they were instructed in such detail that the only thing they had left to decide was whether the defendant actually published the offending statement. Finally, according to Lewis, "[M]odern research suggests that federal judges and marshals packed juries in Sedition Act cases with Federalists."[25] Little was left to either chance or justice.

Politically, the Sedition Act proved to be a disaster. To quote Lewis, "[I]t aroused popular outrage, becoming a campaign issue itself in the election of 1800 and contributing to Jefferson's defeat of Adams."[26] Its constitutionality was never tested in the Supreme Court because the law expired before a case could reach it.[27] Whether or not the authors of the First Amendment intended to eliminate the crime of seditious libel, Lewis notes that 10 years after the Bill of Rights was ratified, the majority of both "informed and popular" opinion was that seditious libel was inconsistent with our Constitution.[28]

WORLD WAR I ESPIONAGE CASES

Before World War I, only a handful of cases had dealt with freedom of expression. Then, suddenly, in 1919, cases addressing issues of freedom of expression became profoundly important and bitterly contested.[29] When the United States entered World War I in 1917, the mood of the country had turned from isolationism to a violent jingoism; dissent from the war was not

---

24. *Id.* at 63.
25. *Id.* at 58.
26. *Id.* at 65.
27. In fairness, Lewis notes that three of the six men who sat on the court in 1800 (Justices Chase, Paterson, and Bushrod Washington) had presided at Sedition Act trials without expressing any constitutional concerns. *Id.* at 65.
28. *Id.*
29. Lewis details much of the history of these cases and chronicles the evolution of Justice Holmes's position on free speech in Chapters 8 and 9 of MAKE NO LAW at 66–89.

tolerated. In that atmosphere, Congress passed a sweeping Espionage Act that, among other measures, made it a crime punishable by up to 20 years in prison for anyone to urge "disloyalty" or inspire insubordination in the military or to "willfully obstruct the recruiting or enlistment service."[30]

Under the Espionage Act, Eugene V. Debs, leader of the Socialist Party and five times its candidate for U.S. president,[31] was sentenced to 10 years in prison for encouraging resistance to the draft in a speech he made in Canton, Ohio in June, 1918. The Espionage Act was the Sedition Act of 1798 reborn. In this and two other cases handed down in March 1919, the Supreme Court, in opinions written by Justice Holmes, unanimously affirmed the convictions.[32] Holmes enunciated the "clear and present danger" test, which has survived to torment generations of law students and judges.[33]

Between March 1919 and October 1919, shortly offer writing those opinions, however, Oliver Wendell Holmes, Jr., then 78 years old, experienced a conversion in his beliefs about freedom of expression.[34] He had been, according to Lewis, exposed to correspondence from Judge Learned Hand that urged a more progressive view of freedom of speech as essential in a democracy; he had also read a timely article from the June 1919 issue of the *Harvard Law Review* by Professor Zechariah Chafee, Jr., titled "Freedom of Speech in War Time."[35] Chafee, instead of criticizing Holmes's three decisions made earlier that year, praised his phrase of "clear and present danger" as a shrewd and deliberate stroke to protect free speech. In fact, Chafee argued that Holmes apparently agreed with Hand and with Scofield, the scholar who wrote a 1914 piece on freedom of speech.[36]

OLIVER WENDELL HOLMES'S DISSENT IN THE ABRAMS CASE

In October 1919, the U.S. Supreme Court heard oral arguments in another Espionage Act case, *Abrams v. United States.*[37] It was a prosecution under the 1918 amendments, which made it a crime to "utter, print, write, or publish any disloyal, profane, scurrilous, or abusive language" about the Constitution, the armed forces, military uniforms, or the flag.[38] The defendants in the case were four refugees from the pogroms and tyranny of Czarist Russia—three anarchists and a socialist—who were outraged at President Wilson's decision

---

30. *Id.* at 69.
31. Eugene Debs actually served 3 years of the 10 year sentence. LEWIS, MAKE NO LAW at 73. While in prison, Debs was to poll almost a million votes as the Socialist Party candidate for president in the 1920 election. KALVEN, A WORTHY TRADITION at 131.
32. The three cases are *Schenck v. United States* 249 U.S. 47 (1919); *Frohwerk v. United States* 249 U.S. 204 (1919); and *Debs v. United States* 249 U.S. 211 (1919).
33. *Schenck v. United States* 249 U.S. 47 (1919) at 51–52. Lewis makes the "perplexed" observation, in which I concur, in MAKE NO LAW at 72.
34. There are a number of biographies of O. W. Holmes, Jr. The classic one is C. D. BOWEN, YANKEE FROM OLYMPUS: JUSTICE HOLMES AND HIS FAMILY (1944). A more current biography is NOVICK, HONORABLE JUSTICE: THE LIFE OF OLIVER WENDELL HOLMES (1989), which discusses the changes between *Schenck* and *Abrams* at 473–474 and is more skeptical about whether there was a significant change in Holmes's position and, if so, whether the causes listed by Lewis account for such a change.
35. *Id.* at 74–77.
36. *Id.* at 76.
37. 250 U.S. 616 (1919).
38. Espionage provisions quoted by Lewis in MAKE NO LAW at 76.

to send U.S. troops into Russia after the Bolshevik Revolution. They had distributed two copies of pamphlets in English and Yiddish that began, "The preparatory work for Russia's emancipation is brought to an end by his majesty, Mr. Wilson, and the rest of the gang; dogs of all colors!"[39] The leaflets urged a general strike in protest. The defendants were convicted and sentenced to terms of 15 and 20 years.[40] The Supreme Court decision in November 1919 affirmed the convictions; the surprise was that Justice Holmes, joined by Justice Louis D. Brandeis, dissented.

Holmes's dissent in the Abrams case is one of the best-known opinions in U.S. law,[41] and it is almost as puzzling as it is well known. Holmes opens by stating that he stood by his earlier decisions in March. Then, he toughens the clear and present danger test by modifying it to read "clear and imminent danger" which will "bring about forthwith certain substantive evils." He then adds that "the best test of truth is the power of the thought to get itself accepted in the competition in the market." He observed near the conclusion of the dissent, "I wholly disagree with the argument of the Government that the First Amendment left the common law as to seditious libel in force. History seems to me to be against the notion."[42] Those lines form the beginning of the modern case law of the First Amendment.

THE CASE OF *NEW YORK TIMES V. SULLIVAN*

The ancient law of libel collided with the modern civil rights movement in a full-page advertisement in the *New York Times* on March 29, 1960. The advertisement, entitled "Heed Their Rising Voices," sought to raise money for the Committee to Defend Martin Luther King and the Struggle for Freedom in the South.[43] L. B. Sullivan, the police commissioner of Montgomery, Alabama, wrote letters on April 9, 1960, to the *Times* and to four black ministers[44] living in Alabama demanding a full retraction.[45] When the four ministers got the letters, it was the first they had heard of the advertisement.[46] However, under Alabama law, their silence in response to Sullivan's demand for retraction

---

39. *Abrams v. United States* 250 U.S. 616 at 621 (1919) as quoted in LEWIS, MAKE NO LAW at 76.
40. Mollie Steimer, 20 years old at the time, was given 15 years; the other three—Jacob Abrams, Hyman Lachowsky, and Samuel Lipman—were sentenced to 20 years. Lewis relates the personal tragedies of these four after conviction in these words:

    The full story of the defendants and the case was told by Professor Richard Polenberg in his book *Fighting Faiths*. The four defendants were released from prison in 1921 on condition that they go to the Soviet Union. There Molly Steimer and Jacob Abrams tangled with a new tyranny and left for Mexico. Hyman Lachowsky and Samuel Lipman stayed in the U.S.S.R. and became victims, one of Stalin's terror, the other of the Nazis. (MAKE NO LAW at 77)

41. Karl Llewellyn asserts that Holmes's dissent in *Abrams*, made under pressure to conform to popular sentiment in wartime, "stands among the papers of our statesmen beside the Gettysburg Address." LLEWELLYN, BRAMBLE BUSH (1930) at 128.
42. *Abrams v. United States* 249 U.S. 616 at 627–631 as quoted in LEWIS, MAKE NO LAW at 78–79.
43. The advertisement is reproduced in full in LEWIS, MAKE NO LAW: THE SULLIVAN CASE AND THE FIRST AMENDMENT (1991) at 2–3. By order of Justice Brennan, it is also reproduced in full as an appendix to *New York Times Co. v. Sullivan* 376 U.S. 254 (1964).
44. The four ministers were Ralph D. Abernathy and S. S. Seay Sr. of Montgomery, Fred L. Shuttlesworth of Birmingham, and J. E. Lowery of Mobile.
45. LEWIS, MAKE NO LAW at 11–12.
46. *Id.* at 12.

operated as an admission of responsibility.[47] The *Times* responded through counsel by letter to Sullivan. The letter admitted a factual error and then asked Sullivan to "let us know in what respect you claim the statements in the advertisement reflect on you."[48]

Anthony Lewis, a two-time Pulitzer Prize–winning journalist,[49] has written a legal history that chronicles not only the path of the Sullivan case to the Supreme Court and its implications for libel law but also covers the entire history of freedom of expression in the United States. This chapter presents a summary of the content of Lewis' 1991 book, *Make No Law: The Sullivan Case and the First Amendment*, as well as critical commentary on it.

Sullivan claimed through his attorneys that, even though the advertisement did not refer to him by name or position, its allegations about police brutality toward Alabama State University students were personally defamatory. He filed suit on April 19, 1960, in the Circuit Court of Montgomery County, an Alabama state court, asking $500,000 in damages.[50] Soon, other public officials of Alabama filed additional lawsuits based on the ad that brought the amount of damages sought to a total of $3 million.[51]

The trial was held in Montgomery, Alabama, in the courtroom of Judge Walter Burgwyn Jones, who was proud that his father had carried Robert E. Lee's colors to Ulysses S. Grant at Appomattox.[52] The *Times* moved to quash service of process on the ground that it could not be subject to personal service in Alabama because of its limited presence in the state. The *Times* had distributed only 394 copies of that issue in Alabama of a total circulation of 650,000.[53] In his passion to reach the merits, Judge Jones held the *Times* subject to his jurisdiction on alternative grounds that it had done enough business in Alabama to be subject to suit and that the *Times* attorney had inadvertently made a general rather than a special appearance—in effect overruling Judge Jones' own book on Alabama pleading and practice.[54]

Such a ruling may have been predictable from a judge who had previously allowed jurors in another trial to be seated in Confederate uniforms, had his bailiffs enforce segregated seating in his courtroom, and had ordered the NAACP to cease doing business in Alabama.[55] The all-White male jury returned a verdict in Sullivan's favor, even though he was not mentioned by name and could not in his testimony identify a single instance of being shunned or ridiculed as a result of the advertisement of which he complained.[56] The jury took 2 hours and 20 minutes to return a verdict for $500,000 against the *New York Times* and the four ministers.[57] Motions for a new trial were denied or held forfeited on procedural grounds by Judge Jones.[58]

---

47. *Id.* at 137.
48. *Id.*
49. Atkin, *Keen Court Observer*, CHRISTIAN SCI. MONITOR, October 1, 1991, at 13.
50. LEWIS, MAKE NO LAW at 12.
51. *Id.* at 14.
52. *Id.* at 25–26.
53. *Id.* at 9.
54. *Id.* at 26.
55. *Id.*
56. *Id.* at 27–29.
57. *Id.* at 33.
58. *Id.* at 43–44.

Sullivan's lawyers began attaching and selling the property of the four ministers.[59] Ralph Abernathy had his 5-year old Buick seized and sold.[60] The Alabama Supreme Court upheld the judgments against the *Times* and the four ministers on August 30, 1962.[61] It "upheld Judge Jones in all respects, using broad language that made the libel case an even greater threat to reporting on the racial issue."[62] In a single sentence, the Alabama Supreme Court rejected the First Amendment argument: "The First Amendment of the U.S. Constitution does not protect libelous publications."[63] In 1962, this statement correctly reflected the federal law.

According to Lewis, "*The New York Times* and the four ministers had one last chance to avoid owing $500,000 to Sullivan—and millions more to other Alabama libel plaintiffs. This was to ask the Supreme Court of the United States to hear the case and reverse the judgment."[64] Lewis recounts that this objective was "anything but easy" because the Supreme Court has no power to correct a state court's decision on matters of state law and libel had always been entirely a matter of state law. Lewis observes that in 1962 "[n]o award of damages for libel, however grotesque the sum or outlandish the legal theory underlying it, had ever been held to violate the First Amendment or any other provision of the Constitution."[65]

The first step was to get the Supreme Court to hear the case—because the Court exercises mostly discretionary jurisdiction—through petition for a writ of *certiorari*. The *Times*, on advice from Louis Loeb, its counsel and a partner in Lord, Day & Lord, chose a distinguished scholar and law professor at Columbia University for this assignment, Herbert Wechsler.[66] Wechsler's first task was to convince a meeting of executives at the *New York Times* that the newspaper should seek review in the Supreme Court at all.[67] He succeeded by invoking Madisonian doctrines of the importance of free debate in a democratic society.[68] On November 21, 1962, the *Times*'s petition for *certiorari*, a 31-page printed pamphlet, was filed.[69] In the section headed "Reasons for Granting the Writ," Wechsler asserted, "[The decision of the Supreme Court of Alabama] transforms the action for defamation from a method of protecting

---

59. *Id.* at 43.
60. Actually, Lewis recounts later that automobiles belonging to Abernathy, Shuttlesworth, and Lowery were sold at auction, as well as a parcel of real estate that Abernathy had inherited from his father. Lowery got his car back when a parish member bought it at the auction and sold it to Lowery's wife for one dollar. *See id.* at 162 for more details and an extended treatment in BRANCH, PARTING THE WATERS: AMERICA IN THE KING YEARS 1954–63 (1988) at 579–580.
61. LEWIS, MAKE NO LAW at 44.
62. *Id.*
63. *Id.* at 45.
64. *Id.* at 103.
65. *Id.*
66. *Id.* at 103–105.
67. *Id.* at 106–107. Some of the senior people at the *Times*, Lewis recounts, wanted to stay with the established policy of never settling libel cases because the *Times* only publishes the truth. When there was an error, the *Times* paid up and accepted it as one of the chances in publishing.
68. Madison's notions of the importance of freedom of information in a democratic society can be found in the Resolutions of the Virginia legislature, which protested the Sedition Act of 1798. In late 1799, Madison expanded on that position with a Report on the Virginia Resolutions in which he declared that under the U.S. Constitution, "The people, not the government, possess the absolute sovereignty." Quoted in LEWIS, MAKE NO LAW at 61. Perhaps, the most telling detail of the Sedition Act of 1798 history is that Thomas Jefferson and James Madison made their attempt to arouse state opposition to the Act in secret for fear of being prosecuted under the Act.
69. LEWIS, MAKE NO LAW at 107.

private reputation to a device for insulating government against attack." Such a rule was "indistinguishable in its function and effect from the proscription of seditious libel."[70]

Professor Wechsler was on sabbatical in the spring of 1963 and devoted himself full-time to writing the brief.[71] Wechsler, his wife, and Marvin Frankel worked tirelessly through the summer of 1963 to finish the brief; at the end, Wechsler would allow no one else to do the cite checking.[72] The brief was filed with the Court on September 9, 1963,[73] and it argued, in part, Madison's view of an absolute privilege to criticize government. It also reviewed the entire history of the Sedition Act of 1798.[74] Oral arguments were held on January 6, 1964[75]; arguments for the four ministers were held over until the morning of January 7th.[76] Oral argument in the Supreme Court of the United States does not play the part it did a century or more ago. At the time of *New York Times v. Sullivan*, advocates were limited to an hour each; this time limit has since been reduced by half.[77]

THE SUPREME COURT REACHES A DECISION

On March 9, 1964, Professor Wechsler was teaching a class in one of the large lecture rooms at the Columbia Law School when his secretary came in and handed him a note that read simply, "Judgment reversed. Decision unanimous."[78] In the interim between argument and decision, William Brennan had written eight separate opinions for the court and had watched his support shift and change up to the night before the decision was announced.[79] The note could hardly suggest the effort involved on Brennan's part in marshaling a unanimous decision, nor could it suggest the sweeping changes the opinion wrought in libel law.

In his opinion for the court, Justice Brennan opened with a summary of the events in Alabama[80] and then disposed of all other issues except the First Amendment issues in a footnote.[81] He stated the Court's decision as follows:

> We reverse the judgment. We hold that the rule of law applied by the Alabama courts is constitutionally deficient for failure to provide the safeguards for freedom of speech and of the press that are required by the First and Fourteenth Amendments in a libel action brought by a public official against critics of his official conduct.[82]

This statement of result was followed by 28 pages of exposition in the U.S. Reports that provides a fascinating and powerful tour through the history and meaning of the First Amendment.[83] Sullivan's legal argument that the

70. *Id.* at 107–108.
71. LEWIS, MAKE NO LAW at 114.
72. *Id.* at 113.
73. *Id.* at 115.
74. *Id.* at 117–119.
75. *Id.* at 129.
76. *Id.* at 137–139.
77. *Id.* at 128.
78. *Id.* at 140.
79. *Id.* at 164–165.
80. *New York Times Co. v. Sullivan* 376 U.S. 254 (1964) at 256–264.
81. 376 U.S. 254 at 264, note 4.
82. 376 U.S. 254 at 264 as quoted in LEWIS, MAKE NO LAW at 141–142 and at 264.
83. 376 U.S. 254 at (1964) 265–292.

Constitution does not protect libelous publications was distinguished on the ground that none of the cases cited sustained the use of libel laws to sanction criticism of the official conduct of public officials. Brennan continued by noting that libel has "no talismanic immunity from constitutional limitations."[84] Throughout the Brennan opinion, there are threads from the briefs and from the oral arguments, starting with Wechsler's argument that the advertisement was a form of speech about public issues and, thus, was entitled to First Amendment protection not available to other commercial advertisements. There followed the most-quoted and perhaps most quotable passage from the opinion:

> Thus we consider this case against the background of a profound national commitment to the principle that debate on public issues should be uninhibited, robust, and wide-open, and that it may well include vehement, caustic, and sometimes unpleasantly sharp attacks on government and public officials. . . . The present advertisement, as an expression of grievance and protest on one of the major public issues of our time, would seem clearly to qualify for the constitutional protection.[85]

Two significant issues directly affecting the extent of Constitutional protection to be given the advertisement remained to be addressed: (1) whether protection was forfeited because the ad contained factual errors and (2) whether protection was affected by the alleged defamation of Sullivan. Brennan addressed these issues in turn.

On the first issue, Justice Brennan quoted Madison's statement in his Report on the Virginia Resolutions: "Some degree of abuse is inseparable from the proper use of everything; and in no instance is this more true than in that of the press."[86] He concluded that "erroneous statement is inevitable in free debate and that it must be protected if the freedoms of expression are to have the 'breathing space' that they 'need . . . to survive.'"[87] On the second issue, Brennan asserted that injury to official reputation affords no more warrant for repressing protected speech than does factual error.

Continuing in this vein, Brennan asserted that government officials, such as elected city commissioners, should be "men of fortitude, able to thrive in a hardy climate."[88] He then moved to bolster these themes with the history of the Sedition Act of 1798. Following the history, he gave Madison's views and noted that the American system was "altogether different" from the British because "the people, not the government, possess the absolute sovereignty."[89] Then, Brennan put the court's approval on the judgment of history, first noted in the Abrams dissent by Justice Holmes, that the Sedition Act (which expired 163 years earlier) was unconstitutional.[90]

---

84. 376 U.S. 254 (1964) at 269.
85. 376 U.S. 254 (1964) at 370–371. Harry Kalven, Jr., in his excellent book on freedom of speech, A WORTHY TRADITION: FREEDOM OF SPEECH IN AMERICA (J. Kalven ed. 1988) at 67 calls the first sentence in this quotation "a perfect and splendid sentence."
86. 4 ELLIOT'S DEBATES ON THE FEDERAL CONSTITUTION (1876) at 571 as quoted in 376 U.S. 254 at 271 (1964) and also quoted in LEWIS, MAKE NO LAW at 144.
87. *N.A.A.C.P. v. Button* 371 U.S. 415 at 433 as quoted at 376 U.S. 254 at 271–272 and also quoted in LEWIS, MAKE NO LAW at 144.
88. *Craig v. Harney* 331 U.S. 367 at 376 as quoted in 376 U.S. 254 (1964) at 272–273.
89. 376 U.S. 254 at 274 and quoted in LEWIS, MAKE NO LAW at 145.
90. 376 U.S. 254 (1964) at 276.

Finally, after embracing the Madisonian position, Justice Brennan turned away from absolute privilege to provide somewhat of a balanced approach in the area of reputation. He held that what was established was a limited immunity from libel suits for erroneous statements honestly made. The formula for balancing these interests follows:

> The constitutional guarantees require, we think, a Federal rule that prohibits a public official from recovering damages for a defamatory falsehood relating to his official conduct unless he proves that the statement was made with "actual malice"—that is, with knowledge that it was false or with reckless disregard of whether it was false or not.[91]

THE AFTERMATH OF THE SULLIVAN DECISION

Alexander Meiklejohn, the philosopher of free speech, said when *New York Times v. Sullivan* was decided that it was "an occasion for dancing in the streets."[92] Lewis, almost 30 years after the decision, cites Robert Bork and Professor Richard A. Epstein for the proposition that the dancing has stopped, supposedly because of the unforeseen problems that have developed with the rule.[93] Lewis writes,

> A good many editors and writers would have agreed. For the prospect that they envisioned in 1964—a country where public debate went on uninhibited by the threat of heavy libel damages—had not come into being. On the contrary, libel suits seemed to be growing in number and size.[94]

This assertion that the progeny of *New York Times v. Sullivan* have unwittingly created a crisis in the litigation of libel by public figures needs some qualification. The rule, which has been extended by later cases to include all public figures, not just government officials, has seriously raised the cost of litigating a public figure libel suit because of the extensive discovery necessary to prove "actual malice." Many of the concerns center on this excessive cost. However, as Lewis points out, the rule also made the investigative reporting of Watergate and of the Pentagon Papers feasible by giving encouragement and protection to the press when it was dealing with public officials and the federal government.[95] Thus, one might question whether the increase in libel verdicts and litigation costs is an unavoidable concomitant of a more vigorous press and not just the accidental product of the Sullivan decision.

DRAFT CARD BURNING, FLAG BURNING, AND CROSS BURNING

When David Paul O'Brien was convicted in 1967 of violating the 1965 amendment to the Universal Military Training and Service Act, the Chaplinsky decision[96] seemed to be healthy. Chaplinsky was a unanimous decision written

---

91. 376 U.S. 254 at 279–280 and quoted in LEWIS, MAKE NO LAW at 147.
92. LEWIS, MAKE NO LAW at 200.
93. *Id.*
94. *Id.*
95. *Id.* at 158.
96. *Chaplinsky v. New Hampshire* 315 U.S. 568 (1942).

by Justice Frank Murphy holding that certain types of speech were beneath First Amendment protection. The "fighting words" exception was cited approvingly by subsequent cases, although, as we have seen, in 1968, the court seems to have indicated some degree of protection for speech judged libelous when it was directed at public officials. Some argue that Chaplinsky was the "last case in which the Court explicitly upheld a conviction only for 'fighting words' directed at public officials."[97]

As to David O'Brien's burning of his Selective Service registration certificate, Chief Justice Warren writing for the Court held,

> This Court has held that when "speech" and "nonspeech" elements are combined in the same course of conduct, a sufficiently important governmental interest in regulating the nonspeech element can justify incidental limitations on First Amendment freedoms.[98]

Further, the opinion held that the incidental restriction on alleged First Amendment freedoms "is no greater than is essential" to further the governmental interest.[99] The court also distinguished "knowing destruction" of Selective Service certificates from "non-possession" of them, which had been made punishable earlier.[100] Somewhat disingenuously, the majority noted that someone could knowingly destroy the Selective Service certificate of another without being guilty of nonpossession.[101] In this case, O'Brien was charged with destroying his own draft card, not one belonging another; and the First Circuit had endorsed his argument that additional punishment was for the public expression of unpopular political sentiment.[102]

Twenty-one years and 31 days later, the Supreme Court, in a bitterly divided 5–4 decision (*Texas v. Johnson*) held that Gregory Lee Johnson's burning of the U.S. flag in Dallas at the 1984 Republican National Convention was "expressive conduct" protected by the First Amendment and conduct that the State of Texas lacked sufficient justification to proscribe.[103] In a majority opinion by Justice Brennan, the Court reasoned,

> If there is a bedrock principle underlying the First Amendment, it is that the government may not prohibit the expression of an idea simply because society finds the idea itself offensive or disagreeable [citations omitted].
>
> We have not recognized an exception to this principle even where our flag has been involved. In *Street v. New York*, 394 U.S.576 (1969), we held that a State may not criminally punish a person for uttering words critical of the flag.... Nor may the government, we have held, compel conduct that would evince respect for the flag. "To sustain the compulsory flag salute we are required to say that a Bill of Rights

---

97. KERMIT L. HALL (ed.), THE OXFORD COMPANION TO THE SUPREME COURT OF THE UNITED STATES (1992) at 135.
98. 391 U.S. 367 at 376.
99. 391 U.S. 367 at 377.
100. 391 U.S. 367 at 381.
101. *Id.*
102. 391 U.S. 367 at 380–381. The Supreme Court implies that nonpossession is a lesser included offense of knowing destruction. However, O'Brien's argument was embraced by the First Circuit Court of Appeals, which held that the Congress had merely sought to punish protesters because the conduct complained of was already punishable. *See O'Brien v. United States* 376 F.2d 538 (1st Cir. 1967).
103. 491 U.S. 397 at 405–406 and 415–416.

which guards the individual's right to speak his own mind, left it open to public authorities to compel him to utter what is not in his mind." (*Id.* [*West Virginia Board of Education v. Barnette* 319 U.S. 624 (1943)] at 634)

The citation of the Street decision is interesting because in that case the Court did not address the act of flag burning, but resolved the dispute presented on narrower grounds.[104] Street had been convicted under a New York statute that made it a crime "publicly [to] defy . . . or cast contempt upon [an American flag] by words." The majority (by a 5–4 vote) in *Street v. New York* overturned the conviction based on over-breadth of the statute and did not address Street's other Constitutional arguments, one of which was that flag burning should be protected as expressive conduct under the 14th Amendment.

Significantly, informed commentators were critical of the uneven results and of what seemed to be unstable constitutional doctrines in the O'Brien, Tinker, and Street decisions as early as 1970.[105] Some attributed the unsatisfying use of the conduct-speech dichotomy to the "excessive aversion" on the Court to balancing First Amendment rights with governmental interests.[106] Another possible explanation may be that a majority of the Supreme Court did not want to address the issue of flag burning in 1969 when the emotional flames surrounding the country's Vietnam involvement were at their peak.

The Court's conjectural desire not to set off a new firestorm of protest centered on the Vietnam War may have also been at the bottom of the Court's consistent refusal to grant certiorari to cases raising the issue of whether involvement in a war without Congressional declaration of war was constitutional. Such a desire might also explain the fairly superficial disposition of O'Brien's First Amendment claim. In 1968 and 1969, the Court may have been trying to avoid condoning what it saw as radical protest while also sending the message that peaceful, nonviolent, nondestructive expressions of protest would receive Court sanction as protected activity.

However, *Street v. New York*[107] was not the bridge to *Texas v. Johnson*[108]; the bridge was the *per curiam* decision in *Spence v. Washington* declaring that a Seattle college student could not be criminally punished for displaying his U.S. flag on private property with a taped-on peace symbol.[109] Chief Justice Burger, Justice Rehnquist, and Justice White dissented.[110]

---

104. 394 U.S. 576 at 590.
105. G. GUNTHER AND N. DOWLING, CONSTITUTIONAL LAW: TEXT AND CASES (1970) at 1208–1209. The intervening case between O'Brien and Street was *Tinker v. Des Moines School District* 393 U.S. 503 (1969). In *Tinker*, Justice Fortas wrote for a divided court that the peaceful wearing of black armbands by students to protest the Vietnam War was protected activity under the Constitution. In *Street v. New York*, Fortas found himself on the dissenting end of a 5–4 split.
106. GUNTHER & DOWLING, CONSTITUTIONAL LAW at 1209 wherein the following observation is also made: "Justice Fortas and Chief Justice Warren were among those generally identified with the libertarian wing during the closing years of the Warren Court; Justice Harlan, by contrast, was a chief target of those who, like Justice Black, saw in 'balancing' a frittering away of First Amendment rights. . . . Is it not ironic, then, that Justice Harlan should write the majority opinion in Street—with Chief Justice Warren as well as Justices Fortas and Black finding little difficulty in sustaining the conviction?"
107. 394 U.S. 576 (1969).
108. 491 U.S. 397 (1989).
109. 418 U.S. 405 (1973).
110. Interestingly, Justice Rehnquist in dissent may have foreshadowed part of the Scalia opinion in the R.A.V. decision in his comment at 418 U.S. 405 at 423, note 7, wherein he says, "It is quite apparent that the Court does have considerable sympathy for at least the *form* of Appellant's message. . . . One would hope that this last observation does not introduce a doctrine

In 1989, *Texas v. Johnson*,[111] the court foreshadowed its 1992 cross-burning decision in some significant ways. The majority opinion by Justice Brennan rejected the idea that the state could compel the use of symbols in one direction or only in a certain orthodox way:

> If we were to hold that a State may forbid flag burning whenever it is likely to endanger the flag's symbolic role, but allow it whenever burning the flag promotes that role—as where, for example, a person ceremoniously burns a dirty flag—we would be saying that when it comes to impairing the flag's physical integrity, the flag itself may be used as a symbol—as a substitute for the written or spoken word or a "short cut from mind to mind"—only in one direction. We would be permitting a State to "prescribe what shall be orthodox" by saying that one may burn the flag to convey one's attitude toward it and its referents only if one does not endanger the flag's representation of nationhood and national unity.
>
> We never before have held that the Government may ensure that a symbol be used to express only one view of that symbol or its referents.[112]

Chief Justice Rehnquist dissented in an opinion joined in by Justices White and O'Connor. Justice Stevens dissented in a separate opinion. I liked what one observer wrote about the Rehnquist dissent:

> It is a little hard to pin down the theory of the Rehnquist opinion. The Chief Justice suggests that Congress can recognize a kind of property interest in the flag, that flag burning, like fighting words, is not an "essential part of any exposition of ideas," that state cases have held that public burning of the flag is inherently inflammatory, and that Johnson could have expressed his ideas by other means.[113]

After reviewing the Stevens' dissent, the same observer lumped it with the Rehnquist dissent and Brennan's majority opinion, concluding with this salvo:

> All the opinions share a feature that speaks volumes about the flag's importance and the expected audience for the opinions. No opinion cites a single law review article or other scholarly work. It is almost as if all the Justices intuitively felt that cluttering their opinions with nice doctrinal distinctions and ample references to authority would detract from the majestic simplicity of the flag and the majestic simplicity of freedom of speech.[114]

The same writer dismissed the rush to overturn *Texas v. Johnson* as being driven more by "political desires not to be outdone in patriotism than with deep conviction."[115] Essentially, the use of the cumbersome amendment process to

---

of 'comparative' expression, which gives more leeway to certain forms of expression when more destructive methods of expression are being employed by others" [italics in original].

111. 491 U.S. 397 (1989).
112. 491 U.S. 397 at 416–417.
113. K. Greenawalt, *O'er the Land of the Free: Flag Burning as Speech*, 37 UCLA LAW REV. 925 (1990) at 942.
114. *Id.* at 943.
115. *Id.* at 947.

reverse an "unpopular, well-publicized, but minor decision" would be "unfortunate" and generate an "unhealthy effect on respect for free speech."[116]

Ten days short of 1 year later, also by a 5–4 vote, the Court invalidated the Congressional Flag Protection Act of 1989 in the 1990 case, *United States v. Eichman*.[117] Justice Brennan wrote the majority opinion in which Justices Marshall, Blackmun, Scalia, and Kennedy joined. Justice Stevens filed a dissenting opinion in which Chief Justice Rehnquist and Justices White and O'Connor joined. The essential thrust of the majority opinion is contained in the following passage:

> Although Congress cast the Flag Protection Act of 1989 in somewhat broader terms than the Texas statute at issue in *Johnson*, the Act still suffers from the same fundamental flaw: It suppresses expression out of concern for its likely communicative impact. Despite the Act's wider scope, its restriction on expression "'cannot be justified without reference to the content of the regulated speech.'" *Boos*, 485 U.S., at 320 [emphasis omitted, citation omitted]; see *Spence v. Washington*, 418 U.S. 405, 414, nn.8,9 (1974) (State's interest in protecting flag's symbolic value is directly related to suppression of expression and thus *O'Brien* test is inapplicable even where statute declared "simply . . . that *nothing* may be affixed to or superimposed on a United States flag.")[118]

Note that the Court wished to avoid imposition of the three-part O'Brien test: whether the law furthers a substantial governmental interest, whether that interest is unrelated to the suppression of free speech, and whether the incidental restrictions on First Amendment speech are no greater than is essential to furtherance of the governmental interest.[119] Somehow, it is predictable that the dissent opens with this point. "The Court's opinion ends where proper analysis of the issue should begin."[120]

On June 22, 1992, the Court, again by a 5–4 vote, reversed the conviction of a Ramsey County, Minnesota, juvenile for burning a cross on the lawn of a Black family in violation of a city ordinance.[121] Surprisingly, the majority opinion, which held that the ordinance censored expressive conduct in violation of the First Amendment, was authored by Justice Scalia, who was joined by Chief Justice Rehnquist and Justices Kennedy, Souter, and Thomas.[122] Justices White, Blackmun, O'Connor, and Stevens joined in the judgment, that is, reversal on the grounds that the city ordinance was fatally overbroad in that it made criminal expression that was both protected and unprotected by the First Amendment.[123]

Thus, on one level, this is a unanimous decision. However, as Justice White makes clear in his dissent, the majority took the decision much further:

> Instead, "find[ing] it unnecessary" to consider the questions upon which we granted review, *ante*, at 2542, the Court holds the ordinance

---

116. *Id.*
117. *United States v. Eichman* 496 U.S. 310 (1990), which invalidated the Flag Protection Act of 1989, 103 Stat. 777, 18 U.S.C. section 700.
118. 496 U.S. 310 at 318.
119. 391 U.S. 367 at 377.
120. 496 U.S. 310 at 319.
121. *R.A.V. v. City of St. Paul, Minnesota* 112 S.Ct. 2538 (1992).
122. *Id.* at 2541 and 2550.
123. *Id.* at 2550.

facially unconstitutional on a ground that was never presented to the Minnesota Supreme Court, a ground that has not been briefed by the parties before this Court, a ground that requires serious departures from the teaching of prior cases.[124]

Scalia declares that the claims adjudicated by the majority are "fairly included" within the questions presented in the petition for *certiorari*[125] and that "[c]ontent-based regulations are presumptively invalid."[126] What Justice Scalia and the majority seem to be after is an unregulated marketplace of ideas in the mold of Chicago School economics, as seen in the following passage:

> Even the prohibition against content discrimination that we assert the First Amendment requires is not absolute. It applies differently in the context of proscribable speech than in the area of fully protected speech. The rationale of the general prohibition, after all, is that content discrimination "rais[es] the specter that the Government may effectively drive certain ideas or viewpoints from the marketplace."[citations omitted][127]

Finally, toward the end of his opinion, Justice Scalia declares,

> The dispositive question in this case, therefore, is whether content discrimination is reasonably necessary to achieve St. Paul's compelling interests; it plainly is not. An ordinance not limited to the favored topics, for example, would have precisely the same beneficial effect. In fact the only interest distinctively served by the content limitation is that of displaying the city council's special hostility towards the particular biases thus singled out.
>
> Let there be no mistake about our belief that burning a cross in someone's front yard is reprehensible. But St. Paul has sufficient means at its disposal to prevent such behavior without adding the First Amendment to the fire.[128]

The dissent labels this approach the Court's "new 'underbreadth' creation."[129] Further, Justice White in dissent declaims,

> [T]he majority offers no reasoned basis for discarding our firmly established strict scrutiny analysis at this time. The majority appears to believe that its doctrinal revisionism is necessary to prevent our elected lawmakers from prohibiting libel against members of one political party but not another and from enacting similarly preposterous ideas. *Ante*, at 2543. The majority is misguided.[130]

We have almost come full circle with this quote in dissent by Justice White.[131] Yes, once in our history, one party did enact a libel law that protected the party in power and not the opposition. However, time has demonstrated

---

124. *Id.* at 2551.
125. *Id.* at 2542, note 3.
126. *Id.* at 2542.
127. *Id.* at 2545.
128. *Id.* at 2550.
129. *Id.* at 2553.
130. *Id.* at 2555.
131. White had announced his intent to retire from the Court at the end of the term. His exasperation with the majority's decision in *R.A.V.* is almost palpable.

the foolishness of that effort, and the wisdom of using that experience as a basis for even-handedness in hate speech laws is surely questionable.

HOW FREE IS THE FREE PRESS?

The mainstream, commercial media do not make much use of the freedom of the press enshrined in our First Amendment. After the election of George W. Bush in November 2000, the press suddenly stopped, for instance, running articles about the wisdom of drilling for oil in the Arctic Wildlife Sanctuary and started running a new series of articles about how *best* to go about the drilling so as to minimize environmental degradation. In other words, the shift of the press' choice of issues deliberately curried favor with the new administration. And if you think the press polishes the apple for the incumbents, just look at what studies show about the hands-off favoritism shown to cash-paying advertisers!

Studies have shown that the newsworthiness of the surgeon general's report on the hazards of smoking was inversely correlated with newspapers' total inches of advertising received from tobacco companies.[132] The local media in Boise, Idaho, used their "news judgment" to sanitize the information that they disseminated. Here is one illustration: When I lived in Boise we had drive-by shootings on a regular basis but not one was ever reported in the local paper. Instead, the only drive-by shootings it reported on were in Caldwell, Idaho, at the far end of the valley, giving the implication that Boise was a safer place to live. Another way to learn about the media biases is to leave the country and read about the United States in a foreign country's press; even subscribing to a Canadian news magazine would be enlightening for the careful reader.

The media are strongly influenced by corporate money, power, and advertising budgets.[133] What information the average American gets on TV, radio, and in the press is only what a power elite wants him or her to get. Anything else is considered unfit to print or run. Here is another example. The student government for 2000–2001 at Boise State University had been conducting a campaign against the treatment that students received; to my mind, it was a

---

132. The tobacco industry is an enormous advertising power in the United States. It buys over $5 billion (or $75 for every adult smoker) of advertising every year. "Censorship in the Media," from *Smoke-Free for Life*, a smoking prevention curriculum supplement from the Nova Scotia Department of Health, Drug Dependency and Tobacco Control Unit, 1996. Accessed at http://www.media-awareness.ca/eng/med/class/teamedia/nfoshti.htm on October 9, 2002. On January 1, 1971, cigarette advertising was outlawed on U.S. television, and advertising revenues began to flow into the print media. Between 1950 and 1969, three leading U.S. news magazines ran a total of 210 articles on the health dangers of smoking. Between 1970 and 1986, the same three magazines included only 64 articles about tobacco and cigarettes, and most dealt with political or business issues, rather than health. Joe Tye, "The STAT Speaker's Guide and Slide Collection" (1991) as cited in "Censorship in the Media," *supra*. Statistically, the drop is from 11.05 articles per year to 3.76 articles per year; a decline of approximately 66% in coverage.

133. According to one source, "*Playboy* is hardly the only mass-circulation magazine going out of its way to be more sensitive to the well-being of tobacco hawkers than human lung tissue. On the rare occasion that either *Time*, *Newsweek*, or *U.S. News & World Report* schedules a negative article about smoking, spokespersons for those magazines reluctantly admitted to us, the policy is to give the cigarette companies advance notice—and the option of moving, or removing, their ads in that issue, lest readers associate them with the unsavory publicity." MARTIN A. LEE & NORMAN SOLOMON, UNRELIABLE SOURCES: A GUIDE TO DETECTING BIAS IN NEWS MEDIA (1992) at 6–7.

significant story about a major institution in that city. For 6 months up to March 30, 2001, not a single word of that story appeared in the local paper, but *The Idaho Statesman* did report that the State Board of Education awarded the president a $150,000 performance bonus.[134]

What value is a free press if the press engages in self-censorship to maintain its finances or to protect its relationships with local and national newsmakers?

CONCLUSION

One respected commentator noted that the O'Brien case is "perhaps the ultimate First Amendment insult."[135] The flag-burning cases seem to go out of their way to avoid having to apply the test from the O'Brien decision, which was applied almost cavalierly so as to confirm the conviction. The balance of the Vietnam era protest cases seem to erect protection for expression of dissent in U.S. society. However, the 1989 decision in *Texas v. Johnson* is difficult for me to reconcile with the O'Brien decision. Surely, if one can be protected in burning the emblem of the country, how can a piece of paper evidencing draft registration be the object of greater governmental interest and protection?

Perhaps the most difficult decision to add to this line of cases is the 1992 *R.A.V. v. City of St. Paul* decision.[136] It may be rationalized as a free market ideological spasm, or it might be excused as a prolonged exercise in *obiter dictum*. As law, Justice Scalia's opinion seems to raise more problems than it solves, and it is devastating to whatever framework has been created over the years in the area of hate speech. Perhaps, it is merely the conservative wing's retaliation for Brennan's flag-burning decisions.

On a grander level, this entire chapter may be understood as an example of the truth of the following assertion by a noted First Amendment scholar, Steven H. Shiffrin: "In fact, it turns out that *no general framework rooted in First Amendment principle exists*. For the most part, the first amendment social engineer just balances the relevant interests and comes to a decision [italics added].[137]

---

134. Patrick Orr, *Ed Board Approves $150,000 Bonus for BSU President Ruch*, ID. STATESMAN (March 24, 2001) at p. 1.

135. STEVEN H. SHRIFFIN, THE FIRST AMENDMENT, DEMOCRACY, AND ROMANCE (1990) at 81.

136. 505 U.S. 377 (1992) on a 5–4 decision, the majority, in an opinion by Justice Scalia, joined by Chief Justice Rehnquist and Associate Justices Kennedy, Souter, and Thomas, reversed the Minnesota Supreme Court's decision upholding an ordinance under which a teenager who allegedly burned a cross inside the fenced yard of a Black family was charged. The majority based its decision to invalidate the St. Paul ordinance on the grounds, *inter alia*, that the hate-crime-style law imposed viewpoint discrimination in that it reached only those who used fighting words to alarm, anger, or otherwise create resentment on the basis of race, color, creed, religion, or gender without imposing similar limits on speech by those who advocated tolerance and equality. Thus, the majority reasoned the ordinance was overbroad and violated the First Amendment.

137. SHIFFRIN, THE FIRST AMENDMENT at 13.

CHAPTER

13

Current Issues in Freedom of Expression

The first casualty when war comes is truth.

—Attributed to Hiram W. Johnson[1]

A profound national commitment to the principle that debate on public issues should be uninhibited, robust, and wide-open.

—Justice William Brennan[2]

Knowledge will forever govern ignorance; and a people who mean to be their own governors must arm themselves with the power which knowledge gives.

—James Madison[3]

Bill Maher had a talk show titled "Politically Incorrect" for a few years on the ABC television network. His show was canceled by ABC in the summer of 2002.[4] According to a report in the *New York Daily News*, "ABC cancelled *'Politically Incorrect'* when several advertisers pulled out after Mr. Maher's comments about Sept. 11 drew criticism from the White House."[5] This action, if the report is true, is reprehensible from a First Amendment perspective. The White House, apparently, achieved by indirection a goal— the silencing of a critic—which it was constitutionally prohibited from doing directly. This conduct seems outrageous, whether or not you agree with Mr. Maher's views.[6]

This silencing of critics seems to be widespread if one looks at corporate conduct. In a real sense, the institution of the law has become an accessory to this silencing. One of the major ways large corporations silence critics is through the use of SLAPP suits. SLAPP is an acronym for "strategic lawsuits against public participation." In addition to silencing critics, a corporations restrict the flow of information to the American people or certain segments of the American people in order to modify their behavior or change their opinion. This screening of information is insidious and undermines what it means to be a free people in the democratic sense. Much of the screening and silencing, although certainly not all of it, is the product of abuse of their vast economic powers by wealthy interests.

Since September 11, 2001, several federal government officials have used the tragic events of that day and our increased fear of international terrorism as a shield to protect themselves from criticism and to chill open discussion of the causes of that attack. This psychological chilling of open expression has only been accelerated by the Bush Administration's decision to invade

---

1. "In 1918 U.S. Senator Hiram Warren Johnson is purported to have said: 'The first casualty when war comes is truth.' However, this was not recorded. In 1928 Arthur Ponsonby's wrote: 'When war is declared, truth is the first casualty.' (Falsehood in Wartime) Samuel Johnson seems to have had the first word: 'Among the calamities of war may be jointly numbered the diminution of the love of truth, by the falsehoods which interest dictates and credulity encourages.' (From The Idler, 1758)." Accessed on http://www.guardian.co.uk/notesandqueries/query/0,5753,-21510,00.html on April 10, 2003.
2. *New York Times v. Sullivan* 408 U.S. 92, 96 (1964)
3. Letter to W. T. Barry, August 4, 1822 (*Madison*, 1865, III, 276). Accessed on http://www.jmu.edu/madison/quote.htm on April 10, 2003.
4. Stephen Battaglio, *Upscale Viewers Tune to NBC*, CINC. ENQUIRER (November 25, 2002) at C4.
5. *Id.*
6. The nature of Mr. Maher's views may be suggested by the title of his recent book, WHEN YOU RIDE ALONE YOU RIDE WITH BIN LADEN, a collection of his thoughts about the war on terrorism. *Id.*

Iraq for the stated goal of ousting the regime of Saddam Hussein. There are some reports on cable news that Peter Arnett lost his job at NBC as a form of "collateral damage" from a head-hunting mission from the White House after he criticized the U.S. war plan on Iraqi television. The result has been disheartening to those who cherish open and robust discussion of matters of public import. This chapter, rather than following a "rights" analysis, analyzes this problem from the perspective of a public good.

SHORT HISTORY OF THE FIRST AMENDMENT

On December 15, 1791, Virginia became the 11th state to ratify the first 10 amendments to the U.S. Constitution, and thus, the Bill of Rights became law.[7] "In most states, Federalist proponents of the Constitution succeeded in securing ratification only by promising that they would seek a bill of rights when the new Congress convened after ratification" [italics added].[8] The First Amendment reads as follows:

> Congress shall make no law respecting an establishment of religion, or prohibiting the free exercise thereof; or abridging the freedom of speech, or of the press; or the right of the people peaceably to assemble, and to petition the Government for a redress of grievances.[9]

After the Civil War (1861–1865), Congress passed and the states ratified the 14th Amendment, which addresses civil rights for former slaves and other matters required as a result of the rebellion. The 14th Amendment, Section 1, declares

> All persons born or naturalized in the United States, and subject to the jurisdiction thereof, are citizens of the United States and of the State wherein they reside. No State shall make or enforce any law which shall abridge the privileges or immunities of citizens of the United States; nor shall any State deprive any person of life, liberty, or property, without due process of law; nor deny to any person within its jurisdiction the equal protection of the laws.[10]

This amendment took effect during Reconstruction and spoke directly to the states. In contrast, the Bill of Rights addresses the new federal government, not the states.

During the struggle by the courts to come to terms with what equal protection means when applied to state governments, the federal courts hit on the idea of selective incorporation. Under that doctrine, the First Amendment protections were applied on a case-by-case basis. Freedom of speech has been upheld against state encroachments since 1968; now an important issue seems to be how to protect freedom of speech, or the larger concept of freedom of expression, against the powers applied by powerful economic forces, by the dominant culture, and—in time of war—by government propaganda, rather than by direct government intervention.

---

7. SAMUEL ELIOT MORISON, THE OXFORD HISTORY OF THE AMERICAN PEOPLE (1965) at 319, note 1.
8. JETHRO K. LIEBERMAN, THE EVOLVING CONSTITUTION (1992) at 76.
9. Amendment I, U.S. Constitution, as quoted in G. GUNTHER & N.T. DOWLING, CONSTITUTIONAL LAW: CASES AND MATERIALS (A70) at lxxxiv.
10. Amendment XIV, U.S. Constitution, as quoted in GUNTHER & DOWLING, *supra* note 3, at lxxxvii.

FREEDOM OF EXPRESSION AS A "PUBLIC GOOD"

Several studies suggest that we, the general public, tend to both underestimate the value or worth of public goods and our fair share required to maintain them. Another problem with public goods is that no one, in general, takes the role of caregiver for them. In one sense, public goods are orphans compared to private goods that "belong" to certain people, who generally take an interest in their care and feeding. One result, as shown in studies done for business ethics, is that public goods tend to suffer, using a bank analogy, from excessive withdrawals and inadequate deposits. For instance, most employers want prospective employees to give them full references from former employers but only a small fraction of them are willing themselves to provide such references out of distrust and fear of litigation.

Free expression is a valuable public good. The Founders protected free speech against federal intrusion because of their very distasteful experience with England and King George III. Criticism of His Majesty's government was grounds, whether true or not, for serious punishment under the doctrine of seditious libel. It was not private conversations that needed protection, but rather public discourse, such as that of the newspaper owner, John Peter Zenger of New York (1735) (see Chapter 12). This public discourse, especially on political topics, needed and received protection under the First Amendment. Both the right to hear and the right to speak were defended.

A free people need a free flow of information. This can be seen as communitarian, but it can also be understood as part of the social contract (e.g., I will respect your right to speak, write, hear, read, publish, and watch whatever you wish if you will respect my right to do the same). This chapter addresses primarily this aspect of free expression: the free flow of information in the so-called marketplace of ideas as a public good, rather than as an individual right, which is a dominant theme in the law. As a public good, it may be that free expression raises as many or more ethical and moral problems than legal issues because in the final analysis the welfare of a society is more a question of what we as members do and respect than it is a matter of what courts will enforce. "As the happiness of man is more a function of morality than law, there may be much unhappiness in society that human laws can undertake to remove."[11] Let us turn to a case in which the dominant social class has proven intolerant of an irreverent parody for commercial profit.

THE POLYGAMY PORTER CASE

We've exhibited much worse taste than this.
—Greg Schirf, President, Schirf Brewing Company (Wasatch Beers)[12]

Good taste and humour are a contradiction in terms, like a chaste whore.
—Attributed to Malcolm Muggeridge[13]

---

11. *Evans v. Evans* I Hag Con 35, 161 Eng. Rep. 466 (Consistory Court of London) (1790).
12. *'Why Have Just One?' Ads for 'Polygamy' Beer Called Offensive*. Accessed at http://abcnews. no.com/sections/us/DailyNews/polvnamvbeer on February 1, 2002.
13. *The Columbia World of Quotations*. 1996. Quotation is attributed to Malcolm Muggeridge, a British journalist and author (1903–1990). Accessed at http://www.bartleby.com/cgi-bin/texis/webinator/sitesearch/+VwwFqAtddmaBw5Bnxzmw on April 11, 2002.

One of the big hits of the 2002 Winter Olympic Games at Salt Lake City was a locally produced beer named "Polygamy Porter." In the context not of marketing, but of business, government, and society, this section discusses how that brand name came to be so popular. It begins with a short history of the Schirf Brewing Company, which produced "Polygamy Porter." I am interested in showing how, in this particular example, a business interacted with its larger community and how the market for a product worked (or in some people's perspective did not work). I am also interested in raising the issue of community and corporate censorship or filtering of free and protected speech[14] in American society.

Raised Roman Catholic in Milwaukee, Wisconsin—the Beer Capital of America—Greg Schirf went west to Park City, Utah, in 1983. He decided that what Utah, a heavily Mormon state, needed was a brewery. The Mormon Church, an informal name for the Church of Jesus Christ of Latter Day Saints, (LDS), frowns on caffeine and is firmly against the use of alcohol or tobacco by any of its members. Thus, it seemed to some observers that Schirf's entrepreneurial quest might have been quixotic or, at least, misplaced.

By 1986, Schirf was able to launch his award-winning brand of beer, Wasatch Beers. Wasatch adopted the motto: "We Drink Our Share and Sell the Rest."[15] Schirf named his beer after "the majestic mountains that provide the pure, natural water." According to the home page of its Web site, "The Wasatch Brew Pub has housed the Schirf Brewing Company, brewers of the new Polygamy Porter, and Park City's most popular restaurant since 1989."[16]

In March 2001, controversy had begun to swirl around some of Wasatch's advertising.[17] One of the elements of the attention-getting campaign urged readers of a billboard to "Baptize your taste buds" with Wasatch Beer. Another ad featured a radio spot in which Elders "Rulon" and "Heber" endure door after door being slammed on them before Heber blurts out "Beer!" and reveals that their mission is of a different kind. "We're here to spread the word about good Beer. . . ." "We're on a mission, sir."[18] These ads, according to the *Salt Lake Tribune*, offended some prominent Utah Mormons, including some legislators and beer distributors.[19] Greg Schirf, in response, said the ad campaign was all meant in good fun: "The campaign really isn't intended to give offense to the prevailing culture." We just want to sell beer and have fun doing it."[20]

People certainly had taken notice and were talking about the ads. In March 2001 phone-in poll on a Mormon-owned radio station, 48% of the callers wanted the billboards taken down, but 52% thought they should stay.[21] A spokesman for the LDS Church was reported in the *Tribune* as having said that it would have no official comment on the campaign.

---

14. Commercial speech, although low on the priority list of protected speech, has enjoyed First Amendment protection since the U.S. Supreme Court decision in *First National Bank v. Belloti* 435 U.S. 765 (1978). In a recent case, the U.S. Supreme Court held that State of Massachusetts regulations of outdoor advertising of smokeless tobacco were overbroad and violated the First and 14th Amendments. *See Lorillard Tobacco v. Reilly* 533 U.S. 121 (2001).

15. Accessed at http://www.wasatchbeers.com/index.html on April 11, 2002.

16. *Id.*

17. *Stephen Beaumont's World of Beer*, "Risking the Mormon's Wrath in Utah" dateline March 5, 2001. Accessed at http://www.worldofbeer.com/briPhtbeer/utah.html on April 11, 2002.

18. *Id.*

19. *Id.*

20. Glen Warchol, *A Blessing or a Curse? Irreverent Beer Ads Brew Plenty of Both; Beer Ads Poke Fun at Local Culture*, SALT LAKE TRIB. (March 4, 2001) at B1.

21. *Id.*

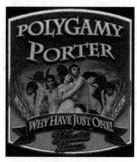

©Wasatch Beer.

Paul Kirwin of Kirwin Communications—the advertising agency located in Park City, Utah, which produced the campaign—took a rather sanguine approach to the controversy surrounding his company's recent pitch for Wasatch Beers. Asked about the potential for offending the state's overwhelming Mormon population, Kirwin replied, "How can you lose a customer you'll never have?"[22]

Apparently the controversy about Wasatch Beers' advertising and the choice of names for its beers was just warming up as Opening Day of the 2002 Winter Olympic Games approached. Schirf Brewing Company had a beer out called "St. Provo Girl Pilsner" featuring an image of a buxom blonde. Next, Schirf came out with "Not 2002 Amber Ale" with an emblem stating Wasatch "Unofficial" NOT 2002 Amber Ale. This number caused a dustup with the Olympic organizers.[23] The real storm came, however, when Wasatch introduced an advertising campaign for its newest beer, Polygamy Porter.[24]

POLYGAMY PORTER AND THE OLYMPIC BREW-HA-HA

As one reporter noted, "With February Winter Olympics crowds about to descend on Salt Lake City, a local brewer has taken a cheeky public poke at Utah's powerful Mormon church by introducing Polygamy Porter with the slogan: 'Why Have Just One?' "[25] The results were spectacular: The beer flew off the shelves, and so did the T-shirts. With the story getting national and international news coverage, Utah brewers' e-commerce sales—mainly Polygamy Porter T-shirts—increased in a few weeks from $1,500 to $57,000 a month.[26]

A newspaper reporter had earlier filed a story that opened with these paragraphs:

> With the Olympics coming to Salt Lake City this winter, only the most optimistic of observers could believe that there won't follow numerous embarrassing situations for the state that controls alcohol more closely than any other. And with the world media eye already focused upon the Utah capital, the fun and games have begun.
>
> Hot on the heels of the Utah Alcoholic Beverage Control Commission's inexplicable decision that hot buttered rum and spiced wine are acceptable drinks for Olympic visitors, but schnapps in hot chocolate and Irish coffee are not, comes word of a controversy surrounding

22. *Id.*
23. Wasatch Beers *Beer List* at 2–3. Accessed at http://www.wasatchbeers.com/pages/beers.html accessed on April 11, 2002 and Candus Thomson, *Utah Beer's Flippant Ads Land Brewmaster in the Suds*, BALTIMORE SUN (November 9, 2001). Accessed at http://www.freerepuiblic.com/focus/fr/567343/sts at p. 2 on April 11, 2002. Schirf says, "I'll never understand that one. Which part did they have licensed? 2002? Unofficial?" *Id.*
24. *See, e.g.*, Candus Thomson, *Utah Beer's Flippant Ads Land Brewmaster in the Suds*, BALTIMORE SUN (November 9, 2001). Accessed at http://www.freerepublic.com/focus/fr/567343/posts on April 11, 2002. AP dispatch titled *Liquor Industry Tangles With the Mormon Church in Mostly Mormon Utah*, dateline Salt Lake City on November 24, 2001. Accessed at http://abcnews.go.com/wire/US/ap20011124_315.html on November 24, 2001. *Stephen Beaumont's World of Beer*, "Utah Beer Follies," dateline November 14, 2001. Accessed at http://www.worldofbeer.com/brightbeer/utah2.html.
25. Michael Valpy, *'Take Some Home for the Wives': Trouble Is Brewing in Salt Lake City Over a Beermaker's Cheeky Campaign.* Accessed at http://globeandmail.workopolis.com/serlet/News/fasttrack/20011227/UBEERM on February 1, 2002.
26. *Id.*

a billboard commissioned by Utah's Schirf Brewing Company, makers of Wasatch beer.

At issue is a brand called Polygamy Porter, the billboards for which poke fun at the Mormon tradition of polygamy. (The Church of Jesus Christ of Latter-Day Saints, known as Mormons, is a powerful political force in Utah.) One billboard, which features a picture of a scantily clad man, cherubs, and a six-pack of wives, advocates that "When enjoying our flavourful beverages please procreate responsibly."[27]

For the record, the LDS Church outlawed polygamy in 1890.[28] This ban on polygamy was a U.S. condition for statehood for Utah. Even so, there are still pockets of practicing polygamists in parts of Utah.[29] There are an estimated 30,000 to 50,000 practicing polygamists in Utah, according to a survey by the *Salt Lake City Tribune*.[30]

In fact, one of the outspoken critics of the beer was Owen Allred, the leader of one of Utah's largest polygamist sects, the Apostolic United Brethren. Mr. Allred was quoted as saying, "I sure don't like it, but I don't think there is anything I can do about it. We do not believe in alcoholic drinks of any kind; it's definitely a slam against the polygamists."[31]

NO BILLBOARDS FOR RENT TO YOU

Schirf and Wasatch Beers ran into serious opposition when the state Alcoholic Beverage Control Commission considered the banning of advertising that makes fun of religion and two local billboard companies refused to run the ad campaign for Polygamy Porter.[32] Civic leaders who were attempting to portray Salt Lake City as having a cosmopolitan flavor in order to attract Olympic visitors were upset that the ads brought up an embarrassing part of Utah's history.[33]

The Reagan Outdoor Advertising Company refused, despite having done previous campaigns for Wasatch Beers, to honor its contract to promote Polygamy Porter.[34] Dewey Reagan of Reagan Outdoor Advertising said, "The entire ad is offensive."[35] Moreover, Mr. Reagan, whose company had contracted to erect the billboard that advised drinkers to "take some home for the wives" and "please procreate responsibly," maintained, "We just do not want to be associated in any way with anything that associates in any way with polygamy. It's not something that is accepted by the majority of society."[36]

Apparently, Reagan Outdoor Advertising had discovered a sensitivity to advertising content that it had not exhibited in years past. The *Salt Lake City Tribune* reported that, 2 years before, Reagan ran a Brighton Ski Resort billboard with the slogan, "Why be wedded to one resort?"—a not-too-subtle

27. "Utah Beer Follies," *supra* note 21.
28. Candus Thomson, *Flippant Ads*, *supra* note 21, at p. 1.
29. *Id.*
30. *Salt Lake City Brewery Creates Olympic Brouhaha with Ads for Polygamy Porter*, THE DENVER POST (November 2, 2001) at p. 2. Accessed at http://ehostvgw11.epnet.com/delivery.asp? on February 1, 2002.
31. *Why Have Just One? supra* note 11.
32. Candus Thomson, *Flippant Ads*, *supra* note 21, at p. 1.
33. *Id.*
34. "Utah Beer Follies," *supra* note 11: and *Why Have Just One? supra* note 11.
35. *Why Have Just One? supra* note 11.
36. *Id.*

nod to Utah's polygamous era.[37] Brighton Marketing Director Dan Mael-
strom said, "We have run boards at Reagan every year. Now it's getting a little
weird."[38] At the time it rejected the Wasatch ads, Reagan had also nixed a
Brighton advertisement featuring free skiing for children 10 years and younger.
That slogan was "Bring'em Young," a word play on the name of the LDS
Church's second president and prophet, Brigham Young, who had numerous
wives.[39] Schirf tried to get other companies to run the billboards for Polygamy
Porter without success. Young Electric Sign Company, based in Salt Lake City,
also rejected the advertisement.[40]

SALT LAKE CITY AND THE MAINLINE MEDIA SPIN

The president of the Salt Lake City Organizing Committee for the Olympics,
Mitt Romney, and others, did a masterful job of selling Salt Lake City as a cosmopolitan city just waiting to be discovered by a world bamboozled by wrong-
headed stereotypes. In fact, Mr. Romney, son of former Michigan governor
George W. Romney,[41] did such a good job that it seemed to jump-start his political career in his home state of Massachusetts.[42] In some nearby towns such
as Boise, Idaho, the media "spin" was so positive as to be almost saccharine.[43]
No mention was made of any logistics problems, and virtually everywhere the
major media outlets praised the Salt Lake City Olympics as possibly the best
ever.

One example from many should provide the flavor. Delta Airlines operates
a major hub in Salt Lake City. In its February 2002 issue of *Sky* magazine, Delta
featured a cover article that ran 10 pages long with photos and quotations that
praised Salt Lake City.[44] The author opened with this confession:

> Salt Lake, I once thought, was just a big city with a small-town mind-
> set, strange liquor laws and a heavy-handed religion. As I met more
> locals over the years, I realized that I had mistaken the stereotype
> for the reality. On the eve of the 2002 Olympic Winter Games, I re-
> turned for a closer look and discovered warm people, civic dynamism,
> a unique history, an active cultural life and an enviable proximity to
> nature.[45]

37. Greg Burton, *Billboard Firm Rejects New Ad Spoofs on Polygamy*, dateline Salt Lake
City on November 8, 2001. Accessed at http://www.broomfieldnews.com/news/statewest/
081poly.html on February 1, 2002.

38. *Id.*

39. *Id.* at p. 1.

40. *Why Have Just One? supra* note 11.

41. George Wilchen Romney (1907–1995) was governor of Michigan from 1963–1969 and then
secretary of Housing and Urban Development from 1969–1973 under President Richard M.
Nixon. Prior to his political career, he was a businessman and the president of American
Motors Corporation. He also held numerous high posts in the Mormon Church. David
Rosenbaum, *George Romney Dies at 88; A Leading G.O.P. Figure*, N.Y. TIMES (July 27, 1995) at
D22.

42. In 1994, when Mitt Romney ran against Edward M. Kennedy for the United States Senate,
Romney's Mormon faith was an issue in the press. By contrast, in November 2002, when
Romney was elected governor of Massachusetts (where less than 0.5% of the residents are
Mormons), his religion received fewer than half as many mentions in the media as it did
in 1994. Michael Paulson, *Romney Win Seen as Sign of Acceptance of Mormons*, BOSTON GLOBE
(November 9, 2002) at B1.

43. *See, e.g.*, Mike Prater, *Drama and Emotion, Successes and Failures*, ID. STATESMAN (February 25,
2002) at 1 (calling the Winter Olympics the "best ever").

44. Roger Toll, *The Soul of Salt Lake City*, SKY (February 2002) at 46–55.

45. *Id.* at 48.

In the next paragraph, the author introduced Mitt Romney (elected Republican governor of Massachusetts in 2002) and his views on Divine Providence's hand in the 2002 Olympic site:

> "God did a good job here geographically," Salt Lake Organizing Committee of 2002 President and CEO Mitt Romney told me. "I was riding up to Park City the other day with Jean-Claude Killy," Romney said of their trip to the nearby ski-resort town, "and he [Killy] started shaking his head. "What's the matter?" I asked. He said "he'd never before seen an eight-lane expressway going to a ski village."[46]

On the facing page in large type, the author quoted former Salt Lake City Mayor Ted Wilson, "The *Mormon Church* has given this community a strong spine: strong families, dedication to clean values, hard work."[47]

The author concluded the article by stating: "[The author] always thought Salt Lake City was a nice place to visit. Now, he's tempted to move there."[48]

One might think it would be newsworthy that a company like Schirf Brewing produced a product legally for sale and could not buy advertising space to promote it in the entire state of Utah in the first years of the 21st century. The story that was not newsworthy in the United States, however, "broke" in *The Economist* with some help from the British Broadcasting Company (BBC). Only then was it imported into the United States.[49]

Other subjects, including an examination of whether Mormon baptism is recognized by the Roman Catholic Church (it is not), were all grist for mainstream journalism's examination in the buildup to the 2002 Winter Olympics.[50] One *Newsweek* article, for example, touched on Mormon church doctrine, history, beliefs about afterlife, Joseph Smith's revelations and murder, the rise of Brigham Young, the controversial 1857 "Mountain Meadows" massacre, and the strict culture in Utah.[51] The tone of these articles, however, was almost jocular; a reader could come away from the issue thinking that the Olympics were going to cause a mild reformation in Utah's Mormon-dominated culture.

Newsweek touched on Wasatch Beer's launching of Polygamy Porter as an example of Utahans having a sense of humor.[52] Schirf Brewing Company's subsequent struggle to find any outdoor advertising company that would run

---

46. *Id.*
47. *Id.* at 49.
48. *Id.* at 55.
49. *See Utah's Holy War*, ECONOMIST (October 27, 2001) at 33.
50. *See* Kenneth L. Woodward, *A Mormon Moment: America's Biggest Homegrown Religion Is Looking More Christian*, NEWSWEEK (September 10, 2001) at 44, 49. Ironically, the introduction of Polygamy Porter was raised in the following passage in a companion article in the same issue:

> In July, the 10th Circuit Court of Appeals struck down a Utah provision that had banned most alcohol advertisements. Salt Lake Mayor Rocky Anderson, looking to shake his hometown's provincial image, has led the effort to make the rules "more hospitable." Anderson, a divorcé and a Democrat, has been something of a lone voice in the wilderness. He won a battle against the city council to allow beer drinking in the park surrounding city hall, and he's now hoping to loosen a law that prohibits dancing till dawn.... Heck, Utahns [sic] even have a sense of humor. Wasatch Brewery has just introduced a new product in time for the Games: Polygamy Porter. It's being promoted with the slogans "Why have just one?" and "Take one home for the wives."

   Ana Figueroa, *Salt Lake's Big Jump: This Sober City is Getting Ready to Party*, NEWSWEEK (September 10, 2001) at 53.
51. *Id.*
52. *Id.*

its ad campaign, however, failed to get similar coverage. In fact, some Utahans did not have a sense of humor about polygamy at all.[53] Mainstream media, controlled by a handful of corporations,[54] did not find this revelation at all worthy of coverage or discussion.

The First Amendment to the U.S. Constitution, passed in 1791 and, in relevant part, declares that Congress shall "make no law . . . abridging the freedom of speech, or of the press. . . ."[55] For almost 190 years, the courts held that commercial speech enjoyed no protection under the First Amendment. Then, in a watershed case, a majority of the court, for the first time, recognized that some commercial speech was entitled to some protection, albeit "a lesser protection" than that given "to other constitutionally guaranteed [forms of] expression."[56]

Of course, no one can deny that the Winter Olympics were very big business.[57] Consequently, the sponsors and other businesses that stood to rake in millions of dollars would not only be sensitive to Salt Lake City's image but would also push hard to ensure that the media spin was extraordinarily positive.[58] Anheuser Busch paid more than $50 million to the Salt Lake City Organizing Committee and the U.S. Olympic Committee in exchange for the exclusive beer-promotion rights during the Winter 2002 Games for its signature brand, Budweiser.[59] This kind of full-court media push can be likened to what the media and Hollywood do when it is time to turn American opinion in favor of a war.[60] In this atmosphere, Wasatch Beer was a small fish swimming against a big current. Through good fortune and a huge amount of free media publicity, however, Wasatch beer did make an unexpected windfall.[61] However, such a result is not the most probable outcome. Wasatch Brewery, under existing law, would have been ill-advised

---

53. The Juab County Attorney and governor's brother, David Leavitt, is a descendent of a polygamist marriage. Holly Mullen, *Tough Prosecutor Seeks to Help Polygamist Green's Victims Rebuild Stolen Lives*, SALT LAKE TRIB. (August 4, 2002) at B1. Recently, Attorney Leavitt successfully prosecuted a prominent polygamist for child rape of his thirteen year-old bride. *Id.* The convicted polygamist, Tom Green, was sentenced to five years to life in prison for the first-degree felony. Kevin Cantera, *Polygamist Gets Five Years to Life; Tearful Defendant Tells Judge He Is Sorry*, SALT LAKE TRIB. (August 28, 2002) at A1.

54. *See infra* Part IV.C.

55. U.S. CONST. amend I.

56. *Cent. Hudson Gas & Elec. Corp. v. Pub. Serv. Comm'n*, 447 U.S. 557 (1980).

57. For example, the Dutch Olympic team paid $180,000 to turn a suburban golf course country club near Park City into the Holland Heineken House. Anheuser-Busch, a $50 million Olympic sponsor, paid an extra $155,000 to lease the Park City-owned Gallivan Center to create a beer garden.

58. To illustrate, on February 13, 2002, the *Denver Post* ran a column by sportswriter Woody Paige who stated: "Salt Lake City has royally screwed up the Olympics." Woody Paige, *Colorado Real Winner of Games*, DENV. POST (February 12, 2002) at D1. After a firestorm of reaction by Utahans, the newspaper editor said the article "should not have been published" and that it represented a " breakdown" in the editing system. Glenn Guzzo, *Paige Column Should Not Have Run*, DENV. POST (February 17, 2002) at C2.

59. Jerry Spangler & Lisa Riley Roche, *This Bud's For You, S.L.: Busch to Sponsor Games*, DESERET NEWS (March 10, 1998) at A1.

60. *See, e.g., The Ad and the Ego* (Parallax Pictures 1997); THE LIFE AND TIMES OF ROSIE THE RIVETER (Clarity Films 1980).

61. By the end of 2001, Greg Schirf, a 49-year-old admitted former hippie, said that "because of the Winter Olympics, they [his opponents] don't seem to realize they are drawing more attention to themselves. I couldn't pay for this kind of publicity." Thomson, *supra* note []. Finally, Schirf, the so-called "life of the party," could not resist one more zinger: "[T]he church has been so helpful, I should tithe 10 percent. It's the only right thing to do.' *Id.* (internal quotation marks omitted).

Greg Schirf © Wasatch Beer.

to sue Reagan Outdoor Advertising for abridging its commercial speech rights. Watsatch Brewery—had it not been the beneficiary of a lucky break courtesy of the BBC – might have had standing and a financial incentive to seek redress and to test the "good taste clause" against the First Amendment rights of consumers in a so-called free market for commercial information.

Since the Olympics, the State of Utah has moved to increase its tax on beer.[62] One member of the Utah legislature said, on the floor of the house, that he was especially offended by Wasatch Brewery's advertisements and thought that beer was a good place to find money for the state budget shortfall.[63] In response, Greg Schirf, dressed as Benjamin Franklin, protested in a fashion reminiscent of the Boston Tea Party by pouring the first few barrels of his First Amendment Amber into the Great Salt Lake.[64] Schirf called the beer tax "brilliant" and compared it to the "Amish raising the tax on gasoline."[65]

In a seemingly unrelated incident, a Utah couple took out billboard space to promote a book that proselytizes polygamy.[66] As an AP writer commented,

62. The beer tax in Utah will rise from $11 per barrel to $12.80 per barrel as a result of a bill passed in the 2002–2003 legislative session. *States' Budget Woes Mean Higher Beer Taxes*, L.A. TIMES (April 6, 2003).

63. Senate Majority Leader Michael Waddoups denied retribution, but promised to point out the billboard to any legislators who were on the fence about the tax increase. Referring to an ad for Wasatch beer in which the "St. Provo Girl" bursting out of her bustier with the caption "Nice Cans!" Waddoups told the *Salt Lake Tribune*, "It's flat out bad taste." Glen Warchol, *Suggestive Ad Campaign Could Result in Beer Tax Hike*, SALT LAKE TRIB. (December 11, 2002) at B1. Waddoups noted that by becoming the majority leader, he would have the "bully pulpit" to increase the beer tax. *Id.* More than 90% of legislators belong to the Mormon faith. *Beer Tax Protest: Utah Brewer Will Dump '1st Amendment Lager' Into Great Salt Lake, at* http://realbeer.com/news/articles/news-001879.php (March 31, 2003).

64. Rene Sanchez, *Entrepreneur Is at Lagerheads With Utah on Taxes*, WASH. POST (April 6, 2003) at A2.

65. *Id.*

66. Catherine S. Blake, *Author: Polygamy Provides for Kids: Billboards Tout New Book, Old Practice*, CINC. ENQUIRER (August 4, 2002) at A3.

"The billboards along Interstate 15 are a glaring reminder that polygamy isn't dead yet."[67] The billboards show somber faces of polygamous Mormon pioneers surrounding the book's title, *More Than One: Plural Marriage—A Sacred Pioneer Heritage*.[68] The book's author, Shane Whelan, calls polygamy "A Promise for Tomorrow."[69]

Our interest in this is not one of censorship. One can, after all, under the First Amendment advocate some far-out, even ridiculous ideas. Rather, we note for the record that the billboard space was unavailable to Wasatch brewery when it wished to advertise a lawful product with the word "polygamy" in the product label. That ad was found "offensive," but other billboards advocating an illegal practice that Mormon leaders have officially renounced were not found to give offense. This situation is ironic, aggravating, and a sad commentary on Corporate America's lack of commitment to good citizenship, fair play, and free expression.

BOISE CASCADE COMPANY CHILLS FREE EXPRESSION[70]

This section will focus on Boise Cascade Company's actions (BCC) in the 15 years from approximately 1988 to 2003. During this period, BCC typified the behavior of transnational corporations in the extractions industry[71] and that industry's alleged general disregard for the environmental welfare of the planet.[72] This section details how BCC's expansion into Mexico became the subject of academic research, and how university administrators under pressure from BCC treated that research.

We note that the author, William Wines, was party to a settlement agreement resulting from litigation between himself, his co-authors, and the University of Denver, arising out of an article he wrote about BCC.[73] This section of the chapter was written based on publicly available sources.

---

67. *Id.*
68. *Id.*
69. *Id.*
70. In an attempt to "re-brand" its image, Boise Cascade shortened its name to "Boise" in 2002. Ken Dey, *'Boise' Lops 'Cascade' Off Its Name; Company Says Change Reflects Current Direction*, ID. STATESMAN (March 15, 2002) at 1. However, many people who had known the company by its old name continue to use "Boise Cascade."
71. Boise Cascade is no longer in the extraction industry after buying Office Max, a large office supply chain, for $1.06 billion in December 2003. Jeff St. John, *Boise Cascade Sells Paper, Timber Assets*, TRI-CITY HERALD (July 28, 2004). Then, in July 2004, BCC agreed to sell its paper and timberland assets to a Chicago-based buyout firm for $3.7 billion and change its name to OfficeMax, Inc., thereby completing its transition to the number three office-products retailer. *Id.* George Harad remained the chief executive. *Id.*
72. The battle between Boise Cascade and the environmental rights group Rainforest Action Network (RAN) over BCC's environmental policies was especially public in 2004. "The . . . company [BCC] accused the group [RAN] of using 'harassment and intimidation' to advance a 'lawless, radical agenda.'" Marc Gunther, *The Mosquito in the Tent; A Pesky Environmental Group Called the Rainforest Action Network Is Getting Under the Skin of Corporate America*," FORTUNE (May 31, 2004) at 158. After RAN persuaded many of BCC's customers (including Kinko's, L.L. Bean, Patagonia, and the University of Texas) to stop buying from BCC, BCC relented and agreed to stop buying wood harvested from endangered forests. *Id.*
73. *Wines v. Univ. of Denver*, No. CIV-00-048-S-EJL (D. Idaho filed at 11:25 a.m. on August 31, 2000). See also Steve Gutterman (AP), *Retraction of Article Prompts Lawsuit*, ID. STATESMAN (September 15, 2000) at D1.

In the late 1990s, BCC was faced with "thinning inventories, toughening environmental regulations, and dogged demonstrators."[74] After the North American Free Trade Agreement was ratified in 1994, BCC became 1 of 15 U.S. wood-products companies to relocate operations to Mexico.[75] BCC closed mills in Joseph, Oregon, in 1994 and Council, Idaho, in 1995.[76] At the same time, BCC opened a new mill in Papanoa, in the Mexican state of Guerrero.[77] A farmer-led protest of BCC's operations led to a massacre on June 28, 1995, when 17 unarmed farmers were killed by police.[78] An attempted cover-up, which involved placing weapons in the hands of those killed, failed when unedited video of the massacre was aired on Mexican television.[79] A special prosecutor jailed 28 police officers, and the governor of the state was forced to resign.[80]

In April 1998, BCC ceased operations in Mexico.[81] Company officials claimed the shutdown was the result of the rainy season and problems with infrastructure.[82] To the contrary, the *Chicago Tribune* reported that local peasant activists, led by Rodolfo Montiel and Teodoro Cabrera, organized trucking blockades that led to BCC's withdrawal.[83] Mexican Army officials arrested Montiel and Cabrera in 1999.[84] They were held incommunicado for 5 days in an army barracks where they were tortured.[85] They eventually signed statements confessing to gun running and illegally cultivating marijuana.[86] The men were convicted of those charges and sentenced to prison terms of 7 to 10 years.[87] During their time in prison, Amnesty International called them prisoners of conscience and Montiel was awarded the prestigious Goldman Prize for environmental activism.[88]

Activist group American Lands Alliance tried to link BCC with the torture and jailing of Montiel in Mexico at the BCC shareholders' meeting in 2000.[89] Company Chairman George Harad replied, "*You may want to think very carefully* about connecting Boise Cascade in any way with the imprisonment of Mr. Montiel."[90] When activists at the shareholder meeting credited

---

74. John Ross, *Treasures of the Costa Grande; U.S. Timber Companies Open Operations in Mexico*, SIERRA (July 1996) at 22.

75. *Id.*

76. *Id.*

77. *Id.*

78. *Id.*

79. Ross, *supra* note [35].

80. *Id.*

81. John Tucker, *Boise Cascade Plan Draws Fire*, ID. STATESMAN (April 21, 2000) at 1D.

82. *Id.*

83. Laurie Goering, *Mexico Frees Environmental Activists; Pardon by Fox Follows Slaying of Their Lawyer*, CHICAGO TRIBUNE (November 9, 2001) at N26.

84. *Id.*

85. During a speech to students at the University of South Florida in 2003, Montiel said he was choked, jumped on, electrically shocked, and had soda injected up his nostrils. Aya Batrawy, *Mexican Activist Shares Stories of Torture at U. South Florida*, U. WIRE (April 15, 2003). According to Montiel, he and Cabrera were forced to sign confessions to three charges and pose with illegal weapons, leading to their convictions on weapons charges. *Id.* Further, Montiel states that they were not permitted to communicate with family members for 15 days after being arrested. *Id*

86. Goering, *supra* note 44.

87. *Id.*

88. *Id.*

89. Tucker, *supra* note 42.

90. *Id.* (emphasis added).

Montiel with BCC's withdrawal from Mexico, Mr. Harad replied, "We had absolutely no knowledge of Mr. Montiel until we read about him in the newspapers."[91]

In 2001, after spending more than 2 years in prison, Montiel and Cabrera were released from prison by Mexican President Vicente Fox.[92] In a statement described as "terse," President Fox said, "With this, we show by our actions, my government's commitment to the promotion and observance of human rights in our country."[93] In response to a question, the U.S. State Department spokesman stated that the United States "applaud[s] this important gesture and the strong reaffirmation of Mexico's commitment to an improved human rights record it signals."[94] Their release came shortly after their lawyer, a prominent human rights lawyer and former nun, Digna Ochoa, was found murdered.[95] Ms. Ochoa's body was found with two bullet wounds, fired from point-blank range, along with an anonymous note threatening further attacks against human rights activists.[96] Incredibly, in spite of the existence of two point blank bullet holes, the Mexican authorities investigating the case concluded that Ms. Ochoa's death was a suicide.[97] The State Department, in its 2004 Annual Human Rights Report on Mexico, took exception to this conclusion, noting that the Mexico City human rights commission had reported that irregularities in the case did not "generate certainty."[98] Prosecutors in Mexico City recently reopened the investigation into Ms. Ochoa's death.[99]

In September 1998, the *Denver Journal of International Law and Policy* published a scholarly article called *The Critical Need for Law Reform to Regulate the Abusive Practices of Transnational Corporations: The Illustrative Case of Boise Cascade Corporation in Mexico's Costa Grande and Elsewhere*.[100] The article was written by William Wines and Mark Buchanan, both then professors from Boise State University, and Donald Smith, an environmental activist.[101] As the article's title suggests, the authors accused BCC of irresponsible corporate behavior in its Mexican operations.[102] In July 1999, and without first contacting the authors, the University of Denver "retracted" the article by publishing an "errata" in the summer 1999 issue of the *Denver Journal of International Law and Policy*.[103] The journal also instructed the Westlaw and Lexis-Nexis legal

91. *Id.*

92. Ginger Thompson, *Fighters for the Forests Are Released From Mexican Jail*, N.Y. TIMES (November 9, 2001) at A12.

93. *Id.*

94. Daily Press Briefing, U.S. Department of State, *Mexico: Release of Environmental Human Rights Activists*, (November 14, 2001), available at http://www.state.gov/r/pa/prs/ps/2001/6127.htm (answering the question "What is the U.S. opinion of the release of Mexican environmentalists Rodolfo Montiel and Teodoro Cabrera?").

95. Ginger Thompson, *Rights Lawyer's Odd Death Tests Mexican Justice*, N.Y. TIMES (June 3, 2002) at A3.

96. *Id.*

97. *Id.*

98. U.S. DEP'T OF STATE MEXICO: COUNTRY REPORT ON HUMAN RIGHTS PRACTICES—MEXICO—2004 (February 28, 2005), available at http://www.state.gov/g/drl/rls/hrrpt/2004/41767.htm.

99. James McKinley, Jr., *Prosecutors in Mexico Reopen Inquiry in Rights Lawyer's Death*, N.Y. TIMES (February 27, 2005) at A8.

100. Peter Monaghan, *A Journal Article Is Expunged and Its Authors Cry Foul*, CHRON. HIGHER EDUC. (December 8, 2000) at A14.

101. *Id.*

102. *Id.*

103. *Id.*

databases to remove the article from their electronic collections.[104] A search on Lexis now yields neither the article nor the errata, but other scholarly articles that cite to the original article are still available.[105]

According to the errata, the article had been retracted because of its "lack of scholarship and false content."[106] The errata also claimed that the article was "not consistent with the editorial standards of the *Journal* or of the University of Denver, and that portions of the article relating to Boise Cascade were clearly inappropriate and required elimination, revision, or correction."[107] The errata also apologized to any individuals who were impacted [sic],[108] and claimed that the withdrawal from Lexis and Westlaw occurred "pending re-editing."[109]

While the University of Denver claims that it did not act under pressure from BCC in withdrawing the article, university officials admit that upset BCC officials contacted the university in October 1999.[110] In a startling admission of acquiescing to corporate censorship, university lawyer Paul Chan responded to a journalist's question about whether the university was threatened with a lawsuit by Boise by answering, "Well, 'threaten' is an interesting word. Let's just say they pointed out that the objections they raised did rise to the level of being actionable."[111]

The authors of the paper filed a lawsuit against the University of Denver for defamation and breach of contract.[112] In late 2001, the parties reached a settlement under which the University of Denver apologized to the authors, returned the copyright to them, and paid an undisclosed sum.[113] As part of its apology, the university stated that it wished to "reiterate its respect for the First Amendment and its legacy of a robust, wide-open, and healthy public discussion of important social issues."[114] Nonetheless, the article on Boise Cascade remains inaccessible on Lexis or Westlaw, despite frequent citations in other scholarly articles.[115] Interestingly, a draft of the article is reported as

104. *Id.*
105. *See, e.g.,* Vincent M. Di Lorenzo, *Legislative and Public Policy Debate: Should the Social Viewpoints of Religious Groups Play No Role?,* 1 MARGINS 489, app. (2001) (citing *The Critical Need for Law Reform to Regulate the Abusive Practices of Transnational Corporations: The Illustrative Case of Boise Cascade Corporation in Mexico's Costa Grande and Elsewhere* in Appendix); Beth Stephens, *The Amorality of Profit: Transnational Corporations and Human Rights,* 20 BERKELEY J. INT'L L. (2002) 45, 53 note 34 (citing subject article); Saman Zia-Zarifi, *Suing Multinational Corporations in the U.S. for Violating International Law,* 4 UCLA J. INT'L L. & FOREIGN AFF. (Spring/Summer 1999) 81, 83 note 5 (citing subject article); Patricia Romano, Comment, *Sustainable Development: A Strategy That Reflects the Effects of Globalization on the International Power Structure,* 23 HOUS. J. INT'L L. (2000) 91 note 4 (citing subject article). The retraction of this article from academic debate is mentioned in Daniel M. Warner, *An Essay on the Market as God: Law, Spirituality, and the Ecocrisis,* 6 RUTGERS J.L. & RELIGION (2004) 1, 28 note 115.
106. Monaghan, *supra* note 100.
107. *Id.*
108. The use of the word "impact" as a verb presents a usage problem. Eighty-four percent of the Usage Panel of the American Heritage Dictionary disapproves of the construction "*to impact on,*" while 95% disapproves of the use of the word "*impact*" as a transitive verb. AMERICAN HERITAGE DICTIONARY OF THE ENGLISH LANGUAGE (4th ed. 2000).
109. Monaghan, *supra* note 100.
110. *Id.*
111. *Id.*
112. *Paper's Authors Sue University,* NAT'L L.J. (September 25, 2000) at A6.
113. Peter Monaghan, *Professors Settle Suit With U. of Denver Over Retracted Article,* CHRON. HIGHER EDUC. (September 7, 2001) at 25.
114. *Id.*
115. *See supra* note 105.

published in volume 26 of the *Denver Journal of International Law and Policy*, and has been available for download on the journal's website.[116]

Academic freedom has been described as "that aspect of intellectual liberty concerned with the peculiar institutional needs of the academic community."[117] "The academic freedom of university professors and researchers is generally understood to be freedom from political, ecclesiastical, or administrative interference with investigation, discussion, or publication in their field of study."[118] Apparently, no one gave much thought to corporations chilling academic freedom before the 1990s.

In 1940, the American Association of University Professors produced the classic statement on academic freedom, the 1940 Statement of Principles on Academic Freedom and Tenure.[119] In relevant part, it reads as follows:

> (a) Teachers are entitled to full freedom in research and in the publication of the results, subject to the adequate performance of their other academic duties; but research for pecuniary return should be based upon an understanding with the authorities of the institution.

> (b) Teachers are entitled to freedom in the classroom in discussing their subject, but they should be careful not to introduce into their teaching controversial matter which has no relation to their subject. Limitations of academic freedom because of religious or other aims of the institution should be clearly stated in writing at the time of the appointment.

> (c) College and university teachers are citizens, members of a learned profession, and officers of an educational institution. When they speak or write as citizens, they should be free from institutional censorship or discipline, but their special position in the community imposes special obligations. As scholars and educational officers, they should remember that the public may judge their profession and their institution by their utterances. Hence they should at all times be accurate, should exercise appropriate restraint, should show respect for the opinions of others, and should make every effort to indicate that they are not speaking for the institution.[120]

In 1967, the U.S. Supreme Court had the opportunity to address academic freedom. The case involved a declaratory judgment action seeking injunctive relief brought by faculty members of Buffalo State University who were

---

116. *See* William A. Wines, et al., *The Critical Need for Law Reform to Regulate the Abusive Practices of Transnational Corporations: The Illustrative Case of Boise Cascade Corporation in Mexico's Costa Grande and Elsewhere*, 26 DENV. J. INT'L. L. & POL'Y, (Spring 1998) [1st page] 453–515, available at http://www.law.du.edu/ilj/online_issues_folder/wines.pdf. Hardcopy editions may be found in various law library holdings.

117. Comment, *Developments in the Law: Academic Freedom*, 81 HARV. L. REV. (1968) 1045, 1048.

118. Susan L. Pacholski, *Title VII in the University: The Difference Academic Freedom Makes*, 59 U. CHI. L. REV. (1992) 1317, 1320 (citing Fritz Malchup, *On Some Misconceptions Concerning Academic Freedom, reprinted in* ACADEMIC FREEDOM AND TENURE 178 (Louis Joughin ed., 1969); Will Herberg, *On the Meaning of Academic Freedom, in* ON ACADEMIC FREEDOM 1 (Valerie Earle ed., 1971) [citing Arthur O. Lovejoy, *Academic Freedom, in* 1 ENCYCLOPEDIA OF THE SOCIAL SCIENCES 384 (Edwin R. A. Seligman ed., 1930)]. Pacholski then adds: "This notion of freedom is bounded by the limits of professional competence and ethical behavior." *Id.* at note 15.

119. AMERICAN ASSOCIATION OF UNIVERSITY PROFESSORS, *1940 Statement of Principles on Academic Freedom and Tenure With 1970 Interpretive Comments, in* POLICY DOCUMENTS & REPORTS (7th ed. 1990), available at http://www.aaup.org/statements/Redbook/1940stat.htm.

120. *Id.*

notified that they would be fired for refusing to sign the "Feinberg Certificate."[121] This certificate declared that the signee was not a Communist and that if he had ever been a Communist, he had communicated that fact to the president of the State University of New York.[122] In a 5–4 decision, the Court, in an opinion by Justice William Brennan, held that the New York statutes requiring the Feinberg Certificate were unconstitutionally overbroad because the state could achieve its objectives, namely preventing seditious speech in classrooms, through less sweeping prohibitions.[123] Brennan wrote, "Our Nation is deeply committed to safeguarding academic freedom, which is of transcendent value to all of us and not merely to the teachers concerned. That freedom is therefore a special concern of the First Amendment, which does not tolerate laws that cast a pall of orthodoxy over the classroom."[124]

The "pall of orthodoxy" in the 1990s and early 21st century seems to be self-imposed in many colleges and universities that are now dependent upon financial contributors to keep operations going. In the 1990s, some state universities changed their names to "state-assisted" universities in order to indicate more accurately their financial relationship with their states.[125] Problems with loyalty oaths and seditious speech are gone. Now the issue is whether a professor's research will offend a major donor,[126] or even a minor donor such as BCC,[127] if that minor donor has annual revenues over $6 billion and the ability to "beggar" a university by SLAPP suit.

One sad conclusion is that the First Amendment means little when university administrators, university professors, and the public press engage in *self-censorship* to appease corporate interests.[128] As another author has noted, "[b]ecause the loss of employment is so damaging, the expectation that they will be fired for expressing their opinions could have a serious chilling effect on individuals' political speech."[129] In the recent episode involving Ward Churchill, a University of Colorado professor, the President of

---

121. *Keyishian v. Bd. of Regents*, 385 U.S. 589 (1967).
122. *Id.*
123. *Id.* at 609.
124. *Id.* at 603.
125. *See* David W. Breneman, *For Colleges, This Is Not Just Another Recession*, CHRON. HIGHER EDUC. (June 14, 2002) at 7.
126. The late Dr. Bong Shin, then his department chairman, explained once that a research grant proposal he had submitted was turned down for full funding by the College of Business in large part for fear that his study might offend the political sensitivities of J. R. Simplot, a substantial donor to higher education (including Boise State University). Simplot's celebrity status was recently affirmed in a glowing feature article in *The Idaho Statesman*. *See* Kristen Moulton, *J.R. Simplot: The Man and the Empire*, ID. STATESMAN (April 11, 1999) at 1D. *See also* George Anders, *At Potato Empire, an Heir Peels Away Years of Tradition: Scott Simplot Tries Updating His Father's Hefty Legacy; Fewer Hunches, More Data*, WALL STREET J. (October 7, 2004) at A1.
127. BCC, for instance, donated $50,000 for environmental scholarships at Boise State University following the publicity of its manner of doing business in Mexico. What BCC obtained in exchange for this donation is unknown. The amount, however, represented approximately 0.0008% of the company's annual sales ($6 billion in 1998) or approximately 6 months of salary and benefits for an American millwright at the Papanoa Mill in Guerrero. *See* Wines, *supra* note 170.
128. *See generally* MARTIN LEE & NORMAN SOLOMON, UNRELIABLE SOURCES: A GUIDE TO DETECTING BIAS IN NEWS MEDIA (1992) (discussing the influence of big business over American news outlets).
129. Dale E. Miller, *Terminating Employees for Their Political Speech*, 109 BUS. & SOC'Y. REV. 225, 229 (2004). *See also* Columbia University President Lee Bollinger, Address at National Press Club Luncheon (April 2, 2003) (explaining that an untenured faculty member who had called for the United States to lose the Iraq war and proclaimed hope for the deaths of U.S.

the University of Colorado felt compelled to resign after she defended Mr. Churchill's academic right of free speech against critics who wanted him fired.[130]

BOVINE HORMONE TREATMENT

> And you don't get rewarded for telling the hard truths about America in a profit seeking environment.
>
> —Bill Moyers[131]

In 1993, the Food and Drug Administration (FDA) approved the use of synthetic bovine growth hormone, an artificial form of growth hormone designed to stimulate milk production in cows.[132] The hormone is injected into cows every 2 weeks, and can increase milk production by 15% per cow.[133] Approximately 22% of cows in the United States receive the growth hormone.[134] In the United States, the hormone is marketed solely by Monsanto, under the brand name Posilac.[135] It is estimated that Posilac generates approximately $250 to $300 million in revenue for Monsanto annually.[136] The use of synthetic bovine growth hormone is controversial.[137] Canada bans the hormone, as does the European Union.[138] Concerns regarding the use of bovine growth hormone treatment range from the onset of early puberty in girls to antibiotic resistance in humans.[139] The FDA continues to insist that the hormone is safe to use and that pasteurization kills the growth hormone in the milk that Americans consume.[140]

In April 1998, news reporter Steve Wilson and his wife Jane Akre filed an unusual lawsuit in Florida state court against WTVT Fox 13, their former employer.[141] The plaintiffs alleged that they had prepared a special report on Monsanto and synthetic bovine growth treatment.[142] The story was supposed to air in 1997, but station executives pulled the story after Monsanto complained.[143] After 10 months and 73 rewrites, the reporters could not obtain

---

soldiers could not be fired because the speech did not occur in the classroom but, rather, at an open "teach-in").

130. *See* Paul Fain, *Under Fire on 2 Fronts, U. of Colorado Chief Resigns*, CHRON. HIGHER EDUC. (March 18, 2005) at A1. "The continuing controversy over Mr. Churchill has received as much if not more attention as the football scandal." *Id.* The football scandal escalated in March 2005 when someone leaked details of a sealed grand-jury report indicating that the grand jury had found an assistant football coach "had sexually assaulted two female athletic trainers." *Id.*

131. Frazier Moore, *Truth-Teller Moyers Retires From TV*, CINC. ENQUIRER (December 14, 2004) at D5.

132. Elizabeth Chang, *Tempest in a Glass: Synthetic Hormones in Milk Don't Speed Puberty, Say Experts*, WASH. POST (October 7, 2003) at F1.

133. *Id.*

134. *Id.*

135. Andrew Pollack, *Maker Warns of Scarcity of Hormone for Dairy Cows*, N. Y. TIMES (January 27, 2004) at C10.

136. *Id.*

137. Chang, *supra* note 186.

138. *Id.*

139. *Id.*

140. *Id.*

141. Walt Belcher, *Reporters Claim Firings Part of Coverup*, TAMPA TRIB. (April 3, 1998) at 1.

142. *Id.*

143. *Id.*

approval for the story from station management.[144] The plaintiffs claim that station management offered the couple $200,000 to walk away and keep the story quiet, but they refused.[145] The reporters were fired, and they filed a claim for wrongful termination and violation of Florida's whistleblower statute.[146]

According to the plaintiffs, Monsanto attorneys sent a letter to the president of Fox News Corporation on the eve of the planned broadcast, which had already been publicized on television and radio.[147] The letter stated that Monsanto was concerned over statements questioning its integrity, and made reference to a recent jury verdict in which ABC News was ordered to pay a grocery chain $5.5 million for reporting that contained some elements of truth.[148]

According to Steve Wilson, the evidence the reporters gathered against Monsanto was damning.[149] Their report asserted that virtually all cows in Florida were injected with synthetic bovine growth hormone.[150] In the report, Florida grocery stores admitted that they had broken pledges made to the public to label milk that had been injected with the hormone.[151] The report confirmed charges from two Canadian regulators that Monsanto had tried to bribe them with $1 to 2 million in exchange for approval of the drug without further testing.[152] The reporters documented millions in research grants from Monsanto to the University of Florida, which conducted some of the testing that eventually led to FDA approval.[153] They interviewed farmers who told them that Monsanto had not properly documented the adverse effects the hormone had on cows.[154] When the reporters challenged David Boylan, the new news manager moved to the station from Fox News Network, he told them, "We'll decide what the news is. The news is what we say it is."[155]

At trial, a unanimous jury found that Fox News had pressured the reporters to broadcast a "false, distorted or slanted news report."[156] The plaintiffs were awarded $425,000, and a short time later they were awarded the Goldman Environmental Prize.[157] In 2003, a state appeals court overturned the jury verdict.[158] The couple is considering further appeals, and in the meantime they have petitioned the FCC to deny renewal of the station's license for "intentionally airing false and distorted news reports."[159]

---

144. *Id.*
145. *Id.*
146. *Id.*
147. Eric Deggans, *Were TV News Bloodhounds Called Off the Case?*, ST. PETERSBURG TIMES (April 12, 1998) at 1F.
148. *Id.*
149. *Id.*
150. Steve Wilson, *Fox in the Cow Barn: Controversial Dairy Hormone News Story Buried by Fox-TV Station WTVT Tampa, Florida*, NATION (June 8, 1998) at 20.
151. *Id.*
152. *Id.*
153. *Id.*
154. *Id.*
155. *Id.*
156. Glen Martin, *American Journalists Win Top Eco Award for Cow Hormone Story*, S. F. CHRON. (April 23, 2001) at A3.
157. *Id.*
158. Walt Belcher, *Ex-WTVT Reporters Take Case to FCC*, TAMPA TRIB. (January 4, 2005) at 2.
159. *Id.*

RESEARCH FUNDING

Professor Tyrone B. Hayes is a developmental endocrinologist in Berkeley's department of integrative biology.[160] Professor Hayes was on the academic fast track.[161] He studied biology on a full scholarship to Harvard University.[162] In 1994, he started teaching at UC Berkeley after finishing his Ph.D. there.[163] He was tenured at the remarkably young age of 30, and 6 years later (June 2004) was still the youngest full professor at Berkeley.[164] But Professor Hayes's career hit a snag when he accepted a funding offer from Ecorisk, Inc.,[165] a consulting company that paid him and other academic scientists to study Atrazine,[166] a widely used weed killer.[167] His findings came out "wrong"—he discovered that Atrazine was harmful to the environment, specifically frogs.[168]

On November 7, 2000, Hayes sent a resignation letter to Syngenta and several of the Ecorisk research panel members.[169] The contracts covering Hayes's work and that of many of the other researchers had given Syngenta (the herbicide's primary manufacturer) and Ecorisk *the final say* over what scientists could research and whether the scientists could publish their findings.[170] In his resignation letter, Professor Hayes, who was still waiting for funding for work he had already begun, expressed concerns about the panel's plan to hold off publishing his results until the following year.[171]

Hayes's letter of November 7, 2000, declared, "It will appear to my colleagues that I have been part of a plan to bury important data. This fear will be particularly realized when independent laboratories begin to publish data similar to data that we [Syngenta and my laboratory] produced together as early as 1999."[172] Some sources claim, "Research has also linked [atrazine] to human prostate and breast cancer."[173] Professor Hayes suggested that there might be a link because "the hormones are the same [and] the mechanisms are the same," in humans and frogs.[174] The Environmental Protection Agency

---

160. Goldie Blumenstyk, *The Price of Research: A Berkeley Scientist Says a Corporate Sponsor Tried to Bury His Unwelcome Findings and Then Buy His Silence,*" CHRON. HIGHER EDUC. (October 31, 2003) at A1.

161. Alison Pierce, *Bioscience Warfare,* S. F. WEEKLY (June 2, 2004) available at 2004 WLNR 15121447.

162. *Id.*

163. *Id.*

164. *Id.*

165. Blumenstyk, *supra* note 212, at A1.

166. *Id.*

167. As of 2003, more than 76 million pounds of atrazine have been applied annually. *Id.* Most of the use has been in agriculture in the Midwest and Southeast. Today, 90% of all sugar cane fields and more than two thirds of all corn and sorghum fields are treated with atrazine, and it is an ingredient in about 130 other products. *Id.* Atrazine is one of the five largest selling herbicides in the United States. *Id.* Sales are estimated at between $500 and 800 million per year. *Id.*

168. At levels as low as 0.1 parts per billion, Professor Hayes's studies started to find atrazine affected the development of sex organs in male frogs. Allison Pierce, *supra* note 214.

169. Blumenstyk, *supra* note 212.

170. *Id.*

171. *Id.*

172. Blumenstyk, *supra* note 217 (internal quotation marks omitted). Novartis Agribusiness has since merged with Syngenta AG, a Swiss corporation. *See Big Biotech Silencing Critics of Pesticides & GE Crops,* Organic Consumers Association at http://www.organicconsumers.org/ge/bigbiotech060304.cfm (last visited May 16, 2005) [hereinafter *Big Biotech*].

173. *Pierce, supra* note 213.

174. Blumenstyk, *supra* note 212, at A1.

(EPA) determined "recently" that atrazine is "not likely to be carcinogenic to humans."[175]

Professor Hayes's experience demonstrated the dangers of corporate research funding in the academe. It has been well said that "the power to tax is the power to destroy."[176] In this context, the power of the purse is the power to control research studies, not only to determine which scientists get funding but also to determine which studies get funded and which results get published and which, under a proprietary data provision, get locked in the corporate safe. [*See generally* JENNIFER WASHBURN, UNIVERSITY, INC.: THE CORPORATE CORRUPTION OF HIGHER EDUCATION (2005); *see also* DEREK BOK, UNIVERSITIES IN THE MARKETPLACE: THE COMMERCIALIZATION OF HIGHER EDUCATION (2003).]

CORPORATE CENSORSHIP: WAR, THE NATIONAL PASTIME, AND THE 2004 PRESIDENTIAL ELECTION

> A popular government without popular information, or the means of acquiring it, is but a prologue to a Farce or a Tragedy, or, perhaps, both.
>
> —James Madison[177]

After the fall of Baghdad, an NPR reporter talked with Iraqis in that nation's capital.[178] The Iraqis talked freely.[179] Some said they hated Saddam; others said they hated the United States.[180] But, the reporter noted they were not as tightlipped as they had been.[181] They openly disagreed and felt free to verbalize opinions.[182] "This free expression," the NPR reporter commented, "is truly a sign that they have been liberated."[183]

That same week *ABC News Tonight* reported that three Cubans who had hijacked a Havana ferry in an attempt to reach the United States were convicted, lost their appeals, and were executed by a firing squad all in the same week.[184] The ferry was overtaken when it ran out of fuel and was towed back to Cuba.[185] The same report noted that the harshest "crackdown" on dissent in Cuba since 1959 was under way.[186] Approximately 80 well-known dissenters, including poets, writers, and intellectuals, were arrested in the prior week.[187] Some had already been sentenced to as many as 20 years in prison for criticizing Fidel Castro's administration.[188] Cuba's spokesman said these measures were necessary because of unrest stirred up in Cuba by the Bush administration.[189]

---

175. *Id.*
176. Chief Justice John Marshall in *McCullough v. Maryland* 4 Wheat 316, 4 L. Ed. 579 (1819).
177. RICHARD K. SHERWIN, WHEN LAW GOES POP: THE VANISHING LINE BETWEEN LAW AND POPULAR CULTURE 23 (2000) (quoting James Madison).
178. *Morning News* on FM 90.9 WGUC Cincinnati's Classical Public Radio broadcast at 8:30 a.m. on April 8, 2003.
179. *Id.*
180. *Id.*
181. *Id.*
182. *Id.*
183. *Id.*
184. *ABC News Tonight with Peter Jennings* (ABC television broadcast, April 11, 2003).
185. *Id.*
186. *Id.*
187. *Id.*
188. *Id.*
189. *Id.*

While reports of censorship and brutal repression of speech are not surprising in totalitarian regimes, they are surprising when they originate in the United States. When the "censor" is not the government, but private corporations, most Americans shrug their shoulders and see no harm in the private market responding to market forces. When the speech is suppressed because of its political content, however, the First Amendment's goals are thwarted. The following is a brief recitation of incidents of corporate citizenship that relate to our national pastime, that have occurred during times of war and during the 2004 Presidential election.

We begin by looking at how corporate citizenship can affect a seemingly innocuous pastime such as baseball. National Public Radio reported that the National Baseball Hall of Fame cancelled a 15th anniversary showing of the baseball movie *Bull Durham*[190] because of the anti-war politics of two of the film's stars, Susan Sarandon and Tim Robbins.[191] Meanwhile, NBC fired Peter Arnett, the media darling of CNN during the first Gulf War, on March 31, 2003 because the network believed he was "wrong" to grant an interview on state-run Iraqi TV in which he said the American war plan had failed because of underestimated Iraqi resistance.[192] Arnett, a New Zealand native and naturalized American citizen, won a Pulitzer Prize for his reporting for the Associated Press during the Vietnam War.[193] NBC initially defended Arnett's interview as a "professional courtesy" and said on Sunday, March 30th, that Arnett's remarks were analytical (i.e., opinion) in character.[194] But the next day, NBC President Neal Shapiro fired Arnett, even after he apologized.[195] This has fueled reports by cable news outlets of White House pressure on NBC.[196]

Not to be outdone by Arnett's blunder, U.S. Senator Jim Bunning (R. KY) said on the floor of the Senate, "I think he [Arnett] should be brought back and tried as a traitor to the United States of America for his aiding and abetting the Iraqi government...."[197] Arnett, who was hired by London's *Daily Mirror* on the same day he was fired, was back on the air and retracted his apology.[198] Apparently, Senator Bunning, whose main qualification for the U.S. Senate seems to be a Major League Baseball career,[199] would have had Arnett targeted by the U.S. Special Forces or brought back forcibly in irons to stand trial for treason and presumably shot for an act of unpopular speech.

---

190. "Bull Durham" (Orion Pictures 1988).

191. Tim Robbins Remarks at the National Press Club Luncheon (April 15, 2003). Robbins' speech was broadcast by *National Public Radio: National Press Club* (National Public Radio broadcast, April 15, 2003) For an audio clip of Robbins' speech as well as a preface by an NPR commentator, *see* http://www.npr.org/programs/npc/2003/030415.trobbins.html. In response, Tim Robbins wrote a letter to the Hall of Fame's administration, saying "you belong with the cowards and ideologues in a hall of infamy and shame." Jeff Jacobs, *Hall's Boss Blows Call on 'Bull,'* CHI. TRIB. (April 12, 2003) at C2.

192. David Bauder, *Arnett's 'Misjudgment' Costs Him Job,* CINC. ENQUIRER (April 1, 2003) at D2.

193. *Id.*

194. *Id.*

195. *Id.*

196. *See, e.g.,* Doug Ireland, *Honesty: The Worst Policy—When Telling the Truth Will Get You Fired From the Networks,* TomPaine common sense (March 31, 2003), at http://www.tompaine.com/scontent/7524.html.

197. Carl Weiser, *Try Arnett for Treason, Senator Says,* CINC. ENQUIRER (April 2, 2003) at C3.

198. *Id.*

199. Jim Bunning was much better than an average ball player. He was only the second pitcher in history, after Cy Young, to win one hundred games in both the National and American Leagues. He played 17 seasons and was elected to the Baseball Hall of Fame in 1996. *See* http://www.pubdim.net/baseballlibrary/ballplayers/B/Bunning_Jim.stm? (last visited April 16, 2003). *See also The Player Page: Jim Bunning* at http://www.thebaseballpage.com/past/pp/bunningjim/ (last visited on July 19, 2005).

Boondocks / by Aaron McGruder

©BOONDOCKS reprinted by permission of Univerisal Press Syndicate.

Baseball has recently had problems with freedom of speech other than canceling a classic movie. In February 2000, former Atlanta Braves relief pitcher John Rocker drew a $20,000 fine and a 3-month suspension from Bud Selig, baseball's commissioner, for racial and ethnic remarks that "offended practically every element in society."[200] On appeal, the arbitrator for Major League Baseball reduced the regular-season part of the suspension from 1 month to 2 weeks and cut the fine to $500, but upheld the requirement that Mr. Rocker attend "sensitivity training."[201] The original suspension was the longest suspension not related to drug use since Lenny Randle was suspended for 30 days for punching his manager, Frank Lucchesi.[202] Here a speech violation, for which Rocker had already apologized, merited three times the suspension for assault and battery.

David Wells, a pitcher with the New York Yankees, wrote a book titled *Perfect I'm Not: Boomer on Beer, Brawls, Backaches, and Baseball.*[203] In the book, among other things, Wells said that he was "half-drunk" when he pitched a perfect game against the Minnesota Twins in 1998.[204] At a February 28, 2003, meeting with the Yankee's manager Joe Torre and the General Manager Brian Cashman about his book, Wells became upset and offered to quit.[205] Torre said that Wells "went over the line" with what he wrote in the book and needed to make amends. Ultimately, Wells agreed to pay a $100,000 fine from the Yankees and apologized to the team and individual players.[206] No one said that what Wells wrote (or had ghost written for him) was untrue or defamatory, just that it "caused problems" and "bothered the team's principal owner, George Steinbrenner."[207]

---

200. Ronald Blum, *Rocker's Words Bring 3 Month Suspension*, ID. STATESMAN (February 1, 2000) at C1.
201. Ken Daley, *Arbitrator Knocks Two Weeks Off Rocker's Ban*, ID. STATESMAN (March 2, 2000) at C1.
202. Blum, *supra* note 253.
203. *Wells Offered to Quit Yankees*, CINC. ENQUIRER (April 13, 2003) at B10.
204. *Id.*
205. *Id.*
206. *Id*
207. *Id.* George Steinbrenner, of course, was convicted of multiple felonies for his role in covering up illegal campaign contributions to CREEP in the days leading up to President Nixon's Watergate crisis and impeachment. FREDERICK D. STURDIVANT, BUSINESS AND SOCIETY: A MANAGERIAL APPROACH (rev. ed. 1981) at 50–51. That may be one reason why he's a sensitive guy.

Meanwhile, Baseball Commissioner Bud (as in "Bud Light") Selig is reported to be considering revoking Pete Rose's lifetime suspension from Major League Baseball. Apparently, Rose, who has even recently denied betting on baseball games as a player and manager despite overwhelming evidence to the contrary, including gambling slips in his handwriting, is still a big celebrity in Cincinnati. Selig's decision seems more motivated by whether the revocation would help the owners at the gate than by any consideration of repentance, remorse, or morality. The Iraq War has generated enough attention in the Cincinnati area to take Pete Rose's future off the headlines.

A Westwood, Ohio, man, James Watters, age 49, became a local celebrity for driving his semi-trailer onto a sidewalk where people were protesting the war in Iraq.[208] Mr. Watters pleaded not guilty to three charges of aggravated menacing, inducing panic and reckless operation in Hamilton County Municipal Court on April 2, 2003. He said, "I'm the hero of my son's battalion. They're all behind me [sic] fighting this."[209] Watters' son, Mark, is a sergeant with the 1st Marine Division, Communications Unit. (Watters was arrested on March 24th when he drove his semi on the sidewalk toward about 40 war protesters, 1 in a wheelchair, who had gathered on an overpass over

---

208. Sharon Turco, *Trucker to Fight Menacing Charges*, CINC. ENQUIRER (April 3, 2003) at C2.
209. *Id.*

Interstate 75. Mr. Watters says he never intended to injure any protestors, only to get them off the bridge.[210]) Co-workers raised $1,100 for his defense fund in the first 48 hours after the incident.[211] A smiling Mr. Watters was pictured on the front page of the "Metro Section" in the local newspaper, receiving a group hug from family after being released from jail.[212]

Although Marines may not be expected in the heat of combat to be free-speech sensitive, Miami University had its own little tempest in the spring of 2003. Aaron Sanders, a student, wrote a column for the *Miami Student* in the January 17th edition that criticized some French Department faculty and was especially harsh on a class session in which a French movie, *Ridicule*, was shown.[213] The film, which was shown in a course on French language and culture, is graphic: The opening scene has a close-up of a man urinating on another man's head. Well, to quote a local newspaper columnist, "Le merde hit le fan."[214] The head of the French Department wrote a lengthy rebuttal, including some personal criticism of Sanders. The faculty advisor for the *Miami Student* sent an e-mail to the student editor calling for Aaron Sanders to be dropped as a columnist. In turn, Sanders lost his unpaid position as a columnist on the student paper.[215]

CONCLUDING OBSERVATIONS

Free speech, free press, and freedom of religion can be inconvenient, embarrassing, and—yes—even messy. However, as one observer has noted, a culture is always an argument as long as it is alive. Sometimes it is easy to fall into the trap of preferring artificial tranquility and superficial agreement to the discomfort of active debate and engagement. Excessive respect for wealth and for celebrities has been a complaint of moralists throughout the ages.[216]

No one ever mistook John Rocker or David Wells for the official spokesman of Major League Baseball. I cannot find it written anywhere that an actor or actress has to be politically correct to be good at his or her trade. Why then should we care that celebrities have opinions different than ours? Why should it be newsworthy that an actress or a baseball player is critical of U.S. foreign policy or that Tiger Woods chooses not to become embroiled in whether Augusta National Golf Course admits women? Does he owe that to us because he is Black? If not, why does no one seem to care that Phil Mikkelson and Ernie Els are not involved?

---

210. *Id.*
211. William A. Weathers, *Trucker Claims He Didn't Aim to Hurt War Protesters*, CINC. ENQUIRER (March 26, 2003) at C1.
212. *Id.*
213. Peter Bronson, *Miami Student Columnist Held Up to Ridicule*, CINC. ENQUIRER (February 17, 2003) at B1.
214. *Id.* at B2.
215. *Id.*
216. Adam Smith said it best: "This disposition to admire, and almost to worship, the rich and the powerful, and to despise, or, at least to neglect persons of poor and mean condition, though necessary both to establish and to maintain the distinction of ranks and the order of society, is, at the same time, the great and most universal cause of the corruption of our moral sentiments. That wealth and greatness are often regarded with the respect and admiration which are due only to wisdom and virtue; and that the contempt, of which vice and folly are the only proper objects, is often most unjustly bestowed upon poverty and weakness, has been the complaint of moralists in all ages." ADAM SMITH, THE THEORY OF MORAL SENTIMENTS (1759), Section III, Chapter 3.

Our very human but imprudent tendency to take ourselves too seriously, both individually and as Americans, makes us good targets for humor. Humor, as the British wit Malcolm Muggeridge noted, is virtually always at odds with the prevailing "good taste." Sometimes our insistence on good taste over fundamental freedoms threatens the latter without significantly advancing the former.[217]

Would Americans be a more civil[218] and a happier people if we were more willing to laugh at ourselves and acknowledge our imperfections? This period in our nation's history may be a critical time, especially if some of our leaders succeed in reducing our highly complex society into just two camps: the true believers and the enemy.[219]

Perhaps, in a limited way and in a limited place, Wasatch Brewery and Greg Schirf are reminding us of the better angels of our nature. In an ideal America, we would honor plainer virtues, such as truth, open debate, and an unblinking honesty.[220] Such virtues would make us ashamed to sweep our embarrassments (both historical and present) under the rug.[221]

The case of Polygamy Porter raises an issue that has been on the back burner in First Amendment circles for ages; namely, the power of large corporate interests to influence and in some cases to control the flow of information to Americans.[222] News judgment is not always unrelated to advertising revenue; in fact, some studies have shown strong correlations. The way in which powerful social and business interests went after Schirf Brewing to squelch the Polygamy Porter campaign should set civil libertarians' teeth on edge. If polygamy is "Utah's dirty little secret," then it might also be fair to say that

---

217. *See, e.g.,* MICHAEL MOORE, STUPID WHITE MEN (2002) and MOLLY IVINS, SHRUB (2000).

218. *See, e.g.,* MARK CALDWELL, A SHORT HISTORY OF RUDENESS: MANNERS, MORALS AND MISBEHAVIOR IN MODERN AMERICA (1999); *see also* William A. Wines & Michael Fronmueller, "American Workers Increase Efforts to Establish a Legal Right to Privacy as Civility Declines in U.S. Society: Some Observations on the Effort and Its Social Context," 78 U. OF NEB. L. REV. 606 (1999) at 611–618.

219. *See, e.g.,* David Corn, "The Fundamental John Ashcroft," MOTHER JONES (March/April2002) at 38ff. Ashcroft declared to the U.S. Senate Judiciary Committee that critics who "'scare peace-loving people with phantoms of lost liberty only aid terrorists, for they erode our national unity and diminish our resolve.'" *Id.* at 39. The author continues, "The journalists in attendance winced. Here was the attorney general of the United States, in wartime, effectively calling his opponents traitors. But no one on the committee challenged Ashcroft on this point." *Id.*

220. The challenge of ethics is "to see life steadily and see it whole." See Matthew Arnold, *To a Friend*, quoted in KENNETH E. GOODPASTER, PERSPECTIVES ON MORALITY: ESSAYS OF WILLIAM F. FRANKENA (1976) 106, 227 note 18.

221. The media did not highlight the news that Salt Lake City was distinguished in January for being one of the 12 meanest American cities in which to be homeless. The press release that accompanied the national survey was dated January 15, 2002, the 73rd anniversary of the birth of Martin Luther King, Jr. Donald Whitehead, "Executive Summary of *Illegal to be Homeless: The Criminalization of Homelessness in the United States.*" Accessed at http://www.nationalhomeless.org/criminalizationrelease.html on April 14, 2002. And *Homeless Group Lists 12 Meanest American Cities,* THE DOMINION POST (March 4, 2002). Accessed at http://www.dominionPOST.COM/A/NEWS/2002/03/04/ao/ on April 14, 2002.

222. Certainly the opening of this subject would almost require scholars to examine the way in which the Department of Defense and the Pentagon "managed" the flow of information to the American people during the 1992 Gulf War and the implications of such "news management" by then General Colin Powell, currently Secretary of State Colin Powell, for the right of the American people to make informed decisions about their government at the polls.

corporate censorship, aided and abetted by for-profit publishers, is the "dirty little secret" of the United States.

I am not ready to suggest any law reform. The nature of the malaise seems more social, cultural, and intellectual (or anti-intellectual) than legal. If rudeness or stupidity were to be made criminal, America could not build prisons fast enough. My conclusion is simply that as a people and as a nation, we face a growing problem of intolerance and lack of respect for dissenting or unpopular views. I believe Justice Brennan and President James Madison would concur.

PART

4

Federal Regulation and Current Workplace Issues

CHAPTER 14
U.S. BUSINESS AND THE DECLINE
OF COMPETITION

CHAPTER 15
RISE OF REGULATION
AND CORPORATE SOCIAL
RESPONSIBILITY

CHAPTER 16
WORKPLACE ISSUES I: EMPLOYMENT
VERSUS PERSONAL DIGNITY

CHAPTER 17
WORKPLACE ISSUES II: DESIGNING
A BETTER ORGANIZATION

U.S. Business and the Decline of Competition

The origins of business in the United States can be traced through at least six stages and probably into a seventh. This chapter examines the history of U.S. business from the beginning of the European invasion of North America to the year 1933. Chapter 15 deals with business history in the United States from 1932 to the present.

The noted business historian, N. S. B. de Gras, divided capitalism into the following six stages[1]:

1. prebusiness capitalism
2. petty capitalism
3. mercantile capitalism
4. industrial capitalism
5. financial capitalism
6. national capitalism

Economic history does not fall neatly into exact divisions; however, in the interest of placing these evolving stages of capitalism into appropriate time periods, I describe them as beginning approximately at a given year and terminating at another approximate date. Keep in mind though that the stages themselves evolved more like new layers on a glacier than as abrupt departures from their predecessors.

Clearly, the study of American business history is intertwined with the development of the later stages of capitalism, the evolution of which I return to shortly. First, we need to briefly examine the nature of capitalism itself. As Maurice Dobb, an economic historian, sagely noted, "It is not altogether surprising that the term Capitalism, which in recent years has enjoyed so wide a currency alike in popular talk and in historical writing, should have been used so variously, and that there should have been no common measure of agreement in its use."[2] Capitalism is often identified with a system of unfettered individual enterprise: a system in which both economic and social relations are governed by contract, individuals are thought to be free agents in pursuing their livelihoods, and legal compulsions and restrictions are thought to be mostly absent or minimal. In this manner, capitalism and *laissez-faire* or free competition are considered virtually synonymous.[3]

Professor Dobb, the Cambridge University economist, goes forward from his observation on the various uses of capitalism to parse out three definitions of capitalism. The first, and most popular, definition seeks the essence of capitalism not in any singular aspect of its construct, but rather in the totality of those aspects represented by the *geist* or *spirit* that has inspired the life of the epoch. This spirit is a synthesis of the spirit of enterprise with the bourgeois spirit of calculation and rationality. In this sense, precapitalist man was a "natural man" who saw economic activity as a simply catering to his natural wants. In contrast, capitalist human uproots the natural man and turns on its head all his primitive life values. Capitalist man sees the amassing of capital as the dominant motive of economic activity and, in a mood of sober rationality and by methods of precise quantitative analysis, subordinates everything in life to this single end.[4]

---

1. N. S. B. GRAS, BUSINESS AND CAPITALISM: AN INTRODUCTION TO BUSINESS HISTORY (1939) as quoted in STURDIVANT & VERNON-WORTZEL, BUSINESS AND SOCIETY: A MANAGERIAL APPROACH (4th ed. 1990) at 98.
2. MAURICE DOBB, STUDIES IN THE DEVELOPMENT OF CAPITALISM (rev. ed. 1963) at 1.
3. *Id.* at 4–5.
4. *Id.*

For a second definition of capitalism, Dobb turns to the German Historical School. This definition virtually identifies capitalism with the organization of production for a distant market. Thus, capitalism would be present as soon as the acts of production and retail sale were separated in time and space by the intervention of a merchant who purchased goods with a view toward subsequent resale at a profit. The emphasis of the German School seems to be on the supplanting of a barter economy with a money economy. This approach seeks the origins of capitalism in the first encroachment of specialized commercial dealings on the "natural economy" of the medieval world.[5]

The third and last definition brought forward by Professor Dobb originated with Karl Marx, who sought the essence of capitalism in a particular mode of production. By mode of production, he did not refer merely to the state of the technique. Capitalism was a system of commodity production under which labor had itself become a commodity and was bought and sold on the market like any other object of exchange. The historical prerequisite for capitalism, thus understood, was the concentration of wealth, the ownership of the means of production in the hands of a few (a class), and the emergence of another property-less class for whom the only means of living was the sale of their labor.[6]

GRAS'S STAGES OF CAPITALISM

Prebusiness capitalism arose in Western Europe in the Middle Ages, the period of European history that began approximately in the year 500 and ended approximately in 1500. In this period, there was very little social mobility; feudalism reigned over the villages and manorial estates. People worked hard and shared under a barter system; thus, by trading goods and services, a condition approximating self-sufficiency was maintained.

Petty capitalism, the second stage according to Gras, dominated the British colonies in North America from the 17th century to about 1750. Petty capitalists were shopkeepers or traveling merchants whose enterprises seldom extended either beyond the village where their shop was located or the route that they traveled. Because little capital was required to set up shop, the fortunes of these petty capitalists frequently soured, although, of course, some did prosper.

The third stage, *mercantile capitalism*, covers the time period of 1750 to roughly 1850 and can be divided into two subparts: *colonial mercantilism* and *wholesale mercantilism*.[7] The colonial merchant, as Chandler noted, was an all-around general business person: "He financed and insured the transportation of these goods. At the same time, he provided the funds needed by the planter and the artisan to finance the production of crops and goods."[8]

In contrast, the wholesaler emerged about the turn of the 19th century when the several functions of the colonial merchant were taken over by specialists, such as importers, insurers, bankers, and wholesalers. Thus, in the second phase of the mercantile period, middlemen replaced merchants as the

---

5. *Id.* at 5–7.
6. *Id.* at 7–8.
7. STURDIVANT & VERNON-WORTZEL, *supra* note 1, at 98–99.
8. A. D. Chandler, Jr., *The Role of Business in the United States: A Historical Survey*, DAEDALUS (Winter 1969) at 24.

integrating force in the economy. During this period, wholesalers controlled the flow of goods from producers to consumers; financed the canals, turnpikes, and early railroads; and supplied capital for early textile mills and steel manufacturers. However, as manufacturing grew in importance, the mercantile capitalists faded.

Industrial capitalism and the rise of factory-based manufacturing followed mercantile capitalism. It was the dominant form of capitalism from 1850 to approximately 1893. The first fully integrated factory in the United States was owned by the Boston Manufacturing Company, a group of Boston merchants who opened a textile plant in Waltham, Massachusetts, in 1814. This company, led by Nathan Appleton and Francis Cabot Lowell, was the first to process completely raw materials into finished consumer goods and sell them. [9] The expansion of highly profitable textile factories into Lowell and Lawrence, Massachusetts, was followed by the rise of iron-processing plants and the agricultural implements businesses. Once the railroads opened up larger regional and then national markets and technology provided significant economies of scale to larger firms, many companies moved to take over their own marketing and financing functions. Some saw the leaders of big businesses as "captains of American industry,"[10] whereas others merely perceived them as "robber barons."[11]

From 1893 to 1933, bankers and investment brokers became the dominant force in American business; this period was known as *finance capitalism*. One major reason for the dominance of bankers and investment brokers was their power to effect industrial combinations through such devices as interlocking directorates and mergers. By 1893, the national railroad system was essentially complete, providing access to all national and regional markets. High tariffs protected nearly every major industry from foreign competition, and the federal government was not aggressively prosecuting trusts or holding companies under the Sherman Act. Finally, the financial capitalists were able to turn enormous (some might say "obscene") profits for those stockholders who entered into trusts and holding company arrangements.

One popular device was to "overcapitalize" assets by combining existing firms into a new corporation and then having a public offering of the "watered" stock. The most visible, if not notorious example, in this period was the formation of U.S. Steel Corporation in 1901. The first billion dollar corporation, U.S. Steel was capitalized at $1,402,846,000, although its constituent parts owned assets worth only $626 million.[12] The American Tobacco Company, the components of which initially cost $50,000, was capitalized for $10 million, then $70 million, and then $180 million in 1904.[13]

One man stood out in this period of finance capitalism as a giant; his name was J. Pierpont Morgan, a banker whose syndicate cleared $57 million

9. STURDIVANT & VERNON-WORTZEL, *supra* note 1, at 99.

10. David McCullough, *PBS: The American Experience: The Presidents Featuring FDR.* Transcript accessed at http://www.pbs.org/wgbh/amex/presidents/nf/resource/fdr/fdrscript.html on May 23, 2003, at 37. In this context: "Roosevelt grew increasingly frustrated as business began to accuse him of meddling with free enterprise. When he regulated the stock exchange and the banks, *the captains of American industry* were outraged" [italics added].

11. JOSEPHSON, THE ROBBER BARONS (1932).

12. FREDERICK LEWIS ALLEN, THE GREAT PIERPONT MORGAN (1949) at 144, as quoted in STURDIVANT & VERNON-WORTZEL, *supra* note 1, at 104.

13. JOSEPHSON, THE ROBBER BARONS (1932) at 387.

for assembling U.S. Steel. The power of Morgan as a financier was unrivaled. Journalist Lincoln Steffens said of him, "In all my time, J. P. Morgan sat on the American throne as the boss of bosses, as the ultimate American sovereign."[14] Gras said of Morgan, "For nearly a generation, Morgan rivaled kings and presidents as an object of interest, respect, and hate."[15] J. P. Morgan rescued the U.S. monetary system in 1895 and prevented the collapse of the American banking system in 1907. On both occasions, the president of the United States sought his advice and followed his directions explicitly. Morgan also aided in the creation of such monolithic corporations as General Electric, International Harvester, and AT&T.

Gras's sixth and last stage of capitalism is *national capitalism*. In this stage, which can be dated from 1933 and the advent of President Franklin Delano Roosevelt's New Deal, we find a dramatic shift away from a strong reluctance of government to intervene in economic affairs toward an expanded use of the federal government's fiscal, monetary, and regulatory powers, initially at least, in an attempt to stem the widespread suffering caused by the Great Depression (roughly 1929–1942).

At least four major movements advocating expanded governmental intervention in the economy fit within Gras's concept of national capitalism: (1) the Progressive Movement of the early 20th century, (2) Franklin Roosevelt's New Deal, (3) the Fair Deal of Harry S. Truman in the late 1940s and early 1950s, and (4) the New Frontier–Great Society programs of John F. Kennedy and Lyndon B. Johnson in the 1960s. According to Gras, these movements "were essentially pragmatic in their approach to the use of state power and were inclined to decide whether or not to invoke the aid of the state in coping with any particular problem on the merits of the case rather than in accordance with some preconceived plan or idea."[16]

Before he died in 1956, Gras predicted that a new stage of capitalism would soon emerge. It is the my considered opinion that we are witnessing the emergence of a seventh stage of capitalism, *global capitalism*, the exact shape and impact of which have yet to be determined.

THE DECLINE IN BUSINESS COMPETITION

Price cutting in the 1870s and the 1880s led to the formation of informal alliances, named *pooling*, by various competitors. One economist attributed the price cutting to the following economic forces:

> The same force of technology which so greatly reduced the costs of production and made it possible to turn out goods of uniform quality in large numbers also required a substantial investment in fixed assets, thereby making the capital-output ratio significantly high. This meant that whenever the demand for a firm's produce [sic] fell, it was under considerable economic pressure to try to expand its sales by cutting its price and in this way spread its overhead costs over a larger volume.[17]

14. LINCOLN STEFFENS, AUTOBIOGRAPHY OF LINCOLN STEFFENS (1931) as quoted in STURDIVANT & VERNON-WERTZEL, *supra* note 1, at 105.
15. GRAS, BUSINESS AND CAPITALISM at 247.
16. *Id.* at 323.
17. ALFRED S. EICHNER, THE EMERGENCE OF OLIGOPOLY: SUGAR REFINING AS A CASE STUDY (1969) at 13 as quoted in STURDIVANT & VERNON-WORTZEL, *supra* note 1, at 101.

Under the mechanism of pooling, rival firms got together to agree on common prices, establish production quotas, and divide market territories. Usually, voting power in the pool was determined by market share, with larger firms having more votes. Pools also tried to establish fines for violations of the pooling arrangements, but this enforcement device proved ineffective because excess capacity encouraged companies to undercut prices and also because the pooling agreements were legally unenforceable.

Let me illustrate how pooling worked. The Gunpowder Trade Association, established in 1872 by Colonel Henry DuPont, comprised of seven so-called competitors and operated by an agreement that set the prices for black gunpowder. The Association set a fine of $1.00 per keg for price cutting. By 1877, DuPont had bought interests in several other firms, and he alone controlled over 50% of the votes.[18] Many members violated the agreement; between 1881 and 1883 there were 230 separate incidents of price cutting by members of the pool.[19] The Gunpowder Trade Association operated until 1907 when the federal government successfully brought suit against DuPont for violating the Sherman Antitrust Act. In 1911, DuPont was divided into three companies: DuPont, Hercules Powder, and Atlas Powder.

The captains of American business and industry quickly solved the problems associated with pools by creating the *business trust*, a legal entity with enforcement powers. This movement followed the pioneering example of John D. Rockefeller in 1879. Under Rockefeller's leadership, the stockholders of 40 companies turned over their stock certificates and voting rights to a group of trustees, who then became the directors of the board of Standard Oil Company. When other companies were bought, they too came under the umbrella of the trust.[20]

The trust device itself is an ancient one that arose in the Courts of Chancery in England about 1500.[21] For centuries, the British have used personal (nonbusiness) trusts for holding land and other assets. Under a trust, one party called the trustor transfers the legal title of a property known as the corpus to the trustee for the benefit of a third party known as the beneficiary. The trustee is obligated by law to manage the corpus for the exclusive benefit of the beneficiary and is also obligated to file periodic reports with the court detailing his or her fiduciary management of the trust properties. Under sophisticated modern property laws, one may form a "voting trust" and have the record owners of the stock transfer only the right to vote their shares to a trustee. Trust agreements are recognized and enforced by law; consequently, the use of a trust avoided the pitfalls of the earlier pooling arrangements.

In the context of finance capitalism, two noted business historians observed the following: "Trusts could appear only in a society in which the

---

18. *See* GERALD COLBY ZILG, DUPONT: BEHIND THE NYLON CURTAIN (1974) at 66–67 as quoted in STURDIVANT & VERNON-WORTZEL, *supra* note 1, at 102.
19. ZILG *supra* at 89.
20. For an abridged version of an early analysis of Rockefeller's methods, see DAVID CHAMBERS (ed.), IDA TARBELL'S THE HISTORY OF THE STANDARD OIL COMPANY (1966).
21. Certainly, the year 1500 CE is a gross approximation. Some sources trace the origins of the pure or private trust doctrine to Roman law and the Justinian Code. Some claim that English use of the trust device came into prominence during the Crusades when a knight or noble of the realm would entrust his legal title to lands and other property to a bishop of the church. The bishop would then manage the estate until the knight's return or death. On his return, assets in the trust reverted to the knight; and on his death, the bishop would transfer title to his heirs, thereby terminating the trust. *See, e.g.,* "The Origin of the Pure Trust." Accessed at http://www.webtrust.com/origins.htm on May 23, 2003.

corporation had become the dominant type of business organization, in which property rights were represented not by land or other physical assets, but by negotiable paper easily converted into other types of negotiable paper."[22]

Soon after the success of Rockefeller's Standard Oil trust, other trusts appeared in whiskey, salt, leather, cottonseed oil, sugar, and many other markets. By 1889, some states had achieved limited success in attacking trusts as being beyond the scope of the corporate charter or being in violation of public policy by enhancing prices to the injury of commerce. In 1890, Congress passed the Sherman Antitrust Act. However, passage of this legislation initially did little to dissolve trusts for various reasons: (a) Some considered the language of the statute to be overly broad and vague; (b) the government did little by way of enforcement; and (c) the federal courts, stacked as they were with judges drawn from and sympathetic to big business, attempted to defeat the purpose of the law at every turn. In the first 14 years of the Act's existence, only one case was successfully prosecuted against a trust.[23]

Theodore Roosevelt (1858–1919) became the 26th president of the United States in 1901 when President McKinley was assassinated. Teddy Roosevelt, the "Rough Rider" or the "Trust Buster" as he was also called, had his Justice Department bring suit against the Northern Securities Company.[24] The Northern Securities Company had been formed by the merger of the assets of the Great Northern, Northern Pacific, and the Chicago, Burlington, and Quincy railroads. People who had a hand in this merger included James J. Hill, J. P. Morgan, Edward H. Harriman, and John D. Rockefeller. Teddy Roosevelt distinguished between "good trusts," which had acquired assets through efficient operation, and "bad trusts," which had resulted from financial manipulation. These latter trusts, Roosevelt called "malefactors of great wealth," and in Roosevelt's mind, the Northern Securities Company was at the head of that list. In a victory for the average American, the U.S. Supreme Court in 1904, by a 5–4 vote, ordered the Northern Securities Company dissolved. By 1911, Standard Oil, American Tobacco, and DuPont were also all ordered to divide into smaller companies.

In the year 1916, an awful war raged in Europe, but in America the Industrial Revolution was in full bloom. America was completing the Progressive Era; laissez-faire capitalism had ended about the turn of the century.[25] Henry Ford was putting Americans into automobiles, employing thousands of workers at good wages and making millions of dollars—while paying little income or other taxes.[26] Mr. Ford had hoped to spread the wealth to the public by building a hospital for his workers and by lowering the price of Model-T

22. THOMAS C. COCHRAN & WILLIAM MILLER, THE AGE OF ENTERPRISE: A SOCIAL HISTORY OF INDUSTRIAL AMERICA (1942) at 142.

23. *Id.* at 190.

24. Interestingly, some social observers see the year 1900 as the approximate demarcation line between the Gilded Age (a term taken from a Mark Twain novel of 1873) and the Progressive Age. For a thorough review of the ills facing American society at that time, see ROBERT D. PUTNAM, BOWLING ALONE: THE COLLAPSE AND REVIVAL OF AMERICAN COMMUNITY (2000) at 367–401. Putnam sees the Gilded Age running from approximately 1870–1900 and the Progressive Era from 1900 to approximately 1915. *Id.* at 367. About the year 1900, Chicago had neighborhoods 300% more crowded than the densest parts of Calcutta, and Pittsburgh had the highest rate of mortality for typhoid in the world. *See Id.* at 373.

25. *See, e.g.,* ROBERT D. PUTNAM, BOWLING ALONE: THE COLLAPSE AND REVIVAL OF AMERICAN COMMUNITY (2000) at 367.

26. The 16th Amendment passed in 1913, but at this time the income tax was a concern only for the very rich and even they paid taxes at a low rate.

Fords from $440 to $380 each, even though some predicted he could sell his total output even at the higher price. The sense about him was that he was a welfare capitalist or, perhaps, a misguided populist, or an eccentric multi-millionaire with a social conscience. Ford described his ambition this way: "to employ still more men, to spread the benefits of this industrial system to the greatest possible number, to have them build up their lives and their homes. To do this, we are putting the greatest share of our profits back in the business."[27]

Enter two truly avaricious capitalists: John and Horace Dodge, two brothers who owned a 10% interest in the Ford Motor Company. They had been receiving dividends of 5% *per month* on their stock, but they sued Henry Ford and Ford Motor Company to have a court declare that the stockholders were entitled to a special dividend from Ford Motor Company's accumulated earnings of $112 million.[28] They also wanted an injunction against plant expansion and against lowering the price of the cars. They got an order for a special dividend of $19,275,385 from the trial court, but lost on the other two issues. The order was affirmed on appeal.[29] Henry Ford became embittered, and his plans for a "sharing of the wealth" with Ford workers and with the general public were shelved.

Imagine how the future of business might have evolved in the United States but for the decision in *Dodge v. Ford Motor Co.* (1916). In the appellate decision, Judge Ostrander wrote, "A business corporation is organized and carried on primarily for the profit of the stockholders. The powers of the directors are to be employed for that end."[30] This classical view of corporations dominated the legal arena for the next four decades.

In 1918, the United States became involved in World War I. A War Industries Board, directed by financier Barnard Baruch, was established to help mobilize war production, and during the war, most of the country believed that the large industrial firms performed well. With the coming of peace in 1919 and the prosperity of the 1920s, antitrust enforcement went onto the back burner. Then, on "Black Monday," October 29, 1929, the stock market collapsed, inaugurating the Great Depression.

The Senate Committee on Banking and Currency held hearings in 1933 to investigate causes of the depression. Committee findings showed widespread manipulation of stock prices; misuse of the holding company approach to business organization; and use of tax dodges, such as phony sales of stock to family members, supposedly at a loss, to eliminate income tax liability.[31] The stage was now set for the advent of extensive regulation of American business under the New Deal.

---

27. *Dodge et al. v. Ford Motor Co. et al.* 204 Mich. 459, 170 N.W. 668 (1919) as quoted in FREDERICK G. KEMPIN, JR. & JEREMY L. WIESEN, LEGAL ASPECTS OF THE MANAGEMENT PROCESS: CASES AND MATERIALS (3rd. ed. 1983) at 508.

28. *Dodge et al. v. Ford Motor Co. et al.* 204 Mich. 459, 170 N.W. 668 (1919) as quoted in KEMPIN & WIESEN, *supra* note 3, at 507.

29. *Id.*

30. *Id.* at 508–509.

31. *See, e.g.*, FREDERICK LEWIS ALLEN, SINCE YESTERDAY: THE 1930's IN AMERICA (1940) as cited and quoted in STURDIVANT & VERNON-WORTZEL, *supra* note 1, at 108.

CHAPTER

15

Rise of Regulation and Corporate Social Responsibility

This chapter deals with the years after 1933 in American business history. In November 1932, Franklin Delano Roosevelt (1882–1945) known popularly as FDR, the Democratic governor of New York State, defeated incumbent President Herbert Hoover by over 7 million votes of a total vote count of 38.5 million. The electoral college victory was even more lopsided with FDR winning by 472 votes to 59 votes for Hoover. On March 4, 1933, FDR was inaugurated the 32nd president of the United States.[1] He served as president for more than 12 years, longer than any other person and was the only person ever elected to that office four times. FDR led this nation through its worst depression and through its worst war. As one source declared, "[P]robably no other President since Abraham Lincoln has been so bitterly hated and so deeply loved."[2]

FDR promised a New Deal: to provide relief to the unemployed, to help farmers, and to balance the budget. He also said that he would end prohibition. John Nance Garner of Texas was FDR's vice president. One of the campaign posters showed FDR on one side, Garner on the other, and a frosty mug of beer between them.[3]

THE OPENING OF THE NEW DEAL

Between the 1932 election and the inauguration in March 1933, the depression had grown steadily worse. About 3 weeks before FDR took office, a banking panic occurred. A "bank run" spread throughout the country as anxious depositors hurried to their banks to get their deposits. The panic ruined many banks. President Roosevelt acted decisively by declaring a bank holiday to begin on March 6, 1933. He ordered all the banks in the United States closed until the Department of the Treasury could examine every bank's books. Banks in good financial condition would be supplied with money from the U.S. Treasury and allowed to reopen. Those in doubtful condition would be kept closed until they could be put on a sound financial footing. Many banks that had been badly run never reopened. This action by FDR restored public confidence and ended the bank crisis.

The stock market crash in 1929 indicated that all was not well in the securities industry. Consequently, shortly after addressing the most pressing problem of the bank panic, the New Dealers turned their attention to securities, as well as unemployment and helping the farmers. On March 9, 1933, Congress began a special session that had been called for by President Roosevelt. This special session of Congress came to be known as the "Hundred Days," although it actually lasted only 99 days from March 9 to June 16.[4] In that session, FDR submitted a large number of reform and recovery laws.

Congress passed nearly all the important bills that FDR requested, most by huge majorities. It passed the Securities Act of 1933, also called the Truth-in-Securities Act, in May 1933. This act required firms issuing new stocks to give investors full and accurate financial information. Congress created

---

1. Franklin D. Roosevelt was the last president to be inaugurated in March. Under the 20th Amendment to the U.S. Constitution, all subsequent inaugurations have been held on noon of the 20th day of January. The 20th Amendment was ratified in 1933.
2. THE WORLD BOOK ENCYCLOPEDIA (1990), vol. 16 at 452.
3. Campaign poster from the Franklin D. Roosevelt Library as shown in THE WORLD BOOK ENCYCLOPEDIA (1990), vol. 16 at 457.
4. *Id.* at 457.

the Securities Exchange Commission (SEC) in 1934 to regulate the sale of securities and to curb unfair stock market practices.

In addition, in May 1934, Congress passed the Agricultural Adjustment Act (AAA). The AAA attempted to raise agricultural prices by limiting production. Funds raised by a tax on processors of farm products were used to pay farmers not to raise crops in the quantities they had previously. Production was limited by a set-aside of farm land, that is, land withdrawn from production. In 1936, the U.S. Supreme Court ruled the AAA unconstitutional. The federal government then paid farmers to leave some land fallow as part of a new soil conservation program.

One of the most important laws passed in the special session was the National Industrial Recovery Act of June 1933. This law created the National Recovery Administration (NRA) to enforce codes of fair practices for business and industry. Representatives of each industry drafted the codes for their respective industries. The industrial codes set minimum wages and maximum hours and supported the right of workers to join unions. However, the codes primarily aided businesses. They allowed member firms to set standards of quality and establish the lowest prices that could be charged for goods.

In 1935, the U.S. Supreme Court declared the NRA unconstitutional.[5] As a result of this case and other cases holding various New Deal acts unconstitutional, FDR and the Congress passed a second wave of legislation. In 1935, Congress enacted several important relief and reform measures that were to be the heart of the New Deal's lasting accomplishments. Most of these new laws were passed during the summer, and consequently some historians refer to this period as the "Second Hundred Days." Three of these laws were the Works Progress Administration (WPA), the National Labor Relations Act (NLRA) and the Social Security Act.

Most scholars agree that the New Deal alleviated economic distress and caused a measure of economic recovery. Yet, almost 8 million Americans were still out of work in 1940. Ultimately, it was the military spending required by World War II, rather than the New Deal, that brought back prosperity. However, the New Deal did bring about major political changes, as the federal government assumed responsibility for the economic security of the American people and for the economic health of the nation. After the New Deal, the government's role in banking and public welfare grew steadily. As a result of the NLRA, organized labor became an important force in national affairs for at least four decades. Under FDR's leadership, the Democratic Party became the major political party in the United States for the first time since the Civil War (1862–1865).

MODERN CORPORATIONS AND FEDERAL REGULATIONS

The New Deal represented a burst of regulatory legislation, brought on by the suffering of the Great Depression. President Franklin Roosevelt's tenure has been divided by historians into two main periods: the New Deal years and the war years (roughly 1940 to his death in April 1945). From 1940 through World War II until the 1960s, there was a lull in the generation of new business regulation. However, government intervention in economic activity expanded dramatically in the 1960s and the 1970s.[6]

---

5. *Schecter Poultry Corp. vs. U.S.* 295 U.S. 495 (1935).
6. MURRAY L. WEIDENBAUM, BUSINESS, GOVERNMENT AND THE PUBLIC (4th ed. 1990) at 20.

With the election of John F. Kennedy (known popularly as JFK) in November 1960, the nation had signaled, albeit by the slimmest of margins,[7] a desire to move forward from the Chamber of Commerce–approved policies promoted by President Eisenhower's two administrations (1953–1961). In moving oratory, the new president told the nation and the world "that the torch has been passed to a new generation of Americans—born in this century, tempered by war, disciplined by a hard and bitter peace, proud of our ancient heritage—and unwilling to witness or permit the slow undoing of those human rights to which this nation has always been committed."[8]

The 1960s proved to be both a time of turmoil and of reexamination. Racial tensions were high, and the civil rights movement had been pressuring JFK to push its legislation. Before he was killed in Dallas on November 22, 1963, JFK had proposed a civil rights bill, but it was stalled in committee. After his death, Lyndon B. Johnson became president and was able to get the bill strengthened and out of committee. It became the 1964 Civil Rights Act and took effect on July 2, 1965. The Equal Employment Opportunity Commission is charged with enforcement of the Act.

In another arena, research showed that state workers' compensation laws no longer functioned as a market-based deterrent to unsafe work conditions. In 1970, Congress passed the Occupational Safety and Health Act, which required all employers in businesses engaging in interstate commerce to provide a safe workplace for their employees. A third area of regulation came about on January 1, 1970, when President Nixon signed into law the National Environmental Protection Act. The most important part of that law is that it requires all federal agencies to prepare an environmental impact statement (EIS) any time they undertake major activity that significantly affects environmental quality. The Environmental Protection Agency has made news since its inception in 1970; among its charges, it is required to monitor environmental practices of industry.

In 1972, Congress established the Consumer Product Safety Commission and gave it the mandate of protecting the public against unreasonable risks of injury associated with consumer products.[9] To accomplish this mandate, Congress directed the Consumer Product Safety Commission to assist consumers in evaluating the comparative safety of consumer products, to develop uniform safety standards for consumer products, and to conduct research into the causes and prevention of product-related casualties.

Murray Weidenbaum of Washington University noted that the New Deal agencies tended to be industry-specific, and he labeled them "vertical regulatory agencies." In contrast, the regulatory agencies created after 1960 tended to be directed toward specific social problems and govern the entire spectrum of business and industry. Weidenbaum called these agencies "horizontal regulatory agencies." Finally, he noted that the passage of the latter did not coincide with repeal of the former; thus, businesses are faced with multiple layers of federal and, in some cases, state regulation.[10] According to Professor Weidenbaum, the number of regulatory agencies climbed

7. JFK's margin of victory over Richard M. Nixon in the popular vote was 34,227,096 versus 34,108,546 or a difference of 118,550 votes— 0.173% of the 68,335,642 votes cast. WORLD ALMANAC AND BOOK OF FACTS 1997 (1996) at 108.

8. MAUREEN HARRISON & STEVE GILBERT (eds.), JOHN F. KENNEDY IN HIS OWN WORDS (1993) at 17.

9. 15 U.S.C. Section 2051 (b).

10. MURRAY L. WEIDENBAUM, BUSINESS, GOVERNMENT AND THE PUBLIC (3rd ed. 1986) at 28–31.

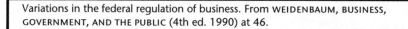

Variations in the federal regulation of business. From WEIDENBAUM, BUSINESS, GOVERNMENT, AND THE PUBLIC (4th ed. 1990) at 46.

■ **FIGURE 15.1**

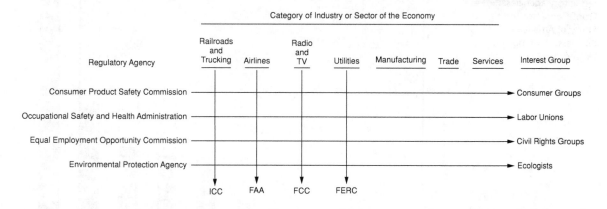

sharply until 1980 when it fell slightly because of attempts at deregulation[11] (Figs. 15.1 and 15.2).

CORPORATIONS TODAY

More than a century after the Sherman Act was passed, the United States finds itself in the midst of a world economy in which competition in many industries takes place on an international scale and where the United States is no longer the dominant economic power. Many people now think that the antitrust laws hinder, rather than help, the ordinary consumer. Members of a new generation have challenged their predecessors' conclusions that certain business practices or market conditions are anticompetitive. They conclude instead that most anticompetitive practices are defeated by market forces. They question the effectiveness of the government's regulation of commerce and markets, arguing that instead of promoting competition, attempts at regulation often increase the anticompetitive structure of the markets.[12]

Does the United States no longer need antitrust regulation? Have the antitrust laws so effectively disassembled the power of the corporation in the 20th century? Many feel that the the oligopolistic corporations are still exploiting consumers and that antitrust laws need to be interpreted more strictly.

As early as the middle of the 19th century, Karl Marx argued that capitalism leads to a concentration of property, resources, and power in a few hands. Exorbitant costs, complex technology, and intense competition all work against the survival of the small firm, said Marx.[13] Many argue that we see the proof of these arguments in today's economy. The economy of America's Industrial Revolution was mostly free and open to competition, but since the time of Carnegie, Morgan, and Rockefeller, the economy is dominated by a relative few enormous companies that can, to some degree, eliminate competition, fix prices, and monopolize an industry.

To illustrate this concentration, Jim Hightower, the Texas Commissioner of Agriculture, came out with figures showing how the merger of firms had

---

11. *See* bar graphs from WEIDENBAUM (4th ed.) at 21.
12. CONSTANCE BAGLEY, THE LEGAL ENVIRONMENT OF BUSINESS (1990) at 396.
13. WILLIAM SHAW, BUSINESS ETHICS (1991).

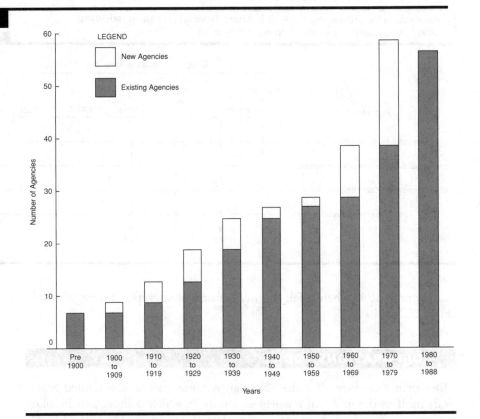

FIGURE 15.2

Growth of federal regulatory agencies. From Center for the Study of American Business, Washington, University.

produced a series of shared monopolies in the food industry.[14] The percentages in this list show the levels of market control by just the top three brands in food preferred by college students:

- Peanut butter: 78.6%
- Canned spaghetti and noodles: 96.0%
- Add-meat dinner mixes: 90.7%
- Frozen dinners: 92.8%
- Corn and tortilla chips: 86.7%

Three top U.S. corporations in sales (in billions of dollars) were

Wal-Mart Stores, Inc.	$285.2[15]
General Electric Co.	$151.3[16]
Proctor & Gambler	$51.4[17]
totaling	$487.9

14. Jim Hightower, *Food Monopoly: Who's Who in the Thanksgiving Business?* TEXAS OBSERVER (Nov. 17, 1978) as quoted in SHAW, *supra* note 13, at 133.

15. Wal-Mart Stores, Inc. of Bentonville, Arkansas listed fiscal year 2005 (ending January 2005) total sales of $285,222 million. *See Hoover's Company Records—Basic Record for Wal-Mart Stores, Inc* at http://web.lexis-nexis.com/universe/printdoc (last visited on July 27, 2005).

16. General Electric Company of Fairfield, Connecticut, listed total sales for the year ending December 2004 of $151,300 million. *See Hoover's Company Records—Basic Records for General Electric* at http://web.lexis-nexis.com/universe/printdoc (last visited on July 27, 2005).

17. The Proctor & Gamble Company of Cincinnati, Ohio listed total sales for fiscal year 2004 (ending June 2004) of $51,407 million. *See Hoover's Company Records—Basic Record for the Proctor & Gamble Company* at http://web.lexis-nexis.com/universe/printdoc (last visited July 27, 2005).

The dollar figures are staggering, but when compared to statistics from *The United Nations' Statistical Yearbook* one can see that corporations are able to compete with the modern nations of this world. These companies were not selected because they were the largest of the big U.S. corporations. Rather, they were selected because they are well-known and are generally representative of large U.S. corporations. Note that P & G will get much larger once it has completed its acqustion of the Gillette Razor Company in 2005. Their total sales (as listed) are $487.9 billion; and if they were combined to make one country, their total sales (as a proxy for GDP) would make them the 17th largest national economy in the world just behind the Netherlands and ahead of such countries as Belgium, Switzerland, Sweden, Turkey, and Poland.[18]

On its own, using similar comparisons, Wal-Mart Stores, Inc. would be the 26th largest national economy, just behind Norway and ahead of such countries as Saudi Arabia, Indonesia, Denmark, and Greece. By itself, General Electric would have the 38th largest national economy, just behind Argentina and ahead of such countries as Malaysia, the Czech Republic, Israel, and Venezuela. Finally, taking P & G by itself, it would rank as the 60th largest economy in the world, just behind Slovakia and ahead of such countries as Vietnam, Luxembourg, and Libya.

For non-publicly traded companies, Forbes listed as the Cargill Corporation of Minnesota as the largest private company in the United States in 2004.[19] Cargill, a crop and seed company, had sales in 2004 in excess of $64 billion. If Cargill were a nation-state, it would have the 56th largest economy—as measured by GDP (nominal), just behind Peru and ahead of Bangladesh, Kuwait, and Morocco. The list of nations by GDP listed the top 180 countries.[20] The United Nations lists 191 members; that number is sometimes mistakenly used as the number of countries in the world.[21] "Mistakenly" is the correct adverb because Vatican City is an independent country and is not a member of the U.N. as is Taiwan — although China considers Taiwan a province.[22] Whatever the final number, it is safe to say that the large corporations of the world have more economic power than most of the countries of the world.

In their book, *The Modern Corporation and Private Property*, Adolph Berle and Gardner Means, two economics professors at Harvard, argue for this point:

> The rise of the modern corporation has brought a concentration of economic power which can compete on equal terms with the modern state—economic power versus political power, each strong in its own field. The state seeks in some aspects to regulate the corporation, while the corporation, steadily becoming more powerful, makes every effort to avoid such regulation. Where its own interests are concerned, it even attempts to dominate the state. The future may see

---

18. Hereinafter, the national GDP (gross domestic product) (nominal, i.e. unadjusted for purchasing power or variations in exchange rates) comes from *List of Countries by GDP (nominal)* accessed at http://encyclopedia. worldvillage.com./s/b/List_of_countries_by_GDP_%28nominal%29 (last accessed on July 27, 2005).

19. *See Largest Private Companies* at http://www.forbes.com/finance/lists/setters/keywordSearch Setter, jhtml?passYear=2004&p . . . (last accessed on July 27, 2005).

20. *See List of Countries by GDP, supra* note 18.

21. *See How Many Countries Are in the World?* At http://geography.about.com/cs/countries/a/ numbercountries.htm (last visited on July 27, 2005).

22. *Id.*

the economic organism, now typified by the corporation, not only on an equal plane with the state, but possibly even superseding it as the dominant form of social organization. The law of corporations, accordingly, might well be considered as a potential constitutional law for the new economic state, while business practice is increasingly assuming the aspect of economic statesmanship.[23]

On July 28, 2005, the House of Representatives approved an $11 billion energy bill with $3 billion in tax incentives for oil and natural gas companies.[24] That was the same day that Exxon-Mobil, the world's largest oil company, announced the biggest one-quarter profits in history: over $15 billion in the second quarter of 2005.[25] One of the likely beneficiaries of a special multi-million dollar fund to underwrite ultra-deep water oil drilling in the Gulf of Mexico is an oil consortium based in Sugarland, Texas (House Speaker Tom Delay's hometown) and including Halliburton, Vice President Cheney's former employer.[26]

THE ARRIVAL OF A PHILOSOPHY KNOWN AS CORPORATE SOCIAL RESPONSIBILITY

In 1972, President Richard Milhous Nixon was running for reelection against a weak but principled Democratic nominee, Senator George McGovern of South Dakota. He was reelected by a landslide.[27] In the summer of the campaign, however, there was a break-in at the Democratic National Headquarters in the Watergate complex in Washington, D.C. Nixon dismissed this event as "a second-rate burglary." Early in the second term, Vice President Spiro Agnew of Maryland resigned rather than be impeached after he was convicted of taking bribes while governor of Maryland. Nixon, in the wake of the House voting articles of impeachment against him, became the first American president to resign, rather than go through the ordeal of a trial in the U.S. Senate. Gerald Ford of Michigan, whom Nixon had appointed vice president to succeed the disgraced Mr. Agnew, then was sworn in as president and granted a full pardon to former President Nixon. The entire seamy affair shocked much of the nation.

Partially in response to the national handwringing over a lack of scruples in high places, colleges and universities began to offer courses in applied ethics. This phenomenon was called cynically "the post-Watergate morality." Courses in legal ethics, medical ethics, and business ethics (just to name a few) surfaced in the curricula of many schools; Figure 15.3 illustrates some of the legal and ethics theories discussed in those classes. In this environment, and also following another round of white-collar crime during the Reagan years (1980–1988), journals in business ethics were founded.[28] A segment—albeit a small

---

23. A. BERLE & G. MEANS, THE MODERN CORPORATION AND PRIVATE PROPERTY (1967) at 313. [The original work came out in 1932.]
24. NPR News at 4 p.m. on WFUC, FM 90-9, Cincinnati's Classical Public Radio Station.
25. *Id.*
26. *Id.*
27. Richard M. Nixon received 47,165,234 votes and 520 electoral college votes in 1972 versus George S. McGovern's 29,170,774 votes and 17 electoral college votes. THE WORLD ALMANAC AND BOOK OF FACTS 1997 (1996) at 108. Nixon received approximately 62% of the votes cast.
28. *The Journal of Business Ethics* made its appearance in 1981. *The Business Ethics Quarterly* came out in 1991.

■ **FIGURE 15.3**

Legal theories and ethics theories. From JOSEPH A. PETRICK & JOHN F. QUINN, MANAGEMENT ETHICS: INTEGRITY at WORK.

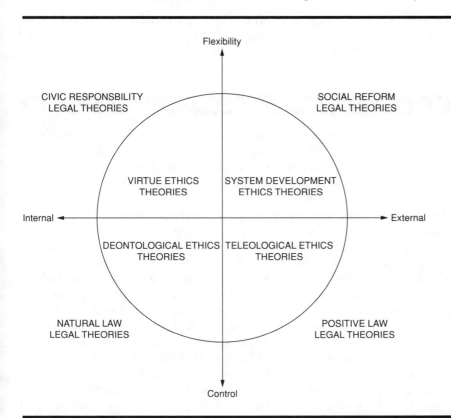

and not very vocal one—of the business school faculty began to cautiously advocate corporate social responsibility, a topic that had been around for ages but had fallen on hard times in the wake of the ascendancy of Chicago-style neoclassical economics.[29]

Robert Holmes, in an important article published in the early 1970s, articulated a spectrum of attitudes toward corporate social responsibility.[30] On the far right is Professor Friedman's extreme position that business's only social responsibility is to maximize profits for shareholders. Next is the position that a corporation *might* be socially responsible *if* such an action were consistent with profit maximization, followed by the position that a corporation *should* be socially responsible when it is consistent with profit maximization. Fourth from right is the position that a corporation *might* be socially responsible *even when it was inconsistent* with profit maximization. Finally, on the far left, is the extreme position for social responsibility, namely that a corporation *must* be socially responsible *even when such an action was inconsistent* with profit maximization. This position is advocated by such academic leaders as Professor Lisa Newton, past president of the Society for Business Ethics. In a nutshell, the debate rages in academic circles, whereas many of this nation's business leaders either ignore it or are oblivious to it. One current concern of business

29. The authors of a popular management textbook argue that the social responsibility position found adherents in print in the early years after World War I (1919 and 1923), but that "few socially responsible programs were actually implemented [by corporate America] until the late 1960s." LESLIE W. RUE & LLOYD L. BYARS, MANAGEMENT THEORY AND APPLICATION (4th ed. 1986) at 60–62.

30. Robert Holmes, *A Spectrum of Attitudes Toward Corporate Social Responsibility*. As quoted in BEAUCHAMP & BOWIE, ETHICAL THEORY AND BUSINESS (1978).

ethicists is that corporate ethics officers may be converted into legal compliance officers in the work of the 2001–2002 Enron melt-down and passage of the Sarbanes-Oxley Acts.[31]

RESPONSIBILITY AND THE ISSUE OF CONTROL

Since the turn of the 20th century, there has been much debate about who actually controls the decisions in corporations. Two basic models attempt to explain the issue of control in corporations: (1) the classic model and (2) the realist model. Both of these models are addressed in this section.

Corporations came into being during the Age of Discovery to encourage investment in exploration. Some of the earliest corporations were the East India Company (1600) and the Hudson Bay Company (1670). With the advent of the Industrial Revolution, large sums of capital were required for railroads, steel mills, and the like. The movement from special acts of the legislation to what is known as "open incorporation" status came about in this period. By turning a small business into a corporation, the owners could separate their personal assets from their business investment and open the door to a vast number of potential investors. According to law, a person could invest money into a corporation by simply purchasing shares of stock in that corporation. By doing so, the investor would share in the profits of the company while at the same time could only lose the amount of money invested, without fear of being sued for wrongdoings of the corporation. This was a very attractive proposition to many business owners and investors. As a result, the size and power of corporations began to grow.

> Since the turn of the twentieth century, modern capitalist economies have been more and more influenced by the rise of large business corporations. The share of total manufacturing assets held by the two hundred largest manufacturing firms in the United States has increased by .5 percent each year from 1900 to the present day; these two hundred corporations now control over half of all manufacturing assets.[32]

The classic view of who has power in these corporations is shown in Figures 15.4. People invest in the corporation and become shareholders; these shareholders then elect a board of directors. The board of directors hires top management and other employees and runs the company on a day-to-day basis. All this is done to help increase shareholder wealth. Types of corporations best exemplified by the classical view are traditional small businesses that are owned by a few people, such as a family. In such businesses, the shareholders play many roles in the business. These positions include owner, CEO, members of the board of directors, and top management, and many times, they make up the largest part of the employees.

The corporation not only gives owners limited liability for the company's actions but it also provides a means of raising large amounts of capital efficiently. This is done by making shares of the company available to investors beyond the original owners. Although going public makes it easier for businesses and entrepreneurs to obtain capital to build their business into the

---

31. Sarbanes-Oxley Act of 2002, 107 Pub. L. No. 204 (July 30, 2002).
32. GIDDENS, INTRODUCTION TO SOCIOLOGY (2d ed. 1996) at 249.

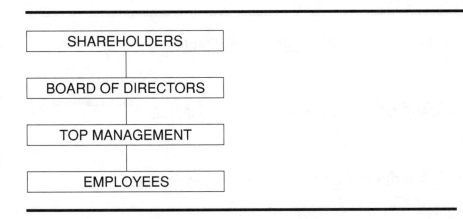

■ FIGURE 15.4

The classical view of corporate structure.

successes they dreamed about, one cost is that it reduces the power of the original owners over the corporation and spreads control over many different investors: "The prevailing view is that the diffusion of ownership in the large corporation among the numerous stock owners has resulted in the separation of ownership and control."[33]

The realist model of the corporate structure (Fig. 15.5) was first explained in the book *The Modern Corporation and Private Property* by Berle and Means (1932). The authors discuss the idea that businesses are not run by the shareholders, but in fact that "companies are management controlled because shareholder dispersion had reached extremes which permitted decisions to be taken by management in disregard of shareholders' interests."[34] The realist point of view believes that, instead of there being a linear and hierarchical relationship among the shareholders, the board of directors, top management, and the employees, there is a bi-linear relationship.

This bi-linear relationship puts the CEO and top management in the controlling positions, with a branch coming off from each. In one branch are the board of directors, who are appointed by the top management, and who then report to the shareholders whatever information that they feel the shareholders should know. The other branch comprises officers appointed by top management, who then hire employees to run the company.

According to the realist structural model, the shareholders (owners) of the corporation have little or no actual power in the decision-making processes that go on in the business itself: "Since share ownership is so dispersed, actual control has passed into the hands of the managers who run firms on a day-to-day basis. Ownership of the corporations is thus separated from their own control."[35] This lack of control has been present for so long that it is believed that "shareholding dispersion has reached extremes which permit decisions to be taken by management in disregard of shareholder's interests."[36]

Berle and Means came up with a five-level classification scheme for businesses based on shareholder concentration. They define control as being distinct from both management and ownership. Control is assumed to lie "in the hands of the individual or group who have the actual power to select the board

33. M. Zeitlin, *Corporate Ownership and Control: The Large Corporation and the Capitalist Class*, 79 AMERICAN JOURNAL OF SOCIOLOGY (no. 5, 1974) 1073—1080, 1089–1108.

34. D. Leech, *Corporate Ownership and Control: A New Look at the Evidence of Berle and Means*, 39 OXFORD ECONOMIC PAPERS (1987), 534–551 at 535.

35. GIDDENS, *supra* note 32, at 249.

36. Leech, *supra* note 34, at 534.

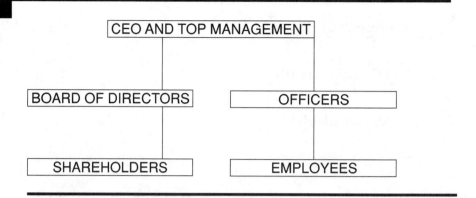

The realist view of corporate structure.

of directors (or its majority), either by mobilizing the legal right to choose them ... or by exerting pressure which influences their choice."[37] Using this definition of control, then all that is needed for a person or people to be in control is the ability to influence the choice of directors in the company. The five types of control are as follows:

1. control through almost complete ownership
2. majority control
3. control through a legal device (pyramiding, nonvoting stock, voting trust)
4. minority control
5. management control[38]

In the first three types, there is no question about who has control because legal and factual controls are the same. However, in the last two control types, legal and factual control do not coincide. The control of shareholders in Type 4 "rests upon their ability to attract from scattered owners proxies sufficient when combined with their substantial minority interest to control a majority of the votes at the annual elections."[39] This assumes that there is no other group with an equal or larger controlling block and therefore requires the shareholders to have the largest voting block.

Type 5, management control, is a residual category in which no individual or small group is in a position to dominate the company through ownership: "By default, control is held by a self-perpetuating and unaccountable group of top managers, usually, equated with the board of directors ... which is able to discount any challenge to its position by shareholders."[40]

In explaining the shift from the classical view to the realist view of corporate power, Berle and Means refer to an evolution process from Type 1 control to Type 5 control. This shift began "in the early 20th century, which was a period of very rapid corporate growth. In many companies, expansion was financed by new share capital supplied by millions of new shareholders and, as a result, concentration fell."[41]

There are critics of this theory. Which structure of organization-the realist or the classical view—best explains corporate behavior. The answer

---

37. BERLE AND MEANS (1967) at 66.
38. Leech, *supra*, note 34, at 535.
39. BERLE AND MEANS (1967) at 750.
40. Leech, *supra* note 34, at 535.
41. *Id.* at 537.

seems to be both. In small corporations and family-owned companies, the shareholders do indeed still own and control the companies in most cases. The classical model best explains their behavior. However, in large publicly traded corporations throughout the nation and the world, top management does control the corporation, and ownership is separate from control. In many cases, the top management and CEOs do not only hold seats in one company, but as C. Wright Mills points out, they hold chairs in the top positions of various other companies as well[42] (Fig. 15.6).

By being in these positions, it is suggested, top management makes decisions for the company that are more for their own benefit than for the good of the shareholders. This is a fear that many potential investors have when it comes to purchasing stock on public exchanges. The concern has not been alleviated by the Enron/Arthur Andersen debacles.

SOCIAL RESPONSIBILITY: THE CASE OF NAPALM AND A USE FOR BUSINESS HISTORY

DOW CHEMICAL AND THE NAPALM CONTROVERSY

When Napalm was developed in 1942, it was done so for the sole purpose of delivering a horrible death. So reported the chemist Louis F. Fieser, the developer of Napalm, in a research paper declassified in 1946. Napalm was used in flame throwers and belly tank bombs to provide an effective means for driving the enemy (the Japanese) out of caves and underground defensive installations. Although Napalm was briefly used against German forces, it was mostly used on the cities of Japan and Saipan. After experiencing several Napalm attacks, thousands of residents of Saipan became panicked and committed suicide because of their fear of the terrible fiery death.[43]

The military held this new weapon in high regard and wanted to use it in future wars. It was very effective and was less costly than the atomic bomb, but they believed that if the chemical material was more dense and sticky that it would burn even more fiercely and possess a higher heat content.

As a result, Napalm-B was developed in 1947 (during peace time) and instead of soap, a plastic called polystyrene was used as the jelling agent. This plastic substance was thin enough to spread great distances and thick enough to stick to anything it hit. A 6-pound bomb could spread Napalm-B over an area the size of a football field and burn at temperatures as hot as 2000 degrees. Just in case burning a victim at 2000 degrees was not enough, it was decided to add magnesium or phosphorous bits to the mixture for skin penetration.

The Air Force came to Dow, the largest American supplier of plastic, to make Napalm-B. In early 1966, the first Napalm-B contracts were awarded to Dow and United Technology Center, a United Aircraft subsidiary. These contracts were for 150 million pounds of Napalm-B. During World War II, the total amount of Napalm dropped on Japan was 194 million pounds. After a year, United got out of the Napalm business.

---

42. C. WRIGHT MILLS, THE POWER ELITE, 1957.
43. ROBERT L. HEILBRONER, et al. IN THE NAME OF PROFIT (1972) at 120. Most of the material in this section has been developed from Chapter 5 of the book written by Saul Friedman at 115–135.

■ **FIGURE 15.6**

Model of the American social structure: the power elite hypothesis. From C. WRIGHT MILLS, THE POWER ELITE (1956) and G. WILLIAM DOMNOFF, THE POWER ELITE AND THE STATE (1990).

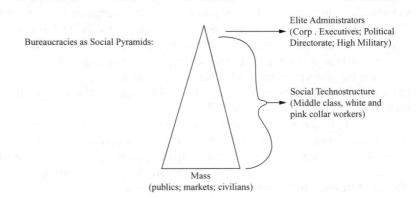

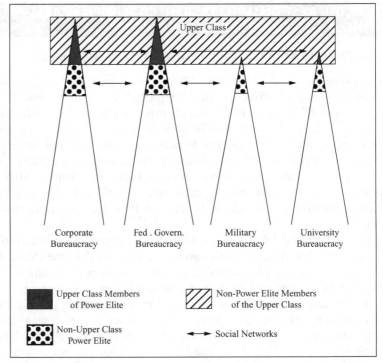

Dow's headquarters are in Midland, Michigan. The organization began to reexamine its production of Napalm-B when protests against its production moved from quiet small protests in New York to more vocal protests in Midland. Herbert (Ted) Dow Doan, president of Dow from 1962 to 1971, stated that he knew nothing of the Napalm contracts until late 1966 because of the team leadership approach Dow had used since 1962. Dow issued statements such as this one:

> Our position on the manufacture of Napalm is that we are a supplier of goods to the Defense Department and not a policy-maker. We do not and should not try to decide military strategy or policy. Simple good citizenship requires that we supply our government and our military

with those goods which they feel they need whenever we have the technology and capability and have been chosen by the government as the supplier.

The protests grew, as reports that Napalm was being used on civilians in the Vietnam War began to surface. Pictures of Napalm victims, including children, were circulated by protestors. Dow's public image was not helped in the least when a Dow public relations man stated the pictures being shown by protesters were "as phony as can be. There are no skin burns from Napalm. It burns right through or kills by concussion and suffocation."[44]

When the Napalm contract came up for bid again in 1969, Dow's board and management team were divided on whether Dow should bid on the contract and, if they did bid, how they should bid on it. Dow did bid on the contract, but deliberately set its price in a way guaranteed to lose the bid. Dow was able to save face when the American Electric Company of Los Angeles decided to bid on the entire contract, including the production of the Napalm filling. American Electric had previously been the government supplier for the canisters that held the Napalm. Rumors began to circulate that Dow helped American Electric with the production or at least supplied the polystyrene in order to get out of the Napalm manufacturing business. In November 1969, American Electric began producing Napalm, but did not become a target for the large-scale protests Dow had faced. In an attempt to shed its Napalm past, Dow moved further into consumer merchandise when Ted Doan resigned as president in 1971 while still remaining on the board.

USE OF U.S. BUSINESS HISTORY IN TEACHING BUSINESS ETHICS

As a vehicle for the teaching of business ethics, the use of business history offers many benefits. In a paper entitled "A Plea for History in Business Ethics Pedagogy," F. Neil Brady argues for the use of business history in teaching and researching business ethics.[45] Dr. Brady looked at 10 available business ethics texts, discovering that the average case presented was approximately 15 years old. He believed the reason for this was that the cases were recent enough to illustrate current concerns, but old enough for all of the "dust to have settled." Brady also believed the same to be true for the professional literature that was being presented. Brady gave several reasons why history was neglected in business ethics literature. One reason was a sense that "like business in general, business ethics is practical; and from a practical point of view, old problems are no longer problems."[46] Another reason given was the absence of a feeling for history within the business ethics field. The third reason he listed was the interest level in the history of the academic field versus the history of business ethics generally. Here, he stressed that business ethics is like many other academic disciplines in which the academic history takes precedence over the general history of the area in the world itself. The last reason was his belief that business ethics scholars do not know American business history.

---

44. *Id.* at 129.
45. F. Neil Brady, "A Plan for History in Business Ethics Prodagogy" (1989). Unpublished paper presented at the annual meeting of the Western Academy of Management, San Francisco, CA.
46. *Id.* at 5.

Brady then gives five reasons why history should be used when teaching business ethics:

1. Through the use of business history, business ethics would appear less "faddish."
2. An increased attention to business history would open students' eyes and enable them to see issues not only as academic entertainment but also as having intrinsic value.
3. Through business history studies, students would become aware that many ethical issues faced in the business world are systemic, rather than idiosyncratic.
4. The study of business history would promote identification of business heroes/heroines. Business heroes and heroines "may offer greater hope for long-term educational influence than the traditional academic approach of issue analysis."[47]
5. An awareness of changing American values would be promoted by providing a historical perspective on business ethics. Comparing a contemporary issue with one from the previous century would enable students to develop a better understanding of ethical issues and autonomy.

CONCLUSION

The Industrial Revolution brought with it urbanization and the reorganization of work. One result was that industrial production became capital intensive. The growth of specialization and the application of capital to industrial production created new wealth, as well as new class distinctions. After the Civil War, corporations increased rapidly in number and in size. This growth was facilitated by a large bounty of natural resources, the availability of cheap labor, and the absence of meaningful regulation.

The results of the price-cutting cycles in 1870s and the 1880s were business combinations in restraint of trade—first pooling arrangements that proved unsatisfactory and then trusts. The use of the trust device, an innovation pioneered by John D. Rockefeller at Standard Oil, led to formation of companies with never before seen power and wealth. The American public was at the mercy of these trusts.

In an initial attempt to regulate the trusts, Congress passed the Sherman Act of 1890, which restricted the trusts' power to monopolize and take advantage of society. "Trust busting" peaked under Teddy Roosevelt in the early 1900s, but disappeared almost entirely between the advent of World War I and the start of the New Deal in 1933. The New Deal of FDR brought about a burst of federal regulation of business in an attempt to alleviate the suffering caused by the Great Depression and to eliminate many of the unscrupulous business practices in banking and the securities industry that had contributed to the economic collapse in the United States.

After 1960, the federal government, responding to single-interest groups, passed laws creating new horizontal regulatory agencies, such as the EEOC, the EPA, CPSC, and OSHA. These agencies regulated the entire band of business and industry, unlike the New Deal vertical agencies that were industry

---

47. *Id.* at 15.

specific. Nonetheless, business in the United States has continued to concentrate and reduce competition.

Today, some argue that antitrust regulation is not healthy for the economy because, instead of promoting competition, it often increases the anticompetitive structure of the markets. As Professor Weidenbaum has noted, regulation of business costs money, and these costs are often passed onto consumers in the form of hidden and regressive taxes. Finally, as Professor Stone has shown, regulation is inherently inefficient because it is aimed at fixing yesterday's problem, a difficulty inherent in the legislative process.[48]

Evidence suggests that indeed corporations do, to some degree, eliminate competition, fix prices, and monopolize markets. Some justify tolerating this condition on the grounds that today's big businesses need enough economic power to compete on equal terms around the globe.

---

48. CHRISTOPHER STONE, WHERE THE LAW ENDS (1975).

CHAPTER 16

Workplace Issues I: Employment versus Personal Dignity

The foregoing cases suggest that specific guarantees in the Bill of Rights have penumbras, formed by emanations from those guarantees that help give them life and substance. [Citation omitted.] Various guarantees create zones of privacy.
—William O. Douglas (1898–1980)[1]

INTRODUCTION

This nation of approximately 280 million Americans manifests a rich diversity of values and attitudes toward work. Some observers have suggested that attitudes toward work can be accurately classified along class lines or by the color of the worker's collar.[2] Many people in the United States see work as an important activity, and, unlike the Biblical[3] or predominant Greek view, work is not merely tolerated as a curse. If anything, the lack of work or unemployment is the modern curse.[4]

The work ethic and secular Calvinism are still endorsed by most people in the United States, but it is probably accurate to say that the Reagan-Bush years (1980–1993) witnessed a small boom in the once-discredited notion that a person's worth may be measured by his or her wealth. Ostentatious displays of wealth were once again fashionable in certain circles in Washington, D.C.[5] A discouraging increase in the negative but related sentiment that poor people are lazy or otherwise undeserving of wealth accompanied such a fashion swing.[6] A better reasoned position might be to praise wealth so long as it is the product of honest labor and also to recognize the importance of compassion.

Americans often see their identity and self-concepts intertwined in their work.[7] Many, if not most, want their work to be interesting, challenging,

---

Chapter 16 is based on a paper written by William Arthur Wines and Michael P. Fronmueller, Ph.D., currently Dean of Management, LeMoyne College, Syracuse, NY, and presented to the Pacific Northwest Academy of Legal Studies in Business, Vancouver, B.C. on April 16, 1999. The author thanks Dean Fronmueller for his graciousness in consenting to allow our joint effort to appear in this work. A revised and expanded version of that paper, footnoted to law review standards, appeared in 78 NEB. L. REV. (no. 3, February 2000), 301–339.

1. *Griswold v. Connecticut* 381 U.S. 479, 484 (1965).
2. *See, e.g.,* SEBASTIAN DE GRAZIA, OF TIME, WORK, AND LEISURE (1962) at 40 and HANNAH ARENDT, THE HUMAN CONDITION (1958) at 77–88.
3. Genesis 3:17–19.
4. *See, e.g.,* WILLIAM JULIUS WILSON, WHEN WORK DISAPPEARS: THE WORLD OF THE NEW URBAN POOR (1996). *See also* JEREMY RIFKIN, THE END OF WORK: THE DECLINE OF THE GLOBAL LABOR FORCE AND THE DAWN OF THE POST-MARKET ERA (1995).
5. *See, e.g.,* WILLLIAM SHAW, BUSINESS ETHICS (3rd ed. 1999) at 83 detailing President Reagan's tax breaks for the rich.
6. ADAM SMITH, THE THEORY OF MORAL SENTIMENTS (1759), Section III, Chapter 3. Adam Smith said it best:

   > This disposition to admire, and almost to worship, the rich and the powerful, and to despise, or, at least to neglect persons of poor and mean condition, though necessary both to establish and to maintain the distinction of ranks and the order of society, is, at the same time, the great and most universal cause of the corruption of our moral sentiments. That wealth and greatness are often regarded with the respect and admiration which are due only to wisdom and virtue; and that the contempt, of which vice and folly are the only proper objects, is often most unjustly bestowed upon poverty and weakness, has been the complaint of moralists in all ages.

7. A 1% rise in unemployment in the United States is associated with an increase in suicides of over 4% and an increase in homicides of over 5%. ID. STATESMAN (December 23, 1998) at 3E. *See also* Kinicki et al., *Socially Responsible Plant Closings,* PERSONNEL ADMINISTRATOR (June 1987) at 116 citing BARRY BLUESTONE AND BENNETT HARRISON, THE DEINDUSTRIALIZATION OF AMERICA (1982), Chapter 3.

and satisfying.[8] Meeting this desire of the American worker provides and will continue to provide serious challenges for managers. Similarly, many workers in the United States—because they see their self-worth tied up in their calling, to use the Calvinist term—are sensitive to wage issues and other conditions of employment. Employment is the central economic relation for every worker. Consequently, much weight attaches to it.

Employment is as central now to an individual's status and ability to survive as the rights to land were 600 years ago in England and Western Europe. In that agrarian society, land was central; all else could be obtained if one had the right to a sufficient quantity of real estate. The result was that the kings, parliaments, and courts erected an elaborate social and legal system to protect and delineate rights in land. In a famous dictum, Sir Henry Maine argued that the progress of societies has been the movement from status to contract.[9] He meant that law had moved from the feudal notion of rights inhering in status to notions of contract and agreed on exchanges. One major shift in Anglo-American law came when the emphasis on property and contract was displaced by a new concern for human rights.[10]

My underlying belief is that the fundamental changes in society away from an agrarian to a postindustrial society demand a fundamental shift in laws, ethics, morals, and customs to protect and delineate the rights of workers in their employment relations. Perhaps, the time has come to dispense with the discredited notion of employment at will[11] and to replace it with a new approach to employment in which workers' human dignity, job security, and health are paramount.[12]

In this chapter, we focus on privacy in employment, an emerging but disputed claim made on behalf of workers who resent being monitored, photographed, and searched in their places of employment and usually as a condition of employment. This chapter addresses the hypothesis that a breakdown in civil society has created a void that the emerging law of workplace privacy is attempting to fill. Because demonstrating an increase in incivility in U.S. society since 1945 cannot be done with scientific accuracy, I use anecdotal evidence, opinions of social observers, and data from selected proxies for incivility, such as divorce, crime rates, and arrests.[13]

A former front-runner for the Republican presidential nomination in 2000, Elizabeth Dole, listed as one of her top priorities the elimination of

8. *See, e.g.,* HAROLD L. SHEPPARD & NEIL Q. HERRICK, WHERE HAVE ALL THE ROBOTS GONE? WORKER DISSATISFACTION IN THE '70S (1972) at 10–11, wherein a University of Michigan study is cited. The Michigan study asked workers to rank the importance of 25 aspects of work. The top seven in order of importance were interesting work, enough help and equipment to get the job done, enough information to get the job done, enough authority to do the job, good pay, opportunity to develop special abilities, and job security.

9. SIR HENRY MAINE, ANCIENT LAW (1901) at 168–170 as quoted in HAROLD J. BERMAN & WILLIAM R. GRIENER, THE NATURE AND FUNCTIONS OF LAW (4th ed. 1980) at 752.

10. Certainly, this is not to imply that there have not been other major shifts in Anglo-American jurisprudence over the centuries.

11. Deborah A. Ballam, *The Traditional View of the Origins of the Employment-at-Will Doctrine: Myth or Reality?*, 33 AM. BUS. L. J. 1, 48–49 (1995).

12. *See, e.g.,* Norm Bowie, *Challenging the Egoistic Paradigm,* 1 BUS. ETHICS Q. 1, 19 (1992). Professor Bowie argues that the underlying reason for corporations is, contrary to Nobel Laureate Milton Friedman's stance of profit maximization, to provide meaningful employment to its workers. This philosophy might well underpin a federal workers' bill of rights some day.

13. For a book-length treatise on the decline of civility in the United States, *see* MARK CALDWELL, A SHORT HISTORY OF RUDENESS: MANNERS, MORALS, AND MISBEHAVIOR IN MODERN AMERICA (1999).

incivility in public life and in the U.S. Congress.[14] Even traditional patterns of etiquette are in decline. Under older formal notions and standards of civility, a gentleman would avert his eyes if a lady accidentally displayed more ankle than was deemed seemly. Many of us were taught not to eavesdrop on the conversations of others—either over a party telephone line or in an adjoining room of the home. These traditional notions of civility, respect, and decency were carried into the American workplace. Now, we seem to have, as a majority, moved toward a much looser, informal standard of civility—one that in the Western states allows cowboy hats and blue jeans at the Philharmonic as well as at the Governor's Inaugural Ball.

As Boy and Girl Scouts, we were schooled to be friendly, courteous, and kind. We men were taught to hold doors open for women, to walk on the curbside when escorting a female companion, to hold chairs for ladies to be seated, and to remove caps and hats when indoors. Alas, chivalry has died. Older, more formal standards of civility have retreated in the face of charges of sexism and elitism. In some instances, good manners have been annihilated by social turmoil. In part, this is one of the social legacies of the 1960s.

A SUMMARY ARGUMENT FOR THE DECLINE OF CIVIL SOCIETY

The traditional role of good manners is to ease potential friction among members of a society by providing norms of respect and deference that ease social interactions. As indicated in the introduction to this chapter, the decline of civility norms has left a vacuum in areas previously covered by etiquette.[15] I do not wish to argue the merits of this social change but merely to note that it has occurred almost entirely since the end of World War II (1945) and principally since 1960.[16] To be sure, some changes have been positive. Some social changes involved elimination of the double standard (and the pedestal) for women. Some of the etiquette was outdated, and in some places it was silent. For instance, there were few social norms dealing with men and women working together on the same job as equals; neither was there much said about e-mail and drug testing. However, social upheaval also eliminated some courtesies[17] that would have eased some of the current problems the law is attempting to confront as it moves into the privacy arena.

---

14. William Saletan, *A Tale of Two Liddys*, MOTHER JONES (May/June 1999) at 29. Saletan writes, "Her [Elizabeth Dole's] ingenious solution is to make Congressional incivility in both parties a moral issue. America faces a plague of 'crime, violence, drugs, illegitimacy, and incivility,' she declares. 'If public life is lacking in civility, then it is our common task to help civilize it.'"

15. *See, e.g.*, Christina Duff, *It's My Party, I'll Cry If I Want to, Cry if I Want to, Cry if I . . .*, WALL STREET J. (June 18, 1998) at A1. Duff writes that the use of RSVP (*respondez, s'il vous plait*) arose about 25 years ago when people stopped automatically writing notes to acknowledge invitations. Now, there is an epidemic of partygoers who do not even respond to the RSVP request. Miss Manners, the *nom de plume* of etiquette umpire, Judith Martin, says, "Party givers should wake up and realize that there is 'simply no recognition any more of hospitality as a social contract between guests and hosts.'" *Id*. Etiquette, morals, and ethics can and usually are distinguished. When we talk about the decline of civil society, in a general sense we are talking about the decline of civility that encompasses all three.

16. *See, e.g.*, H. RAP BROWN, DIE, NIGGER, DIE (1969); TOM HAYDEN, TRIAL (1970); ABBIE HOFFMAN, STEAL THIS BOOK (1971); WILLIAM M. KUNSTLER, MY LIFE AS A RADICAL LAWYER (1994); JERRY RUBIN, DO IT (1970).

17. *See, e.g.*, THE CHRONICLE OF H. ED. (daily@chronicle.com, October 20, 1998) which published the following item: "More evidence of rising incivility for professors: Last week a faculty member at the University of Maryland at College Park reported being threatened with a gun

One social commentator has declared, "In some ways, we have become a numb society. Today almost anything seems endurable, inevitable, or un-scotchable.... Nothing seems offensive any longer in a constitutional sense."[18] Even the perennially upbeat Ann Landers wrote in her 1998 Christmas column, "I am firmly against censorship, but where is the moral outrage against all this filth? It's almost impossible to find a family movie these days. What has happened to plain decency?"[19]

Crime statistics are up,[20] whereas trust levels have dropped in the United States since 1968, a watershed year in American social history.[21] In 1968, polls showed a dramatic decline in American confidence in virtually all of our social institutions.[22] Although there was a small increase in trust/confidence during

by a student who wanted an A in one of the professor's mathematics classes." Note that assault with a deadly weapon is now being lumped with "incivility." As a nation, we have become very insensitive to violence.

18. LEONARD W. LEVY, BLASPHEMY: VERBAL OFFENSE AGAINST THE SACRED, FROM MOSES TO SALMAN RUSHDIE (1993) at 569.
19. Ann Landers, *Peace on Earth, Good Will Still Remain Elusive*, ID. STATESMAN (December 25, 1998) at 2E.
20. *See, e.g.*, STEVEN DONZIGER (ed.), THE REAL WAR ON CRIME: THE REPORT OF THE NATIONAL CRIMINAL JUSTICE COMMISSION (1996).
21. *See, e.g.*, FREDERICK STURDIVANT, BUSINESS AND SOCIETY: A MANAGERIAL APPROACH (rev. ed. 1981) at 32–36.
22. Lance Morrow, *1968: The Year That Shaped a Generation*, TIME (January 11, 1988) 16 at 23–24. "What died with Martin Luther King Jr., and later, in great finality, with Robert Kennedy, was a moral trajectory, a style of aspiration. King embodied a nobility and hope that all but vanished. With King and Kennedy, a species of idealism died—the idealism that hoped to put America back together again, to reconcile it to itself."

the Reagan administrations, the levels of trust have not since risen anywhere near the high pre-1968 levels.

In 1990, the divorce rate hit 50%.[23] Other studies indicate that one third of all marriages now break up in less than 4 years, and a child in the 1990s had a 1 in 5 chance of experiencing two parental divorces before reaching the age of 18 years. Crime statistics seem to parallel divorce in some areas. For instance, children younger than 10 were 3 to 40 times more likely to suffer parental abuse if living with a stepparent and a biological parent than with two biological parents.[24] In urban Canada in the 1980s, a child under age 2 was 70 times as likely to be killed by a parent if living with a stepparent and a biological parent than if living with two natural parents.[25] Some social commentators argue that childhood itself, a product of the Enlightenment, has virtually disappeared.[26]

Another way at looking at the problem is to note that divorce rates per 1,000 women have more than doubled between 1951 and 1993[27] (Fig. 16.1). The results are a bit less dramatic if we use 1945 and 1998 as the benchmark years. First, 1945 appears to be an anomaly because of the backlog of divorces that was cleaned up when the troops returned home at the end of World War II. Second, there has been a slight decline in divorce rates since 1991, which may be caused in part by Americans waiting longer to marry and by the increased number of couples living together without benefit of marriage. In any event, the doubling of divorce, although it has multiple and complex causes, may be seen as a proxy for a general decline in civility because, at one level, it manifests a disregard for ritual commitments and breaking of solemn promises.

Political discourse seems to have hit an all-time low for America with the Starr Report on President Clinton and the Lewinsky affair,[28] with President Clinton's impeachment,[29] and with the overwhelmingly negative and often vicious political campaigning of 2004.[30] One contrast is the so-called gentleman's agreement under which the press never showed President Franklin D. Roosevelt in his wheelchair or using crutches.[31] Another contrast was the silence in the press during the 1960s about President Kennedy's notorious

---

23. Robert Wright, *Our Cheating Hearts*, TIME (August 15, 1994) at 44, 51.
24. *Id.* at 51.
25. *Id.*
26. *See, e.g.*, NEIL POSTMAN, THE DISAPPEARANCE OF CHILDHOOD (1982, Vintage Books ed. 1994).
27. STATISTICAL ABSTRACT OF THE UNITED STATES (U.S. Census Bureau, 1998).
28. THE STARR REPORT: THE FINDINGS OF INDEPENDENT COUNSEL KENNETH W. STARR ON PRESIDENT CLINTON AND THE LEWINSKY AFFAIR (released by U.S. Congress on September 11, 1998).
29. *See, e.g.* David Rogers & Jeffrey Taylor, *A President Impeached and A Congress Torn—The Show Must Go On*, WALL STREET J. (Dec. 21, 1998) at A1.
30. For example, the Swift Boat Veterans attack ads questioning Senator Kerry's Vietnam service and medals were particularly egregious. Senator Kerry's campaign filed a complaint with the Federal Election Commission alleging the ads were "inaccurate." See *Kerry Group Files Complaint Against Swift Boat Group*. Accessed at http://www.cnn.com/2004/ALLPOLITICS/08/20/kerry.swiftboat/ on September 23, 2004. *See also Cheney says Kerry can't effectively fight terror*. Accessed at http://www.freep.com/index/politics.htm accessed on September 23, 2004. *See* further *The Bush Watch* (detailing dirty tricks that then-candidate George W. Bush and Karl Rove dusted off after the New Hampshire primary in 2000 to "get" Senator John McCain). Accessed at http://www.bushwatch.com/negative.htm on September 23, 2004). These tricks included so-called push polls designed to besmirch Sen. McCain's war record, his alleged womanizing, and his wife's ties to organized crime. *Id.*
31. DAVID HALBERSTRAM, THE POWERS THAT BE (1979) at 10.

■ **FIGURE 16.1** Divorce rates in the United States from 1945–1995.

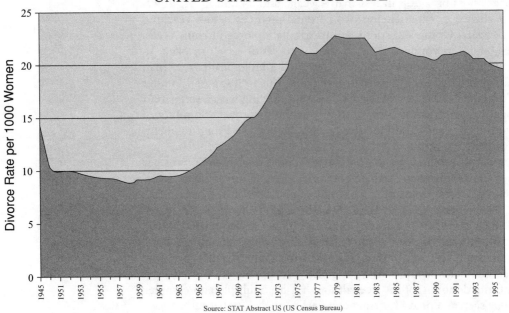

UNITED STATES DIVORCE RATE

Source: STAT Abstract US (US Census Bureau)

womanizing,[32] a subject then not thought appropriate for reporting.[33] To quote one scholar, "The event that did the most to redefine the relationship not only between the news media and the President, but also between the media and all major institutions, was Watergate."[34]

In 1940, the unemployment rate in the United States was 14.6%, and 47.5 million Americans were working.[35] Virtually all of the workers were men. In 1995, 124.9 million Americans were working, and the unemployment rate was officially 5.6%.[36] Of the 103 million women 16 years or older in this country, 61 million were labor-force participants—that means working or looking for work—in 1995.[37] Women represented 46% of the civilian labor force in 1995 and accounted for 59% of the labor-force growth between 1985 and 1995.[38]

---

32. WESLEY O. HAGOOD, PRESIDENTIAL SEX: FROM THE FOUNDING FATHERS TO BILL CLINTON (1995) at 135–180.
33. "The media knew about Kennedy's philandering but looked the other way. One former Associated Press reporter said, 'There used to be a gentlemen's agreement about reporting such things.' The same sentiment was echoed by another observer, who said, 'There was a sort of gentlemen's agreement in Washington that you don't talk about my private life and I don't talk about yours .'" *Id.* at 138–39.
34. FREDERICK STURDIVANT, BUSINESS AND SOCIETY: A MANAGERIAL APPROACH (rev. ed. 1981) at 76. *See also* BOB WOODWARD AND CARL BERNSTEIN, ALL THE PRESIDENT'S MEN (1974).
35. THE WORLD ALMANAC AND BOOK OF FACTS [FOR] 1997 (1996) at 165.
36. *Id.*
37. *Id.* at 172.
38. *Id.*

Arrest rates in the United States from 1966–1997. ■ FIGURE 16.2

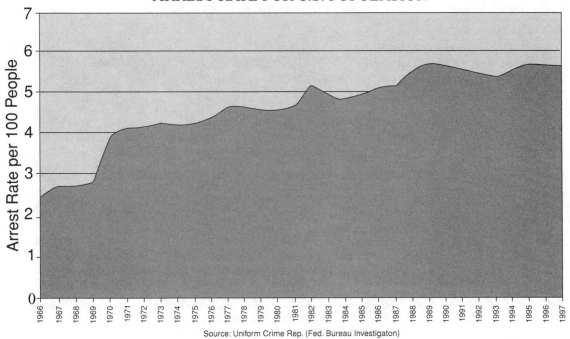

ARREST RATE FOR U.S. POPULATION

Source: Uniform Crime Rep. (Fed. Bureau Investigaton)

The average American worker earned $25,852 in 1994.[39] However, the economist's assumption of *ceteris paribus* did not apply at the pay window: Male workers earned $32,087 compared to the female average of $18,684, and White workers took home $26,696 in contrast to the average for Black workers of $19,772 and for Hispanics of only $18,568.[40] In addition to being a focal point for discrimination and gender stereotyping, the American workplace is not terribly safe. Assaults and violent acts accounted for 20% of workplace deaths in 1995, a figure second only to the category of transportation incidents that collectively accounted for 40% of workplace deaths.[41]

These statistics do not reflect a Norman Rockwell America at work. The arrest rate for the general U.S. population has more than doubled between 1966 and 1997[42] (Fig. 16.2). Certainly, arrest does not indicate guilt, but it is fair to say that the vast majority of people who get arrested have been severely uncivil to at least one other person.

Respect for property seems to be in decline, even anecdotally, if one considers the increase in graffiti, littering, and trespassing. Bumper stickers proclaim, "Keep honking, I'm reloading" and "Horn broken, watch driver's finger." Road rage is a new phenomenon on the American scene. Some may argue against a decline in civility, but they do not even offer

39. *Id.* at 167.
40. *Id.*
41. *Id.* at 168 citing U.S. Department of Labor sources.
42. UNIFORM CRIME REPORTS (FBI, 1998).

■ **FIGURE 16.3**   Property crime rates in the United States from 1960–1996.

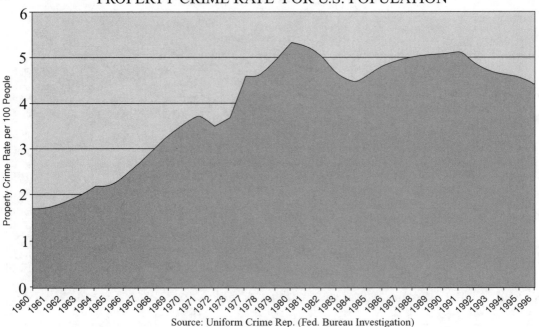

Source: Uniform Crime Rep. (Fed. Bureau Investigation)

anecdotal evidence to bolster their argument.[43] Property crime rates in the United States, however, have more than doubled between 1960 and 1996[44] (Fig. 16.3).

As women increasingly entered the workplace, a male-dominated arena, sexual harassment increased. On July 2, 1965, the U.S. Civil Rights Act of 1964, Title VII,[45] took effect and outlawed employment discrimination based on race, color, religion, national origin, or sex (meaning gender). Yet, 20 years after the effective date of this law, the battle about justice on the job for women and Americans of color raged across the second Reagan administration and its judicial appointments.[46] The defeat of President Reagan's nomination of Robert Bork to the U.S. Supreme Court on October 23, 1987, can be understood as a plebiscite on what Americans wanted from their Supreme Court.[47] In this light, the American people, on the bicentennial of the Constitution, determined by a vast majority that it approved of the directions that the court

---

43. Tom Dunfee, Kolodny Professor at Wharton School of Business, University of Pennsylvania, and Director of the Ethics Center, made this argument at the Huber Hurst Seminar on February 20, 1999, at the University of Florida. He offered no support for it, however.
44. UNIFORM CRIME REPORTS (FBI, 1998).
45. Civil Rights Act of 1964, 42 U.S.C. sections 2000e-15 (1976).
46. "To claim that there is strict color and gender blindness in a society that is not color and gender-blind only perpetuates discrimination and circumvents the law," asserted Congressman Don Edwards of California. *Quotes*, A.B.A.J. (August 1985), at 35 as quoted in William A. Wines, *Title VII Interpretation and Enforcement in the Reagan Years (1980–1989): The Winding Road to the Civil Rights Act of 1991*, 77 MARQ. L. REV. 645 at 653.
47. Wines, *supra*, note 38 at 657.

had taken—especially in the areas of equality, privacy, and free speech.[48] The passage of the Civil Rights Act of 1991 during the Bush Administration further strengthens this argument because its principal effect was to reverse some of the more extreme employment discrimination decisions of the Rehnquist Court and reinstate the earlier court positions.[49]

The awareness of the impending arrival of global capitalism, coupled with the discovery by investment bankers that they could make a fortune or two using junk bonds for leveraged takeovers, fueled a merger binge in the 1980s. The result was some serious "collateral damage"—a large number of middle managers and other workers were laid off and experienced for the first time "downward mobility."[50] Principally, it was the down sizing and threat of job loss that caused the average American worker to increase his or her work year by 163 hours in the years between 1969 and 1987.[51] By the end of the 1990s, even the custom of waiting until after the holidays to announce layoffs so as not to spoil workers' Christmases fell into the garbage can of history.[52]

ATTITUDES TOWARD WORK

To see life steadily and see it whole[53] is a challenge for each of us; it is the perspective that Aristotle argued was essential to the moral position. Aristotle argued that avoiding extremes by hewing to a "golden mean" was the path of virtue.[54] More modern commentators phrased this path this way:

> *Ethics* [italics in original] is, first of all, the quest for, and the understanding of, the good life, living well, a life worth living. It is largely a matter of *perspective*: putting every activity and goal in its place, knowing what is worth doing and what is not worth doing, knowing what is worth wanting and having and knowing what is not worth wanting and having. It is keeping in mind the place of a business

---

48. *Id.*
49. Civil Rights Act of 1991, Pub. L. No. 102-166, 105 Stat. 1071. For a discussion of the impact of the Act, *see* Wines, *supra* note 38, at 710–712.
50. Rick Brooks, *Those Were the Days Before We Had to Lay You Off*, WALL STREET J. (May 5, 1998) at A1. For instance, the $19.8 billion takeover of CoreStates Financial Corporation by First Union Corporation of N.C. resulted in 7,000 of the bank's 19,200 employees losing their jobs.
51. JULIET SCHOR, THE OVERWORKED AMERICAN: THE UNEXPECTED DECLINE OF LEISURE (1991) at 28–32.
52. Kristine Henry (The Baltimore Sun), *Holiday Pink Slips No Longer Are Taboo*, ID. STATESMAN (December 20, 1998) at 1D. Henry states, "There is no wonderful time for a company to declare that it is cutting jobs, but December announcements may be the worst. There's nothing like a pink slip to ruin someone's holiday festivities, and there's nothing like being compared to the Grinch who stole Christmas to make a company look bad. . . . This year, U.S. companies have cut nearly 575,000 jobs—the highest number since 1993—and many came in the month that traditionally is reserved for parties, bonuses and good cheer."
53. Matthew Arnold, *To a Friend*, as quoted in KENNETH E. GOODPASTOR (ed.), PERSPECTIVES ON MORALITY: ESSAYS OF WILLIAM FRANKENA (1976) at 106.
54. *See, e.g.*, J. A. K. THOMSON (TRANS.), THE ETHICS OF ARISTOTLE: THE NICHOMACHEAN ETHICS at 101–107 (rev. ed. 1976) (Hugh Tredennick, ed.). At 102, Aristotle declares "It [virtue] is a mean between two kinds of vice, one of excess and the other of deficiency; . . . virtue discovers the mean and chooses it. Thus from the point of view of its essence and the definition of its real nature, virtue is a mean; but in respect of what is right and best, it is an extreme."

career in our life as a whole, not allowing limited business successes
or even business success in general to eclipse our awareness of the rest
of life.[55]

This is no small task and a goal not easily reached. Maintaining a balanced perspective on one's work has historically defied Western civilization. Overwork
has been a chronic problem for many in the West, and now research suggests
it may be epidemic.[56]

An uplifting view of work is offered by an English economist who worked
in India. In his book, *Small Is Beautiful*, E. F. Schumacher argues in his chapter
on Buddhist economics that the function of work "is at least threefold: to give a
man a chance to utilize and develop his faculties; to enable him to overcome his
ego-centeredness by joining with other people in a common task; and to bring
forth the goods and services needed for a becoming existence."[57] Buddhist
economics is very different from modern materialism because "the Buddhist
sees the essence of civilization not in the multiplication of wants but in the
purification of character."[58] Character is formed primarily by work, and "work,
properly conducted in conditions of human dignity and freedom, blesses those
who do it and equally their product."[59]

Moral philosophy recognizes three major approaches to ethical problems:
consequential ethics,[60] the ethics of duty,[61] and the ethics of virtue.[62] Each has
a distinct theoretical approach to the question of how we can know whether
an act is good or bad. The consequential position is that an act is good if it
produces good results, which is frequently measured by utility. Duty-based
ethics measures the quality of the act by moral yardsticks that are constructed
on rules of moral duties. If an act fulfills the actor's duty, it is moral. Third,
the ethics of virtue concentrates on the character of the actor, grounded
on the premise that we tend to become what we do. Hence, we are always
in the process of defining ourselves. Our objective should always be to become
a good person, "especially the kind of person who performs right actions by
habit and by desire."[63] A good act, then, would be one that complies with the
rules, promotes good ends, and—most important—moves us in the direction
of becoming a good person.[64]

One synthesis of these different ethical schools is that all tend to promote
human dignity. Utilitarianism strives to produce the greatest good for the
greatest number of those affected by the act.[65] Immanuel Kant (1724–1804)
asserts that we must always treat humanity, whether in ourselves or in others,
as an end and never merely as a mean.[66] Aristotle argues that we should seek to

---

55. ROBERT C. SOLOMON & KRISTINE R. HANSON, ABOVE THE BOTTOM LINE: AN INTRODUCTION TO
     BUSINESS ETHICS (1983) at 9.
56. JULIET SCHOR, THE OVERWORKED AMERICAN: THE UNEXPECTED DECLINE OF LEISURE (1991).
57. E. F. SCHUMACHER, SMALL IS BEAUTIFUL: ECONOMICS AS IF PEOPLE MATTERED (1973) at 54–55.
58. *Id.* at 55.
59. *Id.*
60. *See, e.g.,* JOHN STUART MILL, ON UTILITARIANISM (1861) as discussed in AMES RACHELS, THE
     ELEMENTS OF MORAL PHILOSOPHY, (2nd ed. 1993) at 90–116.
61. *See, e.g.,* IMMANUEL KANT, THE FUNDAMENTAL PRINCIPLES OF THE METAPHYSICS OF MORALS (1785
     orig., Prometheus ed. 1988, trans. by T. K. Abbott).
62. *See, e.g.,* THE NICHOMACHEAN ETHICS, *supra* note 55.
63. LISA H. NEWTON, DOING GOOD AND AVOIDING EVIL: PRINCIPLES AND REASONING OF APPLIED ETHICS
     (1992) at 39.
64. *Id.*
65. RICHARD T. DE GEORGE, BUSINESS ETHICS (5th ed. 1999) at 61.
66. WILLIAM SHAW, BUSINESS ETHICS (2nd ed. 1996) at 61.

define ourselves as ones who habitually and by desire perform right actions—right actions being those that make us better human beings.[67] Consequently, any work that degrades human personality, causes pain, or prevents someone from reaching his or her potential violates basic ethical precepts.

Motivation theory states that the factors affecting job performance fall into two categories: hygiene factors and motivation factors.[68] The absence of hygiene factors leads to dissatisfaction and unhappiness, and can prevent motivation.[69] However, according to the theory, only motivational factors can motivate.[70] Motivation factors include achievement, recognition, responsibility, advancement, and the characteristics of the job. These factors tend to be associated with esteem or ego needs and with self-actualization.[71] The findings of a Michigan study[72] seem to be consistent with this theory.

What attitudes toward work would a socially responsible employer then foster among its workers?[73] Here are five standards that I believe a socially responsible employer would want to provide its workers and to endorse in its culture:

1. moderation in the expected amount of work
2. pride in the work product and in the employer
3. voice in the management and direction of the work
4. some freedom in the performance of the work
5. conditions of human dignity in both performance of the work and in the organizational climate

Yet, how does one define or even describe the concept of human dignity? One starting point, of course, might be a dictionary. Dignity means "the quality or state of being worthy, honored or esteemed."[74] In turn, worthy is defined as "having worth or value."[75] Synonyms for worthy are given as "estimable, honorable, or meritorious."[76] The opposite of worthy is worthless, which denotes "lacking worth: *syn.* valueless, useless; low: *syn.* despicable."[77] Direct substitution leads to the statement that human dignity means "having the value of a human being."

---

67. MANUEL G. VELASQUEZ, BUSINESS ETHICS: CONCEPTS AND CASES (4th ed. 1998) at 133–138.
68. FREDERICK HERZBERG, THE MANAGERIAL CHOICE: TO BE EFFICIENT AND TO BE HUMAN (rev. 2nd ed. 1982) at 53–60.
69. LESLIE W. RUE & LLOYD L. BYARS, MANAGEMENT THEORY AND APPLICATION (4th ed. 1986) at 361–362.
70. *Id.* at 361.
71. *Id.* at 362–363.
72. *See supra* note 8.
73. *See* Norman Bowie, *A Kantian Theory of Meaningful Work*, J. OF BUS. ETHICS (July 1998) at 1083–1092. Bowie states,

> A Kantian would endorse the following six characteristics as characteristics of meaningful work: 1. Meaningful work is work that is freely entered into; 2. Meaningful work allows the worker to exercise her autonomy and independence; 3. Meaningful work enable [sic] the worker to develop her rational capacities; 4. Meaningful work provides a wage sufficient for physical welfare; 5. Meaningful work supports the moral development of employees; and 6. Meaningful work is not paternalistic in the sense of interfering with the worker's conception of how she wishes to obtain happiness. *Id.* at 1083–1084.

74. WEBSTER'S SEVENTH NEW COLLEGIATE DICTIONARY (1963) at 233.
75. *Id.* at 1031.
76. *Id.*
77. *Id.*

What then is the value or worth of a human being? The term "value" comes from the Latin word *valere*, meaning to be worthy, to be strong.[78] After various definitions and usages of "value" involving exchange, such as to "give value," and relative worth, its seventh definition is "something intrinsically valuable or desirable."[79] Thus, by substitution, human dignity would mean having the intrinsic value of a human being. Social psychology would support this definition because, at a minimum, there is substantial evidence for a taboo against "intra-species killing."[80] From a Jungian perspective, a strong ancestral memory declares it is wrong to kill one of our own kind.

Moral philosophy supports this approach. A minimalist approach to duties to third parties (i.e., strangers) requires that one refrain from injuring a stranger, that one tell the truth to strangers, and that one treat strangers fairly.[81] Fairness can be equated with justice, that is, giving a person his or her due.[82] What is due? The essentials are not injuring anyone. From a legal perspective, it would require no offensive touching and also not putting one in fear of being touched offensively. This can be understood as respecting the stranger's person and personal space. Using simple tort concepts, we have derived an elemental notion of right to privacy as part of human dignity.

Suppose we reason backward in an elementary binary manner from a negative stance. the stance of worthlessness. Human dignity would require that we *not* treat a human being as low or despicable. Slavery and involuntary servitude would not be compatible with human dignity, neither would racism or sexism or other forms of categorizing human beings as inferior or possessed of inferior qualities based on group membership.[83] Neoclassical economics, strictly construed, would violate the concept of human dignity because it treats human labor and thus human lives as interchangeable at the margins with machinery and capital.[84] The folk story of John Henry's competition with the steam engine illustrates a devaluing of human dignity. Some religious faiths have a theology that decrees, "There is that of God in every human being."[85] For believers, then, to hold human labor exchangeable or fungible with equipment and capital is to demean the sacred or to engage in idolatry.[86]

---

78. *Id.* at 980.

79. *Id.*

80. *See, e.g.,* DAVID GROSSMAN, ON KILLING: THE PSYCHOLOGICAL COST OF LEARNING TO KILL IN WAR AND SOCIETY (1996).

81. WILLIAM H. SHAW & VINCENT BARRY, MORAL ISSUES IN BUSINESS (7th ed. 1998) at 358–359.

82. SHAW, BUSINESS ETHICS (2nd ed.), *supra* note 60, at 88.

83. *See, e.g., Schware v. Board of Bar Examiners* 353 U.S. 232 (1957) at 244 wherein the court held that the First Amendment precluded New Mexico from barring an applicant from the practice of law because he had once been a member of the Communist Party.

84. *See, e.g.,* LARUE TONE HOSMER, THE ETHICS OF MANAGEMENT (3rd ed. 1996) at 32–50; and R. Larry Reynolds & William A. Wines, "The Ethical Implications of Various Schools of Economic Thought" (August 7, 1992), (unpublished paper, presented at Society for Business Ethics annual meeting, Las Vegas, NV).

85. *See, e.g.,* NORTH PACIFIC YEARLY MEETING OF THE RELIGIOUS SOCIETY OF FRIENDS (Quakers), FAITH AND PRACTICE (1991).

86. The next question of whether modern employment under capitalism is compatible with a healthy notion of human dignity will not be pursued. That inquiry, although intriguing, is clearly beyond the scope of this book. The old form of denoting an employment relationship was to talk about "master and servant." Looking at the root for servant, we find that it is the Latin participle *servir,* coming from the Latin word *servire,* meaning to be a slave or a member of a menial class. WEBSTER'S SEVENTH NEW COLLEGIATE DICTIONARY (1963) at 793. The

Law, philosophy, theology, and social psychology provide arguments for an expanded notion of human dignity. Buddhist economics contributes the concept of a "becoming existence."[87] We can say that human dignity means being accorded the respect and status appropriate to a human being, being treated in a way that allows or enables one to live a becoming existence (i.e., a life that "looks good" on a human being).

HISTORY OF LEGAL EFFORTS LEADING TO WORKPLACE PRIVACY

One of the central tenets of human dignity is a right to privacy. Although not an absolute right, it is a substantial right that yields only on a showing of a greater good. When the Founders drafted the Bill of Rights, the right to privacy—that is the right to be left alone in your person, papers, dwelling, and effects—motivated the First, Third, Fourth, and Fifth Amendments. In 1890, Warren and Brandeis wrote a ground-breaking article for the *Harvard Law Review* in which they advocated a right to privacy as being required by the evolution of technology.[88] However, academic argument did not find any Constitutional traction[89] in the courts until 75 years later when Justice William O. Douglas used it in deciding *Griswold v. Connecticut*.[90]

In his 1965 Griswold decision, Justice Douglas wrote, "We deal with a right of privacy older than the Bill of Rights—older than our political parties, older than our school system."[91] In a concurring opinion, Chief Justice Earl Warren, Justice Arthur Goldberg, and Justice William Brennan argued that the Ninth Amendment, which reserves rights not specifically delegated or enumerated to the people, had been made applicable to the states through the 14th Amendment.[92]

Justices Hugo Black and Potter Stewart filed strong dissenting opinions.[93] Black indicated that he agreed with all of the criticism aimed at the Connecticut statute by the majority, "except their conclusion that the evil qualities they see in the law make it unconstitutional."[94] Furthermore, Justice Black argued, "The Court talks about a constitutional 'right of privacy' as though there is some constitutional provision.... But there is not."[95] Taking aim at the

---

synonym is subservient. Hence, when the International Workers of the World ("Wobblies") talked about "wage slaves," it was quite literally accurate. A position of servitude would clearly violate conditions of human dignity, at least under our working definition. For an excellent history of the IWW, *see* MELVYN DUBOFSKY, WE SHALL BE ALL: A HISTORY OF THE INDUSTRIAL WORKERS OF THE WORLD (2nd ed. 1988).

87. *See supra* material accompanying note 58 [Schumacher].

88. Warren and Brandeis, *The Right to Privacy*, 4 HARV. L. REV. 193 (1890). The advances in technology that they had in mind were newspapers and photography.

89. The common law tort of invasion of privacy was well established as early as 1905, according to some authorities. Pauline T. Kim, *Privacy Rights, Public Policy, and the Employment Relationship*, 57 OHIO STATE L. J. 671 at 683, note 53 in which Kim states "the common law right to privacy was decisively recognized in 1905 by the Georgia Supreme Court in *Pavesich v. New England Life Ins. Co.* 50 S.E. 68 (Ga. 1905). See KEETON ET AL., *supra* section 117, at 851."

90. 381 U.S. 479 (1965).

91. *Id.* at 486.

92. *Id.* at 490–493.

93. *Id.* at 507–527 and 527–531, respectively. Each also joined in the other's dissenting opinion.

94. *Id.* at 507.

so-called right of privacy, Justice Black opined,

> "Privacy" is a broad, abstract and ambiguous concept that can easily be shrunken in meaning but which can also, on the other hand, easily be interpreted as a constitutional ban against many things other than searches and seizures. . . . For these reasons I get nowhere in this case by talk about a constitutional "right of privacy" as an emanation from one or more constitutional provisions [footnote omitted]. I like my privacy as well as the next one, but I am nevertheless compelled to admit that government has a right to invade it unless prohibited by some specific constitutional provision.[96]

Justices Warren, Goldberg, and Brennan's position did not gain any further advocates and so remains a concurring theory to reach the same result that Douglas reached without recourse to the obscure Ninth Amendment. Mr. Justice White filed an opinion concurring in the result, but not using the majority's reasoning.[97] Justice Harlan also filed an opinion concurring in the judgment.[98] The Griswold decision, a 6–2 vote with six separate opinions, laid the foundation for rights to privacy in the marital bed and ultimately a right to privacy in reproductive decisions, most prominently *Roe v. Wade*.[99]

In this chapter, I am looking to find a path to workplace rights to privacy on behalf of workers. This road has landmarks in the Coors Brewery case[100] and the question of polygraph testing,[101] as well as in the federal act giving workers the right to see their personnel records.[102]

Most efforts to develop privacy legislation begin with "fair information practices," which can be understood as sets of privacy principles. Fair information practices are guidelines for the collection, use, disclosure, retention, and disposal of personal information. Sets of fair information practices vary, but they usually include the following principles:

- ensuring public awareness and transparency (openness) of information policies and practices
- establishing necessity and relevance of the information collected

---

95. *Id.* at 508.
96. *Id.* at 509–510.
97. *Id.* at 502–507. Justice White argued that the Connecticut statute failed to pass the strict scrutiny test for laws abridging liberty under the 14th Amendment. The statute failed because it was unnecessarily and overly broad in view of the law's stated objective, which was to prevent the use of contraceptives by persons engaging in illicit sexual relations to the end that such relations would be discouraged. *Id.* at 506–507.
98. "I fully agree with the judgment of reversal, but find myself unable to join the Court's opinion. . . . In my view, the proper constitutional inquiry in this case is whether this Connecticut statute infringes the Due Process Clause of the Fourteenth Amendment because the enactment violates basic values 'implicit in the concept of ordered liberty,' *Palko v. Connecticut*, 302 U.S. 319, 325. For reasons stated at length in my dissenting opinion in *Poe v. Ullman*, *supra*, [367 U.S. 497, 539–545.] I believe that it does." *Id.* at 499–500.
99. 410 U.S. 113 (1973) [*Roe v. Wade*].
100. *See The Case of Adolph Coors Company*, FREDERICK D. STURDIVANT, THE CORPORATE SOCIAL CHALLENGE: CASES AND COMMENTARIES (4th ed. 1990) at 456–476.
101. *See* the Employee Polygraph Protection Act of 1988 that prohibited most employers from using polygraphs in preemployment testing.
102. *See, e.g.*, Privacy Act (PL 93-579, 1974). The purpose of the Privacy Act was to allow individuals to learn what information the government maintains on them and to correct or amend any false data. Additionally, the act enables public and private sector employees to review their personnel files.

- building in finality (establishing the uses of the information in advance and eventually destroying it)
- identifying the person who has responsibility for protecting personal information within an organization
- obtaining informed consent from the individual
- maintaining accuracy and completeness of records
- providing access to the information and a right of correction

PRIVACY RIGHTS IN OTHER WESTERN NATION STATES AND THE EC

PRIVACY RIGHTS IN GERMANY

The notion that privacy is a fundamental right can be traced to Germany's Constitution, the Grundgesetz.[103] Article 10 of this "Basic Law" provides that the privacy of letters, posts, and telecommunications shall be inviolable.[104] A preface provided by German President Richard von Weizaeker in the amendment of the Grundgesetz, required by German unification in 1990, underscores the importance of this basic right:

> For more than forty years, the Basic Law has determined the development of the polity of the Federal Republic of Germany. In its area of application, it has bestowed on the citizens a life in liberty, democratic self-determination and personal responsibility, protected by law and justice.[105]

The Federal Data Protection Act (*Bundesdatenschutzgesetz*, BDSG) is designed to protect the privacy of data that have been collected about an individual. This statute governs data collection, processing, and dissemination of data by all public or quasi-public agencies and in a more select way also governs some data collection by private entities. Application of this law to private entities is restricted to data that are collected in a systematic fashion or automatically and/or are processed or stored by automatic/electronic means.[106]

Germany has an extensive system of data protection officials (*Datenschuetzer*) at the federal, state, and county government levels and in most public institutions down to the department level. There is formal training for such officials, and there are associations/committees formed by data protection officials. They generally have subpoena powers and the right to examine and secure data and can make recommendations regarding data storage and disposal.

Although most of Germany's efforts to secure privacy used to be restricted to ensuring privacy in relation to public institutions, major inroads have been and continue to be made to ensure privacy in the public sector. Current laws regarding privacy in the workplace rest on two pillars. The first pillar is individual specific and emanates from the federal legislation, the (BDSG). In addition to the BDSG, there are also a number of sectoral

---

103. Parliamentary Council F.R.G. (1949, May 23) Basic Law F.R.G.: Article 10.
104. *Id.*
105. Preface to Basic Law for the Federal Republic of Germany as amended by the Unification Treaty, August 31, 1990, and federal statute of September 23, 1990, FEDERAL LAW GAZETTE II at 885.
106. BDSG [*Bundesdatenschutzgesetz*], December 1990.

laws and relevant labor court rulings, such as those providing for examination of employment and other files by the employee. One requirement for the employer who systematically gathers data is that the data be "objectively" necessary for the regular conduct of business.[107] Even if the employee grants permission, an objective need must still be shown. Yet, another basis for privacy rights is found in the Personnel Records Law.[108] It goes beyond the data collection that is systematic and/or automatic to include all collections of data about an employee. The employee has the right to examine any record and to receive a printout, in an easily understood format, of all the data kept on him or her.[109] The employee has the further right to add items to the record, and in some cases, the employee may have the record corrected.[110]

The second pillar of privacy rights is a collective legal protection provided by the right of participation in data collection and privacy protection granted to the workers' councils *(Betriebsrat)* found in German industry. This right is further enhanced by specific arrangements found in union-industry contracts and many company-specific agreements.[111] The *Betriebsrat* has the right to determine whether the employer is in compliance with the laws. It also participates in the design of data collection instruments, such as questionnaires. Co-determination in regard to the control of observation equipment is also provided; this equipment includes cameras and PC-based controls, etc.[112] However, even though the law prescribes an objective need for the data, it is not clear whether that standard is followed in actual practice.[113] This is a gray area that justifies additional legislation. An Employee Privacy Law has been in development, but it has yet to be enacted.[114]

PRIVACY RIGHTS IN THE EUROPEAN COMMUNITY (EC)

Directive 95/46/EC of the European Parliament and of the Council of 24, promulgated in October 1995, on the protection of individuals with regard to the processing of personal data and on the free movement of such data is an important foundation for privacy in Europe and is likely to lead to major advances in member countries and those countries that aspire to membership in the EC. It states,

> 1. In accordance with this Directive, Member States shall protect the fundamental rights and freedoms of natural persons, and in particular their right to privacy with respect to the processing of personal data.
>
> 2. Member States shall neither restrict nor prohibit the free flow of personal data between Member States for reasons connected with the protection afforded under paragraph 1.[115]

---

107. *Id.*
108. PARA. 83 BetrVG.
109. *Id.*
110. *Id.*
111. *Id.*
112. *Id.*
113. *Id.*
114. Directive 95/46/EC of the Parliament and of the Council of 24, October 24, 1995.
115. Art. 8 Abs.2 der Europaischen Konvention zum Schutz der Menschenrechte und Grundfreiheiten (BGB1.Nr.210/1958).

PRIVACY IN AUSTRIA

As cosigner of the European Convention for the Protection of Human Rights and Basic Rights (1958), Austria has taken steps to implement privacy rights. The Austrian *Datenschutzgesetz* guarantees to each citizen the privacy of data collected and stored by all public entities. In one case that challenged application of this law, the Austrian Supreme Court affirmed the "protection of privacy [as] an inborn right."[116] However, in the same 1978 ruling, the court declared that although privacy is a basic right it must be balanced against all interests endangered by it, as well as the interests of the collective (i.e., the employer and the larger society).[117]

PRIVACY IN CANADA

Canada's Federal Privacy Law (1982) applies to all federal government departments, most federal agencies, and some federal Crown corporations.[118] The Privacy Commissioner of Canada oversees the Act and has powers to receive complaints, conduct investigations, and attempt to resolve disputes, among others.[119]

Privacy rights in the private sector are another matter entirely. Only Quebec has a comprehensive privacy act for the private sector. Quebec's Act Respecting the Protection of Personal Information in the Private Sector[120] provides a detailed framework for the collection, use, and disclosure of personal information. The Quebec Commission on Access to Information is responsible for conducting investigations, settling disputes, and generally overseeing the Act's enforcement.[121]

In the other provinces, protection of privacy in the private sector is sporadic and uneven. Many industries are not subject to any rules regarding the collection, use, and disclosure of personal information. A few industries, however, are covered by what the privacy commissioner of Canada has termed "a patchwork" of laws, regulations, and codes.[122] The patchwork is made up of various federal and provincial laws that result in incomplete and possibly inconsistent protections. Effective as the patchwork may be in particular sectors, it does not establish common principles. This incompleteness causes uncertainty for business managers and spotty protection for consumers. This patchwork becomes even more inadequate in the face of new developments in electronics, computers, and communications technology.[123]

However, the Canadian government has recently introduced legislation to protect privacy in the private sector.[124] This proposed law would apply to all personal information in the federally regulated sector (i.e., banking, telecommunication, and transportation). Interestingly, the bill was drafted based on a consensus among consumers and industry regarding the need for and the

---

116. OGH 24.10.1978 SZ 51/146.
117. *Id.*
118. Privacy Act, Legislative History: 1980-81-82-83, c.111, SCU II "1."
119. *Id.*
120. Task Force on Electronic Legislation (1998). Privacy: The Protection of Personal Information. *Legislation.*
121. *Id.*
122. Privacy Commissioner of Canada, Rep. Fed. Commission CAN. 1998.
123. *Id.*
124. *Id.*

nature of such legislation.[125] In addition, the government actually conducted research into the subject.[126]

WORKPLACE PRIVACY

ESSENTIAL ELEMENTS OF PRIVACY

When Samuel Warren and Louis Brandeis announced their novel thesis in 1890,[127] the authors saw the advent of modern newspapers and photography as a leap in technology that threatened the privacy of ordinary citizens.[128] Their main points can be summarized as follows:

> They argued that the existing common law recognized a principle of "inviolate personality" which could be invoked to protect the privacy of the individual [citation omitted]. Although arguing eloquently for explicit recognition of a right to privacy, they offered little in the way of definition, beyond locating privacy as "part of the more general right to the immunity of the person—the right to one's personality."[129]

In 1905, the Georgia Supreme Court "decisively recognized" the common law right of privacy in a case that was to become a landmark.[130]

Dean William L. Prosser (1898–1972) of the College of Law at the University of California–Berkeley addressed privacy in 1960 in a well-known law review article and declared that it had four elements.[131] "The law of privacy comprises four distinct kinds of invasion of four different interests of the plaintiff, which are tied together by the common name, but otherwise have almost nothing in common."[132] Despite vigorous debate about the nature, definition, and value of a common law concept of privacy,[133] the common law tort of invasion of privacy is now understood to apply in four distinct but interrelated situations: (1) "unreasonable intrusion upon the seclusion of another"; (2) "appropriation of the other's name or likeness"; (3) "unreasonable publicity given to the other's private life"; or (4) "publicity that unreasonably places the other in a false light before the public."[134] Clearly, from the perspective of the authors of the *Restatement of Torts*, Dean Prosser's analysis from his 1960 article carried the debate.[135]

---

125. *Id.*
126. *Id.*
127. 4 HARV. L. REV. 193, *supra* note 72.
128. *Id.* at 195.
129. Pauline T. Kim, *Privacy Rights, Public Policy, and the Employment Relationship*, 57 OHIO STATE L. J. 671, 682 (1996).
130. *Id.* at 683, note 53 citing *Pavesich v. New England Life Ins. Co.*, 50 S.E. 68 (Ga. 1905) and W. PAGE KEETON ET AL., PROSSER AND KEETON ON THE LAW OF TORTS (5th ed. 1984) section 117, at 850–51.
131. William L. Prosser, *Privacy*, 48 CAL. L. REV. 383 (1960).
132. *Id.* at 389.
133. For an excellent discussion as well as a collection of this literature, see Kim, *supra* note 129, material accompanying notes 2 through 135.
134. RESTATEMENT (SECOND) OF TORTS (1977) section 652.
135. *See, e.g.*, Edward J. Bloustein, *Privacy as an Aspect of Human Dignity: An Answer to Dean Prosser*. 39 N.Y.U.L. REV. 962 (1964). Bloustein argues that the single interest, protection of human dignity, underlines the broad diversity of cases collected under invasion of privacy. *Id.* at 1000–1003.

In a parallel but not unrelated development, the concept of privacy has been recognized in constitutional jurisprudence.[136] Although not named in the Constitution, a right to privacy has been held protected by the "penumbras" of the Bill of Rights, as well as by several specific amendments.[137] Penumbra is defined as "a space of partial illumination (as in an eclipse) between the perfect shadow on all sides and the full light."[138] The word itself is derived from the Latin words meaning "almost shadow."[139] Because of Douglas' opinion, the word has come to mean "a body of rights held to be guaranteed by implication in a civil constitution."[140] In a sense, these would be rights that exist on the fringe, in the partial light or shadow from the emanations of the rights that are granted directly in the Bill of Rights. Consequently, when workers seek protection in the alleged rights of privacy, it is no stretch to say that they are seeking shelter in the shadows of the law.

REDUCED EXPECTATIONS OF PRIVACY IN THE WORKPLACE

Clearly, a person has an expectation of privacy in his or her person and home.[141] However, what expectations of privacy exist for a worker in a workplace belonging to the employer? Whatever they are, surely such expectations must be lower than the expectations of privacy in the home. In 1890, Warren and Brandeis wrote that the right of privacy was a "general right of the individual to be let alone."[142] However, the employer when it provides work has certain legitimate interests in monitoring the employees' performance and in not just letting them alone. For instance, the employer wants to monitor productivity, employee morale, and its ownership interest (property) to protect it from pilferage and sabotage.

Courts that have rendered decisions in this area have tended to use a balancing of interests approach.[143] In addition, courts have noted that a long history of intensive government regulation of an industry, say banking, would tend to weaken expectations of privacy of officials working in such industries.[144] One author states, "[T]he overall purpose of the business of the employer and the

---

136. One of the most unfortunate results of this parallel jurisprudence is that public sector employees enjoy more protection against invasions of their privacy than do comparable private sector employees. *See, e.g.*, Laura B. Pincus and Clayton Trotter, *The Disparity Between Public Sector and Private Sector Employee Privacy Protections: A Call for Legitimate Privacy Rights for Private Sector Workers*, 33 AM. BUS. L. J. 51 (1995). Professors Pincus and Trotter conclude, "Consistent federal protection of privacy in the private sector is warranted" and note that it has been called for by various authors since the mid-1970s. *Id.* at 55.

137. See *Griswold v. Connecticut, supra* note 3.

138. MERRIAM WEBSTER'S COLLEGIATE DICTIONARY (10th ed. 1995) at 860.

139. *Id.*

140. *Id.*

141. Amendment IV [1791] to the U.S. Constitution states, "The right of the people to be secure in their persons, houses, papers, and effects, against unreasonable searches and seizures, shall not be violated, and no Warrants shall issue, but upon probable cause, supported by Oath or Affirmation, and particularly describing the place to be searched, and the persons or things to be seized."

142. 4 HARV. L. REV. 193, 205, *supra* note 72.

143. *See, e.g.*, Kim, *Privacy Rights, Public Policy, and the Employment Relationship*, 57 OHIO STATE L. J. 671 (1996) at 698–709 and cases cited therein.

144. *See, e.g., In re Gimbel*, 77 F3d 593 (2d Cir.) cert. denied, 117 S. Ct. 62 (1996) and discussion of case in Katherine Scherb, *Administrative Subpoenas for Private Financial Records: What Protection for Privacy Does the Fourth Amendment Afford?* 1996 WIS. L. REV. 1075 at 1096–1098.

■ **FIGURE 16.4** | Growth in the number of pages of key numbers, *Decennial Digests.*

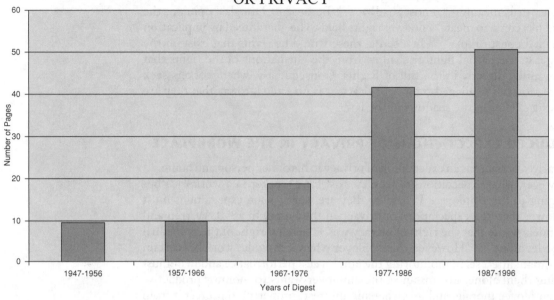

PAGES OF KEY NUMBER 8,
INVASION OF PERSONAL SAFETY, COMFORT
OR PRIVACY

nature of the employee's specific job are relevant considerations in determining which intrusions violate socially sanctioned claims of privacy."[145] Although avoiding the word "balancing" entirely, the author also declares, "The more closely an employer's inquiries trench on interests at the recognized core of individual privacy, the greater the need for some specific justification."[146] Yet, the initial inquiry for the court, writes the same commentator, was to determine "general societal understandings" of privacy.[147]

As judges wrestled with balancing the legitimate interests of employers in workforce supervision with the equally important rights of workers to be free from unnecessary and outrageous intrusions, workers took their complaints in increasing numbers to the courtrooms of America. I used West Publishing key number 8, invasion of personal safety, comfort, or privacy, as a proxy for the amount of litigation in the privacy area. Turning to the *Decennial Digests* published by West, I measured the number of pages under key number 8 and found a dramatic increase in privacy cases between 1947 and 1996 (Fig. 16.4). This material indicated an absolute increase in the number of privacy cases. I also wanted to know whether privacy cases had increased relative to the increase in litigation over the same time period. Consequently, I determined the total number of pages in the same *Decennial Digests* (Fig. 16.5) and divided that by the number of pages for key number 8 to determine the

---

145. *Id.* at 707.
146. *Id.* at 706.
147. *Id.* at 705.

Growth in the number of pages of the *Decennial Digests*. ■ **FIGURE 16.5**

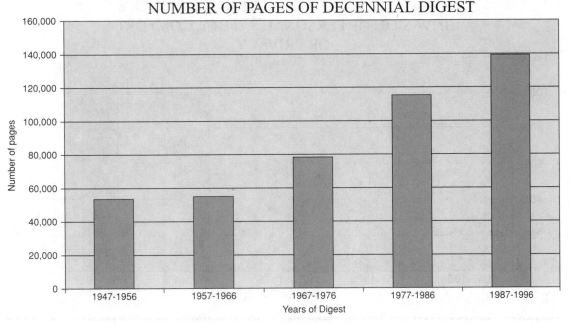

relative importance of privacy cases to litigation in the United States. Privacy cases nearly doubled in significance as part of the overall litigation between 1947 and 1996 (Fig. 16.6).

PROBLEM AREAS FOR WORKPLACE PRIVACY CONCEPTS

Despite the conservative approaches to the right of privacy that have prevailed in most courts, courts have applied more caution in ruling against employees in several areas in which the courts find that employer actions may intrude on the employees' right to be let alone.[148] This section addresses some of the most blatantly intrusive inquiries into employee behavior and personal histories.

DRUG TESTING. Drug tests fall into five categories: random, periodic, suspicion-based, post-accident, and preemployment. In some jurisdictions, mandatory random drug tests have, under certain circumstances, been held to be actionable invasions of privacy.[149] Generally, these decisions support the observation that drug testing invades an employee's privacy if either (a) safeguards are not incorporated into the tests to protect the employee's privacy or (b) the test is used to reveal other private medical facts (in addition to drug use), especially when such facts are embarrassing and unrelated to workplace

---

148. *See* Steven C. Bennett and Scott Locke, *Privacy in the Workplace: A Practical Primer,* LABOR LAW J. (January 1998) 781 at 784.
149. *See, e.g., Hennessey v. Coastal Eagle Point Oil Co.* 609 A2d 11 at 19 (N.J. 1992) and *Folmsbee v. Tech Tool Grinding & Supply, Inc.* 630 N.E. 2d 586 at 589 (Mass. 1994).

■ **FIGURE 16.6**   Growth in the relative occurrence of privacy cases.

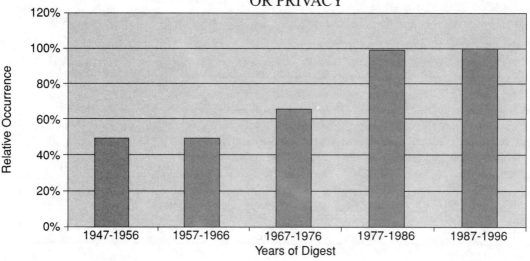

RELATIVE OCCURRENCE OF KEY NUMBER 8,
INVASION OF PERSONAL SAFETY, COMFORT
OR PRIVACY

performance (e.g., pregnancy). Two lawyers who practice in this area summarize the state of the law in these words:

> The analysis in these cases involves balancing employee and employer interests. To require an employee to disclose his drug status obviously involves some intrusion into the employee's right to be let alone [citation omitted]. A court will weigh this invasion against the employer's need to know whether the employee is a drug user [citation omitted]. Thus, drug testing may be an invasion in some settings (e.g., the entertainment industry) and not in others (e.g. the defense industry).[150]

Another author uses these words to capture much the same idea: "Privacy norms are contextually determined."[151] She goes on to argue that privacy "is not only culturally contingent, but relationally contingent as well, for the meaning of an apparent encroachment on the 'territories of the self' turns on the social relationship of the parties."[152]

Courts, which have to administer the laws, seem less delicate in the manner in which they deal with privacy claims. For instance, Robert Gilmore, an engineer, had been a long-time employee of Mustang Fuel. Mustang, a company that had no drug testing policy, was acquired by Enogex, a company that did have a random drug testing program. Gilmore was selected randomly and ordered to have a drug test. He refused, claiming a right to privacy, and was fired. After his firing, Gilmore voluntarily submitted to a drug test (at the same hospital). His results were negative, but Gilmore was not rehired. He

---

150. Bennett and Locke, *supra* note 107, at 784.
151. Kim, *Privacy Rights, Public Policy, supra* note 143, at 695.
152. *Id.*

sued and lost. The Oklahoma Supreme Court in 1994 upheld Enogex's right to impose random drug testing, even though Gilmore was not in a safety-sensitive position and despite Gilmore's many years as a satisfactory employee.[153]

One review of the Gilmore decision stated,

> Mr. Gilmore lost his job ... because he conscientiously objected to being tested, on grounds of privacy. It is debatable whether or not the Company's policy actually conduced toward a drug free workplace; but the Company's policy certainly did insure a workforce resigned to the surrender of its privacy [citation omitted].[154]

An enormous growth in the testing of applicants and of incumbent employees by corporate America for metabolites of certain controlled substances, primarily marijuana and cocaine, was fostered by the so-called War on Drugs. This drug screening triggered a batch of cases alleging violations of the right to privacy.[155] It also precipitated legislation: 15 states have regulated workplace drug testing primarily to ensure the accuracy of test results [citation omitted], Montana limits applicant screening to safety-sensitive jobs [citation omitted], and Iowa and Vermont limit screening of applicants to ensure that drug screens are done as a part of preemployment medical examinations [citation omitted].[156] The Supreme Courts of Massachusetts, New Jersey, and West Virginia have limited drug screening to safety-sensitive positions.[157]

SEARCHING EMPLOYEE WORK AREAS. Searches of employee work areas, such as desks and lockers, and of mail necessarily raise privacy concerns. Again the context and the relationship are important considerations. However, the fact that an employer owns the desk or locker does not confer an unlimited power to search the same. The rulings, however, are inconsistent. For instance, one court held that a jury could find an employer liable for examining confidential materials found on top of an employee's desk.[158] Yet, in another decision, an employer who discreetly and covertly searched an employee's unlocked desk, located in an open area, for employee-owned documents was held not liable for the invasion of privacy.[159] Another court held that searching an employee's locker to which the company allowed the employee a key might be an invasion of privacy.[160] Yet, other courts have held that searching an employee's lunch bucket[161] or a car parked on the company lot[162] would not.

Although the Fourth Amendment comes into play only when government actions threaten an individual's "reasonable expectations of privacy,"[163] developments under the Constitutional standard shed some light on social

---

153. *Gilmore v. Enogex, Inc.* 878 P.2d 360 (Okla. 1994) at 364.
154. Matthew W. Finkin, *Employee Privacy, American Values, and the Law*, 72 CHI-KENT L. REV. 221 (1996) at 232.
155. *Id.* at 230.
156. *Id.* at 230–231.
157. *Id.* at 231 citing *Webster v. Motorola* 637 N.E. 2d 203, 208 (Mass. 1994); *Hennessey v. Coastal Eagle Point Oil Co.* 609 A.2d 11, 21 (N.J. 1992); and *Twiggs v. Hercules Corp.* 406 S.E.2d 52, 55–56 (W. Va. 1990).
158. *Doe v. Kohn Nast & Graf, P.C.* 862 F. Supp. 1310, 1326 (E.D.Pa. 1994).
159. *O'Bryan v. KTIV Television* 868 F. Supp. 1146, 1159 (N.D. Iowa 1994), aff'd in part, rev'd in part, 64 F. 3d 1188 (8th Cir. 1995).
160. *K-Mart Corp. Store No. 7441 v. Trotti* 677 S.W. 2d 632, 637 (Tex. App. 1984).
161. *Simpson v. Unemployment Compensation Bd. of Rev.* 450 A.2d 305, 309 (Pa. Commw. Ct. 1982).
162. *Terrell v. Rowsey* 647 N.E.2d 662, 665 (Ind. Ct. App. 1995).
163. *Terry v. Ohio* 392 U.S. 1, 9 (1968).

expectations. The Fourth Amendment threshold test has been treated as a two-prong inquiry, asking first whether the individual "exhibited an actual (subjective) expectation of privacy" and second, whether that expectation is "one that society is prepared to recognize as 'reasonable.' "[164] In a Fourth Amendment challenge to an employer's search of an employee's desk and file cabinets, the Supreme Court held that an employee had a reasonable expectation of privacy when the employee did not share the desk or file cabinets, had occupied the office for more than 17 years, and had kept personal materials in the office.[165] Granted the Fourth Amendment brings its own weight and history to a decision, we nonetheless find it difficult to reconcile these cases, because the starting point for all of them is an expectation of privacy stemming from the same U.S. society.

SURVEILLANCE OF EMPLOYEES.   Surveillance of employees takes many forms. Everything from monitoring telephone calls,[166] checking e-mail,[167] eavesdropping on conversations,[168] and using hidden cameras[169] has been subject at various times to claims of invasion of privacy. Surveillance alone does not violate an employee's right to privacy. Again, the critical issue is whether the employee has a reasonable expectation of privacy.[170] Let us examine some of the issues in the following subsections.

Capturing Conversations.   A starting point for this discussion is the 1968 federal law on wiretapping that was designed to regulate interception of wire and oral communication.[171] The Electronic Communications Privacy Act (ECPA) of 1986 was an amendment to the 1968 wiretap statute and was created to regulate and control forms of electronic communications that had been invented since 1968, primarily computer systems.[172] Voice-activated recording machines attached to company telephones have been held to generate liability and did not qualify under the "business extension" exception to federal law.[173]

---

164. *Katz v. United States* 389 U.S. 347, 361 (1967) (Harlan, J., concurring).
165. *O'Connor v. Ortega* 480 U.S. 709, 718-19 (1987).
166. See, e.g., *Watkins v. UPS, Inc.* 797 F. Supp. 1349 (S.D. Miss.), aff'd 979 F. 2d 1535 (5th Cir. 1992) and *Jackson v. Nationwide Credit, Inc.* 426 S.E. 2d 630 (Ga. Ct. App. 1992).
167. *See, e.g., Bohach v. City of Reno* 932 F. Supp. 1232 (D. Nev. 1996); *Smyth v. Pillsbury Co.* 914 F. Supp. 97 (E.D. Pa. 1996); and *Restuccia v. Burk Tech. Inc.*, No. 95–2125 (Mass. App. Ct. 1996).
168. *See, e.g., Brazinski v. Amoco Petroleum Additives Co.*, 6 F.3d 1176 (7th Cir. 1993); *Speer v. Ohio Dep't of Rehabilitation & Correction*, 624 N.E. 2d 251 (Ohio Ct. App. 1993); Steve Casimiro, *The Spying Game Moves into U.S. Workplace*, FORTUNE (March 30, 1998) at 152–153. Casimiro describes offices being equipped with microphones hidden in pens, warehouses, and stockrooms; he also discusses hidden video cameras in employee break-rooms. Technology has made the tools for eavesdropping cheap, small, powerful, and accessible. A 1997 survey by the American Management Association found that nearly two thirds of employers conduct electronic surveillance of employees and that about one quarter of those conducting surveillance do not inform their employees. *Spying on Workers Common and Usually Legal, Group Reports*, BOSTON GLOBE (May 23, 1997) at A3 as quoted in David C. Yamada, *Voices From the Cubicle: Protecting and Encouraging Private Employee Speech in the Post-Industrial Workplace*, 19 BERKELEY J. OF EMPLOYMENT AND LABOR LAW 1 (1998) at 16.
169. *See, e.g., Saldana v. Kelsey-Hayes Co.* 443 N.W. 2d 382 (Mich. Ct. App. 1988) wherein the court held that use of a high-power camera lens to look into an employee's home did not violate a right to privacy. *Id.* at 384.
170. Bennett and Locke, *Privacy in the Workplace: A Practical Primer*, *supra* note 107, at 785.
171. The Omnibus Crime Control and Safe Streets Act of 1968.
172. ECPA amended Title III of the 1968 Act, *supra* note 130.
173. *Pascale v. Carolina Freight Carriers Corp.* 898 F. Supp. 276 (D.N.J. 1995).

Conducting surveillance in a restroom was ruled to invade privacy,[174] but conducting similar surveillance outside the entrance to a restroom did not, in the absence of any person being seen undressed.[175]

Monitoring Telephone Calls.

Federal law prohibits the willful interception of any "wire, oral, or electronic" communication through the use of "any electronic, mechanical or other device" except under specified circumstances.[176] Thus, eavesdropping on an employee's telephone conversations is broadly prohibited. Two exceptions to this blanket prohibition are generally applicable to employers. First, interception is expressly permitted when "one of the parties to the communication has given prior consent."[177] Second, the business extension exception excludes any component of a "telephone or telegraph instrument" used in the ordinary course of its business from the definition of "electric, mechanical, or other device." Consequently, monitoring with a "business extension" does not violate the law. Interceptions of telephone calls that are not covered by these exclusions can result in fines and imprisonment and also subject the employer to civil liability.

The consent exception, although seemingly straightforward, has been held to include so-called implied consent. If an employee is aware that the employer monitors or records telephone conversations on its lines, yet uses such a line, most courts will find implied consent, and no liability attaches under federal law.[178] As for the business extension exception, courts have held that clandestine, indiscriminate monitoring that picks up both personal and business calls does not qualify because such monitoring is not a valid part of a business operation.[179]

E-mail and Computer Monitoring.

Federal law treats telephone and e-mail communications very differently. Federal law prohibits the interception of private messages. However, once a message is stored in an electronic format, a different federal statute applies. That statute prohibits unauthorized access to electronically stored messages, but also provides a blanket exception for service providers.[180] Consequently, employees have very little chance of prevailing on a privacy violation in the area of computer e-mail.

Unlike telephone conversations that disappear into the ether in the absence of any recording device, e-mail and voice mail messages are routinely and of necessity saved on computer hard drives and are frequently backed up to tape or some other form of long-term storage device. System administrators or anyone else with access to these sources are free to review all of the stored messages without any need for any individual user passwords. Courts have

---

174. *Speer v. Ohio Dept. of Rehabilitation & Correction*, 624 N.E.2d 251, 254 (Ohio Ct. of App. 1993) as cited in Matthew W. Finkin, *Employee Privacy, American Values, and the Law*, 72 CHI-KENT L. REV. 221 (1996) at 225.

175. *Brazinski v. Amoco Petroleum Additives Co.*, 6 F.3d 1176, 1183 (7th Cir. 1993) as cited in Matthew W. Finkin, *Employee Privacy, etc., supra* note 133, at 125.

176. 18 U.S.C.A. section 2511(1)(a).

177. 18 U.S.C.A. section 2511(2)(d).

178. William C. Martucci and Jeffrey M. Place, *Privacy Rights and Employee Communication in the Workplace*, EMPLOYMENT RELATIONS TODAY (Summer 1998) 109, 110.

179. *See, e.g., Sanders v. Robert Bosch Corp.* 38 F.3d 736 (4th Cir. 1994). But *cf. Knight v. City of New Orleans* No. 89-3409, 1991 WL 126387 (E.D. La., July 1, 1991). In that case, a police chief was fired when his racial comments, captured by a telephone monitoring system, were made public. In the ensuing litigation, the recording was held legal because the monitored conversation was a business one and the chief was aware of the department's policy of recording telephone conversations.

180. 18 U.S.C.A. section 2701(c)(1).

held that employers qualify as "service providers" and have also held that employees cannot have any "reasonable expectation" of privacy in any messages sent over such systems.[181]

Although my reading of the cases convinces me that the dominant view is one of no expectation of privacy, there is no consensus in the courts that no one could, under any circumstances, ever have a reasonable expectation of privacy in either e-mail or voicemail.[182]

Regulating Personal Associations.   Numerous employers have policies that address some aspect of their employees' personal associations—off the premises. Litigation not infrequently follows job actions taken against employees who violate such policies or who commit off-duty acts that the employer finds objectionable. Recent examples include employees who have been fired for living with someone of the opposite sex without benefit of marriage,[183] smoking,[184] drinking,[185] and riding a motorcycle.[186] As Professor Dworkin, an expert in this area, concludes,

> At present, marriage discrimination statutes, lifestyle protection statutes, and Title VII's protection against religious discrimination offer employees the most likely avenues to successful vindication of their associational rights. Common law theories, including the tort of invasion of privacy, have proved less successful although they are growing in use and success.[187]

CONCLUSIONS

PRUDENCE OF USING THE LAW TO GUARANTEE PRIVACY?

Writers, law professors, and judges do not agree on any specific definition of the right to privacy.[188] Some noted scholars have argued that the entire construct is a mistake, others have declared that it is so unwieldy that it collapses from its own weight, and still others have praised it in almost exalted terms as necessary to human dignity. Other writers have declared that it is only derivative, coming from other better-defined torts and concepts, and some

181. *See, e.g., Bohach v. City of Reno* 932 F. Supp. 1232 (D. Nev. 1996); *see also Payne v. Norwest Corp.* 911 F. Supp. 1299 (D. Mont. 1995) wherein the court held that voicemail was not protected from recording and dissemination to others.

182. *See* William C. Martucci and Jeffrey M. Place, *Privacy Rights etc., supra* note 137, at 114 and cases cited therein.

183. *See, e.g., Meltebeke v. Bureau of Labor & Industries* BOLI 903 P.2d 351 (Or. 1995) wherein plaintiff used a theory of religious harassment to recover when employer told him he was a sinner and going to hell because he lived with his girlfriend; State ex rel. *Johnson v. Porter Farms, Inc.* 382 N.W. 2d 543 (Minn. App. 1986).

184. *See, e.g., City of North Miami v Kurtz* 653 So. 2d 1025 (Fla 1995). The tobacco industry fired up a campaign for state laws protecting employees who smoked off the job. This campaign has been expanded to cover other off-duty behaviors. Now, 29 states have enacted some version of "off-the-job" privacy protection laws. Terry Morehead Dworkin, *It's My Life— Leave Me Alone: Off-the-Job Employee Associational Privacy Rights*, 35 AMER. BUS. L. J. 47, 51 (1997).

185. *See, e.g., Best Lock Co. v. Review Board* 572 N.E. 2d 520 (Ind. App. 1991).

186. *See, e.g.,* cases cited in Lewis L. Maltby & Bernard J. Dushman, *Whose Life Is It Anyway— Employer Control of Off-Duty Behavior*, ST. LOUIS U. PUB. L. REV. 645, 646 no. 7 (1994) as cited in Dworkin, *It's My Life—Leave Me Alone, etc. supra*, note 184.

187. *See* Terry Morehead Dworkin, *It's My Life—Leave Me Alone, etc., supra* note 184, at 98.

188. *See* Kim, *Privacy Rights, Public Policy, etc., supra* note 143, at 683–685 and works cited therein.

have dismissed it as a "petty tort."[189] I am reminded of the limits of law to effect social changes as I read the cases and commentary.[190] Law is a social institution, and in many ways it cannot rise above its source.

PROBLEMS OF SOCIAL AND HUMAN COSTS LEFT OUT OF BUSINESS EQUATIONS

The double-entry accounting system used in American business has no place for so-called externalities on the balance sheet or income statement. Thus, the increase in human suffering, alcohol abuse, suicides, batteries, and homicides that flow in the wake of plant closings and layoffs does not reflect adversely on the financial statements of the companies that fire people and move plants/mills to Third World countries. If business performance is measured in quarterly and annual financial reports, as virtually all of it is these days, then businesses are free to have no conscience or social responsibility.[191]

My initial thesis was that workers are striving to erect a privacy structure in an effort to offset the decline in civility in U.S. society. If that is so, one of the largest causes of incivility in this country is business conduct.[192] The principal apologists for insensitive behavior toward workers (and the environment) are the neoclassical economists, many from the University of Chicago school of thought, who legitimatize greed and indifference toward human suffering. Ultimately, this behavior is sanctified by accountants who fail to see beyond their beloved double-entry system and GAAP (Generally Accepted Accounting Practices).

DECLINE OF CIVILITY AND INCREASED CLAIMS OF WORKPLACE PRIVACY: CORRELATION, CAUSE, OR COINCIDENCE?

A wag once declared that in the United States the incidence of cancer correlates almost perfectly with milk drinking. His point was that correlation and causation are two entirely different concepts, even though they are sometimes conflated in people's thinking. Thus, even if we were to quantify a decline in civility and an increase in worker's privacy claims, it might be merely coincidence or simple correlation. Consequently, we have only advanced a hypothesis that workers are seeking shelter from incivility in the workplace by making claim to workplace privacy rights.

---

189. "I suspect that fascination with the great Brandeis trademark, excitement over the law at a point of growth, and appreciation of privacy as a key value have combined to dull the normal critical sense of judges and commentators and have caused them not to see the pettiness of the tort they have sponsored." Harry Kalven, Jr., *Privacy in Tort Law—Were Warren and Brandeis Wrong?* 31 LAW & CONTEMP. PROBS. 326, 328 (1966).

190. "Courts of Justice do not pretend to furnish cures for all the miseries of human life. They redress or punish gross violations of duty but they go no farther; they cannot make men virtuous; and as the happiness of the world depends upon its virtue, there may be unhappiness in it which human laws cannot undertake to remove." Lord Stowell in *Evans v. Evans* (1790).

191. *See, e.g.*, Oliver Edwards, *Will Europe Reform Its Corporate Governance?*, EUROBUSINESS (April 1999) at 65–66 in which the author interviews business guru Peter Drucker. Drucker asserts that the key to financial success in the United States and United Kingdom is that corporations exist for the benefit of their shareholders. He apparently believes that Japan, Germany, and Italy face financial ruin unless they convert to this corporate dogma.

192. *See, e.g.*, MARTHA BANTA, TAYLORED LIVES: NARRATIVE PRODUCTIONS IN THE AGE OF TAYLOR, VEBLEN, AND FORD (1993).

ROOT CAUSE IN AT-WILL RULE AND THE NEED FOR A WORKERS' BILL OF RIGHTS?

Another author suggests that the real cause of workplace problems with privacy is the underlying dominant rule of employment in the United States, employment-at-will.[193] This author details the relationship between privacy and the at-will rule in the following words:

> Although the common law tort of invasion of privacy *does* offer protection against all manner of unreasonable intrusions on employee privacy, its application in the workplace is complicated by the conflicting right of the employer to terminate the relationship at will. Most courts that have considered the issue agree that an employer may be liable in tort for unreasonable intrusions on employee privacy *after the fact*.... However, when the employer gives notice *in advance* [sic] that it intends to engage in the same intrusive practices, the protection offered by the common law tort is problematic. If the employee accedes to the employer's intrusive practices (or merely continues to work after receiving notice), her employer will likely assert that she consented to the intrusion as a defense to her claim that her privacy was wrongfully invaded. If, on the other hand, she objects to the intrusion and is fired as a result, the common law privacy tort provides no relief because no invasion of her privacy has occurred. She has suffered the loss of her job, but no loss of privacy. It is at this point that the interpretation of the at-will doctrine becomes crucially important. If applied strictly, the employee cannot recover for the loss of her job either, and will be left without recourse, regardless how invasive the employer's threatened actions were, or how justified her refusal to comply with her employer's demands.[194]

CIRCULARITY OF CIVILITY AND PRIVACY: NO SHELTER HERE

If the law were to provide a meaningful refuge for the lack of civility in the workplace, it would need to be both independent of the declining level of civility and be able to provide a bulwark against the decline as pegged to an independent standard. Unfortunately, the current state of the law regarding the so-called right to privacy does neither. The benchmark for the right to privacy is the social standard or norm of civility.[195] Consequently, when civility declines in U.S. society, so too does the protection provided by the law. The result is that the refuge provided is somewhat illusory—at least in general legal theory.

The tort of invasion of the right of privacy requires an "outrageous" invasion of a "reasonable expectation" of privacy. In both the question of

---

193. *See* Kim, *Privacy Rights, Public Policy, etc., supra* note 143.
194. *Id.* at 675–676.
195. An interesting illustration of how social norms actually can be more effective than regulation is discussed in Michele L. Tyler, *Blowing Smoke: Do Smokers Have a Right? Limiting the Privacy Rights of Cigarette Smokers*, 86 GEO. L. J. 783 at 808–811. She notes that a significant number of smokers agree that they should not smoke in the presence of nonsmokers and that many smokers voluntarily refrain from smoking at work or in many indoor public places. Ms. Tyler concludes that a civility norm "is almost in place with regard to many indoor public places." *Id.* at 809.

outrage[196] and the issue of reasonableness, the only standards are those brought to these issues from society. The result is that the current law does not provide a meaningful shelter from the nationwide decline of civility. As one authority movingly declares,

> A robust legal commitment to privacy would recognize that all the above predicate conditions are invasive—to be surveilled [sic] by a hidden camera wherever one sits, to have one's desk rifled for whatever is read, to be questioned about one's private affairs however seemingly trivial—and it would then require a showing of a specific business need sufficient to overcome that intrusion, which condition may or may not be satisfied in these cases. But such is not the law.[197]

Some writers suggest codes of privacy.[198] That idea is beyond the scope of this chapter. However, I believe that it merits serious further research. One obvious advantage of such an approach would be to level the current privacy inequity between public sector workers and private sector workers. Another advantage would be to disconnect the law of privacy from the declining American norms of civility. My proposal is to examine and move toward advocating creation of a federal worker's bill of rights, predicated on the Commerce Clause[199] that, among other things, would do the following:

■ guarantee employment termination only for good cause after a probationary period of 6 months[200]
■ limit drug testing to safety-sensitive positions, security-sensitive positions, and for good cause
■ limit searches of employee desks, lockers, lunch buckets, and automobiles to situations in which legitimate business reasons outweigh the invasion
■ require all monitoring of employees be with both notice to employees and consent of employees
■ include speech protections for employees, with exceptions only for disloyal, disruptive, insubordinate, and legally unprotected types of speech

Otherwise, the tendency of the law of privacy to decline in tandem with American civility standards, combined with the lopsided power granted employers by the employment-at-will rule, will continue to rob American workers of their human dignity. This review of the state of privacy laws in Germany, Canada, and the European Community suggests that those countries lead the United States in protecting privacy, mainly because of national concerns and

---

196. Matthew W. Finkin, *Employee Privacy, American Values, and the Law*, 72 CHI-KENT L. REV. 221 (1996) at 228 states succinctly, "The inescapable conclusion is that what the law of intrusion actually regulates is not privacy, but outrage [citation omitted]. The law protects freedom from emotional distress, not freedom of informational control."
197. *Id.* at 228–229.
198. *See, e.g.*, Kevin J. Conlon [District Counsel for Communication Workers of America], *Privacy in the Workplace*, LABOR LAW J. (August 1997) 444 at 447–448 suggests an eight-point list of legislative reforms to protect employee privacy in the workplace; David C. Yamada, *Voices From the Cubicle: Protecting and Encouraging Private Employee Speech in the Post-Industrial Workplace*, 19 BERKELEY J. OF EMPLOYMENT AND LABOR LAW 1, 58 (1998) lists a *Model Private Employee Free Speech Statute*; and Kevin J. Baum, *Comment: E-Mail in the Workplace and the Right to Privacy*, 42 VILL. L. REV. 1011 (1997) at 1036–1040 discusses considerations and provisions that should be in any e-mail monitoring policy.
199. Article I, Section 8 of the U.S. Constitution.
200. Model Employment Termination Act (META) (1991) proposes a 1-year waiting period before an employee is entitled to protection of "good-cause" standard. PATRICK J. CIHON & JAMES O. CASTAGNERA, EMPLOYMENT AND LABOR LAW (3rd ed., 1999) at 20–23.

legislation. I believe that in the near term American workers will continue to increase their use of the judiciary to try to establish meaningful protections against the incivility and outrageous invasions of privacy that they encounter in the workplace. However, until and unless there is meaningful law reform, American workers will be forced to choose between their dignity and their economic well-being. The blows to workers' dignity are part of what Studs Terkel had in mind in this passage from *Working* (1972):

> *This book, being about work, is, by its very nature, about violence*—to the spirit as well to the body. It is about ulcers as well as accidents, about shouting matches as well as fistfights, about nervous breakdowns as well as kicking the dog around. It is, above all (or beneath all), about daily humiliations. To survive the day is triumph enough for the walking wounded among the great many of us [italics added].[201]

---

201. STUDS TERKEL, WORKING (Avon Books, 1972, 1974) at xiii.

CHAPTER 17

Workplace Issues II: Designing a Better Organization

INTRODUCTION

People act differently when they are in groups than when they are not. In one study, 85% of managers used a different set of moral values at work than they used at home.[1] Aware of this dichotomy, Reinhold Neibuhr, the noted theologian,[2] wrote a book entitled *Moral Man and Immoral Society.*[3] One of the common tests of integrity is whether we are the same regardless of whom we are with.[4] Several fields actually have developed based on this phenomenon: organizational behavior and organizational development, industrial psychology, social psychology, sociology, and others. One of the shortcomings, until recently, of business ethics has been its failure or reluctance to acknowledge the truth of this axiom.[5]

Ferrell and Fraedrich, in their well-established textbook on business ethics,[6] were among the first, if not the first, to include chapters on how the organization influences ethical decision making.[7] In a chapter on how organizations influence behavior, Ferrell and Fraedrich look at two broad categories of organizational structures: centralized and decentralized[8] (Table 17.1).

This chapter is based on a paper written by J. Brooke Hamilton III and William Arthur Wines and presented to the Association for Practical & Professional Ethics, Charlotte, North Carolina, on February 28, 2003. The author wishes to thank Professor Hamilton for his graciousness in consenting to allow our joint effort to appear in this work. A revised and expanded version, fully footnoted to law review standards, of this work appeared in 29 DEL. J. OF CORP. LAW (no. 1, August 2004) at 43–82.

1. Investigators found that only 15% of a sample of business managers maintained the same moral philosophy in both work and nonwork ethical decision making. John Fraedrich and O.C. Ferrell, *Cognitive Consistency of Marketing Managers in Ethical Situations,* 20 J. OF THE ACADEMY OF MARKETING SCIENCE (Summer 1992) at 245–252 as cited in FERRELL, FRAEDRICH & FERRELL, BUSINESS ETHICS: ETHICAL DECISION MAKING AND CASES (2000) at 101.

2. Niebuhr, pronounced "NEE boor," was the family name of two brothers who became influential American Protestant theologians. Reinhold (1892–1971) won fame as an author and teacher. He was Dean of the Union Theological Seminary in New York from 1950 to 1960. He started his career as a pastor to a church in Detroit and was an active Socialist and leader of the "social gospel" liberal wing of Christians. By 1939, he had changed his mind and was a leader of the anti-social gospel wing. He graduated from Yale Divinity School in 1915. His brother, H. Richard Neibuhr (1894–1962), was an authority on Christian ethics and the history of Christian thought. He was a professor at Yale Divinity School from 1931 until his death. THE WORLD BOOK ENCYCLOPEDIA (1990), vol. 14 at 409–410.

3. REINHOLD NEIBUHR, MORAL MAN AND IMMORAL SOCIETY (1932).

4. William Stringfellow (1928–1985), in an early book of his, wrote that (paraphrasing here) what is important is not so much who you are but that you be the same person wherever you find yourself. I believe this is a key insight into the moral issue of personal integrity. *See William Stringfellow.* Accessed at http://www.victorshepard.on.ca/Heritage/Stringfellow.htm on May 20, 2003.

5. A short list of all the business ethics books that do not even mention environmental factors that influence business decisions would easily fill a page. I cite only one outstanding scholar in the field: Robert C. Solomon, the Quincy Lee Centennial Professor of Business and Philosophy at the University of Texas at Austin. In 1999, Oxford Press published his new book: A BETTER WAY TO THINK ABOUT BUSINESS: HOW PERSONAL INTEGRITY LEADS TO CORPORATE SUCCESS (1999). I cite Professor Solomon, not because I dislike his work, but merely to point out that leading people in the field write book-length works that do not mention the powerful effects of organizational and environmental factors.

6. *See* FERRELL & FRAEDRICH, BUSINESS ETHICS (1991); FERREL & FRAEDRICH, BUSINESS ETHICS (2nd ed. 1994); FERRELL & FRAEDRICH, BUSINESS ETHICS (3rd ed. 1997); and FERRELL, FRAEDRICH, & FERRELL, BUSINESS ETHICS: ETHICAL DECISION MAKING AND CASES (4th ed. 2000).

7. *See, e.g.,* 3rd ed., *supra,* Chapter 6 at 110–132.

8. *Id.* at 112–115. I modified the box by the addition of the last line on communication filtering based on our own experiences and readings.

	Emphasis	
Characteristic	**Decentralized**	**Centralized**
Hierarchy of authority	Decentralized	Centralized
Flexibility	High	Low
Adaptability	High	Low
Problem recognition	High	Low
Implementation	Low	High
Dealing with changes in environmental complexity	Good	Poor
Rules and procedures	Few and informal	Many and formal
Division of labor	Ambiguous	Clear cut
Use of managerial techniques	Minimal	Extensive
Coordination and control	Informal and personal	Formal and impersonal
Communication (up and down structure)	Less filtered	Highly filtered

Two Categories of Organizational Structure ■ **TABLE 17.1**

Later on, they state,

> Management's sense of the organization's culture may be quite different from the values and ethical beliefs that are actually guiding the firm's employees. Ethical issues may arise because of conflicts between the cultural values perceived by management and the ones actually at work in the organization.[9]

One essential for ethical behavior on the job is that employees think critically and creatively. However, it is equally important for managers to recognize that employees must work and communicate "inside the box"[10]; that is, within the organizational structure and culture of the company that employs them. Even while managers encourage employees to think outside of the limitations of the existing structure and culture, they need to design a better box in which their employees can work.

SHORT REVIEW OF THE LITERATURE

One of the foundational works in this area is Amitai Etzioni's *Modern Organizations* (1964). In that work, Professor Etzioni covers the history of thought in the sociology of organizations. He starts with the definition of organizations from Talcott Parsons,[11] explains the contributions of the formal (Scientific

---

9. *Id.* at 117.
10. Our title was suggested by Professor Patricia Werhane's concern that corporate executives use moral imagination to think outside the box. P. WERHANE, MORAL IMAGINATION AND MANAGEMENT DECISION MAKING (1999). She may have seen a similar suggestion in an earlier book. MARK PASTIN, THE HARD PROBLEMS OF MANAGEMENT: GAINING THE ETHICS EDGE (1986).
11. Organizations may be defined as

> social units (or human groupings) deliberately constructed and reconstructed to seek specific goals. Corporations, armies, schools, hospitals, churches, and prisons are included; tribes, classes, ethnic groups, friendship groups, and families are excluded. Organizations are characterized by: (1) divisions of labor, power, and communication responsibilities, divisions which are not random or traditionally patterned, but deliberately planned to enhance the realization of specific goals; (2) the presence of one or more power centers which control the concerted efforts of the organization and direct them toward its goals; these power centers must also

Management) school, presents the contributions of the informal (Human Relations) schools, discusses the emerging synthesis represented by the Structuralist approach, summarizes Max Weber's theory of bureaucracy (Early Structuralist), and then concludes with applications of the Structuralist approach to organizations as they relate to clients and the larger environment.[12]

Organizations, for our purposes, are social units deliberately constructed and maintained to seek specific goals. They are characterized by three attributes: (1) divisions of labor, power, and communication responsibilities; (2) one or more power centers directing the organization toward its goals; and (3) the free substitution of personnel through removal, promotion, or recombination/transfer.[13] In Chapter 2 of *Modern Organizations*, Etzioni raises the issue of whether modern organizations are masters or servants. He discusses various ways in which goals become either distorted or displaced, stating that "one of a larger categories of distortions" arises from the overmeasurement of some aspects of an organization's output to the detriment of others.[14] He suggests that this problem may be particularly acute in organizations, such as churches and schools, in which the output is not material and, hence, their efficiency is extremely difficult to measure.[15]

The formal (Scientific Management) school assumes no conflict between humans and the organization.[16] Its perspective is taken from a strong managerial stance, and its underlying assumption is that what is good for management is good for the workers. In contrast, the informal (Human Relations) school teaches that workers have many needs other than pure economic ones, and it argues that the formal school approach benefited neither the workers nor the management.[17] It posits approaches under which management—by acknowledging the noneconomic, social, and cultural needs of workers—could both increase worker satisfaction and raise productivity. However, one finding that suggests incompleteness in the informal school is that, although social rewards have proven important in organizations, they do not reduce the importance of material (formal) rewards.[18]

The Structuralist school comes down on the side of viewing some conflict and tension between workers and the organization as inevitable and not always undesirable. It raises systematically the issue of the relationship between formal and informal organizations by promoting a synthesis of the formal and informal approaches, drawing also on the work of Max Weber, and, to a limited extent, of Karl Marx.[19] Structuralist writers were the first to fully recognize the organizational dilemma: the inevitable strains between organizational needs and personal needs, between rationality and nonrationality,

---

review continuously the organization's performance and re-pattern its structure, where necessary to increase its efficiency; (3) substitution of personnel, i.e., unsatisfactory persons can be removed and others assigned their tasks. The organization can also recombine its personnel through transfer and promotion.

TALCOTT PARSONS, STRUCTURE AND PROCESS IN MODERN SOCIETIES (1960) at 17 as cited in AMITAI ETZIONI, MODERN ORGANIZATIONS (1964) at 3.

12. AMITAI ETZIONI, MODERN ORGANIZATIONS (1964) at 4.
13. See note 10 *supra*.
14. AMITAI ETZIONI, *supra* note 11, at 9–10.
15. *Id.* at 9.
16. *Id.* at 21.
17. *Id.*
18. *Id.* at 48 citing M. S. VITELES, MOTIVATION AND MORALE TO INDUSTRY (1953) at 27; and C. R. WALKER & R. H. GUEST, THE MAN ON THE ASSEMBLY LINE (1952) at 91.
19. *Id.* at 41.

between discipline and autonomy, between formal and informal relations, and between management and workers, or (more generically) between ranks and divisions.[20]

One of the best, if not the best, empirical studies of designing business organizations that are more moral is found a recent book published by Stanford University and written by Linda Trevino and Gary Weaver.[21] The authors declare that normative scholars and empirically oriented business scholars should (note the normative judgment) pay attention to each other, even though doing so raises problems because of different perspectives, training, and styles of scholarship.[22] In fact, they write that attempts to integrate the two types of work "always tempts a facile rejection" of the normative principles.[23] I commend this work to readers, even as I revert to my nonintegrated normative-style scholarship.

CENTERS OF CONTROL IN ORGANIZATIONS

The formal (Scientific Management) school, which had its foundations in the scientific management theories of Frederick Winslow Taylor,[24] emphasized the division of labor as its "central tenet."[25] However, this division of labor had to be balanced by a unity of control.[26] To explain, the tasks of the organization had to be broken down into components by a central authority in line with a central plan of action, the efforts of each unit needed to be supervised, and the various job products leading to the final product had to be coordinated. Because each supervisor had a limited span of control, it was necessary to have so many first-line supervisors, so many second-line supervisors, and so on. There is much written on the span of control, but, according to most classical writers, the optimal span of control was 5 to 10 workers, with higher numbers of 8 to 10 appearing at the top of the organization chart where the greater resources needed to support diverse decision making were likely to be found.[27]

Using this classical (formal model), we can see how armies, churches, universities, and many corporations are organized and why it is appropriate, but not necessarily ideal, to lump armies with churches and schools. From the centers of control arise orders, job descriptions, bonus decisions, and production and sales quotas. Then comes a need to motivate, manipulate, or coerce workers and their supervisors into meeting these demands and expectations.

---

20. *Id.*
21. LINDA KLEBE TREVINO & GARY R. WEAVER, MANAGING ETHICS IN BUSINESS ORGANIZATIONS: SOCIAL SCIENTIFIC PERSPECTIVES (2003).
22. *Id.* at 3–4.
23. *Id.* at 40–42.
24. Adam Smith in his THE WEALTH OF NATIONS (1776) provides the first classic illustration of the effect of division of labor when he described a pin factory. Smith noted that a worker by himself might produce 20 pins per day. By breaking the task of pin production down into 18 different tasks, Smith showed that a pin factory could produce 48,000 pins in a day using 10 workers. This represents 4,800 pins per worker or a productivity increase of 240 times. *See* ADAM SMITH, THE WEALTH OF NATIONS (1776, Modern Library Ed. 1937) at 4–5. Also discussed in AMITAI ETZIONI, *supra* note 11, at 22–23.
25. ETZIONI, *supra* note 10, at 22.
26. *Id.* at 23.
27. JOHN B. MINER, THE CHALLENGE OF MANAGEMENT (1975) at 159. *See also* ETZIONI, *supra* note 11, at 23, wherein he concurs that by "using a pyramid of control" the whole organization could be run from one center of authority without having one supervisor control more than "5 to 10 subordinates."

It is frequently at this exact juncture that a number of serious business ethics issues and dilemmas arise, some conscious and visible, some neither conscious nor readily apparent. Very powerful forces of environment/context, peer pressure, and role assignments/expectations assist the supervisor in "motivating" the worker at this juncture.

BRIEF INTRODUCTION TO THE PSYCHOLOGY OF AUTHORITY, PEER PRESSURE, AND ROLES

Stanley Milgram of Yale University did some ground-breaking studies on authority in the early 1960s.[28] Professor Milgram discovered that a simple white lab coat and an instruction "that the experiment requires you continue" were sufficient to get subjects to apply increased doses of electricity to supposedly suffering human subjects. As Professor Milgram notes in the postscript to one of his articles,

> With numbing regularity good people seemed to knuckle under the demands of authority and perform actions that were callous and severe. Men who are in everyday life responsible and decent were seduced by the trappings of authority, by the control of their perceptions, and by the uncritical acceptance of the experimenter's definition of the situation, into performing harsh acts. . . .
>
> The results, as seen and felt in the laboratory, are to this author disturbing. They raise the possibility that human nature, or – more specifically – the kind of character produced in American democratic society, cannot be counted on to insulate its citizens from brutal and inhumane treatment at the direction of malevolent authority. A substantial portion of people do what they are told to do, irrespective of the content of the act and without limitations of conscience, so long as they perceive that the command comes from a legitimate authority.[29]

In the 1970s, Phillip Zimbardo of Stanford did an incredible experiment using the psychology building on campus as a makeshift prison. He and two graduate assistants assembled a group of college-age volunteers, sorted them for emotional stability, and randomly assigned them to positions as guards or prisoners. Within a few days, the guards assumed the roles of guards, and the prisoners started to display the attributes of "first-timers" at real prisons. Within 6 days, the experiment had to be called off because the situation became "too real" and too intense, with several prisoners having to be dismissed because of psychological trauma. Zimbardo's experiment unmasked the amazing power of role expectations in how people make decisions and a major factor in how people see their situations.

The power of context and environment in determining how people perceive others, as well as in determining the underlying assumptions they make about other people was demonstrated dramatically by another Stanford

---

28. S. Milgram (1963). *Behavioral Study of Obedience,* 67 JOURNAL OF ABNORMAL and SOCIAL PSYCHOL-OGY 371–378. S. Milgram (1965). *Some Conditions to Obedience and Disobedience to Authority,* HUMAN RELATIONS (18 no. 1) 57–75.

29. Stanley Milgram, *"Some Conditions of Obedience and Disobedience to Authority,"* 18 HUMAN RE-LATIONS (no. 1) 57–75 (1965) at 74–75.

experiment.[30] In that experiment, healthy investigators got themselves admitted to various mental hospitals under false names with false diagnoses. The physicians and other hospital workers treated them as mentally ill—even though they were not—because they were, after all, inmates in wards for the insane. The power of the underlying assumption (they would not be here if they were not mentally ill) prevented the staff from recognizing mentally healthy patients.

WHEN GOOD PEOPLE DO BAD THINGS

I am an optimist about human nature. Certainly, some illegal and unethical business activities are carried out by bad people. However, most people are part of social networks that encourage following the law and being ethical. Most people live in communities to which they have ties. They have friends, raise families, care for their parents, practice their religion, vote, pay taxes, and follow the law. However, when the business in which they work threatens their welfare *unless* they act illegally or unethically, or conditions the rewards they seek on their doing illegal or unethical actions, *good people will do bad things*.

Many recent cases of business misconduct support this view: the Sears auto repair scandal and collection attempts from bankrupt customers, State Farm's medical claims denials, and Bausch & Lomb's accounting and sales frauds, to name a few. An analysis of how basically good companies can pressure basically good employees to do such wrongs is helpful in designing a better box for your companies.

Our upbringings and experiences—in higher education, in business, and in the military—have taught us that the hard work of ethics goes far beyond learning the right thing to do. Although it is important to know what is right, the more daunting challenge in ethics is to discover how to get yourself and others to do the right thing and to avoid doing the wrong thing. Such an undertaking or inquiry into "moral dynamics" requires an understanding of human nature, of the influence of the environment on human choices, and of how humans are motivated to do good and to do evil.

So, in doing research and teaching about law and ethics, focusing just on discovering and teaching what is legal and ethical, although essential, is woefully inadequate. We must examine how to get people who have to work "inside the box (cubicle)" in organizations to do what is legal and right and avoid doing what is illegal and wrong. To do this we need to understand how businesses are organized and operate and how the individuals in these businesses make decisions and are motivated.[31] We need to discover how to keep businesses out of the back seat of the car on the back row of the drive-in movie because, as our priests, teachers, and parents used to tell us, if you go there, putting yourself in that near occasion of sin, you are going to fall. If businesses go there, if they organize themselves in certain ways, those businesses are going to fall into illegal and unethical conduct. This chapter suggests how to help businesses design better boxes. As a beginning point for this effort, it

---

30. D. L. Rosenhan, *On Being Sane in Insane Places* 179 SCIENCE (New Series) (January 19, 1973) at 250–258.

31. *See, e.g.*, Stanley Milgram's work on the power of authority at Yale and Zimbardo's discovery of the tremendous power of role expectation in his Stanford Prison experiment.

offers four analytical frameworks for examining the causes of legal and ethical failures in business and explores briefly some solutions that might help in the design of better business structures and company cultures.

UNDERSTANDING THE CHANGING SOCIAL MANDATES FOR BUSINESS

One cause of legal and ethical failures in businesses is a lack of understanding of the changing social mandates for business. One scholar suggests that in return for granting businesses their franchise to operate, society has expectations of what businesses will provide and how they will behave.[32] These expectations develop and change as society's needs and the relations among its members change. With the rapid growth of industrialization in the United States after the Civil War, businesses were expected to add to the wealth of the society by producing more, cheaper, and higher-quality goods so that the standard of living would rise.

By the early 1900s, this mandate had expanded to include the expectation that businesses would protect the health and safety of their workers and allow them to bargain collectively in order to raise their standard of living. Businesses were also required to respect the operation of free markets by antitrust laws and fair trade practices acts. Beginning in the late 1950s, the expectation that businesses would protect the environment was added.[33] The decade of the 1960s saw the advent of demands for consumer information and protection. In the 1980s, "stakeholder" language began to recognize the concerns of society that hostile takeovers not harm workers and communities and that corporate decision makers acknowledge other constituencies that contribute to corporations.

These changes in society's expectations were reflected in a *Business Week* poll conducted during 2000.[34] Only 4% of respondents agreed with Milton Friedman and the neoclassical economists that the sole purpose of business is to increase the wealth of its stockholders. Ninety-six percent thought that the purpose of business included benefiting workers and communities.

Because social mandates do change, following the law is not enough to keep businesses out of trouble with society. Another reason that merely obeying the law is inadequate is that the law continually regulates yesterday's business abuses.[35] The law does not usually change fast enough to reflect society's current expectations.[36] Suggestions by the experts and excuses by the participants to the effect that neither Enron executives nor their Arthur Andersen auditors broke the law have not blunted their near-universal condemnation. Our society has also begun to recognize that the current political system allows corporate money to influence the writing of laws and their enforcement to the corporations' and not always to society's benefit.

The Enron affair has heightened this recognition and may have provided the tipping point for a new social mandate that society expects businesses to

---

32. RICHARD DEGEORGE, BUSINESS ETHICS (3rd ed. 1990).
33. For one benchmark, Rachel Carson's book, *Silent Spring* was published in 1962.
34. A. Bernstein, *Too Much Corporate Power*, BUS. WEEK (September 11, 2000).
35. CHRISTOPHER D. STONE, WHERE THE LAW ENDS: THE SOCIAL CONTROL OF CORPORATE BEHAVIOR (1975).
36. For instance, Arthur Andersen lost its license to practice in the State of Texas, but was fined only $1,000—the maximum permitted.

restrain themselves from harming others, even if it is legal to do so. *Society may be developing a view that law and ethics should be combined into a single system* that would provide guidance for managers, restrain the abuses of economic power, promote the general welfare, and prevent harm to others. According to this view, conduct within the law is no longer seen as self-justifying or positivistic rules of the game because the law is not seen as a complete system. Ethics completes the law in that promotion of the general good and avoidance of harm to others are seen as the overall purposes of law. When following the law does not advance these purposes and when others are harmed by following the law, society expects companies to restrain their conduct by applying ethical standards.

If this new mandate to operate under the guidance of law *and* ethics, rather than justifying conduct by its legality, has in fact come into general acceptance, then businesses should be wary of using the legality of an action—"We did not break any laws"—as a defense when the following conditions apply:

- when others' interests are seriously harmed by following the law (Enron and Andersen)
- when large segments of the population reject the law or its purpose (Freeport MacMoran in Indonesia)
- when the political institutions making or enforcing the law are unjust or corrupt (Exxon in Grand Bois, Louisiana)
- when the law and its good consequences are threatened by outrage over its bad consequences in that instance (Exxon in Grand Bois, Louisiana)
- when enactment or enforcement of the law is significantly influenced by the company's or its industry's involvement (Enron)

A second social mandate that may be evolving in this new century is the concern that *businesses respect the institution of the law as a means of resolving disputes and compensating the injured.*[37] Corporations should aim to benefit stockholders and other inside stakeholders by winning their legal battles, but they should employ legal tactics that respect rather than weaken rules of procedure in the legal system itself. Although society recognizes that both sides in our adversarial system should put on their best case and attempt to discredit the case of their adversary, the use of scorched earth litigation tactics, such as the reliance on endless motions designed to bankrupt less well-financed adversaries (as has been suggested of Exxon in the Valdez case and others), renders the courts less effective and weakens society's confidence in their ability to serve their purpose.

Businesses that ignore changing social mandates and operate contrary to society's expectations may see their franchises chipped away bit by bit. They may be subjected to larger and larger jury awards and settlement demands, as Exxon has in recent cases in Alabama and Louisiana. Their actions may also trigger a change in the regulatory and political climate as the Enron/Andersen situation and the recent Merrill Lynch securities analysts' compensation settlement show.

---

37. *See* Robert Prentice, *Lessons Learned in Business School* (N.Y. TIMES, August 20, 2002). I believe that Professor Prentice may be about half-right in his observations of the need for a renewed respect ("fear") of the law. His attempt to portray evolving ethics courses, which are offered in a minority of business schools as displacing business law courses, is at best misguided.

ORGANIZATIONAL STRUCTURES THAT BLOCK GOOD CONDUCT

Legal and ethical failures in business are also caused by organizational structures that are instituted to promote efficient operation of the firm, but have the consequences of blocking legal and ethical action by employees. This effect may be unintended both on the part of the company and the employees. The management of the company may well understand the costs of illegal and unethical activities, ranging from criminal penalties, loss of reputation, the opportunity costs of investigating and remedying wrongdoing, and their corrosive effects on the internal morale and employee retention at the company. Management staff can also be committed to doing the right thing in their personal and professional lives. Employees may also share this commitment to doing what is legal and ethical. Yet, in organizing the work processes within the company, management may put pressure on employees to do what is illegal or unethical. James Waters suggests a number of these blocks to legal and ethical action in his analysis of price fixing at General Electric.[38]

AMBIGUITY ABOUT PRIORITIES

When employees are not sure how high a priority the company attaches to acting legally and ethically, especially when these actions conflict with productivity and short-term profits, they may feel pressured to fulfill the measurable or "hard" criteria at the expense of following the law and ethics. The company may give a high priority to both profits and good conduct, but not provide guidance on how to reconcile conflicts between them. Andersen employees who were told to follow the law but to shred "excess" documents may have felt pressure to widen their view of what was really "excess" in order to protect the company and their own jobs from another auditing failure. State Farm employees, in their zeal to keep rates low for policyholders, may have lost sight of their company's commitment to making those policyholders whole if they were injured in an accident. When Dan Gill told his Bausch & Lomb managers to "make the numbers but don't do anything stupid!" they may have gotten the message that it would be stupid not to make the quotas by whatever means possible, because that was what would be measured and rewarded. Exxon may be committed as a corporation to following the rules of legal proceedings, but winning lawsuits is what is measurable whereas playing fair is not.

SEPARATION OF POLICY DECISIONS FROM IMPLEMENTATION

Decision making within large corporations is often divided into functions, with upper managers setting the policies and goals, middle managers deciding how to implement these policies and goals, and the lower managers getting the work done. Much discussion in management circles has focused on combining these functions as much as possible to create flatter, more horizontal organizations, thereby connecting the making of policy with its implementation. When this connection does not exist, managers may unwittingly make policies that require illegal or unethical actions to carry them out. Exxon's upper managers' cost-cutting goals may have pressured field managers to seek the cheapest

---

38. L. Waters, *Catch 20.5 Corporate Morality as an Organizational Phenomenon*, ORGANIZATIONAL DYNAMICS (Spring, 1978).

disposal of hazardous wastes, despite potential harms to local residents. Dan Gill's insistence on impossibly high sales growth numbers may have pressured division managers to resort to means that Gill would have considered wrong. Keeping the revenues generated by Enron's consulting contracts may have pressured Andersen auditors to look the other way at questionable partnerships. "Welcome to the Hotel Cramitdown. When 'the suits' arrive, have your alibis ready."

STRICT LINE OF COMMAND

A one-over-one command structure with no access to managers higher up the chain prevents employees from reporting wrongdoing by their managers. For example, although concern about questionable partnerships was general water-cooler talk among Enron managers, none dared take their concerns to Kenneth Lay as long as President Jeffrey Skilling was in charge.

STRONG ROLE MODELS

If training in how to do a job comes primarily from those already doing that function, new employees may be taught that there are no alternatives to illegal or unethical means to get the job done. Company values and alternative methods may not be learned. For example, new hires in the turbine division at General Electric were taught that price fixing was the only way to meet sales goals. The fact that Arthur Andersen did not rotate its auditors may have meant that those working on the Enron account were given a significant amount of their training by the one partner who managed the account.

DIVISION OF WORK

Dividing tasks by specialization or geographical division may generate efficiency, but it also may prevent employees from reporting suspected wrongdoing in other divisions. Because employees in one division may not understand fully what goes on in another, they may be reluctant to report perceived wrongdoing for fear of looking foolish. An employee's direct supervisor may not feel responsible for what happens in other divisions and may discourage reporting the perceived violation.

TASK GROUP LOYALTY

Employees working within a group may feel pressured not to report wrongdoing by group members because of loyalty to the group or fear of punishment by the group. Studies of social and market disasters, such as the Equity Funding debacle and Morten-Thiokol's part in the Challenger disaster, indicate that a number of otherwise good and decent people "went along" because of their loyalty to the group and their desire not to see colleagues and friends hurt, even though their choices injured tens of thousands of investors and killed seven astronauts.

PROTECTION FROM OUTSIDE INTERVENTION

Employees may hesitate to report wrongdoing within the company for fear that an internal investigation of the incident may be leaked to the outside and cause harm to the company.

BELIEVING YOUR OWN STORY TOO MUCH

Employees can justify departures from law and ethics because of the good that the company is doing. Enron's belief that it was totally redesigning the way energy and other commodities were sold to the great benefit of these markets may have led it to overlook its methods of financing these operations.

GIVING YOURSELF TOO MUCH CREDIT

Psychological test data indicate that because individuals are more familiar with their own contributions they tend to give themselves more credit than they objectively deserve. Thus, companies and individuals within companies may be willing to engage in illegal or unethical behavior in order to continue to operate because of an exaggerated sense of their own importance to the marketplace or to their company.

CIRCLING THE WAGONS AND DEMONIZING CRITICS

This block is related to protection from outside intervention. In this case, companies may react to any criticism from outside as a threat to the continued existence of the company. It is also related to task group cohesiveness in that members of the company do not see criticisms from outside as an opportunity to learn from others, but as an opportunity to show loyalty to the company by ignoring them.

PRAISING A AND REWARDING B

This behavior is related to ambiguity about priorities in that a company may expect legal compliance and ethical behavior, but have no mechanisms for rewarding either type of conduct in its evaluation or compensation systems. Behavior that gets the job done may be rewarded, whereas legal practices and ethical conduct are only talked about.

During the Vietnam years, I received this order: "Lieutenant, just get the job done; I don't care how you do it, and I don't want to know." Demands like these are not found just in the military. Many colleges and universities pay lip service to the importance of good teaching, but pay salaries and promotions that correlate heavily to the amount of publications. Some companies may send similar signals by spending only minimal funds on environmental compliance or ethics staffing and training while featuring one or both prominently in their mission statements or ethics codes.

UNDERVALUING THE PUBLIC GOOD

Social psychology literature has repeatedly pointed out that each of us as individuals, when asked to estimate our share of a public good, such as state parks, schools, or highways, tends to undervalue our fair share of what it costs for the state to provide that good. In a sense, this is the psychological basis for the "tragedy of the Commons." I believe that this mind-set extends to the issue of how corporate managers should rate or value good will, the company's public image, clean water, and cleaner air. Consequently, it follows that these considerations frequently come up short when decisions are made about company plans and priorities.

For example, top managers at one large timber company shared the mind-set that a tree only had value when it was converted into pulp or board feet. This perspective became part of the corporate culture and was displayed repeatedly in various public forums. That a tree or a stand of trees could have esthetic value or could help prevent erosion on a mountainside or could help in the oxygen cycle never rose to consciousness for them. The same managers expressed shock when their company was chosen as the target for an environmental campaign.

There are certainly more organizational blocks to legal and ethical actions to be discovered based on the analysis of companies that have failed. Were there organizational factors that made it difficult for individuals in those companies to do the right thing? Another question is whether these factors are different for smaller companies or for entrepreneurial companies.

RULES FOR A SUCCESSFUL CAREER IN THE ORGANIZATION

A third level of analysis of the causes of illegal and unethical behavior in businesses examines the rules of behavior for building a successful career in large organizations. Robert Jackall suggests that, to negotiate the "moral mazes" in large corporations, individual managers must strip themselves of their ordinary sense of law and ethics and adopt new ways of thinking about doing the right thing.[39] To have a successful career, these new rules require that executives take the actions described in the next sections.

LOOK UP AND LOOK AROUND—BUT DO NOT LOOK OUTSIDE THE COMPANY

The actions of individual managers have very little effect on the outcomes of large corporations—on their financial performance and on how they affect consumers or the environment. Market forces—such as the state of the global, national, or regional economy; changes in the regulatory or competitive environment; and technological developments—largely determine financial performance. All of these forces are totally outside the control of individual managers or even the company as a whole. The company's responses to these market forces are determined by a series of fragmented and bureaucratized decisions into which individual managers have little input. This lack of control over outcomes creates a constant anxiety in managers about the security of their jobs. A recession, a change in ownership, or a decision to close a plant or a division of the company may result in a premature end to an individual's career, whereas good conditions can provide good career development opportunities. The individual can only hope that he or she has the good luck to be in the right place at the right time.

The one factor over which the individual can exercise some control is his or her relationships with others. Being networked with the right individuals in higher management and the right peers can mean that the individual will move up when this network is favored by luck to move up. The first rule requires that managers look up to develop relationships with mentors and look around at peers, and not be concerned with the effects of the company's actions on the society or on the environment. These effects on others outside the company, however, are the primary focus of law and ethics, both of which are aimed

---

39. ROBERT JACKALL, MORAL MAZES: THE WORLD OF CORPORATE MANAGERS (1988).

at doing good and avoiding harm to others, respecting others' rights, and regulating behavior in a way that is just for all. If individual managers perceive that they have little control over these effects on others, they will never focus on the legal and ethical aspects of the company's behavior.

FIT IN BY MAKING OTHERS COMFORTABLE WITH YOU

Success at networking—looking up and around—requires fitting into the style of the company so that others will be comfortable that the individual manager is one of them. Having the proper style, appearance, and manner of team play allows the manager to put others at ease. If discussions about legal compliance and ethical conduct are not a part of the corporate culture, if talking about these subjects makes others uncomfortable, then career success will require managers to forego talking about ethics and the law. One can imagine that individual managers hide their ethical principles behind a glass door like the old-fashioned fire extinguishers, with a label reading, "Ethics Principles. Break glass only in severe crisis! Ethics discussions are embarrassing to your bosses and peers. Mentioning ethics or law may be hazardous to your career!"

GET THE JOB DONE

Successful managers are those who get the job done, even if they have to do what is unpleasant, unethical, or even illegal. The individual may have to break a few eggs, but the omelet gets made. The law and ethics can come to be seen as barriers that the successful manager has to be tough enough to overcome.

The rules for career success can prevent the law and ethics from being discussed or used as serious factors in corporate decision making. Managers will not raise legal or ethical questions because they are not related to the network of relationships that make for a successful career or can work against relationships by making others uncomfortable or can interfere with getting the work done.

What this analysis is suggesting is that working inside the corporate box can lead good individuals to do bad things by changing the factors that are used to make decisions. A misunderstanding of society's mandates can focus the individual manager on goals and values that are incompatible with or do not include all of society's expectations for businesses. Organizational structures designed for efficient workflow inside the box can block individuals from being ethical or following the law. The rules for career success within the box can make operating on the basis of or even discussing law and ethics a risky business for individual managers.

Because of these three conditions for working inside the box, management decision making is not a series of choices between following the law and ethics on the one hand versus personal and corporate power and gain on the other. Managers do not see their decisions as requiring a choice between the benefit of consumers and society and the benefit of the company. Rather, decision making inside the box is much more complex than "us against them" or illegal and unethical versus legal and ethical. Managers focus on goals and values that are not in themselves illegal or unethical, but in a way that excludes consideration of the law and ethics. Decisions are made to increase shareholder value to the exclusion of other societal expectations, or they focus on corporate goals and groups and not on the effects that cutting costs or protecting their task group will have on others. Decisions are governed by the need to look up and around, to fit in, and to get the job done, rather than on the importance of looking out. The law and ethics are effectively left out of corporate decision making by these factors.

ACKNOWLEDGING THE POWER OF GROUP DYNAMICS AND ROLE EXPECTATIONS

In addition to the first three frameworks for analyzing causes of ethical and legal failures in organizations, many businesses fail to appreciate and respect the tremendous psychological power of role expectations within the organization and its corporate culture. Aristotle taught, "We tend to become what we do." It is sage advice, but the gradual effects can often be insidious. People are easily influenced by the unspoken admonitions of the situation and what they perceive as the demands of the organization and their role in it.

Over 20 years ago, I watched a local chapter of the National Education Association (NEA) struggle with an anti-teacher Board of Education in a small town in the upper Midwest. The union's lawyer and the NEA local organizer decided to run "one of their own" for the board in a nonbargaining election year. They backed a college professor who was married to one of the union activists. Their hope was that by getting an educator on the otherwise hostile board they could, at a minimum, have someone who understood and was sympathetic to their position inside the school board. This, they hoped, would improve their chances for negotiating a favorable agreement without a strike.

This tactic backfired. The professor soon was acting and talking like any other elected board member and trying to impress the other board members with his concern for the taxpayers' dollars. Within a year, the professor was elected president of the board. That year, the town experienced its first teachers' strike in history. The household of the college professor was torn; a line went down the middle of the kitchen separating management and labor. The town was divided. Social scars still linger in the teachers' lounges two decades later. What happened? The college professor had become "one of them." He was no longer playing the role; the role was playing him.

The power of such a situation was vividly demonstrated in Zimbardo's famous Stanford Prison experiment.[40] In 1972, Professor Zimbardo and two graduate assistants, Banks and Haney, conducted an experiment in the psychology building at Stanford University. A group of 24 paid college volunteers, all white men and all screened for mental health and stability, were selected for an experiment in which they would serve either as a prisoner or a guard. The prisoner and guard roles were determined by a flip of a coin.

The experiment was to last 2 weeks, but it had to be called off after 6 days because the situation had become too real. Guards had become sadistic and aggressive and, at least in one case, were abusing the prisoners. The guards enjoyed the exercise of power and volunteered for extra duty without additional pay. The prisoners had started to act like "first-timers" in real prisons, experiencing "a loss of personal identity" and displaying signs of "passivity, dependency, depression, and helplessness." In less than 36 hours, one of the prisoners showed signs of severe psychosomatic disturbance and had to be released early. Four other prisoners who developed signs of severe psychological

---

40. F. Neil Brady & J. M. Logsdon, *Zimbardo's 'Stanford Prison Experiment' and the Relevance of Social Psychology for Teaching Business Ethics*, 7 JOURNAL OF BUSINESS ETHICS (July 1988) at 703–710.

symptoms were also released. When the experiment was terminated early, the guards were disappointed, whereas the remaining prisoners were elated.[41]

In 1982, Professor Zimbardo explained his observations and why the experiment had to be terminated in these words:

> At the end of only six days we had to close down our mock prison because what we saw was frightening. It was no longer apparent to most of the subjects (or to us) where reality ended and their roles began. The majority had indeed become prisoners or guards, no longer able to clearly differentiate between role playing and self. There were dramatic changes in virtually every aspect of their behavior, thinking and feeling. In less than a week the experience of imprisonment undid (temporarily) a lifetime of learning, human values were suspended, self-concepts were challenged and the ugliest, most base, pathological side of human nature surfaced.[42]

If we can induce such major behavior changes in volunteers who were paid minimum wage and playing at prison, imagine what is possible in a real situation where a person's livelihood and the economic welfare of his or her family is at stake. These situational imperatives drive such scenarios as Equity Funding, Ford Motor Company's Pinto gas tank design, Arthur Andersen's shredding of Enron documents, Rely Tampon, the Challenger disaster, and numerous others. Good people will do bad things if we make their cubicle (box) too much like Stanford's prison. The opposite is an open environment that promotes independent thinking and tolerates questioning and dissent. In short, we need to design organizations more like town meetings and less like the hierarchical organizational charts derived from military models if we really want our employees to be good citizens on the job as well as after work.

REDESIGNING THE BOXES

If this analysis of managers' decision making is correct, then we need to look for ways to redesign the corporate box so that working there does not exclude law and ethics as decision factors. These remedies will be different from those designed to prevent the greedy or the power-obsessed or the completely self-interested from breaking the law or acting unethically. For those bad individuals, the remedies would be to change their character by reeducation or exhortation or to change the balance of self-interest by significantly raising the penalties for bad actions. Both of these remedies do have a place. The federal uniform sentencing guidelines have motivated companies to educate workers in compliance by raising the penalties for not doing so. However, companies with these programs still break the law and act unethically. For instance, Enron touted the success of its RICE[43] program. Therefore, what we also need to

---

41. Brady and Logsdon (1988), *supra* note 37, citing C. Haney, C. Banks, and P. Zimbardo, *Interpersonal Dynamics in a Simulated Prison*, 1 INTERNATIONAL JOURNAL OF CRIMINOLOGY AND PENOLOGY (1973) 69–97, at 63.

42. Peter Zimbardo, *Pathology of Imprisonment*, in D. KREBS (ed.), READINGS IN SOCIAL PSYCHOLOGY: CONTEMPORARY PERSPECTIVES (2nd ed. 1982) at 249–251, at 249 as quoted in BRADY & LOGSDON (1988).

43. The acronym for Enron's Code of Ethics and standing for Respect, Integrity, Communication, and Excellence.

figure out is how to change some of the conditions for working inside the corporation.

One change would be to ensure that all levels of the organization focus on society's goals and values, as well as on the corporation's goals and values. This would require not only training throughout the corporation but also a sustained commitment by boards of directors and top managers to keep in touch with the changes in society's expectations—not that corporations cannot attempt to influence or even change these expectations, as corporations have done in promoting deregulation, and not that they should give in to changing whims. Long-running societal and cultural changes, however, should be recognized and accommodated.

To mitigate organizational blocks, companies should adopt strong ethics codes based on benchmarking with successful practices. Legal compliance and ethics vocabularies need to be developed within companies so that managers and employees will be as comfortable raising issues of law and ethics as they are now are in raising concerns about worker safety. Corporate cultures should be examined, and where necessary strong corporate cultures might be deliberately weakened and individual voices strengthened. Companies should also adopt methods for internal whistleblowers to report perceived violations without risking their job or the acceptance of their peers. Many companies have ethics action lines for this purpose.

Companies also need to figure out how to change the rules for career success in the company. Executives need to be focused on how their company's actions affect both internal and external stakeholders—look out and not just up and around. Pay and promotion policies need to incorporate accountability for the long-term as well as short-term effects of executive decisions. Consistent efforts from the boardroom on down must be made to incorporate law and ethics into the everyday decision making of corporate managers. Some companies have been able to do this through the adoption and constant reference to company values and by annual awards for employees who creatively utilize these values in their work.

There is a rich literature on organizational structures and behavior, on leadership, and on corporate culture, which can be mined for creative ways to redesign the work environment to promote legal compliance and ethical behavior. The four frameworks for analysis presented here are only a small part of what is a much-needed focus on organizational factors that contribute to ethical and legal failures in business. In a recent article about how Enron pursued the "Talent Myth," which meant that it promoted on merit but failed to provide guidance, Malcolm Gladwell noted, "They were there looking for people who had the talent to think outside the box. It never occurred to them that, if everyone had to think outside the box, maybe it was the box that needed fixing."[44]

---

44. M. Gladwell, *The Talent Myth*, THE NEW YORKER (July 22, 2002) at 28–33.

PART 5

The Environment, Wealth, and Success

CHAPTER 18

Environmental Issues

PEOPLE AND THE POPULATION ISSUE

In the year 2000, the human population of the planet Earth exceeded 6 billion people, that is, 6,000 million.[1] Some argue that the human population explosion may be the single biggest threat to the environment. To gain a perspective on that issue, examine the rate of human population growth. In mid-year 1999, the world's population was estimated at 5.996 billion; projections for 2025 and 2050 were 7.895 billion and 9.289 billion, respectively.[2] In mid-year 1999, one out of every five people on the planet lived in China.[3]

BIRTH OF AMERICAN CONSERVATIONISM: TEDDY ROOSEVELT

Humankind's dependence on the resources of the planet threatens the earth; we produce ravished forests, extinct species, polluted air, and undrinkable water, just to name a few by-products of our so-called progress. Without the pioneering efforts of John Muir, Teddy Roosevelt, George Bird Grinnell, Rachel Carson, and dozens of other activists, this country would be a much more polluted and barren place to live.

As a youth, Teddy Roosevelt developed a keen interest and love for the environment. He read widely, and such books as *Missionary Travels and Researches in South Africa* by David Livingston and *The Boy Hunters, Afloat in the Forest,* and *Wild Life or Adventures on the Frontier* by Captain Mayne Reid were among the young naturalist's favorites. Family outings to the country each summer influenced his values, and young Roosevelt always regretted his return to the dullness of city life each fall.

Roosevelt carried his love of nature with him into his adult life and professional activities. In 1887, he, along with George Bird Grinnell,[4] established the Boone and Crockett Club, and Teddy became its first president. "The Boone and Crocket Club, in time, became a powerful instrument in furthering the preservation of our nation's natural resources."[5] The Club outlined the following goals in its constitution:

- to promote manly sport with the rifle
- to promote travel and exploration in the wild and unknown
- to work for the preservation of the large game of this country and to further legislation for that purpose and to assist in enforcing the existing laws

---

1. THE WORLD ALMANAC AND BOOK OF FACTS (1999) at 878 says, "According to estimates by the UN Population Information Network, the world population reached 6 billion on October 12, 1999, having doubled in about 40 years."
2. *Id.* at 879.
3. *Id.* at 878. China has an estimated population of 1.25 billion.
4. George Bird Grinnell (1849–1938) served in 1874 as a naturalist on Custer's expedition to the Black Hills. He developed an interest in Native American tribes and was eventually adopted into the Pawnee Tribe. Some of his writings in anthropology are considered among the best of that period. In 1886, he founded the first Audubon Society. He was an editor of an outdoors magazine and suggested a system of game wardens financed by hunting and fishing licenses. He supported the preservation of Yellowstone and spent his lifetime working to preserve the land. *See, e.g., George Bird Grinnel.* Accessed at http://www.mnsu.edu/emuseum/information/biography/fghij/grinnell_george_bird.html on February 14, 2005.
5. PAUL RUSSELL CUTRIGHT, THEODORE ROOSEVELT: THE MAKING OF A CONSERVATIONIST (1985) at 169.

- to promote inquiry into and to record observations on the habits and natural history of the various wild animals
- to bring among the members interchange of opinions and ideas on hunting, travel, and exploration; on the various kinds of hunting rifles, on the haunts of game animals, etc.[6]

The club grew rapidly, and its members were instrumental in lobbying for and in the enactment of several environmental bills, including the following:

- Vest Bill—protection and maintenance of the Yellowstone National Park, opposition to right-of-way travel for private railroads through the Park
- Formation of Glacier National Park
- Lacey Act (National Park Protection Act)—prohibition of all game hunting on the Yellowstone preserve and of marketing of the hides or heads in the United States
- Forest Reserve Act—"an Act to Repeal Timber Culture Laws" that gave the President power to set aside and reserve forest lands from private or commercial entry[7]

Vice-President Theodore Roosevelt succeeded President McKinley and became the 26th president of the United States on September 14, 1901.[8] McKinley, a pro-business Republican from Ohio, died 8 days after an anarchist shot him in Buffalo, New York, where he had been greeting the public at the Pan American Exposition.[9] Roosevelt had been camping in the Adirondacks when McKinley was shot and was unable to reach Buffalo until after the president died. He immediately took the oath of office.

On December 3, 1901, President Roosevelt delivered his first annual address to the Congress. He declared, "The forest reserves should be enlarged and 'set apart forever, for the use and benefit of our people as a whole and not sacrificed to the shortsighted greed of a few.'"[10] Roosevelt proposed a three-fold conservation program: "(1) reclaiming arid lands through irrigation; (2) setting aside additional timberlands as forest reserves; [and] (3) creating wildlife refuges."[11]

In conjunction with the above program, Roosevelt implemented the Reclamation Act of 1902 that enabled the government to begin constructing dams and resulted in the start of 16 projects by 1904. He also signed the Antiquities Act that authorized the president to create or designate national monuments. With this power, President Roosevelt doubled the number of national parks from 5 to 10 and created 18 national monuments.[12] In addition, he established the first federal wildlife refuge and organized the National Conservation Commission.

---

6. *Id.* at 173.
7. MICHAEL COLLINS, THAT DAMNED COWBOY (1989) at 124–126.
8. THE WORLD BOOK ENCYCLOPEDIA (1990), vol. 16 at 465. Theodore Roosevelt (1858–1919) was the youngest man to become president when he assumed the duties at the age of 42 years.
9. THE WORLD BOOK ENCYCLOPEDIA (1990), vol. 16 at 465.
10. PAUL RUSSELL CUTRIGHT, *supra* note 5, at 211.
11. *Id.* at 213.
12. For a current article arguing that the United States should again double the size (not necessarily number) of national parks, *see* William A. Wines, *A Proposal to Greatly Expand National Parks in the Lower 48 States: An Investment in Our Planet's Future*, 12 MO. ENVTL. L. & POL'Y REV. (no. 2, March 2005) 130–148.

During his term in office, President Roosevelt accomplished what he had set forth as his goals in his first presidential address to the Congress:

> Some at least of the forest reserves should afford perpetual protection to the native fauna and flora, safe havens of refuge to our rapidly diminishing wild animals of the larger kinds, and free camping grounds for the ever-increasing number of men and women who have learned to find rest, health and recreation in the splendid forests and flower-clad meadows of the mountains.[13]

As one observer noted so well, "The creed of conservation was gaining acceptance in the United States as national policy, and the persistent efforts of Roosevelt and his friends played no small role in shaping this historic development."[14]

JOHN MUIR AND THE SIERRA CLUB

One of Roosevelt's contemporaries was the memorable Scot, John Muir. It has been said of Muir that "he single-handedly sparked a preservationist attitude among people in influential positions."[15] Muir's influence sprang from his intense love of nature and respect for the environment. He understood the delicate balance between humans and the wilds of nature and expressed that view in his writings:

> When he began to write about the forests, and the Sequoia forests in particular, Muir attempted to demonstrate that Nature's realm was self-perpetuating and worth protecting. Men needed forests for water, lumber, and more. Their health depended on the well-being of an entire community of life.[16]

Muir concluded that there were two paths to improvement of Americans' relations with their environment: (1) educating the public to Muir's out-of-doors gospel with its cornerstone of "compulsory recreation"[17] based on his free wandering in nature; and (2) getting the federal government to protect the natural resources of America, a path that would require government control over land resources.

In 1892, Muir, along with 27 other men, founded the Sierra Club as "a guardian for the Yosemite reservation."[18] The Sierra Club was instrumental in defending the California forest and lobbied Congress for and against various bills that would have potentially aided or been harmful to Yosemite and that area.

Eventually, the Sierra Club became involved in the battle over Hetch Hetchy, a proposed dam site that would destroy a pristine forest area in order to supply more water to the San Francisco area. Muir believed that the area to be inundated with a reservoir was comparable to a minor Yosemite. Despite his protestations and the opposition of the Sierra Club, Hetch Hetchy was pushed through. The loss of this battle further eroded Muir's already dim

---

13. *Id.* at 211.
14. MICHAEL COLLINS, *supra* note 7, at 126.
15. WILLIAM L. GRAF, WILDERNESS PRESERVATION AND THE SAGEBRUSH REBELLIONS (1990) at 13.
16. MICHAEL P. COHEN, THE PATHLESS WAY (1984) at 191.
17. *See, e.g.*, John Muir's writings (Herald Wood, ed., as found at http://www.yosemite.ca.us/john-muir-writings/favorite_quotations.
18. HOLWAY JONES, JOHN MUIR AND THE SIERRA CLUB (1965) at 11.

view of government. Muir lived long enough to see American government become the chief destroyer of American lives and American wilderness.

In addition to his environmental activism, Muir also opposed much of the popular economic philosophies of his day, including Social Darwinism and William Graham Sumner's Naturalistic Calvinism, which proposed "the industrious, temperate and frugal man of the Protestant ideal...capable of winning the hard struggle against Nature."[19] Conversely, Muir believed that "man's problems were a result not of the hardness of Nature, but of the inequities of society" and that compulsory recreation was a solution.[20] John Muir's active role in the development of the environmental movement continues to have an impact today at the same time that his messages echo through time and society.

Ultimately, Theodore Roosevelt and John Muir shared the same concerns about the quality of the environment that the people of this nation have to live in and get to enjoy. Water quality and air quality are on the top of the list.

RACHEL CARSON AND *SILENT SPRING*

One of the landmarks of the American movement to protect our environment was the publication in 1962 of Rachel Carson's book, *Silent Spring*. This book called public attention to the wasteful and destructive use of pesticides.[21] In her writings, Rachel Carson (1907–1964) stressed the interrelationship of all living things and the dependence of human welfare on natural processes.

Carson, who held a master's degree from Johns Hopkins University (1932), worked for the U.S. Fish and Wildlife Service most of her adult life. She warned that pesticides were poisoning the food supply of animals and killing large numbers of birds and fish. She explained that pesticides could also contaminate human food supplies. Her arguments led to restrictions on the use of pesticides in the United States and in other parts of the world.[22]

CESAR CHAVEZ, THE UFW, AND THE PROBLEM OF PESTICIDES

Cesar Estrada Chavez (1927–1993) organized migrant farm workers under the banner of the United Farm Workers. He was born on a farm near Yuma, Arizona. In the depths of the Great Depression when Cesar was 10 years old, his parents lost their farm, and the family became migrant workers in California.[23]

Chavez first began to organize grape pickers in California in 1962, when he established the National Farm Workers Association. His union merged with another union in 1966 and became the United Farm Workers Organizing Committee (UFWOC). Both unions had been on strike against California grape growers since 1965. After the merger, California wine grape growers agreed to accept UFWOC as the legitimate bargaining agent for the pickers. However, the table grape growers refused to recognize the union.

Cesar Chavez then organized a successful nationwide boycott of California table grapes. In 1970, most table grape growers agreed to accept the union,

---

19. COHEN, *supra* note 16, at 202.
20. *Id.* at 203.
21. THE WORLD BOOK ENCYCLOPEDIA (1990), vol. 3 at 250.
22. *Id.*
23. THE WORLD BOOK ENCYCLOPEDIA (1990), vol. 3 at 389.

and the boycott was called off. In 1973, the union changed its name to the United Farm Workers of America (UFW).[24]

Chavez was steadfast in his commitment to nonviolence, despite pressures to abandon it and despite the occasional outbreak of violence in the fields and during organizing campaigns. "He declared that the 'truest act of courage, the strongest act of manliness, is to sacrifice ourselves for others in a totally non-violent struggle for justice.' "[25] Senator Robert Kennedy called Cesar Chavez "one of the heroic figures of our time."

In the late 1980s, Cesar Chavez and the UFW brought public attention to the negative health impact on farm workers of the growers' use of pesticides in the fields. The Unitarian Universalist Association resolution on the Grape Boycott (1986) endorsed the "Wrath of Grapes" boycott and reported that over 300,000 farm workers were being poisoned each year by pesticides.[26] From July through August 1988, Chavez, now 61 years old, conducted his last and longest public fast. He fasted (water only) for 36 days in Delano, California, to call attention to the plight of farm workers and their children, all of whom had been stricken by pesticides.

About his 1988 fast, Cesar said,

A fast is first and foremost personal. It is a fast for the purification of my own body, mind and soul. The fast is also a heartfelt prayer for purification and strengthening for all those who work beside me in the farm worker movement. The fast is also an act of penance for those in positions of moral authority and for all men and women activists who know what is right and just, who know that they could and should do more. The fast is finally a declaration of non-cooperation with supermarkets who promote and sell and profit from California table grapes. *During the past few years I have been studying the plague of pesticides on our land and our food. The evil is far greater than even I had thought it to be, it threatens to choke out the life of our people and also the life system that supports us all. This solution to this deadly crisis will not be found in the arrogance of the powerful, but in solidarity with the weak and helpless.* I pray to God that this fast will be a preparation for a multitude of simple deeds for justice. Carried out by men and women whose hearts are focused on the suffering of the poor and who yearn, with us, for a better world. Together all things are possible [italics added].[27]

On April 23, 1993, Chavez spent the day at a trial in Yuma helping UFW attorneys defend the union against a lawsuit brought by Bruce Church, Inc., a giant Salinas, California–based lettuce and vegetable producer. He had just finished 2 days of grueling examination by attorneys for Church, who had selected Arizona as a result of venue shopping for an agribusiness-friendly jurisdiction. After a short staff meeting, Cesar went to bed. The next morning, he was found in bed with his shoes off, but with his clothes from the day before still on. He had apparently died in his sleep at 66 years and 23 days of age.[28]

On April 29, 1993, approximately 40,000 mourners marched behind Cesar Chavez's plain pine casket during funeral services at Delano. Cardinal

24. *Id.* at 390.
25. *Id.*
26. *Grape Boycott: 1986 UUA Board Resolution.* Accessed at http://www.uua.org/actions/ agriculture/86grape.html on April 10, 2001 and citing the World Resources Institute for the statistic on stricken farm workers.
27. *The Story of Cesar Chavez.* Accessed at http://www.ufw.org/cecstory.htm on April 10, 2001.
28. *Id.*

Roger M. Mahoney, who celebrated the funeral mass, called Chavez "a special prophet for the world's farm workers."[29] On August 8, 1994, at a White House ceremony, President Clinton presented Helen Chavez, Cesar's widow, with the Medal of Freedom, this country's highest civilian honor that was awarded posthumously. Clinton praised Chavez for having "faced formidable, often violent opposition with dignity and nonviolence."[30]

VARIOUS U.S. ENVIRONMENTAL LAWS

Congress passed the National Environmental Policy Act (NEPA) in 1970. The declared purposes of NEPA were

> [t]o declare a national policy which will encourage productive and enjoyable harmony between man and his environment; to promote efforts which will prevent or eliminate damage to the environment and biosphere and stimulate the health and welfare of man; to enrich the understanding of the ecological systems and natural resources important to the Nation; and to establish a Council on Environmental Quality.

NEPA did not mandate any specific or concrete steps to protect the environment; but in response to heavy public pressure, it did establish a federal policy that environmental issues were to be of the highest priority and concern.

Perhaps, the most important feature of NEPA is the requirement that an environmental impact statement (EIS) be prepared for each "major federal action significantly affecting the quality of the human environment." A second important section created the Council on Environmental Quality (CEQ), a three-member council whose members are appointed by the President and approved by the Senate. The CEQ and its staff advise the President on environmental issues. The CEQ also attempts to coordinate programs of the various federal agencies that deal with the environment.

In 1970, President Nixon (R. Ca.) reorganized several existing agencies into the Environmental Protection Agency (EPA). By combining some 15 departments from 5 agencies, Nixon effectively created the primary federal regulatory body addressing environmental issues. The EPA is an independent agency within the executive branch of the federal government; its administrator serves at the pleasure of the president. Since 1970, the EPA has expanded significantly, unlike the CEQ, which has remained a small advisory body. The EPA is now the largest federal agency.[31]

The Clean Air Act is now the primary federal statute aimed at eliminating air pollution. The current act combines more than 10 separate acts of Congress passed between 1955 and the 1990 amendments. The Act requires the EPA to establish standards for substances that contribute to air pollution; these standards, called national ambient air quality standards (NAAQS), set the maximum permissible amount of each air pollutant. The Act also calls for each state to design its own state implementation plan (SIP).

In 1899, the federal government first became involved in combating water pollution with the passage of the Rivers and Harbors Act. However, significant government involvement did not occur until passage of the Federal Water Pollution Control Act of 1948, which was substantially amended in 1972,

---

29. *Id.* at p. 5.
30. *Id.*
31. BIXBY ET AL., THE LEGAL ENVIRONMENT OF BUSINESS: A PRACTICAL APPROACH (1996) at 426.

1977, and 1987. The combined law, as it now stands on the U.S. Code, is commonly called the Clean Water Act (CWA).

Finally, for our short survey, let us take a look at a very controversial piece of legislation passed in 1973, the Endangered Species Act. Under this act, the secretary of the interior is required to list those animals and plant species that are either "endangered" or "threatened" (less serious) and to define the critical habitat of those species. The Act goes on to mandate that all federal agencies will not take any action likely to jeopardize the continued existence of such species or result in destruction or have an adverse impact on its habitat. The spotted owl case in Oregon in the 1990s is just one example of the nature of the debate and the protests against the economic impact of this environmental act.

THE GLOBAL ENVIRONMENT AND OTHER DEVELOPMENTS

Similar developments are taking place to clean the environment on the international level.[32] These efforts include the array of multinational environmental agreements, such as the Convention on International Trade in Endangered Species (CITIES), the Basil Convention on Transboundary Movements of Hazardous Wastes, and the Montreal Protocol on Substances That Deplete the Ozone Layer. Recent events include the ongoing negotiation of a global warming treaty[33] and the call by environment ministers from 19 countries for a global convention on forest protection that would establish a worldwide regulatory framework applying to both developed and developing countries.[34] Although the efficacy of these and other international agreements is in dispute, the trend discussed an earlier chapters about strengthening labor rights is similarly evident here.

Unrelated to labor or the environment, but quite relevant to the discussion of the government control of corporate conduct, are recent advances in the U.S. campaign against bribery. The United States has pursued this campaign to the full extent of its jurisdiction through the Foreign Corrupt Practices Act. However, the constraints of this Act have long been blamed for hindering U.S. competitiveness abroad as other countries do not seek to limit bribery by their corporations and even facilitate it by allowing payments to foreign officials to be deducted against income. In May 1997, the 29 Organization for Economic Cooperation of Development (OECD) member countries agreed to negotiate a binding convention to criminalize the bribing of foreign officials, with the treaty to be concluded by the end of the year and domestic implementation to be accomplished by the end of 1998.[35] At the request of the United States, the issue of corruption in the context of government procurement was also on the agenda of the 1996 WTO Ministerial Meeting. The WTO members agreed to establish a working party to explore transparency in government procurement, which could include the effects of corruption.

---

32. The balance of Chapter 18 relies heavily on an earlier work, William A. Wines, Mark A. Buchanan, and Donald J. Smith, *The Critical Need for Law Reform to Regulate the Abusive Practices of Transnational Corporations: The Illustrative Case of Boise Cascade Corporations in Mexico's Costa Grande and Elsewhere*, 26 U. DENV. J. INT'L L. & POL'Y (no. 3, September 1998) 453–515. I am especially indebted to Professor Buchanan for his keen insights into international law and policy. Anyone interested in seeing the full article and complete footnotes should see the article, which is available on-line.

33. *See Global Warming Treaty Faces Host of Political Clouds*, WALL STREET J. (May 27, 1997).

34. *International Environmental Report*, BNA (April 2, 1997).

35. *OECD Ministers Agree to Ban Bribery as Means for Companies to Win Business*, WALL STREET J. (May 27, 1997).

In summary, although the United States has clearly led in efforts to regulate corporate and commercial behavior both domestically and internationally, in an increasingly globalized economy such efforts run aground on issues of jurisdiction, competitiveness, and capital flight. International solutions in international forums are needed. As a caveat, however, it must be understood that international forums are also being used in efforts to resist local control or regulation of corporate behavior.[36] To this extent, public policy processes are as apparent in these forums as in domestic ones, and actual outcomes are dependent on the relative power of various constituencies and interest groups. The battle is merely being extended to another level in which the immediate parties are nations and transnational corporations and nongovernment organizations are backroom players.

SUMMARY OF POSSIBLE REFORM ALTERNATIVES

This examination of the manner in which transnational corporations (TNCs) operate leads me to agree with David Korten's assessment: Corporations have emerged as the dominant force on the planet earth and it is the corporate interest rather than the human interest that increasingly defines the agenda of municipal corporations, nationstates, and international bodies.[37] As William Greider suggested in metaphors, the storm is already on us because the machinery of modern capitalism "driven by the imperatives of a global industrial revolution" is out of control and promises to spew forth vast changes that will "destabilize" political order in every corner of the planet.[38] My assessment is that TNCs cannot be regulated effectively because the nation-states lack effective long-arm jurisdiction and the international law mechanisms currently in place are ineffective. Thus, without reform, we should expect capital to flow to countries where both labor and natural resources are abundant, cheap, and not protected by regulation from abuse or exploitation; or as is the case in Mexico and most of Southeast Asia, capital will flow to countries where laws are on the books but are either unenforced or selectively enforced and where government officials are corrupt. The exporting of jobs and capital will cause other nationstates to provide tax breaks and weaker environmental and labor laws so as to become competitive, and all of these so-called reforms will be defended as required by the forces of the marketplace. *The race to the bottom will be on.*

---

36. For instance, one of the more recent initiatives in the OECD is the draft of the OECD Multilateral Agreement on Investment (MAI). This agreement, which would be open for signature to both OECD and non-OECD countries, is aimed at investment protection and sets standards that protect traditional investor rights, prohibits discrimination (both through most favored nation and national treatment obligations), expropriation, investment incentives, and performance requirements. It would also provide for direct action by investors against host countries through international arbitration or in domestic courts. Even in the United States, the primary proponent of the agreement, it is recognized as having serious implications for sovereignty and will curtail the powers of both national and subnational governments. *See The Western Governor's Association Report: Multilateral Agreement on Investment: Potential Effects on State and Local Government.* Accessed at http://www.westgov.org/ wga/publicat/maiweb.htm. The WTO Ministerial Declaration following the December 1996 WTO meeting resolved to establish a working group to study the relationship between trade and investment. The working group first met in June 1997. The idea of an MAI has been seriously challenged as adverse to developing county interests. *See* Bhagirath Lal Das, *A Critical Analysis of the Proposed Investment Treaty in the WTO,* Third World Network. Accessed http://www.twnside.org.sg/souths/twn/title/ana-ch.htm.
37. *See, supra* note 4.
38. Greider, *supra* note 4, at 11–12.

Firms that disregard the welfare of labor also seem to be quite capable of disregarding the health of the environment in which we live, the quality of the air we breathe, and the purity of the water we drink. Current regulation of TNCs is inadequate, and some significant legal reforms are desperately needed. Although I do not gainsay the problems of abuse of economic power within the United States, I believe that any triage-type analysis would mandate that international restraints be looked at as well.

An initial step might be to address the power imbalances that currently exist between large corporations and labor. The literature in this area, even within the United States, demonstrates that it is cost effective to break labor unions by violating the National Labor Relations Act.[39] It is also cost effective, probably far more so, to export jobs to Mexico to avoid meaningful environmental legislation. The Foreign Corrupt Practices Act (FCPA) has been held to reach overseas and regulate corporate conduct abroad in the area of corruption.[40] Congress might consider extending such a long arm to environmental laws, labor laws, and antidiscrimination laws. It might make labor laws interactive with employment discrimination laws.[41] Thus, discrimination and unfair labor practices might potentially be merged into a new category such as illegal labor and employment practices (ILEP).

Penalties and enforcement budgets would need to be vastly increased to get the attention of the new breed of robber barons spawned by the merger binge of the 1980s and 1990s within the United States.[42] However, whether one nation can possibly reach nonresident firms and whether it should make the attempt unilaterally are significant legal and political issues.

An extension of environmental quality standards to U.S. multinationals and their wholly owned subsidiaries would be another positive step in preventing the exporting of jobs to poorer countries that are at the mercy of TNC wealth. I am reminded of a judge's dictum made famous by H. L. Mencken: "Corporations have no pants to kick or soul to damn" and "by God, they ought to have both."[43]

---

39. *See, e.g.*, James B. Atleson, *Reflections on Labor, Power and Society*, 44 MD. L. REV. 841 (1985) in which the author makes the point that labor laws tend to keep a labor dispute localized by preventing secondary activity, etc. when frequently the employer is a national organization. The history of Boise Cascade Corporation and its ability to use its vast economic powers to "cram down" a labor settlement over the objections of nine unions at International Falls Mill also supports this conclusion. *See, supra*, Wines et al., note 32. *See also* William A. Wines, *The Long March to Bildisco and the 1984 Bankruptcy Amendments: Establishment of a Limited Right to Reject Collective Bargaining Agreements*, 20 GONZAGA L. REV. 187 (1985) in which the power of corporations to legally and unilaterally reject labor contracts that were bargained under the NLRA is documented.

40. *See, supra*, Wines et al., note 32 at 471–475.

41. *See, e.g.*, William A. Wines, *The Case of the Willmar Eight: Is Leviticus Still Good Law in Employment Discrimination?*, 6 HAMLINE L.R. (1983) at 215–246 in which this suggestion for reform is made based on the outcome of the employment disputes at Citizens National Bank, Willmar, Minnesota.

42. *See, e.g.*, William A. Wines, *Title VII Interpretation and Enforcement in the Reagan Years (1980–1989): The Winding Road to the Civil Rights Act of 1991*, 77 MARQ. L.R. 647 (1994) in which the author details the impact of budget reductions and policy shifts that virtually gave the green light to corporations to ignore employment discrimination laws during the decade of the 1980s.

43. H. L. MENCKEN, A DICTIONARY OF QUOTATIONS ON HISTORICAL PRINCIPLES FROM ANCIENT AND MODERN SOURCES (1942) at 223. Mencken's reported quip has long historical roots. Sir Edward Coke in the Case of Sutton's Hospital (1613) declared that corporations cannot commit treason, nor be outlawed, or excommunicated, for they have no souls. 10 Coke 23A, 77 ENG. REP. 960 (K.B. 1613).

Congress might enact a long-arm statute covering environmental abuses by U.S. corporations, their subsidiaries, and subcontractors anywhere on the planet. Treble damages plus actual costs and attorney fees would be a good start to encourage private attorney generals (civilian plaintiffs) to bring individual actions to protect the impoverished of this planet from dealing away their children's inheritance and from polluting the air and water all living things need to survive.

This is not an appropriate place for an extended discussion of the details of such regulations; however, some sketching out of the nature of possible laws might provide their flavor. Suffice it to say that crimes against the earth (CATEs) should include clear-cutting and any other logging that is not at a sustainable level, eliminating wetlands that support waterfowl or provide significant flood plains, destroying spawning streams for trout and salmon, fishing on a nonsustainable yield basis, and failing to restore the environment after any mining activity or toxic chemical spill. This does not begin to exhaust the possibilities, but should demonstrate the scope of the legal reform I have in mind.

The resources of this planet, including the lives and health of its workers, should not be sold to the highest bidder at fire sales necessitated by the poverty and corruption of some of its nations. Some will object to these proposals for law reform on the grounds that morality cannot be legislated. Others may object to what they see as draconian measures. I dispute neither the inability of law reform to promote morality nor the vast sweep of these proposals. I would like the U.S. Congress to take the profits out of the abuses of power as have been practiced over the past two decades by TNCs.

A full-scale review of possible reform measures is beyond the scope of this chapter. My purpose here is to encourage vigorous public debate, intense media attention, and focused social science research on the coming storm. What alternatives might be explored? I suggest that the dichotomy between jobs and the health of the planet be deleted as an operative assumption, and that the role of corporations be reexamined from a populist or progressive stance that vigorously insists on corporate accountability. After all, society existed for many centuries without business corporations. Corporations were allowed to exist only because it was thought they might contribute to the improvement of the quality of life on this planet. Maybe that conclusion needs to be revisited. Perhaps a people- and planetary-centered accounting system needs to be implemented so that human costs and other so-called externalities are reflected on the income sheets of corporations and reparations might be required.

At the very least, some attention needs to be paid to the flaws in the current global government structures. Why does the United Nations seem to be ineffective when it addresses human welfare issues? What should be done to make the ILO (International Labor Organization) more relevant to the lives of working people? Is there a way to impose sanctions for General Agreements on Tariffs and Trade (GATT) violations and other trade misdeeds other than the self-defeating approach of countervailing tariffs? Let us approach these issues with some sense of urgency.

Other challenges lie ahead as well. Our political and social structures have not yet fully grasped the lessons of the 19th century and have not fully engaged the challenges of the 20th century,[44] but must be brought up to speed if misery

---

44. BRUCE CATTON, WAITING FOR THE MORNING TRAIN (1972) at 18–19 stated prophetically: "There is no twentieth-century culture; the twentieth century is simply a time of transition, and the noise of things collapsing is so loud that we are taking the prodigious step from the nineteenth

on a global scale and bloody revolutions are to be averted, as Noam Chomsky states:

> It seems to me that several tendencies can be detected. One is the tendency towards centralization power in high-level planning and decision-making institutions, as epitomized in the EU executive. More generally, as the international business press has pointed out, a 'de facto world government' is taking shape with its own institutions: the International Monetary Fund (IMF). World Bank, G-7, the General Agreements on Tariffs and Trade (GATT), *et cetera*. These are becoming the governing institutions of a 'new imperial age'.[45]

Edward W. Soja describes five characteristics of TNCs and the reach of international capitalism.

1. One prevailing trend has been the increasing centralization and concentration of capital ownership, typified by formation of huge corporate conglomerates combining diversified industrial production, finance, real estate, information processing, entertainment and other service activities.
2. Added to the corporate conglomeration of ownership has been a more technologically-based integration of diversified industrial, research, and service activities that similarly reallocates capital and labor into sprawling spatial systems of production linking centers of administrative power over capital investments to a constellation of parallel branches, subsidiaries, subcontracting firms, and specialized public and private services.
3. Linked to increased capital concentration and oligopoly has been a more pronounced internationalization and global involvement of productive and finance capital, sustained by new arrangements for credit and liquidity organized on a world scale.
4. The weakening of local controls and state regulation over an increasingly 'footloose' and mobile capital has contributed to an extraordinary global restructuring of industrial production.
5. In the USA and elsewhere, the accelerated geographical mobility of industrial and industry-related capital has triggered and intensified territorial competition, among government units for new investments (and for maintaining existing firms in place.)[46]

These five characteristics have resulted in

> the self-perpetuating spiral of economic and ecological decline ... rooted in a fundamental and growing contradiction between an unbalanced system of production, veering towards chaos, and an increasingly fragile biosphere. And oceans to rain forests to the atmosphere, cannot sustain for long a capitalist industrialism driven toward endless material expansion, generalized domination, and the conversion of human beings and nature into commodities.[47]

---

century to the twenty-first century without a moment of calm in which we can see where we are going."

45. *Noam Chomsky: Nationalism and the New World Order: An Interview by Takis Fotopulos*, SOCIETY AND NATURE, THE INTERNATIONAL JOURNAL OF POLITICAL ECOLOGY (no. 2, 1994) at 1.

46. Edward W. Soja, *Postmodern Geographies: The Reassertion of Space in Critical Social Theory*, VERSO (1989) at 185–186.

47. *Id.*

According to Carl Boggs, another consequence of the dominance of TNCs is the exclusion of 90% of the earth's population from the material benefits of the globalizing economy, in which the "search for integrated markets rooted in easy access to raw materials, cheap labor, and stable high-tech infrastructure is expected to give rise to nearly one billion affluent consumers by the year 2020; the rest will be consigned to underclass status."[48] This rapid and overwhelming development of a global economic and integrated system affects not only the sustainability of the biosphere but also has an impact on labor. The mobility of capital leads to "restructuring processes" that "derigidify long-established spatial divisions of labour at virtually every geographical scale," according to Soja.[49] He provides the following descriptive analysis:

- Paralleling what has been happening at the global scale, the regional division of labor within countries has been changing more dramatically than it has over the past hundred years.
- Accompanying these processing are major changes in the structure of urban labor markets. Deeper segmentation and fragmentation is occurring, with a more pronounced polarization of occupations between high pay/high skill workers, and an increasing specialized residential segregation based on occupation, race, ethnicity, immigrant status, income, lifestyle, and other employment related variables.
- Job growth tends to be concentrated in those sectors which can most easily avail themselves of comparatively cheap, weakly organized, and easily manipulated labour pools and which are thus better able to compete within an international market (or obtain significant protection against international competition from the local or national state.)[50]
- Under these prevailing circumstances, "few governments seem willing to step forward, to take initiatives that might challenge corporate power, frighten capital markets, or undermine competitive advantage. Governments of diverse ideological labels, from Britain to China, from Italy to Brazil, remain captive to both the logic of transnational growth as well as the ideology of a self-correcting market.[51]

According to principles established in GATT, the best means to address environmental damages that transcend national boundaries is through domestic policies, rather than trade policies. Yet, as Paul Ekins points out, this approach is probably not politically feasible as long as it has serious negative implications for the competitiveness of domestic environments. Failure to protect domestic industry from competitors who do not conform to environmental regulations so would permit only the countries with the strongest economies to maintain domestic environmental protections, which would then be under continual siege from parties concerned with international competitiveness.[52]

In effect, whether in Mexico or elsewhere in less developed countries, the development of domestic environmental protections is unlikely because

---

48. Carl Boggs, *The New World Order and Social Movements*, SOCIETY AND NATURE (no. 2, 1994) at 96.
49. Soja, *supra* note 46, at 186.
50. *Id.* at 171.
51. Boggs, *supra* note 48, at 125.
52. Paul Ekins, *The Future of the World Trade Organization: Proposals for Fair and Environmentally Sustainable Trade*, DEMOCRACY AND NATURE, THE INTERNATIONAL JOURNAL of POLITICAL ECOLOGY (no. 3, 1997) at 81.

of the negative consequences for competition on the international level both in exporting products and services and in attracting foreign investment. One informed observer calls for "an environmental nationalism which can harness the legitimate anger against global capitalism to carry out the massive transformations necessary to create an environmentally sustainable civilization."[53] I believe that such a step would work only if accompanied by an international cooperative effort, such as in the WTO, that would both establish global environmental standards and share the necessary resources to make enforcement a reality. Note that this approach would couple nationalism with global cooperation, rather than the global competition that now characterizes the race toward the bottom.

Because no international corporate juridical framework exists and because international economic competition supercedes domestic environmental protection, Ekins calls for "environmentally orientated trade restrictions."[54] The situation is all the worse in that domestic environmental (and labor) protections are hampered by the growing transcendence of such nation-states by a globalizing economy.

Furthermore, nations, in seeking a comparative advantage on the international market, are pressured to reduce environmental protection or refrain from implementing or enforcing it. The same is true for labor standards, human rights, and the gamut of controls on corporate and commercial behavior. The results include the unraveling of the prevailing theory of "comparative advantage," a trademark of international trade. Among other things, the theory of comparative advantage ignores environmental externalities, in which prices do not reflect the full social cost of production.

The theory also rests on the assumption that capital and labor remain immobile, "producing for the country's advantage."

> With free mobility of factors of production, comparative advantage becomes a much less relevant concept because factors from different countries will instead flow across borders according to the logic of absolute advantage or simple price competitiveness. Countries without such advantage will experience pressure on wage rates, working conditions, environmental regulations and anything else perceived to hinder competitiveness.[55]

Under such conditions, reform of the system of production, domestically and internationally, appears all the more impossible. The environmental movement has fallen drastically short, both nationally as well as internationally, in addressing these conditions and providing workable structures for the resolution of the various environmental crises on the planet. In sum, the outlook for positive reform of environmental degradation seems very unlikely in the short term.

---

53. A. E. GARE, POSTMODERNISM AND THE ENVIRONMENTAL CRISIS (1995) at 145. Gare makes this argument, in part, because he believes that "only by cultivating nationalist sentiments will it be possible to mobilize people to bear the costs of the struggle" to regain control over their economies and their environments. *Id.*
54. *Id.* at 69.
55. *Id.* at 60.

CHAPTER 19

Wealth, Hunger, and Poverty

> Know then thyself, presume not God to scan: The proper study of mankind is man.
>
> — Alexander Pope, *Essay on Man*, Epistle II, line 1[1]

> A decent provision for the poor is the true test of civilization.
>
> —Boswell's *Life of Dr. Johnson*, Vol. 1, p. 396[2]

> To those peoples in the huts and villages across the globe struggling to break the bonds of mass misery, we pledge our best efforts to help them help themselves, for whatever period is required—not because the Communists may do it, not because we seek their votes, but because it is right. *If a free society cannot help the many who are poor, it cannot save the few who are rich* [italics added].
>
> — President John F. Kennedy, 1961 Inaugural Address[3]

Sophie Tucker, a vaudeville star, reportedly once remarked, "I've been rich and I've been poor. Rich is better."[4] Yet, the stark truth is that the odds overwhelmingly favor our being poor; the earth contains so many more poor people than rich that the odds of being rich are slimmer than the odds of winning a lottery. In the United States, that richest of all nations, the U.S. Census found that 57% of all households earned less than $50,000 in the year 2001; yet, the mean household income was $58,208. By that measure, it is probable that over 60% of American households were below average as measured by household income.[5]

Yet, even in the United States, household incomes are not color-blind; of the 13.3 million households headed by people denominated "Black," the mean household income was $39,248. Over 72% of Black households failed to make $50,000 annually.[6] In the year 2001, the number of middle-class households fell for the first time in 10 years, and the proportion of Americans living in poverty rose significantly for the first time in 8 years.[7] This figure rose to 11.7%, up from 11.3% in 2000. In real terms, that means there were 32.9 million poor Americans in 2001. However, poverty, American style, may seem relatively well off to people in other countries and in other parts of the globe.[8]

---

1. As quoted in FAMILIAR QUOTATIONS BY JOHN BARTLETT (13th ed. 1955) at 316.
2. As quoted in FAMILIAR QUOTATIONS BY JOHN BARTLETT (13th ed. 1955) at 340. When asked to name a Bible verse on the poor, many Americans respond, "For you always have the poor with you." JIM WALLIS, GOD'S POLITICS: WHY THE RIGHT GETS IT WRONG AND THE LEFT DOESN'T GET IT (2005) at 209. Wallis notes that this is only the first part of a longer verse (Mark 14:7) that continues to urge the disciples to show kindness to the poor. *Id.* at 209–211. In fact, Wallis argues that a major theme in both the Old and New Testaments is care for the poor and opposing injustice. *Id.* at 212–215.
3. John F. Kennedy, Inaugural Address (Friday, January 20, 1961). Accessed at http:www.bartleby.com/124/pres56.html on February 1, 2005.
4. MARGARET MINER & HUGH RAWSON, AMERICAN HERITAGE DICTIONARY OF AMERICAN QUOTATIONS (1997) at 436. The authors add this annotation: "Some think Joe E. Lewis said it first but, as Ralph Keyes pointed out in *Nice Guys Finish Seventh* [1992], Lewis and Tucker often performed together and either might have borrowed it from the other." *Id.*
5. U.S. Census Bureau, *Money Income in the United States: 2001* (September 2002) at 15 (Table A–1).
6. *Id.* at 16.
7. Robert Pear, *Number of People Living in Poverty Increases in US*, N.Y. TIMES (September 25, 2002). Accessed at http://www.globalpolicy.org/socecon/inequal/2002/0925census.htm on March 21, 2003.
8. *See supra*, Chap. 5 at 5–10 to 5–11 (Fall 2004).

It is estimated that the average American spends about $16,500 per annum, yet, in Somalia, the average per capita expenditure is $17 per year.[9] Two researchers working for the World Bank, after studying poverty in 83 countries, found a net decrease in the incidence of consumption poverty[10] over 1987–1998, "but that it was not enough to reduce the total number of poor," using various definitions of poverty.[11] They cite two main reasons for the disappointing rate of poverty reduction: too little economic growth in the poorest countries and persistent inequalities that restrained the poor from participating in whatever growth did take place.[12] Let us now take a look at how "We the People" spend our discretionary money.

U.S. DISCRETIONARY BUDGET

The federal budget of the United States runs on fiscal years (FYs) from October 1st to September 30th. Some expenditures, such as Social Security and Medicare/Medicaid, are mandated by law and hence are considered nondiscretionary (Fig. 19.1). That is, Congress *must* fund those items. Whether or not we consider these social welfare items as part of the budget has a *very dramatic* impact on the shape of the budget and, particularly, whether Defense Department spending appears dominant (Fig. 19.2).

If we include the social welfare programs, *just the interest* alone on the national debt runs about 15% of the federal budget.[13] From FY 1963 through FY 1997, the federal government operated on deficit budgets; from FY 1998 through FY 2001, it posted surpluses. However, in FY 2002, which ended September 30, 2002, the government's budget dropped dramatically back into deficit spending.[14] The full amount of the national debt in 2003 was estimated at $6.4 trillion.[15] That is approximately $22,400 for every man, woman, and child in the United States.[16]

CEO PAY IN PERSPECTIVE

One of the subjects that usually comes up when we talk about income or wealth or distributive justice is the size of CEO pay, particularly in the United States. For starters, Dr. David Korten notes that "the 1,000 largest companies in

9. *The Distribution of Wealth and Resources in the World Is Unequal.* Accessed at http://www.courseworkhelp.co.uk/GCSE/RE/10.htm on March 22, 2003.
10. Consumption poverty uses the amount people spend on food, clothes, medicines, and other items directly related to maintaining life to determine poverty rather than using comparisons of income or wealth. *See, e.g.,* David S. Johnson, *Measuring Consumption and Consumption Poverty* (unpubl. paper dated November 18, 2004 prepared for the American Enterprise Institute) accessed at http://www.welfareacademy.org/pubs/poverty/Johnson.pdf (last visited on July 28, 2005.).
11. Shaohua Chen and Martin Ravallion, *How Did the World's Poor Fare in the 1990's?* Working Paper No. 2409. Accessed at http://econ.worldbank.org/programs/poverty/library/doc?id=1164 on March 22, 2003.
12. *Id.*
13. *Current Budget Percentages.* Accessed at http://www.kowaldesign.com/budget/percentages.html on April 14, 2003.
14. *Id.*
15. *The Debt to the Penny*, source: Bureau of the Public Debt. Accessed at http://www.publicdebt.treas.gov/opd/opdpenny.htm on April 14, 2003.
16. Using a population figure of 288 million people.

■ **FIGURE 19.1**   2003 federal nondiscretionary budget.

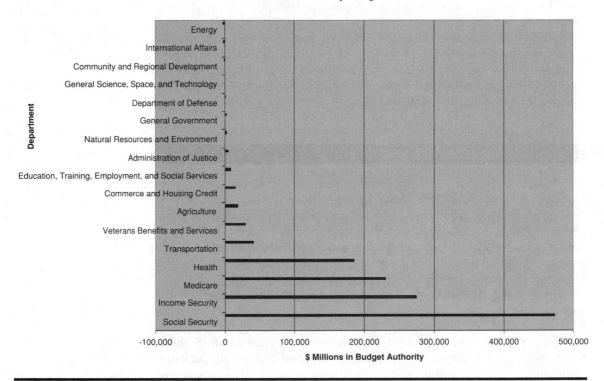

2003 Federal Mandatory Budget

America account for over 60% of the Gross National Product (GNP), leaving the balance to 11 million small businesses."[17] He then compares today's outsourcing of contracts to the relationship between core and peripheral countries during the days of the colonial empires: "The tyranny of state colonialism worked very well for a rather small percentage of the world's population. It was disastrous for the rest. Modern corporate colonialism is little different."[18]

Warming to his subject, Dr. Korten continues with the following:

> Thus we witness the paradox that when the world's largest corporations unceremoniously shed well-educated, loyal, and hardworking employees, they are increasing their economic power. From 1980 to 1993, the Fortune 500 industrial firms shed nearly 4.4 million jobs, more than one out of four that they previously provided. During the same period, their sales increased by 1.4 times and assets by 2.3 times. The average annual chief executive officer (CEO) compensation at the largest corporations increased by 6.1 times to $3.8 million.[19]

The explosion of CEO pay is not a global phenomenon. According to a 1991 study, U.S. CEOs made almost twice what CEOs made in Japan.[20]

17. DAVID C. KORTEN, WHEN CORPORATIONS RULE THE WORLD (1995, 1996) at 217–218 citing PAUL HAWKEN, THE ECOLOGY OF COMMERCE (1993) at 14.

18. *Id.* at 218.

19. *Id.*

20. *Bosses' Pay: Worthy of His Hire?*, THE ECONOMIST (February 1, 1992) 19, at 20.

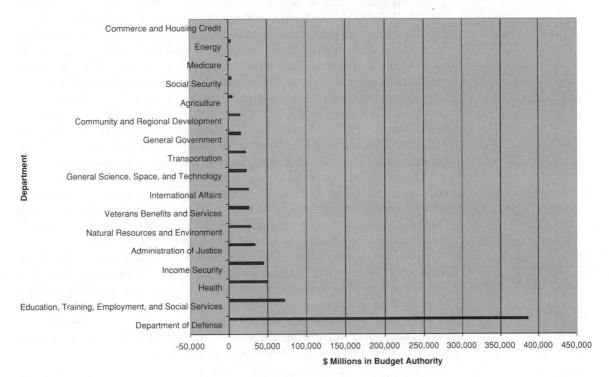

■ FIGURE 19.2

2003 federal discretionary budget.

In the spring of 1992, when CEO pay was a hot topic, there were two bills introduced in Congress on the subject.[21] One would have given shareholders the right to participate in setting executive salaries, and the second would have removed corporate tax breaks if an executive's salary exceeded 25 times the compensation of the company's lowest-paid employee.[22] Neither bill got out of committee.

In the spring of 2003, the hue and cry over excess executive compensation was heating up again, "especially in badly battered industries, such as the airlines."[23] A study done for the *Wall Street Journal* found that total direct compensation for chief executives rose 15% in calendar year 2002 to a median of $3,022,505.[24] This salary increase was augmented by a median realized gain from stock options exercised of $1,683,509, down from the prior year's $2,057,580.[25] The median unrealized gain from options (so-called paper profits) was $3.1 million during 2002, down from $4.96 million in 2001.[26]

---

21. Carol Smith, *Shareholders Are Targeting CEO Salaries*, SEATTLE POST-INTELLIGENCER (April 3, 1992) at E1.
22. *Id.*
23. Joann S. Lublin, *Why the Get-Rich-Quick Days May Be Over*, THE WALL STREET J. (April 14, 2003) at R1.
24. *Id.* Note: this is based on a sample of 350 "large companies"—not necessarily members of the Fortune 500.
25. *Id.*
26. *Id.*

Consequently, the total median compensation (direct plus exercised options) was $4.7 million, not bad for 12 months of work.

The figures just cited relate to median (the middle figure in the sample) compensation. In fact, some CEOs did quite a bit better than their counterparts. J. C. Barbakow of Tenet Healthcare Corp. made $116.4 million in 2002. Mr. Barbakow also owned shares valued at $82.9 million when his company's fiscal year ended on May 31. By contrast, Tenet Health System's agreement to purchase four hospitals in which employees were covered by collective bargaining contracts did not obligate the hospital chain to honor sick leave days that employees had accrued prior to the purchase. That decision was announced by a panel of the U.S. Court of Appeals for the Third Circuit on September 20, 2004, and related to the acquisition of the hospitals in November 1998. The court held for Tenet, even though it was not free to ignore the collective bargaining agreements in force at the time of the purchase.[27]

Overall, total compensation for chief executives rose 15% in 2002.[28] By contrast, white-collar staffers were not as fortunate. "Paychecks of nonunion salaried employees increased 3.5% in 2002. U.S. wages and benefits in general rose only 3.2% last year, a rate down from the 4.2% increase posted in 2001.[29] It seems safe to say that it pays to be the boss in more ways than one.

In 1999, *Business Week* reported that top executives earned 419 times the average wage of a blue-collar worker, up from 326 times in 1998. Compare these figures to the 1980 ratio of 42:1.[30] These statistics bring to mind the quotation from President Kennedy at the beginning of this chapter: If we cannot "help" the many who are poor, how can we "save" the few who are rich? Does government have a legitimate role in ensuring that vast income and wealth inequalities do not persist in a free society?

WEALTH DISTRIBUTION IN THE UNITED STATES

DISTRIBUTION OF HUNGER AND POVERTY

Hunger can be understood as "an unpleasant, often painful sensation caused by the body's need for food"[31] when that need is not met. The most familiar hunger pains are stomach cramps, produced by strong contractions of the stomach muscles. Certain chemicals in the brain and other parts of the central nervous system regulate the sensation of hunger in humans.[32] In addition to glucose (sugar) levels in the blood that influence hunger, people also need vitamins, minerals, and amino acids. These substances may trigger internal chemoreceptors in the brain, kidneys, digestive system, and elsewhere in the body.[33] Nerve impulses from these receptors reach a region in the brainstem called the hypothalamus, where the impulses are translated into a detection of

---

27. *See Employee Benefits: Tenet Not Liable for Sick Leave Accrued by Workers Prior to Purchase of Hospitals,* BNA DAILY LABOR REPORT. Accessed at http://www.pubs.bna.com/IP/BNA/DLR.NSF/SearchAllViews/51F984D72505E85A85256F1800 on September 23, 2004.
28. *Id.*
29. *Id.*
30. *Wealth Distribution Statistics 1999.* Accessed at http://www.cooperativeindividualism.org/wealth_distribution1999.html on April 14, 2003.
31. THE WORLD BOOK ENCYCLOPEDIA (1990), vol. 9, 435.
32. *Id.*
33. *Id.*

a need for the missing substances. In short, this is the sensation called hunger.[34] Many Americans never actually experience it. However, many Americans do experience hunger on a regular basis, and worldwide hunger is a major social problem.

Hunger and poverty are related. In the United States in 2001, the number of people living below the poverty line increased by 1.3 million to 32.9 million people.[35] For a benchmark, that number exceeded the total populations of California and Arizona in the 1990 census.[36] It also exceeded the total population of our neighbor to the north, Canada.[37]

In 2001, the Census Bureau's annual report on income and poverty stated that 13.4 million Americans were "severely poor," an increase from 12.6 million in the year 2000.[38] People are considered severely poor when their family incomes are less than half the official poverty level.[39] The official poverty levels are updated each year to reflect changes in the Consumer Price Index. In 2001, a family of four was classified as poor if it had cash income less than $18,104 last year.[40] A family of three had a poverty level of $14,128; for a family of two (a married couple), it was $11,569; and for an individual, the poverty line was $9,039.[41]

The distribution of poverty was not even handed—neither geographically nor racially. Increases in poverty in 2001 were concentrated in the suburbs, in the South, and among non-Hispanic Whites.[42] Non-Hispanic Whites were the only group for whom poverty showed a significant increase, rising to 7.8% in 2001 from 7.4% the year before. Otherwise, the Census Bureau stated that poverty rates remained at "historic lows" for Blacks (22.7%), Hispanics (21.4%), and Asian Americans (10.2%).[43]

DISTRIBUTION OF INCOME

In February 2003, real disposable personal income decreased 0.2%, when seasonally adjusted.[44] Per capita real disposable income dropped $68 in February 2003 (at a seasonally adjusted annual rate).[45] The median income in the United States in 2001 was $42,228, a drop of 2.2% from the year 2000 in real terms.[46]

The median income of Hispanic-origin households remained unchanged in 2001 at $33,565, but the real income of every other racial group declined.[47] Real median household income declined 1.3% for households with a

---

34. *Id.*

35. *Economics Statistics Briefing Room.* Accessed at http://www.whitehouse.gov/fsbr/income.html on April 14, 2003.

36. THE WORLD BOOK ALMANAC AND BOOK OF FACTS FOR 2000 (1999) at 385. For those with an historical bent, that number exceeded the total population of the United States in the 1870 census. *Id.* at 384.

37. *Id.* at 782.

38. Robert Pear, *Number of People Living in Poverty Increases in US*, N.Y. TIMES (September 25, 2002). Accessed at http://www.globalpolicy.org/socecon/inequal/2002/095census.htm on March 21, 2003.

39. *Id.*

40. *Id.*

41. *Id.*

42. *Id.*

43. *Id.*

44. *Economic Statistics Briefing Room.* Accessed at http://www.whitehouse.gov/fsbr/income.html on April 14, 2003.

45. *Id.*

46. *Id.*

47. *Id.*

non-Hispanic White householder to a level of $46,305; there was a 3.4% decline for Blacks to $29,470 and a 6.4% decline for Asians and Pacific Islanders to $53,635.[48]

Real earnings (adjusted for inflation) of women who worked full time, 12 months a year, increased 3.5% to $29,215 in 2001.[49] Men's comparable earnings did not change. As a result, women's gross earning as a ratio of men's gross earnings rose to 76%.[50]

With its customary caution, the Census Bureau reported that data did not conclusively establish an annual increase in income inequality.[51] However, there has been a clear trend toward increased inequality in income figures since 1985. The most affluent 20% of the U.S. population received half of all household income last year, up from 45% in 1985.[52] The poorest one-fifth of the population received 3.5% of total household income, down from 4% in 1985.[53]

Average income for the top 5% of American households rose by $1,000 in calendar year 2001 to $260,464, but the average declined or stayed the same for most of the other income brackets.[54] Robert Greenstein, executive director of the Center on Budget and Policy Priorities, said, "The census data show that income inequality either set a record in 2001 or tied for the highest level on record."[55]

DISTRIBUTION OF WEALTH

The White House web site shows the median household net worth in the United States as of the year 1995 at a level of $40,200, a figure not significantly different from the 1993 median household net worth of $39,590 (in 1995 dollars).[56] As of 1995, the Federal Reserve found that the wealth of the top 1% of Americans was greater than the combined wealth of the bottom 95%. In 1992, the ratio was 1% to the bottom 90%.[57]

From 1983–1995, only the top 5% of households saw an increase in net worth, and only the top 20% experienced an increase in income.[58] Wealth projections through 1997 suggested that 86% of stock market gains between 1989 and 1997 went to the top 10% of households, whereas 42% went to the wealthiest 1%. Consequently, stock market participation in the United States can be said to be "broad but remarkably shallow."[59] Seventy-one percent of American adults own no stock shares at all or hold less than $2,000 worth.[60]

Adjusted for inflation, the net worth of the median American household fell 10% between 1989 and 1997, declining from $54,600 to $49,900. The net worth of the top 1% in 1999 was 2.4 times the combined wealth of the

48. *Id.*
49. *Id.*
50. *Id.*
51. Robert Pear, *supra* note 31.
52. *Id.*
53. *Id.*
54. *Id.*
55. The *New York Times* felt it necessary to qualify Mr. Goldstein's remarks by noting that the Center on Budget and Policy Priorities is a "liberal research institute." *Id.*
56. *Id.*
57. *Wealth Distribution Statistics 1999.* Accessed at http://www.cooperativeindividualism.org/wealth_distribution1999html on April 14, 2003.
58. *Id.*
59. *Id.*
60. *Id.* This estimate includes mutual funds and the popular 401 (k) plans.

Household Wealth Distribution

Policy Quick Take No. 1

By Bernard Wasow

Policy Ideas is a project of The Century Foundation. Nothing written here is to be construed as necessarily reflecting the views of The Century Foundation or as an attempt to aid or hinder the passage of any bill before Congress.

A household's wealth—its net worth, or the value of its assets minus its debts—is in some ways more important than its income. Wealth provides security against the year to year income fluctuations that plague many families as members move into and out of various jobs. A family with a big house, a small mortgage, and money in the bank is in an enviable position.

The two figures below summarize the latest data on wealth compiled by Professor Edward N. Wolff of New York University from U.S. Bureau of the Census data for 1998.

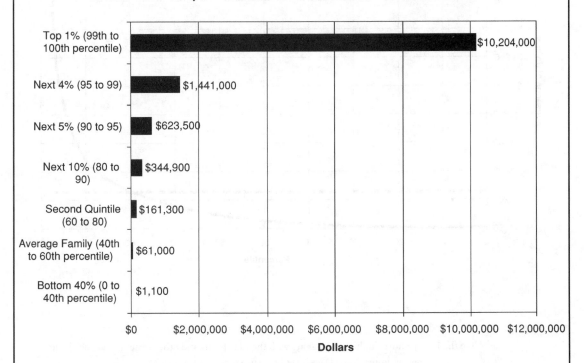

Figure 1 shows the average wealth at various percentiles of the wealth distibution. The top 1 percent of families averaged $10.2 million in wealth, while a family in the middle of the wealth distribution has a net worth of $61,0000, and the bottom 40 percent averaged $1,100 in wealth.

Policy Ideas is a project of The Century Foundation, formerly the Twentieth Century Fund, a research foundation that undertakes timely and critical analyses of major economic, political, and social institutions and issues. Nonprofit and nonpartisan, TCF was founded in 1919 and endowed by Edward A. Filene.

Headquarters: 41 East 70th Street * New York, NY 10021 * 212.535.4441 * 212.535.7534 (fax) * info@tef.org
DC Office: 1755 Massachusetts Ave., NW * Washington, D.C. 20036 * 202.387.0400 * 202.483.9430 (fax) * info@tef.org
www.tef.org   www.policyideas.org

(Continued)

Figure 2 shows this information differently. Here, the percentile of the wealth distribution is on the horizontal axis while the wealth of families at that point in the wealth distribution is on the vertical axis. For example, families below about the thirteenth percentile have almost no wealth—their debt was about the same size as the value of their assets—while a family at the sixtieth percentile has about $100,000 in wealth.

The horizontal line in this figure represents average wealth of all families (total wealth divided by the total number of households), $270,000. It hits the graph at the eightieth percentile: 80 percent of families have less than $270,000 in net worth.

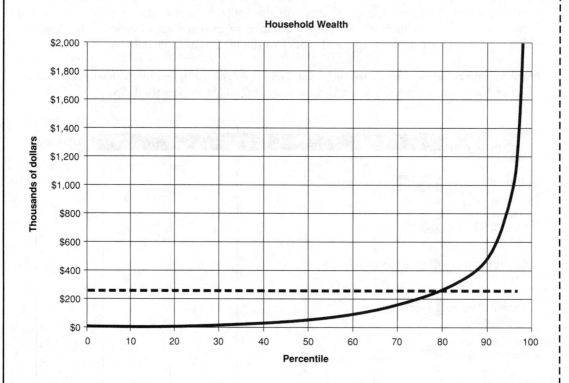

All of the Policy Shorts in this series, along with the Idea Briefs and other materials, are available on the Policy Ideas Website at http://www.policyideas.org.

For more information, please contact Tina Doody at 212-452-7750 or doody@tef.org.

poorest 80%.[61] The modest net worth of White families was 8 times that of African Americans and 12 times that of Hispanics. The median net worth of African Americans (net worth less home equity) was $200 or 1% of the median net worth of $18,000 for Whites; the median net worth of Hispanics was zero.[62]

The average net worth in the United States, as reported by the U.S. Census Bureau in 2001, was $270,000.[63] Microsoft CEO Bill Gates has more wealth than the bottom 45% of American households combined.[64] The top 1% averaged $10.2 million in wealth, and the bottom 40% averaged $1,100 in wealth.[65] If we were to graph the net worth of American families, we would not reach the average wealth of $270,000 until the 80th percentile: in other words, 80% of American families have below-average net worths.[66]

DISTRIBUTION OF POVERTY, HUNGER, AND WEALTH ON THE PLANET

In 1998, the United Nations Development Program (UNDP) reported that 100 countries were worse off than 15 years ago.[67] For a benchmark, 188 nations were members of the United Nations,[68] and the U.S. Census Bureau did population projections for 192 nations titled "Projections for All Countries" in 1999.[69] The conclusion would seem to be unavoidable that a majority of nations are worse off than they were in 1985.

The UNDP also reported that in 1998 the world's wealthiest 225 people had a combined wealth of $1 trillion, an amount equal to the combined annual income of the 2.5 billion poorest people on the planet.[70] *Additionally, the wealth of the three most well-to-do individuals exceeded the combined GDP of the 48 least developed countries.*

In 1998, the 20% of the world's population living in the highest-income countries accounted for 86% of total private consumption expenditures, whereas the poorest 20% accounted for only 1.3%. That consumption figure was down from 2.3% three decades ago.[71] Three billion people lived on less than $2 per day, whereas 1.3 billion got by on less than $1 per day. Seventy percent of those living on less than $1 per day were women.[72]

Two billion people worldwide suffer from anemia, including 55 million in industrial countries. Given today's hoarding of wealth and current trends in population growth, three decades from now the world could have 3.7 billion people suffering from anemia.[73] UN development experts have observed that the planet is heading toward "grotesque inequalities" and that

61. *Id.*
62. *Id.*
63. Bernard Wasow, *Household Wealth Distribution* (Century Foundation, November 16, 2001).
64. *Id.*
65. *Id.*
66. *Id.*
67. *Wealth Distribution Statistics 1999.* Accessed at http://www.cooperativeindividualism.org/wealth_distribution1999html on April 14, 2003.
68. THE WORLD BOOK, *supra* note 29.
69. *Id.* at 878–879.
70. *Wealth Distribution Statistics 1999, supra* note 50.
71. *Id.*
72. *Id.*
73. *Id.*

development "that perpetuates today's inequalities is neither sustainable nor worth sustaining."[74]

CONCLUDING OBSERVATIONS

The statistics presented in this chapter convey a dramatic picture. Some time ago, a futurist predicted, "The next war will be over oil; and the one after that will be over food." I remember the prediction, but hope it is wrong. In the Book of Revelation, the Apostle John describes the four horsemen of the Apocalypse, writing, "So I looked, and behold a pale horse. And the name of him who sat on it was Death, and Hades followed with him. And power was given to them over a fourth of the earth, to kill with the sword, with hunger, with death, and by the beasts of the earth."[75] At the rate we are proceeding, such a prophesy may seem too real. To avoid an apocalypse, what we may need is a transformation of the system on a global scale to root out the inequities and to ensure security through justice. Such a transformation has also been prophesied.[76]

Finally, the words of America's greatest civil rights leader, Martin Luther King, Jr., ring through time as we attempt to comprehend this incomprehensible planetary division between the haves and the have-nots. He spoke these little-noticed sentiments at Riverside Church in New York on April 4, 1967, 1 year to the day before he was martyred in Memphis:

> I am convinced that if we are to get on the right side of the world revolution, we as a nation must undergo a radical revolution of values. We must rapidly begin the shift from a "thing-oriented" society to a "person-oriented" society. When machines and computers, profit motives and property rights are considered more important than people, the giant triplets of racism, materialism, and militarism are incapable of being conquered....
>
> One day we must come to see that the whole Jericho road must be transformed so that men and women will not be constantly beaten and robbed as they make their journey on life's highway. True compassion is more than flinging a coin to a beggar; it is not haphazard and superficial. It comes to see that an edifice which produces beggars needs restructuring. A true revolution of values will soon look uneasily on the glaring contrast of poverty and wealth.... A true revolution of values will lay hands on the world order and say of war: 'This way of settling differences is not just.'...A nation that continues year after year to spend more money on military defense than on programs of social uplift is approaching spiritual death.[77]

---

74. *Id.*
75. Revelation 6:8.
76. *See* Isaiah 2:4: "And they shall beat their swords into plowshares, and their spears into pruning hooks; nation shall not lift up sword against nation, neither shall they learn war anymore" (RSV). *See also* R. C. EDWARDS, REICH, & WEISSKOPH, THE CAPITALIST SYSTEM (1986) at 3 for a more secular prophesy.
77. Martin Luther King, Jr., *A Time to Break Silence*, JAMES M. WASHINGTON (Ed.), A TESTAMENT OF HOPE: THE ESSENTIAL WRITINGS AND SPEECHES OF MARTIN LUTHER KING, JR. (1986) at 231–244, 240–241.

CHAPTER

20

The Good Life and Its Discontents

"I don't get it," Bill cried out, "what can money buy?"

"Money can buy everything," I said, not being inclined to mitigate the paradox of human life on earth. "Money can buy everything. The only thing it can't buy is meaning."

—Jacob Needleman[1]

One might do well to ask, "If we Americans are so well off, as most of the incumbent politicians said in the last election year, why am I not happy?" Or, "Why aren't I happier than I am?" At first blush, these questions may not seem terribly deep, but, on reflection, they deserve a serious answer. As a friend said so well, the so-called good life is relative and not absolute; it is not so much a place in time as it is a place of the mind.[2]

This chapter addresses the issue of American discontent or malaise. There are several theories about its causes:

- The American Dream has mutated into one of entitlement from one of opportunity.
- Americans are having a spiritual crisis and are suffering from a virtual emptiness of spirit.
- American individualism, as de Tocqueville warned, has evolved into a radical individualism that is destroying our national culture and impoverishing our individual lives.
- Corporations and the free market are dominating American society and culture, depriving it of any moral force or cohesiveness.
- The sense of community or "social capital" (its social science cousin) is at a 100-year low, causing all manner of social ills.
- The huge and expanding economic gap between the haves and the have-nots has contributed to higher rates of violent crime and incarceration and greater social dislocation.[3]

As Professor Putnam documented so thoroughly, U.S. social capital is at its lowest point in 100 years.[4] This single fact has broad implications for other aspects of American life, such as mental health, life expectancy, and crime rates. Trust in our fellow Americans, as in answering yes to this question—"Do you believe that most people can be trusted?"—fell from a high of 50% in 1952 to a low of just over 25% in 1998.[5] We do not trust each other not to lie to us nor to keep our promises or to respect our property. This is a breakdown in the social fabric of immense significance. Our trust in our government to "do the right thing" fell from a high of 76% in 1961 to a current low of 19% in the year 2000.[6] Family dinners have declined 33% in the past 25 years.

---

1. JACOB NEEDLEMAN, MONEY AND THE MEANING OF LIFE (1991) at 239.
2. Conversation with the Rev. Mr. Don Sower in Boise, March 28, 2001.
3. One public health expert has written that the gap between the so-called haves and the have-nots has had a negative impact on American public health. *See* Stephen Bezrucha, M.D., "Is Our Society Making You Sick?" NEWSWEEK (February 26, 2001) at 14. Dr. Bezrucha writes, "We expend almost half of all the money spent on medical care" in the world, but comprise only "about 4 percent of the world's total population." Yet, the United States has slipped from about 15th in world health in 1970 to "around 25th in recent years. *Id.* He believes that both current data and archeological records support the proposition that "people's life span depends on the hierarchal structure of their society" (i.e., the size of the gap between the rich and the poor). *Id.*
4. ROBERT D. PUTNAM, BOWLING ALONE: THE COLLAPSE AND REVIVAL OF AMERICAN COMMUNITY (2000).
5. *Id.* at 137–139 (Putnam).
6. TIME MAGAZINE survey, quoted by U.S. Senator McCain on the *Jim Lehr Newshour* (PBS) on Monday, April 2, 2001.

The Glutted Mind

While it is a blessing that a man no longer has to be rich in order to enjoy the masterpieces of the past—for paperbacks, first-rate color reproductions, and stereo phonograph records have made them all available to all but the very poor—this ease of access, if misused—and we do misuse it—can become a curse. We are all of us tempted to read more books, look at more pictures, listen to more music, than we can possibly absorb; and the result of such gluttony is not a cultured mind but a consuming one; what it reads, looks at, listens to, is immediately forgotten, leaving no more traces behind it than yesterday's newspaper.

W. H. Auden, SECONDARY WORLDS (1968) at 128.

It may be that Professor Bellah and his co-authors were right when they predicted a movement to radical individualism.[7] Radical individualism has as its goal "aloneness." A person caught up in radical individualism simply wants to be left alone; he or she has no desire to carry the burden of any commitments—even the simplest one of attending a bowling league or going to a neighborhood association meeting. In a sense, Americans are having a spiritual crisis. Fewer of us attend temple/church/synagogue/mosque services, although more of us claim to believe in a Supreme Being. We are also bombarded with over 1,500 advertisements per day that tell us "You are *not* okay! But you might be okay, if you buy this one item or service or drink the right beer."

This advertising message is the opposite of therapy; it is designed to make us unhappy with ourselves. Ultimately, this message drives the materialist society we inhabit, and it is devastating. One of its contributions is the creation of a mantra for teenage girls in the United States: "I hate my body."[8]

Not trusting our neighbors and not feeling good about ourselves make it easy for us to fall into the trap of being discourteous to others. America is experiencing an unprecedented amount of incivility.[9] The incivility goes beyond rudeness to actual physical violence. It has gotten so bad that assault with a deadly weapon was reported as "incivility" in one trade paper. The divorce-rate is up to 50%. Children are killing other children, and our irrational response is to further eliminate childhood by turning children, whom we deem out of control, over to the adult corrections industry.

The communications revolution also keeps us informed almost instantaneously of the problems in the world and at home. We know about the ozone layer and the hole in it. We know about the annihilation of the Brazilian rain forests. We know about genocide and war and rebellion and the "powder keg" conditions in the Middle East.

This information makes some of us simply uncomfortable, it makes others of us irritable, and it makes others guilty or afraid. The point is that knowing

---

7. ROBERT N. BELLAH ET AL., HABITS OF THE HEART: INDIVIDUALISM AND COMMITMENT IN AMERICAN LIFE (1985) at 142–163.

8. JOAN JACOBS BRUMBERG, THE BODY PROJECT (1997) as quoted in Laura Shapiro, *Fear and Self-Loathing in Young Girls' Lives*, NEWSWEEK (September 22, 1997) at 69.

9. MARK CALDWELL, A SHORT HISTORY OF RUDENESS: MANNERS, MORALS AND MISBEHAVIOR IN MODERN AMERICA (1999).

©DOONESBURY reprinted with permission of Universal Press Syndicate.

about all the problems in the world is not always conducive to peace of mind, particularly when the media follow their old adage, "If it bleeds, it leads." Many people worry about the gap between rich and poor, not only in the United States but also in the other nations of the world. We know that humanity, all 6 billion of us, is *not* flourishing.[10]

The "trickle down" theory of is not so much a theory as a myth. Wealth has not found its way into the middle class in the United States, much less

---

10. For example, witness the following information disseminated by email and attributed to a professor at Stanford Medical School: "If Earth's population were shrunk into a village of just 100 people (n = 100)—with all the human ratios existing in the world still remaining—what would this tiny village look like? That's exactly what Dr. Phillip Harter of the Stanford University School of Medicine attempted to figure out. This is what he found.

- 57 would be Asian
- 21 would be European
- 14 would be from the Western Hemisphere
- 8 would be Africans
- 52 would be female; 48 would be male
- 70 would be non-White; 30 would be White
- 70 would be non-Christian, 30 would be Christian
- 89 would be heterosexual; 11 would be homosexual
- 6 people would possess 59% of the entire world's wealth—and all 6 would be from the United States
- 80 would live in substandard housing
- 70 would be unable to read
- 50 (read "half") would suffer from malnutrition
- One would be near death and one near birth
- One person would have a college education
- One person would own a computer

Forwarded by Matthew B. Houser. Accessed at housermb@whitman.edu on April 4, 2001. Mr. Houser further notes that "if you have money in the bank, in your wallet, and spare change in a dish someplace, you are among the top 8%" of the wealthy people in the world. Dr. Harter's site is http://gbgm-umc.org/units/treasurer.html accessed on April 18, 2001.

Public domain.

the lower income classes. Most of the wealth that had been generated by the Reagan and George W. Bush tax cuts has centralized in the top 1% of the wealthy families in the country. Such a concentration of wealth, coupled with the diminishing of the middle class, is not an example of human flourishing because most of humanity is left out.

What might be one characteristic, perhaps even a defining characteristic, of a good and just society? I believe that it might be *human thriving*. A society that genuinely promotes human thriving would seem to me to be on the road to both goodness and justice.

WHAT HUMAN THRIVING MIGHT MEAN

One business ethicist, Paul Camenish, suggested over 20 years ago that any adjustment of any major social institution should focus on the central reason for its existence: the production of life-sustaining and enhancing goods and services that "contribute to human flourishing."[11] My definition of human thriving is very similar, I suspect, to what Paul Camenish meant by "human flourishing." In fact, Webster lists "flourish" and "prosper" as synonyms for thrive.[12] Thrive means "1. To make steady progress: prosper; 2. To grow vigorously: flourish."[13] It comes from the Middle English word *thriven*, which derives from an Old Norse word, a reflexive of a word that means "to seize." I rather like that etymology—*carpe diem*. Seize the day. Squeeze the entire flavor out of life. Work and play vigorously but take time to smell the roses. We should strive to live a life in balance, but we should also live passionately. Human thriving means having the freedom and the opportunity that the above sentiments imply.

11. Paul F. Camenish, *Business Ethics: On Getting to the Heart of the Matter*, BUS. & PROFESSIONAL ETHICS J. 1 as quoted in W. SHAW & V. BARRY, MORAL ISSUES IN BUSINESS (5th ed. 1992) at 253–258.
12. WEBSTER'S II NEW RIVERSIDE UNIVERSITY DICTIONARY (1984) at 1206.
13. *Id.*

I would expand Camenish's suggestion by adding "life-sustaining and enhancing employment" to the production of goods and services. E. F. Schumacher, the British economist, says that work conducted under conditions of freedom and human dignity blesses both the worker and the product.[14] Yet, this lesson escapes many managers in today's stress-filled workplace. An MBA student recently told me that her company had posted a huge profit this past year after 9 years of red ink because, in her opinion, the new CEO acknowledged the humanity of the labor force. He did this by speaking with the workers on the service floor in a manner that reflected genuine concern for them.[15]

More than three decades ago, Robert F. "Bobby" Kennedy declared, "Some people see things that are and ask 'Why?' I dream of things that have never been and ask 'Why not?'"[16] To achieve human thriving means that 4.5% of the earth's population can no longer continue to consume over 40% of its resources.[17] Human thriving means it is not acceptable to have 5.5 million children die each year from starvation and related diseases.[18] Such levels of death and pestilence must be ruled unacceptable when the world has the resources to feed all its people, but merely lacks the will.

An official national level of unemployment of 6.4% with pockets of unemployment exceeding 40% is not acceptable in a society in which human thriving is paramount. My travels to Vietnam convince me that there is much moral good in labor-intensive work that eliminates unemployment and reaffirms people's sense of worth. Employment should be provided for everyone who wants to work.[19]

That everyone in this country does not have access to the minimum amount of medical assistance necessary to promote human dignity is a national disgrace.[20] People in the final stages of AIDS are dying on the sidewalks a few blocks from the U.S. Capitol in Washington, D.C.[21] Have we no sense of shame?[22] Is this tolerated because their skin is dark? The lack of health care, quality education, adequate housing, and elder care on our Indian reservations

---

14. E. F. SCHUMACHER, SMALL IS BEAUTIFUL: ECONOMICS AS IF PEOPLE MATTERED (1973) at 55.
15. Interview with anonymous MBA students after class, in Jepson Center, GU, Spokane on September 9, 1999.
16. Robert F. Kennedy used this expression as his campaign slogan in 1968. President John Kennedy used it first in 1963. The quotation originated with George Bernard Shaw. RALPH KEYES, "NICE GUYS FINISH SEVENTH": FALSE PHRASES, SPURIOUS SAYINGS, AND FAMILIAR MISQUOTATIONS (1992) at 92.
17. U.S. population in 1976 was 4.52% of the earth's population. Our resource consumption was 39.47% of the earth's consumption. Calculations based on the U.S. DEPARTMENT OF COMMERCE STATISTICAL ABSTRACT (1998).
18. Estimate from executive director of the United Nation's Children's Fund (UNICEF) as quoted in JAMES RACHELS, ELEMENTS OF MORAL PHILOSOPHY (3rd ed. 1999) at 82.
19. See Appendix A-4, Section 23 at 609–610.
20. Apparently Bill Bradley, one of the top contenders for the Democratic nomination for president in 2000 also shares this view because he has proposed a way to provide health care for 95% of U.S. population. See Ronald Brownstein (LA Times), *Democratic Contenders Trade Barbs*, ID. STATESMAN (November 1, 1999) at 7A. Mr. Bradley made his proposal claiming it would cost $65 billion a year. *Id.* Even the GOP is getting into the health care arena, belatedly and marginally, with a so-called Patient's Bill of Rights addressed to HMOs. See Robin Toner (N.Y. Times), *Health Care Fight Renewed*, SPOKESMAN-REVIEW (October 4, 1999) at A1.
21. See Rick Wartzman, *AIDS Heaps Hardship on Washington Slum Called 'the Graveyard,'* WALL STREET J. (November 4, 1987) at A1.
22. See Chapter 7 "The Eight Ages of Man" in ERIK H. ERIKSON, CHILDHOOD AND SOCIETY (1985).

and in our cities is a national disgrace, yet, hardly anyone notices.[23] These conditions must be addressed if human beings are going to thrive in our society.

Human thriving excludes warfare and unnecessary[24] violence. Killing someone or his or her children or killing a neighbor's child will never change that person's mind. As a people, we need to outgrow our penchant for violence and its use as a supposed tool for problem solving.[25] Moreover, we should stop selling violence as a form of entertainment. Businesses can lead the way here even if the government lacks the will. No excuse can justify the manufacture, testing,[26] or deployment of nuclear weapons, nerve gas, chemical weapons, landmines, bacteriological weapons, or Napalm. President Dwight Eisenhower on April 16, 1953, declared:

> Every gun that is made, every warship launched, every rocket fired signifies, in the final sense, a theft from those who hunger and are not fed, those who are cold and are not clothed.
>
> This world in arms is not spending money alone. It is spending the sweat of its laborers, the genius of its scientists, the hopes of its children.
>
> The cost of one modern heavy bomber is this: a modern brick school in more than 30 cities. It is two electric power plants, each serving a town of 60,000 population. It is two fine, fully equipped hospitals. It is some 50 miles of concrete highway.
>
> We must pay for a single fighter plane with a half-million bushels of wheat.
>
> We pay for a single destroyer with new homes that could have housed more than 8,000 people.
>
> This, I repeat, is the best way of life to be found on the road the world has been taking.
>
> This is not a way of life at all, in any true sense. Under the cloud of threatening war, it is humanity hanging from a cross of iron.[27]

Yet, more than 50 years later, our national budget makes a statement that indicates we did not hear President Eisenhower's lament, then or now. The United States has less than 5% of the world's population, but is responsible for more than 30% of the military spending on the planet! This spending—some $267 billion in FY 1997—constitutes more than our government spends on all other discretionary programs combined, on justice, health, Medicare, and education. These underfunded programs are the heart of real national security, and they represent the best hope of a prosperous future for our children and

23. *See, e.g.,* Louis Romano, *Indian Health Care in America's Cities Lacks Money, Facilities,* SEATTLE TIMES (December 21, 1996) at A15.

24. Necessary violence would include such things as open heart surgery, amputation of a gangrenous limb, cutting a victim out of a collapsed automobile, self-defense, extraction of bad teeth, etc.

25. For an excellent discussion of the mythology underlying the concept of so-called redemptive violence, *see* WALTER WINK, ENGAGING THE POWERS (1992).

26. *See* William Neikirk (Chicago Tribune), *Senate Defies Clinton, Rejects Test Ban Treaty,* SPOKESMAN-REVIEW (October 14, 1999) at A1.

27. President Dwight D. Eisenhower, *The Chance for Peace,* a speech delivered to the American Society & Newspaper Editors, April 16, 1953, at the Statler Hotel in Washington, D.C., as found at http://www.eisenhower.archives.gov/content.htm, and last visited on July 29, 2005.

grandchildren.[28] The most dangerous people in the world are those who have nothing to lose.

Human thriving can be seen as a global condition in which children are fed, clothed, housed, and educated and have reasonable access to health care, and a condition in which adults have meaningful work, economic security, freedom from war and violence, and access to reasonable health care. Human thriving means that old people receive the respect and care that they need to tell their stories, share their visions, and die good deaths. Human thriving in its broadest sense means a world in which happiness, love, and freedom from fear are preeminent; it means a world in which people might strive to establish an ideal human community.

WHO GETS TO DO THE HEAVY LIFTING?

The age-old question confronts us: "Whom shall I send, and who will go for us?"[29] Many of us devoutly seek a world in which human beings thrive. Yet, the issue of who should do the heavy lifting separates us into political groups and splinters our potential community. There is enough work to go around. Government has a legitimate role; nonprofit organizations, churches, and charities have important roles to play. Yet, I believe that government is not situated to take on ambitious social agendas. The popular mood of the past two decades has been toward more local control and less top-down federal programs. The nonprofit sector and the churches are overwhelmed. The unions are dwindling in numbers.[30] That leaves one major, well-financed, very talented social institution that has not fully accepted its role in human thriving: business.

American business has been myopic.[31] This myopia is caused mainly by acceptance of the ideology that businesses, especially large publicly traded corporations, should be run exclusively to benefit their shareholders by maximizing wealth.[32] This choice to run corporations for the benefit of one segment of

---

28. Data from Office of Management and the Budget as cited by Friends Committee on National Legislation in a 1997 publication.

29. Isaiah 6:8. "Also I heard the voice of the Lord, saying, Whom shall I send, and who will go for us? Then said I, Here *am* I; send me."

30. Nancy Cleeland (LA Times), *Hard Work Lies Ahead for Labor*, SPOKESMAN-REVIEW (October 11, 1999) at A1. "With only about 10 percent of private [sector] workers in unions—less than half the share of twenty years ago—labor has little muscle with which to fight back. And despite tripling the resources spent on organizing under Sweeney, unions have not kept pace with the growth of new jobs—adding just 100,000 members last year while the economy expanded by nearly 2 million jobs." *Id. See also* Barbara Ehrenreich, *Tiny Labor*, PROGRESSIVE (August 2005), 16–17.

31. For instance, 75% of American corporations do not make any donations to charity. (AP) *Top CEOs Want Giving to Be Way to Do Business*, ORLANDO SENTINEL (November 19, 1999) at B1. In the United States in 1998, charitable donations amounted to $174.65 billion. Individual donations accounted for over 77% of those donations. *NBC Nightly News*, November 26, 1999, at 6 p.m., Channel 6 in Spokane. Paul Newman and other top CEOs are organizing to increase corporate giving by 10% per year through the year 2004, which would increase corporate donations by $6 billion. *See Giving as Good as He Gets*, U.S. NEWS & WORLD REPORT (November 29, 1999) at 14.

32. *See, e.g.*, MILTON & ROSE FRIEDMAN, FREE TO CHOOSE (1980, 1979) wherein the authors declare in the Introduction:

> We must understand the fundamental principles of our system, both the economic principles of Adam Smith, which explain how it is that a complex, organized,

society is an arbitrary moral decision; business does not have to operate that way. Indeed, the choice is highly questionable when one reviews the development of capitalism and the corporate form.

THE ROLE OF BUSINESS IN OUR SOCIETY

> Ill fares the land, to hastening ills a prey,
> Where wealth accumulates, and men decay
> —Oliver Goldsmith (1730–1774)[33]

Business is the dominant social institution in U.S. society today and soon will be the dominant institution on the planet.[34] The number of corporations in the United States has increased from about 500,000 in 1940 to over 4.47 million in 1995, an increase of almost 900%(Fig. 20.1). [35] Assets controlled by U.S. corporations have increased from about $300 billion in 1935 to $26 trillion in 1995, an increase of 8,600% (Fig. 20.2).[36]

Institutions that control significant social assets and wield awesome financial power have a corresponding responsibility to use those assets and that power in ways that make good sense for the society generally. In other words, responsibility or duties accompany any grant of power.[37] This is true in the legal world, but it also is true in society generally. A grant of a power of attorney carries with it certain fiduciary obligations. Similarly when one takes a commission as an officer in the Armed Forces, the authority granted carries with it serious responsibilities. In a representative society, the irresponsible use of power, over time, results in the loss of that power or the reduction of it by regulation and law.[38] Financial power carries social responsibility. It is unavoidable. Figures 20.1 and 20.2 graphically show the growth of business.[39]

---

smoothly running system can develop and flourish without central direction, how coordination can be achieved without coercion (Chapter 1); and the political principles expressed by Thomas Jefferson (Chapter 5). We must understand why it is that attempts to replace cooperation by central direction are capable of doing so much harm (Chapter 2). We must understand also the intimate connection between political freedom and economic freedom.

See also Milton Friedman, *The Social Responsibility of Business Is to Increase Its Profits*, N.Y. TIMES (Sunday Supplement) (September 13, 1970) at 32 ff. Friedman declares "there is one and only one social responsibility of business—to use its resources and engage in activities designed to increase its profits so long as it stays within the rules of the game." *Id.* at 124 quoting from FRIEDMAN'S CAPITALISM AND FREEDOM (1970).

33. *The Deserted Village*, (1770) l.51 as quoted in ANGELA PARTINGTON, THE CONCISE OXFORD DICTIONARY OF QUOTATIONS (3rd ed. 1993) at 154.
34. *See, e.g.*, WILLIAM GREIDER, ONE WORLD, READY OR NOT: THE MANIC LOGIC OF GLOBAL CAPITALISM (1997).
35. Data from the U.S. Bureau of the Census.
36. *Id.*
37. *See* WESLEY NEWCOMB HOHFELD, FUNDAMENTAL LEGAL CONCEPTIONS (Walter Wheeler Cook, ed., 1923). Hohfeld produced works on analytical jurisprudence, and one of his propositions can be loosely rendered, "creation of a right simultaneously creates a corresponding duty."
38. "In the long run, those who do not use power in a manner that society considers responsible will tend to lose it." This is the "Iron Law of Responsibility" according to KEITH DAVIS & ROBERT L. BLOMSTROM, BUSINESS AND SOCIETY: ENVIRONMENT AND RESPONSIBILITY (1975) at 50 as quoted in DONNA J. WOOD, BUSINESS AND SOCIETY (1990) at 123.
39. Data for the graphs came from the following sources: Years 1930–1970 from U.S. DEPT. OF COMMERCE, BUREAU OF THE CENSUS, HISTORICAL STATISTICS OF THE UNITED STATES (Bicentennial ed. Sept. 1975) at 914, 924–925; the year 1975 from U.S. DEPT. OF COMMERCE, BUREAU OF THE CENSUS, STATISTICAL ABSTRACTS OF THE UNITED STATES (110th ed. 1990) at 525; and for years

| ■ **FIGURE 20.1** | Growth in the number of corporations, 1930—1995. |

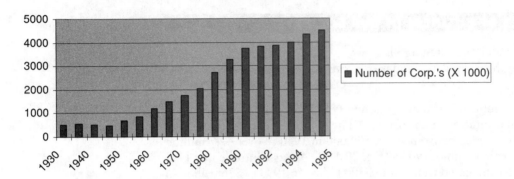

Ethics requires perspective.[40] Thus, I would be remiss not to acknowledge that we have one of the strongest economies, if not the strongest, in the history of Western civilization. Our vast natural resources, coupled with American labor and know-how, have generated unparalleled wealth.[41] However, if we do nothing else to continue the project of building our economy, if we become complacent and only stand back and admire, the backlash from global capitalism or some other similar social upheaval will catch us unprepared. Moreover, we may miss an opportunity to provide nonviolent and progressive solutions to some of the planet's pressing needs. I see no other social institution, no part of government, and no one in the nonprofit sector that seems as capable as business to provide these solutions.

No one is suggesting that profits are dirty or that business needs to stop making money. Yet, a healthier society might well result from trade-offs at the margin between maximum profits and decisions designed to promote community health. Profits are, as Kenneth Mason, the former CEO of Quaker Oats, argued, a necessary condition of corporate existence in the same way that getting enough to eat is a necessity of life.[42] Life's purpose, once existence is ensured, is higher, grander, and nobler than simply eating; the same goes for

1980–1995 from U.S. DEPT. OF COMMERCE, BUREAU OF THE CENSUS, STATISTICAL ABSTRACTS OF THE UNITED STATES (118th ed. 1998) at 544.

40. "In Aristotle's terms, ethics may be defined as the quest for, and the understanding of, the good life, living well, a life worth living, or, from the Greek, *eudaimonia*. The pursuit of *eudaimonia* is largely a matter of attempting to gain and maintain a balanced perspective on life." W. A. WINES, READINGS IN BUSINESS ETHICS AND SOCIAL RESPONSIBILITY (rev. ed. 1999) at 9.

41. Some divisions exist relative to America's prosperity:

> Consider two Asian views of America—perspectives an American in Asia learns to recognize as commonplace. One sees a land vast, rich, hard-driving, and innovative, fired by strange but intriguing democratic ideals, diversity and individual drive....
>
> Another view is less rosy and today is exploding in acceptance. It sees America as a nation of sloppy, loud-mouthed, poorly schooled people, quick to gripe and slow to work, a people grown unworthy of their national wealth and international position.

Tom Ashbrook, *Has U.S. Gotten Lazy?* THE BOSTON GLOBE (September 3, 1989).

42. Kenneth Mason, *Responsibility for What's on the Tube*, BUS. WEEK (August 13, 1979) at 14.

Growth in the assets controlled by U.S. corporations, 1930–1995.   ■ **FIGURE 20.2**

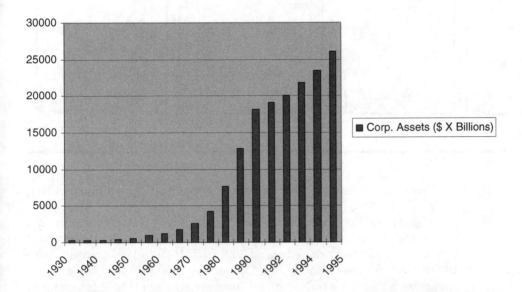

Corp. Assets ($ X Billions)

corporate profits. The pursuit of profits with no concern for the flourishing of the society is short-sighted and ultimately counterproductive.

American business history is replete with examples of this short-sighted pursuit of profits. For instance, closing plants in the so-called Rust Belt to move to the Southwest for lower taxes, no labor unions, and reduced regulation in the 1980s resulted in about 30 states passing plant-closing laws.[43] "I work for my shareholders, the public be damned," declared William Henry Vanderbilt (1821–1885), one of the robber barons, over a century ago.[44] Such attitudes brought about the passage of antitrust regulations and fair trade laws. Yet, Vanderbilt's disdain for the general society seems to be enjoying a revival, courtesy of Milton Friedman and other neoclassical economists.[45]

FALLOUT FROM THE DOMINANT PARADIGM

An United Nations Report released on Labor Day, 1999, indicated that the U.S. worker had passed the Japanese worker in hours worked per year in 1993.[46] On average in calendar year 1997, the American worker labored 1,966 hours or 83 hours more than in 1980 and 77 hours more than our nearest counterpart, the Japanese worker.[47]

---

43. *See* Angelo Kinicki et al., *Socially Responsible Plant Closings*, PERSONNEL ADMINISTRATOR (June 1987) at 116–128.
44. As quoted in a letter from A. W. Cole to the N.Y. TIMES (August 25, 1918).
45. *See, e.g.*, Milton Friedman, *The Social Responsibility of Business Is to Increase Its Profits*, N.Y. TIMES, Sunday Supplement, September 13, 1970 at 32 ff.
46. J. JOHNSON ET AL., KEY INDICATORS OF THE LABOR MARKET (1980–1997) as cited in Geir Moulson (AP), *Americans Work Harder, but Not Better*, SPOKESMAN-REVIEW (September 6, 1999) at A1.
47. *Id.*

THATCH/Jeff Shesol

French and German workers averaged 1,656 and 1,574 hours, respectively, in 1997.[48] In 1980, they worked 1,809 hours and 1,742 hours.[49] Yet, significantly, this trend toward fewer hours of work per year[50] was accompanied by a higher rate of increase in productivity than experienced in the United States.[51] U.S. labor productivity surged ahead 20% from 1980 to 1996 compared to a 38% increase for the Japanese, 31% for Germany, and 30% for France.[52] One possibility is that the layoffs in middle management and cuts in research and development (R & D) meant to make American business "leaner and meaner" have generated burnout, as well as a paucity of new product and promotion ideas.[53] The only employee sector that has really prospered is that of U.S. CEOs, whose pay has risen almost 500% between 1990 and 1998.[54]

Harvard economist Juliet Schor has already pointed out that the rising American workload "has contributed to a variety of social problems,"[55] including an increase in stress-related diseases, sleep deficits, sleep disorders, marital distress, child neglect, and a decline in leisure despite a tremendous advance in labor-saving technologies and appliances.[56] Almost half of couples with young children have one partner in the labor force at other than regular daytime hours.[57] This exacerbates the usual problems of poorer communication and

48. *Id.* at A8.

49. *Id.*

50. In France, legislation is pending that will decrease the national workweek from 39 to 35 hours. The maximum of 39 hours per week is enforced by government inspectors. If the legislation passes, companies will be required to maintain worker pay at the 39 hour per week level, an 11% wage increase. Thomas Sancton, *French Revolution: A Proposed 35-Hour Workweek Infuriates Bosses*, TIME (October 18, 1999) at 76.

51. *Id.*

52. *Id.*

53. America still leads the world in labor productivity, but the lead is smaller. Co-author of the study, Jeff Johnson, raised the possibility of burnout as one factor. *Id* at A1. For the impact of layoffs and decreased workplace privacy, *see* Wines and Fronmueller, *American Workers Seek to Establish a Right to Workplace Privacy in Law: Some Observations on the Social Context* (forthcoming) 78 NEB. L. REV. (Spring 2000).

54. *See* Susan English, *Consider This*, SPOKESMAN-REVIEW (September 26, 1999) at F10. "Is this what Reagan intended when he said, 'We're the party that wants to see an America where people can still get rich'? And we thought he meant all people, as in any one of us." *Id.*

55. JULIET B. SCHOR, THE OVERWORKED AMERICAN: THE UNEXPECTED DECLINE OF LEISURE (1991) at 11.

56. Id. at 11–15 ff.

57. *Id.* at 12.

less time together found in two-earner households. Researchers have found that having less time together reduces happiness and satisfaction in a marriage.[58] When one of the partners works the swing shift, the sense of "two ships passing in the night" is greatly heightened. Studies indicate that up to one in every three children spends time alone at home caring for him- or herself, and at least 500,000 preschoolers are thought to be left alone at home each day in this country.[59] We have become a nation of children raising children.[60]

The divorce rate reached 50% in the United States in the year 1990.[61] One third of all marriages now dissolve within 4 years.[62] In a sense, children get caught in the crossfire. A child in the 1990s had a one-in-five chance of experiencing two parental divorces before the age of 18 years.[63] Crime statistics[64] seem to parallel divorce rates in some areas. For instance, children under 10 years were 3 to 40 times more likely to suffer parental abuse if living with a stepparent and a biological parent than with two biological parents.[65] Some commentators have argued that childhood itself, a product of the Enlightenment, has virtually disappeared.[66]

So, what is human thriving? I believe that the essentials of human thriving are that everyone on the planet would have access to basic needs, such as clean water, an adequate diet, clean air, education, medical care, participatory government, freedom of movement, the right to private property, and—perhaps, most important of all—meaningful employment. The only social institution on the planet that can move us in that direction is business.

DEPARTURE FROM A DYSFUNCTIONAL PARADIGM

Reliance on a strict Friedmanian view[67] of corporate governance and strategy formulation has, as this discussion shows, not yielded the desired outcomes. Several decades of corporate "externalization" of social and ethical concerns, should, according to the classical model, have left its impact on the overall welfare of society. Thus, the desirability of this paradigm as a means for maximizing societal welfare must be questioned. Even for the purpose of achieving

---

58. *Id.*
59. *Id.*
60. *See, e.g., Revisiting 'The Baby Trap'*, PEOPLE WEEKLY (October 11, 1999) at 54–76. This was a 5-year follow-up on an article entitled *Babies Who Have Babies*, PEOPLE WEEKLY (October 24, 1994), cover story, bringing readers up to date on the lives of the 25 unwed teenagers profiled in the original story.
61. Robert Wright, *Our Cheating Hearts*, TIME (August 15, 1994) at 44, 51.
62. *Id.*
63. *Id.*
64. Professor L. R. Reynolds of the Economics Department at Boise State University has brought to my attention a study showing a high positive correlation between wealth distribution (the gap between haves and have-nots) and crime rates in industrialized nations; such wealth disparity also correlates with high numbers of imprisoned citizens.
65. *Id.*
66. *See, e.g.,* NEIL POSTMAN, THE DISAPPEARANCE OF CHILDHOOD (1982, Vintage Books ed. 1994).
67. Milton Friedman's view is that corporations are morally inert and that corporations have no social responsibility other than to maximize profits for stockholders within the boundaries of the law. *See, e.g.* Milton Friedman, *The Social Responsibility of Business Is to Increase Its Profits*, N.Y. TIMES (Sunday Supplement, September 13, 1970), as reprinted with permission in WINES (ED.), READINGS IN BUSINESS ETHICS AND SOCIAL RESPONSIBILITY (rev. ed. 1999) at 138–142.

corporate and shareholder wealth maximization, serious questions are raised by the slew of corporate catastrophes and disasters of the recent past.

Johns Manville Corporation, in its steadfast denial of the dangers of asbestos despite overwhelming scientific evidence to the contrary that included internal company documents, is one such example of a corporation that followed the Friedmanian view. Although clearly an example of unethical business practices because of the company's deception and outright lies, it is also one of the classical cases of an attempt to externalize the true costs of doing business. Not only are the costs of asbestos remediation and the human costs in terms of suffering and lost lives staggering but Johns Manville also represents a failure in terms of the alleged shareholder wealth maximization benefit. Shareholders in fact lost their wealth because Johns Manville ended up in Chapter 11 bankruptcy.

The pharmaceutical company R.H. Robbins, in a mistaken attempt to gain market leadership, ignored safety warnings in the development of its intrauterine device and, when evidence of is failure became widespread, refused to take responsibility for its actions. The resulting legal actions, although doing little to remedy the true social cost of this corporate failure, brought the company to near bankruptcy.

The major U.S. tobacco companies are yet another case where the Friedmanian paradigm appears to fail. Granted, several of these companies have attained economic dominance of gargantuan proportion. Some, such as Phillip Morris and R. J. Reynolds, have even managed to transfer this dominance into other related industries. It remains to be seen, however, what the final impact of tobacco litigation will be on these corporate giants. Even Phillip Morris, I suggest, will be negatively affected by a series of monetary judgments in the hundreds of millions.

To overcome these obvious failures of the Friedmanian paradigm, a new approach to corporate strategy is needed. This new approach must explicitly recognize the need for ethical behavior and social responsiveness. Moreover, the new approach must move beyond the mere recognition of ethics and include the active pursuit of ethical and responsive behavior. Some believe that a stakeholder approach to management would be the right approach; others see no inherent superiority to stakeholder management and no ethical basis for it.

SOME CONCLUSIONS

In his book, *The Good Life and Its Discontents*, Robert J. Samuelson discusses the change in attitude among Americans after the end of World War II in 1945.[68] Samuelson writes that our current pessimism is a direct reaction to the excessive optimism—euphoria, if you will—of the early postwar decades. He claims that Americans now display an entitlement attitude that contributes to the current malaise, entitlement as in "I didn't get the promotion/bonus/raise that I was entitled to." The change, according to Samuelson, is profound. The earlier understanding of the American Dream had to do with opportunity; that is, "America is great because I have the opportunity to succeed." Now, many Americans are bitter whenever they fail to experience uninterrupted

---

68. ROBERT J. SAMUELSON, THE GOOD LIFE AND ITS DISCONTENTS: THE AMERICAN DREAM IN THE AGE OF ENTITLEMENT 1945–1995 (1995).

personal and social progress. People feel entitled to results and are not happy with "just" the opportunity to succeed. The result is a psychological dance that dallies with perpetual disappointment. Samuelson suggests that the cure is a sense of proportion that evokes an ethic of responsibility.[69]

Additionally, it seems that Americans are experiencing a spiritual crisis, even as they fail to recognize it as such. At least two writers[70] suggest that we Americans (a generalization with significant exceptions to be sure) have elevated the free market to the position of God. Neil Postman declares that we cannot address the crisis in American schools until we recognize that it is first and foremost a spiritual emptiness rather than an engineering or mechanical problem that we need to fix.[71] Yet, whenever people speak of how we should go about improving public education, someone invariably suggests that competition (i.e., the free market) is the solution.

Instead, I suggest that despair and disillusionment are the problem and that more free market ideology is not the solution. Indeed, the blind, uninformed faith in the free market is a big part of our social problems. Americans live in a frenzied, almost an end-of-the-world-the-sky-is-falling haste. I believe this springs from a sense of isolation and from a lack of any spiritual anchor. I am reminded of two men I knew: one a Catholic priest and the other a candidate for a ministerial post. The first, believing that the end of the world was at hand from his readings of Revelation and because of his emotional problems, began to have sexual relations with two simple-minded young women who were entrusted to him for spiritual guidance. He ended up disgraced and in prison. The second lived his life as though he never was in a hurry. He walked, never ran, and always took time to help those in need or those who asked his help. His serenity was his witness. He lived out his life quietly as a pastor in small-town America, caring for those he believed were his spiritual brothers and sisters, and trusting that his times were in the hands of the Almighty.

Do not misunderstand what I propose. I am not proselytizing for any brand of organized religion. Indeed, the opposite might be the case. I am suggesting that the answers to our discontents lead us toward an outward manifestation of a sense of community rooted in an inner discipline and a spiritual faith. I also agree with Gandhi that "there must be more to life than merely increasing its speed." If we wish, as a nation, to address our discontents, we should slow down our lives, get more involved with family, participate in community activities, and strive to restrain our tendencies toward workaholism and materialism.

---

69. *Id.* at 218–231.
70. THOMAS FRANK, ONE MARKET UNDER GOD (2000); and Harvey Cox, *The Market as God: Living in the New Dispensation*, THE ATLANTIC MONTHLY (March 1999) at 18–23.
71. NEIL POSTMAN, THE END OF EDUCATION (1995).

CHAPTER
21

Success and the American Dream

The moral flabbiness born of the exclusive worship of the bitch-goddess SUC-CESS. That—with the squalid cash interpretation put on that word success—is our national disease.

—William James[1]

I believe this now without question: income, position, the opinion of one's friends, the judgment of one's peers and all the other traditional criteria by which human beings are generally judged are for the birds.

—James A. Michener[2]

Success is a lousy teacher. It seduces smart people into thinking they can't lose. And it's an unreliable guide to the future.

—Bill Gates[3]

INTRODUCTION

Ralph Waldo Emerson reportedly observed, "It is to that itch to succeed that never gives us a moment's rest that we owe the best and the worst of what is in us."[4] This chapter explores various competing notions of what it means to be a successful human being in a society that is dominated by the institution of business,[5] that is corrupted by materialism,[6] and that is obsessed with sex.[7] Does the one who dies with the most toys win? Is winning what human life is about? Could cooperation rather than competition be the basis for modern society?[8] Where does happiness fit in? Could success involve process, rather than product or destination? Is it conceivable that such a process might involve a dynamic balance between public and private life, as well as between our material and spiritual natures? Might it also be true that success involves movement on the moral and spiritual development planes?

After examining the threshold issue of whether life has meaning, this chapter explores these and related questions. At the outset, let me note that the prestigious "Great Books" series[9] does not list "success" as one of the 102 great ideas that are the topics of the "Great Conversation."[10] By way of contrast, it does list "happiness" and "virtue."[11]

---

1. William James, letter to H. G. Wells (September 11, 1906) as quoted in AMERICAN HERITAGE DICTIONARY OF AMERICAN QUOTATIONS, Margaret Miner & Hugh Rawson, eds. (1997) at 478.
2. James A. Michener, *On Wasting Time*, READER'S DIGEST (October, 1974) at 196.
3. BILL GATES, THE ROAD AHEAD (1995) at 35.
4. EMERSON as quoted in P. SETHI, UP AGAINST THE CORPORATE WALL (4th ed. 1982) at vi.
5. Sharon Daloz Parks, *Is It Too Late? Young Adults and the Formation of Professional Ethics*, THOMAS R. PIPER, ET AL., CAN ETHICS BE TAUGHT: PERSPECTIVES, CHALLENGES, AND APPROACHES AT HARVARD BUSINESS SCHOOL (1993) 13–72 at 16.
6. *See, e.g.*, EARL SHORRIS, A NATION OF SALESMEN: THE TYRANNY OF THE MARKET AND THE SUB-VERSION OF CULTURE (1994).
7. *See, e.g.*, Paul Recer (AP), *Sex More Important Than Job Satisfaction, Survey Finds*, ID. STATESMAN (April 30, 1999) at 7A, wherein the author cites the results of a national survey by a professor of medicine at Columbia University.
8. *See, e.g.*, WILLIAM F. ALLMAN, THE STONE AGE PRESENT (1994, Touchstone ed. 1995) for one argument that human society is dominated by cooperation, rather than competition.
9. THE GREAT BOOKS OF THE WESTERN WORLD (Phillip W. Goetz, editor-in-chief, 2nd ed. 1990, 3rd printing 1992).
10. THE GREAT CONVERSATIONS: A READER'S GUIDE TO GREAT BOOKS OF THE WESTERN WORLD (Phillip W. Goetz, editor-in-chief, 2nd ed. 1990, 3rd printing 1992) at 99.
11. *Id.*

Non-Sequitur   Wiley Miller

©Universal Press Syndicate.

SOME PRELIMINARY MATTERS

The poet Matthew Arnold challenged us to "see life steadily and see it whole."[12] If we adopt that notion and seek an ethical perspective, we must include modern scientific knowledge as an important aspect of our perspective. We live in a universe that is expanding at the speed of light—186,000 miles per second.[13] Our planet is not the center of the universe as the ancient and medieval world thought[14]; it is not even close to the center. We live on the "third rock from the Sun"[15] in a remote corner of a galaxy[16] that is in a remote corner of a

12. Matthew Arnold, *To a Friend*, as quoted in PERSPECTIVES ON MORALITY: ESSAYS OF WILLIAM K. FRANKENA (Kenneth E. Goodpaster, ed., 1976) at 106.

13. The discovery of the fact that light travels at a finite but very high speed dates to 1676 and the work of the Danish astronomer, Ole Christensen Roemer. STEPHEN W. HAWKING, A BRIEF HISTORY OF TIME: FROM THE BIG BANG TO BLACK HOLES (1988) at 18–19. The current or modern value of the speed of light is 186,000 miles per second. *Id*. at 19. As noted by Professor Hawking, "Our modern picture of the universe dates back to only 1924 when the American astronomer Edwin Hubble demonstrated that ours was not the only galaxy." *Id*. at 36. Then in 1929, Hubble discovered that the universe was not static but expanding. This was "one of the great intellectual revolutions of the twentieth century." *Id*. at 39.

14. "Aristotle thought that the earth was stationary and that the sun, moon, and stars moved in circular orbits around the earth." He also believed that the earth was the center of the universe. Ptolemy in the second century A.D. elaborated this theory into a complete cosmological model. STEPHEN HAWKING, *supra* note 12 at 2. This model was endorsed by the Christian church and enforced until the 16th and 17th centuries when Copernicus, Kepler, Galileo, and Newton established through a series of discoveries that the earth orbited the sun. *Id*. at 3–5.

15. *See, e.g.*, THE WORLD BOOK ENCYCLOPEDIA (1990) vol. 6, at 18. Mercury and Venus are the two planets that are closer to the sun than is the earth. The earth is 93 million miles from the sun. *Id*.

16. The earth is a huge sphere, with an equatorial circumference of 24,901.55 miles; it is one of nine planets that orbit our sun. The sun is a star, one of billions that make up a galaxy called the Milky Way. The Milky Way and billions of other galaxies make up the known universe. THE WORLD BOOK ENCYCLOPEDIA (1990) vol. 6, at 16–17.

cosmos that is over 16 billion light years across.[17] In the view of some distinguished scientists, our planet is about as significant in this cosmos as a grain of sand is on a huge beach.[18] This information about the cosmos and our virtual insignificance is mind-boggling.

Despair and disillusionment are the avenues that many follow once they have truly gotten a grasp of the insignificance of humankind in the larger scheme of things. How can anyone who understands the significance of our relationship to cosmos still believe that humankind is the crowning achievement of a Creator who has generated this awesome creation?[19] In response, one segment of the existentialists, led by Albert Camus[20] and others, argued that life is absurd.[21] If life is absurd, then it would make no sense to talk about a successful life—in business or anywhere else. However, as one pair of authors point out, "The suicidal renunciation of life under this condition stems from a failure to realize that we can live in conscious defiance of this absurdity."[22] They go on to argue that Camus asserted that such acts of defiance create value and can ultimately make our lives worthwhile.[23]

Another group of philosophers argue that life can only have meaning within the context of the existence of a much larger enterprise. Metaphysicians and religious writers often seek to discover life's meaning in something that either embraces or transcends all existence.[24] "According to the theistic answer," E. D. Klemke writes, "the meaning of life is found in the existence of a God—a supremely benevolent and all-powerful being, transcendent to the natural universe, but who created the universe, and fashioned man in his image and endowed him with a preordained purpose."[25] In this view, as Klemke notes, life has no meaning and no purpose without the existence of God or without faith in God.[26] This position is seldom defended from a purely philosophic position, but almost always rests on, at least partially, some religious tenet.

Julian Huxley advances a nontheistic position of scientific humanism in an essay entitled "The Creed of a Scientific Humanist."[27] He argues that life can be worth living, but not necessarily so; that humanity can find a satisfying purpose in existence, without one inhering in the universe; and that many people have lived noble lives without belief in either a deity or a hereafter. Ultimately, Huxley says he believes in a hierarchy of values and has faith in a concrete and comprehensive idea of life, both its abundance and its progress.[28]

At one point, Huxley states that the meaning of life is one of a "number of questions that it is no use our asking, because they can never be answered."[29] He says the attempt to answer the question of the meaning of life reminded him of the story about a philosopher and a theologian. "[T]he theologian used the old quip about a philosopher resembling a blind man, in a dark room, looking

17. THE WORLD BOOK ENCYLCOPEDIA, (1990), vol. 20 at 195.
18. *See, e.g.*, CARL SAGAN, COSMOS (1980).
19. *See, e.g.*, MARK TWAIN, LETTERS FROM THE EARTH (1974, originally published 1909).
20. ALBERT CAMUS, THE STRANGER (English translation for Knopf Everyman ed., 1993).
21. THE MEANING OF LIFE: QUESTIONS, ANSWERS, AND ANALYSIS (Steven Sanders & David R. Cheney, ed. 1980) at 7–8.
22. *Id.* at 8.
23. *Id.*
24. *Id.* at 5.
25. E. D. Klemke, *Introduction to the Question of the Meaning of Life*, THE MEANING OF LIFE (E. D. Klemke, ed., 2nd ed. 2000) at 3.
26. *Id.*
27. *Id.* at 78–83.
28. *Id.*
29. *Id.* at 79.

Desiderata

Go placidly amid the noise and the haste, and remember what peace there may be in silence. As far as possible without surrender be on good terms with all persons. Speak your truth quietly and clearly; and listen to others, even to the dull and the ignorant, they too have their story. Avoid loud and aggressive persons, they are vexations to the spirit.

If you compare yourself with others, you may become vain or bitter; for always there will be greater and lesser persons than yourself. Enjoy your achievements as well as your plans. Keep interested in your own career, however humble; it is a real possession in the changing fortunes of time.

Exercise caution in your business affairs, for the world is full of trickery. But let not this blind you to what virtue there is; many persons strive for high ideals, and everywhere life is full of heroism. Be yourself. Especially do not feign affection. Neither be cynical about love; for in the face of all aridity and disenchantment it is as perennial as the grass.

Take kindly the counsel of the years, gracefully surrendering the things of youth.

Nurture strength of spirit to shield you in sudden misfortune. But do not distress yourself with dark imaginings. Many fears are born of fatigue and loneliness. Beyond a wholesome discipline, be gentle with yourself. You are a child of the universe, no less than the trees and the stars; you have a right to be here. And whether or not it is clear to you, no doubt the universe is unfolding as it should.

Therefore, be at peace with God, whatever you conceive Him to be. And whatever your labors and aspirations in the noisy confusion of life, keep peace in your soul. With all its sham, drudgery and broken dreams; it is still a beautiful world. Be cheerful.

Strive to be happy.

—Max Ehrmann (1927).

for a black cat—which wasn't there. 'That may be,' said the philosopher: 'but a theologian would have found it.'"[30]

Klenke's well-known anthology on the meaning of life divides its selections into three sections: (1) those that give a theistic answer, such as an essay by Leo Tolstoy; (2) those that give a nontheistic answer, such as essays by Camus, Schopenhauer, Bertrand Russell, and Julian Huxley; and (3) those that question the question of meaning itself, such as essays by R. M. Hare and A. J. Ayer.[31] Another anthology also divides its selections into three, somewhat differently labeled groups: (1) essays raising questions about the meaning of life, (2) essays that provide answers to the questions of life, and (3) essays not directly concerned with either of the above two approaches, but providing a line of inquiry into examining key concepts and presuppositions of claims about the meaning of life.[32]

Whether or not we should question asking the question about the meaning of life is a matter that I leave to the reader. Certainly, this chapter cannot resolve what is perhaps the most profound question of human existence. Some of the great philosophers and theologians have grappled with this issue for millennia. The question of life's meaning must be acknowledged certainly. If life itself has no meaning, then an essay on how to lead a successful life would be pointless. For our purposes, I simply acknowledge that some agree with the theistic position and some agree with the nontheistic position, and then *I posit axiomatically that life has meaning* and move on.

30. *Id.*
31. THE MEANING OF LIFE (E. D. Klemke, ed., 2nd ed. 2000).
32. Sanders & Cheney, *supra* note 22, at ix.

A final philosophical issue that must be acknowledged before we can proceed is the one of determinism.[33] Some scholars, notably Paul Edwards and John Hospers, hold that human beings do not make valid choices and that choice is an illusion.[34] This is the position of determinism. If one takes that position, then one must be prepared either to radically restructure the moral institutions of life or drop the idea of moral philosophy (i.e., the "good life") altogether because without meaningful choice the entire field of morality disappears.[35] If we choose determinism, this chapter ends here. Some philosophers posit two variations of determinism: loose determinism and nondeterminism (indeterminism).[36] Consequently, I axiomatically state my belief that human beings do make real choices, either under loose determinism or nondeterminism. Having made that statement, let us now turn to the enduring and evolving American Dream.

THE EVOLVING AMERICAN DREAM

The elusive American Dream changes and evolves with American society. It used to be relatively simple: The American Dream was to be free and to have the opportunity to compete for the available wealth. One observer writes that since the end of World War II in 1945 the American Dream has become a fantasy that is based on the perfectionist elimination of social ills and on notions of entitlement.[37] Under the old dream, Americans were given opportunity, albeit imperfect and uneven, but opportunity nonetheless, and if they failed to achieve material success, no one blamed America. Now, under the prevailing fashion of "victimology," any failure must be seen as the fault of others—the schools, government, big business, the legal system, or the "isms," such as sexism, racism, etc. Thus, the notion of entitlement to the American Dream's goal of success[38] has replaced notions of freedom and opportunity and rugged but accountable individualism.[39] Citizens get their due—namely success—or else get to claim they have been victims of social injustice. This, of course, simplifies the picture, but it does lay out in broad strokes a significant change in social attitudes.[40] Putting aside for now the issue of entitlement and

---

33. For a general discussion of determinism, see WILLIAM K. FRANKENA, ETHICS (2nd ed. 1973) at 71–78.
34. *Id.* at 76.
35. *Id.*
36. *See, e.g.,* JOSEPH B. MCALLISTER, ETHICS: WITH SPECIAL APPLICATION TO THE MEDICAL AND NURSING PROFESSIONS (1955) at 25–27.
37. ROBERT J. SAMUELSON, THE GOOD LIFE AND ITS DISCONTENTS (1995) at xiii, 16–17.
38. Of course, many do not share this goal of success. One of the best counterculture odes against success is a folk song written by Malvina Reynolds:

> I don't mind wearing raggedy britches
> Because them that succeeds are sons of bitches.
> I don't mind failing in this world.
> I'll stay down here with the raggedy crew
> If gettin' up there means steppin' on you.

Quoted in STUDS TERKEL, AMERICAN DREAMS: LOST & FOUND (1980) at 41.
39. *Supra*, note 1.
40. Myths can be powerful forces for good or evil. Values are transmitted very effectively to the next generation by stories and myths; some are benign, some positive, and others pernicious. To quote two observers of the American scene: "All mythologies contain a vision of what we aspire to be and have within them the purgatory of destructive thoughts. Myth illuminates and projects a light in the darkness of reality and the haze of misperception over the glow of

whether the thesis is sound, let us turn our attention to the question, What is success?

One dictionary definition of success is reaching a goal, whatever that goal may be.[41] As we descend the list of definitions, success is defined as "favorable or desired outcome; *also:* the attainment of wealth, favor, or eminence."[42] Finally, the last definition of success is "the one that succeeds."[43] At this stage, the person, rather than the activity, becomes a "success." In the White male consciousness, the opposite of success is "poor." In our society, dominated by business (a White male institution), corrupted by materialism, and obsessed with sex, this equation of success with wealth and poverty with failure is the ultimate simplification—a grotesque reduction of human life to material acquisition.

Calvin Coolidge, the 30th president of the United States said, "The chief end of man is wealth."[44] This is, at one level, blasphemous because it is a play on words of the Presbyterian Catechism that teaches that the "chief end of man is to worship God and abide with Him forever."[45] In another way, this statement takes us full circle to the central issues of classical education: What are the nature and the destiny of humankind?[46] Coolidge's answer, and we can hope that he spoke in jest, was that humans live exclusively to accumulate wealth. Such an answer would, if seriously given, suggest that capitalism had replaced both religion and ethics.

This severing of the human spirit from the definition of what it means to be successful contributes to the impoverishment of American life and culture. However, the separation predates U.S. culture, even as it finds its apotheosis in it. The early Christian Church renounced wealth in its teachings, even as it attempted to deal with the spiritual mystery of a messiah who was both man and God.[47] The mystery is that of understanding spirit and physical being (i.e., biological matter) fused into one. Greek thinking that had for centuries taught the dichotomy of spirit and matter rebelled at such teaching. One philosopher asserts, "The challenge of economic life, the challenge of living in a way that is adequate for our material needs, is to make that life serve the spiritual aspirations."[48] He continues as follows:

> In sum, the Christian Church presented a picture of hypocrisy and corruption. Condemning the sexual nature of man, the leaders of the Church indulged their sexual needs. Warning against greed and

truth. It is our task to distinguish between those myths that give us light and those that blind our vision." H. I. LONDON & ALBERT L. WEEKS, MYTHS THAT RULE AMERICA (1981) at xvii.

41. WEBSTER'S COLLEGIATE DICTIONARY (10th ed. 1995) at 217. *See also* WEBSTER'S NEW WORLD DICTIONARY (3rd college ed. 1994) at 1337. This idea of success as the achievement of a goal may have become corrupted in popular thought among adolescents to be understood as celebrity or fame. In an interview, the internationally acclaimed author Salman Rushdie stated, "A graduating class of high school kids [in England] was asked what they wanted to be, and something like three-quarters of them answered that they wanted to be famous. I mean, as if that were a career. Famous for *what* didn't occur to them....Anything would do. Performing a blow job on the president or murdering your wife. Albert Schweitzer or Monica Lewinsky, same thing. It is the curse of our time." Salman Rushdie, MOTHER JONES (July/August 1999) at 64.
42. *Id.*
43. *Id.*
44. DAVID E. SHI, THE SIMPLE LIFE (1985) at 217.
45. *Id.*
46. *See, e.g.*, ALLEN BLOOM, THE CLOSING OF THE AMERICAN MIND (1987).
47. JACOB NEEDLEMAN, MONEY AND THE MEANING OF LIFE (1991) at 68 ff.
48. *Id.* at 69.

avarice, the Church and monasteries amassed wealth and political power which they were unable to deal with in ethically balanced ways. Much later in history—in the early part of the twentieth century—the question of sex became largely excluded from the rule of religious influence. That is what the Freudian revolution effected. But as for the material desires of man, these became separated off from the influence of the Christian teaching much earlier, under the banner of Protestantism. The earliest name for this state of affairs in which the conduct of economic life became cut off from the influence of spiritual ideals was and now still is: *Capitalism* [italics in original].[49]

OUTCOME OR PRODUCT MODELS OF SUCCESS

In a number of circles, it is fashionable to think about success as a goal or a destination. This is true especially in business circles where managers and others are exhorted to succeed. It may be a reflection of American business's domination for so long by White males that an "outcome" is frequently the first thing that comes to mind when the subject of success is broached. The following are seven models or paradigms of success:

1. materialism or the accumulated wealth model (Bill Gates or Andrew Carnegie)
2. Emersonian or *mensch* model (Fred Rogers of "Mr. Rogers' Neighborhood" fame)
3. sainthood or step 6 of the Kohlberg scale (prophetic morality) or the universalizing faith model (Gandhi or Mother Teresa)
4. self-actualization as in Abraham Maslow's top step in his hierarchy (Nelson Zink)
5. "hero/heroine" model (Charles Lindbergh or Audie Murphy)
6. biological/genetic success model (spawning salmon or Brigham Young)
7. top of the heap/competitive—one sport model (Clarence Darrow, Wilt Chamberlain, Babe Ruth)

Let us examine these models in turn to ascertain the nature, strengths, and weaknesses of each. This discussion is intended to be neither definitive nor exhaustive, but seeks rather to promote critical thought about models of success that many of us have inherited or have been programmed culturally to accept.

MATERIALISM OR ACCUMULATED WEALTH MODEL

Under this model, the "one who dies with the most toys wins." Naturally, the next question is, Wins what? Dickens lampooned this idea in his *A Christmas Carol*.[50] Ebeneezer Scrooge is confronted by the ghost of his dead partner Jacob Marley, who scolds him for his penny-pinching ways. When Scrooge says that Marley was always a good man of business, the apparition responds in these words: "Mankind was my business. The common welfare was my business; charity, mercy, forbearance, and benevolence were, all, my business.

---

49. *Id.* at 69–70.
50. CHARLES DICKENS, A CHRISTMAS CAROL AND OTHER CHRISTMAS STORIES (Children's Classics ed., 1987; first published in 1843) at 30.

The dealings of my trade were but a drop of water in the comprehensive ocean of my business!"[51]

A search of the catalogue holdings of the Boise State University library disclosed 610 titles under the subject of success; of those titles, the single largest subheading contained 165 that dealt with success in business. In contrast, 37 treated the subject of self-realization, 6 dealt with success in literature, and only 2 titles contained information on success in teaching. Clearly, the implication is that, in the area of success, the Big Kahuna is business success, and in business, people keep score with dollars.

The American Dream, many people believe, is to amass a comfortable amount of wealth, to enjoy the so-called good things in life. A variation of this idea is that we should live and work to guarantee that our children are better off (usually in the financial sense) than we were. Some would call this progress, rather than success. There are some indications that the American Dream has more appeal to those emigrating to the United States than to natives.[52] Taking the above measures literally and in their simplest configurations, they are purely materialistic measures of success. Moreover, such measures lack any referent to community, to a spiritual dimension of life, or to any dimension of humanity other than work and wealth accumulation.

EMERSON OR *MENSCH* MODEL

Ralph Waldo Emerson proposed that success involved such things as "toiling on that plot of ground which is given to [you] to till."[53] One quote, frequently misattributed to Emerson, advocated that one could be a success merely by "appreciating beauty; finding the best in others; giving one's self; leaving this world a bit better whether by a healthy child, a garden patch, or a redeemed social condition; playing and laughing with enthusiasm and singing with exultation; or by knowing that even one life breathed easier because of you."[54]

---

51. *Id.*
52. *See, e.g., Nora, Maria and the American Dream,* THE ECONOMIST (March 9, 2000). Accessed at http://www2.economist.com/surveys/PrinterFriendly.cfm?Story_ID=289853 on August 3, 2004.
53. Ralph Waldo Emerson, *Essay on Self-Reliance,* as found in CARL BODE AND MALCOLM COWLEY (EDS.), THE PORTABLE EMERSON (1981) at 139.
54. Actually, this quotation is often attributed to Ralph Waldo Emerson, but he did not write it. The quotation in full is:

> To laugh often and much; to win the respect of intelligent people and the affection of children; to earn the appreciation of honest critics and endure the betrayal of false friends; to appreciate beauty; to find the best in others; to leave the world a bit better, whether by a healthy child, a garden patch or a redeemed social condition; to know that even one life has breathed easier because you have lived. This is to have succeeded.

These words were written in 1905 by Bessie A. Stanley (b. 1879) in an essay that won first place in a contest sponsored by *Modern Women,* a magazine. It is possible that Ms. Stanley was influenced by these lines written by Robert Louis Stevenson:

> He has achieved success who has lived well, laughed often and loved much; who has enjoyed the trust of pure women, the respect of intelligent men and the love of little children; who has filled his niche and accomplished his task; who has left the world better than he found it, whether by an improved poppy, a perfect poem, or a rescued soul; who has never lacked appreciation of earth's beauty or failed to express it; who has always looked for the best in others and given them the best he had; whose life was an inspiration; whose memory is a benediction.

Accessed at http://www.chebucto.ns.ca/~ac230/emerson/success.html on November 30, 1999.

This definition of success is idealistic but also holistic in the sense that it provides a universal standard that is available to all of humanity, regardless of circumstance. It incorporates notions of community as well as self. In short, it seems to prescribe a formula, if taken metaphorically or literally, that can be said to make one fully human, (i.e., a *mensch*). The weakness of this approach seems to lie in its deceptive easiness, for in fact, as a daily formula for living the Emerson approach, it presents significant challenges.

Defining success as "leaving this world a better place whether by a garden patch, a healthy child or a redeemed social condition" is nontraditional and perhaps even countercultural. Emerson also argued, "Whoso would be a man must first be a nonconformist."[55] Further, he essayed, "Nothing is at last sacred but the integrity of your own mind"[56] and "Few and mean as my gifts may be, I actually am, and do not need for my own assurance or the assurance of my fellows any secondary testimony."[57] These lines and the accompanying essay suggest that life is not a race and that a good life should be measured by its integrity and virtue, not its accumulation.

Focusing on success in the sense of what it means to lead a successful life or to be a success as a human being narrows our inquiry. In a deeper sense it makes the inquiry more difficult because it requires us to confront eternal questions. The Yiddish word *mensch* is defined as "a sensible, mature, responsible person."[58] The derivation given is from Old High German, *mannisco*, meaning human. The translation is inadequate because to call someone a *mensch* is to bestow high praise, to declare that such a person is fully human in all the best senses of that term.[59]

The Talmud tells of a dying rabbi surrounded by his students. As he lay dying, one of the students asked him, "Rabbi, do you have any thoughts of the next life?" The rabbi replied, "Yes, in the next world, I will not be asked why I was not Moses but why I was not a better version of myself." This seems to be a view toward which Emerson would be sympathetic. Success lies in taking an honest and fearless inventory of your strengths and weaknesses and of the work to which you find a calling. This approach is not entirely inconsistent with the 1960s counterculture that challenged the values of the "Establishment" and urged a greater sense of community and a deemphasis on material success.[60]

In his book, *The Simple Life*, David Shi characterizes Emerson and the Transcendental movement as working to simplify their material and institutional needs so that they could devote more time and energy to "spiritual truths, moral ideals, and aesthetic impulses."[61] Their credo, as expressed by William Henry Channing, was "to live content with small means; to seek elegance rather than luxury, and refinement rather than fashion; to be worthy, not respectable, and wealthy, not rich; to study hard, think quietly, talk gently, act frankly."[62] In sum, the simple life for Emerson and his disciple Thoreau

---

55. *Self-Reliance, supra* note 54, at 141.
56. *Id.*
57. *Id.* at 143.
58. WEBSTER'S NEW WORLD DICTIONARY (3rd college ed., 1972) at 847.
59. Reportedly, years ago, a former Israeli prime minister was asked about Ariel Sharon, the current prime minister of Israel and an authentic military hero and replied, "Sharon is a brilliant general but he will never be a *mensch*." Achieving *mensch-hood* can be considered the hallmark of success as a human being.
60. ANNIE GOTTLEIB, DO YOU BELIEVE IN MAGIC? THE SECOND COMING OF THE 60's GENERATION (1987) at 124–162.
61. DAVID E. SHI, THE SIMPLE LIFE (1985) at 127–128.
62. *Id* at 128.

involved grafting a form of religious free thinking, philosophical idealism, and literary romanticism onto the trunk of the core of their Puritan heritage in order to transcend the limits of Lockean rationalism and penetrate the inner recesses of the self.[63] In many ways, this movement paralleled the earlier Quaker movement.

At the start of this chapter, a James A. Michener quote debunks "traditional criteria by which human beings are judged." Michener does not advocate much beyond venturing to try out as many pursuits as one finds interesting and possible before one reaches the age of 35 years. He then suggests that a person settle down into a calling if that person means to make a constructive contribution to society.[64] After debunking traditional criteria of success, Michener writes that the only important question is whether a person "can hang on through the crap" the world throws at him or her without losing either freedom or good sense.[65]

The poet Gray makes a similar point, but somewhat more directly than Michener: "Success lies not in doing what others think great but in what you think is right." Because this approach emphasizes moral duty, it should be distinguished from Emerson and more properly labeled a Kantian approach to success.[66] A singular devotion to moral duty rejects the holistic, mystic, and individualistic approach of Emerson and reflects the moral rigidity of Immanuel Kant's ethics. If rightness is, for some, equated with justice, then we might invoke Lawrence Kohlberg's work[67] and talk of moral development along the path of righteousness as success. Alternatively, we might examine Carol Gilligan's ethics of care[68] and take a feminist approach to moral development.[69] Although this approach is still nontraditional, it might then pick up some of the flavor of the Psalms and also echo some of the strains of spiritual development from Fowler.[70]

SAINTHOOD, PROPHETIC MORALITY, AND UNIVERSALIZING FAITH

Success could also be achieved in the minds of many by a person reaching sainthood. For secularists, anyone reaching Step 6 of Lawrence Kohlberg's scale for moral reasoning might qualify; others would be happy to accept anyone reaching John Fowler's Step 6 of faith development, the universalizing faith. Sainthood, for our purposes, is used more broadly than canonization in the Roman Catholic Church, although that might well be included. Sainthood would include all those who lived lives remarkable for piety or virtue, regardless of religious affiliation or lack thereof. Subsets of the sainthood category of success might include (a) asceticism (monks and hermits of the early Christian Church, the Greek ascetics/stoics, the Buddhist and Hindu ascetics, Hebrew

---

63. *Id.* at 126.
64. James A. Michener, *On Wasting Time*, READER'S DIGEST (October, 1974) at 194.
65. *Id.* at 196.
66. *See, e.g.*, IMMANUEL KANT, THE FUNDAMENTAL PRINCIPLES OF THE METAPHYSICS OF MORALS (1785, Prometheus ed. 1988, transl. by T.K. Abbott).
67. *See, e.g.*, BRENDA MUNSEY (ed.), MORAL DEVELOPMENT, MORAL EDUCATION, AND KOHLBERG (1980).
68. CAROL GILLIGAN, IN A DIFFERENT VOICE (1982).
69. For an excellent discussion of feminism and the ethics of care, see JAMES RACHELS, THE ELEMENTS OF MORAL PHILOSOPHY (4th ed. 2003) at 160–172.
70. JAMES W. FOWLER, STAGES OF FAITH: THE PSYCHOLOGY OF HUMAN DEVELOPMENT AND THE QUEST FOR MEANING (1981).

©The Nobel Foundation.

ascetics of the Qumran community[71] in the first century BCE, etc.); (b) Simple Living advocates (modern environmentalists); and (c) altruists who practice the self-sacrificing love ethic of Jesus.

Agnes Gonxha Bojaxhiu. Agnes Gonxha Bojaxhiu was born on August 27, 1910, in Skopje, Albania. She grew up in a well-off Christian family. While in high school, Agnes sensed her vocation and decided to become a missionary in India. In 1928, she joined the Sisters of Loreto. Thereafter, she went to Ireland for training and arrived in India in 1929. On taking her final vows, she took the name "Teresa," after the patroness of missionaries, St. Teresa of Lisieux.

In India, Mother Teresa worked as a principal and school teacher. It was in 1946 that Mother Teresa experienced her second vocation. She described the experience by saying, "I opened my eyes to suffering and understood the true essence of my calling." She founded an order of nuns in Calcutta, India, called the Missionaries of Charity.

Mother Teresa spent the rest of her life caring for the sick and needy. For Mother Teresa, it did not matter whether an individual was suffering from leprosy or AIDS. Of those in pain and suffering, Mother Teresa saw Jesus. She said, "They are Jesus. Each one is Jesus in a distressing disguise."

Although many called her a living saint, Mother Teresa saw herself as merely a servant of God. She dedicated her life to helping the poor, and that earned her the Nobel Prize for Peace in 1979. When she died on September 5, 1997, in her convent in India, the order that she started had grown from

---

71. *See, e.g.*, SHUSAKU ENDO, A LIFE OF JESUS (Richard A. Schuchert, S.J., trans. 1973) at 26–27 and KAREN ARMSTRONG, A HISTORY OF GOD (1993) at 71 and 80.

© Courtesy of the Pennsylvania Academy of the Fine Arts, Philadelphia.

12 nuns in Calcutta to over 3,000 in 517 missions spread throughout 100 countries worldwide.[72]

Thomas C. Eakins. Thomas Cowperthwait Eakins was born on July 25, 1844. After finishing high school, Eakins became a student at the Pennsylvania Academy of the Fine Arts in Philadelphia. He was very interested in the dynamics of the human body and took anatomy courses at Jefferson Medical College where he received the thorough anatomical training given to the medical students. Eakins then traveled to Paris to study art at Ecole des Beaux-Arts, which was viewed as the leading art academy of its day.

Eakins spent nearly 4 years studying in France and Spain. After returning to the United States, Eakins' primary goal was to succeed as a professional painter. Success as an American artist was difficult in 1870. American collectors prefered European art, and the American artists who did make names for themselves often imitated European styles.

Eakins began painting *The Gross Clinic* in 1875. The very descriptive painting portrays a surgical team, headed by a Dr. Gross, removing a piece of dead bone from the thigh of a patient in the amphitheater of Jefferson Medical College. Eakins felt this painting was far better than anything he had ever done. However, the painting was not well received and remained unsold for 2 years until it was purchased by the Alumni of Jefferson College. The price paid for the painting barely would have covered the cost of its frame.

Eakins became a professor of drawing and painting at the Philadelphia Academy in 1879 and later went on to become director of the schools.

> Caring far less about his public reputation than about his freedom to paint as he pleased, Eakins tenaciously upheld his principles, no matter what the cost. His candor regarding the nude led to his expulsion from his teaching position at the Pennsylvania Academy of the Fine Arts, prevented him from continuing his beneficial influence in art education, tarnished his personal reputation, and exiled him from the social and art-political circles in Philadelphia where he could have exerted considerable leadership.[73]

72. http://www.catholic.net/RCC/people/mother/teresa/teresa.html; http://www.catholic.net/RCC/Periodicals/Inside-0995/12-96/TERESA_WORD.html

73. WILLIAM INNES HOMER, THOMAS EAKINS: HIS LIFE AND ART (1992) at 8.

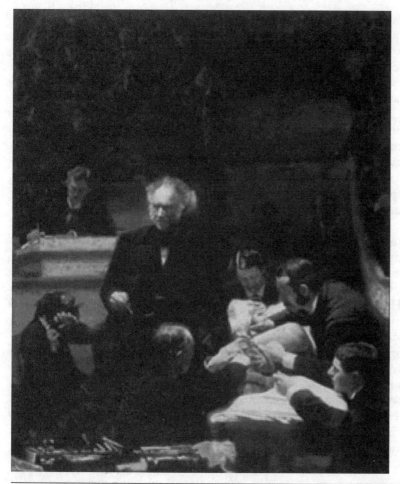

©*The Gross Clinic* by Thomas Eakins Metropolitan Museum of Art.

From 1875 through 1886, Eakins did not sell many paintings or win many portrait commissions. He received negative criticisms and rejections from critics in both New York and Philadelphia. For example, President Rutherford B. Hayes was not pleased with the commissioned portrait by Eakins, and it appeared in public only briefly.

Eakins died of heart failure in 1916. His reputation as an artist grew just after his death. Despite the lack of critical success, Thomas Eakins worked very hard throughout his life to become an accomplished painter, and he is now considered to be one of the best American painters of his time.

George Gershwin. George Gershwin was born in 1898 in Brooklyn of immigrant parents who had come to the United States from Russia. Gershwin had three other siblings, the oldest of whom was Ira Gershwin. It was Ira with whom George would spend his life creating music.

Gershwin began his musical career in 1914 working for a music publishing company. The company became "one of the most important publishers in Tin Pan Alley, the center for popular music in New York and the nation."[74] In his position selling sheet music, Gershwin spent much time playing the piano, and

---

74. CHARLES SCHWARTZ, GERSHWIN, HIS LIFE AND MUSIC (1973) at 21.

as his playing ability increased, so did his reputation. From there, Gershwin worked as a pianist with theatre productions, and he soon began writing his own music. By 1922, when he was just 24 years old, Gershwin's talent was widely recognized.

Gershwin "had always aspired to write a full-length, American musical drama" and had always searched for the right story.[75] In 1926, Gershwin read DuBose Heyward's *Porgy and Bess*, and in 1933 the Theatre Guild signed Gershwin and Heyward to make an opera out of it. The pre-Broadway performances in Boston were well received. The New York opening, however, was met with harsh criticism. The New York production closed after 124 performances, and box office receipts "earned him $10,000 in royalties, less than he had spent on having the music copied." The folk opera was revived in the 1940s and 1950s, and it was very successful in Milan. In 1985, 50 years after its premier, *Porgy and Bess* had a sold-out debut season at the Metropolitan Opera. Today, the opera "remains the single outstanding American theatre piece of the twentieth century."[76]

One of Gershwin's biographers notes, "Taking stock of his situation early in 1936, Gershwin would have admitted that Broadway was not treating him kindly. He had been working harder than at any time in his life, yet had scored three failures in succession: *Pardon My English* and *Let 'Em Eat Cake* in 1933 and now *Porgy and Bess*."[77] Gershwin died a year later in 1937 at the age of 38 following surgery for a brain tumor. His entire professional career spanned a mere two decades.

His real fame came after his death with a revival of *Porgy and Bess*. Now, critics say that George Gershwin is "among that hapless group of famous composers—Mozart, Schubert, Bellini, Mendelssohn, Chopin—whose lives ended when young, at the height of their creative powers."[78] George Gershwin is considered by many to be one of the greatest composers of all time and, perhaps, the greatest of all American composers.

SELF-ACTUALIZED INDIVIDUAL OF MASLOW'S HIERARCHY

Success is represented as ascension of Abraham Maslow's hierarchy of needs.[79] The only individual who comes to mind here as an example of this model of success is a psychologist/author named Nelson Zink. I am sure that there are others, but I do not know any. I suppose we could also accept in this classification anyone who negotiated the five stages of ego development proposed by Jane Loevinger[80] or the eight life stages of Erik Erikson.[81] All of these have achieved a psychological maturity and all of them have scaled pinnacles.

---

75. RODNEY GREENBERG, GEORGE GERSHWIN (1998) at 166.

76. *Id* at 196.

77. *Id* at 200.

78. *Id* at 9.

79. ABRAHAM H. MASLOW, MOTIVATION AND PERSONALITY (1954). The hierarchy starts with lower-level needs and rises to self-actualization; Maslow's premise is that a satisfied need does not motivate behavior. The lowest level is physiological needs (food, water, etc.) and rises sequentially through safety and security, love and belonging, esteem and self-esteem, to self-actualization.

80. JANE LOEVINGER, EGO DEVELOPMENT (1976) at 24–25. In order, the stages are impulsive, self-protective, conformist, self-aware, and conscientious.

81. ERIK ERIKSON, IDENTITY AND THE LIFE CYCLE (1959, 1980). Some serious scholars (e.g., H. Straub) believe that sub-stages within the Erikson stages were identified by DANIEL J. LEVINSON, THE SEASONS OF A MAN'S LIFE (1978).

"HERO/HEROINE" MODEL

In this model, success is equated to achieving the mythic hero's journey, so well described by Joseph Campell in several of his works. There are six elements of the hero's journey: (1) the call to adventure or signs of the vocation of hero; (2) the unsuspected, usually supernatural, aid that comes to one who undertakes his or her proper adventure; (3) the crossing of the first threshold, such as Caesar's crossing the Rubicon; (4) the passage into the realm of night, as in Jonah's descending into the belly of the whale; (5) the stage of trials and victories of initiation; and (6) the return and reintegration with society.[82] The hero is a "personage of exceptional gifts."[83] Sometimes, the hero is honored by his society on his or her return, but just as likely, the hero is not recognized or even disdained. Campbell writes as follows:

> Whether the hero be ridiculous or sublime, Greek or barbarian, gentile or Jew, his journey varies little in essential plan. Popular tales represent the heroic action as physical; the higher religions show the deed to be moral; nevertheless, there will be found astonishingly little variation in the morphology of the adventure, the character roles involved, the victories gained.[84]

Sometimes, fame and celebrity attach to the hero/heroine and sometimes not. If the hero is a prominent sports or entertainment figure in the United States in this century, celebrity usually attaches; witness John Wayne, Knute Rockne, Mickey Mantle, Greta Garbo, Marilyn Monroe, Picabo Street, and a host of others. In many of these cases, the public relations mythology overtakes the life of the real person.[85] For instance, many Americans find it difficult or impossible to believe that John Wayne is dead because he was so indestructible on the movie screen.[86]

BIOLOGICAL STANDARDS FOR SUCCESS

The biological standard of success is that one has succeeded if one has perpetuated his or her genetic heritage for another generation; conversely, one has failed biologically if one does not pass on one's gene pool. Some of my students find the "spawning salmon" model mildly humorous, but this is serious material. In this model, it is easy to define success. However, it is a most narrow and rigid standard, one that does not appear to withstand serious intellectual challenge, especially in the age of cloning and DNA engineering.[87]

---

82. J. CAMPBELL, THE HERO WITH A THOUSAND FACES (2nd ed. 1968) at 36.
83. *Id.* at 37.
84. *Id.* at 38.
85. *See, e.g.,* G. WILLS, JOHN WAYNE'S AMERICA: THE POLITICS OF CELEBRITY (1997).
86. *Id.* at 43.
87. Spawning salmon is a topic of serious interest in the Pacific Northwest. Salmon usually spawn at the headwaters of mountain rivers, such as the South Fork of the Salmon River near Warm Lake, Idaho, and then die. The eggs are fertilized by the males and usually develop in the interstices of gravel beds in the stream, protected there from other aquatic life that would feed on the fry. The smolt find their way downstream hundreds or thousands of miles to the ocean and there grow to maturity. At maturity, these salmon return to the exact location they hatched and reproduce and die—unless, of course, they are first caught by fishermen, eaten by bears, or chopped up in the giant turbines that produce hydroelectric power on the many dams along the rivers. Some anadromous fish runs, such as the sockeye salmon that run to Redfish Lake in Idaho's Sawtooth Mountains, are endangered or on the verge of extinction. Shall we declare the species a failure if it becomes extinct? Would it be more accurate to say

Some people believe that the social institution of marriage is designed for the sole purpose of reproduction. In that case, those people would declare a childless marriage to be a failure. Yet, recent studies in the United States indicate that one in three marriages have to deal with issues of infertility.[88] Other studies show that more couples are deciding not to have children because of career and other considerations. It seems too simplistic to declare that members of childless marriages, those who choose not to marry, or those who do not share a heterosexual orientation are failures in life.

For illustration, we need only look to the Windsors, the royal family of Great Britain, to see the huge emphasis put on Princess Diana's ability to conceive an heir to the crown. Clearly, reproduction was *the* screening emphasis, along with noble lineage. Many Americans put more emphasis on mating their hunting dogs than they do on their choice of parenting partners. Yet, some families and some religions consider the production of a male heir to be a significant duty either for carrying on the family name, taking over the family farm, or running the family business. The brutal injustices that Henry VIII of England inflicted on his wives for not giving him sons have not entirely disappeared into the dustbin of history.

This biological model awards the success label to any creature that succeeds in passing its genetic heritage onto another generation. Although at first this may be lampooned as a spawning salmon model, it figures prominently in many beliefs about the purpose of marriage and the sex act. No one who ever listened to a parent's diatribe about wanting grandchildren could seriously doubt that there is some validity to this notion. What it may lack in depth and sophistication, it apparently makes up for in staying power.

THE TOP OF THE HEAP MODEL

In this model, success attaches to "winning" through a singular attachment or devotion to the pursuit of a calling, a virtue, or a native talent—frequently a talent at the level of genius. Some of the names that come to mind in this model include Pablo Casals, Sojourner Truth, Thomas Eakins, Clarence Darrow, Marian Anderson, Thomas Jefferson, Mother Teresa, Grandma Moses, Alice Walker, Thomas Wolfe, John Steinbeck, Maya Angelou, and Oliver Wendell Holmes, Jr. Some might add sports and entertainment celebrities, such as Michael Jordan or, in an earlier era, Wilt Chamberlain and Bob Cousey, Babe Ruth and Joe DiMaggio, Marilyn Monroe and Humphrey Bogart. This approach to success in life is too one-dimensional to qualify as Aristotelian. Yet, we should be cautious in rejecting this approach because some human beings have such singular focus and drive that to argue for a well–balanced, Aristotelian life of virtue would be to deny the essence of their beings.

For example, Clarence Darrow was a brilliant trial lawyer and social justice crusader, but he was not a "nice" man in the sense that term carries in everyday conversation.[89] His life would be judged successful from this perspective of the top of the heap model, but it would fail other broader developmental, self-actualizing standards. Based on the material on individualism,[90] Darrow's

---

that the extinction of such a native fish is a moral failure of humankind to protect the ecology generally and endangered species specifically?

88. S. Begley, *The Baby Myth* [cover story], NEWSWEEK (September 4, 1995) at 38–45.

89. *See, e.g.*, IRVING STONE, CLARENCE DARROW FOR THE DEFENSE (1941, Signet ed., 1971).

90. ROBERT N. BELLAH et al., HABITS OF THE HEART: INDIVIDUALISM AND COMMITMENT IN AMERICAN LIFE (1985) at 147–155.

DOONESBURY

©DOONESBURY reprinted with permission of Universal Press Syndicate.

life was much too focused to meet the standards of Walt Whitman's "deeper and richer life experience."

A possible variant of the materialism theme is based on notions of winning in an accumulation contest that keeps score by net worth. The emphasis here is on winning![91] Americans love winners. Colleges and universities actively compete for the top places in rankings, such as *U.S. News & World Report*'s lists of the best colleges. Attendance goes up at ballparks that are homes to winning teams just as applications go up to schools that feature winning athletic teams.[92] *This clearly is one manifestation of White male consciousness at work.*[93] Some men need not only endure but they must prevail, and for some of us to feel like winners, someone else needs to lose. With our national fixation on wealth and market success, can it be any surprise that *Fortune* magazine and others print lists of the wealthiest people in the United States and in the world? Wealth accumulation is presumed by many to be a proxy for success, even though some of the wealthiest individuals and families have sorry histories of criminal convictions for tax fraud or other felonies. The commonality of this felony-fortune link leads us to agree with Balzac that behind every great fortune lies a crime.[94]

In a recent book, two scholars emphasize the impoverishment that accompanies a culture that has become overly fixated on competition and winning.[95]

91. Many proverbs as well as essays argue against this position; perhaps, the best known is a rhyme by Grantland Rice: "For when the One Great Scorer comes to write against your name, He writes not that you won or lost, But how you played the game." Grantland Rice, *Alumnus Football* (1925) as quoted in RANDOM HOUSE WEBSTER'S QUOTATIONARY (Leonard Ray Frank, ed., 1999) at 233.

92. For instance, "After winning the NCAA basketball championship in 1983, North Carolina State University experienced a 40 percent rise in applications for admission. Boston College applications went up from 12,500 in 1984 to 16,200 in 1985 after Doug Flutie won the Heisman Trophy for the 1984 season." ROBERT H. FRANK & PHILLIP J. COOK, THE WINNER-TAKE-ALL SOCIETY: HOW MORE AND MORE AMERICANS COMPETE FOR FEWER AND BIGGER PRIZES, ENCOURAGING ECONOMIC WASTE, INCOME INEQUALITY, AND AN IMPOVERISHED CULTURAL LIFE (1995) at 135.

93. ANN WILSON SCHAEF, WOMEN'S REALITY (1981) at 99–145.

94. Honore de Balzac (1799–1850) as quoted in THE OTHER 637 BEST THINGS ANYBODY EVER SAID (Robert Byrne, ed., 1984) at entry 221.

95. R. H. FRANK AND P. J. COOK, THE WINNER-TAKE-ALL SOCIETY: HOW MORE AND MORE AMERICANS COMPETE FOR EVER FEWER AND BIGGER PRIZES, ENCOURAGING ECONOMIC WASTE, INCOME INEQUALITY, AND IMPOVERISHED CULTURAL LIFE (1995).

The distortion of labor markets caused by a combination of excessive rewards, psychological dispositions toward winning, and technological innovations generates vast income inequalities, huge economic inefficiencies, and an impoverished cultural life for millions of Americans.

A PROCESS APPROACH TO SUCCESS

An alternative approach with an emphasis on process rather than product challenges much of the traditional models of success. This approach suggests that success is *not* a place or a person or a pinnacle to be scaled, but rather that it's much like true happiness, and is a by-product of what Buddhists would call "right living."[96] This philosophy parallels Aristotle's theory of *eudamonia* in which happiness, as in an enduring sense of well-being, is the by-product of a life lived in pursuit of virtue. Under this process model, one succeeds by living well; that is, by living a life that is becoming to a fully human person who has character, commitment, a sense of community, and the like.

Accordingly, by applying a process approach, individuals who do their best every day to live their calling according to their spiritual beliefs are a success, even if they are not famous or wealthy. One of my favorite examples is what is written on an old tombstone in an English country churchyard: "Here lies Thomas Cobb, who mended shoes in this village for thirty years to the greater glory of God." Socrates seems to concur, if one trusts the dialogues written by Plato. In *The Crito*, Socrates admonishes his disciple "that the really important thing is not to live, but to live well."[97] This, of course, is process. Socrates says living well includes living honorably and rightly.[98] Consequently, we can argue that the ancients saw success as living well and that it is a manner or style or journey, rather than a destination, an accumulation, or public adulation.[99] Moreover, such a concept gets us away from zero-sum contests that are implicit in wealth and power definitions and encourages everyone to pursue an honorable and upright life—because the only competition is with ourselves, the complex, multifaceted human being who hears many voices within his or her own head.

THE INWARD AND THE OUTWARD JOURNEYS

Life involves two journeys; one is outward and material, and the second is the spiritual journey, the inward journey of the soul.[100] If we accept the notion of success as a process or a journey, then we should, at least briefly, explore the nature of the process. The outward journey is fairly easily understood.

---

96. For a somewhat fluffy but readable book-length treatise along this line of argument, *see, e.g.,* T. MORRIS, TRUE SUCCESS: A NEW PHILOSOPHY OF EXCELLENCE (Berkeley ed. 1995).

97. PLATO, THE LAST DAYS OF SOCRATES (Hugh Tredennick, trans., 1954, 1957, Penguin Classic ed., reprinted 1966) at 87.

98. *Id.*

99. "During the classical period, for instance, there were many types of simple living, including the affluent temperance of the Stoics, Cicero, Seneca, and Marcus Aurelius; the more modest 'golden mean' of Socrates, Plato, and Aristotle; the ascetic primitivism of Diogenes, and the pastoral simplicity of Virgil and Horace." DAVID E. SHI, *supra* note 45, at 5.

100. *See* DAVID E. SHI, *supra,* note 45 at 125–28. Shi says that the Transcendentalists professed a more spiritual approach to spending and getting that evoked little sympathy among New England's social and economic elite. This mystical emphasis also inevitably led them to withdraw from the market and the society in order to find something "worthy to do." Such a journey is clearly inward, a journey of the soul.

How did we live our material existence? Did we pursue justice, truth, mercy, and virtues? Did we pursue wealth in the form of wisdom or in possessions? There are two main paths in U.S. society for the outer journey: the material emphasis that features appearances, such as the trappings of wealth and power or celebrity, and the pursuit of virtue and substance without regard for fame or notoriety.[101]

The inward journey is more difficult to describe. The Transcendentalists sought to simplify their material needs in order to devote themselves to the inward journey. So did Buddha, Gandhi, Jesus, and Mother Teresa. The inward journey is toward spiritual goals, such as peace, serenity, love, justice, freedom from fear, compassion, and community. Fowler has documented a linear, developmental scale for faith development, analogous to Kohlberg's moral reasoning scale.

Are we growing spiritually? Have we reconciled our inward journey with our outward journey? Have we balanced our private life with our public life? These are some of the questions that confront us in thinking about success as process. Being a *mensch* requires integrity; one must be a fully human being, and that means being whole and devoid of fundamental internal conflicts. The popular refrain of many managers that "they are really nice people away from the job" does not work. It is a sad admission that they compromise their values and their integrity on the job every day. Ultimately, if Bellah and Aristotle and others are correct, a life lived in balance brings happiness, and happiness, in the best sense of the word, is the only goal or end that humans seek for itself.

THE EASTERN AND THE PSYCHOTHERAPEUTIC PATH

In a powerful book, Sheldon B. Kopp argues that "no meaning that comes from outside ourselves is real."[102] Kopp declares,

> This search for enlightenment, pursued in a secular context by today's psychotherapy patient, has in the past been cast in religious terms. Whatever the metaphors in which the pilgrim experiences his quest, any trip involving a search for spiritual meaning is an allegorical journey through life, a journey that can renew and enrich the quality of the rest of the pilgrim's daily living.[103]

Kopp makes a comprehensive analogy to the religious pilgrimages of the past. He notes that many pilgrimages to shrines of local saints were undertaken because the pilgrim had been ill, sought a cure, and then recovered and went to fulfill an oath of gratitude. Or, the pilgrim went to expiate his or her sins as a communal expression of penance.[104] Regardless of the initial motive, the journey often gave pilgrims new perspectives on the meaning of their lives. Frequently, one pilgrim was helped by other pilgrims. Many did not return. However, Kopp emphasizes, the important thing "is to begin."[105] In addition,

---

101. To that effect, Zeno, an ancient stoic, was asked by a skeptic if virtue and justice were real; he replied "as real as that table." *See* BERTRAND RUSSELL, HISTORY OF WESTERN PHILOSOPHY (1945) at 253. Also, Bias of Priene reportedly advised his students: "Make wisdom your provision for the journey from youth to old age, for it is a more certain support than all other possessions." MORRIS, *supra* note 89, at 18.

102. SHELDON B. KOPP, IF YOU MEET THE BUDDHA ON THE ROAD, KILL HIM: THE PILGRIMAGE OF PSYCHOTHERAPY PATIENTS (1972) (Bantam ed. 1976) on front cover.

103. *Id.* at 8.

104. *Id.* at 9.

105. *Id.* at 10.

one is well advised to start out with a professional pilgrim as a guide; Kopp states that these guides are easily recognized because they are adorned with many tokens as the heroes of many adventures.[106]

Life, to be sure, involves choices—for virtually all of us. Kopp turns the tables on the reader and describes the choice *not* to be a pilgrim in this passage:

> And remember, too, you can stay at home, safe in the familiar illusion of certainty. Do not set out without realizing that "the way is not without danger. Everything is costly, and the development of the personality is one of the most costly of all things." It will cost you your innocence, your illusions, your certainty.[107]

All choices involve consequences. The cost of avoiding the danger of the inward journey is that we become stunted; we live out our lives without realizing our potential, condemning ourselves to a life lived in the certainties and illusions of a type of childhood, safe but ultimately deformed.

BALANCE BETWEEN PUBLIC AND PRIVATE LIVES

Research by sociologists at the University of California and elsewhere strongly indicate that no one can be happy in a meaningful sense unless they find a balance in their lives between their private life and their public life.[108] An active public life involves the person in service to the larger community.[109] Yet, recent studies show that American social capital is at an all-time low.[110] Social capital can be defined as "the collective value of all 'social networks' [who people know] and the inclinations that arise from these networks to do things for each other ['norms of reciprocity']."[111] Putnam uses the symbolism of bowling alone to demonstrate the decline in social capital because decades ago thousands of Americans bowled in organized leagues; yet by 1995, an American was more likely to bowl alone (roughly rendered, not-in-a-league) than with others.[112] This tendency to avoid organized bowling leagues, in view of the almost 100 million Americans who bowl each year, results in a serious loss of social capital.[113]

Thus, we might well be leery of definitions of success that are one-dimensional or entirely introspective or exclusively devoted to materialism on the one hand or selflessness on the other.[114] Our study of Aristotle suggests a vision of a well-lived life as one lived in balance and in pursuit of patterns of virtuous behavior. This model and perhaps the Emersonian one seem most

---

106. *Id.*
107. *Id.* at 95 citing for the quotation, THE SECRET OF THE GOLDEN FLOWER, A CHINESE BOOK OF LIFE (Harvest Book ed., Richard Wilhelm, trans. 1962).
108. ROBERT N. BELLAH ET AL., HABITS OF THE HEART: INDIVIDUALISM AND COMMITMENT IN AMERICAN LIFE (1985).
109. *Id.* at 163.
110. *See* ROBERT D. PUTNAM, BOWLING ALONE: THE COLLAPSE AND REVIVAL OF AMERICAN COMMUNITY (2000).
111. *Social Capital: What Is it?* Accessed at http://www.bowlingalone.com/socialcapital.php3 on July 29, 2004.
112. ROBERT D. PUTNAM, *supra* note 103 at 112–113, wherein Putnam notes that although more Americans are bowling than ever before, the amount of league bowling has dropped dramatically since about 1960. League bowling declined more than 40% between 1980 and 1993 alone. *Id.*
113. *Id.*
114. ROBERT N. BELLAH ET AL, *supra* note 101, at 294–296.

SHOE/Jeff MacNelly

compatible with what we have learned from sociology and developmental psychology.

SYNTHESIS: BUDDHA AND EMERSON

The process model has much appeal, especially when we combine the inward journey with the external journey and balance the public with the private life while insisting on integrity. One is reminded of the Chinese symbols of *yin* and *yang*, the female and male elements in the universe or in the individual in tension.[115] The *yin* (or "shaded" part) represents the female in the social system and stands for darkness, softness, and inactivity. The *yang* (or "sunlit") principle is male and symbolizes light, hardness, and activity. To quote one authority,

> The events on earth consist in the interplay of two opposed forces, the *yin* and the *yang*, the female and male principles respectively.... The *yin* and the *yang*, represented by divided and undivided lines in the I-Ching, are cosmic forces; from their interplay come all social, as well as all physical developments, all ideas, all institutions, cultures and civilizations.... There is a metaphysics here as well as a social philosophy, in effect a two-tiered universe, just as there is in Plato's philosophy, every event in the visible world being an image of an idea in the world of abstract forms."[116]

Modern philosophy teaches us that all human beings have a male and a female nature. In midlife, the man often needs to "get in touch" with his heretofore suppressed female side.[117] Women at midlife often experience a certain "yeastiness" that may, in part, reflect getting in fuller touch with their male, competitive side.[118] Balance is required, but achieving this balance is not a simple matter. Achieving it might well be the best measure of success, as well as of health and happiness. Interestingly, the I-Ching teaches that "[o]ne *yin* and one *yang* together equal the Tao (the Great Ultimate)."[119] The Tao

115. *See, e.g.,* JAMES K. FEIBLEMAN, UNDERSTANDING ORIENTAL PHILOSOPHY (rev. ed. 1984) at 86.
116. *Id.*
117. DANIEL J. LEVINSON, THE SEASONS OF A MAN'S LIFE (1978) at 197–200.
118. GAIL SHEEHY, PASSAGES: PREDICTABLE CRISES OF ADULT LIFE (1976, Bantam ed. 1981).
119. *Id.*

may be understood as a seamless eternity; and we gain tranquility, if not peace, when we can see our proper place in this eternal circle of being.

The Buddha taught the Middle Way, Aristotle taught the "golden mean" of virtue, and Emerson helped lead the Transcendental movement, which urged simplicity and an inner spiritual journey. The Transcendentalists sought to "transcend" rationality in order to explore the inner recesses of the self. Their spiritual approach to getting and spending did not find much favor or evoke sympathy among New England's social and economic elite.[120] Aristotle's *Ethics*, although dominant in philosophy for over a millennia, lacked an emotional dimension, which evoked severe criticism.[121] Moreover, some of Aristotle's arguments for virtues being found in the middle between deficiency and excess were not persuasive; some were downright disingenuous.[122]

Leaving Aristotle, we have the Buddha and Ralph Waldo Emerson for guidance, the gurus, if you will, for our pilgrimage of life. The combination has a certain attractiveness. Emerson is an American original, a "mind on fire." The Buddha has influenced spiritual practice for billions of people over thousands of years. Yet, their wisdom is, at certain levels and in specific perspectives, compatible and even reinforcing. The Buddha urges "right livelihood" as a way of making work a meaningful part of our spiritual journey.[123] Emerson argues that we must transcend the economic rationality of our time and find an inner peace as an anchor in the stormy seas of our lives. The Buddha taught that we must overcome fear and desire in order to be free. Emerson found and practiced that freedom—intellectually, materially, and spiritually. If we are able to go and do likewise, perhaps, we may lead successful lives.

CONCLUSION

Most people, however, live "lives of quiet desperation."[124] In an updated version of this observation, Studs Terkel writes, "To survive the day is triumph enough for the walking wounded among the great many of us [Americans who work for a living]."[125] Capitalism is soulless, and when it exploits workers as merely another input in the production process, it alienates human beings and produces a rage that seeks outlets in many inappropriate ways. The result is that many who succeed in the American way of business have denied their inward beings and negated their inward journeys.[126] A definition of success that talks of a process in which the inner journey is compatible with the outward journey and the public life is balanced with the private life presents a

---

120. DAVID E. SHI, *supra* note 45, at 125–128.

121. *See, e.g.,* BERTRAND RUSSELL, A HISTORY OF WESTERN PHILOSOPHY (1945), especially chapter titled "Aristotle's Ethics," in which Lord Russell declaims about Aristotle's *Ethics*, "More generally, there is an emotional poverty in the *Ethics*, which is not found in the earlier philosophers.... For these reasons, in my judgement [sic], his *Ethics*, in spite of its fame, is lacking in intrinsic importance." *Id.* at 184.

122. For a more complete discussion of Aristotle's theory of virtue ethics, including its strengths and weaknesses, *see* JAMES RACHELS, THE ELEMENTS OF MORAL PHILOSOPHY (4th ed. 2003) at 175–190.

123. For an excellent discussion of "right livelihood" in the context of Buddhist economics, *see* E. F. SCHUMACHER, SMALL IS BEAUTIFUL: ECONOMICS AS IF PEOPLE MATTERED (1973) at 50–58.

124. HENRY DAVID THOREAU, WALDEN (1854, Signet Classic ed. 1960) at 10.

125. STUDS TERKEL, WORKING (1972, paperback ed. 1974) at xiii.

126. *See, e.g.,* Lisa Miller, *Can You Go Back? More Professionals Return to Church or Synagogue; Having It All Isn't Enough,* WALL STREET J. (April 10, 1998) at W1.

difficult standard. Yet, it is an idea that should be vigorously advocated to help Americans reclaim the quality of life that is missing for many millions of us. Some critics have questioned whether capitalism in its present form could survive if the mass of people on the planet embraced such a definition of success. The answer may be not; however, the reformation of capitalism would be a beneficial by-product of a healthier, happier, and saner society.[127]

---

127. *See, e.g.*, William A. Wines, *A Call for American Businesses to Move Human Thriving to the Head of the Line* (November 4, 1999), an unpublished manuscript delivered as the 9th John L. Aram Lecture on Business Ethics, at the Spokane Club, Spokane, Washington. (Copy in possession of the author.)

PART

6

Appendices

APPENDIX A1
THE DECLARATION OF INDEPENDENCE

APPENDIX A2
THE U.S. CONSTITUTION

APPENDIX A3
ABRAHAM LINCOLN'S GETTYSBURG ADDRESS, NOVEMBER 19, 1863

APPENDIX A4
UNIVERSAL DECLARATION OF HUMAN RIGHTS

The Declaration of Independence

IN CONGRESS, JULY 4, 1776

THE UNANIMOUS DECLARATION OF THE THIRTEEN UNITED STATES OF AMERICA

When in the Course of human events, it becomes necessary for one people to dissolve the political bands which have connected them with another, and to assume among the powers of the earth, the separate and equal station to which the Laws of Nature and of Nature's God entitle them, a decent respect to the opinions of mankind requires that they should declare the causes which impel them to the separation.

We hold these truths to be self-evident, that all men are created equal, that they are endowed by their Creator with certain unalienable Rights, that among these are Life, Liberty and the pursuit of Happiness.—That to secure these rights, Governments are instituted among Men, deriving their just powers from the consent of the governed,—That whenever any Form of Government becomes destructive of these ends, it is the Right of the People to alter or to abolish it, and to institute new Government, laying its foundation on such principles and organizing its powers in such form, as to them shall seem most likely to effect their Safety and Happiness. Prudence, indeed, will dictate that Governments long established should not be changed for light and transient causes; and accordingly all experience hath shewn, that mankind are more disposed to suffer, while evils are sufferable, than to right themselves by abolishing the forms to which they are accustomed. But when a long train of abuses and usurpations, pursuing invariably the same Object evinces a design to reduce them under absolute Despotism, it is their right, it is their duty, to throw off such Government, and to provide new Guards for their future security.—Such has been the patient sufferance of these Colonies; and such is now the necessity which constrains them to alter their former Systems of Government. The history of the present King of Great Britain is a history of repeated injuries and usurpations, all having in direct object the establishment of an absolute Tyranny over these States. To prove this, let Facts be submitted to a candid world.

> He has refused his Assent to Laws, the most wholesome and necessary for the public good.
>
> He has forbidden his Governors to pass Laws of immediate and pressing importance, unless suspended in their operation till his Assent should be obtained; and when so suspended, he has utterly neglected to attend to them.
>
> He has refused to pass other Laws for the accommodation of large districts of people, unless those people would relinquish the right of Representation in the Legislature, a right inestimable to them and formidable to tyrants only.
>
> He has called together legislative bodies at places unusual, uncomfortable, and distant from the depository of their public Records, for the sole purpose of fatiguing them into compliance with his measures.
>
> He has dissolved Representative Houses repeatedly, for opposing with manly firmness his invasions on the rights of the people.
>
> He has refused for a long time, after such dissolutions, to cause others to be elected; whereby the Legislative powers, incapable of Annihilation, have returned to the People at large for their exercise; the State remaining

in the mean time exposed to all the dangers of invasion from without, and convulsions within.

He has endeavoured to prevent the population of these States; for that purpose obstructing the Laws for Naturalization of Foreigners; refusing to pass others to encourage their migrations hither, and raising the conditions of new Appropriations of Lands.

He has obstructed the Administration of Justice, by refusing his Assent to Laws for establishing Judiciary powers.

He has made Judges dependent on his Will alone, for the tenure of their offices, and the amount and payment of their salaries.

He has erected a multitude of New Offices, and sent hither swarms of Officers to harrass our people, and eat out their substance.

He has kept among us, in times of peace, Standing Armies without the Consent of our legislatures.

He has affected to render the Military independent of and superior to the Civil power.

He has combined with others to subject us to a jurisdiction foreign to our constitution, and unacknowledged by our laws; giving his Assent to their Acts of pretended Legislation:

For Quartering large bodies of armed troops among us: For protecting them, by a mock Trial, from punishment for any Murders which they should commit on the Inhabitants of these States:

For cutting off our Trade with all parts of the world:

For imposing Taxes on us without our Consent:

For depriving us in many cases, of the benefits of Trial by Jury:

For transporting us beyond Seas to be tried for pretended offences

For abolishing the free System of English Laws in a neighbouring Province, establishing therein an Arbitrary government, and enlarging its Boundaries so as to render it at once an example and fit instrument for introducing the same absolute rule into these Colonies:

For taking away our Charters, abolishing our most valuable Laws, and altering fundamentally the Forms of our Governments:

For suspending our own Legislatures, and declaring themselves invested with power to legislate for us in all cases whatsoever.

He has abdicated Government here, by declaring us out of his Protection and waging War against us.

He has plundered our seas, ravaged our Coasts, burnt our towns, and destroyed the lives of our people.

He is at this time transporting large Armies of foreign Mercenaries to compleat the works of death, desolation and tyranny, already begun with circumstances of Cruelty & perfidy scarcely paralleled in the most barbarous ages, and totally unworthy the Head of a civilized nation.

He has constrained our fellow Citizens taken Captive on the high Seas to bear Arms against their Country, to become the executioners of their friends and Brethren, or to fall themselves by their Hands. He has excited domestic insurrections amongst us, and has endeavoured to bring on the inhabitants of our frontiers, the merciless Indian Savages, whose known rule of warfare, is an undistinguished destruction of all ages, sexes and conditions.

In every stage of these Oppressions We have Petitioned for Redress in the most humble terms: Our repeated Petitions have been answered only by repeated injury. A Prince whose character is thus marked by every act which may define a Tyrant, is unfit to be the ruler of a free people.

Nor have We been wanting in attentions to our Brittish brethren. We have warned them from time to time of attempts by their legislature to extend an unwarrantable jurisdiction over us. We have reminded them of the circumstances of our emigration and settlement here. We have appealed to their native justice and magnanimity, and we have conjured them by the ties of our common kindred to disavow these usurpations, which, would inevitably interrupt our connections and correspondence. They too have been deaf to the voice of justice and of consanguinity. We must, therefore, acquiesce in the necessity, which denounces our Separation, and hold them, as we hold the rest of mankind, Enemies in War, in Peace Friends.

We, therefore, the Representatives of the United States of America, in General Congress, Assembled, appealing to the Supreme Judge of the world for the rectitude of our intentions, do, in the Name, and by Authority of the good People of these Colonies, solemnly publish and declare, That these United Colonies are, and of Right ought to be Free and Independent States; that they are Absolved from all Allegiance to the British Crown, and that all political connection between them and the State of Great Britain, is and ought to be totally dissolved; and that as Free and Independent States, they have full Power to levy War, conclude Peace, contract Alliances, establish Commerce, and to do all other Acts and Things which Independent States may of right do. And for the support of this Declaration, with a firm reliance on the protection of divine Providence, we mutually pledge to each other our Lives, our Fortunes and our sacred Honor.

The 56 signatures on the Declaration appear in the positions indicated:

Column 1	Column 2	Column 3	Column 4	Column 5	Column 6
Georgia:	**North Carolina:**	**Massachusetts:**	**Pennsylvania:**	**New York:**	**New Hampshire:**
Button Gwinnett	William Hooper	John Hancock	Robert Morris	William Floyd	Josiah Bartlett
Lyman Hall	Joseph Hewes	**Maryland:**	Benjamin Rush	Philip Livingston	William Whipple
George Walton	John Penn	Samuel Chase	Benjamin Franklin	Francis Lewis	**Massachusetts:**
	South Carolina:	William Paca	John Morton	Lewis Morris	Samuel Adams
	Edward Rutledge	Thomas Stone	George Clymer	**New Jersey:**	John Adams
	Thomas Heyward, Jr.	Charles Carroll of Carrollton	James Smith	Richard Stockton	Robert Treat Paine
	Thomas Lynch, Jr.	**Virginia:**	George Taylor	John Witherspoon	Elbridge Gerry
	Arthur Middleton	George Wythe	James Wilson	Francis Hopkinson	**Rhode Island:**
		Richard Henry Lee	George Ross	John Hart	Stephen Hopkins
		Thomas Jefferson	**Delaware:**	Abraham Clark	William Ellery
		Benjamin Harrison	Caesar Rodney		**Connecticut:**
		Thomas Nelson, Jr.	George Read		Roger Sherman
		Francis Lightfoot Lee	Thomas McKean		Samuel Huntington
		Carter Braxton			William Williams
					Oliver Wolcott
					New Hampshire:
					Matthew Thornton

From The National Archives Experience. Accessed at http://www.archives.gov/national_archives_experience/charters/declaration_transcript.html on September 22, 2004.

The U.S. Constitution

We the People of the United States, in Order to form a more perfect Union, establish Justice, insure domestic Tranquility, provide for the common defence, promote the general Welfare, and secure the Blessings of Liberty to ourselves and our Posterity, do ordain and establish this Constitution for the United States of America.

ARTICLE I

SECTION 1

All legislative Powers herein granted shall be vested in a Congress of the United States, which shall consist of a Senate and House of Representatives.

SECTION 2

Clause 1: The House of Representatives shall be composed of Members chosen every second Year by the People of the several States, and the Electors in each State shall have the Qualifications requisite for Electors of the most numerous Branch of the State Legislature.

Clause 2: No Person shall be a Representative who shall not have attained to the Age of twenty five Years, and been seven Years a Citizen of the United States, and who shall not, when elected, be an Inhabitant of that State in which he shall be chosen.

Clause 3: Representatives and direct Taxes shall be apportioned among the several States which may be included within this Union, according to their respective Numbers, which shall be determined by adding to the whole Number of free Persons, including those bound to Service for a Term of Years, and excluding Indians not taxed, three fifths of all other Persons [*see note 2*]. The actual Enumeration shall be made within three Years after the first Meeting of the Congress of the United States, and within every subsequent Term of ten Years, in such Manner as they shall by Law direct. The Number of Representatives shall not exceed one for every thirty Thousand, but each State shall have at Least one Representative; and until such enumeration shall be made, the State of New Hampshire shall be entitled to chuse three, Massachusetts eight, Rhode-Island and Providence Plantations one, Connecticut five, New-York six, New Jersey four, Pennsylvania eight, Delaware one, Maryland six, Virginia ten, North Carolina five, South Carolina five, and Georgia three.

Clause 4: When vacancies happen in the Representation from any State, the Executive Authority thereof shall issue Writs of Election to fill such Vacancies.

Clause 5: The House of Representatives shall chuse their Speaker and other Officers; and shall have the sole Power of Impeachment.

SECTION 3

Clause 1: The Senate of the United States shall be composed of two Senators from each State, chosen by the Legislature thereof [*see note 3*], for six Years; and each Senator shall have one Vote.

Clause 2: Immediately after they shall be assembled in Consequence of the first Election, they shall be divided as equally as may be into three Classes. The Seats of the Senators of the first Class shall be vacated at the Expiration of the second Year, of the second Class at the Expiration of the fourth Year, and of the third Class at the Expiration of the sixth Year, so that one third may be chosen every second Year; and if Vacancies happen by Resignation, or otherwise, during the Recess of the Legislature of any State, the Executive thereof may make temporary Appointments until the next Meeting of the Legislature, which shall then fill such Vacancies. [*See note 4*].

Clause 3: No Person shall be a Senator who shall not have attained to the Age of thirty Years, and been nine Years a Citizen of the United States, and who shall not, when elected, be an Inhabitant of that State for which he shall be chosen.

Clause 4: The Vice President of the United States shall be President of the Senate, but shall have no Vote, unless they be equally divided.

Clause 5: The Senate shall chuse their other Officers, and also a President pro tempore, in the Absence of the Vice President, or when he shall exercise the Office of President of the United States.

Clause 6: The Senate shall have the sole Power to try all Impeachments. When sitting for that Purpose, they shall be on Oath or Affirmation. When the President of the United States is tried, the Chief Justice shall preside: And no Person shall be convicted without the Concurrence of two thirds of the Members present.

Clause 7: Judgment in Cases of Impeachment shall not extend further than to removal from Office, and disqualification to hold and enjoy any Office of honor, Trust or Profit under the United States: but the Party convicted shall nevertheless be liable and subject to Indictment, Trial, Judgment and Punishment, according to Law.

SECTION 4

Clause 1: The Times, Places and Manner of holding Elections for Senators and Representatives, shall be prescribed in each State by the Legislature thereof; but the Congress may at any time by Law make or alter such Regulations, except as to the Places of chusing Senators.

Clause 2: The Congress shall assemble at least once in every Year, and such Meeting shall be on the first Monday in December [*see note 5*], unless they shall by Law appoint a different Day.

SECTION 5

Clause 1: Each House shall be the Judge of the Elections, Returns and Qualifications of its own Members, and a Majority of each shall constitute a Quorum to do Business; but a smaller Number may adjourn from day to day, and may be authorized to compel the Attendance of absent Members, in such Manner, and under such Penalties as each House may provide.

Clause 2: Each House may determine the Rules of its Proceedings, punish its Members for disorderly Behaviour, and, with the Concurrence of two thirds, expel a Member.

Clause 3: Each House shall keep a Journal of its Proceedings, and from time to time publish the same, excepting such Parts as may in their Judgment require Secrecy; and the Yeas and Nays of the Members of either House on any question shall, at the Desire of one fifth of those Present, be entered on the Journal.

Clause 4: Neither House, during the Session of Congress, shall, without the Consent of the other, adjourn for more than three days, nor to any other Place than that in which the two Houses shall be sitting.

SECTION 6

Clause 1: The Senators and Representatives shall receive a Compensation for their Services, to be ascertained by Law, and paid out of the Treasury of the United States [*see note 6*]. They shall in all Cases, except Treason, Felony and Breach of the Peace, be privileged from Arrest during their Attendance at the Session of their respective Houses, and in going to and returning from the same; and for any Speech or Debate in either House, they shall not be questioned in any other Place.

Clause 2: No Senator or Representative shall, during the Time for which he was elected, be appointed to any civil Office under the Authority of the United States, which shall have been created, or the Emoluments whereof shall have been encreased during such time; and no Person holding any Office under the United States, shall be a Member of either House during his Continuance in Office.

SECTION 7

Clause 1: All Bills for raising Revenue shall originate in the House of Representatives; but the Senate may propose or concur with Amendments as on other Bills.

Clause 2: Every Bill which shall have passed the House of Representatives and the Senate, shall, before it become a Law, be presented to the President of the United States; If he approve he shall sign it, but if not he shall return it, with his Objections to that House in which it shall have originated, who shall enter the Objections at large on their Journal, and proceed to reconsider it. If after such Reconsideration two thirds of that House shall agree to pass the Bill, it shall be sent, together with the Objections, to the other House, by which it shall likewise be reconsidered, and if approved by two thirds of that House, it shall become a Law. But in all such Cases the Votes of both Houses shall be determined by yeas and Nays, and the Names of the Persons voting for and against the Bill shall be entered on the Journal of each House respectively. If any Bill shall not be returned by the President within ten Days (Sundays excepted) after it shall have been presented to him, the Same shall be a Law, in like Manner as if he had signed it, unless the Congress by their Adjournment prevent its Return, in which Case it shall not be a Law.

Clause 3: Every Order, Resolution, or Vote to which the Concurrence of the Senate and House of Representatives may be necessary (except on a question of Adjournment) shall be presented to the President of the United States; and before the Same shall take Effect, shall be approved by him, or being disapproved by him, shall be repassed by two thirds of the Senate and House of Representatives, according to the Rules and Limitations prescribed in the Case of a Bill.

SECTION 8

Clause 1: The Congress shall have Power To lay and collect Taxes, Duties, Imposts and Excises, to pay the Debts and provide for the common Defence and general Welfare of the United States; but all Duties, Imposts and Excises shall be uniform throughout the United States;

Clause 2: To borrow Money on the credit of the United States;

Clause 3: To regulate Commerce with foreign Nations, and among the several States, and with the Indian Tribes;

Clause 4: To establish an uniform Rule of Naturalization, and uniform Laws on the subject of Bankruptcies throughout the United States;

Clause 5: To coin Money, regulate the Value thereof, and of foreign Coin, and fix the Standard of Weights and Measures;

Clause 6: To provide for the Punishment of counterfeiting the Securities and current Coin of the United States;

Clause 7: To establish Post Offices and post Roads;

Clause 8: To promote the Progress of Science and useful Arts, by securing for limited Times to Authors and Inventors the exclusive Right to their respective Writings and Discoveries;

Clause 9: To constitute Tribunals inferior to the supreme Court;

Clause 10: To define and punish Piracies and Felonies committed on the high Seas, and Offences against the Law of Nations;

Clause 11: To declare War, grant Letters of Marque and Reprisal, and make Rules concerning Captures on Land and Water;

Clause 12: To raise and support Armies, but no Appropriation of Money to that Use shall be for a longer Term than two Years;

Clause 13: To provide and maintain a Navy;

Clause 14: To make Rules for the Government and Regulation of the land and naval Forces;

Clause 15: To provide for calling forth the Militia to execute the Laws of the Union, suppress Insurrections and repel Invasions;

Clause 16: To provide for organizing, arming, and disciplining, the Militia, and for governing such Part of them as may be employed in the Service of the United States, reserving to the States respectively, the Appointment of the Officers, and the Authority of training the Militia according to the discipline prescribed by Congress;

Clause 17: To exercise exclusive Legislation in all Cases whatsoever, over such District (not exceeding ten Miles square) as may, by Cession of particular States, and the Acceptance of Congress, become the Seat of the Government of the United States, and to exercise like Authority over all Places purchased by the Consent of the Legislature of the State in which the Same shall be, for the Erection of Forts, Magazines, Arsenals, dock-Yards, and other needful Buildings;—And

Clause 18: To make all Laws which shall be necessary and proper for carrying into Execution the foregoing Powers, and all other Powers vested by this Constitution in the Government of the United States, or in any Department or Officer thereof.

SECTION 9

Clause 1: The Migration or Importation of such Persons as any of the States now existing shall think proper to admit, shall not be prohibited by the

Congress prior to the Year one thousand eight hundred and eight, but a Tax or duty may be imposed on such Importation, not exceeding ten dollars for each Person.

Clause 2: The Privilege of the Writ of Habeas Corpus shall not be suspended, unless when in Cases of Rebellion or Invasion the public Safety may require it.

Clause 3: No Bill of Attainder or ex post facto Law shall be passed.

Clause 4: No Capitation, or other direct, Tax shall be laid, unless in Proportion to the Census or Enumeration herein before directed to be taken [*see note* 7].

Clause 5: No Tax or Duty shall be laid on Articles exported from any State.

Clause 6: No Preference shall be given by any Regulation of Commerce or Revenue to the Ports of one State over those of another: nor shall Vessels bound to, or from, one State, be obliged to enter, clear, or pay Duties in another.

Clause 7: No Money shall be drawn from the Treasury, but in Consequence of Appropriations made by Law; and a regular Statement and Account of the Receipts and Expenditures of all public Money shall be published from time to time.

Clause 8: No Title of Nobility shall be granted by the United States: And no Person holding any Office of Profit or Trust under them, shall, without the Consent of the Congress, accept of any present, Emolument, Office, or Title, of any kind whatever, from any King, Prince, or foreign State.

SECTION 10

Clause 1: No State shall enter into any Treaty, Alliance, or Confederation; grant Letters of Marque and Reprisal; coin Money; emit Bills of Credit; make any Thing but gold and silver Coin a Tender in Payment of Debts; pass any Bill of Attainder, ex post facto Law, or Law impairing the Obligation of Contracts, or grant any Title of Nobility.

Clause 2: No State shall, without the Consent of the Congress, lay any Imposts or Duties on Imports or Exports, except what may be absolutely necessary for executing its inspection Laws: and the net Produce of all Duties and Imposts, laid by any State on Imports or Exports, shall be for the Use of the Treasury of the United States; and all such Laws shall be subject to the Revision and Controul of the Congress.

Clause 3: No State shall, without the Consent of Congress, lay any Duty of Tonnage, keep Troops, or Ships of War in time of Peace, enter into any Agreement or Compact with another State, or with a foreign Power, or engage in War, unless actually invaded, or in such imminent Danger as will not admit of delay.

ARTICLE II

SECTION 1

Clause 1: The executive Power shall be vested in a President of the United States of America. He shall hold his Office during the Term of four Years, and, together with the Vice President, chosen for the same Term, be elected, as follows:

Clause 2: Each State shall appoint, in such Manner as the Legislature thereof may direct, a Number of Electors, equal to the whole Number of Senators and Representatives to which the State may be entitled in the Congress: but no Senator or Representative, or Person holding an Office of Trust or Profit under the United States, shall be appointed an Elector.

Clause 3: The Electors shall meet in their respective States, and vote by Ballot for two Persons, of whom one at least shall not be an Inhabitant of the same State with themselves. And they shall make a List of all the Persons voted for, and of the Number of Votes for each; which List they shall sign and certify, and transmit sealed to the Seat of the Government of the United States, directed to the President of the Senate. The President of the Senate shall, in the Presence of the Senate and House of Representatives, open all the Certificates, and the Votes shall then be counted. The Person having the greatest Number of Votes shall be the President, if such Number be a Majority of the whole Number of Electors appointed; and if there be more than one who have such Majority, and have an equal Number of Votes, then the House of Representatives shall immediately chuse by Ballot one of them for President; and if no Person have a Majority, then from the five highest on the List the said House shall in like Manner chuse the President. But in chusing the President, the Votes shall be taken by States, the Representation from each State having one Vote; A quorum for this Purpose shall consist of a Member or Members from two thirds of the States, and a Majority of all the States shall be necessary to a Choice. In every Case, after the Choice of the President, the Person having the greatest Number of Votes of the Electors shall be the Vice President. But if there should remain two or more who have equal Votes, the Senate shall chuse from them by Ballot the Vice President [*see note 8*].

Clause 4: The Congress may determine the Time of chusing the Electors, and the Day on which they shall give their Votes; which Day shall be the same throughout the United States.

Clause 5: No Person except a natural born Citizen, or a Citizen of the United States, at the time of the Adoption of this Constitution, shall be eligible to the Office of President; neither shall any Person be eligible to that Office who shall not have attained to the Age of thirty five Years, and been fourteen Years a Resident within the United States.

Clause 6: In Case of the Removal of the President from Office, or of his Death, Resignation, or Inability to discharge the Powers and Duties of the said Office [*see note 9*], the Same shall devolve on the Vice President, and the Congress may by Law provide for the Case of Removal, Death, Resignation or Inability, both of the President and Vice President, declaring what Officer shall then act as President, and such Officer shall act accordingly, until the Disability be removed, or a President shall be elected.

Clause 7: The President shall, at stated Times, receive for his Services, a Compensation, which shall neither be increased nor diminished during the Period for which he shall have been elected, and he shall not receive within that Period any other Emolument from the United States, or any of them.

Clause 8: Before he enter on the Execution of his Office, he shall take the following Oath or Affirmation:—"I do solemnly swear (or affirm) that I will faithfully execute the Office of President of the United States, and will to the best of my Ability, preserve, protect and defend the Constitution of the United States."

SECTION 2

Clause 1: The President shall be Commander in Chief of the Army and Navy of the United States, and of the Militia of the several States, when called into the actual Service of the United States; he may require the Opinion, in writing, of the principal Officer in each of the executive Departments, upon any Subject relating to the Duties of their respective Offices, and he shall have Power to grant Reprieves and Pardons for Offences against the United States, except in Cases of Impeachment.

Clause 2: He shall have Power, by and with the Advice and Consent of the Senate, to make Treaties, provided two thirds of the Senators present concur; and he shall nominate, and by and with the Advice and Consent of the Senate, shall appoint Ambassadors, other public Ministers and Consuls, Judges of the supreme Court, and all other Officers of the United States, whose Appointments are not herein otherwise provided for, and which shall be established by Law: but the Congress may by Law vest the Appointment of such inferior Officers, as they think proper, in the President alone, in the Courts of Law, or in the Heads of Departments.

Clause 3: The President shall have Power to fill up all Vacancies that may happen during the Recess of the Senate, by granting Commissions which shall expire at the End of their next Session.

SECTION 3

He shall from time to time give to the Congress Information of the State of the Union, and recommend to their Consideration such Measures as he shall judge necessary and expedient; he may, on extraordinary Occasions, convene both Houses, or either of them, and in Case of Disagreement between them, with Respect to the Time of Adjournment, he may adjourn them to such Time as he shall think proper; he shall receive Ambassadors and other public Ministers; he shall take Care that the Laws be faithfully executed, and shall Commission all the Officers of the United States.

SECTION 4

The President, Vice President and all civil Officers of the United States, shall be removed from Office on Impeachment for, and Conviction of, Treason, Bribery, or other high Crimes and Misdemeanors.

ARTICLE III

SECTION 1

The judicial Power of the United States, shall be vested in one supreme Court, and in such inferior Courts as the Congress may from time to time ordain and establish. The Judges, both of the supreme and inferior Courts, shall hold their Offices during good Behaviour, and shall, at stated Times, receive for their Services, a Compensation, which shall not be diminished during their Continuance in Office.

SECTION 2

Clause 1: The judicial Power shall extend to all Cases, in Law and Equity, arising under this Constitution, the Laws of the United States, and Treaties made, or which shall be made, under their Authority;—to all Cases affecting Ambassadors, other public Ministers and Consuls;–to all Cases of admiralty and maritime Jurisdiction;—to Controversies to which the United States shall be a Party;—to Controversies between two or more States;—between a State and Citizens of another State [*see note 10*];—between Citizens of different States,—between Citizens of the same State claiming Lands under Grants of different States, and between a State, or the Citizens thereof, and foreign States, Citizens or Subjects.

Clause 2: In all Cases affecting Ambassadors, other public Ministers and Consuls, and those in which a State shall be Party, the supreme Court shall have original Jurisdiction. In all the other Cases before mentioned, the supreme Court shall have appellate Jurisdiction, both as to Law and Fact, with such Exceptions, and under such Regulations as the Congress shall make.

Clause 3: The Trial of all Crimes, except in Cases of Impeachment, shall be by Jury; and such Trial shall be held in the State where the said Crimes shall have been committed; but when not committed within any State, the Trial shall be at such Place or Places as the Congress may by Law have directed.

SECTION 3

Clause 1: Treason against the United States, shall consist only in levying War against them, or in adhering to their Enemies, giving them Aid and Comfort. No Person shall be convicted of Treason unless on the Testimony of two Witnesses to the same overt Act, or on Confession in open Court.

Clause 2: The Congress shall have Power to declare the Punishment of Treason, but no Attainder of Treason shall work Corruption of Blood, or Forfeiture except during the Life of the Person attainted.

ARTICLE IV

SECTION 1

Full Faith and Credit shall be given in each State to the public Acts, Records, and judicial Proceedings of every other State. And the Congress may by general Laws prescribe the Manner in which such Acts, Records and Proceedings shall be proved, and the Effect thereof.

SECTION 2

Clause 1: The Citizens of each State shall be entitled to all Privileges and Immunities of Citizens in the several States.

Clause 2: A Person charged in any State with Treason, Felony, or other Crime, who shall flee from Justice, and be found in another State, shall on Demand of the executive Authority of the State from which he fled, be delivered up, to be removed to the State having Jurisdiction of the Crime.

Clause 3: No Person held to Service or Labour in one State, under the Laws thereof, escaping into another, shall, in Consequence of any Law or Regulation therein, be discharged from such Service or Labour, but shall be delivered up on Claim of the Party to whom such Service or Labour may be due [*see note 11*].

SECTION 3

Clause 1: New States may be admitted by the Congress into this Union; but no new State shall be formed or erected within the Jurisdiction of any other State; nor any State be formed by the Junction of two or more States, or Parts of States, without the Consent of the Legislatures of the States concerned as well as of the Congress.

Clause 2: The Congress shall have Power to dispose of and make all needful Rules and Regulations respecting the Territory or other Property belonging to the United States; and nothing in this Constitution shall be so construed as to Prejudice any Claims of the United States, or of any particular State.

SECTION 4

The United States shall guarantee to every State in this Union a Republican Form of Government, and shall protect each of them against Invasion; and on Application of the Legislature, or of the Executive (when the Legislature cannot be convened) against domestic Violence.

ARTICLE V

The Congress, whenever two thirds of both Houses shall deem it necessary, shall propose *Amendments* to this Constitution, or, on the Application of the Legislatures of two thirds of the several States, shall call a Convention for proposing Amendments, which, in either Case, shall be valid to all Intents and Purposes, as Part of this Constitution, when ratified by the Legislatures of three fourths of the several States, or by Conventions in three fourths thereof, as the one or the other Mode of Ratification may be proposed by the Congress; Provided that no Amendment which may be made prior to the Year One thousand eight hundred and eight shall in any Manner affect the first and fourth Clauses in the Ninth Section of the first Article; and that no State, without its Consent, shall be deprived of its equal Suffrage in the Senate.

ARTICLE VI

Clause 1: All Debts contracted and Engagements entered into, before the Adoption of this Constitution, shall be as valid against the United States under this Constitution, as under the Confederation.

Clause 2: This Constitution, and the Laws of the United States which shall be made in Pursuance thereof; and all Treaties made, or which shall be made, under the Authority of the United States, shall be the supreme Law of the Land; and the Judges in every State shall be bound thereby, any Thing in the Constitution or Laws of any State to the Contrary notwithstanding.

Clause 3: The Senators and Representatives before mentioned, and the Members of the several State Legislatures, and all executive and judicial Officers, both of the United States and of the several States, shall be bound by Oath or Affirmation, to support this Constitution; but no religious Test shall ever be required as a Qualification to any Office or public Trust under the United States.

ARTICLE VII

The Ratification of the Conventions of nine States, shall be sufficient for the Establishment of this Constitution between the States so ratifying the Same.

Done in Convention by the Unanimous Consent of the States present the Seventeenth Day of September in the Year of our Lord one thousand seven hundred and Eighty seven and of the Independence of the United States of America the Twelfth In witness whereof We have hereunto subscribed our Names,

GO WASHINGTON—Presidt. and deputy from Virginia

[Signed also by the deputies of twelve States.]

Delaware

Geo. Read
Gunning Bedford jun
John Dickinson
Richard Bassett
Jaco. Broom

Maryland
James MCHenry
Dan of St Tho. Jenifer
DanL Carroll.

Virginia

John Blair—
James Madison Jr.

North Carolina

WM Blount
RichD. Dobbs Spaight.
Hu Williamson

South Carolina

J. Rutledge
Charles 1ACotesworth Pinckney
Charles Pinckney
Pierce Butler.

Georgia

William Few
Abr Baldwin

New Hampshire

John Langdon
Nicholas Gilman

Massachusetts

Nathaniel Gorham
Rufus King

Connecticut
WM. SamL. Johnson
Roger Sherman

New York

Alexander Hamilton

New Jersey

Wil: Livingston
David Brearley.
WM. Paterson.
Jona: Dayton

Pennsylvania

B Franklin
Thomas Mifflin
RobT Morris
Geo. Clymer
ThoS. FitzSimons
Jared Ingersoll
James Wilson.
Gouv Morris

Attest William Jackson Secretary

NOTES

Note 1: This text of the Constitution follows the engrossed copy signed by Gen. Washington and the deputies from 12 States.

The Constitution was adopted by a convention of the States on September 17, 1787, and was subsequently ratified by the several States, on the following dates: Delaware, December 7, 1787; Pennsylvania, December 12, 1787; New Jersey, December 18, 1787; Georgia, January 2, 1788; Connecticut, January 9, 1788; Massachusetts, February 6, 1788; Maryland, April 28, 1788; South Carolina, May 23, 1788; New Hampshire, June 21, 1788.

Ratification was completed on June 21, 1788.

The Constitution was subsequently ratified by Virginia, June 25, 1788; New York, July 26, 1788; North Carolina, November 21, 1789; Rhode Island, May 29, 1790; and Vermont, January 10, 1791.

In May 1785, a committee of Congress made a report recommending an alteration in the Articles of Confederation, but no action was taken on it, and it was left to the State Legislatures to proceed in the matter. In January 1786, the Legislature of Virginia passed a resolution providing for the appointment of five commissioners, who, or any three of them, should meet such commissioners as might be appointed in the other States of the Union, at a time and place to be agreed upon, to take into consideration the trade of the United States; to consider how far a uniform system in their commercial regulations may be necessary to their common interest and their permanent harmony; and to report to the several States such an act, relative to this great object, as, when ratified by them, will enable the United States in Congress effectually to provide for the same. The Virginia commissioners, after some correspondence, fixed the first Monday in September as the time, and the city of Annapolis as the place for the meeting, but only four other States were represented, viz: Delaware, New York, New Jersey, and Pennsylvania; the commissioners appointed by Massachusetts, New Hampshire, North Carolina, and Rhode Island failed to attend. Under the circumstances of so partial a representation, the commissioners present agreed upon a report (drawn by Mr. Hamilton, of New York), expressing their unanimous conviction that it might essentially tend to advance the interests of the Union if the States by which they were respectively delegated would concur, and use their endeavors to procure the concurrence of the other States, in the appointment of commissioners to meet at Philadelphia on the second Monday of May following, to take into consideration the situation of the United States; to devise such further provisions as should appear to them necessary to render the Constitution of the federal government adequate to the exigencies of the Union; and to report such an act for that purpose to the United States in Congress assembled as, when agreed to by them and afterward confirmed by the Legislatures of every State, would effectually provide for the same.

Congress, on the 21st of February, 1787, adopted a resolution in favor of a convention, and the Legislatures of those States which had not already done so (with the exception of Rhode Island) promptly appointed delegates. On the 25th of May, seven States having convened, George Washington, of Virginia, was unanimously elected president, and the consideration of the proposed constitution was commenced. On the 17th of September, 1787, the Constitution as engrossed and agreed upon was signed by all the members present, except Mr. Gerry of Massachusetts, and Messrs. Mason and Randolph, of Virginia. The president of the convention transmitted it to Congress, with a resolution stating how the proposed federal government should be put in operation, and an explanatory letter. Congress, on the 28th of September, 1787, directed the Constitution so framed, with the resolutions and letter concerning the same, to "be transmitted to the several Legislatures in order to be submitted to a convention of delegates chosen in each State by the people thereof, in conformity to the resolves of the convention."

On the 4th of March, 1789, the day which had been fixed for commencing the operations of Government under the new Constitution, it had been ratified by the conventions chosen in each State to consider it, as follows: Delaware, December 7, 1787; Pennsylvania, December 12, 1787; New Jersey, December 18, 1787; Georgia, January 2, 1788; Connecticut, January 9, 1788; Massachusetts, February 6, 1788; Maryland, April 28, 1788; South Carolina, May 23, 1788; New Hampshire, June 21, 1788; Virginia, June 25, 1788; and New York, July 26, 1788.

The president informed Congress, on the 28th of January, 1790, that North Carolina had ratified the Constitution November 21, 1789; and he informed Congress on the 1st of June, 1790, that Rhode Island had ratified the Constitution May 29, 1790. Vermont, in convention, ratified the Constitution January 10, 1791, and was, by an act of Congress approved February 18, 1791, "received and admitted into this Union as a new and entire member of the United States."

Note 2: The part of this Clause relating to the mode of apportionment of representatives among the several States has been affected by Section 2 of amendment XIV, and as to taxes on incomes without apportionment by amendment XVI.

Note 3: This Clause has been affected by Clause 1 of amendment XVII.

Note 4: This Clause has been affected by Clause 2 of amendment XVIII.

Note 5: This Clause has been affected by amendment XX.

Note 6: This Clause has been affected by amendment XXVII.

Note 7: This Clause has been affected by amendment XVI.

Note 8: This Clause has been superseded by amendment XII.

Note 9: This Clause has been affected by amendment XXV.

Note 10: This Clause has been affected by amendment XI.

Note 11: This Clause has been affected by amendment XIII.

Note 12: The first ten amendments to the Constitution of the United States (and two others, one of which failed of ratification and the other which later became the 27th Amendment) were proposed to the legislatures of the several States by the First Congress on September 25, 1789. The first ten amendments were ratified by the following States, and the notifications of ratification by the Governors thereof were successively communicated by the president to Congress: New Jersey, November 20, 1789; Maryland, December 19, 1789; North Carolina, December 22, 1789; South Carolina, January 19, 1790; New Hampshire, January 25, 1790; Delaware, January 28, 1790; New York, February 24, 1790; Pennsylvania, March 10, 1790; Rhode Island, June 7, 1790; Vermont, November 3, 1791; and Virginia, December 15, 1791.

Ratification was completed on December 15, 1791.

The amendments were subsequently ratified by the legislatures of Massachusetts, March 2, 1939; Georgia, March 18, 1939; and Connecticut, April 19, 1939.

Note 13: Only the 13th, 14th, 15th, and 16th articles of amendment had numbers assigned to them at the time of ratification.

Note 14: This sentence has been superseded by section 3 of amendment XX.

Note 15: See amendment XIX and section 1 of amendment XXVI.

Note 16: Repealed by section 1 of amendment XXI.

As found on The United States House of Representatives web site. Accessed at http://www.house.gov/Constitution/Constitution.html on September 22, 2004.

APPENDIX

A3

Abraham Lincoln's Gettysburg Address, November 19, 1863

Note: This version is known as the "Bliss" copy, the widely adopted version of Lincoln's Gettysburg Address. However, this was a copy written after November 19, a gift from Lincoln to Colonel Alexander Bliss. The original of the Bliss version is now in the Lincoln Room of the White House.

Fourscore and seven years ago our fathers brought forth on this continent a new nation, conceived in liberty and dedicated to the proposition that all men are created equal.

Now we are engaged in a great civil war, testing whether that nation or any nation so conceived and so dedicated can long endure. We are met on a great battlefield of that war. We have come to dedicate a portion of that field as a final resting-place for those who here gave their lives that that nation might live. It is altogether fitting and proper that we should do this.

But, in a larger sense, we cannot dedicate, we cannot consecrate, we cannot hallow this ground. The brave men, living and dead who struggled here have consecrated it far above our poor power to add or detract. The world will little note nor long remember what we say here, but it can never forget what they did here. It is for us the living rather to be dedicated here to the unfinished work which they who fought here have thus far so nobly advanced. It is rather for us to be here dedicated to the great task remaining before us—that from these honored dead we take increased devotion to that cause for which they gave the last full measure of devotion—that we here highly resolve that these dead shall not have died in vain, that this nation under God shall have a new birth of freedom, and that government of the people, by the people, for the people shall not perish from the earth.

Accessed at the Fifties Web site, http://www.fiftiesweb.com/usa/gettysburg-address.htm on September 28, 2004.

APPENDIX

A4

Universal Declaration
of Human Rights

On December 10, 1948, the General Assembly of the United Nations adopted and proclaimed the Universal Declaration of Human Rights, the full text of which appears in the following pages. Following this historic act the Assembly called on all Member countries to publicize the text of the Declaration and "to cause it to be disseminated, displayed, read and expounded principally in schools and other educational institutions, without distinction based on the political status of countries or territories."

PREAMBLE

Whereas recognition of the inherent dignity and of the equal and inalienable rights of all members of the human family is the foundation of freedom, justice and peace in the world,

Whereas disregard and contempt for human rights have resulted in barbarous acts which have outraged the conscience of mankind, and the advent of a world in which beings shall enjoy freedom of speech and belief and freedom from fear and want has been proclaimed as the highest aspiration of the common people,

Whereas it is essential, if man is not to be compelled to have recourse, as a last resort, to rebellion against tyranny and oppression, that human rights should be protected by the rule of law,

Whereas it is essential to promote the development of friendly relations between nations,

Whereas the peoples of the United Nations have in the Charter reaffirmed their faith in fundamental human rights, in the dignity and worth of the human person and in the equal rights of men and women and have determined to promote social progress and better standards of life in larger freedom,

Whereas Member States have pledged themselves to achieve, in co-operation with the United Nations, the promotion of Universal respect for and observance of human rights and fundamental freedoms,

Whereas a common understanding of these rights and freedoms is of the greatest importance for the full realization of this pledge,

Now, Therefore THE GENERAL ASSEMBLY proclaims THIS UNIVERSAL DECLARATION OF HUMAN RIGHTS as a common standard of achievement for all peoples and all nations, to the end that every individual and every organ of society, keeping this Declaration constantly in mind, shall strive by teaching and education to promote respect for these rights and freedoms and by progressive measures, national and international, to secure their universal and effective recognition and observance, both among the peoples of Member States themselves and among the peoples of territories under their jurisdiction.

ARTICLE 1

All human beings are born free and equal in dignity and rights. They are endowed with reason and conscience and should act towards one another in a spirit of brotherhood.

ARTICLE 2

Everyone is entitled to all the rights and freedoms set forth in this Declaration, without distinction of any kind, such as race, color, sex, language, religion, political or other opinion, national or social origin, property, birth or other status. Furthermore, no distinction shall be made on the basis of the political, jurisdictional or international status of the country or territory to which a person belongs, whether it be independent, trust, non-self-governing or under any other limitation of sovereignty.

ARTICLE 3

Everyone has the right to life, liberty and security of person.

ARTICLE 4

No one shall be held in slavery or servitude; slavery and the slave trade shall be prohibited in all their forms.

ARTICLE 5

No one shall be subjected to torture or to cruel, inhuman or degrading treatment or punishment.

ARTICLE 6

Everyone has the right to recognition everywhere as a person before the law.

ARTICLE 7

All are equal before the law and are entitled without any discrimination to equal protection of the law. All are entitled to equal protection against any discrimination in violation of this Declaration and against any incitement to such discrimination.

ARTICLE 8

Everyone has the right to an effective remedy by the competent national tribunals for acts violating the fundamental rights granted him by the constitution or by law.

ARTICLE 9

No one shall be subjected to arbitrary arrest, detention or exile.

ARTICLE 10

Everyone is entitled in full equality to a fair and public hearing by an independent and impartial tribunal, in the determination of his rights and obligations and of any criminal charge against him.

ARTICLE 11

(1) Everyone charged with a penal offence has the right to be presumed innocent until proved guilty according to law in a public trial at which he has had all the guarantees necessary for his defence.

(2) No one shall be held guilty of any penal offence on account of any act or omission which did not constitute a penal offence, under national or international law, at the time when it was committed. Nor shall a heavier penalty be imposed than the one that was applicable at the time the penal offence was committed.

ARTICLE 12

No one shall be subjected to arbitrary interference with his privacy, family home or correspondence, nor to attacks upon his honour and reputation. Everyone has the right to the protection of the law against such interference or attacks.

ARTICLE 13

(1) Everyone has the right to freedom of movement and residence within the borders of each state.

(2) Everyone has the right to leave any country, including his own, and to return to his country.

ARTICLE 14

(1) Everyone has the right to seek and to enjoy in other countries asylum from persecution.

(2) This right may not be invoked in the case of prosecutions genuinely arising from non-political crimes or from acts contrary to the purposes and principles of the United Nations.

ARTICLE 15

(1) Everyone has the right to a nationality.

(2) No one shall be arbitrarily deprived of his nationality nor denied the right to change his nationality.

ARTICLE 16

(1) Men and women of full age, without any limitation due to race, nationality or religion, have the right to marry and to found a family. They are entitled to equal rights as to marriage, during marriage and at its dissolution.

(2) Marriage shall be entered into only with the free and full consent of the intending spouses.

(3) The family is the natural and fundamental group unit of society and is entitled to protection by society and the State.

ARTICLE 17

(1) Everyone has the right to own property alone as well as in association with others.

(2) No one shall be arbitrarily deprived of his property.

ARTICLE 18

Everyone has the right to freedom of thought, conscience and religion; this right includes freedom to change his religion or belief, and freedom, either alone or in community with others and in public or private to manifest his religion or belief in teaching, practice, worship and observance.

ARTICLE 19

Everyone has the right to freedom of opinion and expression; this right includes freedom to hold opinions without interference and to seek, receive and impart information and ideas through any media and regardless of frontiers.

ARTICLE 20

(1) Everyone has the right to freedom of peaceful assembly and association.

(2) No one may be compelled to belong to an association.

ARTICLE 21

(1) Everyone has the right to take part in the government of his country, directly or through freely chosen representatives.

(2) Everyone has the right of equal access to public service in his country.

(3) The will of the people shall be the basis of the authority of government; this will shall be expressed in periodic and genuine elections which shall be by universal and equal suffrage and shall be held by secret vote or by equivalent free voting procedures.

ARTICLE 22

Everyone, as a member of society, has the right to social security and is entitled to realization, through national effort and international co-operation and in accordance with the organization and resources of each State, of the economic, social and cultural rights indispensable for his dignity and the free development of his personality.

ARTICLE 23

(1) Everyone has the right to work, to free choice of employment, to just and favourable conditions of work and to protection against unemployment.

(2) Everyone, without any discrimination, has the right to equal pay for equal work.

(3) Everyone who works has the right to just and favourable remuneration ensuring for himself and his family an existence worthy of human dignity, and supplemented, if necessary, by other means of social protection.

(4) Everyone has the right to form and to join trade unions for the protection of his interests.

ARTICLE 24

(1) Everyone has the right to rest and leisure, including reasonable limitation of working hours and periodic holidays with pay.

ARTICLE 25

Everyone has the right to a standard of living adequate for the health and well-being of himself and of his family, including food, clothing, housing and medical care and necessary social services, and the right to Security in the event of unemployment, sickness, disability, widowhood, old age or other lack of livelihood in circumstances beyond his control.

(2) Motherhood and childhood are entitled to special care and assistance. All Children, whether born in or out of wedlock, shall enjoy the same social protection.

ARTICLE 26

(1) Everyone has the right to education. Education shall be free, at least in the elementary and fundamental stages. Elementary education shall be compulsory. Technical and professional education shall be made generally available and higher education shall be equally accessible to all on the basis of merit.

(2) Education shall be directed to the full development of the human personality and to the strengthening of respect for human rights and fundamental freedoms. It shall promote understanding, tolerance and friendship among all nations, racial or religious groups, and shall further the activities of United Nations for the maintenance of peace.

(3) Parents have a prior right to choose the kind of education that shall be given to their children.

ARTICLE 27

(1) Everyone has the right freely to participate in the cultural life of the community, to enjoy the arts and the share in scientific advancement and its benefits.

(2) Everyone has the right to the protection of the moral and material interests resulting from any scientific, literary or artistic production of which he is the author.

ARTICLE 28

Everyone is entitled to a social and international order in which the rights and freedoms set forth in this Declaration can be fully realized.

ARTICLE 29

(1) Everyone has duties to the community in which alone the free and full development of his personality is possible.

(2) In the exercise of his rights and freedoms, everyone shall be subject only to such limitations as are determined by law solely for the purpose of securing due recognition and respect for the rights and freedoms of others and of meeting the just requirements of morality, public order and the general welfare in a democratic society.

(3) These rights and freedoms may in no case be exercised contrary to the purposes and principles of the United nations.

ARTICLE 30

Nothing in this Declaration may be interpreted as implying for any State, group or person any right to engage in any activity or to perform any act aimed at the destruction of any of the rights and freedoms set forth herein.

From the United Nations web site accessed at http://www.un.org/Overview/right.html on September 22, 2004.

AUTHOR INDEX

This index is limited to authors quoted in the main body of the text.

SUBJECT INDEX